ALTERNATIVE TRAVEL DIRECTORY

The Complete Guide To
Travel, Study, & Living Overseas

GENERAL EDITORS

David Cline

Clayton A. Hubbs

CONTRIBUTING EDITORS

Andrew Gerard, Susan Griffith, Cynthia Harriman,
Deborah McLaren, William Nolting, Vanessa Relli-Moreau
Susan Sygall, Kathy Widing, Arline K. Wills

Transitions Abroad Publishing, Inc.
Amherst, MA

Contributing editors:
Kathy Widing (Chapter 1), Arline K. Wills (Chapter 3),
Cynthia Harriman (Chapter 5), Susan Sygall (Chapter 6),
Deborah McLaren (Chapter 8), William Nolting (Chapter 10),
Vanessa Relli-Moreau (Chapter 15), Andrew Gerard (Internet resources)

Published by Transitions Abroad Publishing, Inc.
P.O. Box 1300, Amherst, MA 01004-1300

Manufactured in the United States of America

ISBN 1-886732-06-x
Fifth Edition

Cover and book design by David Cline
Cover photo by Peter Keegan
Typesetting and editorial assistance by Janis G. Sokol
Proofreading by Sheila Gilmartin

CONTENTS

Preface to the Fifth Edition, 7

Introduction, 9: *Be a traveler, not a tourist. Travelers leave home at home, bringing only themselves and a desire to see, hear, and feel new cultures, and to grow and learn from the experience.*

INDEPENDENT TRAVEL

The Changing Times of Travel, 16: *The majority of travelers today are exploring the world on their own, not as part of an organized tour or bus trip. That means there is a greater demand for good information and new and better opportunities for direct access to other cultures. The editors have selected the best choices from the growing number of resources and programs for independent travel.*

Preface to the Fifth Edition

The *Alternative Travel Directory,* produced by the editors of *Transitions Abroad* magazine annually since 1993, is a one-volume selection of the most essential practical information on the overseas alternatives to "packaged" tourism: independent travel, ecotravel, study abroad, and living overseas. Opportunities for working overseas, along with a selection of placement and training programs, are collected separately in the biannual *Work Abroad: The Complete Guide to Finding a Job Overseas.* Ordering information is on page 388.

The growth in the number and variety of listings in each new volume of the *Alternative Travel Directory* indicates a burgeoning interest in avoiding the international tourist trails and traps that tend to isolate travelers from the people and culture of the host country. Readers of *Transitions Abroad* magazine are among the growing number of visitors to other countries who recognize the enormous rewards that come from seeing the world from the hosts' perspective—whether we are independent travelers, students, volunteers, or guests in private homes. The result of the increase in immersion travel is that more people are meeting more people than at any time in history.

For a variety of reasons, our readers are spending longer periods of time abroad. Some go as "working travelers," who pay for their extended journeys with short-term jobs. Others go abroad to find more permanent positions in the new global economy. So this year we've added a final section on living abroad. Everyone from diplomats to students preparing to spend a year in Europe will benefit from this wealth of tools for overseas living.

To stay up to date on all the latest practical information on work, study, independent travel, and living abroad subscribe to *Transitions Abroad* magazine. For an examination copy call 800-293-0373 or go to our continuously updated web site, www.transabroad.com. Just click on *"Where do you want to go?"* or *"What do you want to do?"*

INTRODUCTION

In 1977 I launched *Transitions Abroad,* a magazine of practical information for independent travelers who go abroad to live, work, study, or travel for reasons other than those connected with mass tourism. The title "Transitions" was meant to suggest the changes that occur when travelers leave home behind and truly immerse themselves in a new environment.

Many of the first writers for *Transitions Abroad* were students, just back from a semester or year of travel and study abroad. Writing in the first issue, Gary Langer, then a student at the Univ. of New Hampshire, described staying at the Jerusalem guesthouse of an elderly Armenian called Mr. A. Those who sought out Mr. A were travelers, not tourists:

"Travelers and tourists, the distinction is simple: Tourists are those who bring their homes with them wherever they go, and apply them to whatever they see. They are closed to experience outside of the superficial. Travelers left home at home, bringing only themselves and a desire to see and hear and feel and take in and grow and learn. Tourists do not go to Mr. A's. They would not appreciate him, nor he them. And the main reason travelers go to Mr. A's is for Mr. A."

Taken out of context, Langer's contrast between travelers and tourists may sound a bit exaggerated and smug (after all, we are all in one sense tourists when we travel to another country). But the distinction has long been made between those who seem to travel more to confirm what they already know than to gain new understanding of themselves and of others. One thinks of Mark Twain's 1860s satirical novel on American travelers who brought so much cultural (and other) baggage with them that they were only "In-a-Sense" Abroad.

The stereotypical tourist—whether of Twain's time or ours—doesn't so much abandon his own familiar environment for the sake of engaging with a new one as have himself transported to a foreign place, taking with him as much of his familiar environment as possible. He views the unfamiliar people, places, and culture through the windows or walls of the familiar and pretends that he is still at home. If he must speak to the natives he does so loudly, thereby giving them every opportunity to understand him.

The modern traveler, on the other hand, is increasingly interested in experiencing new people, places, and cultures on their own terms and precisely because they are unfamiliar. The transition is not simply a passage from one place to another; it is a change in perspective and perception.

Interest in alternative travel, or travel for enrichment, grew rapidly in the 1970s and 1980s, in part a result of international air travel becoming affordable to a much larger group of people. In 1989 *Travel & Leisure* magazine commissioned Louis Harris Associates, Inc. to survey thousands of traveling Americans to find out why they traveled. To their surprise, the interviewers found that three travelers out of four took their last trip to improve their minds, to gain new perspectives, and to meet new people. Asked to name their dream vacation, only 10 percent named a place in the U.S. The conclusion of the pollsters was that international travel for personal growth was increasing more rapidly than any other form of nonbusiness travel.

In 1991 Arthur Frommer wrote: "After 30 years of writing standard guidebooks, I began to see that most of the vacation journeys undertaken by Americans were trivial and bland. . . . Travel in all price ranges is scarcely worth the effort unless it is associated with people, with learning and ideas. To have meaning at all, travel must involve an encounter with new and different outlooks and beliefs. . . . At its best, travel should challenge our preconceptions and most cherished views, cause us to rethink our assumptions, shake us a bit, make us broader-minded and more understanding."

"Not to have met the people of other cultures in a nontouristic setting," Frommer concludes in *The New World of Travel,* "is not to have lived in this century."

Detailing the ways and the means to meet people of other cultures in a nontourist setting has been the major purpose of *Transitions Abroad* since its beginning 20 years ago. In each issue of the magazine we select and publish the most important sources of information on alternative travel along with a selection of programs and other opportunities for the curious and independent-minded.

We revise and update this information continuously. At the end of each year we bring it all together in one volume: the *Alternative Travel Directory.* The three sections—Independent Travel, Study Abroad, and Living Abroad—contain our selection of the major alternatives to mass tourism.

Alternative Travel. The experience of travel involves a continuum or a progression from the familiar to the new. On the one extreme are the unadventurous packaged tourists or mass tourists described above who spend a good portion of their trip in a literal bubble being whisked along on a guided tour, usually in an air-conditioned bus. They make virtually no decisions on their own and are taken, on a fixed schedule, from one attraction (often man-made for their benefit) to another. They observe and photograph but rarely actively experience their surroundings.

On the other extreme are those relatively few travelers who avoid the tourist scene altogether and strike out on their own. They are on no fixed schedule or itinerary and settle where they like for as long as they like, finding casual work when necessary to cover their modest expenses or to pay for moving on.

Between these two extremes are those of us in that growing group of travelers who like to go on our own, often to pursue a particular interest, but only after enough planning and preparation to insure that our limited time and money will be well spent. We don't want to be bound to a group or have our experience spoiled by hordes of tourists; on the other hand, we want to be comfortable and feel sufficiently secure to accomplish our goals.

In recent years the most rapid area of growth in alternative travel has been ecotourism. As contributing editors Deborah McLaren and Rob Ramer write in the introduction to Responsible Travel Resources (Chapter 7), "Experiencing the richness of tropical ecosystems is one of the purest 'highs' of traveling. Yet are the tourists and tour operators giving anything back to preserve the natural beauty we are traveling to enjoy?"

In other words, are we traveling responsibly? Or do we, by the very act of flying to a faraway place, contribute to the destruction of its environment and culture? The editors of *Transitions Abroad* and of this volume are proud that for more than 20 years we have provided readers with the best and most comprehensive information on ways to travel responsibly, to preserve the world's natural and human environment.

Independent Travel Abroad. The travel resources and programs in the first nine chapters are grouped under the heading of independent or "life-seeing travel." The latter term comes from the concept of the Scandinavian School for Life (adult continuing education schools to enrich the mind, sometimes but not always to teach a vocational skill) which we described in the first issue of *Transitions Abroad* in 1977. Axel Dessau, director of the Danish Tourist Office, is credited with applying the concept to tourism. Visitors to Denmark are able to engage in activities that match their particular interests—for example, educators may visit schools and stay in the homes of teachers.

The fact that similar home and hospitality exchanges are proliferating throughout the world–as more of us travel from one foreign host's home to another rather than to tourist hotels–is just one indication of the increasing desire on the part of international travelers for an authentic engagement with the local people. For more and more travelers, including the readers of *Transitions Abroad*, life-seeing has replaced sightseeing.

Chapter 1 is a country-by-country guide to the best guidebooks and background reading to consult as you begin to make your overseas travel plans. Chapter 2 lists the best opportunities and resources for combining a trip overseas with your interest or hobby, say by taking Italian cooking classes in Tuscany or birdwatching in the Amazon. Chapters 3 through 6 cover the best travel information resources and selected programs for seniors, for families traveling with children, and for persons with disabilities. Chapters 7 and 8 cover the major resources and programs exemplifying culturally and environmentally responsible travel, the fastest growing of all forms of alternative travel. How precisely one defines responsible travel and how one travels responsibly is a central topic of each issue of *Transitions Abroad*. Chapter 9 lists volunteer programs around the world for travelers who want to work and live with local people while contributing to the host community.

Study Abroad. In Chapter 10 we list the most useful resources for learning opportunities abroad. Whereas all travel is at least potentially educational, the programs and resources for people of all ages described in chapters 12 through 16 are structured learning experiences. Those organized for undergraduates carry academic credit. Older adults are welcome to take part in most academic programs for no credit, usually at a reduced price.

Living Abroad. In Chapter 17 Gina Doggett, herself an expatriate American living in Paris, has put together an incredibly comprehensive list of where to find everything you need to know about living abroad: organizations for Americans abroad (Democrats, Republicans, women, etc.), guides for individual countries, books on cross-cultural adjustment and health and safety and language learning, home and hospitality exchange organizations, and other publications on living abroad and reentry and retirement abroad. As in the earlier chapters, we include up-to-date e-mail addresses and web sites where available.

Whatever your age, whatever your reason for travel, we think you'll find the overseas travel alternative you're looking for here. If not, let us know and we'll try to include it in the next issue of *Transitions Abroad* and next year's edition of the *Alternative Travel Directory*. Our address is Transitions Abroad, P.O. Box 1300, Amherst, MA 01004-1300; info@transabroad.com; www.transabroad.com.

Clay Hubbs
Amherst, MA
December 1998

INDEPENDENT TRAVEL

Today's travelers are much more independent than in past decades. They tend to travel with specific goals and become more involved with people and surroundings. More and more people today travel with a purpose—whether it be teaching English in Korea, volunteering in Guatemala, cooking in Tuscany, studying in Russia, or learning French in Provence.
—KATHY WIDING, PAGE 16

The Times Are A Changin'

Travelers Are Much More Independent and Goal Oriented

by Kathy Widing

Travel is changing, and over the last decade the changes have been increasingly reflected in travel books. Today's traveler is not only looking for an informative, all-round travel guide, but also for cultural, historical, and background information—including help in communicating in the local language.

In short, today's travelers are much more independent than in past decades. They tend to travel with specific goals and become more involved with people and surroundings. More and more people today travel with a purpose—whether it be teaching English in Korea, volunteering in Guatemala, cooking in Tuscany, studying in Russia, or learning French in Provence. As a result, more titles are appearing that focus on combining work or study with travel, ecotourism, and nature or "green" travel.

The thirst to become more familiar with one's destination has led to a huge expansion of background titles, such as the Insight Guides series which combines essays on history and culture with destination material and beautiful photography. The Traveller's History series offers a historical perspective, and the Culture Shock! series provides an understanding of customs and behavior.

The recent increase in travel narratives and anthologies indicates the value that travelers now find in travel literature as a supplement to practical research. Travel literature imparts a sense of place and a cognizance of a people or culture; it also offers the reader a perspective on a country or region from an individual author's personal perspective.

Lonely Planet, long associated with practical guidebooks, has launched a new literature series called Journeys. Beginning with just four books only two years ago, the company now offers 14 titles with stories on countries and areas as diverse as Central America, India, Jordan, New Guinea, and Zimbabwe.

Travel anthologies have recently come to the forefront of travel literature, the best known being the Travelers' Tales and the Literary Companion series. Each give the reader a look at an area or a theme through the eyes of multiple authors.

Practical, down-to-earth guides have held their place. Established guide-book publishers such as Frommer, Fodor, and Michelin continue to provide solid material, as do the younger companies such as Lonely Planet, Moon Publications, Rough Guides, Cadogan, and many publishers of single titles. Each strives to provide the best information, constantly updating and improving. It's no longer enough to just list sights and accommodations. A good guide will also cover history, cultural happenings, and issues such as festivals and etiquette, architectural notes, and outdoor adventures.

Particularly important to travel publishing are the "active" adventure enthusiasts, whose major reason to travel is to experience nature and take on physical and spiritual challenges. The range of outdoor opportunities is enormous, and active travel guides have become more and more specialized. There are now guides for kayaking in Baja, diving in Scotland, walking in the Italian Alps, cycling in the Netherlands, backpacking in Bolivia, observing wildlife in the Galapagos, and climbing Kilimanjaro.

In fact, the most remarkable change in travel publishing in general is the specialization of titles. Where 10 years ago we were lucky to find information on specific areas tucked away in a larger more general volume, today we can find half a dozen books on Sicily alone, a shelf on Provence, a dozen books on Cuba. As travelers head further off the beaten path, we now find books on Bulgaria, Antarctica, Mongolia, Oman, Albania, Eritrea, and Malawi.

Another trend is the desire of travelers to see "real life," break down barriers, and get closer to the people. Travelers are looking for lodgings with local flavor, and there has been an increase in guides devoted to exclusively to bed and breakfasts, inns, castles, farms, monasteries, and small family run-hotels, homestays, home exchanging, and rentals.

In order to help you make informed choices from the key titles below, an asterisk (*) indicates the best of the best, in both individual books and series guides—the most in-depth practical and cultural coverage to enhance your planning and ultimately your travel experience. Two references for further reading worth seeking out are Maggy Simony's **Traveller's Reading Guide** (Facts on File) and **Anderson's Travel Companion** by Sarah Anderson (Scolar Press), both guides to travel fiction and non-fiction. And don't miss the list of Key Web Sites, compiled by Andrew Gerard, on page 50.

*The authentic **American** certificates...*

Worldwide Teachers Professional Certificates

Do you want to Travel and Teach English?
Your TEFL Certificate will be your ticket
to the world's most interesting places!

CTEFL (Certificate In Teaching English as a Foreign Language)

The Boston TEFL Certificate Method® is a three-week immersion course (150 hours) offered monthly. Part-time courses are also available. Emphasis is on practice rather than theory.

- **Limited enrollment**
- **Second career persons are welcome**
- **No second language is necessary**
- **Global placement guidance**
- **Supervised teacher training on-site**
- **Features a special module on "Teaching Young Learners"** (no extra cost)

Cert.TBE (Certificate In Teaching Business English)

Sponsored by The American English Language Foundation

This intensive ,one-week, 50 hour course is specially designed for qualified EFL/ESL teachers and offered monthly. This training course is targeted toward developing practical skills and teaching American Business English. The course is specifically designed to expand the repertoire of classroom activities and techniques and to help build a substantial file of immediately usable American Business English material.

If one chooses to take this course upon completion of The Boston TEFL Course®, the tuition will be reduced by 50%. Alumni of The Boston TEFL Course® will also enjoy this 50% tuition reduction. RSA/Cambridge TEFL Certificate graduates will receive a 25% tuition reduction.

CTEFL/DL (Certificate In Teaching English as a Foreign Language / Distance Learning)

Internationally approved programs invite you to become part of the technological revolution. This course may be completed via the internet (on-line training) or traditional correspondence. A practical teaching component is required and may be fulfilled in the student's local area. This is the only Distance Learning TEFL course in North America or South America authorized by the Accreditation Council for TESOL Distance Education Courses. *Tuition covers all materials and access to faculty via e-mail. Call for special brochure.*

Course Director: Thomas A. Kane, Ph.D. Appointed Visiting Scholar at Harvard University, is Director of the Boston TEFL Certificate Course®. Dr.Kane is author of the recent best-seller, *Teach American English Around the World. (ISBN#1-888811-10-2)* The International Employment Gazette and The American Language Review recognize him as the American authority on "teaching English abroad."

♦**All courses at Worldwide Teachers Development Institute are eligible for Professional Development Points for recertification by the Massachusetts Department of Education. We welcome on-site visits by any prospective students, educators, or language industry professionals.**

Visit our Web site for more information! **www.bostontefl.com**

Worldwide Teachers Development Institute
Boston, USA / Guadalajara, Mexico
Toll free (within the USA): 1-800-875-5564 Boston Admissions office: (617)262-5766
Fax: (617) 262-0308 Email: BostonTEFL@aol.com Web site: www.bostontefl.com
Guadalajara, Mexico: [011] 52 3 614-4883 E-mail: teflmexi@hotmail.com

CHAPTER 1

INDEPENDENT TRAVEL: THE KEY RESOURCES

Whether you intend to go abroad for a week, a month, or a year, every trip requires planning. The more you learn about your destination, the better equipped you are to embark on your adventure. We hope the extensive resources that follow will help you choose which road to follow. Those marked with an asterisk are particularly recommended. Happy travels!

Guidebook Series

*Access Guides (Harper Collins). Well-organized guides with informative walking routes. Titles on London, Paris, Rome, Venice, Milan, Florence, Mexico, Caribbean, Budget Europe, Montreal and Quebec City, French Wine Country.

Around the World Program (McDonald and Woodward). A new series sponsored by the American Geographical Society provides substantive introductions to single countries. Titles include: Japan, Switzerland, Fiji, Australia, Malta, and Brazil.

*Blue Guides (W. W. Norton and Co.). Incredibly detailed British series covering history, culture, walks, driving tours, etc. Titles include Egypt, Istanbul, Jerusalem, Morocco, Denmark, Barcelona, Tuscany, Amsterdam, Albania, Southwest France, Sweden, Tunisia, Jordan, Budapest, Thailand, Rhodes and Dodecanese, Vienna, Madrid. New this year: Bulgaria.

Berlitz Travel Guides (Berlitz Publishing). **Discover Series**: lots of good background and pre-trip information. Titles include: France, Italy, Prague, Israel, Singapore, Portugal, Tuscany. The classic series: **Berlitz Pocket Guide.** Titles for over 100 destinations including Budapest, Cuba, Dublin, South Africa, Egypt, Thailand.

Bradt Guides (Globe Pequot Press). Reliable guides originating in the U.K. covering unusual and less traveled destinations for the adventurous traveler. Titles include: Albania, Burma, Estonia, Lebanon, Senegal, Zanzibar,

Africa by Road, Eritrea, Malawi, Madagascar Wildlife, Venezuela, Hiking in Romania, Antarctica, Mozambique, Greece by Rail, Backpacking in Mexico. New this year: Ghana, Namibia, Cape Verde, Zanzibar.

*Cadogan Guides (Globe Pequot Press). Excellent, all-purpose guidebooks at moderate prices. Titles include detailed country and regional guides to the Caribbean, India, Turkey, Morocco, Amsterdam, Southern Spain, Mexico, Paris, Sicily, Cyprus, Malta, Germany, Southwest France, Brussels, London, Southwest Ireland, Andalucia, Henry Kelly's West of Ireland, London Markets, The Algarve, Crete, Northern Spain, Central Asia, Tuscany, Provence, China: The Silk Route, Loire, Belize, Lombardy and Italian Lakes, Antarctica and The Falklands. New this year: Southern African on the Wild Side, Brittany, Yucatan.

*Culture Shock! Series (Graphic Arts). Guides to customs and etiquette of various cultures. Titles include: Thailand, China, Pakistan, France, Britain, Israel, India, South Africa, Burma, Canada, Philippines, Australia, Korea, Nepal, A Globe-Trotter's Guide, Ireland, Morocco, Switzerland, Syria, Vietnam, Successful Living Abroad: Wife's Guide, Turkey, Germany, Denmark, Bolivia, United Arab Emirates, Czech Republic, Living and Working Abroad. New this year: Mexico, Netherlands, Egypt.

Customs and Etiquette in... (Global Books). Pocket guides to customs, manners, and culture of individual countries. Available for: Arabia and the Gulf States, China, Germany, Russia, Greece, Hungary, Japan, England, India, Israel, Thailand, Singapore, Holland, Italy, Ireland, Vietnam.

Day Trips Series by Earl Steinbecker (Hastings House). Oriented to public transportation. Titles: Day Trips in France, Germany, Holland/Belgium/Luxembourg, Italy, Israel. Daytrips from London, Ireland, Spain/Portugal. New this year: Switzerland.

Driving Tours (Macmillan). Interesting regional driving routes with lots of tips and sightseeing information. Titles include: Britain, France, Ireland, Mexico, Scotland, Austria, Australia, Scandinavia, Switzerland.

Exploring Rural Europe Series (Passport Books). Driving tours of 1 day to 1 week acquaint the traveler with the history, character, and cuisine of the region. Titles for Austria, France, England, Germany, Ireland, Greece, Portugal, Spain.

Eyewitness Guides (Dorling Kindersley Publishing). Well-designed with lots of color and illustrations, many in 3-D. Good for art and architecture. Titles include: London, Paris, Rome, Prague, Vienna, France, Provence, Venice, Italy, Loire Valley, Seville and Andalucia, Greece, Greek Islands. New this year: Istanbul, Naples, and Campania.

Fielding's Guides (Fielding Worldwide). Good general guidebooks for all budget levels. Titles: Europe, Italy, France, Caribbean, Portugal, Amazon, Southeast Asia, Vietnam, Borneo, Thailand. Also a series of Fielding's pocket-sized guides called **Fielding's Agenda.** Titles include: London, Paris, Rome, Asia's Top Dive Sites, Diving Indonesia, Surfing Indonesia, Sydney Agenda.

Fodor's Guides (Fodor's Travel Publications/Random House). The **Fodor's Gold Guides** and **Pocket Guides:** The largest all-purpose series with over 100 titles covering countries, cities, and regions all over the world. **Fodor's Exploring Guides:** Well-organized guides with good maps, color photos, detailed information on sights, and lots of interesting facts. Titles include: Paris, Germany, Spain, Rome, Thailand, Australia, Caribbean, Florence, Mexico, Prague, Turkey, China, Egypt, Israel, Greek Islands, Costa Rica, South Africa.

Fodor's Affordable Guides for the cost-conscious traveler include: France, Germany, Great Britain, Italy, Caribbean. **Fodor's Citypacks,** pocket-sized guides with fold-out maps, include: Amsterdam, Berlin, Florence, Hong Kong, Montreal, Paris, Prague, Venice. New to the Fodor family: **Up CLOSE** guides. For budget and adventurous travelers oriented to getting off the beaten path. Available for: Europe, Great Britain, Italy, London, France, Paris.

*Footprints Handbooks (NTC Publishing). The original book in the series is the old reliable South American Handbook. Now the series has changed its name to **Footprints Handbooks**. Other titles following the same format include: Caribbean Islands, Mexico/Central America, India, North Africa, East Africa, Egypt, Sri Lanka, South Africa, Indonesia, Burma, Andalucia, Namibia, Tunisia/Libya. New this year: Argentina, Colombia, Cuba, Goa, Venezuela.

Frommer's Guides (Macmillan). Solid, all-purpose favorite of many travelers. Frommer's comprehensive series covers all price ranges from deluxe to inexpensive for several countries and regions. The **Dollar-a-Day** series is more budget oriented. City guides available for many major cities. New this year: Singapore/Malaysia, China, Provence. **Walking Tour Series** includes: Paris, London, Berlin, Venice, Tokyo, Spain's Favorite Cities. **Food Lover's Companion** Series includes: France, Italy. **Frommer's Irreverent Guides** include: Amsterdam, London, Paris, Virgin Islands. **Frommer's Driving Tours** (Macmillan) present interesting regional driving routes with lots of tips and sightseeing information. Titles include: Britain, France, Ireland, Mexico, Scotland, Austria, Australia, Scandinavia, Switzerland, Western Europe.

*Insight Guides (APA Publications). In-depth background, historical, cultural discussion with good destination information. Over 150 guides to most international destinations. **Insight Pocket Guides** include a fold-out map and cover over 100 locales including Alsace, Corsica, Maldives, Sabah, Sikkim, Algarve, Brussels, Nepal. New this year: Amsterdam, Denmark. **Insight Compact Guides** have expanded beyond Europe to include Bahamas, Bali, Beijing, Cotswolds, Devon, Italian Riviera, Italian Lakes, York, Yorkshire Dales. New this year: Kenya, Jerusalem, Shakespeare Country.

Karen Brown's Country Inns and Itineraries Series (Random House). Offers some great choices throughout Western Europe. Primary selections, organized as part of an itinerary, can be quite expensive but there are usually moderate and sometimes low-cost alternatives as well. Titles include: Austria, France, England, Germany, Ireland, Italy, Spain, Switzerland. New this year: Portugal.

Knopf Guides (Knopf). Heavy focus on art and architecture with lots of photos, drawings, and plans. Titles include: Amsterdam, Istanbul, London, Vienna, Egypt, Provence, Ireland, Louvre, Bali, Loire Valley. New this year: Italy, Seville/Andalusia. New this year are the **Knopf City Guides** for Berlin, Lisbon, London, Madrid, Milan, Paris.

*Let's Go Guides (St. Martin's Press). Still the best all-purpose budget guides around. Thoroughly updated annually. Titles available: Europe, Britain/Ireland, France, Greece, Israel/Egypt, Italy, Mexico, Spain/Portugal/Morocco, Germany/Austria/Switzerland, London, Paris, Eastern Europe, Southeast Asia, Central America, India/Nepal, Ecuador and Galapagos Islands. New this year: Australia, New Zealand.

*Lonely Planet Guides (Lonely Planet Publications). **On a Shoestring Guides:** Ultra-low-budget guides of considerable reputation. Titles: Africa on a Shoestring and similar titles on Eastern Europe, Northeast Asia,

South America, Southeast Asia, West Asia, Central America, Western Europe, Mediterranean Europe, Scandinavian and Baltic Europe, and Middle East. **Travel Survival Kits:** Excellent guides for the adventurous traveler. All-purpose, all price ranges with plenty of low-cost choices. Wide range of titles throughout Africa, Asia, Europe, Australasia, South America. New this year: Bahamas/Turks/Caicos, Germany, Canary Islands, Romania/Moldova. **City Guides** new this year: Cairo, Berlin, Kyoto, Lisbon. **Walking/Trekking Guides** titles include: Australia, New Zealand, Nepal, Patagonia, Switzerland, Turkey. New this year: Walking in Italy. New line of travel literature, **Journeys,** with titles on Australia, Japan, New Guinea, Syria, Jordan, Africa, Central America. New to the Lonely Planet family is a series of diving guides, **Pisces: Diving and Snorkeling Guides** to destinations such as the Great Barrier Reef, Belize, Fiji, Cuba, Honduras, etc.

Maverick Guides (Pelican Publishing). General guidebooks covering accommodations, sights, background, etc. Titles include: Australia, New Zealand, Thailand, Bali and Java, Prague, Berlin, Great Barrier Reef. New this year: Oman, Scotland, Barcelona.

*Michelin Green Guides (Michelin Guides & Maps). Sightseeing guides with maps and historical notes. English language titles cover countries and cities of Western Europe and regions of France, plus Mexico and Canada. New this year: Sicily, Alps. **Michelin Red Guides** are comprehensive, symbol-oriented guides to restaurants and hotels throughout Western Europe. Also: 21 titles in the new **In Your Pocket** series.

*Moon Travel Handbooks (Moon Publications). These guides provide thorough cultural, historical, and political coverage, as well as exhaustive practical information aimed at getting travelers the best value for money. Titles include: Bali, Nepal, Indonesia, Southeast Asia, South Pacific, Tahiti, New Zealand, Fiji, South Korea, Micronesia, Belize, Jamaica, Outback Australia, Thailand, Tibet, Virgin Islands, Costa Rica, Honduras, Dominican Republic, Cuba, Japan, Mexico (plus individual regional guides), Vietnam/Cambodia/Laos, Australia, Alberta and Northwest Territories, Singapore. New this year: Ecuador.

Nelles Guides (Seven Hills Books). Cover culture and history plus basics on lodgings, sights, and getting around. Good maps. Titles available: Cyprus, Morocco, Paris, Spain (North and South), Turkey, India (North and South), Provence, China, Cambodia/Laos, Bali, Philippines, Moscow/St. Petersburg, Corsica, Israel, Portugal, South Africa, Scotland. New this year: Brazil, Norway, Burma (Myanmar), Croatia, Syria/Lebanon.

Off the Beaten Track (Globe Pequot). Good for driving itineraries. Titles include: Spain, Austria, Switzerland, France, Scandinavia, Czech and Slovak Republics, Poland, Western Canada, Greece, Germany.

Passport Regional Guides (Passport Books). This series divides countries/continents into several areas and provides detailed information. Countries/continents regionalized: Africa, China, France, Italy, Indonesia, India, Great Britain, Malaysia, Portugal, Russia.

*Rick Steves' Backdoor Series (John Muir). Offers annually updated budget travel insights by *Transitions Abroad* contributing editor on the cities and regions of Europe and more. Also tips on transport, lodging, and dining. Titles include: Europe, Italy, Scandinavia, France, Great Britain, Baltics and Russia, Asia.

*Rough Guides (Penguin). For independent budget travelers. Rough Guides are written with a political awareness and a social and cultural sensitivity that makes them unique. Titles include many European destinations plus Mexico, Kenya, Morocco, Peru, Yugoslavia, Czech Republic, Poland, Nepal, Holland, Belgium/Luxembourg, Prague, Barcelona, Egypt, Thailand, Tunisia, England, Corsica, Pyrenees, Tuscany/Umbria, Sicily, London, India, Moscow, Romania, Germany, Canada, Costa Rica, Goa, West Africa, China, Sweden, Norway, New Zealand, Jamaica, South Africa. New this year: South Africa, Austria, Central America, Syria. Also new Rough Guide mini series: Dublin, Edinburgh, Madrid.

Sierra Club Adventure Guides (Sierra Club Books). Fine guides to every adventure under the sun. Titles available: **Adventuring in:** Australia, Belize, Caribbean, Central America, East Africa, the Pacific, North Africa, Trekking in Nepal, West Tibet and Bhutan, Indonesia. New this year: Southern Africa.

Time Out (Penguin) From the editors of Time Out in London, these guides detail the practical facts of lodging and eating out as well as arts and entertainment, plus sections for students, gays, lesbians, business travelers. Titles include: London, Paris, Barcelona, Rome, Budapest, Dublin, Sydney.

Travelers' Tales (O'Reilly and Assoc.). Not regular guidebooks with sights and lodgings, but a collection of travelers' tales from experienced travelers. Titles include: Mexico, France, Paris, Thailand, Gutsy Women, India, A Woman's World, Brazil, Hong Kong, Spain, Food, Nepal, Italy. New this year: Italy, Road Within, Dog's World.

Travellers' History Series (Interlink). Concise background on cities and countries. Easy reference. Titles include: England, Scotland, France, Paris, Spain, China, Japan, India, Turkey. New this year: North Africa, London, Italy, the Carribean, Greece, Ireland, Russia.

Treasures and Pleasures of... (Impact Publications). New series designed for people who want to appreciate local cultures by shopping from artists and craftspeople: Caribbean, Hong Kong, Thailand, Indonesia, Singapore and Malaysia, China, Italy, Paris, and the French Riviera.

Ulysses Travel Guides (Ulysses Travel Publications). Thorough guides for the independent traveler exploring all aspects of travel from the practical to outdoor adventures, complemented by a well-researched cultural perspective. Titles include: Canada's Maritime Provinces, Western Canada, Cuba, Portugal, Guadeloupe, Martinique, Panama.

Walking Easy (Globe Pequot). Titles for recreational walkers of all ages include: Austrian Alps, Italian Alps, Swiss Alps, French Alps.

Planning Guides

1998 International Travel Health Guide by Stuart R. Rose. ($19.95 plus s/h from Travel Medicine, Inc., 351 Pleasant St., Suite 312, Northampton, MA 01060; 800-872-8633). Updated annually in spring; recommended by U.S. State Department.

Adventure Holidays 1998: Your Complete Guide to Thousands of Active Vacations Worldwide (Vacation Work). Bicycling, windsurfing, canoeing, and more.

Adventures in Good Company: The Complete Guide to Women's Tours and Outdoor Trips by Thalia Zepatos (The Eighth Mountain Press). Profiles more than 100 companies worldwide that offer trips for women.

Air Courier Bargains: How to Travel Worldwide for Next to Nothing by Kelly Monaghan (6th ed. $17.50 postpaid from

The Intrepid Traveler, P.O. Box 438, New York, NY 10034). Complete guide to courier travel in U.S. and around the world.

Archaeology Abroad, 31-34 Gordon Sq., London WC1H 0PY, England. Three annual bulletins list worldwide archaeological digs with details of staffing needs and costs; (011) 44-171-504-4750, fax (011) 44-171-383-2572; arch.abroad@ucl. ac.uk, www.britarch.ac.uk/cba/archabroad.

The Archaeology Handbook: A Field Manual and Resource Guide by Bill McMillon (John Wiley & Sons). Comprehensive how-to and where-to guide for volunteers.

Big Book of Adventure Travel, by James Simmons (John Muir Publications). A source book of worldwide guided adventure tours.

Bugs, Bites and Bowels by Dr. J. Howarth (Globe Pequot). A Cadogan series guide on healthy travel covering prevention, diagnosis, and cure.

Campus Lodging Guide (Campus Travel Service). Details on hundreds of inexpensive accommodations on university campuses throughout the world.

Consolidators: Air Travel's Bargain Basement. A 73-page list of U.S. and Canadian companies that buy blocks of seats from the airlines at discounts and pass savings on to the consumer. $9.95 postpaid from The Intrepid Traveler, P.O. Box 438, New York, NY 10034.

Damron Address Book by Ian Phillips. (Damron Co., annual). The original gay travel guide, published since 1964. Lists over 10,000 gay-friendly B and Bs, bars, cafes, and more, in North America and major European cities.

Do's and Taboos Around the World: A Guide to International Behavior by Roger Axtell (John Wiley & Sons). Advice for the business and pleasure traveler on what to do and not to do in other cultures. Titles include: Gestures: Do's and Taboos of Body Language Around the World, Do's and Taboos of Using English Around the World.

Foiling Pickpockets and Bag Snatchers and Other Travel Related Crimes or Scams. A guide to traveling safely, 24 pp. Covers over 200 scams, pickpocket tricks, and other safety tips. Order from: Travel Companion Exchange, Inc., P.O. Box 833, Amityville, NY 11701-0833. One copy $4, two copies $6.

Ford's Freighter Travel Guide (Ford's Travel Guides). Very informative. Updated semi-annually.

Hostelling International (Hostelling International—International Youth Hostel Federation). Lists nearly 5,000 hostels in over 70 countries for all ages. Two annual volumes: Europe and Africa/Americas/Asia/Pacific.

Hostels Canada by Paul Karr (Globe Pequot Press). At-a-glance ratings of 200 hostels for overall quality as well as hospitality, safety, cleanliness, and setting.

Hot Spots. (Fielding Worldwide). Compendium of stories complementing World's Most Dangerous Places (see below).

International Assn. for Medical Assistance to Travelers; iamat@sentex.net, www.sentex.net/~iamat.Provides a directory of English-speaking doctors in 500 cities in 120 countries. Also information on health risks and immunizations worldwide, detailed information on tropical disease, climatic, and sanitary conditions.

International Travel and Health 1998 (World Health Organization, 49 Sheridan Avenue, Albany, NY 12210; www.who.org). Vaccination requirements and health advice.

*A Journey of One's Own: Uncommon Advice for the Independent Woman Traveler by

Thalia Zepatos (The Eighth Mountain Press). 2nd ed. Detailed advice on practical matters for women traveling abroad alone.

Ordnance Survey Maps, Atlases and Guides Catalogue 1998. Ordnance Survey Customer Orders: (011) 44-1703-792910, fax (011) 44-1703-792602; paulsahrp@ordsvy.gov.uk, www.ordsvy. gov.uk. Britain's national mapping agency produces detailed maps and atlases for U.K. and Commonwealth countries as well as specialty guides—cycling, motoring, etc.

Passport to World Band Radio (International Broadcasting Services). Hour-by-hour, country-by-country listings for world band radio programming.

The Pocket Doctor: Your Ticket to Good Health While Traveling by Dr. S. Bezruchka (Mountaineers). 2nd ed. A compact health guide for the traveler.

The Practical Nomad: How to Travel Around the World by Edward Hasbrouck (Moon Travel Handbooks). Essential information on airfare strategies, travel documents, information sources, and more.

Rough Guide: First Time Europe and **Rough Guide: First Time Asia** (Rough Guides). Practical information providing lots of tips and advice for the novice traveling in these two areas.

Rough Guide to the Internet and World Wide Web (Rough Guides). Listings and web sites on many topics, including much travel-related information.

Shawguides (www.shawguides.com). Shaw Guides' educational travel guides are now available exclusively on the internet: descriptions of more than 2,500 cooking schools, photo workshops, writers' conferences, art and craft workshops, learning and language vacations, and golf, tennis, and water sports,

schools and camps worldwide. Searchable by keyword, name, state, country, region, month, and specialty. Site also provides a calendar of over 5,000 upcoming programs and lists organizations and publications relating to each subject.

Single-Friendly Travel Directory, edited by Dianne Redfern. Frequently updated listing of hundreds of tour companies, cruise lines, lodges, spas, resorts, and travel clubs whose functions and pricing are attractive to single and solo travelers. Included with membership to Connecting: Solo Travel Network. Connecting, P.O. Box 29088, 1996 W. Broadway, Vancouver, BC V6J 5C2, Canada; (800) 557-1757; www.travel-wise.com/solo.

Specialty Travel Index. Biannual directory/magazine of special interest and adventure travel listing over 600 tour operators worldwide including addresses, phone, and fax numbers. $10 per year for 2 issues from Specialty Travel Index, 305 San Anselmo Ave., San Anselmo, CA 94960; (415) 459-4900, fax (415) 459-4974; www.specialtytravel.com.

Tips for the Savvy Traveler by Deborah Burns and Sarah May Clarkson (Storey Publishing). Hundreds of valuable tips from planning to coming home.

Tips on Renting a Car. Council of Better Business Bureau, 4200 Wilson Blvd., Arlington, VA 22209; (703) 276-0100. $2 with long SASE. Guide to getting the most service for your money from car rental companies. Ask for their other "Tips On" publications.

Transcultural Study Guide. Volunteers in Asia. 1987. $7.95 plus $1.70 postage from VIA Press, P.O. Box 4543, Stanford, CA 93409; www.volasia.org. Hundreds of questions that lead a traveler toward an understanding of a new culture.

Transformative Adventures, Vacations and Retreats by John Benson (New Millennium).

Worldwide organizations offering programs for personal change—meditation retreats, health spas, etc.

Travel Alone & Love It: A Flight Attendant's Guide to Solo Travel by Sharon B. Wingler. (Chicago Spectrum Press, $14.95). Instructions on how to plan your own successful solo journey.

Travel and Learn by Evelyn Kaye (Blue Panda). Describes more than 2,000 vacations in arts, archaeology, language, music, nature, and wildlife.

Travel by Cargo Ship (Cadogon).

Vacation Home Exchange and Hospitality Guide by John Kimbrough (Kimco Communications). Call (503) 524-0956; JCKimb@aol.com. Guide to opportunities for vacation home exchanges all over the world. Information on associations/agencies that will put you in touch with contacts.

Volunteer Vacations by Bill McMillon (Chicago Review Press). 5th ed. More than 500 opportunities worldwide.

Women's Traveller '97 by Gina M. Gatta, Ian Philips. (Damron Company). 8th ed.

Work your Way Around the World by Susan Griffith (Peterson's Guides). 7th ed. Excellent first-hand information, by country, on short-term jobs. By *Transitions Abroad*'s contributing editor.

World's Most Dangerous Places by Robert Young Pelton and Coskun Aral (Fielding Worldwide). First-hand experiences, advice on avoiding scams, regions to be aware of, protecting yourself, etc. Some areas covered: Gulf States, Golden Triangle, Cuba, Eastern Turkey.

Africa

Series: Bradt, Berlitz, *Blue Guides, *Cadogan, *Culture Shock!, Customs and Etiquette, Fodor, *Footprints, Frommer, Knopf, Insight, *Let's Go, *Lonely Planet (Pisces), *Michelin, Nelles, *Rough Guides, Sierra Club, Traveller's History.

Africa's Top Wildlife Countries by Mark W. Nolting (Global Travel Publishers). Excellent reference by an authority on African wildlife.

Africa: Literary Companion by Oona Strathern (Passport Books). Compilation of literature, background, and cultural information.

African Customs and Manners by E. Devine and N. Braganti (St. Martin's Press). Dos and taboos on the African continent.

Beyond Safaris by Kevin Danaher (Africa World Press). A guide to building people-to-people ties with Africans.

Bicycling in Africa by David Mozer (International Bicycle Fund, 4887 Columbia Dr. S., Apt. T-8, Seattle, WA 98109-1919; Tel./fax (206) 767-0848; ibike@ibike.org, www.ibike.org). How to do it, with supplements on 17 separate countries.

Guide to South Africa by Philip Briggs (Bradt Publishing). Comprehensive guide to the new South Africa.

Kilimanjaro and Mount Kenya: Climbing and Trekking Guide by Cameron M. Burns. (Mountaineers).

Namibia: Independent Traveler's Guide by Scott and Lucinda Bradshaw (Hippocrene). Essential for anyone making their way across the country's vast expanse.

Rafiki Books, (45 Rawson Ave., Camden, ME 04843; 207-236-4244, fax 207-236-6253): Distributors of over 200 titles on Africa.

The Safari Companion: A Guide to Watching African Mammals by Richard Estes (Chelsea Green Publishing). Good reference.

The Budget Travel Top Five
Choosing Countries to Explore Independently

By Terry Redding

Everyone, from friends to guidebook editors, has an opinion about the "best" countries for independent, low-budget travel. My own criteria for choosing my next destination include overall diversity of things to see and do, ease of travel, history, geography, cost, safety, and a nebulous "fun factor."

Thailand. Thailand comes in at number one. The food and accommodations are abundant and cheap. There is much to explore in the ruins of Sukhothai and Ayutthaya. Colorful Buddhist temples dot the country. Buses, trains, boats, and hitchhiking are all excellent. The south coast has beaches, islands, and small villages to explore. The north has mountains with fascinating hill tribe villages to visit, and there are a number of national parks throughout the country.

Outside of Bangkok traveling alone is relatively safe and most things run smoothly. Even in crowded Bangkok you should have few problems. The local people—especially those beyond the few cities—enjoy talking to visitors. Bring a phrasebook and dictionary and you'll never be bored.

Turkey. Toss *Midnight Express* out the window. The Turks are friendly, generous, kind, hospitable, and outgoing—again, once you get outside the big cities. The area's fascinating past is always laid out in front of you. You can pull off the road and walk among the ruins of an ancient Greek city, joining goats and sheep wandering nonchalantly across 2,500-year-old cobblestones. The country includes lovely coastlines and such compelling oddities as the "Cotton Castles" at Pamukkale and windswept pinnacles and peaks in the Cappadocia valley region.

You are expected to bargain for everything in Turkey, but the amounts bargained are usually small. Accommodations in people's homes ("Pensiyons") can be had for a few dollars. Buses go everywhere, all the time. Hitching is quite good in certain areas, and you can often catch a passing truck or tractor to take you to sites off the main roads. The food is spicy and ranges far beyond kebabs. The coffee is thick and delicious.

People will offer you tea and sometimes a meal in their home and will help you if you appear to be in distress. "You can pay me tomorrow" is a phrase you will hear more than once in the smaller towns. Although the country is safe, women travelers should dress conservatively. A dictionary and phrasebook make a significant difference. Someone will always show you the way to a bus, pension, or restaurant.

New Zealand. New Zealand is about as close to paradise as I have found. This would not be an unusual day: You hitchhike in the morning and the first car takes you out of the way to see a beautiful panorama. The second ride offers to buy you lunch. The third ride gives you the names of several interesting places to visit as well as the addresses of a few friends. The last ride of the day puts you up for the night and tosses in a hearty dinner or breakfast for good measure.

The country remains mostly unspoiled. National parks dot both main islands and offer plenty of walking and overnight bunkhouses. New Zealand is not only the home of bungee jumping and blackwater rafting, it is one of the rare colonized countries where the natives were not exiled to reservations.

Bus transport can be a bit limited but hitching is great. Budget accommodations in youth hostels and backpackers (private hostels) are around $15 per night. There is also abundant camping at the motor camps and wherever else you may want to pitch a tent. You can drink the water in most places—right out of the streams and lakes.

Ireland. The pubs are the main social focus, although there are plenty of parks and other public areas to enjoy. The countryside can be breathtaking and the history is fascinating. Music plays a vital part in the culture.

The few drawbacks are the weather and occasional expensiveness. The food is filling (if not exciting) and there are plenty of hostels, campgrounds, and B and Bs. Train lines and buses are plentiful and hitchhiking is renowned.

Costa Rica is easily accessible, affordable, and especially beloved by nature fans. Mountains, beaches, jungles, volcanoes, islands, parks, parks, and more parks are all main attractions. The country is a very safe haven in a recently unsettled region. The climate varies from the Pacific coast to the central rainforest mountains to the Caribbean jungle coast.

Buses get you around efficiently and hitching is great, although the locals don't really understand the concept and will often take you to the bus station. National park tours can be arranged from San Jose, or you can do them on your own. The country in general is inexpensive except for the $15 fee to enter the parks. Accommodations are usually in small hotels or family pensions for under $10. Food is an interesting mix in San Jose, but expect mostly rice and beans outside the large towns. This is probably the safest country south of the border and single women should have few problems.

At least a dozen countries could fit into the next five places on the list. Malaysia is inexpensive, very easy to get around in, and beautiful. Hungary is a place with lots to see and do and eat. Australia is of course a place where you can experience amazing nature. Germany offers much: castles, cathedrals, culture, great hitchhiking, and camping. But it's costly. Italy is a personal favorite of mine for the food, wine, history, art, and everything else. France, Spain, and Portugal are also on my list. Mexico is vastly underrated as an independent destination. It would probably be on most people's top five list; I just haven't explored enough there yet for it to qualify. The only way to find your favorite place is to go yourself and find out.

Planning Your Trip: The Practical Details

Costa Rica. You can easily get by with $30 daily, with the exception of park fees. Accommodations run $5-$15 (hot water costs more), meals are $2-$6, and buses to anywhere are rarely more than $10. Stop in San Jose at the National Parks office, Avanida 8 and Calle 25, next to the offices of the Ministerio de Recursos Naturales, Energia y Minas for maps and brochures. Look for flight bargains on Aero Costa Rica, (800) 237-6274. For more information call the Costa Rica Tourism Board at (800) 327-7033.

Ireland. A daily budget is $20-$35. Bring rain gear and lightweight luggage. Accommodations start at $10 and can go quite a bit higher. The youth hostels are a bit less and are close to their traditional roots. Cycling is a favorite way to get around and rentals are available. Best bet for food is to buy it yourself in the supermarkets and shops. The buses will steadily nip at your budget, so look for discounts and passes. For more details contact the Irish Tourist Board, 757 Third Ave., 19th Floor, New York, NY 10017; (800) 223-6470.

New Zealand. Daily budgets will depend on how rough you want to go. You can get by camping and hitching and spend $10 a day. Hosteling will cost up to $20 a day, and eating at restaurants will tack on at least another $10. Accommodations run from free camping to $10 hostels to $20 B and Bs. Bus trips can cost $5-$20, and various deals are available on private buses (such as Kiwi Experience) that loop the islands. Bring all-weather gear. Stop at the visitor's information center at Aotea Square in Auckland for information and maps. For brochures contact the New Zealand Tourist Board at (800) 388-5494, or write them at 501 Santa Monica Blvd., Suite 300, Santa Monica, CA 90401. Call between 8 a.m. and 5 p.m. Pacific Standard Time to speak with a trip consultant; they are open 24 hours for brochure requests.

Thailand. Unless you are extravagant, you can live well in Thailand for $10-$20 a day. Accommodations are usually under $5 at basic but clean guest houses. Food should only cost you a couple of dollars at street stalls and simple restaurants, and trains and buses will only be a few dollars for most day trips. The food available at the street stalls is generally safe. There are some really nice guesthouses scattered around the country, and in the beach areas you can find some good values. For details contact the Tourist Authority of Thailand, 5 World Trade Center, Suite 3443, New York, NY 10048; (212) 432-0431.

The tourist office in Bangkok, which is reasonably helpful, is on Ratchadamnoen Nok Avenue (011-66-282-1143). Consult the English-language Bangkok Post for items of interest to travelers. Spend a few dollars on the Thailand Highway Map published by the Highway Department Club of the Thailand Department of Highways. The "Tour'n Guide" maps are cheaper but less accurate.

Turkey. You can spend as little as $10 a day and get by quite well. Accommodations can be a couple of dollars in the off season, meals are a dollar or so, and buses run $5-$10 for most medium destinations (second class). Lonely Planet Publications puts out a good guidebook as well as a trekking guide. For more details and region-specific booklets, try the Turkish Government Tourist Office, 821 U.N. Plaza, New York, NY 10017; (212) 687-2194, fax (212) 599-7568.

Spectrum Guides (Interlink Publishing). Beautifully photographed, good cultural and background information. Available for: Uganda, Jordan, United Arab Emirates, Maldives, Pakistan, India, Mauritius, Tanzania.

Touring Southern Africa (Thomas Cook) Independent holidays in South Africa, Botswana, Namibia, Lesotho, Swaziland, Mozambique, Zimbabwe.

Albania

Series: *Blue Guides, Bradt.

Antarctica

Series: Bradt, *Cadogan, *Lonely Planet.

Asia

Series: *Blue Guides, *Cadogan, *Culture Shock!, Customs and Etiquette, Fielding, Fodor, *Footprints, Frommer, *Insight Guides, *Let's Go, *Lonely Planet (Pisces), *Moon Handbooks, Passport Regional Guides, Sierra Club, *Rough Guides, Traveler' Tales, Travellers' History, Treasures and Pleasures of. . .

*****Asia Through the Back Door** by Rick Steves and Bob Effertz (John Muir Publications). Inexpensive ways to experience the region.

Asia Overland by Mark Elliott and Will Klass (Trailblazer). Routes and planning for overland options across Asia.

First-Time Asia (Rough Guides) Complete trip planning for low budget independent travelers.

Southeast Asia : Literary Companion by Alistair Dingwell (Passport Books). Compilation of literature, background, and cultural information.

Teaching English in Southeast Asia by Jerry O'Sullivan (Passport Books). Practical information on finding a job, teaching and living in Cambodia, Hong Kong, Indonesia, Malaysia, Singapore, Thailand, Laos, Philippines, and Vietnam.

Thailand, Malaysia, Singapore by Rail by Brian McPhee (Bradt).

The Traveler's Guide to Asian Customs and Manners by Elizabeth Devine and Nancy Braganti (St. Martin's Press).

Australia

Series: Berlitz, *Culture Shock!, Driving Tours, Eyewitness, Fielding, Fodor, Frommer, *Insight Guides, Let's Go, *Lonely Planet (Pisces) Maverick, *Moon, Nelles, *Rough Guides, Sierra Club, Time Out, Treasures and Pleasures of... (Lonely Planet also covers each state plus regions: Victoria, N.S.W. and A.C.T., Queensland, Northern Territory, South Australia, Western Australia, Tasmania and the Outback, Great Barrier Reef, and Sydney and Melbourne.)

Australia and New Zealand by Rail by Colin Taylor (Bradt Publishing).

The Australian Bed and Breakfast Book by J. and J. Thomas (Pelican). Stay in private homes, on farms, and in guest houses with friendly hosts.

Bushwalking in Australia by John and Monica Chapman (Lonely Planet Publications).

Cycling Australia by Ian Duckworth (Bicycle Books).

Stepping Lightly on Australia by Shirley LaPlanche (Globe Pequot). Traveler's guide to ecotourism in this land of diverse flora and fauna.

A Traveler's Literary Companion edited by Robert Ross (Whereabouts Press). Modern short stories by Australian authors.

Austria

Series: Berlitz, *Blue Guides, Citywalks, Driving Tours, Exploring Rural Europe, Eyewitness, Fodor, Frommer, Insight Guides, Karen Brown, Knopf, *Let's Go, *Lonely Planet, *Michelin, Off the Beaten Track, *Rick Steves, *Rough Guides.

Austria: Charming Small Hotels by Paul Wade (Hunter). A selection of small hotels with character.

Walking Easy in the Austrian Alps (Globe Pequot). Hiking guide for active adults.

Baltic Countries

Series: *Bradt, *Insight Guides, *Lonely Planet, *Rick Steves.

Bulgaria

Series: *Rough Guides.

Essential Bulgaria by David Ash (Passport Books). Pocket size guide.

Canada

Series: *Access, Berlitz, *Culture Shock!, Fodor, Frommer, *Insight Guides, *Let's Go, *Lonely Planet, *Michelin, *Moon, Off the Beaten Track, Nelles, *Rough Guides, Sierra Club, Ulysses.

Canada Campground Directory (Woodall/Globe Pequot). Complete guide to campgrounds and RV parks.

Canada Compass Guide (Random House). History, background, maps, and resource information. Nicely illustrated.

Canadian Bed & Breakfast Guide by Gerda Pantel (Penguin). 1,500 choices including chalets, farmhouses, and city homes.

Canadian Rockies by Graeme Pole (Altitude). Informative and thorough guide.

Cycling Canada by John M. Smith (Bicycle Books).

Guide to Eastern Canada and **Guide to Western Canada** by Frederick Pratson (Globe Pequot). Both guides provide thorough information on all aspects of travel in Canada.

Maritime Provinces Off the Beaten Path by Trudy Fong (Globe Pequot).

Nova Scotia & The Maritimes by Bike: 21 Tours Geared for Discovery by Walter Sienko (Mountaineers).

Series of Canadian Guides (Formac Publishing/Seven Hills). Titles available for Nova Scotia, New Brunswick, Prince Edward Island, Manitoba, Halifax, Ottawa, Toronto.

Toronto Ultimate Guide and **Vancouver Ultimate Guide** (Chronicle). Comprehensive guides covering all aspects of travel to these 2 Canadian cities.

Trans-Canada Rail Guide by Bryn Thomas (Trailblazer).

Vancouver Best Places by K. Wilson (Sasquatch Books). 2nd ed.

Caribbean/West Indies

Series: *Access, Baedeker, Berlitz, *Cadogan, Fielding, Fodor, *Footprints,

Frommer, *Insight Guides, *Lonely Planet (Pisces), *Moon, Nelles, *Rough Guides, Sierra Club, Traveller's History, Treasures and Pleasures of..., Ulysses.

Adventure Guide to ... Barbados, Bermuda, Dominican Republic, Jamaica, Puerto Rico Trinidad/Tobago, and **the Virgin Islands** (Hunter Publications). Practical guides for the adventurous traveler.

Best Dives in the Caribbean by J. and J. Huber (Hunter Publications). 2nd ed. Covers 24 islands.

Caribbean Literary Companion by James Ferguson (Passport Books). Compilation of literature, background and cultural information.

Caribbean Ports of Call by Kay Showker (Globe Pequot). A guide to the ports of the Caribbean.

Diving Bermuda by Jesse Cancelmo and Mike Strohofer (Aqua Quest Publications). Diving sites, information on marine life, shipwrecks, and travel in Bermuda.

Diving Off the Beaten Track by Bob Burgess (Aqua Quest Publications). Diving in various Caribbean destinations.

Undiscovered Islands of the Caribbean by Burl Willes (John Muir Publications). Undiscovered is a relative term, but good ideas abound.

Central America

Series: Bradt, *Culture Shock!, Fodor, *Footprints, Frommer, *Insight Guides, Knopf, *Let's Go, *Lonely Planet (Pisces), *Moon, *New Key, *Rough Guides, Sierra Club, Ulysses.

Adventures in Nature Series... (John Muir) Available for Guatemala, Belize, Costa Rica and Honduras. Focus on adventure and outdoor travel.

Choose Costa Rica by John Howells (Gateway Books). Wintering and retirement in Costa Rica (includes Guatemala).

Costa Rica Traveler's Literary Companion by B. Ras (Whereabouts Press). Compilation of short stories by Costa Rican authors.

Costa Rica's National Parks and Preserves: A Visitor's Guide by Joseph Franke. (Mountaineers).

Costa Rica: A Natural Destination by Ree Strange Sheck (John Muir). Focus on nature travel.

The Costa Rica Traveler by Ellen Searby (Windham Bay Press). 4th ed. Good background notes. All price ranges. User-friendly. Over 500 hotels, lodges. Nature travel.

Diving Belize by Ned Middleton (Aqua Quest Publications). Diving sites, information on marine life and travel in Belize.

Explore Belize by Harry S. Pariser (Hunter Publications). 4th ed. Practical guide for the adventurous traveler.

***Guatemala Guide, Belize Guide, Costa Rica Guide** by Paul Glassman and Travel Line Press. (Open Road). Comprehensive guides for these 3 countries.

Honduras and Bay Islands Guide by J. Panet (Open Road). Good all-around guide.

Latin America by Bike: A Complete Touring Guide by W. Siekno (Mountaineers). From Mexico through Central America to the tip of Argentina.

Maya Road by J. Conrad (Hunter Publications). Covers Yucatan, Belize, and Guatemala. Thorough guide to travel.

New Key to Belize by Stacy Ritz (Ulysses). Good detailed information on Belize.

On Your Own in El Salvador by Jeff Brauer. New. Comprehensive.

* **The New Key to Costa Rica** by Beatrice Blake and Anne Becher (Ulysses Press). Good all-around guide to Costa Rica, now in its 11th edition. Blake is a resident of Costa Rica and gives knowledgeable, up-to-date advice.

Traveller's Survival Kit: Central America by Emily Hatchwell and Simon Calder (Vacation Work). Extensive practical information and town-by-town guide to the 7 countries of this region.

China/Hong Kong

Series: Berlitz, *Blue Guides, *Culture Shock!, Customs and Etiquette, Fodor, Frommer, *Insight, *Lonely Planet, Maverick, *Moon Handbooks, Nelles, *Rough Guides, Travelers' Tales, Traveller's History, Treasures and Pleasures of....

China Bound by Anne F. Thurston (National Academy Press). Prepares long- and short-term visitors for everyday life in China.

China by Bike: Taiwan, Hong Kong, China's East Coast by Roger Grigsby (Mountaineers).

China by Rail by Douglas Streatfeild-James (Trailblazer).

China Regional Guides (Passport Books). Includes Fujian, Xian, Beijing, Yunnan.

Essential Chinese for Travelers by Fan Zhilong (China Books). Basic phrasebook, dictionary, and cassette, includes sections on hotels, transportation, money, food, and business. Rev. 1996.

Silk Route by Rail by Dominic Streatfeild-James (Trailblazer).

Trekking in Russia and Central Asia: A Traveler's Guide by Frith Maier (Mountaineers).

Cuba

Series: Berlitz, Bradt, *Footprints, *Insight Guides, *Lonely Planet (Pisces), *Moon, Passport, Ulysses.

Guide to Cuba by Stephen Fallon (Bradt Publishing).

Reader's Companion to Cuba edited by Alan Ryan (Harcourt Brace). Selection of travel writing about the island.

Czech and Slovak Republics

Series: Berlitz, *Blue Guides, Citywalks, *Culture Shock!, Customs & Etiquette, Eyewitness, Fodor, Frommer, *Insight Guides, Knopf, *Let's Go, *Lonely Planet, *Michelin, Nelles, Off the Beaten Track, *Rough Guides, Time Out.

Prague Traveler's Literary Companion by P. Wilson (Whereabouts Press). Compilation of short stories by Prague writers.

Europe

Series: *Access, Berlitz, *Blue Guides, Bradt, *Cadogan, Fielding, Fodor, Frommer, *Insight Guides, *Let's Go, *Lonely Planet, *Michelin, Nelles, *Rick Steves, *Rough Guides.

Best European Travel Tips by John Whitman (Harper Collins). 2,001 tips for saving money, time, and trouble in Europe.

Cambridge Guide to the Museums of Europe (Cambridge Univ. Press). Over 2,000 entries, includes art collections and cathedral treasures.

Central & Eastern Europe: Literary Companion by James Naughton (Passport Books). Compilation of literature, background, and cultural information.

Eastern Europe by Rail by Rob Dodson (Globe Pequot). Practical guide.

Euroad: Complete Guide to Motoring in Europe by Bert Lief (VLE Ltd.). Maps include driving times and distances in miles; documents required.

***Europe 101: History and Art for the Traveler** by Rick Steves and Gene Openshaw (John Muir Publications). Wonderful.

Europe by Bike: 18 Tours Geared for Discovery by Karen and Terry Whitehill (Mountaineers). 2nd ed.

Europe by Eurail, 1998-99 by G. and L. Ferguson (Globe Pequot). How to tour Europe by train.

Europe for Free: Hundreds of Free Things to Do in Europe by Brian Butler (Mustang Publishing).

***Europe Through the Back Door** by Rick Steves (John Muir Publications). The best "how-to" and preparation book for Europe with lots of useful hints and information.

***Europe Through the Back Door Travel Newsletter**, Rick Steves, ed. Quarterly. Free from Europe Through the Back Door, Inc., 120 4th Ave. N., Edmonds, WA 98020. Our favorite travel newsletter.

Exploring Europe by RV by Dennis and Tina Jaffe (Globe Pequot). Practical guide to RV travel in Europe.

Europe's Wonderful Little Hotels & Inns: The Continent by Hilary Rubinstein and Carolyn Raphael (St. Martin's Press).

First-Time Europe: Everything You Need to Know Before You Go by Louis CasaBianca (Rough Guides). Complete trip-planning resource for low-budget independent travelers.

***Mona Winks: A Guide to Enjoying Europe's Top Museums** by Rick Steves and Gene Openshaw (John Muir Publications).

Moto Europa by Eric Bredesen (Seren Publishing). P.O. Box 1212, Dubuque, IA 52004; (800) 387-6728. In-depth details on renting, driving, buying, and selling a car.

On the Rails Europe edited by Melissa Shales (Passport Books). Routes, maps, transport information.

***Rick Steve's Europe Through the Back Door Phrase Books** (John Muir). French, Italian, German, Spanish/Portuguese, and French/Italian/German (3 in 1).

Ski Europe by Charles Leocha (World Leisure). Rev. 1997.

Teaching English in Eastern and Central Europe by Robert Lynes (Passport Books). Practical information on finding a job, teaching and living in Czech Republic, Slovakia, Poland, Hungary, Romania, and Bulgaria.

Thomas Cook European Timetable. $27.95 plus $4.50 shipping from Forsyth Travel Library, Inc., 1750 E. 131 St., P.O. Box 480800, Kansas City, MO 64146; (816) 942-9050, (800) 367-7984; www.forsyth.com. Rail schedules for over 50,000 trains on every European and British main line.

Travel Guide to Jewish Europe by Ben Frank (Pelican). Jewish historical sites, Holocaust memorials, neighborhoods, restaurants, etc.

Traveler's Guide to European Camping by Mike and Teri Church (Rolling Homes Press). Explore Europe economically at your own pace using an RV or tent. Lots of campground listings; Call (425) 822-7846.

Traveling Europe's Trains by Jay Brunhouse (Pelican). Detailed itineraries.

Understanding Europeans by Stuart Miller (John Muir Publications). Insights into European behavior, historical and cultural heritage.

Walking Europe from Top to Bottom by Susan Margolis and Ginger Harmon (Sierra Club Books). Follows the Grande Randonnée Cinqu on a 107-day journey. (You can do smaller portions.)

Walks (VLE Ltd.). Street-by-street walking maps through 13 principal European cities.

France

Series: *Access, Berlitz, *Blue Guides, *Cadogan, Citywalks, *Culture Shock!, Customs and Etiquette, Driving Tours, Daytrips, Exploring Rural Europe, Eyewitness, Fielding, Fodor, Frommer, *Insight Guides, Karen Brown, Knopf, *Let's Go, *Lonely Planet, *Michelin, Nelles, Off the Beaten Track, Passport Regional Handbooks, *Rick Steves, *Rough Guides, Time Out, Traveller's History, Ulysses.

Alastair Sawday's Special Paris Hotels / Alastair Sawday's French Bed & Breakfast (Alastair Sawday Publishing). Accommodations with character, comfort, and value.

Bed and Breakfasts of Character and Charm in France (Rivages Guides).

Camping and Caravaning France (Michelin Publications). Campgrounds, town plans, location information, plus facilities.

Cheap Sleeps in Paris and **Cheap Eats in Paris** by Sandra A. Gustafson (Chronicle). Guides to inexpensive lodgings, restaurants, bistros, and brasseries.

France by Bike: 14 Tours Geared for Discovery by Karen and Terry Whitehall. (Mountaineers).

France: Literary Companion by John Edmondson (Passport Books). Compilation of literature, background, and cultural information.

Hotels and Country Inns of Charm and Character in France (Rivages Guides).

An Insider's Guide to French Hotels: $50-$90 a Night for Two by Margo Classé (Wilson Publishing). Covers centrally located hotels in many French cities.

Literary Cafés of Paris by Noel Riley Fitch (Starrhill Press). Sit in Parisian cafes and read about the writers who made them famous.

On the Rails Around France, Belgium, Netherlands and Luxembourg by Roger Thomas (Passport Books). Routes, maps, transport information.

Paris for Free (Or Extremely Cheap) by Mark Beffart (Mustang Publishing).

Paris Inside Out by Anglophone S.A. An insider's guide for resident students and discriminating visitors on living in the French capital.

Paris-Anglophone by David Applefield. Print and online directory of essential contacts for English speakers in Paris.

The Unknown South of France: A History Buff's Guide by Henry and Margaret Reuss

(Harvard Common Press). A guide to the history and culture of the south of France.

Walking Easy in the French Alps (Globe Pequot). Hiking guide.

Germany

Series: Berlitz, *Blue Guides, *Cadogan, Citywalks, Customs and Etiquette, Daytrips, Driving Tours, Exploring Rural Europe, Fodor, Frommer, Insight Guides, Karen Brown, *Let's Go, *Michelin, Off the Beaten Track, *Rick Steves, *Rough Guides, Traveller's History.

Germany by Bike: 20 Tours Geared for Discovery by Nadine Slavinski (Mountaineers).

Traveler's Guide to Jewish Germany by Hirsch and Lopez (Pelican). Sites, synagogues, memorials, and exhibitions.

Greece

Series: Berlitz, *Blue Guides, *Cadogan, Customs and Etiquette, Exploring Rural Europe, Eyewitness, Fodor, Frommer, *Insight Guides, Knopf, *Let's Go, *Lonely Planet, *Michelin, Nelles, Off the Beaten Track, *Rough Guides, Traveller's History.

Greece: A Traveler's Literary Companion, edited by Artemis Leontis (Whereabouts Press). Modern short stories by Greek authors.

Greek Island Hopping by Richard F. Poffley (Passport Books). Valuable advice on ferries, island itinerary planning.

Hungary

Series: Berlitz, *Blue Guides, Customs and Etiquette, Fodor, Frommer, *Insight Guides, *Lonely Planet, Nelles, *Rough Guides, Time Out.

People to People Czech-Slovakia, Hungary, Bulgaria by Jim Haynes (Zephyr Press). Latest in a series of books on Eastern Europe for travelers who want to experience life as locals live it. Lists over 1,000 locals to contact.

Indian Subcontinent

Series: Berlitz, *Cadogan, *Culture Shock!, Customs and Etiquette, Fodor, *Footprints, Frommer, *Insight, *Let's Go, *Lonely Planet, *Moon Handbooks, Nelles, Passport Regional Guides, *Rough Guides, Travelers' Tales, Traveller's History.

Bhutan: Himalayan Kingdom by Booz (Passport Books). Focuses on background, history, etc. (not the practical).

India by Stanley Wolpert (Univ. of California Press). A concise and comprehensive guide to Indian history and culture by an authority.

India by Rail by Royston Ellis (Bradt).

India by Rail (Hunter Publishing).

India: Literary Companion by Simon Weightman (Passport Books). Compilation of literature, background, and cultural information.

Passport Regional India Guides (Passport Books). All-purpose guides with planned itineraries and good orientation. Titles include: Museums of India, Bhutan and Bombay/Goa, Delhi, Agrand Pakistan, Jaipur, The Hill Stations of India, The Kathmandu Valley.

Silk Route by Rail by Dominic Streatfeild-James (Trailblazer).

Driving in Europe
Rent, Lease, or Buy? Plus the Rules of the Road

By Rick Steves

Every year, as Europe's train prices go up, car rental becomes more economical. Two-somes pay about the same whether they rent a car or buy railpasses; three or four people travel cheaper by car. Consider renting if your trip is less than three weeks, leasing if your trip is three weeks or longer, or getting a rail and drive pass if you'd like to mix train and car travel.

Rentals are cheapest when arranged in the U.S., either through a travel agent or directly with the car company. For the best deal, ask for a weekly rate with unlimited mileage. Prices vary from company to company, month to month, and country to country. Shop around, using the toll-free numbers below. If you're older than 70 or younger than 23, check all the car companies (ages vary) or consider leasing, which has less stringent age restrictions. Take advantage of "open jaws" possibilities to save you rental days and avoid big-city driving.

Pick Up Options

You can normally pick up and drop off a car at any of the rental company's offices in a country. Know the location of all the offices so you'll understand your options. There is usually about a $100 fee to drop in another country. You'll find some pleasing and some outrageous exceptions.

Rental cars come with enough insurance and paperwork to cross borders effortlessly in virtually all of Western Europe. Ask for specific limitations if you're driving through Eastern Europe. Don't count on being allowed to take your rental car from England to Ireland or the continent. High ferry costs make renting two separate cars a better deal anyway, since two single weeks of car rental usually cost the same as two weeks in a row.

Get an international driver's license if you'll be driving in Portugal, Spain, Italy, Austria, Germany, Greece, or Eastern Europe. An international driver's license provides a translation of your American license, making it easier for the cop to write out the ticket. Exactly where you need an international driver's license depends on whom you talk to. Vendors say you need them almost everywhere. Car rental agents say you need them almost nowhere. Police can get mad and fine you if you don't have one. International licenses are easy to get from your local AAA office for $10 and two passport-type photos.

Hidden Costs of Car Rental

Outside of the weekly rate, you'll pay: taxes, generally 18 to 25 percent; gas, about $130 a week (1,000 miles); tolls for autoroutes in France and Italy (about $5 per hour), $30 for a highway permit in Switzerland, and $10 for a permit in Austria; parking, $20 a day in big cities; theft protection, required in Italy, about $12 a day; CDW insurance supplement, $10 to $15 a day.

A rental car comes with basic insurance but a huge deductible. For peace of mind, get the collision damage waiver (CDW) insurance. In return for dropping the deductible down to nothing, you'll pay $10 to $15 a day, depending on the country, car, and company. Figure roughly $100 a week. Some credit cards include CDW coverage if you charge the rental on their card. In the case of an accident, you might have to settle with the rental company and then fight to get reimbursed by your credit card company when you get home. Ask your credit card company about the worst-case scenario. Insurance companies, such as Travel Guard, sell CDW for $5 a day. CDW is worth the cost. It's a comfort to know you can return a wrecked car with an apologetic "Oops!" and just walk away.

Rail and Drive Passes
If you'd like to mix rail and car travel—using the train for long hauls and a car for exploring the countryside—consider the various rail and drive passes. These offer a set number of days of car rental and a set number of days of train travel (e.g., any four rail days and three car days within a two-month period). Euraildrive covers 17 countries in Western Europe (except Britain); Europass Drive covers France, Germany, Switzerland, Italy, and Spain (with an extra-cost option to add adjacent countries); and country passes are offered by Britain, France, Germany, Spain, Switzerland, and Scandinavia.

Leasing and Buying
Cheaper than renting, leasing is a better choice for travelers needing a car for three weeks or more (though Europe by Car now leases cars in France for as few as 17 days for $500). Lease prices include all taxes and CDW insurance. Companies that rent cars usually also lease.

The most popular places to buy cars are London, Amsterdam, Frankfurt, and U.S. military bases. Before your trip, or once in Europe, you can check the classified ads in the armed forces Stars and Stripes newspaper. In London, check the used-car market on Market Road (Caledonian Road Underground stop), and look in London periodicals such as TNT, Law, and New Zealand-UK News.

Vans and Motor Homes
Whether buying or renting, consider a van or motor home, which gives you the flexibility to drive late and just pull over and camp for free. Campanje, a Dutch company, rents and sells used VW campers fully loaded for camping through Europe. Rates vary from $500 to $750 per week including tax and insurance. For a brochure, write P.O. Box 9332, 3506 GH Utrecht, Netherlands; (011) 31/30-244-7070, fax 242-0981; campanje@xs4all.nl. In Copenhagen, Rafco rents all sizes of cars and fully-equipped motorhomes. The manager, Ken, promises my readers a 10 percent discount (Englandsvej 380, DK-2770 Kastrup, Denmark; 011 45/32 51 15 00, fax 10 89; rafco@dk-online.dk, www.rafco.dk). For more information, read Europe by Van and Motor Home by David Shore and Patty Campbell ($16 postpaid from the authors, 1842 Santa Margarita Dr., Fallbrook, CA 92028; 800-659-5222, fax 760-723-6184; shorecam@aol.com).

Road Rules
Europe is a continent of frustrated race car drivers. The most dangerous creature on the road is the timid American. Be aggressive, fit in, avoid big-city driving when pos-

sible, wear your seat belt, learn the signs, and pay extra for CDW insurance.

All of Europe uses the same simple set of road symbols. Just take a few minutes to learn them. Many major rest stops have free local driving almanacs (or cheap maps) that list signs, roadside facilities, and exits. You can drive in and out of strange towns fairly smoothly by following a few basic signs. Most European towns have signs directing you to the "old town" or the center (such as centrum, centro, centre ville, stadtmitte). The tourist office, normally right downtown, will usually be clearly signposted (i, turismo, VVV, or other abbreviations that you'll learn in each country). The tallest church spire often marks the center of the old town. Park in its shadow and look for the information booth. To leave a city, look for freeway signs (distinctive green or blue, depending on the country) or "all directions" (toutes directions) signs.

The shortest distance between any two European points is on the autobahn, autostrada, or autoroute. After a few minutes, you'll learn not to cruise in the passing lane. Although tolls can be high in Italy and France ($30 from Paris to the Italian border), the gas and time saved on European super highways justifies the expense. Park rather than drive your car in big cities. Don't use a car for city sightseeing, unless it's Sunday, when big cities are great fun and nearly traffic-free. Otherwise, park your car and use public transportation or taxis. City parking is a pain. Find a spot as close to the center as possible, grab it, and keep it. For overnight stops, choose a safe, well-lit, and well-traveled spot. Ask your hotel receptionist for advice. In cities where traffic is heavy, look for cheap, government-sponsored parking lots on the outskirts. A bus or subway will zip you easily into the center. It's often worth parking in a garage ($10 to $30 a day).

On the continent you'll be dealing with kilometers. To convert kilometers to miles, cut the total in half and add 10 percent (90 km per hour = 45 + 9 miles: 54 mph—not very fast in Europe). Britain uses miles instead of kilometers. Gas is sold by the liter (roughly four to a gallon).

Instead of intersections with stop lights, the British have roundabouts. These work wonderfully if you take advantage of the yield system and don't stop. Stopping before a roundabout is as bothersome and dangerous as stopping on freeway on-ramps. For many, roundabouts are high-pressure circles that require a snap decision about something you really don't completely understand—your exit. Make it standard operating procedure to make a 360-degree case-out-your-options circuit, discuss the exits with your navigator, and then confidently wing off on the exit of your choice.

Car Rental/Leasing Companies
Auto Europe (800) 223-5555
Avis (800) 331-1084
Budget (800) 472-3325
DER Tours (800) 782-2424.
Dollar (800) 800-6000
Europcar (800) 227-3876
Europe by Car (800) 223-1516
Hertz (800) 654-3001
Kemwel (800) 678-0678

Tibet: Roof of the World (Passport Books). 3rd ed. Good overall coverage, focuses more on background, history, etc., than on practical travel information.

Trekking in the Annapurna Region by Bryn Thomas (Trailblazer).

Trekking in Indian Himalayas by G. Weare (Lonely Planet).

Trekking in Nepal: A Traveler's Guide by Stephen Bezruchka (Mountaineers, 7th ed.).

Trekking in the Everest Region by Jamie McGuinness (Trailblazer).

Trekking in Tibet: A Traveler's Guide by Gary McCue (Mountaineers).

Indonesia, Malaysia, Singapore

Series: Berlitz, Bradt, *Culture Shock!, Customs and Etiquette, Fielding, *Footprints, *Insight Guides, Knopf, *Lonely Planet, Maverick, *Moon Handbooks, Nelles, Passport Regional Guides, *Rough Guides, Treasures and Pleasures of…

Eat Smart In Indonesia by Joan and David Peterson (Gingko Press) Cuisine, menu guide, market foods, and more.

Passport Regional Indonesia Guides (NTC Publishing). Excellent coverage of the islands of the Indonesian Archipelago. Titles include **Bali, Java, Spice Islands, Sumatra, Underwater Indonesia**, and more.

Thailand, Malaysia, Singapore by Rail by Brian McPhee (Bradt).

Italy

Series: *Access, Berlitz, *Blue Guides, *Cadogan, Citywalks, Customs and Etiquette, Daytrips, Driving Tours, Exploring Rural, Eyewitness, Fielding, Fodor, Frommer, *Insight Guides, Karen Brown, Knopf, *Let's Go, *Lonely Planet, *Michelin, Nelles, Off the Beaten Track, Passport Regional Guides, *Rick Steves, *Rough Guides, Time Out, Travelers' Tales, Traveller's History.

Cento Citta: A Guide to the "Hundred Cities and Towns" of Italy by Paul Hofmann (Henry Holt). Beyond the major tourist cities.

Hotels and Country Inns of Character and Charm in Italy (Rivages Guides).

Independent Walker's Guide Italy by Frank Booth (Interlink). Planning and preparation for 35 great walks throughout Italy.

An Insider's Guide to Italian Hotels: $40-$75 a Night for Two by Margo Classé (Wilson Publishing). Covers centrally located hotels in many Italian cities.

Northern Italy: A Taste of Trattoria by Christina Baglivi (Mustang). Eat with the locals.

Teaching English in Italy by Martin Penner (Passport Books). Practical information on finding a job, teaching, and living in Italy.

Touring Club of Italy Guides (Monacelli Press). Established series of Italian guidebooks recently translated into English. Excellent maps. Titles for: Italy, Rome, Venice, Florence.

Undiscovered Museums of Florence by Eloise Danto (Surrey Books). Guide to little-known, hard-to-find (and major) museums and galleries.

Walking and Eating in Tuscany and Umbria by James Lasdun and Pia Davis (Penguin). The title says it all!

Walking Easy in the Italian Alps (Globe Pequot). Hiking guide.

Japan

Series: Berlitz, *Cadogan, *Culture Shock!, Customs and Etiquette, Fodor, Frommer, *Insight Guides, *Lonely Planet, *Moon Handbooks, Traveller's History.

Cycling Japan by B. Harrell (Kodansha).

Hiking in Japan by Paul Hunt (Kodansha). Mountain trails, maps, great geological notes.

Japan-Think, Ameri-Think by Robert J. Collins (Penguin). An irreverent guide to understanding the cultural differences.

Japan: A Literary Companion by Harry Guest (Passport Books). Compilation of literature, background and culture.

Ski Japan! by T.R. Reid (Kodansha).

Teaching English in Japan by Jerry O'Sullivan (Passport Books). Practical information on finding a job, teaching, and living in Japan.

Korea

Series: *Culture Shock!, Fodor, *Insight Guides, *Lonely Planet, *Moon Handbooks.

Malta

Series: Berlitz, *Blue Guides, *Cadogan, *Insight Guides.

Mexico

Series: *Access, Berlitz, Birnbaum, Bradt, *Cadogan, *Culture Shock!, Daytrips, Driving Tours, Fielding, Fodor, Footprints, Frommer, *Insight Guides, Knopf, *Let's Go, *Lonely Planet (Pisces), *Michelin, *Moon Handbooks, Nelles, *New Key, *Rough Guides, Travelers' Tales, Ulysses.

Adventures in Nature: Mexico by Ron Mader (John Muir). Excellent details and recommendations for outdoor activities.

Baja by Kayak: The Ultimate Sea Kayaking Guide to Baja by Lindsay Loperenza (White Cloud).

Bicycling Mexico by E. Weisbroth and E. Ellman (Hunter Publications).

Choose Mexico by J. Howells and D. Merwin (Gateway Books). Guide for those interested in retiring or residing in Mexico.

Diving Cozumel by Steve Rosenberg (Aqua Quest Publications). Diving sites, information on marine life, archaeological sites, and travel.

Mexico: A Hiker's Guide to Mexico's Natural History by Jim Conrad (Mountaineers). Steers hikers through Mexico's natural landscape while illuminating its natural history.

Mexico by Rail by G. Poole (Hunter Publications).

***The People's Guide to Mexico** by Carl Franz (John Muir Publications). A wonderful read—full of wisdom, too.

***The People's Guide to RV Camping in Mexico** by Carl Franz (John Muir Publications). Extensive camping information and advice.

Traveler's Guide to Camping in Mexico by Mike and Terri Church (Rolling Homes Press). Explore Mexico with RV or tent.

The Yucatan: A Guide to the Land of Maya Mysteries by Antoinette May (Wide World Publishing). $10.95. Now includes Tikal,

Belize, Copan. A respected guide focusing on cultural considerations, history, Mayan legends. Includes photographs.

Middle East

Series: Bradt, Berlitz, *Blue Guides, *Cadogan, *Culture Shock!, Customs and Etiquette, Fodor, *Footprints, Frommer, Knopf, Insight, *Let's Go, *Lonely Planet (Pisces), Maverick, *Michelin, Nelles, *Rough Guides.

The Bazak Guide to Israel and Jordan 1996-1997 by Avraham and Ruth Levi. (Sterling). Detailed practical guide, includes map.

Guide to Lebanon by Lynda Keen (Bradt Publishing).

Israel on Your Own by Harriet Greenberg (Passport Books). 2nd ed. All-purpose guide to independent travel.

Israel: Traveler's Literary Companion edited by M. Gluzman and N. Seidman (Whereabouts Press). Short stories by Israeli authors.

Lebanon: A Travel Guide by Reid, Leigh and Kennedy (Pelican Publishing). General guide.

Petra: A Traveller's Guide by Rosalyn Maqsood (Garnet Publications) Guide to Jordan's most famous historical attraction.

Spectrum Guides (Interlink Publishing). Beautifully photographed, good cultural and background information. Available for: Jordan, United Arab Emirates.

Myanmar (Burma)

Series: Bradt, *Culture Shock!, Fielding, *Footprints, *Insight Guides, *Lonely Planet,

*Moon Handbooks, Nelles. (*Transitions Abroad* urges you not to travel to Burma.)

Netherlands, Belgium, Luxembourg

Series: Berlitz, *Blue Guides, *Cadogan, *Culture Shock!, Customs and Etiquette, Daytrips, Eyewitness, Fodor, Frommer, *Insight Guides, Knopf, *Lonely Planet, *Michelin, *Rick Steves, *Rough Guides, Time Out.

Backroads of Holland by Helen Colijn (Bicycle Books). Scenic excursions by bicycle, car, train, or boat.

Cycling the Netherlands, Belgium & Luxembourg by Katherine and Jerry Widing (Bicycle Books). Planning, preparation, touring information, and routes through the three most bicycle-friendly countries in Europe.

On the Rails Around France, Belgium, Netherlands, and Luxembourg by Roger Thomas (Passport Books). Routes, maps, transport information.

New Guinea

Series: *Lonely Planet , Passport Regional Guides.

Bushwalking in Papua New Guinea by Riall Nolan (Lonely Planet Publications).

New Zealand

Series: Berlitz, Fielding, Fodor, Frommer, *Insight Guides, Let's Go, *Lonely Planet, Maverick, *Moon, Nelles, Sierra Club.

Australia and New Zealand by Rail. (Bradt Publishing).

The New Zealand Bed and Breakfast Book by J. and J. Thomas (Pelican). Lists over 300 private homes and hotels.

New Zealand by Bike: 14 Tours Geared for Discovery by Bruce Ringer (Mountaineers, 2nd ed.).

Pacific

Series: *Lonely Planet, Frommer, Pisces, *Moon Handbooks, Sierra Club. Lonely Planet and Moon Handbooks have many titles that focus on this area by island groups and individual islands. Titles include: **South Pacific Handbook** (Moon Handbooks), **Micronesia** (both publishers), **Fiji** (both publishers), **New Caledonia** (Lonely Planet), **Samoa** (Lonely Planet), **Tahiti** (both publishers), **Tonga** (Lonely Planet), **Vanuatu** (Lonely Planet). Lonely Planet's imprint Pisces has diving & snorkeling guides to areas of the Pacific such as Fiji, Guam, Palau, etc.

Adventuring in the Pacific (Sierra Club). For the adventurous traveler.

Hidden Tahiti and French Polynesia by Robert Kay. (Ulysses). Practical guide emphasizing highlights off the beaten track.

Philippines

Series: *Culture Shock!, *Insight Guides, *Lonely Planet, *Moon Handbooks, Nelles.

Poland

Series: Bradt, Customs and Etiquette, Eyewitness, *Insight Guides, *Lonely Planet, Off the Beaten Track, *Rough Guides.

Hiking Guide to Poland and Ukraine by Tim Burford (Bradt).

People to People Poland by Jim Haynes (Zephyr Press). One of a series of books on Central Europe for travelers who want to experience life as the locals live it. Lists over 1,000 locals to contact.

Polish Cities (Pelican). A guide to Warsaw, Krakow, and Gdansk.

Portugal

Series: Berlitz, *Blue Guides, *Cadogan, Citywalks, Daytrips, Exploring Rural Europe, Fielding, Fodor, Frommer, *Insight Guides, Karen Brown, *Let's Go, *Lonely Planet, *Michelin, Off the Beaten Track, Passport Regional Guides, *Rick Steves, *Rough Guides, Ulysses.

Special Places to Stay in Spain and Portugal by Guy Hunter-Watts (Alastair Sawday Publishing). Accommodations with character, comfort, and value.

Romania

Series: Bradt, *Lonely Planet, *Rough Guides.

Hiking Guide to Romania. (Bradt).

Russia and the NIS

Series: Baedeker, Berlitz, *Blue Guides, *Cadogan, Customs and Etiquette, Fodor, Frommer, *Insight Guides, Knopf, *Lonely Planet, *Rough Guides, Traveller's History. **Distributors:** Russian Information Services, 89 Main St., Montpelier, VT 05602; (800) 639-4301. Free Access Russia and Central Europe catalog.

Georgian Republic by Roger Rosen (Passport Books). First comprehensive guide in English.

Hiking Guide to Poland and Ukraine by Tim Burford (Bradt).

Language and Travel Guide to Ukraine by L. Hodges (Hippocrene). Revised edition.

Russia: People to People by Jim Haynes (Zephyr Press). One of a series of books on Central Europe for travelers who want to experience life as locals live it. Lists over 1,000 locals to contact.

Russia Survival Guide by Paul Richardson (Russian Information Services). Comprehensive guide with practical information.

Russian Life Magazine (Russia Information Services). A monthly (10 issues per year) color magazine on Russian travel, culture, history, business, and life. One-year subscription $29 (U.S.), $53 (foreign). Contact publisher for free trial subscription: (800) 639-4301, fax (802) 223-6105; sales@rispubs.com.

Siberian Bam Rail Guide by Athol Yates (Trailblazer). The second Trans-Siberian Railway.

Trans-Siberian Handbook by Bryn Thomas (Trailblazer). Solid information.

Trekking in Russia and Central Asia: A Traveler's Guide by Frith Maier (Mountaineers).

Where in St. Petersburg by Scott McDonald (Russian Information Services). Practical information, maps, and information on the city.

Scandinavia

Series: Berlitz, *Blue Guides, Bradt, *Culture Shock!, Driving Tours, Fodor, Frommer, *Insight Guides, *Lonely Planet, Nelles, Off the Beaten Track, *Rick Steves, *Rough Guides.

South America

Series: Berlitz, Bradt, *Cadogan, Fielding, Fodor, *Footprints, Frommer, *Insight Guides, *Let's Go, *Lonely Planet, *Moon, *New Key, *Rough Guides, Travelers' Tales, Ulysses.

Backpacking and Trekking in Peru and Bolivia by Hilary Bradt (Bradt).

Eat Smart In Brazil by Joan and David Peterson (Gingko Press). Cuisine, menu guide, market foods and more.

Latin America by Bike: A Complete Touring Guide by W. Sienko (Mountaineers). From Mexico through Central America all the way to the tip of Argentina.

South America's National Parks: A Visitor's Guide by William Leitch (Mountaineers). A long-needed introduction to South America's great ecological treasures.

South and Central America: Literary Companion by Jason Wilson (Passport Books). Compilation of literature, background and cultural information.

Traveler's Guide to Latin America Customs & Manners by N. Braganti and E. Devine (St. Martin's Press). An important aid in understanding Latin American culture.

Trekking in Bolivia: A Traveler's Guide by Yossi Brain (Mountaineers).

Spain

Series: *Access, Berlitz, *Blue Guides, *Cadogan, Citywalks, *Culture Shock!, Daytrips, Driving Tours, Exploring Rural Europe, Eyewitness, Fielding, Fodor, *Footprints, Frommer, *Insight Guides, Karen Brown, *Let's Go, Maverick, *Michelin, Nelles, Off the Beaten Track, *Rick Steves,

*Rough Guides, Time Out, Travelers' Tales, Traveller's History.

An Insider's Guide to Spain Hotels: $40-$80 a Night for Two by Margo Classé (Wilson Publishing). Covers centrally located hotels in many Spanish cities.

Special Places to Stay in Spain and Portugal by Guy Hunter-Watts. (Alastair Sawday Publishing). Accommodations with character, comfort, and value.

Trekking in Spain by Marc Dubin (Lonely Planet Publications). Gives both day hikes and overnight treks.

Switzerland

Series: Berlitz, *Blue Guides, Bradt, *Culture Shock!, Daytrips, Driving Tours, Fodor, Frommer, *Insight Guides, Karen Brown, *Let's Go, *Lonely Planet, *Michelin, Off the Beaten Track, *Rick Steves.

Switzerland by Rail by Anthony Lambert (Bradt Publishing).

Switzerland: The Smart Traveler's Guide to Zurich, Basel and Geneva by Paul Hofmann (Henry Holt).

Walking Easy in the Swiss Alps by C. and C. Lipton (Globe Pequot). Hiking guide for active adults.

Walking Switzerland the Swiss Way: From Vacation Apartments, Hotels, Mountain Inns, and Huts by Marcia and Philip Lieberman. (Mountaineers). 2nd ed.

Taiwan

Series: *Culture Shock!, *Insight Guides, *Lonely Planet.

Thailand

Series: Berlitz, Bradt, *Culture Shock!, Eyewitness, Fielding, Fodor, *Footprints, Frommer, *Insight Guides, *Let's Go, *Lonely Planet, Knopf, Maverick, *Michelin, *Moon Handbooks, Nelles, Passport Regional Guides, *Rough Guides, Travelers' Tales, Treasures and Pleasures of...

Chiang Mai: Thailand's Northern Rose (Passport Books). Good planning information.

Diving in Thailand by Collin Piprell (Hippocrene). Best diving sites with information on preparation, facilities, etc.

Thailand, Malaysia, Singapore by Rail by Brian McPhee (Bradt).

Turkey

Series: Berlitz, *Blue Guides, *Cadogan, *Culture Shock!, Fodor, Frommer, *Insight Guides, Knopf, *Let's Go, *Lonely Planet, *Michelin, Nelles, *Rough Guides, Traveller's History.

Eat Smart In Turkey by Joan and David Peterson (Gingko Press). Cuisine, menu guide, market foods and more.

United Kingdom and Ireland

Series: *Access, Berlitz, *Blue Guides, *Cadogan, Citywalks, Customs and Etiquette, Daytrips, Driving Tours, Exploring Rural Europe, Eyewitness, Fielding, Fodor, Frommer, *Insight Guides, Karen Brown, Knopf, *Let's Go, *Lonely Planet, *Michelin, Nelles, Off the Beaten Track, Passport Regional Guides, *Rick Steves, *Rough Guides, Time Out, Traveller's History, Treasures and Pleasures of...

Alastair Sawday's Special Irish Hotels / Alastair Sawday's French Bed & Breakfast (Alastair Sawday Publishing). Accommodations with character, comfort, and value.

The Best of Britain's Countryside: The Heart of England and Wales by Bill and Gwen North (Mountaineers). Two-week drive and walk itinerary for northern England and Scotland, southern England, and the heart of England and Wales.

Bed and Breakfast Ireland by Elsie Dillard and Susan Causin (Chronicle). Guide to over 300 of Ireland's best B and Bs.

Brit-Think, Ameri-Think by Jane Walmsley (Penguin). An irreverent guide to understanding the cultural differences.

Best Bed and Breakfasts: England, Scotland, Wales 1997-98 by Sigourney Wells (Globe Pequot). Alphabetical by county.

Cheap Eats in London and Cheap Sleeps in London (Chronicle Books). 100 inexpensive places to eat and sleep.

CTC Route Guide to Cycling in Britain and Ireland by Christa Gausden and Nicholas Crane (Haynes Publishing). First rate. Not available in U.S.

Cycle Tours in the U.K. (Ordnance Survey). Sixteen different guides, each describing around 24 different one-day trips in the U.K.

Cycling Great Britain by Tim Hughes (Bicycle Books).

Cycling Ireland by Philip Routledge (Bicycle Books).

England by Bike: 18 Tours Geared for Discovery by Les Woodland (Mountaineers).

English and Scottish Tourist Board Publications (distributed by Seven Hills). Selection includes titles on Hotels, B and Bs, Self-Catering, Staying on a Farm, Activity Breaks.

Europe's Wonderful Little Hotels and Inns: Great Britain and Ireland by Hilary Rubinstein and Carolyn Raphael (St. Martin's Press).

Free Mini Guide to Ireland. All the facts necessary to jump-start your perfect trip to Ireland. Available by mail order only. Send your name and address (or an address label) plus $1 for s/h to Mini Guide to Ireland, Dept. 606, P.O. Box 862194, Marietta, GA 30062.

Holidays at British Universities. Free brochure from British Universities Accommodation Consortium, Ltd., Box H98, University Park, Nottingham, England NG7 2RD; fax (011) 44-115-942-2505; buac@nottingham.as.uk. Lists all universities that offer accommodations during vacation periods and those that offer noncredit summer classes for visitors.

Hotels and Restaurants of Britain, 1998 by British Hospitality Association (Globe Pequot).

Ireland by Bike: 21 Tours Geared for Discovery by Robyn Krause (Mountaineers).

Ireland: Complete Guide and Road Atlas (Globe Pequot). Comprehensive guide, organized by regions, color road and street maps.

Irish Bed & Breakfast Book by Frank and Fran Sullivan (Pelican).

Joyce's Dublin: A Walking Guide to Ulysses by Jack McCarthy (Irish Books & Media). Fascinating.

Literary Villages of London by Luree Miller (Starrhill Press). The author has mapped her

Hitting the Road Solo
Rewards Can Be Great for Women Going it Alone

By Kate Galbraith

Solo travel can be intimidating in prospect. But traveling alone—particularly if you're a woman—can actually increase interaction with local people along the way. Confronted with the peculiar sight of an unaccompanied female traveler, people tend to react first with surprise, then curiosity, then friendship.

In countless trips across the Balkans, I have always been warmly welcomed, invited to drink Turkish coffee, and seen and heard first-hand the nuances of individual lives. Solo travel is a form of direct, grassroots cultural exchange.

On a trip to Belgrade, for example, I hopped aboard a bus from Sarajevo with someone I'd met the day before. Sonja, a Serbian woman who works for a human rights organization in Belgrade, took me under her wing and acted as my guide as the bus crept along the winding mountain road. When we finally reached Belgrade, Sonja whisked me off to her house for the night because she didn't want me to find a hotel by myself. The next day, she showed me around the city and introduced me to her colleagues at work, who carefully instructed me on how to change money on the black market and how to orient myself in the city.

Were I accompanied by a traveling companion, I would have conversed with my friend on the bus, rather than sitting with Sonja. Two is a closed crowd, dependent mostly upon each other. Traveling with another person makes it much easier to bypass local culture and thus the reason for travel in the first place.

For the solo traveler, open, uninhibited interaction with locals is particularly easy in developing countries, where visitors are not taken for granted as they are in Western Europe.

If people are surprised to see a lone foreign traveler, they are stunned to see a woman alone. In traditional societies, few women venture off independently. Again and again, people have asked me in astonishment, "You are alone?" I reply "Yes" without fear. In my experience, people offer more courtesy and guidance to a woman. My male friends have also been welcomed by locals, but not to the same extraordinary extent.

Challenges and Pitfalls

It is important, though, to proceed with caution. Westerners, particularly women, have been subject to various forms of harassment in areas where they really stand out. A different hair or skin color, a different way of dressing, and other subtle indentifying traits can signal the locals that a foreigner is among them. In areas including the Middle East, India, and Africa, solo Western women are frequently hassled by men. The best precaution is to stay constantly alert—know where you are, don't wander too far off into deserted areas, and, if you have taken a self-defense class, brush up on those skills before you go. (A Let's Go researcher in Jordan, a small, wiry woman, fended off an aggressive man with a few well-placed kicks that left him reeling. A "Model Mugging" course, that she took before leaving the U.S., helped out her moves.)

Of course the challenges and pitfalls of traveling seem more acute when you're alone—there is no companion to consult or to joke nervously with when you miss a train connection in Siberia or get a flat tire in rural Guatemala, and it can be exhausting to draw always from your own resources and stamina. But in the end the challenges are stimulating and the resolutions are exhilarating exercises in self-reliance.

Traveling alone requires a certain level of assertiveness, something that begins to come naturally after a little practice. For example, if you arrive in a new town and need a room for the night but have not planned ahead, ask the people immediately around you. The grocer or taxi driver is likely to know about hotels and where to eat. After six months on the road, I have lost my inhibitions about asking for help. When I ask for directions, people often change their own direction and lead me to the place themselves.

Knowing the local language—even a few words—can greatly facilitate these interchanges. A phrasebook (with pronunciation tips) is essential.

Particularly in countries with "exotic" tongues—like Uzbek or Basque—people will be amazed and gratified that you know their language, or are at least trying to learn. Time and again I've seen people's faces light up with delight when I utter the few Serbo-Croatian words I know. Using the language demonstrates a respect for the culture and paves the way to friendship.

The main challenge of traveling alone is loneliness. Regardless of how many people you meet, there is a prevailing sense of transience, the knowledge that you must eventually push onward to a new destination and leave new friends behind. But, as they say, memories are golden—and you will always remember the man who took time to show you around the town or the woman who offered you coffee.

Safety Tips for Solo Female Travelers

Stay in touch with friends and family back home. The Internet can be especially useful in this regard. Most large cities, from Bombay to Irkutsk, have terminals at "cybercafes" or other locations, where, for a small fee, you can log into your e-mail account and send messages back home. Checking e-mail also helps alleviate loneliness.

Size up the people you meet carefully. First impressions are not everything, but if you're not comfortable with someone, there may well be a reason. Trust your instincts.

Don't walk down dark alleys at night. The old adage is not only worth remembering—it can be expanded and improved. Other deserted or dubious venues, such as parks, are also wisely avoided after dark. Stick to lighted streets—if you must walk at all.

For budget travelers: If staying safe means paying a little bit of extra money, do so with a clear conscience. Take a taxi rather than walk late at night if your apartment or room is far.

Try to dress like the local populace. The more you blend in, the less likely it is that you will be targeted for crime. Bear in mind, however, that clothes are not the only mark of a foreigner. No matter how closely you emulate local attire, you may be given away by your coloring or the way you walk.

Be particularly alert on transportation routes. Trains in Eastern Europe, for example, have notoriously high crime rates. Plan your trip carefully, and do not take a lot of valuables.

Finally, don't be afraid—it's adventure and excitement that awaits.

(go down in history)

Don't drop down to Mexico without an **AT&T Direct**® Service wallet guide.

It's a list of access numbers you need to call home fast and clear from around the world,

using an AT&T Calling Card or credit card. What an amazing culture we live in.

Dial **1 888 259-3505** for your free guide, or visit our Web site

at **www.att.com/traveler**

I t ' s   a l l   w i t h i n   y o u r   r e a c h .

favorite walks past the London homes and haunts of celebrated writers.

London for Free by Brian Butler (Mustang Publishing).

National Trust Handbook (Trafalgar Square). Lists National Trust properties including homes, gardens, castles, lighthouses.

On the Rails Around Britain and Ireland edited by Neil Wenborn (Passport Books). Routes, maps, transport information.

On the Rails Britain & Ireland (Thomas Cook). Rail itineraries and advice.

Passport Guide to Ethnic London by Ian McAuley (Passport Books). A guide to history, food, culture—neighborhood by neighborhood.

Scotland Bed and Breakfast (British Tourist Authority). Over 2,000 B and Bs listed.

Special Places to Stay in Britain by Alastair Sawday (Alastair Sawday Publishing). Accommodations with character, comfort, and value.

Undiscovered Museums of London by Eloise Danto (Surrey Books). Guide to little-known, hard-to-find (and major) museums and galleries.

Vietnam, Laos, Cambodia

Series: Bradt, *Culture Shock!, Customs and Etiquette, Fielding, *Footprints, *Insight Guides, *Lonely Planet, Maverick, *Moon, Nelles, *Rough Guides.

Guide to Vietnam by John R. Jones (Bradt). Every province and area of interest is described in detail, along with fascinating ethnic and cultural information.

Vietnam: Traveler's Literary Companion edited by J. Balaban and N. Qui Duc (Whereabouts Press). Compilation of short stories by Vietnamese writers.

Worldwide

Amateur's Guide to the Planet by Jeannette Belliveau (Beau Monde Press). Reports on 12 adventure journeys reflect author's responses to diverse cultures and how people live. Good background reading for responsible travelers.

Gay Travels: A Literary Companion edited by Lucy Jane Bledsoe (Whereabouts Press). Short stories by contemporary gay male writers.

Going Abroad? Superintendent of Documents, U.S. Government Printing Office, Washington, DC 20420; (202) 512-1800. Free pamphlet with safety tips; includes order form for other U.S. government publications on foreign travel and residency.

Jewish Travel Guide by Stephen Massil (ISBS). Lists Jewish organizations throughout the world.

More Women Travel (Penguin). From Rough Guide series.

The Thrifty Traveler, P.O. Box 8168, Clearwater, Fl 34618; (800) 532-5731, fax (813) 447-0829; editor@thriftytraveler.com, www.thriftytraveler.com. Eight-page monthly newsletter filled with resources, tips, and budget travel strategies. Also publishes **The Over-50 Thrifty Traveler** monthly newsletter; **Net News for the Thrifty Traveler** monthly newsletter. All newsletters are $29 for a 1-year subscription; a sample issue is $3.25 postpaid. Also available is a 464-page book entitled **Thrifty Traveling: Your Step-by-Step Guide to Bar-**

gain Travel in the U.S., Canada, and Worldwide. $15.95 plus s/h.

Travel Books Worldwide: The Travel Book Review. $36 per year (10 issues), Canada $48, rest of the world $72 or £42 per year from: Travel Keys Books/Travel Books Worldwide, P.O. Box 162266, Sacramento, CA 95816-2266; (916) 452-5200. A 12- to 20-page newsletter devoted to new travel books.

Travel Smarts: Getting the Most for Your Travel Dollar by H. Teison and N. Dunnan (Globe Pequot). Some useful tips and advice.

Traveler's Handbook: Essential Guide for Every Traveler (WEXAS/Globe Peqout). Good resource.

U.S. State Department Travel Advisories. Periodic advisories alert U.S. travelers to health and safety risks worldwide; (202) 647-5225; http://travel.state.gov.

Wild Planet! 1,001 Extraordinary Events for the Inspired Traveler by Tom Clynes (Visible Ink). Thorough compendium of festivals, cultural events, and holidays spanning the globe.

The World Awaits: Comprehensive Guide to Extended Backpack Travel by Paul Otteson (John Muir Publications). Practical book with details for life on the road.

World Music from the Rough Guides Series. (Penguin). References and information on music spanning the globe. Titles available: Reggae, Rock & Opera.

Web Sites

1travel.com, www.1travel.com. Helps cost-conscious consumers find the best rates for airfares and accommodations worldwide.

They take airline and/or hotel requests and deliver them to travel agents who, in turn, e-mail the best itinerary options back to the consumer.

AAA: All Aboard Africa, www.allaboard. co.za/aaa. Great place to find information on travel and tourism in South Africa.

Airhitch, www.airhitch.org. Get to Europe cheaply by taking advantage of seats left empty on commercial flights.

Amerispan's Latin America Resources, www.amerispan.com/resources/ default.htm. Links to trusted travel guides, tourist information and Spanish language programs.

Artoftravel.com, www.artoftravel.com. Information on pre-departure preparation, includes traveler's checklist.

Arthur Frommer's Outspoken Encyclopedia of Travel, www.frommers.com. Information on budget and alternative travel.

Budget Travel, www.budgettravel.com. Geographically indexed contact information for travelers who "don't want to pay 5-star prices."

Budget Travel: The Mining Company, http://budgettravel.miningco.com. The Mining Company's Budget Travel page is a collection of links to some of the most important sites on the web.

City Rail Transit, http://pavel.physics. sunysb.edu/RR/metro.html. Information and links for train and subway travelers just about everywhere on the globe: maps, timetables, etc.

The Civilized Explorer, www.cieux.com/ index.html. A "jumping off page" for adventuresome, independent travel. Find web site reviews on their Travel Information Page.

CNN Travel Guide, www.cnn.com/TRAVEL. The capital letters are necessary.

The Comfort Zone, www.global travelapartments.com. A choice of 200,000 furnished apartments in 125 cities in 26 countries around the world.

The Cybercafé Search Engine, http://cybercaptive.com. Cybercafés offer a multitude of services for the international traveler. As of May 1998, the database contained listings for 1,803 cybercafés in 105 countries.

Deutsche Bahn AG, http://bahn.hafas.de/english.html. Up-to-date timetables for train services all around Europe. Well-designed site has options for text-only browsers and English or German language.

Dollar Saver Vacations, www.dollar savertravel.com. This site can help you find cheap flights and hotels worldwide.

Ecola Newsstand, www.ecola.com. Published on the World Wide Web since March 1995, Ecola has links to more than 6,600 English language newspapers and magazines worldwide.

Eco-Source, www.podi.com/ecosource. Managed by working professionals, Eco-Source is a dynamic global resource for anyone interested in ecotourism.

Epicurious Traveler, http://travel4.epicurious.com. Conde Nast's site has budget travel info and discussion forums, as well as other resources for travelers.

European Travel Network, www.etn.nl/index.html. Good place to find budget travel information such as cheap fares and hotels. A non-profit, so no on-site ads.

Eurostar, www.eurostar.com. Good information on rail travel in Europe such as timetables, fares, and individual stations.

Everything's Travel, http://members.aol.com/trvlevery. Quite possibly the largest collection of travel links available. Also has bookstore.

EXES Travel Search Engine, www.exes.com. Only indexes travel related pages.

Federal Travel Service Web Site, www.federaltravel.com. Site for business, family and vacation travel, as well as for those who are traveling to adopt. A full service travel agency.

Fern Modena's Timeshare & Travel Page, www.geocities.com/RodeoDrive/1060. If you are looking for a place to network and find information on timeshares, this is Mecca.

Global On-line Travel, www.got.com. An all-purpose information/service site for world travelers. One can book a flight or hotel room, get information on a travel destination, or browse their web links.

HomeExchange.com, www.HomeExchange.com. A big database of homes for exchange. Extensive worldwide listings. For $30, they'll list your home for one year. Browsing their listings is free.

Home Free, www.homefree.com/homefree/index.html. Home Free offers Home Exchange and Travel Companion Matching Services.

Hostelling International, www.iyhf.org. Lists hostels in 74 countries, along with current news in hostelling.

Hostels of Europe, www.hostelwatch.com. Lists Europe's finest youth hostels and hotels and offers budget travel links, a travel bookstore, a free electronic newsletter, and more.

The Hotel Guide, www.hotelguide.com. Find a room anywhere in the world using

The Hotel Guide's database of 60,000 hotels.

InfoHub Specialty Travel Guide, www.infohub.com. Comprehensive, easily searchable database of specialty travel programs.

International Hospitality Exchange, http://shell.ggg.net/~nyara. Membership is free, and profiles contain information to make sure you find like-minded people to contact.

International Society of Travel Medicine, www.istm.org. The largest organization of professionals dedicated to the advancement of the specialty of travel medicine; online directory of travel clinics.

Internet Guide to Hostelling, www.hostels.com. Among the largest directories of hostels in the world, also a list of guidebooks, provide a bulletin board and travel links.

Izon's Backpacker Journal, www.izon.com. An extensive list of links and a modest but useful list of free Youth/Budget Travel Guides for several destinations.

Journeywoman Online, www.journeywoman.com, is an online magazine for women who love to travel. Sign on for a free e-mail newsletter and it's delivered to you in minutes.

Le Travel Store, www.letravelstore.com. Travel gear and accessories including travel packs, money belts, duffles, day bags, voltage converters and more. Their San Diego storefront has been in business since 1976.

Let's Go, www.letsgo.com. The well-organized and snazzy looking web site of Let's Go Guidebooks.

Lonely Planet, www.lonelyplanet.com. Lonely Planet is one of the premier publishers in the travel book industry. Their site has a whole bunch of great content–and a great sense of humor.

Maiden Voyages, http://maidenvoyages.com. Maiden Voyages is a literary consumer magazine for women; web site contains a large directory of tour operators who cater to women.

Netscape Guide, by Yahoo, http://netscape.yahoo.com/guide/travel.html. Skip this one. What content it has it borrows from Traveolcity (see below).

No Shitting in the Toilet, www.noshit.com.au. "A celebration of everything that is perverse about travel."

Passport to Web Radio (International Broadcasting Services, www.passport.com). Explains how to hear hundreds of local AM/FM stations audible worldwide over the internet.

Places to Stay, www.placestostay.com. An extensive online reservation service for hotels, bed and breakfasts, inns, and resorts worldwide with up-to-the-minute information on prices and availability.

Preview Travel, www.previewtravel.com. Fare-finding and ticket-booking sites are now commonplace; this one has on-line version of Fodor's travel guides for over 80 destinations worldwide.

RailServe, www.railserve.com. A vast amount of practical resources and web links for rail travelers worldwide.

Rec.Travel Library, www.travel-library.com. Good resource information for travelers not looking for a packaged tour.

Roadnews, www.roadnews.com. Has everything you need to stay connected to the "cyberworld" while traveling in the real one.

Shoestring Travel, www.stratpub.com. A great E-Zine with lots of links and an emphasis on the exchange of information among budget travelers.

Third World Traveler, www.infoasis.com/people/stevetwt. Provides alternative travel information for developing countries, opportunities for travelers to act on behalf of social and economic justice in the Third World.

Transitions Abroad, www.transabroad.com. The central hub of alternative travel online with links to the web sites of everyone listed in our resource and program directories. You can purchase books reviewed in our resource directories and read articles from recent editions of *Transitions Abroad* magazine.

Travel & World Section/LinkEase, www.linkease.com/travel.htm. A great number of links, some of which are rated.

Travel Document Services, www.traveldocs.com. Provides visa services for U.S. citizens for most countries for which an entry visa is required; web site also has up-to-date information on most countries. You can browse their impressive list of travel resources and purchase relevant books.

Travel Source, www.travelsource.com. A database of travel links. Almost as many categories as actual listings.

Travel Whiz, www.travelwiz.com. Resources for car rentals and hotels.

Traveler's Medical and Vaccination Center, www.tmvc.com.au. Worldwide information on how to travel healthy and a good selection of links to other organizations.

Travelocity, www.travelocity.com. Huge selection of options for airline tickets, hotel and car rental reservations, and packaged tours. Not budget-minded or alternative.

Traveloco, www.traveloco.com. Includes forums wherein you can see what others have to say about their study and travel abroad experiences and contact them.

TravLang, www.travlang.com. Provides useful tools for the traveler and those interested in learning a foreign language, also links to other places on the net providing related services.

Travelmag, www5.red.net/travelmag, An online alternative travel magazine with articles and links to many other sites of interest.

U.S. State Department: Travel Warnings and Consular Information, http://travel.state.gov/travel_warnings.html. The U.S. State Department issues warnings and advisories to travelers about destinations to avoid and dangers to watch out for. Consular Information Sheets include U.S. Embassy or Consulate locations, health conditions, political disturbances, currency and entry regulations, crime and security information, etc.

World Travel Guide, www.wtgonline.com/info.html. Provides, besides climate, a wealth of information about each country.

For more listings of resources for independent travel, and for bargains worldwide, travel tips, and all sorts of information on learning, living, working, and traveling abroad, see *Transitions Abroad* magazine. To order a single copy or a subscription, please call 1-800-293-0373 or visit the *Transitions Abroad* web site at www.transabroad.com.

CHAPTER 2

SPECIAL INTEREST VACATIONS

The following listing of special interest programs was supplied by the organizers in 1998 and is updated in each March/April issue of Transitions Abroad *magazine. Contact the program directors to confirm costs, dates, and other details. Please tell them you read about their programs in this book! Programs based in more than one country or region are listed under "Worldwide."*

Africa

The African Magic ESL Training and Placement. Eight-day trips, all accommodations in hotel. Discover the African magic practiced by the populations of Togo and Benin—voodoo in the South and the traditional animisim in the north.

Dates: Flexible. Cost: For groups of at least 5, $680 per person, double room. Single supplement: $130. Includes full board. Contact: TRANSAFRICA, B.P. 265 Lome, Togo, Africa; (011) 228-21-68-23, fax (011) 228-21-88-52; transafr@cafe.tg.

Culture and the Arts. An introduction to the rich history, culture, and the arts of the very diverse and ancient people of Senegal and The Gambia. The focus will be on the visual and performing arts. Meet new people, learn new artistic techniques, attend ceremonies and performances, and expand your understanding of West African art and culture.

Dates: May 28-Jun 24 (1998). Cost: $2,690. Includes airfare, hotel accommodations, 2 meals per day, tuition for 3 credits. Contact: Rockland Community College, Center for International Studies, 145 College Rd., Suffern, NY 10901; (914) 574-4205, fax (914) 574-4423; study-abroad@sunyrockland.edu.

Americas

Sea Kayaking with Whales. Sea Quest Kayak Expeditions provides biologist guides for 1-day to 1-week sea kayak adventures in the world's premier whale and wildlife areas: Baja Mexico, San Juan Islands of Washington, and Southeast Alaska.

Dates: Year round. Cost: $50-$100 per day depending on length and location. Contact: Mark Lewis, P.O. Box 2424, Friday Harbor, WA 98250; (360) 378-5767; seaquest@ pacificrim.net, www.sea-quest-kayak.com.

Trek America. Small group adventure camping tours. USA, Canada, Alaska, Mexico, Guatemala, and Belize. We do the driving and supply all the camping equipment. National and state parks, big cities and small towns, famous places and hidden wonders. Tours from 7 days to 9 weeks from 14 cities. Hike, bike, horseback ride, raft and more.

Dates: Year round. Cost: $40-$120 per day (avg. $60 per day). Contact: Jeff Hall, Trek America, P.O. Box 189, Rockaway, NJ 07866; (800) 221-0596, fax (973) 983-8551; trekamnj@ix.netcom.com.

Argentina

Instituto de Lengua Española (ILEE). Located downtown in the most European-like city in Latin America, Buenos Aires. Dedicated exclusively to teaching Spanish to foreigners. Small groups and private classes year round. All teachers hold Master's degrees in Education or Literature and have been full-time Spanish professors for years. Method is intensive, conversation-based. Student body is international. Highly recommended worldwide. Ask for individual references in U.S.

Dates: Year round. Cost: Four-week intensive program (20 hours per week) including homestay $1,400; 2 weeks $700. Private classes $19 per hour. Registration fee (includes books) $100. Contact: Daniel Korman, I.L.E.E., Director, Lavalle 1619 7° C (1048), Buenos Aires, Argentina; Tel./fax (011) 54-1-375-0730. In U.S.: David Babbitz; (415) 431-8219, fax (415) 431-5306; ilee@overnet.com.ar, www.study abroad.com/ilee.

Asia

Star Clippers Exotic Far East. Experience the Far East on a voyage to Singapore, Malaysia, and Thailand aboard the modern clipper ship Star Flyer. Sail under 36,000 square feet of white billowing sails with only 170 guests. Enjoy open seating dining, thrilling watersports, nautical sailing classes, and much more.

Dates: Nov 14-Dec 19. Cost: From $1,475-$2,475, 7-night cruises. Contact: Lori Bell, Star Clippers, 4101 Salzedo St., Coral Gables, FL 33146; (800) 442-9550, fax (305) 442-1611; http://star-clippers.com.

Australia

The Adventure Company. The Adventure Company, Australia specializes in top quality adventure and nature tours for individuals and groups. We run a variety of scheduled trips, all of which involve a strong nature element. Many of the tours take place in World Heritage Listed National Parks. Hike along ancient Aboriginal rainforest trails, sea kayak along pristine coastline and deserted islands, mountain bike through small country villages on the Atherton Tablelands or visit Aboriginal art sites dating back 40,000 years.

Dates: Call program for information. Join 1- to 12-day trips. Cost: $50-$1,500, including all trips departing from Cairns. Contact: Gary Hill, The Adventure Company, Australia, P.O. Box 5740, Cairns, Queensland 4870, Australia; (011) 61-7-4051-4777, fax (011) 61-7-4051-4888; adventures@adventures. com.au, www.adventures.com.au. In U.S.: (800) 388-7333.

Chinese and Thai Cooking Classes. Eight-week courses in basic and advanced Chinese and Thai cuisines. Australia's foremost Chinese cooking school, established over 21 years.

Dates: Call for details. Cost: Call for details. Contact: Harry Quay, Harry's Chinese Cooking Classes, 47 Bruce St., Brighton-Le-Sands 2216, NSW Australia; (011) 61-2-9567-6353.

WWOOF-Australia. Learn organic growing while living with host family. Nine hundred hosts in Australia or travel the world with over 600 hosts on all continents.

Dates: Year round. Cost: $30 single, $35 double. Contact: WWOOF Australia, Buchan, Victoria 3885, Australia; (011) 61-3-5155-0218; wwoof@ozemail.com.au.

Canada

Bowers Homestay Services. Come to Canada and learn about our culture. Live with warm and hospitable Canadian families, become a member of the family rather than a tourist, and improve your conversational English skills. The host family provides a safe place for you to live while being immersed in the use of English language and culture with Canadian family. The host family provides students with breakfast and dinner daily as well as a clean private room. Many language and credit high school courses are available and may be taken in conjunction with the homestay program.

Dates: Year round. Cost: $680 per 4-week session including 2 meals daily; $800 per 4-week session for ESL programs. Contact: Bowers Homestay Service, 1 Holswade Rd., Scarborough, ON, M1L 2G1, Canada; (416) 751-0698, fax (416) 751-3670; rbowers@arcos.org, www.arcos.org/rbowers/homestay/index.htm.

Circle VH Enterprises. Located in the middle of the Yukon Territory, Circle VH offers a cozy trapper-style cabin with breakfast or meals in the main house, horses by the hour or day, boat trips down the Pelly River.

Dates: Year round. Cost: Packages range from CAN$525 per person for 3 days to CAN$1,775 for 10 days. Add 7 percent tax. Contact: Circle VH Enterprises, P.O. Box 204, Farc. Yukon, Canada Y0B 1K0; Tel./fax (403) 994-2055.

Language Studies Canada Montréal. Using a multi-skill approach students develop effective communication skills in French. Classes are informative, practical, and enjoyable. Seven levels of 4 weeks each: intensive, 6 hours daily or semi-intensive, 4 hours daily. Maximum of 14 students per class. Audio-visual equipment, multi-media Student Resource Center. Optional activity program. Homestay and alternate accommodations available.

Dates: Year round. Two-week courses begin any Monday. Other programs offered: one-to-one instruction, year round; 2-week. Group 5 executive courses, Jun-Oct; Summer Language Adventure (13- to 17-year-olds), 2-9 weeks in Jul and Aug. Cost: Two weeks intensive program $545 (1998); homestay accommodations $365 (1998). Cost of other services available upon request. Contact: Language Studies Canada Montréal, 1450 City Councillors, Montréal, PQ, H3A 2E6, Canada; (514) 499-9911, fax (514) 499-0332.

Palaeontology in Canada. Join scientists from the world-renowned Royal Tyrrell Museum at a field research site in fossil-rich Alberta. You'll prospect for and collect fossils, study the rocks for clues about ancient environments, and learn how the fossils formed. The fossils you find and the information you gather will be used in published scientific studies. On-site training and tools provided. Ages 18 and over.

Dates: Jun 7-Aug 30 (1998). Cost: CAN$800 per week. Includes meals and accommodations. Discounts for booking multiple weeks. Contact: Becky Kowalchuk, Royal Tyrrell Museum, P.O. Box 7500, Drumheller, AB T0J 0Y0, Canada; (888) 440-4240 or (403) 823-7707, fax (403) 823-7131; rtmp@dns.magtech.ab.ca, www.tyrellmuseum.com.

Wilderness Guide Training. Licensed guide outfitting business conducts 1- and 2-week training programs in guiding and outdoor adventure tourism. Programs include: horsehandling, western mountain riding, guiding, horse packing/shoeing/logging, back country living, and operational procedures. Acquire skills for pack horse trips, guest ranch adventures, alpine fishing, ecotourism, big game viewing, and photo safaris.

Dates: Two-week guide training: May 2-14, May 16-28, May 30-Jun 11; 1-week guide training: Jul 4-10, Aug 15-21. Cost: All inclusive packages: 2-week guide training CAN$2,056; 1-week guide training CAN$1,067. Contact: Sylvia Waterer or Kevan Bracewell, Chilcotin Holidays Guest Ranch, Gun Creek Road, Gold Bridge, BC V0K 1P0, Canada; Tel./fax (250) 238-2274; chilcotin_holidays@bc.sympatico.ca, www.chilcotinholidays.com.

Wilderness Lodging. Purcell Lodge is Canada's finest remote mountain lodge. It sets a new environmental standard in sustainable tourism development. A few miles beyond the crowds of Banff and Lake Louise lies true solitude. A spectacular helicopter flight leaves the familiar far behind. Inside, the comfort of a fine country manor. Outside, your own natural paradise. Peaceful walks in alpine meadows, guided ski tours in stunning surroundings.

Dates: Late Jun-early Sep, Dec-Apr. Cost: All-inclusive American plan $85-$140 per night. Contact: Russ Younger, Manager, Purcell Lodge, Places Less Travelled Ltd., P.O. Box 1829, Golden, BC, Canada V0A 1H0; (250) 344-2639, fax (250) 344-5520; places@rockies.net, www.purcell.com.

Working Landscape Micro-Tours. Short educational tours that introduce participants to community-based, environmentally sustainable economic models being explored in Cape Breton as alternatives to the traditional resource-based industrial economy. Individuals and/or small groups stay in local bed and breakfast and enjoy the spectacular beauty of Cape Breton.

Dates: Jun-Sep. Cost: CAN$1,259 (3 days); CAN$1,950 (5 days). Contact: Working Landscape Micro-Tours, R.R. #4, Baddeck, NS B0E 1B0, Canada; (902) 929-2063, fax (902) 929-2348; rschneid@sparc.uccb.ns.ca.

Caribbean

Sonrise Beach Retreat. Jamaica's best ecotourism project: affordable cottages on idyllic private white sand cove, unspoiled wilderness, great swimming, snorkeling, hiking, camping, birding, eco-adventure tours, empty beaches, waterfalls, ruins, rivers, mountains, popular weekend family beach party. Experience the best of Jamaica's natural, cultural, and spiritual life. Special interest low group rate.

Dates: Year round. Cost: From $280 up with accommodations and meals for 1 week. Contact: Robert or Kim Chase, Sonrise Beach Retreat, Robins Bay, St. Mary, Jamaica, WI; Tel./fax (876) 999-7169; www.in-site.com/sonrise.

Costa Rica

Adventure Beachfront Resort Hotel. Fishing, horseback riding, waterskiing, relaxing about the large pool or your hammock outside your room, yacht tours/charters, scuba, bird, butterfly, small animal watching in preserved virgin forest, snorkeling, playing (volleyball, horseshoes, minigolf, soccer, badminton). Enjoy continental and Costa Rican menu—air conditioning if desired. In Costa Rica (011) 506-381-2296.

Dates: Through Jun 99. Cost: $30 per person, double occupancy; $45 single occupancy (includes breakfast). Contact: U.S. Agents, Bahia Luminosa; (800) 700-7768 or (530) 842-3322; bahia-luminosa@getawaynow.com, www.getawaynow.com/bahia-luminosa.

Costa Rica Rainforest Outward Bound School. Our organization promotes environmental, personal, and cultural integrity through experiential wilderness education in 15-, 24-, and 30-day courses, custom-made courses, and an 85-day tri-country semester course that explores Costa Rica, Ecuador, and Peru. Activities include backpacking, whitewater rafting, kayaking, waterfall rappelling, caving, surfing, and more.

Dates: Year round. Cost: Fifteen days $1,695, 24 days $2,495, 30 days $2,895, 85 days $6,800. Contact: (800) 676-2018, fax (011) 506-777-1222; crrobs@sol.racsa.co.cr, www.centralamerica.com/cr/crrobs.

Costa Rican Language Academy. Costa Rican-owned and-operated language school offers first-rate Spanish instruction in a warm and friendly environment. Teachers with university degrees. Small groups or private classes. Included free in the programs are airport transportation, coffee and natural refreshments, excursions, Latin dance, Costa Rican cooking, music, and conversation classes to provide students with complete cultural immersion.

Dates: Year round (start anytime). Cost: $135 per week or $220 per week for program with homestay. All other activities and services included at no additional cost. Contact: Costa Rican Language Academy, P.O. Box 336-2070, San José, Costa Rica; (011) 506-221-1624 or 233-8914 or 233-8938, fax (011) 506-233-8670. In the U.S.: (800) 854-6057; crlang@sol.racsa.co.cr, www.crlang.co.cr/index.html.

Instituto de Lenguaje "Pura Vida." Only minutes from the capital in the fresh mountain air of Heredia. Intense total immersion methods of teaching. Morning classes and daily cultural activities all conducted in Spanish, maximum 5 students per class. Teachers hold university degrees. Latin music and dance lessons, tours, trips, parties. Learn Spanish fast.

Dates: Classes for all levels start every Monday year round. Cost: Language only, 20 hours

per week $230; total immersion, 35 hours per week with homestay $370; children's classes with homestay $370 per week, daycare available. Contact: Instituto de Lenguaje "Pura Vida," P.O. Box 730, Garden Grove, CA 92842; (714) 534-0125, fax (714) 534-1201; BS7324@aol.com, www.arweb.com/puravida.

Learn Spanish While Volunteering. Assist with the training of Costa Rican public school teachers in ESL and computers. Assist local health clinic, social service agencies, and environmental projects. Enjoy learning Spanish in the morning, volunteer work in the afternoon/evening. Spanish classes of 2-5 students plus group learning activities; conversations with middle-class homestay families (1 student per family). Homestays and most volunteer projects are within walking distance of school in small town near the capital, San Jose.

Dates: Year round, all levels. Classes begin every Monday, volunteer program is continuous. Cost: $345 per week for 28 hours of classes and group activities plus Costa Rican dance and cooking classes. Includes tuition, 3 meals per day, 7 days per week, homestay, laundry, all materials, and airport transportation. $25 one-time registration fee; $100 additional one-time registration fee for volunteer program. Contact: Susan Shores, Registrar, Latin American Language Center, 7485 Rush River Dr., Suite 710-123, Sacramento, CA 95831; (916) 447-0938, fax (916) 428-9542; lalc@madre.com.

Rainforest Bird Watching. Beautiful, small-scale, environmentally conscious rainforest lodge. Trilingual guide leads custom-tailored bird watching tours daily and is usually available for consultation. See updated bird list on Internet, or request via mail, e-mail, or fax. Beginners welcome. Lodge offers additional activities, including natural history tours and tree climbing.

Dates: Year round except Dec 15-Jan 30. Group reservations only (6-14 people). Cost:

$310 (3 days/2 nights) to $640 (6 days/5 nights) per person, double occupancy. Includes transportation, lodging, all meals, taxes, all birding, natural history and horseback tours, and personal birding guide (prices subject to change). Contact: Selva Bananito Lodge, Apdo. 801-1007, Costa Rica; Tel./fax (011)506-253-8118; conselva@sol.racsa.co.cr, www.selvabananito.com.

Turtle Tagging in Costa Rica. Travel to Tortuguero on the northern Caribbean coast for 6 nights or 13 nights tagging endangered sea turtles along the secluded black sand beach, the largest nesting site of endangered turtles in the Western hemisphere. Contribute to the efforts of the oldest sea turtle research program in the world, the Caribbean Conservation Corporation (CCC), a U.S.-based nonprofit organization dedicated to the preservation of endangered sea turtles. Participants in this service program check for old tags, measure the shells, watch the egg-laying process, and count the eggs as they drop in the nest.

Dates: Departures each Saturday in Mar, Apr, Jun, Jul, Aug, and Sep. Cost: From $1,585 for 9 days; From $1,985 for 16 days. Contact: Holbrook Travel, Inc., 3540 NW 13th St., Gainesville, FL 32609; Tel./fax (800) 451-7111; www.holbrooktravel.com.

Europe

Bicycle and Walking Tours. North Sea Jazz Festival tour in Holland; guided and self guided tours in Austria, France, Italy, and Holland; tulip tours; Normandy tour.

Dates: Apr-Oct (1998). Cost: $500-$1,700 (1998). Contact: Michael Sorgi, VanGogh Tours, P.O. Box 57, Winchester, MA 01890; vangogh@vangoghtours.com, www.vangoghtours.com.

Bike Riders Tours. Bike Riders specializes in small group (maximum 16) bicycle tours with unique itineraries throughout Italy, Ireland, Spain, Portugal, Canada, and New England.

Guest chef tours in Umbria and Sicily. Self-guided European tours.

Dates: Mar-Nov. Cost: $355-$3,000. Contact: Eileen Holland, Bike Riders Tours, P.O. Box 254, Boston, MA 02113; (800) 473-7040, fax (617) 723-2355; info@bikeriderstours.com, www.bikeriderstours.com.

Carefree Tour du Mont-Blanc. A 6-day classic tour visiting France, Italy, and Switzerland on foot. Minibus support will take your heavy bags while you enjoy the splendor of the Alps.

Dates: Every Sunday from mid-Jun-mid-Sep (1998). Cost: FF3,250 (1998). Contact: Promotions Manager, La Compagnie Des Guides de Chamonix Mont-Blanc, 190 Place de L'Eglise, 74400 Chamonix, France; (011) 33-4-5053-00-88, fax (011) 33-4-5053-48-04; chamonix.guides@mont-blanc.com.

Cooking in Florence. Learn the art of cooking and wine appreciation in the heart of Florence. Group classes from 1 week to a year; individual classes available all year round. Possible combination with Italian language, art history, studio art.

Dates: Year round. Cost: From LIT180,000. Contact: Dr. Gabriella Ganugi, "Apicius," Via Faenza 43, 50123 Florence, Italy; (011) 39-55-287143, fax (011) 39-55-2398920; ldm@dada.it, www.dada.it/ldm.

Cuisine International. Week-long culinary experiences in Europe to learn about regional cuisine and culture.

Dates: Year round. Cost: From $1,800-$5,000 excluding airfares. Contact: Judy Ebrey, Cuisine International, P.O. Box 25228, Dallas, TX 75225; (214) 373-1161, fax (214) 373-1162; cuisineint@aol.com, www.cuisineinternational.com.

Cultural Hiking in the Alps. Hiking village to village in the Alps through a breathtaking region of great cultural diversity. Moderate hiking. Two weeks under $2,000 all inclusive.

Dates: Jun-Sep. Cost: $1,995 plus airfare.

Contact: Bill Russell's Mountain Tours; (800) 669-4453, fax (203) 255-3426.

Issue-Specific Travel Courses. Visit 1 to 4 cities. Topics include International Business and Economics, Comparative Education, Historical Literature, Social Service Systems, and other crosscultural studies. Emphasis on personal interaction between students and European professionals and providing a holistic cultural experience. Two- to 5-week programs. Three to 6 credit hours—undergraduate, graduate, or audit basis—through the Univ. of Missouri-Kansas City.

Dates: Early Summer. Cost: Approx. $2,000 (does not include airfare). Contact: People to People International, Collegiate and Professional Studies Abroad, 501 E. Armour Blvd., Kansas City, MO 64109-2200; (816) 531-4701, fax (816) 561-7502; collegiate@ptpi.org, www.ptpi.org/studyabroad.

Language, Arts, and Sports. Active learning vacations. French, Spanish, Italian; cooking, painting, drawing, photography workshops. Combine programs or interests in one vacation. Learn French and sailing or skiing; Spanish and golfing. Bicycle tours with language lessons. We match individual needs and interests with programs and options: family stay, residence, apartment, hotel; intensive to total immersion (no English); group or one-on-one (including studying and living in your teacher's home).

Dates: Programs run from 1 week to months. Cost: Include room and board, tuition. Contact: Mary Ann Puglisi, eduVacations, 1431 21st St. NW, Suite 302, Washington, DC 20036; (202) 857-8384, fax (202) 835-3756.

Opera Tours. Bayreuth, Salzburg, La Scala, Verona, London, Munich, etc. Daily lectures by cultural historian.

Dates: Vary. Cost: Varies. Contact: OEI Tours, 400 Yale Ave., Berkeley, CA 94708-1109; (800) OPLOVER, (510) 526-5244, fax (510) 524-5999; opga@wenet.net, www.operalover.net.

Rentals in Italy (and Elsewhere!). Villa, farmhouse, apartment, and castle rentals in Italy and France. We've been in business for 14 years. For catalogs, comments, impressions, and opinions on the various properties—as well as very personal help—contact us!

Dates: TBA. Cost: TBA. Contact: Rentals in Italy (and Elsewhere!), 1742 Calle Corva, Camarillo, CA 93010; (800) 726-6702, fax (805) 482-7976; mail@rentvillas.com, www.rentvillas.com.

Residential Yoga Holidays. Held in country retreats throughout the British Isles. All levels of ability are catered to. A chance to unwind and recharge vital energies. In quiet country mansions away from worldly hustle and bustle.

Dates: Two retreats every month. Cost: £115 for a weekend includes everything. Contact: Ruth White, Yoga Centre, Church Farm House, Spring Close Ln., Cheam, Surrey SM3 8PU, U.K.; (011) 44-181-644-0309, fax (011) 44-181-287-5318.

Villa and Apartment Rentals. Europe's finest villas and apartments in all the most desirable locations. Modest to most luxurious. One-week minimums.

Dates: Year round. Cost: $700 per week and up. Contact: Scott Stavrou, European Escapes, LLC, 487 2nd Ave., San Francisco, CA 94118; (888) 387-6589, fax (415) 386-0477; EuroEscape@aol.com, http://members.aol.com/EuroEscape.

France

Arts in a French Country House. "La Maison Verte" in the south of France offers weekly workshops throughout the summer. Examples include pottery, yoga, singing, Alexander technique, painting, wine tasting, and cooking. Very French, very rural.

Dates: Jun-Sep. Cost: £350 includes accommodations, tuition, some meals. Contact: Linda Garnett, 55 High St., Herringford Grey, Huntingdon PE18 9BN, U.K.; Tel./fax (011)

44-1480-495364.

Fine Arts on the French Riviera. Workshop, courses for 1 week and more. Watercolor, painting, drawing, lithography, monotypes, etching classical and modern. The studio is situated next to the Picasso Museum on the seafront. The studio and its gallery work with professional and beginner artists of different levels. Students are given a choice of 3 hotel accommodations or a family residence or only courses.

Dates: Year round. Cost: FF2,600 (1 week) plus half-board accommodations. Tuition fee FF1,500. Contact: Atelier du Safranier, Mme. Prevost, 2 bis rue de Cannet, Antibes 06600, France; (011) 33-06-09-55-91-58, fax (011) 33-04-93-34-74-30.

French and Cookery in a Château. Live and study in 18th-century château with relaxed, convivial atmosphere. Residential French language and Provençal cooking for adults. Comfortable single/twin and shared rooms. Good food and wine at the heart of France's loveliest areas, near Lyon.

Dates: Two weeks in Feb, and every Sunday May-Nov. Cost: From $800 full board and classes in château. Contact: Michael Giammarella in U.S.; (800) 484-1234 ext 0096 or Ecole des Trois Ponts, Château de Matel, 42300 Roanne, France; (011) 33-477-70-80-01, fax (011) 33-477-71-53-00; info@3ponts.edu, www.3ponts.edu.

French in France. Among the ways to learn French, total immersion is the most enjoyable and the most effective. We have been doing it for 20 years in a small historical city located in Normandy (west of Paris, close to the seaside). We welcome people at any age and any level in 1- to 10-week programs, intensive or vacation type, from mid-March to mid-November.

Dates: Spring: Mar 23-May 29; Summer: Jun 15-Aug 28; Fall: Sep 7-Nov 13 (1998). Cost: From $525 per week (tuition, room and board, and excursions). Contact: Dr. Almeras, Chairman, French American Study Center, 12, 14, Blvd. Carnot, B.P. 176, 14104 Lisieux Cedex, France (011) 33-2-31-31-22-01, fax (011) 33-2-31-31-22-21; centre.normandie@wanadoo.fr.

The French Traveler. Enjoy various regions of France for 8-9 days on theme trips focusing on art, wine and cuisine, spas, architecture, etc. Small groups (12-15); simple or deluxe trips, affordable. Particular specialties: affinity groups, family reunions, alumni, special events. Trips all year round. Fax for free brochure: (617) 484-2309.

Dates: Year round. Cost: $1,850-$2,950. Contact: Valerie Sutter, The French Traveler, 206 Claflin St., Belmont, MA 02178; (617) 484-1673, fax (617) 484-2309; frenchtraveler@juno.com.

Horizons Art and Travel. Provençe evokes images of grape vines, olives, sun-filled landscapes, and a profusion of antique monuments-it is all this and more. A week in the stunning hilltop village of Venasque, ringed by Roman monuments, sleepy wine villages, red ocher cliffs and mountains. Lodging in a charming bed and breakfast. Workshops include Painting, Photography, Fabric Printing, Faux Finishes.

Dates: Apr 9-16, Sep 25-Oct 1. Cost: $1,425 (lodging, all meals except 1 lunch, tuition, and field trips). Contact: Karen Totman-Gale, Horizons, 108 N. Main St.-T, Sunderland, MA 01375; (413) 665-0300, fax (413) 665-4141; horizons@horizons-art.org, www.horizons-art.org.

"Le Marmiton" Cooking School. Le Marmiton cookery school offers its clients the chance to learn about Provençal cuisine. Lessons are given in a 19th century kitchen, and we invite only the best chefs from around the region to teach. The pupils prepare a delightful meal which is then enjoyed by the whole class and any friends they might wish to invite.

Dates: Five classes per month except in Jan,

Jul, and Aug (1998). Cost: From FF400 per person per day. Contact: Martin Stein, Hotel de la Mirande, 4, place de La Mirande, F-84000 Avignon, France; (011) 33-4-90-85-93-93, fax (011) 33-4-90-86-26-85; www.la-mirande.fr.

Modernism in Paris. You will explore the world of the writers and artists who lived and worked in Paris in the early 20th century. Highlights include visits to museums, sites of artists' salons, and more. The course is open to anyone with an interest in art, literature, and the nature of creativity.

Dates: May 25-Jun 8. Cost: $1,960. Includes airfare, hotel, breakfast, program costs, and tuition (1998). Contact: Jody A. Dudderar, Rockland Community College, 145 College Rd., Suffern, NY 10901; (914) 574-4205, fax (914) 574-4423; study-abroad@sunyrockland. edu.

Pottery Courses. Throwing, glazing, firing.

Dates: Jul and Aug. Cost: FF5,000 for 2-week courses, FF2,800 for 1-week courses. Includes lodging and meals (1998). Contact: Simonot, Mas Cassac, F-30500 Allegre, France; (011) 33-4-66-24-8565, fax (011) 33-4-66-24-8055.

REMPART—Preserving the Past. REMPART aims to preserve the French cultural heritage through the restoration of threatened buildings and monuments. It consists of a grouping of more than 140 autonomous associations organizing workcamps providing a wide variety of work projects involving the restoration of medieval towns, castles, churches, ancient walls, wind/watermills, and industrial sites. Work includes masonry, excavations, woodwork, stone cutting, interior decorating, and clearance work. Opportunities for sports, exploring the region, and taking part in local festivities. Minimum age is 13. Previous experience is not necessary. Some knowledge of French required.

Dates: Workcamps last from 2 to 3 weeks. Most of them are open during Easter holidays and from Jul to Sep. A few camps are open throughout the year. Cost: FF220 for insurance, FF40-FF50 per day for food and accommodations. Volunteers help with camp duties, pay their own fares, and should bring a sleeping bag. Contact: REMPART, Foreign Secretary: Sabine Guilbert, Union des Associations pour la réhabilitation et l'Entretien des Monuments et du Patrimoine Artistique, 1 rue des Guillemites, 75004 Paris, France; (011) 33-1-42-71-9655, fax (011) 33-1-42-71-7300.

Six-Month Painting Course. Spend 6 months in France in a rural village of the Loire Valley drawing and painting. Enjoy the peaceful environment of the French country: 30 hours of class per week, American instructor.

Dates: Call for details. Cost: $3,000 for 6 months instruction and accommodations from $300 and up per month (1998). Contact: Ateliers Sans Frontières, J. Tilkin, 49310 Les Cerqueux s/s Passavant, France; fax (011) 33-2-41-59-55-57.

Summer Workshops France. Since 1981, painting, drawing, and French language workshops in Montaigut-le-Blanc, a medieval hill village in the rugged Auvergne region of France. The art courses include all media and levels; the French courses include intermediate and advanced levels. Optional guided stay in Paris is also offered in July.

Dates: Two workshops: 1 in Jul and 1 in Sep. Cost: July only: $2,645 (subject to change) 19-day workshop (3 courses), accommodations, all meals, drinks, and 4 excursions (no travel). Contact: Continuing Education Dept., Capilano College, 2055 Purcell Way, N. Vancouver, BC V7J 3H5, Canada; (604) 984-4901, fax (604) 983-7545; ctang@capcollege. bc.ca or Cindy Horton, Infinity Travel (888) 986-2262 or (604) 986-2262; infinity@ ibm.net.

Germany

Collegium Palatinum Heidelberg. A German language institute, located in downtown Heidelberg, offering German at all levels from beginner to advanced. Two-, 4- and 8-week courses year round. Combination courses, one-on-one tuition and customized courses for groups. Recreational and cultural program. Accommodations: residential, guest family, private arrangement, or hotel.

Dates: Year round. Cost: Four weeks DM2,370; 8 weeks DM1,730. Activity program extra. Contact: Mrs. Martine Berthet-Richter, PR Director, Adenauerplatz 8, D-69115 Heidelberg, Germany; (011) 49-6221-46289, fax (011) 49-6221-182023; SchillerUS@ aol.com.

German as a Foreign Language. Various levels of German year round; intensive, crash, and long-term courses, individual tuition. Special feature: German and theater. Special programs: business German for professionals, German for teachers, German in a teacher's home, German for special purposes. Academic year for high school students, international study year, internship, guest studentship, homestays for groups, courses for firms and other institutions (banking, insurance, doctors, lawyers, etc.), residential language camps for juniors, examination preparation. Various types of accommodations. Full range of activities.

Dates: Year round. Cost: Contact school for details. Contact: GLS Sprachenzentrum, Barbara Jaeschke, Managing Director, Kolonnenstrasse 26, 10829 Berlin, Germany; (011) 49-30-787-41-52; fax (011) 49-30-787-41-92; gls.berlin@t-online.de, www.gls-berlin.com.

Greece

An Archaeological Tour of Greece. Obtain first-hand knowledge of the art and architecture of ancient Greece through on-site archaeological visits and museum tours. This is the only course of its kind in which students are invited to have one of their lectures inside the Parthenon. Other highlights include visits to Sparta, Corinth, Mycenae, the Olympia Grounds, Delphi, Thermopylae, and Mystra, the world's best-preserved medieval city. The trip ends with 4 days on the island of Mykonos and a visit to the "birthplace" of Apollo.

Dates: Jun 7-Jun 29 (1998). Cost: $2,800 (3 credits) includes roundtrip airfare, double occupancy rooms, breakfast daily, bus, ship, and airport transfers. Contact: Dora Riomayor, Director of International Studies, School of Visual Arts, 209 E. 23rd St., New York, NY 10010-3994; (212) 592-2543, fax (212) 592-2545.

Art School of the Aegean. Art classes and Greek studies in a small seaside village on the island of Samos. Classes: Pinhole Camera, Mosaic/Tile Making, Landscape Painting, Paper Making and Installation Project, Multi Media Sculpture. Evening program: Classical Greek Studies, Art History, and an informal introduction to the Greek Language and Contemporary Greek culture. For adult and college students.

Dates: Tour: Jun 15; Art classes: Jun 20. Payment due by Apr 1. Cost: $1,970. Contact: Susan Trovas, Director, Art School of the Aegean, P.O. Box 1375, Sarasota, FL 34230-1375; (941) 351-5597; greece3@gte.net, www.studyabroad.com/aegean.

Guatemala

Art Workshops in Guatemala. Provides 10-day art classes as backstrap weaving, photography, beading, papermaking, creative writing, in the visual, fiber, book arts, and much more. All classes are held in Antigua, Guatemala. (Will be expanding to other countries soon.)

Dates: Classes held during Jan, Feb, Mar, Apr, and Nov. Cost: Approx. $1,700 including airfare from U.S., lodging, tuition, field trips, and all ground transportation. Contact: Liza Fourre, Director, Art Workshops in Guatemala, 4758 Lyndale Ave. S, Minneapolis, MN 55409-2304; (612) 825-0747, fax (612) 825-6637; info@artguat.org, www.artguat.org.

Iceland

Iceland 1999. Specialized active vacations in Iceland.

Dates: May-Aug. Cost: TBA. Contact: Dick Phillips, Dick Phillips Icelandic Travel, Whitehall House, Nenthead, Alston CA9 3PS, U.K.; Tel./fax (011) 44-1434-381440.

India

Kolam Tours. Personalized tour programs for groups and individuals are people oriented, culturally sensitive, ecologically aware, and politically conscious.

Dates: Individually customized tours from Aug to Mar. Cost: From $75 per person per day for group tours for accommodations (3-star), most meals, all surface travel (road and rail), tours with guides. No hidden costs. Contact: Ranjith Henry, Kolam, Responsible Tours and Soft Travel, B22 Bay View Apts., Kalakshetra Colony, Besant Nagar, Chennai/Madras 600 090 India; (011) 91-44-4913404/4919872, fax (011) 91-44-4900939/4915767; http://ourworld.compuserve.com/homepages/kolam.

Indonesia

The Back Roads of Bali. Go where the tourists aren't! Intellectually curious adventurers, trekkers, and water sport enthusiasts: explore misty volcano, shimmering jungle forests, native villages, national parks and wildlife, meandering rice fields, monuments, excavations, and the colorful underwater life of Bali. Stay in traditional bungalows. In-depth seminars on Balinese customs/culture.

Dates: Feb 28-Mar 11; Aug 16-30. Cost: $2,750 includes air. Contact: Danu Enterprises, P.O. Box 156, Capitola, CA 95010; (831) 476-0543; danu@earthlink.net.

Experiencing the Arts in Bali. Providing insight and practice into Bali's arts and craft. Based in the cultural center, includes island tours, traditional dance performances, and 10 classes in Gamelan music, dance, painting, batik, or mask carving, taught by Balinese artists in family compounds. A life-changing experience created by quality guides with 16-year track record.

Dates: Jul 4-24; Jul 25-Aug 14. Cost: $3,100 includes air. Contact: Danu Enterprises, P.O. Box 156, Capitola, CA 95010; (831) 476-0543; danu@earthlink.net.

The Healing Arts of Bali. Research Bali's traditional healing practices, observe the work of folk doctors, study herbal medicines, temple offerings, traditional massages, and herbal body revitalization experiences. Besides this, participants visit all Bali's top attractions on island tours, attend dance performances and trance rituals, visit artists, and enjoy expert seminars on Balinese culture and religion.

Dates: Mar 10-25; Aug 1-15. Cost: $2,800 includes air. Contact: Danu Enterprises, P.O. Box 156, Capitola, CA 95010; (831) 476-0543; danu@earthlink.net.

Israel

Tel Dor Excavation Project. The Tel Dor Excavation Project is devoted to investigating one of the largest coastal cities in ancient Israel. Volunteers will be engaged in all facets of field archaeology, and in some of the preliminary work of artifact analysis.

Dates: May 30-Aug 11. Cost: $28 per day and $65 participation fee per week. Contact: Dr. I. Sharon, Tel Dor Excavation Project, Institute of Archaeology, Hebrew Univ., Jerusalem, Israel.

Italy

Art and Design in Florence. The Accademia Italiana is an international, university-level

Special Interest Vacations

institute of art and design. The Accademia offers courses in art, fashion, interior, industrial and textile design during the autumn and spring semesters and fashion design, fashion illustration, drawing and painting, window display design and Italian language during the months of June and July.

Dates: Jan 14-May 22, Jun, Jul, Sep 9-Dec 22. Cost: Depends on course chosen. Contact: Barbara McHugh, Accademia Italiana, Piazza Pitti n. 15, 50125 Florence, Italy; (011) 39-55-284616/211619, fax (011) 39-55-284486; modaita@tin.it, www.gamut.it/accademia.

Art Workshop Int'l., Assisi. Live and work in a 12th-century hilltown surrounded by the Umbrian landscape. Instructional courses: painting, drawing, artmaking, all media, art history, creative writing, fiction, poetry. Independent program for professional painters/writers. Two- to 6-week sessions Jun-Aug. Visiting artists. New York painters/instructors.

Dates: TBA. Cost: Vary. Contact: Bea Kreloff, 463 West St., 1028H, New York, NY 10014; Tel./fax (800) 835-7454; www.vacation-inc.com/workshops/artworkshop.html.

Arte/Vita Workshops. Immerse yourself in artmaking for 2 weeks in Tuscany. Arte/Vita workshops encourage your artistic growth in a structured, open atmosphere. Draw and paint from observation, make paper, bind books, learn about Renaissance art materials, and visit hidden treasures in Florence while developing a project of your own conception.

Dates: May 22-Jun 5. Cost: $2,100. Includes homemade meals, studio space, ground transportation, admission fees, and reading materials. Airfare and art supplies not included. Contact: Arte/Vita, 1081 High Falls Rd., Catskill, NY 12414; (212) 726-1379; jph340@columbia.edu; www.artevita.net.

Biking and Walking Tours. Specializing in Italy for over 10 years, Ciclismo Classico distills the "Best of Italy," offering more unique Italian destinations than any other active vacation company. Educational, active tours for all abilities in Umbria, Tuscany, Piedmont, the Dolomites, Puglia, Sicily, the Amalfi Coast, Cinque Terre, Sardegna, Abruzzo, Campania, Corsica, and Elba. Ireland, too. Charming accommodations, expert bilingual guides, cooking demonstrations, wine tastings, support vehicle, detailed route instructions, visits to local festivals, countryside picnics—an unforgettable cultural indulgence.

Dates: Apr-Nov (70 departures). Call for specific dates. Cost: $1,500-$3,000. Contact: Lauren Hefferon, Director, Ciclismo Classico, 13 Marathon St., Arlington, MA 02174; (800) 866-7314 or (781) 646-3377.

Italiaidea. Italiaidea is a center for comprehensive Italian instruction. We offer every level and format of Italian study from intensive short-term "survival" Italian courses to advanced, semester-long courses meeting once or twice a week. We offer on-site lectures and visits to historic sites in Italian, conversation, and flexible scheduling. For over 10 years we have been offering college credit courses at numerous U.S. college and university programs in Italy; we now offer both academic assistance and travel/study assistance to our client institutions. Homestays are offered as well as accommodations in shared apartments.

Dates: Year round. Cost: Sixty-hour group course LIT780,000; 25-hour one-on-one program LIT1,200,000; 15 hour-specific purposes or culture LIT1,330,000 (taxes not included). Contact: Carolina Ciampaglia, Co-Director, Piazza della Cancelleria 5, 00186 Roma, Italy; (011) 39-6-68307620, fax (011) 39-6-6892997; italiaidea@italiaidea.com, www.italiaidea.com.

Italian Courses for Foreigners. Italian language courses for foreigners, from beginner to proficiency, open all year round. Courses: G-20 group courses in the morning 20 hours per week; GK-25 combination courses 25 hours per week; GK-30 combination intensive courses 30 hours per week. Cultural courses: Italian cooking, business Italian, commercial correspondence, history of art, Italian wines. Accommodations: family, flat, small hotels.

Dates: Jan 4, Jan 18; Feb 1, Feb 15; Mar 1, Mar 15; Apr 6, Apr 19; May 3, May 17; Jun 7, Jun 21; Jul 5, Jul 19; Aug 2, Aug 16, Aug 30; Sep 13, Sep 27; Oct 11, Oct 25; Nov 8, Nov 22; Dec 6. Cost: Two weeks: LIT560,000 (G20), 1,130,000 (GK25), 1,640,000 (GK30); 4 weeks: LIT820,000 (G20), 1,880,000 (G25), 2,820,000 (GK30). Contact: Prof. Bruno Fabbri, "I Malatesta," Corso d'Augusto 144, 47900 Rimini, Italy; (011) 39-541-56487, fax (011) 39-541-21088; imalatesta@rn.nettuno.it, www.akros.it/imalatesta.

Italian Renaissance. Based in Florence and Rome, explore the achievements of writers, painters, sculptors, and architects of the Italian Renaissance. Highlights include visits to the David, the Duomo, Giotto's Bell Tower, the Vatican Museums, the Sistine Chapel, and St. Peter's Basilica. Experience Italian Renaissance literature, art, and architecture where it was created.
Dates: May 28-Jun 11 (1998). Cost: $2,190. Includes airfare, hotel, breakfast, program costs, and tuition. Contact: Jody A. Dudderar, Rockland Community College, 145 College Rd., Suffern, NY 10901; (914) 574-4205, fax (914) 574-4423; studyabroad@sunyrockland. edu.

Italiano a Modo Mio. Sixth consecutive year: Castiglione della Pescaia/Tuscany; Marzabotto/ Bologna; Sulmona. Eight-day customized programs of "breakfast-to-bedtime" full immersion in Italian. Limited to 8 well-motivated adults per class. Studies reinforced by practical application to real-life situations while enjoying Italian food and culture.
Dates: May 9-30; Aug 29-Sep 19; Oct 3-17 (8-day programs). Cost: $2,000-$3,500 includes single occupancy, classes, meals, activities. Airfare not included. Contact: Sergio Stefani, 33 Riverside Dr., 1E, New York, NY 10023; (212) 595-7004; annamaria@italianmyway.com, www.italianmyway.com.

Learn Italian in Italy. Study Italian in a 16th century Renaissance palace in the center of Florence, or in a classic Tuscan town just 30 minutes from the sea. Koiné Center's professional language teachers and small class sizes encourage active participation by each student. Cultural program, guided excursions, choice of accommodations including host families.
Dates: Year round; starting dates each month. Cost: Two-week intensive program $290; 3 weeks $390; homestay accommodations from $115 per week. Contact: In Italy: Dr. Andrea Moradei, Koiné Center, Via Pandolfini 27, 50122 Firenze, Italy; (011) 39-055-213881. In North America: (800) 274-6007; homestay@teleport.com; www.koine center.com.

Myth and Movement. Jeanne Bresciana, renowned dancer, educator, and director of the Isadora Duncan International Institute, combines movement with history, art, music and poetry in a sensory odyssey through locales rich in myth and beauty. Using movement, you will explore the creative forces within yourself and the Tuscan landscape, lush with vineyards awaiting harvest.
Dates: Sep 20-26 (1998). Cost: $2,045 includes meals and local ground transportation. Airfare not included. Contact: Tuscany Institute for Advanced Studies, c/o Ellen Bastio, 4626 Knoy Rd., #7, College Park, MD 20740; (800) 943-8070.

Tuscany: Horizons Art and Travel. Tuscany is studded with panoramic landscapes, ancient walled villages, olive groves and vineyards... and capped by the gorgeous cities of Florence and Siena. Lodging in a charming country inn/ villa in the heart of Chianti country, perfectly situated to see the sites of the region. Workshops include painting, glass beads, mosaics, book arts, jewelry, photography.
Dates: Apr 17-Apr 24, Oct 2-Oct 9. Cost: $1,425 (lodging, all meals except 1 lunch, tuition, and field trips). Contact: Karen Totman-Gale, Horizons, 108 N. Main St.-T, Sunderland, MA 01375; (413) 665-0300, fax (413) 665-4141; horizons@horizons-art.org, www.horizons-art.org.

Malta

Prehistory in Mediterranean Malta. Archaeology is adventure in Malta, where 7,000 years of human history continues. New and important discoveries are on the horizon. We'll visit megalithic temples that are the oldest buildings still standing on earth and talk with experts who know the sites intimately. Conservation of this remarkable heritage is a global responsibility.

Dates: Varies. Call for availability. Cost: From $1,387 land cost for 8 nights first-class accommodations, nearly all meals, full program of presentations, field trips, and excursions. All program proceeds support historic conservation efforts in Malta and Gozo. Contact: The OTS Foundation Education and Historic Preservation in Malta, P.O. Box 17166, Sarasota, FL 34276; (800) 680-2766, fax (941) 918-0265; otsf@aol.com, www.swift-tourism.com/ots.htm.

Mediterranean

Sailing Yacht Charters. GPSC offers group and individual charters of crewed and bareboat sailing yachts, motorsailers, and motor yachts from 27' to 250'. GPSC also offers "learn to sail" programs in Greece, and 10-14 day all-inclusive packages. Ideal for those with a variety of interests (exploring sailing, snorkeling, racing, archaeology, hiking, naturalism, gastronomy) who seek adventure off the beaten path.

Dates: Ongoing. Cost: Varies. Contact: Ginny Heyer, Chartering Manager, GPSC Charters Ltd., 600 St. Andrews Rd., Philadelphia, PA 19118; (800) 732-6786, (215) 247-3903, fax (215) 247-1505; ginny@gpsc.com, www.gpsc.com.

Mexico

Intensive Language Programs. Intensive Spanish immersion program in groups, 40 class hours per week including Spanish class, lectures, and Hispano-American courses. Executive, semester, and specialized programs for teachers, professionals, nurses, and adults continuing education. Live with Mexican family or in student residence. Excursions to historical and archaeological sites.

Dates: Year round starting every Monday. Cost: Tuition $190 per week; lodging $154 per week. Contact: The Center for Bilingual Multicultural Studies, Javier Espinosa, San Jeronimo #304, Cuernavaca, MOR-62179, Mexico; (011) 52-73-17-10-87, fax (011) 52-73-17-05-33; admin@bilingual-center.com, www.bilingual-center.com.

Language and Culture in Guanajuato. We work with innovative teaching techniques, tailoring instruction to each student's needs. Spanish, Mexican history, politics, culture-cuisine, folk dancing, and Latin American literature.

Dates: Year round. New classes begin every Monday. Cost: $925. Includes 4 weeks of classes and homestay with 3 meals daily. Contact: Director Jorge Barroso, Instituto Falcon, A.C., Guanajuato, Gto. 36000 Mexico; Tel./fax (011) 52-473-1-0745, infalcon@redes.int.com.mx, www.infonet.com.mx/falcon.

Latin American Studies, Spanish. Intensive Spanish language study in small groups at all language levels, taught by native speakers. Latin American studies courses in history, literature, Mexican arts and crafts, current events, Mexican cuisine, anthropology of Mexico, extensive program of field study excursions led by Cemanahuac anthropologists. Academic credit available; professional seminars arranged; family homestay highly recommended.

Dates: Classes begin each Monday year round. Cost: Registration, tuition, room and board with Mexican family for 2 weeks: $756. Contact: Vivian B. Harvey, Educational Programs Coordinator, Cemanahuac Educational Community, Apartado 5-21, Cuernavaca, Morelos, Mexico; (011) 52-73-18-6407, fax

Vacations in Ecuador
Combine Language Immersion with Ecotoursim

By Clay and Joanna Hubbs

In a recent issue of *Transitions Abroad* magazine we called Quito, Ecuador, perhaps "the best city in the world for Spanish language study" and emphasized that Ecuador "offers some of the best ecotourism in the Western Hemisphere." With a few days on our hands and other reasons to take us in this direction, my wife and I investigated for ourselves the opportunities to combine the two—language study and ecotourism—in one vacation. On our first day we found ourselves happily lost in a rainforest, attempting to speak Spanish, and already planning a return trip.

We found—not to our surprise—that combining language learning and adventure is a remarkably inexpensive and richly rewarding way to spend a vacation. And it's also a great deal of fun. Many of the more than 60 language schools in Quito include, as part of their program, outings to the mountains, jungles, and rainforests that surround the city.

Language immersion in Quito means living with a host family whose members can (or will) speak only Spanish, spending from four to seven hours a day with your own tutor, learning at your own pace, developing the vocabulary that's important to you, and making periodic excursions—in most schools with your own tutor and always speaking Spanish—to local places of interest.

Our host family welcomed us like long-lost relatives, made us feel at home, and gave us a key to the door so we could come and go as we pleased. Because of our limited time, we selected only one school for an extended visit, the **Academia Latinamericano** (Jose Queri 2 y Eloy Alfaro, P.O. Box 17-17-593, Quito; from U.S. call 011-593-2-433-820; in U.S. contact Suzanne Bell at 801-268-4608, fax 801-265-9156; latinoa1@spanish.com. ec, http://ecnct.cc/academia/learnspa.htm). The atmosphere at the Academia is that of a warm and close-knit family. Hours of individualized study are from 8 a.m.-12:30 or 1:15 p.m. with a short break when students place their orders for lunch, send money out to be changed, etc. The school provides a variety of services so that student are free to concentrate on learning Spanish.

We were amazed by the personal attention that every student receives. Each member of the del Coral family—the parents; the children, Sandra, Patty, and Diego; and Sandra's and Patty's small children—are at the school throughout the day and often take part in the twice-weekly excursions. At least one family member meets every student at the airport when they arrive, regardless of the time. Diego and Patty were both Rotary Foundation exchange students in the U.S. They say they know what it's like to arrive in a strange country for the first time, and they want every student to feel secure and relaxed from the moment they step off the plane.

The school is in a large and elegant home inside a walled garden in a green and affluent neighborhood. Amenities include a heated indoor swimming pool, sauna, hot tub, lounges with a TV-VCR system and a stock of educational and travel tapes, and a large eat-in kitchen where students can join the family for lunch.

As at other schools we visited, activities are organized at the Acadamia Latinamericano according to the interests of the students—dancing lessons, cooking lessons, etc. You can even take lessons with a professional golfer while you learn Spanish.

Students themselves decide where to go on optional twice-weekly outings, always accompanied by their tutors and always speaking only Spanish. On the day we arrived, the destination was Aldea Salamandra, a spectacular nature reserve in the lush tropical rainforest on the western slopes of Pichincha, 140 km northwest of Quito. We spent the day trekking with Darwin, a 15-year-old local guide, who not only introduced us to the flora and fauna of the rainforest but took us to his home and showed us how he and his family lived off the forest's products.

Another group at the school was bound for a week in the Galapagos Islands. Afterwards, they would return to the Academia for a week of intensive Spanish instruction before going down to the Amazon basin for yet another week of ecotouring. Here, as at other schools we visited, schedules are flexible and can be customized for groups as well as for individuals. (Weekly rates at the Academia Latinamericano range from $296 for fours hours of one-on-one instruction five days a week with seven nights' host family accommodations to $362 for seven hours of daily instruction plus family stay.)

Diego del Coral arranged transportation to an ecolodge above Otavalo—just two hours to the north—where we spent the weekend hiking around the Mojanda lakes at a breathtaking altitude high above the town. In the evenings we were entertained by, and provided entertainment for, the local villagers who came to the Casa Mojanda. The men played their handmade instruments and the young women coaxed us to join them in their dance.

Amazon Trips

Visitors to Ecuador who want to combine a week-long adventure in the rainforest with professional Spanish instruction can enroll in the Spanish Program Anaconda sponsored by the **Academia de Espanol Quito**, the first language school in Quito, founded in 1982. (Contact: Edgar J. Alverez, Director, Academia de Espanol, Quito, P.O. Box 17-15-0039-C, Quito, Ecuador; from the U.S. call 011-293-2-553-647; in the U.S. contact Kay Rafool at Language Link Inc., P.O. Box 3006, Peoria, IL 61612; (800) 552-2051, fax (309) 692-2926; info@langlink.com, www.langlink.com.)

The curriculum includes four hours of tutoring each day and a daily excursion accompanied by the language teacher and a group of native guides. Students stay in Cabanas Anaconda on Anaconda Island in the Amazon basin. Excursions from base camp include a trip by motorized canoe up the Arajuno River to learn about medicinal plants, a trip to a native village, a rafting trip on the Napo or Arajuno River on a raft built by the students themselves using native techniques, and a gold-panning expedition led by indigenous people. The cost, including roundtrip transportation from Quito, is $408.

The Anaconda program is organized in cooperation with the Fundacion Jatun Sacha, a nonprofit Ecuadorian organization that supports biological conservation, research, and education. (JS also offers volunteer opportunities. See sidebar.) Some knowledge of Spanish is essential for the Anaconda program.

Academia de Espanol also offers intensive one-on-one instruction—in its own six-story building (with roof terrace bar) near the business center of Quito—for either four or seven hours per day. Students who choose the half-day option (Espanol Activa) can join daily afternoon excursions with teachers acting as guides. Group courses with seven students or less (two weeks, 10 days of classes, 50 hours) cost $440 with full board with a family or $170 for tuition only; one-on-one instruction costs $6 per hour;

two weeks of individual classes seven hours daily (10 days) with 14 days of family stay costs $700.

Galapagos Islands trips are discounted approximately 30 percent for students at Academia de Espanol Quito. Several schools offer similar ecotour packages.

Other language schools we visited in Quito—all of which have been consistently praised by South American Explorers Club members for teachers' competence and enthusiasm, quality of facilities, location, extracurricular activities, and other services—include: **Bipo & Toni's**, J. Carrion 300 y Leonidas Plaza; Tel./fax (011) 593 2 540-618; bipo@ pi.pro.ec, http//homepage.iprolink. ch/~bipo/. $5 per hour. Dancing lessons $4 per hour, cooking lessons $6 per hour. Free e-mail service. Weekly excursions. Bipo & Toni's is involved in a development project for the poor in Pomasqui, on the outskirts of Quito, and a reforestation project on the extinct volcano Casitahua. Volunteer workers are needed. **Instituto Superior de Espanol**, Ulloa 152 y J. Carrion (also at Darquea Deran 1650 y 10 de Agosto); 011-293-2-223-242 (Ecuadorian owned). $5 per hour, $10 inscription fee. Excursions and group cooking organized every week. Can arrange voluntary work. **Simon Bolivar**, Leonidas Plaza 690 y Wilson; (011) 293-2-226-635; khaugan@aol.com, www.studyabroad.com/simon. $5 per hour. The school has an in-house travel agency. It offers salsa lessons and excursions every weekend.

All schools in Quito can place you with a family for a cost of $9-$15 per day.

Quito Travel Info

Independent travelers to Quito are fortunate to have available the services of the non-profit **South American Explorer's Club**. At its clubhouses in Quito and Lima, Peru and its U.S. headquarters in Ithaca, New York, the club collects and makes available to its members volumes of up-to-date travel information on Central and South America.

For a membership fee of $40 per year ($60 for couples) members have access to the club's knowledgeable staff and trip reports on just about every subject: language schools, volunteering, local tour operators, visiting the Galápagos, etc. Reports are available by mail (for a small photocopying fee) from the U.S. address: 126 Indian Creek Rd., Ithaca, NY 14850; (607) 227-0488, fax (607) 277-6122; explorer@samexplo.org, www.samexplo.org (9 a.m.-5 p.m. weekdays).

Ecolodges in Ecuador

Casa Mojanda (Apartado 160, Otavalo, Ecuador; Tel./fax 011-593-9-731737; mojanda@ uio.telconet.net, www.casamojanda.com) an ecologically oriented inn located three miles from Otavalo in the Andes of northern Ecuador overlooking the sacred father and mother mountains, Imbabura and Cotacachi. Guests stay in adobe cottages with spectacular mountain views. The owners, who built the inn and moved from New York to run it two years ago, are exploring ways for environmentally and socially aware travelers to interact with local communities in positive ways. Volunteers are needed to assist in environmental protection and community development projects.

Fundacion Jatan Sacha (Rio Coca 17-34, Casilla 1712867, Quito, Ecuador; Tel./fax 011-593-2-441-592; jatsacha@sacha.ec) offers volunteer opportunities in a variety of conservation projects under the supervision of resident researchers, environmental education instructors, and administrators at each of their three reserves. Volunteers live with families or in cabins with other volunteers. Cost ranges from $220 to $300 per month including all meals and lodging. Contact: David Neill.

Cerro Golondrinas Cloudforest Conservation Project, Isabel La Catolica 1559y Salazar, Quito, Ecuador; fax (011) 593-2-222-390; manteca@uio.satnet.net. Contact: Piet Sabbe. A project in northwestern Ecuador to conserve 25,000 acres of highland forest and introduce new agroforestry techniques. Volunteers help with collecting seeds, planting trees, clearing trails, etc. and work with local farmers problems of deforestation and soil conservation.

Yachana Lodge, Ancrade Marín 188 y Diego de Almagro, Quito, Ecuador; (011) 593-2-543-851, fax 220-362; dtm@pi.pro.ec. Part of the Funedesin Foundation Mondaña Project—which is helping 30 indigenous communities build schools and a medical clinic, install running water, and more—the lodge provides a beautiful and comfortable setting for visitors to experience the Amazon and learn about the endangered ecosystem. Located two hours by motorized canoe from Misahualli. Nonvolunteer visitors pay $70 per day for lodging, meals, and guide. Contact: Douglas McMeekan.

Black Sheep Inn, Apartado 04-01-240, Latacunga, Cotopaxi, Ecuador. An ecologically friendly inn located at 10,000 feet on the furthest west edge of the western cordillera of the Ecuadorian Andes overlooking Rio Toachi Canyon, the "Grand Canyon" of Ecuador, it provides a comfortable base for hiking and visiting indigenous markets. Guests pay $30 per day single, $15 shared room; includes two meals. Contact Andréas Hammerman and Michelle Kirby. For work opportunities at Black Sheep Inn e-mail heals@socrates.berkeley.edu.

For more information on volunteering and jungle stays in Ecuador, including programs hosted by indigenous communities, contact the South American Explorers Club in Quito at Jorge Washington 311; Tel./fax (011) 593-2-225-228.

(011) 52-73-12-5418; 74052.2570@compuserve. com, www.cemanahuac.com. Call (800) 247-6641 for a brochure.

Study or Work-Study in Cuernavaca. Intensive written and conversational Spanish classes given by credentialed and experienced native teachers. Six hours of classes daily with no more than 4 students to a class. Hotel is optional but homestay is highly recommended for maximum advancement and cultural exposure. Activities and excursions are offered in addition to classes each week. Register for any length of time.

Dates: Year round. New classes begin every Monday. Cost: Under $1,200. Includes registration fee, 4-week tuition, room and board for 30 days. Contact: C.R. Roberts, Personal Tours International, 12976 Sycamore Village Dr., Norwalk, CA 90650-8334; fax (562) 920-0121; per.tours@worldnet.att.net.

Nepal

Explorations in Medicine and Culture. An extraordinary opportunity to learn from experts: a variety of Asian healing systems while you trek through breathtaking vistas of the Himalayas, encounter a variety of cultures and their rituals, visit Chitwan Wildlife Sanctuary, and explore the wondrous city of Kathmandu. Regular and CME tours. Free brochure; (800) 833-2444.

Dates: Mar 14-Mar 31; Apr 2-Apr 27; Sep 3-Sep 21; Oct 4-Oct 19; Nov 5-Nov 23. Cost: $2,295-$3,295 plus airfare depending on 16- or 19-day tour and season. Includes breakfast, 3 banquets, lodging, air and land transportation in Nepal, guides and fees. Contact: Explorations, P.O. Box 130465, Ann Arbor, MI 48113; (313) 971-4754, fax (313) 971-0042; emcnepal@worldnet.att.net, www.explorations-altmed.com.

New Zealand

Serious Fun New Zealand. Serious Fun has operated hiking oriented, small group adventure tours of New Zealand since 1987. The 14-day Best of the South Island Tour (departures Nov-Mar) is highlighted by a swim with the dolphins at Kaikoura and a 3-day tramp along the Routeburn Track.

Dates: Jan 18-31; Feb 22-Mar 7; Mar 22-Apr 4; Nov 22-Dec 5, 1999; Dec 20, 1999-Jan 2, 2000; Jan 17-30; Feb 21-Mar 5, Mar 20-Apr 2, 2000. Cost: 1998: $2,800 (11-day $2,200). Includes ground transportation, meals, lodging, activities, guide, t-shirt. Contact: Stu Wilson, c/o Outland Adventures, 3103 Whiteway Dr., Austin, TX 78757; (800) 411-5724, fax (512) 459-0990; outland@bga.com, www.seriousfun newzealand.com.

Papua New Guinea

Trans Niugini Tours. Nature and culture programs are offered in 3 areas: the Highlands, the Sepik Area, and a marine environment on the North Coast. Each area has its own distinct culture and environment, with comfortable wilderness lodges.

Dates: Weekly departures. Cost: $889-$3,570 per person (land cost). Contact: Bob Bates, Trans Niugini Tours, P.O. Box 371, Mt. Hagen, Papua New Guinea; (800) 521-7242 or (011) 675-542-1438, fax (011) 675-542-2470; travel@pngtours.com, www.pngtours. com.

Peru

Amazon and Andes Exploration. Scholar escorted, small group adventures to the Amazon rainforest and Cuzco, Machu Picchu in the Andes. Amazon jungle safaris and treetop canopy walkway, riverboat cruises. Inca archaeology and colonial history.

Dates: Monthly departures, year round. Cost: Varies. Approx. $2,000 from Miami for an 8-day program. Contact: Charlie Strader, Explorations Inc., 27655 Kent Rd., Bonita Springs, FL 34135; (800) 446-9660, fax (941)

992-7666; cesxplor@aol.com, http://members.aol.com/xplorper.

Russia and the NIS

Off the Beaten Path. Unique, flexible, and affordable travel opportunities for individuals and small groups. MIR is a 12-year veteran specialty tour operator with representation in Moscow, St. Petersburg, Kiev, Irkutsk, Ulan Ude and Tashkent. Homestays, Trans-Siberian rail journeys, Central Asian explorations, Mongolian adventures, European brewery adventures. Customized independent and group travel.

Dates: Year round; scheduled departures for tours. Cost: Homestays from $40 a night; full packaged tours from $1,175. Contact: MIR Corporation, 85 S. Washington St., Suite 210, Seattle, WA 98104; (800) 424-7289 or (206) 624-7289, fax (206) 624-7360; mir@igc.apc.org, www.mircorp.com.

South Africa

South Africa after Mandela. Assess firsthand the progress and problems of a new South Africa. Meet activists in education, health, labor, media, human rights, and the church. Focus on grassroots development in Soweto/Johannesburg, Durban/Kwazulu and Capetown regions.

Dates: Aug 1-22. Cost: $3,995 from NY. Includes airfare, 2 meals daily, simple lodging, land transport, and facilitators. Contact: Vic Ulmer, Our Developing World, 13004 Paseo Presada, Saratoga, CA 95070-4125; (408) 379-4431, fax (408) 376-0755; vic_ulmer@vval.com.

Spain

Cortijo Romero. Year round alternative holidays in Andalucia, Spain. Each week includes a 20-hour personal development course.

Dates: Begins every Saturday, year round. Cost: £355-£370 includes full board, course, full day excursion. Contact: Janice Gray, Cortijo Romero, Little Grove, Grove Lane, Chesham HP5 3QQ, U.K.; (011) 44-1494-782720, fax (011) 44-1494-776066; bookings@cortijo-romero.co.uk, www. cortijo-romero. co.uk.

CP Language Institutes. A Spanish language institute located in the town center of Madrid. Two- to 8-week standard and intensive courses, 4 hours per day. One-on-one instruction, customized courses for groups and combination courses. All levels available. Classes are small and thus offer a great deal of attention to the student. Cultural activities are an integral part of the program. Accommodations in selected guest families.

Dates: Year round (except for the month of Aug). Cost: PTS22,500 per week, 20 hours tuition; PTS23,000 (approx.) half-board accommodations in guest family. Contact: Mrs. Maria Dolores Romero, CP Language Institute, c/o Schiller International Univ., Calle San Bernardo 97/99, 28015 Madrid, Spain; SchillerUS@aol.com.

Painting in Barcelona. A celebrated Spanish faculty made up of Tom Carr and Carme Miquel will conduct a 3-week advanced painting workshop at the spacious studio of Escola d'Arts Plastiques i Disseny "Llotja." Included are 3 museum tours to the Antonio Tapies Foundation, the Miro Foundation, and the Picasso Museum. Three credits.

Dates: Jul 3-Jul 25 (1998). Cost: $2,850. Includes airfare, double occupancy rooms, continental breakfast daily, and 3 tours. Contact: Dora Riomayor, Director of International Studies, School of Visual Arts, 209 E. 23rd St., New York, NY 10010-3994; (212) 592-2543.

Sweden

Backroad Travel in Sweden. Bicycling and walking vacations in the unspoiled and beautiful countryside of Sweden. Follow Viking trails. Experience the rich Swedish culture with a native guide. Vacations include charming accommodations, breakfast and dinners, support vehicle, bilingual guides, and guided tours.

Dates: Jul 1-Aug 31. Cost: Call for details. Contact: Backroad Travel in Sweden, 18 Lake Shore Dr., Arlington, MA 02474; (888) 648-3522 or (781) 646-2955, fax (781) 648-3522; cfranzel@aol.com, http://members.aol.com/cfranzel/backroad.htm.

Switzerland

CP Language Institute. The language school is located in Leysin, a beautiful mountain resort above Lake Geneva in a former Grand Hotel. CP offers 2- to 32-week intensive French language courses at all levels. International student body, highly experienced teachers, and a unique atmosphere. Classes are small and thus offer a great deal of personal attention. Activity and recreational programs offered. Courses can be taken in conjunction with university courses at the American College of Switzerland.

Dates: Year round. Cost: Per week: Tuition SFR775 including 24 hours tuition and full board accommodations. Contact: Mrs. Françoise Bailey, CP Language Institutes, c/o American College of Switzerland, CH 1854 Leysin, Switzerland; (011) 41-24-494-22-23, fax (011) 41-24-494-1346.

Tanzania

Wildlife Safaris. We organize wildlife safaris to Lake Manjara, Ngorongoro Crater, Tarangire (lodge and camping safaris), Mt. Kilimanjaro-Mt. Meru climb with professional guides. Cultural tourism and walking safaris in the wildness. Agent for precious stones. Budget student safari program.

Dates: Advance booking program. Cost: Available on request. Contact: Mr. Herman

Kimaro, Polly Adventure and Safaris, Ltd., P.O. Box 8008, Arusha, Tanzania, Africa; fax (011) 255-57-8360/4454; polly@whiteyellow.com, www.whiteyellow.com/polly.

United Kingdom and Ireland

Anglia Summer Schools. Residential Theater Performance Holidays for 8 to 19 year olds arranged by age groups. Six-, 9-, and 13-day stays during Apr, Jul, and Aug. Students are immersed in every aspect of theater—acting, singing, dance, mime, etc., always with the emphasis on enjoyment. It's time to act.

Dates: Call for details. Cost: Call for details. Contact: J.R. Lucas, Anglia Summer Schools, 15 Inglis Rd., Colchester, Essex C03 3HU, U.K.; (011) 44-1206-540111, fax (011) 44-1206-766944.

Art Tour and Workshop. A perfect opportunity to tour magnificent England off the beaten path or to develop your artistic skills and creative insights in beautiful Buckingham.

Dates: Jul and Aug. Cost: Inquire. Contact: Rockland Center for the Arts, 27 S. Greenbush Rd., West Nyack, NY 10994; (914) 358-0877, fax (914) 358-0971; www.rocklandartcenter.org.

Cycling, Walking, Leisure Breaks. A variety of short breaks and longer holidays in Britain's largest area of outstanding natural beauty. Self-guided or guided, we use quiet lanes and plan the trips to reveal the secret and best of each area. Excellent accommodations and a warm welcome guaranteed.

Dates: Year round. Cost: From £70 1 night, 2 days. Contact: Angie Petkovic, Compass Holidays, 48 Shurdington Rd., Cheltenham, Gloucestershire GL53 0JE; (011) 44-1242-250642, fax (011) 44-1242-529730; compassholidays@bigfoot.com, www.gibp.co.uk/cycling.

Edinburgh Univ. Summer Courses. Scotland past and present: Art, Architecture, History,

Literature, Archaeology, Presentation skill, Ethnology, Gaelic, Music, Drama, Creative Writing, Film, Ecology, the Edinburgh Festival. Courses last 1-4 weeks each. Instruction by University professors: highest academic standards. Integral field trips; theatre/concert/cinema tickets provided. Social program. Choice of accommodations.

Dates: Jun-Sep. Cost: Inquire. Contact: Elaine Mowat, Univ. of Edinburgh, Centre for Continuing Education, 11 Buccleuch Pl., Edinburgh EH8 9LW, U.K.; (011) 44-131-650-4400, fax (011) 44-131-667-6097; CCE@ed.ac.uk, www.cce.ed.ac.uk/summer.

Field Studies Council Courses. The Field Studies Council offers a wide range of day, weekend, and 5- to 7-day special interest courses in art and environmental subjects. The 12 centers are situated in some of the finest locations in England and Wales, each with its own character and many in historical buildings.

Dates: Jan-Dec. Cost: From £102 for a weekend (1998). Full board, tuition, and accommodations. Contact: Cathy Preston, Field Studies Council, Head Office, Preston Montferd, Shrewsbury SY4 1HW, U.K.; (011) 44-1743-850674, fax (011) 44-1743-850178; fsc.headoffice@ukonline.co.uk.

Fine Art Courses. Two-year portrait diploma, foundation and portfolio course, continuing studies. Open studio. Day and evening courses, Easter and summer courses: sculpture, painting, drawing, printmaking, water color, portraiture, life drawing, still life—full time, part time.

Dates: Sep-Dec, Jan-Apr, Apr-Jul, Jul-Sep. Cost: £110-£5,400 depending on course and duration. Contact: Ms. Andrea Giebeler, Registrar, The Heatherley School of Fine Art, 80 Upcerne Rd., London SW10 0SH; (011) 44-171-351-4190, fax (011) 44-171-351-6945.

Green Wood Working. Traditional coppice woodland craft courses and holidays. One-day to 8-day courses in the woodland and rural environment of the Old Hall syndecat community.

Dates: Jul-Sep. Cost: £30 per day tuition (1998). Contact: Richard King, Old Hall, E. Bergholt, Colchester, Essex CO7 6TG, U.K.; (011) 44-1206-298045.

An Irish Idyll. From historic Dublin to mountain landscapes, fields of green to quaint villages and dramatic ocean views...this evocative country has a beauty all its own. Lodging in a charming bed and breakfast in the gorgeous seaside village of Kinsale—perfectly situated to see the diversity of the Irish panorama. Workshops include painting, jewelry, hats and bags, fiber arts and felting, photography.

Dates: Jun 12-Jun 19, Oct 2-Oct 9. Cost: $1,425 (lodging, meals, tuition, and field trips). Contact: Karen Totman-Gale, Horizons, 108 N. Main St.-T, Sunderland, MA 01375; (413) 665-0300, fax (413) 665-4141; horizons@horizons-art.org, www.horizons-art.org.

Irish Language and Culture. Irish language programs at all learning levels for adults are offered by Oideas Gael, which also offers cultural activities, learning programs in hillwalking, dances of Ireland, painting, tapestry weaving, Raku-Celtic pottery, and archaeology.

Dates: Weekly, Apr-Sep. Cost: $150 plus accommodations (from $90 per week). Contact: Liam O'Cuinneagain, Director, Oideas Gael, Gleann Cholm Cille, County Donegal, Ireland; (011) 353-73-30248, fax (011) 353-73-30348; oidsgael@iol.ie.

Issues in Public Safety in Ireland. Explore historic and current public safety issues in Ireland. Field study will take place at Dublin Castle, the courts, Probation, Aftercare and Correction Services, and Garda Police College. Tours of historic Dublin will enhance your understanding of Ireland's history and the relationship to the challenges in public safety today.

Dates: Jul 7-21 (1998). Cost: $1,850. Includes airfare, housing, program costs, and tuition. Contact: Jody A. Dudderar, Rockland Community College, 145 College Rd., Suffern, NY 10901; (914) 574-4205, fax (914) 574-4423; study-abroad@sunyrockland.edu.

Landscape Painting in the Burren. Professional art tutors take groups outdoors on location for sketching and painting in the famous Burren country of North Clare: rockscapes, seascapes, streetscapes. Media include oils, watercolors, pastel, gouache, acrylics. Accommodations in Irish Tourist Board B and B. Studio, materials, and equipment available.
Dates: May-Oct weekly and weekends. Cost: From $375 per week. Includes tuition, accommodations, and full breakfast. Contact: Christine O'Neill, The Burren Painting Centre, Lisdoonvarna, Co. Clare, Ireland; (011) 353-74208, fax (011) 353-74435; isclo@indigo.ie.

London Summer Theatre Workshop. Foundation Course: An ideal pre-drama school/university course which also caters for the needs of mature students as a refresher, it focuses on the core skills. Theatre Workshop: A program including scene study, classes in voice, movement and dance, improvisation, acting, etc.
Dates: Foundation Course: 10 weeks from Apr 20. Theatre Workshop: 1 month from mid-Jul-mid-Aug. Cost: Foundation Course: £2,608.50. Theatre Workshop: £895. Contact: Miriam Anderson, Webber Douglas Academy, Theatre Workshop, 30 Clareville St., London SW7 5AP, U.K.; (011) 44-171-370-4154, fax (011) 44-171-373-5639.

Lower Shaw Farm. Program of weekend and weeklong courses including crafts, well-being, children's events, and celebrations. Semi-rural setting; good vegetarian food; relaxed, informal atmosphere. Opportunities for volunteering.
Dates: Vary. Cost: From £75. Contact: Andrea Hirsch, Lower Shaw Farm, Old Shaw Ln.,

Shaw Swindon, SN5 9PJ, U.K.; Tel./fax (011) 44-1-793-771080.

New House Organic Farm. Family-run organic farm in an area of outstanding natural beauty. The farm has a wide variety of animals, vegetable gardens, and orchards. Offering paying holidays, free working holidays, camping, and program of courses such as dowsing, alternative health care, etc.
Dates: Call for details. Cost: Call for details. Contact: Bob or Mary Smail, New House Farm, Kniveton, Ashbourne, Derbyshire DE6 1JL, U.K.; (011) 44-1335-342429.

Poplar Herb Farm. Bed and breakfast on small holding/herb nursery in rural England on Somerset Levels. Good for walking and cycling. Seven miles west of Glastonbury (ancient Isle of Avalon), full of myths and legends. Exclusively vegetarian, herb gardens, meditation room, astrology, and friendly rescued animals.
Dates: Mar-Nov. Cost: £17 per person B and B (en-suite shower). Contact: Chris or Richard Fish, Poplar Herb Farm, Burtle, Bridgewater, Somerset TA7 8NB, U.K.

Pottery and Painting Summer School. The painting course covers all media and techniques: oil, watercolor, pastel, pen and ink, drawing and an appreciation of composition, line, tone, and color mixing. The pottery course covers every aspect of making pots with emphasis on throwing. Each student has their own seater wheel, only small numbers allows for individual tuition of all levels.
Dates: Three-day weekends May/Jun, weekly Jul/Aug. Cost: From £229 all inclusive. Contact: Tina Homer, Martin Homer Pottery, Aston Bank, Knighton-On-Teme, Tenbury Wells, Worcs, WR15 8LW, U.K.; (011) 44-1584-781-404.

Residential Pottery Workshops. Highly educational, fun 5-day pottery activity residential workshops. One hour from London in the beautiful rural village of Somersham in Suffolk. Courses offer a huge range of clays, glazes, and temperatures. Food included.

Dates: Five-day courses throughout the summer every week. Cost: £290 all inclusive (workshop and residence). Contact: Alan Baxter Pottery Workshop, The White House Pottery, Somersham, Ipswich, Suffolk IP8 4QA, U.K.; Tel./fax (011) 44-1473-831256; abaxter@netcomuk.co.uk, www.ecn.co.uk/alanbaxter/index.htm.

Scottish Clan and Theme Tours. Arranged trips for those interested in visits to individual clan lands or in Scotland. Trips also available for those who want to see the highlands and lowlands areas of beauty. Castles, lochs, palaces, cathedrals, battlefields, gardens, etc.

Dates: $2,500-$3,000 per person. Cost: Summer. Contact: Caledonian Travel, Inc., 2563 River Knoll Dr., Lilburn, GA 30047; (770) 979-1010, fax (770) 978-6119; kategraham@opa.com.

Summer Music School. An 8-day summer school at Ardindly College, Sussex, England, for string players and aolo and choral singers. Ages 14 and above. Single and double bedrooms. String coaching, orchestra, opera, oratorio, piano accompaniment, story writing.

Dates: Aug 22-30 (1998). Cost: £255 (1998) plus value added tax. Contact: Summer Music, 22 Gresley Rd., London, U.K; Tel./fax (011) 44-171-272-5664.

Teach English as a Foreign Language. Courses in central London leading to the Cambridge/RSA Certificate (CELTA), regarded internationally as the ideal qualification in TEFL. International House has 40 years experience in training teachers and can offer jobs to those recently qualified in its 110 schools in 27 countries.

Dates: Four-week (110 hours) intensive courses begin Jan 5, Feb 2, Mar 2, Apr 14, May 11, Jun 8, Jul 6, Aug 3, Sep 1, Sep 28, Oct 26, Nov 23 (1998). Cost: £944 includes Cambridge/RSA registration. Contact: Teacher Training Development, International House, 106 Piccadilly, London W1V 9FL, England; (011) 44-171-491-2598, fax (011) 44-171-499-0174; teacher@dial.pipex.com.

Traditional Chinese Silk Painting. A unique course for silk painters. This ancient technique enables far more painterly and subtle effects to be achieved through the application of many layers of color to both sides of natural silk. Includes a river boat cruise in the Broads National Park to collect design ideas for translation onto silk back in the studio.

Dates: Aug 23-Aug 28 (1998). Cost: £275 (1998) includes 4 days tuition (9:30-5), plus boat excursion and lunches/snacks. Contact: Angela Dammery, Course Director, NDD, ATC, 43 The Crossways, Westcliff on Sea, Essex SS0 8PU, U.K.

Univ. of Cambridge International Summer Schools. Largest and longest established program of summer schools in the U.K. Intensive study in Cambridge as part of an international community. Term I (6 weeks) and Term II (2 weeks) of the International Summer School offer over 60 different courses. Three-week specialist programs: Art History, Medieval Studies, History, English Literature, and Shakespeare. Wide range of classes on all programs. U.S. and other overseas institutions grant credit for study at the Univ. of Cambridge Summer School. Guidelines available.

Dates: Jul 5-Aug 15 (1998). Cost: Tuition from £460-£625 (2 to 4 weeks), accommodations from £240-£925 (2 to 4 weeks). Six-week period of study also possible by combining 2 Summer schools. Contact: Sarah Ormrod, Director, International Division, Univ. of Cambridge Board of Continuing Education, Madingley Hall, Madingley, Cambridge CB3 8AQ, England; (011) 44-1954-210636, fax (011) 44-1954-210677; rdi1000@cam.ac.uk, www.cam.ac.uk.

Walking Adventure. Spend a week walking through wild, ancient landscapes of Wales and England. Camp gear and luggage travel ahead.

Personal tours. Acclaimed vegetarian cuisine. Let your spirit soar!

Dates: Call for details. Cost: Call for details. Contact: Laurence Golding, Head for the Hills, Garth, Builth, Piwys LD4 4AT, Wales; (011) 44-1591-620-388.

Walking Holidays. Guided independent tours throughout England, Scotland, Wales, and Ireland from 2 to 14 days and from easy to tough.

Dates: Year round. Cost: Seven nights in Devon £489. Dinner, bed, and Sunday breakfast. Contact: Philip S. Criver, English Wanderer, 6 George St., Ferryhill, Co. Durham, DL17 0DT, U.K; (011) 44-1740-653169; englishwanderer@btinternet.com.

Walking/Hiking Holidays in Ireland. Week-long fully inclusive holidays. Relaxing, carefree with international groups through the beautiful green land of Ireland. Quality accommodations with excellent Irish dinner each evening. Local Irish guide.

Dates: Year round. Cost: $400 part board to $660 full board plus guide (7 days). Contact: John Ahern, Southwest Walks Ireland, 40 Ashe St., Tralee, Kerry, Ireland; swwi@iol.ie, www.limerich-ireland.com/activity-holidays.

United States

Columbia River Barter Faire. A unique outdoor village in remote setting. On the Columbia River on Canadian border in eastern Washington. Friends and neighbors camp-out and barter arts, crafts, music, skills, mountain lore, healing arts, antiques, second-hand items, almost anything you can think of.

Dates: Second weekend in Apr, Jun, and Oct. Cost: $10 per person; $10 for camp spot. Contact: Columbia Barter Faire, P.O. 296, Northport, WA 99157; (509) 732-6130.

Dolphin Camp. Dolphin Camp is the ultimate experience for anyone who has ever dreamed of watching and being with these gentle crea-

tures. Days are spent intensively with dolphins, up close and in various settings. Dolphin Camp is the finest dolphin interaction-personal development program offered anywhere.

Dates: Jul 10-Jul 15, 1998. Cost: $1,995 includes room (based on double occupancy), meals, activities, and transportation during Dolphin Camp. Transportation to Marathon, FL is not included. Contact: Bill DeLano, Triangle Training Center, 1654 Hamlct Chapel Rd., Pittsboro, NC 27312; (800) 451-2562; www.dolphin.com

Summer Internship and Seminar Programs. Internship program in Washington, DC with Middle East organizations, dealing with such issues as Palestine, U.S.-Arab relations, and trade. Supplementing the internship are lectures from scholars and government employees familiar with the issues facing the Arab world.

Dates: Jun-Aug. Cost: Call for information. Contact: National Council on U.S.-Arab Relations, (202) 293-0801; internship@ncusar.org.

Worldwide

American-Int'l Homestays. Stay in English-speaking foreign homes in over 30 countries. Explore foreign cultures responsibly. Learn foreign languages. Perfect for families or seniors. Learn how other people live by living with them in their homes.

Dates: Year round. Cost: From $59 per night. Contact: Joe Kinczcl, American-Int'l Homestays, P.O. Box 1754, Nederland, CO 80466; (303) 642-3088 or (800) 876-2048, fax (303) 642-3365; ash@igc.apc.org.

Coral Cay Conservation Expeditions. Volunteers needed to join major expeditions to help survey and protect coral reefs and tropical forests in the Caribbean, Asia-Pacific, Philippines, Indonesia, Red Sea. No previous experience required. Full accredited training provided (including scuba certification if required). Thousands of CCC volunteers have already helped establish 8 new marine reserves and wildlife sanctuaries worldwide.

Dates: Expeditions depart monthly throughout the year. Cost: From $995 (2 weeks) to $4,415 (12 weeks) excluding flights. Contact: Coral Cay Conservation Ltd., 154 Clapham Park Rd., London SW4 7DE, U.K.; (305) 757-2955 (U.K. office 011-44-171-498-6248, fax 011-44-171-498-8447); ccc@coralcay.demon. co.uk, www.coralcay.org.

The Culinary Travel Company. Cooking vacations to wonderful destinations. Small groups. One-on-one cooking classes. Visit wineries, olive oil factories, fresh food markets, historical and gastronomic landmarks, first-class hotels.

Dates: Year round. Cost: Starts at $1,950 per person (dbl. occup.) Includes meals, cooking classes, accommodations, excursions, and ground transportation. Contact: Dan Strebel, The Culinary Travel Company, 210 W. Pickwick, Arlington Heights, IL 60005; (888) 777-0760.

Destination Tanzania Safaris. We organize wildlife safaris to all game parks. Hotel/lodges and camping, Mt. Kilimanjaro/Mt. Meru treks: 5-8 day professional guided treks; nature trails, 5-15 days adventure walking safaris; beach holidays; Zanzibar Spice Island and Mafia.

Dates: Year round. Cost: Available on request. Contact: Ostrich Tours & Safaris Ltd., Aloyce Joseph Assey, Managing Director, P.O. Box 12752, Arusha, Tanzania; Tel./fax (011) 255-57-4140.

¿?don Quijote In-Country Spanish Language Schools. Intensive Spanish language courses using the communicative method are combined with an intensive immersion in the social and cultural life of some of Spain's most interesting cities (Salamanca, Barçelona, Granada, Malaga). Airport pick-up service, study counseling, homestay or student flats, excursions, access to recreational facilities,

touring, and sightseeing opportunities. donQuijote now offers intensive Spanish language courses through partner schools in Latin America: Cuernavaca and Mèrida, Mexico; Antigua, Guatemala; Alajuela, Costa Rica; and Quito, Ecuador.

Dates: Year round—Fall, Spring, Winter, and Summer. Cost: Inquire. Contact: ¿?don Quijote, Apartado de Correos 333, 37080 Salamanca, Spain; (011) 34-923-268-860, fax (011) 34-923-268-815; donquijote@offcampus.es, www.teclata.es/donquijote.

Earthwatch Institute. Unique opportunities to work with leading scientists on 1- to 3-week field research projects worldwide. Earthwatch sponsors 160 expeditions in over 30 U.S. states and in 60 countries. Project disciplines include archaeology, wildlife management, ecology, ornithology and marine mammalogy. No special skills needed—all training is done in the field.

Dates: Year round. Cost: Tax deductible contributions ranging from $695-$2,800 support the research and cover food and lodging expenses. Airfare not included. Contact: Earthwatch, 680 Mt. Auburn St., P.O. Box 9104-MA, Watertown, MA 02272; (800) 776-0188, (617) 926-8200; info@ earthwatch.org, www.earthwatch.org.

Free Spirit Travel. Activity holidays in unspoiled destinations. Perfect for those traveling on their own, as well as with friends. Activities include: painting, walking, pottery, yoga, Tai Chi, mosaics, self development, cycling, swimming with dolphins, crafts. Fantastic locations throughout Europe and beyond.

Dates: Year round. Cost: From £159-£2,500 including half/full board. Contact: Jillian Batchelar, Free Spirit Travel, 153 Carden Avenue, Brighton BN1 8LA, U.K.; (011) 44-1273-504230, fax (011) 44-1273-504076.

Garden Tours. Travel to international destinations on a first-class garden tour. Visit stately homes and gardens and meet garden owners. Small groups led by professional guides. Custom tours available. Call for a brochure: (800) 448-2685.

Dates: Vary. Cost: Varies. Contact: Cindy Steinman, Director of Sales, Expo Garden Tours, 70 Great Oak, Redding, CT 06896; (203) 938-0410, fax (203) 938-0427.

Global Volunteers. "An adventure in service." The nation's premier short-term service programs for people of all ages and backgrounds assist mutual international understanding through ongoing development projects in 19 countries throughout Africa, Asia, the Caribbean, Europe, the South Pacific, North and South America. Programs of 1, 2, and 3 weeks, range from natural resource preservation, light construction, and painting to teaching English and assisting with health care. No special skills or foreign languages are required. Ask about the Millennium Service Project.

Dates: Over 130 teams year round. Cost: Tax-deductible program fees range from $400 to $2,095. Airfare not included. Contact: Global Volunteers, 375 E. Little Canada Rd., St. Paul, MN 55117; (800) 487-1074, fax (651) 482-0915; email@globalvolunteers. org, www.globalvolunteers.org.

Green Volunteers. The World Guide to Voluntary Work in Nature Conservation lists more than 100 projects and organizations worldwide where you can volunteer from 1 week to 1 year. Projects on marine mammals, primates, sea turtles, African wildlife, birds, and on conservation work in general are listed. Some of the projects do not require a financial contribution from the volunteers.

Dates: Year round. Cost: $16 plus $5 postage. Contact: Green Volunteers: in the U.S.: 1 Greenleaf Woods Dr., #302A, Portsmouth, NH 03810; (800) 525-9379. In Europe: P.O. Box 23, Sandy, Bedfordshire SG19 2XE, U.K.; (011) 44-1767-262481, fax (011) 44-1767-260901; info@greenvol.com, www.greenvol.com.

Italian Language Courses. Atrium Institute of Italian Language and Culture, located in the heart of Italy, offers Italian language courses at 6 levels. Our students study the Italian language immersed in a small Italian hill town in constant contact with the local people. Various types of accommodations are available. School open all year.

Dates: Year round. Cost: Regular language course (4 weeks) LIT700,000 includes registration fee and text. Accommodations from LIT500,000 (4 weeks). Contact: Donna Galletta, Atrium, P.zza Papa Giovanni XXIII, n. 3 61043 Cagli (PS), Italy; Tel./fax (011) 39-721-790321; atrium@info-net.it, www.info-net.it/atrium.

LA County Natural History Museum Travel Program. Tour the world with one of the exciting travel programs offered by the Natural History Museum of Los Angeles county. Itineraries include exotic and fascinating destinations such as the incomparable wonders and wildlife of Malaysia: Tunisia, a mosaic of ancient civilizations; and the silk road of Central Asia. Most tours are escorted by the museum's own staff. Twenty-five destinations.

Dates: Inquire. Cost: Vary. Contact: Christine Robison, Natural History Museum of LA County, 900 Exposition Blvd., Los Angeles, CA 90007; (213) 763-3350, (213) 744-1042; crobison@nhm.org, www.nhm.org/travel.

Language Immersion Programs. Learn a language in the country where it's spoken. Intensive foreign language training offered in Costa Rica, Russia, Spain, France, Italy, Germany, and Ecuador for students aged 16 and older. Classes are taught in up to 8 different proficiency levels and are suitable for beginners as well as people with advanced linguistic skills. All courses include accommodations and meals. Lots of extracurricular activities available. Students can earn college credit through Providence College.

Dates: Courses start every second Monday

year round. Year programs commence in Sep, semester programs in Jan, May, and Sep. Cost: Varies with program, approx. $950 per 2-week course. Contact: Stephanie Greco, Director of, Admissions, EF International Language Schools, EF Center, 1 Education St., Cambridge, MA 02142; (800) 992-1892, fax (617) 619-1701; ils@ef.com.

Myths and Mountains. Educational tours and custom trips focused on 4 learning themes: culture and crafts, traditional medicines, religion, holy sites and history, the environment and wildlife. Group departures, individual custom trips, nonprofit association trips. Destinations: Asia and South America.

Dates: Year round. Cost: From budget to deluxe. Free catalog. Call for estimate. Contact: Myths and Mountains, 976 Tee Court, Incline Village, NV 89451; (800) 670-6984, fax (702) 832-5454; travel@mythsandmountains.com, www.mythsandmountains.com.

Nature Expeditions International. Educational adventure programs to 6 continents: Africa, Asia, South America, North America, Antarctica and Australia (and the South Pacific). Focus is on wildlife, natural history, and cultural experiences in a small group setting with expert leaders. Upcoming special programs include Mundo Maya with homestays; New Zealand by Foot; and Tapati Rapa Nuli. Special Chile and Easter Island expeditions.

Dates: Year round. Cost: Call for details. Contact: Nature Expeditions, International, 6400 E. El Dorado Cir., Suite 210, Tucson, AZ 85715; (800) 869-0639, fax (520) 721-6719; naturexp@aol.com, www.naturexp.com.

Outer Edge Expeditions. We specialize in small group expeditions: 1-10 people, to remote wilderness and cultural destinations. Visit Africa, the Amazon, Argentina, Australia, Borneo, Canada, Chile, Indonesia, Irian Jaya, New Zealand, Patagonia, and Peru. Activities include biking, kayaking, trekking, caving, rafting, and more.

Dates: Year round. Cost: Varies. Contact: Brian Obrecht, Outer Edge Expeditions, 45500 Pontiac Trail, Walled Lake, MI 48390; (800) 322-5235, fax (248) 624-6744; adventure@outer-edge.com, www.outer-edge.com.

Penn Summer Abroad. Academic programs granting Univ. of Pennsylvania credits. Courses focusing on language, culture, economics, theater, anthropology, Jewish studies, cinema, art history, traditional folk medicine, performing arts, and religion. Several programs offer homestays, some offer internships.

Dates: Mid-May-late Aug (2-8 weeks). Cost: Tuition: $1,484 per course. Living costs vary. Contact: Elizabeth Sachs, Penn Summer Abroad, College of General Studies, Univ. of Pennsylvania, 3440 Market St., Suite 100, Philadelphia, PA 19104-3335; (215) 898-5738, fax (215) 573-2053.

Sugarcraft School. Squires Kitchen's 5-day international school. A week of fun and sugarcraft with the country's top tutors. Royal icing, floral, and novelty work. Take home fantastic pieces of work and plenty of inspiration. All levels welcome. Early booking advisable.

Dates: Mar 16-20, 1999. Cost: £250 plus cost of additional equipment and accommodations. Contact: Vicki Moore, Squires Kitchen School, 3 Waverley Ln., Farnham, Surrey GU9 8BB, U.K. (011) 44-1252-711749, fax (011) 44-1252-14714.

Univ. of California Research Expeditions Program-UREP. Adventure with a purpose. Join research expeditions in archaeology, anthropology, environmental studies and more. Get off the beaten track, help in research that benefits local communities. No special experience necessary. Free brochure. Dates: May-Sep (2 weeks). Cost: From $700-$1,700 (tax deductible). Contact: Univ. of

California Research Expeditions Program (UREP); (530) 252-0692, fax (530) 752-0681; urep@ucdavis, www.mip.berkeley.edu/ure.

Variety Vacation Opportunities. America's most complete all around climbing school and climbing area located at Rocky Mountain National Park also offers expeditions to Mexico, Ecuador, Bolivia, Argentina, Africa, and Alaska on a year-round basis.

Dates: Mexico: Nov-Feb, 9-12 day trips; Ecuador: Jan-Feb, 15-day trips. Special trip dates can be arranged (1998). Cost: Mexico $1,595, Ecuador $2,495 (1998). Contact: Colorado Mountain School, P.O. Box 2062, Estes Park, CO 80517; (970) 586-5758, fax (970) 586-5798; cms-climb@sni.net, www.sni.net/homepage/cms.

Villa Vacation Service. At Home Abroad offers a personalized villa vacation service offering upscale properties in Europe (France, Spain, England, Ireland, Italy), Caribbean, and Mexico. Most homes have been personally inspected by AHA. The company, established in 1960, commissions 10 percent on most properties.

Dates: Call for details. Cost: Call for details. Contact: Claire Packman, President, At Home Abroad, Inc., 405 E 56th St., Suite 6-H, New York, NY 10022; (212) 421-9165, fax (212) 752-1591; athomabrod@aol.com, http://members.aol.com/athomabrod/index.html.

Youth International. An experiential education program focusing on international travel and intercultural exchange, community service, adventure, and homestays. Teams of 12, aged 18-25, travel together for 1 semester to East Asia and India/Nepal, or East Africa and the Middle East. Assist refugees, hike the Himalayas, build water tanks in Africa, scuba dive, and much more. Also looking for leaders.

Dates: Jan 19-May 30, 1999 (4 1/2 months) and Sep 2-Dec 16, 1999 (3 1/2 months).

Cost: Spring $6,900; Fall $5,900 (1998). Prices may change as of Fall '99. Contact: Brad Gillings, Youth International, 1121 Downing St., #2, Denver, CO 80218; Tel./fax (303) 839-5877; youth. international@bigfoot.com, http://home.att. net/~youth-international.

For more listings of opportunities for special interest travel, and for bargains worldwide, travel tips, and all sorts of information on learning, living, working, and traveling abroad, see *Transitions Abroad* magazine. To order a single copy or a subscription, please call 1-800-293-0373 or visit the *Transitions Abroad* web site at www.transabroad.com.

CHAPTER 3

SENIOR
TRAVEL
RESOURCES

The dynamics of travel have changed in the last several years – for seniors as well as for the general population. Older travelers once wanted a comfortable tour of castles and churches in familiar territory; foreign travel meant a tour of the Continent. Today they are heading for exotic destinations like Sulawesi and Zimbabwe.

Now that they have the time and the energy, seniors also want more interesting and intellectually challenging traveling experiences. They want to get out and meet people in the countries they visit–people with ideas and experiences to enrich their own lives. They like to combine travel with homestays, volunteer work, teaching, and language study.

The travel industry is aware of this growing demand for travel for enrichment, and more and more tour operators are gearing their offerings in this direction. Instead of three countries in 10 days, operators offer longer stays in one area, opportunities to meet families and take part in hands-on programs.

And seniors traveling in unfamiliar territory who want to experience more than just the usual sightseeing activities should look into a homestay program. Much more than merely a convenient solution to the room and board problem, living in your own quarters in a private home with the resident owners adds a valuable dimension to travel.

While apartment or house rentals or exchanges are gaining in popularity for extended stays, homestays offer the further advantages of actually learning first-hand how the host families go about their daily affairs: their work and eating habits, entertainments, holiday observances. How else could a traveler learn what Russian or French or Japanese people think about politics, child rearing, education, or world affairs? Only by living with them on a daily basis is this possible.

Homestay programs usually ask you to fill out forms outlining your preferences as to location, living arrangements (bed size, separate or shared bathroom, kitchen privileges, etc.), length of stay, language requirements, occupation, and cultural interests. Then they try to match you with carefully selected hosts in the designated area—or areas if you choose to go from one homestay to another.

The obligations of the host families vary according to those who arrange the homestay. Some families leave you on your own to find your way around while relying on them to make suggestions and provide general guidance. Other families commit to being your personal daily guides to places and events not covered by traditional tours.

Joining families for meals, calling on their friends or relatives, visiting their workplace, shopping, attending sporting events—all add to mutual understanding among people of different cultures and persuasions. Such an experience is not possible when you spend precious travel days in hotel surroundings.

Finally, there is the comfort and convenience, especially for seniors, of staying in one place. And, if your new family members become real friends you'd like to see again, you may end up becoming hosts to them in your stateside home.

The following programs can send you on your way. And the additional resources will not only help seniors get ready to go but will help assure a safe and pleasant journey.

— *By Arline K. Wills*

Homestay Organizations

Alliances Abroad, 2222 Rio Grande, Austin, TX 78705; (888) 622-7623 or (512) 457-8062, fax (512) 457-8132; alliancesa@aol.com, www.studyabroad.com. Offers opportunities to live with a family in 40 cities in 16 countries on six continents.

American International Homestays, Box 1754, Nederland, CO 80466; (303) 642-3088, (800) 876-2048, fax (303) 642-3365; www.spectravel.com/home. Specialized in homestays in over 30 countries since 1988. They offer every other travel arrangement as well, such as air and train tickets, group trips, apartment rentals, and special language pro-

grams. Full-service homestays start at $179 for double private room and bath, home-cooked breakfast and dinner, personal guides, and interpreter to introduce you to others with similar areas of interest.

AmeriSpan Unlimited, P.O. Box 40007, Philadelphia, PA 19106; (800) 879-6640; info@AmeriSpan.com, www.AmeriSpan.com. Family, teen, senior, and adult language programs in 12 countries in Mexico, Spain, Central and South America. Housing with a host family.

Amigos Travel Services, 500 Del Verde Circle #1, Sacramento, CA 95833; (916) 648-1617. Live with Mexican families or American expatriates throughout Mexico. The company will also arrange art, educational, and retirement tours as well as participation in language, art, and photography classes.

Asesoria Gerencial, S.A., P.O. Box 7309-1000, San Jose, Costa Rica; (011) 506-240-9430, fax (011) 506-236-2249; agsamac@sol.racsa.co.cr, www.studyabroad.com/asesoria. Individual and family homestays in Tibas, a suburb of San Jose, the capital of Costa Rica. For $18 per person a night, an ecotourism program is offered to explore, sometimes by horseback, places of interest and astonishing beauty.

Bell's Home Hospitality, Dept 1432, PO Box 025216, Miami, FL 33102-5216; (011) 506-225-4752, fax (011) 506-224-5884; homestay@sol.racsa.co.cr, www.ilisa.com/bells. A homestay program in Costa Rica where all homes are personally inspected and selected and each host is anxious to share "Costaricana" with welcomed guests.

Elderhostel Homestays are offered in Europe, Asia, and New Zealand for people over 55. Prices range from $2,300 to $3,500 including air, lodgings, meals, classes, and field trips with just a few days spent in host family homes. Elderhostel, Dept. M2, Box 1959, Wakefield, MA 01880-5959.

Elderhostel, 75 Federal St., Boston, MA 02110; (617) 426-7788. Educational adventures for older adults. Sponsors over 2,000 nonprofit, short-term programs in 70 countries. Must be 55 or over; younger companions are allowed; www.elderhostel.org.

Eldertreks, 597 Markham St., Toronto, Ontario, Canada M6G 2L7; (800) 741-7956, fax (416) 588-9839; passages@inforamp.net, www.eldertreks.com. Exotic adventures for travelers 50 and over. Experienced local guides and Western escort. Group size limited to 15 participants. No mandatory single supplement charge.

FAMILYHOSTEL, 6 Garrison Ave., Durham, NH 03824; (800) 733-9753; www.learn. unh.edu/INTERHOSTEL/IH_FH.html. Ten-day learning and travel programs in foreign countries for families (parents, grandparents, school-age children).

Friends in France, 40 E. 19th St., New York, NY 10003-1303; (212) 260-9820, fax (212) 228-0576; stay@friends-in-france.com. Short-term homestays in chateaux, manor houses, farmhouses, and villas throughout France. Personally selected French families offer hospitality and local expertise to their guests year round. English spoken in most homes. Furnished apartments in Paris also available.

Friends Overseas, 68-04 Dartmouth St., Forest Hills, NY 11375. For a $25 fee, you get a list of Finnish people who want to meet Americans. They can also arrange connections with people in other Scandinavian countries and in Australia.

Friendship Force, 75 Forsyth St., NW, Suite 900, Atlanta, GA 30303; (404) 522-9490, (800) 688-6777, fax (404) 688-6148; www.friendship-force.org. A nonprofit, private organization founded in 1977, under President Carter's direction, whose goal is to promote peace through international friendships. Matches travelers and overseas families. The member-ship fee is $18 per year. Members also act as hosts for overseas visitors.

Global Social Venture Network, 721 Monticello Rd., San Rafael, CA 94903; (714) 752-9036. Arranges homestay trips to Poland and Russia.

Hospex (Hospitality Exchange), P.O. Box 561, Lewistown, MT; (406) 566-2500, fax (406) 566-2612; http://hospex.icm.edu.pl. A traveler's directory of 250 members in 26 countries. Some can offer overnight accommodations; others will hook you up with local families. $20 annual membership.

Idyll, Ltd., Box 405, Media, PA 19063; (610)565-5242, fax (610) 565-5142; info@untours.com, www.untours.com. Idyll arranges apartment rentals for two or four weeks, typically in a private home, with separate entrance, bathroom, kitchen, bedroom(s), living room. The owner provides contacts and help in getting around. Unlike other apartment rental agencies, Idyll provides a package of air, car rental or rail pass; escort from airport arrival to destination; maps and planning guides describing day trips, hikes, things to do, and places to go. "Untour" arrangements are for travelers who want to be free from the restrictions of a scheduled tour and from the uncertainties of do-it-yourself travel. Areas include Austria, Belgium, Germany, Holland, Prague/Budapest/Vienna, Tuscany, Spain, Switzerland, and Venice.

INNter Lodging Co-op, Box 7044, Tacoma, WA 98407; (253) 756-0343. Members pay $100 to join, $30 per year, and agree to make their homes available to guests at least four months a year. Located in England, Germany, Switzerland, Belgium, Australia, and Indonesia.

Inside Russia Sojourns, 4697 Rich Mountain Rd., Boone, NC 28607; Tel./fax (704) 297-4653, for orders only (800) 892-5409; http://gccrafts.com/inruss. One week homestays in St. Petersburg, $525 single, $700 couple includes breakfast and dinner. Live with a caring host family as an honored guest and family member. Extended stays with guided tours also available.

Japan Home Visit System. For short-term visits with Japanese families of compatible interests, you must fill out a profile form at least 24 hours ahead and contact Japan National Tourist Organization, 1 Rockefeller Plaza, Suite 1250, New York NY 10020; (212) 757-5640, fax (212) 307-6754; jntonyc@interport.net.

Labo (011-82-2-817-4625, fax 813-7047) is a homestay program in Korea with 2,500 homes registered, set up by the Korea National Tourist Organization and connected with its Language Laboratory, a non-governmental agency for international exchanges.

LEX America offers homestay programs in Japan where participants live as members of a Japanese family and take part in daily activities. Contact: Steffi Samman, Program Manager, Lex America, 68 Leonard St., Belmont, MA 02178; (617) 489-5800, fax (617) 489-5898; exchange@lexlrf.com, www.lexlrf.com/LEX.htm.

Russian Home. A homestay and service program operated by Host Families Association (HOFA) in Russia, the Baltic countries, Georgia, Ukraine, Belorussia, and Central Asia. All host families are carefully selected, mostly from the faculty or research staff of local universities, matched with guests by language, age, and other requested preferences. Services include transfers, home meals, walking guide, car with driver, cultural programs, laundry, or simply a day-host arrangement for hotel visitors. Contact: HOFA, 5-25 Tavricheskaya, 193015 St. Petersburg, Russia; Tel./fax (011) 7-812 275-1992; hofa@usa.net, www.spt.ru/homestays.

Seniors Abroad International Homestays 12533 Pacato Circle North, San Diego, CA 92128; (619) 485-1696, fax (619) 487-1492;

haev@pacbell.net. Homestays are organized for active people over 50 between residents of the U.S. and New Zealand, Australia, Scandinavia, and Japan.

SERVAS, 11 John St., Suite 407, New York NY 10038; (212) 267-0252, fax (212) 267-0292; http://servas.org. Founded in Denmark in 1948 and affiliated with the United Nations. An international cooperative system of hosts and travelers to help build world peace, goodwill, and understanding—the largest and best organized group of its kind. Families and individuals are welcome. Annual membership fee is $55.

Sleeping Booklet. Aimed at touring cyclists who need rest stops and wish to meet other cyclists. Contact: Stefan Barthez, Staffelweg 3, Erlangen, Germany.

The Warm Shower List is a list of Internet and off-Internet persons who offer hospitality to touring cyclists. The extent of the hospitality depends on the host. Contact: Roger Gravel at wsl@intercime.qc.ca.

The World for Free, Box 137, Prince St. Station, New York, NY 10012; mqb8130@acfcluster.nyu.edu. A hospitality club started by a touring musician who then interested his friends in the idea, so many musicians and artists are in the group, but there is no restriction.

Women Welcome Women, 88 Easton St., High Wycombe, Buckinghamshire HP11 1LT, U.K.; or 2 Michallan Court, Donvale 3111, Australia. A nonprofit trust whose objective is to further international friendship by encouraging and facilitating women of different nationalities to visit one another.

WWOOF (Willing Workers on Organic Farms), 3231 Hillside Rd., Deming, WA 98244; Mt. Murrindal Reserve, W. Tree, Via Buchan 3885, Australia; 19 Bradford Rd., Lewes BN17 1RB, Sussex, U.K.; Stettingerstrasse 3, 6301

Pohlheim, Germany; Ballymalone, Tuamgraney, Co. Clare, Ireland. An exchange group that gives you a place to stay and something to eat in return for your help in managing an organic farm or smallholding. Stay for a weekend or a month—whatever you work out with your hosts. Membership is very cheap and there are lots of member groups to choose from. Check out www.cityfarmer.org/wwoof.html.

Health and Safety

1998 International Travel Health Guide by Stuart R. Rose. ($19.95 plus s/h from Travel Medicine, Inc., 351 Pleasant St., Suite 312, Northampton, MA 01060; 800-872-8633). Updated annually in spring; recommended by U.S. State Department.

American Lung Association. Advice on traveling with oxygen; call (800) 586-4872.

Citizens' Emergency Center, U.S. Dept. of State, 2201 C St., NW, Washington, DC 20520; (202) 647-5225. Handles emergency matters involving U.S. citizens abroad.

Doctor's Guide to Protecting Your Health Before, During and After International Travel by Dr. W. Robert Lange. 1997. Addresses travelers' health issues with particular emphasis on seniors; includes a special section on retiring or relocating abroad, as well as tips and precautions for travelers with chronic health problems, disabilities and handicaps. $9.95 plus $2 s/h from Pilot Books, 127 Sterling Ave., P.O. Box 2102, Greenport, NY 11944; (800) 79PILOT.

Health Information for International Travel, Supt. of Documents, U.S. Government Printing Office, PO Box 371954, Pittsburgh, PA 15250-7950; (202) 512-1800, fax (202) 512-2250. Stock # 017-023-00197-3. $20 (prepaid, Visa/MC accepted). Discusses health precautions and immunizations for travelers to foreign countries.

International Assn. for Medical Assistance to Travelers. Provides a directory of English-speaking doctors in 500 cities in 120 countries. Also information on health risks and immunizations worldwide, detailed information on tropical disease, climatic, and sanitary conditions; iamat@sentex.net, www.sentex.net/~iamat.

International SOS. Emergency medical evacuation coverage; (800) 523-8930.

Wordwide Assistance Services, Inc. (800) 821-2828. The largest global support system for travelers. Provides emergency medical payments, transportation, referrals, monitoring, and interpretation services. Also insurance for medical, trip cancellation, baggage, accidental dismemberment, evacuations, repatriations, return of mortal remains, and death.

Senior Organizations

Accessible Kiwi Tours New Zealand, Ltd. Adventure or leisure tours for all, including disabled or elderly. Group or individual tours New Zealand-wide. Accessible Kiwi Tours New Zealand, Ltd., P.O. Box 550, Opotiki, New Zealand; (011) 64-7-315-7867, fax (011) 64-7-315-5056; kiwitour@wave.co.nz.

Alaska Snail Trails. Ten-day, 5-day, and 1-day Alaskan tours; (800) 348-4532, (907) 337-7517, fax (907) 337-7517.

Gadabout Tours, 700 E. Tahquitz, Palm Springs, CA 92262; (800) 952-5068.

Golden Age Travelers, Pier 27, The Embarcadero, San Francisco, CA 94111; (800) 258-8880, fax (415) 776-0753.

Grand Circle Travel, 347 Congress St., Boston, MA 02210; (800) 248-3737. More than 200 programs worldwide. Free booklet: "101 Tips for Mature Travelers."

Insight International Tours, 745 Atlantic Ave., Boston, MA 02116; (617) 482-2000.

Interhostel, 6 Garrison Ave., Durham, NH 03824; (800) 733-9753. Over 50 educational travel programs per year worldwide for mature travelers age 50 and up.

Photo Explorer Tours has three programs: a 15-day tour to Tibet and two 16-day tours to China, all led by English-speaking photographer-guides. Tours include programs in the Guilin area and in Longsheng with custom arrangements, all transportation in China, hotels, meals, and fees. Prices are $3,595 for Tibet and $2,995 for China, plus air. Photo Explorer Tours, 2506 Country Village, Ann Arbor, MI 48103; (800) 315-4462, fax (313) 996-1481.

Safari Travel offers a tour of the wine country of South Africa plus an optional week to Victoria Falls, Zimbabwe, and Chobe Game Lodge in Botswana. Non-smokers only. Safari Travel, P.O. Box 5901, Maryville, TN 37802; (888) 445-8340, fax (423) 981-1706.

Saga Holidays, "Road Scholar" Educational Travel Programs, 222 Berkeley St., Boston, MA 02116; (617) 262-2262 or (800) 621-2151.

Seventy Plus Ski Club, (518) 399-5458.

Sterling Tours offers an 11-day Performing Arts tour featuring theater and music in London and the Edinburgh festival. $2,353 plus airfare. Sterling Tours, 2707 Congress St., Suite 2-G, San Diego, CA 92110; (800) 727-4359, fax (619) 299-5728.

Travelearn. Ten-day to 3-week programs for adults in 17 countries on 6 continents. On-site lectures and field experiences by local resource specialists. Travelearn, P.O. Box 315M, Lakeville, PA 18438; (800) 235-9114.

Senior Publications

The 50+ Traveler's Guidebook (Thorndike large print self-help) by Anita Williams, Merrimac Dillon. Thorndike Press. 1992. $15.95.

Adventures Abroad: Exploring the Travel/ Retirement Option by Allene Symons and Jane Parker (Gateway Books, see below). Introduction to vacation and retirement living in 17 countries with first-hand experiences of people living abroad. Information on housing, medical, cost of living, laws, finances, etc.

Auto Europe Wallet Card. Toll-free telephone access codes to reach AT&T, MCI, and Sprint in 20 countries; (800) 223-5555.

Britain on Your Own: A Guide for Single Mature Travelers by Dorothy Maroncelli. West Wind Books. 1997. $12.95.

Dept. of State Publications. Travel Tips for Older Americans, Tips for Americans Residing Abroad, Your Trip Abroad, and **A Safe Trip Abroad** are $1.25 each from Superintendent of Documents, U.S. Government Printing Office, Washington, DC 20402; (202) 647-1488, fax on demand (202) 647-3000; http://travel.state.gov.

Get Up and Go: A Guide for the Mature Traveler by Gene and Adele Malott, 1989. $10.95 from Gateway Books, 2023 Clemons Rd., Oakland, CA; (800) 669-0773.

Hostelling Directory (Hostelling International—International Youth Hostel Federation). Two annual volumes: Europe and Africa/Americas/Asia/Pacific. Lists nearly 5,000 hostels in over 70 countries for all ages.

The Mature Traveler. Monthly 12-page newsletter listing discounts and destinations

Travel on Your Own
All You Need is Determination and Desire
By Mike Dannen

Seniors, don't write off traveling on your own. Tours might provide sightseeing, comfort, and convenience, but you're also tied to the tour schedule. You can't spend the extra hour needed to explore Saint Peters or enjoy a relaxing cup of cappuccino while people watching on the Piazza Navona.

And, barring a holdup, it's unlikely you'll experience real adventure. You won't meet the Kyoto diplomat who took us to Osaka to see its spectacular "Golden Castle" or share the Palestinian taxi driver's breakfast at Jerusalem's Jaffa Gate.

Desire and determination are the two keys to a great on-your-own travel adventure. First, determine to enjoy the trip no matter what. Handling the dollar exchange, finding meals and lodging within your budget—these are the tasks that transform you into a world traveler. This is where you meet the people and experience their customs. The minor difficulties you overcome are the tales you'll repeat and the experiences you'll remember.

What about age? On reaching 60, I told Doris, three years my junior, that I wanted to travel during the next 10 years while we were healthy enough to do it on our own. I am now 76. I underestimated.

What of the language barrier? European cities pose no problem, nor do any of Britain's former colonies. English is the second language in Japan and much of Asia. Elsewhere, a smile will do wonders, and some of your most humorous moments will occur during attempts to bridge the language barrier.

As for desire: Plan a trip you would like to take in a year or two. Plan it in detail—the places you will visit, what you want to see and do there, the transportation, the time of the year, the cost, the documents and shots required, and how you'll arrange the time to go. Then change your reading to the history, customs, and art of each country you plan to visit. At this point you'll be hooked.

As for cost, try this: Decide how much of your savings you are willing to use and how much you could save during the coming year on a belt-tightening budget. To this add the at-home expenses which will be reduced.

Next, go over your plan to determine what you will eliminate or change if you have to. Join SERVAS and Hostelling International and plan the trip so as to stay with host families or at hostels, YMCAs, and the Salvation Army as much as possible. Here you will meet and converse with travelers from all parts of the world. If you're in the market for a new car, consider buying one for delivery overseas. If Europe is your destination, a Volkswagen camper will cut food and lodging costs dramatically.

Just about every city has a tourist information office located at the railroad station. These have a list of hotels, homes, and bed and breakfasts to fit every budget.

If you're traveling by rail, schedule your trip at night. The Eurail pass also includes ferry crossings. If you rent a car, be sure it has reclining seats.

A house swap is another possibility. Join Intervac U.S., The Invented City, Teacher Swap, Vacation Exchange Club, or others. On three occasions we rented our home—furnished. I screened the renters by contacting their employer or previous residence.

Investigate becoming a sales representative for a local business. This not only provides a tax write-off but also adds to your income. Travel writing also provides a write-off. Keep extensive notes and take your pictures with this in mind.

for the mature traveler. Send $2 for a random sample copy or $29.95 for a 12-month subscription. P.O. Box 50400, Reno, NV 89513-0400.

The Mature Traveler's Book of Deals. More than 140 pages of discounts especially for the mature traveler throughout the world. $7.95 plus $1.95 s/h. Call (800) 466-6676 for credit card purchases or send check to PS1. 8803 Tara Ln., Austin, TX 78737.

Old Age is Another Country: A Traveler's Guide by Page Smith. Crossing Press. 1995. $12.95.

Season of Adventure: Traveling Tales and Outdoor Journeys of Women Over 50 (Adventura Series, No. 10) by Jean Gould, ed. 1996. $15.95 from Seal Press Feminist Publishers.

The Seasoned Traveler by Marcia Schnedler. Country Roads, 1992, $10.95.

Secrets Every Smart Traveler Should Know by Wendy Perrin (Fodor's), 1997. Specific ways to smooth the traveler's path by the former ombudsman of Condé Nast Traveler.

The Story of Elderhostel by Eugene S. Mills. Univ. Press of New England. 1993. $25.

Taken by Surprise: Travel after 50 ($5.95) and Taken by Surprise: Travel after 60, both by Esther Mock ($6.95). R & E Publishers, 1991.

Unbelievably Good Deals and Great Adventures That You Absolutely Can't Get Unless You're Over 50 by Joan Rattner Heilman. Contemporary Books, 9th ed., 1997, $10.95.

Single Travelers

Handbook for Women Travelers by Maggie and Gemma Ross. Piatkus Books, 5 Windmill St., London W1P 1HF, England; (011) 44-631-0710.

Mesa Travel Singles Registry, P.O. Box 2235, Costa Mesa, CA 92628; (714) 546-8181.

Travel Alone & Love It: A Flight Attendant's Guide to Solo Travel by Sharon B. Wingler. (Chicago Spectrum Press, $14.95). Instructions on how to plan your own successful solo journey.

Travel Companion Exchange, P.O. Box 833, Amityville, NY 11701; (516) 454-0880 or (800) 392-1256. $48 yearly, $6 sample newsletter. Widely recommended listings and outstandingly useful newsletter for senior travelers seeking companions. The only major nationwide service of this nature. Includes travel health and solo travel tips in each issue.

Transportation

American Society of Travel Agents. Call their Consumer Affairs department at (703) 706-0387 if you need their help to mediate a travel dispute.

Berlitz Complete Guide to Cruising and Cruise Ships by Douglas Ward (Berlitz Publishing), 1996. $21.95.

How to Select a Package Tour. U. S. Tour Operators Assn., 342 Madison Ave., Suite 1522, New York, NY 10173; (212) 599-6599. Free.

Ocean and Cruise News. Ratings, classifications, and features of ships. World Ocean and Cruise Liner Society, P.O. Box 92, Stamford, CT 06904. $28 for a year's subscription (12 issues).

TravLtips Association. Unusual cruises: freighters, yachts, expeditions. Membership includes magazine and free reference book.

$15 a year. P.O. Box 580218-C9S, Flushing, NY 11358; (800) 872-8584.

Volunteering and Other Options

Archaeology Abroad, 31-34 Gordon Sq., London WC1H OPY, England. Three annual bulletins lists worldwide archaeological digs with details of staffing needs and costs.

Earthwatch Expeditions, 680 Mt. Auburn St., Watertown, MA 02172; (617) 926-8200. Be a paying volunteer on scientific expeditions worldwide.

Golden Opportunities: A Volunteer Guide for Americans over 50 by Andrew Carroll. Peterson's Guides, 1994, $14.95.

National Senior Sports Association, (800) 282-6772. Golf vacations.

Over the Hill Gang, 3310 Cedar Heights Dr., Colorado Springs, CO 80904; (719) 685-4656. Skiing, hiking, and biking for those over 50.

Smart Vacations: The Traveler's Guide to Learning. 1993. 320 pp. $14.95 plus s/h from Council-Pubs Dept., 205 E. 42nd St., New York, NY 10017-5706; (888) COUNCIL. Adult traveler's guide to learning abroad includes, in addition to study tours, opportunities for voluntary service, field research and archaeological digs, environmental and professional projects, fine arts, and more.

Volunteer Vacations by Bill McMillon. Chicago Review Press, 6th ed., 1997, $16.95. Includes 2,000 opportunities worldwide plus personal stories.

Senior Web Sites

Access-Able Travel Source, www.accessable.com. A free Internet information service for mature and disabled travelers: accessibility guide for countries, states and provinces, and cities; also accommodations, transportation, attractions, adventures, doctors and equipment rental and repair, specialty travel agents, and a comprehensive list of disability links and publications. Pages include discussion forums and *What's News*, an online newsletter. (303) 232-2979 (Voice), fax (303) 239-8486; www.accessable.com.

Senior News Network: Travel, www.seniornews.com/travel.html. A compilation of articles by senior travelers. Most articles have contact and resource information for planning your own trip. Also see www.seniornews.com/new-choices/travel.html, for the *New Choices* travel newsletter.

SeniorsSearch.com Travel Section, www.seniorssearch.com/stravel.htm. A search directory exclusively for the over 50 age group, it has links to web sites with information and resources for senior travelers.

For more listings of resources for senior travel, and for bargains worldwide, travel tips, and all sorts of information on learning, living, working, and traveling abroad, see *Transitions Abroad* magazine. To order a single copy or a subscription, please call 1-800-293-0373 or visit the *Transitions Abroad* web site at www.transabroad.com.

CHAPTER 4

SENIOR TRAVEL PROGRAMS

The following listing of senior travel programs was supplied by the organizers in 1998 and is updated in each July/August issue of Transitions Abroad *magazine. Contact the program directors to confirm costs, dates, and other details. Please tell them you read about their programs in this book! Programs based in more than one country or region are listed under "Worldwide."*

Central America

Panama Canal Transit. Travel the Panama Canal, explore Panama's history, culture, and rich ecological diversity. Trek through rainforests and visit indigenous tribes. High adventure, learning, leisure and shopping tours available. Visit the only natural rainforest within a city's limits. See ruins from the Spanish colonial era and discover American history in the Panama Canal Zone.

Dates: Once a month. Cost: Eight-day tour, double occupancy $1,118 per person. Contact: Panama Discovery Tours, P.O. Box 130, Clarita, OK 74535; (800) 813-3115, fax (580) 428-3499; pdt@iamerica.net; www.panamacanal.com.

Costa Rica

Casa Rio Blanco Rainforest Reserve. If adventure and learning is the nature of your journey, then volunteer to work in one of the most complex ecosystems in the world—the rainforest. Meet nice people while participating in rainforest conservation projects and environmental education. The emerald green classroom is right outside your door. Send 3 international reply coupons.

Dates: Four-week sessions throughout the year. Cost: $100 downpayment, $400 upon arrival. Includes meals, cabin and, laundry. Contact: Dee Bocock (new owner), Casa Rio Blanco, Apdo 241-7210, Guapiles Pococi, Costa Rica.

Learn Spanish While Volunteering. Assist with the training of Costa Rican public school teachers in ESL and computers. Assist local health clinic, social service agencies, and environmental projects. Enjoy learning Spanish in the morning, volunteer work in the afternoon/evening. Spanish classes of 2-5 students plus group learning activities; conversations with middle-class homestay families (1 student per family). Homestays and most volunteer projects are within walking distance of school in small town near the capital, San Jose.

Dates: Year round, all levels. Classes begin every Monday, volunteer program is continuous. Cost: $345 per week for 28 hours of classes and group activities plus Costa Rican dance and cooking classes. Includes tuition, 3 meals per day, 7 days per week, homestay, laundry, all materials, and airport transportation. $25 one-time registration fee; $100 additional one-time registration fee for volunteer program. Contact: Susan Shores, Registrar, Latin American Language Center, 7485 Rush River Dr., Suite 710-123, Sacramento, CA 95831; (916) 447-0938, fax (916) 428-9542; lalc@madre.com.

Europe

Senior Group Program Tours. Destinations available: Algarve-Portugal, Dubrovnik, Montecatini, Tuscany, Amalfi Coast, Malta, Athens and Vravrona, Madeira-Portugal, classical Greece. Group size varies from 25-30 passengers. All inclusive tours feature roundtrip airfare from NYC. Trips range from 9 to 15 days.

Dates: Most programs valid through May 31, 1999. Cost: From $935-$1,549 (all-inclusive). Contact: Sergio Bigini, Central Holidays, 120 Sylvan Ave., Englewood Cliffs, NJ 07632; (800) 935-5000, ext 260, fax (201) 222-7899; group@centralh.com, www.centralholidays.com.

France

France Langue Schools in Paris/Nice. Delightful private language institute blocks from the Champs Elysees, Paris, or the sunny beaches of the French Riviera. Year round, all ages and levels. Specialty classes: commerce, cuisine, business, au pair, tourism, DELE, DALF. Custom-designed programs for teachers and high school groups. University credit available. Family stay, residence halls, apartments, or hotel accommodations.

Dates: Contact for information. Cost: Contact for information. Contact: Mr. De Poly, France Langue, 22 ave. Notre Dame, 06000 Nice, France; (011) 33-4-93-13-7888, fax (011) 33-4-93-13-7889; frlang_n@club-internet.fr, www.france_langue.fr.

French and Cookery in a Château. Live and study in 18th-century château with relaxed, convivial atmosphere. Residential French language and Provençal cooking for adults. Comfortable single/twin and shared rooms. Good food and wine at the heart of France's loveliest areas, near Lyon.

Dates: Two weeks in Feb, and every Sunday May-Nov. Cost: From $800 full board and classes in château. Contact: Michael Giammarella in U.S.: (800) 484-1234 ext 0096 or Ecole des Trois Ponts, Château de Matel, 42300 Roanne, France; (011) 33-477-70-80-01, fax (011) 33-477-71-5300; info@3ponts.edu, www.3ponts.edu.

French Language Immersion. International institute on Mediterranean coast. Short- and long-term French courses. Modern air-conditioned premises in large park. Restaurant with terrace. Top-quality homestay, hotels, apartments. Minimum age 17, maximum unlimited. Students, business people, employees, airline staff, retired people. Charming medieval town linking Provence to Riviera, lively marina, unspoiled beaches.

Dates: Year round. Cost: From FF1,200 per week (tuition). Contact: Institut ELFCA, 66 ave. du Toulon, 83400 Hyeres, France; (011) 33-4-94-65-03-31, fax (011) 33-4-94-65-81-22; elfca@elfca.com, www.elfca.com.

Learn French in France (IFG). Whatever the need, whatever the level, IFG Langues has the experience, the skill, and the resources to provide the optimum courses in French. Our team of highly qualified teachers offers individually tailored programs. Courses concentrate first on general language, then on specific professional needs. Host family or hotel on request.

Dates: Courses begin any Monday. Cost: FF470.34 per hour, all taxes included. Contact: Aline Pernot, IFG Languages, 37, quai de Grenelle, 75015 Paris, France; (011) 33-1-40-59-31-38, fax (011) 33-1-45-75-14-43.

India

Project India. A unique 3-week service program open to people of all ages and backgrounds run by a highly qualified staff of educators, social workers, and cultural advisers. Positions include health care, education, social development, arts/recreation, and more. No skills or experience required.

Dates: Three-week programs run year round. Longer term placements can be arranged. Cost: $1,750 covers all India-based expenses. International airfare, insurance, and visa not included. Program fee is tax deductible. Contact: Cross-Cultural Solutions, 47 Potter Ave., New Rochelle, NY 10801; (914) 632-0022 or (800) 380-4777, fax (914) 632 8494; info@crossculturalsolutions.org, www.crossculturalsolutions.org.

Italy

Florence Discovery. Two-week program, 2 hours daily Italian language in small groups (max. 8 people) plus activities. Accommodations in single room with Italian family.

Dates: Every 2 weeks. Cost: $290 includes course, accommodations, and activities for 2 weeks. Contact: Alberto Del Mela, Scuola Toscana, via Benci 23, Florence 50122, Italy; Tel./fax (011) 39-55-244583; scuola.toscana@firenze.net, www.waf.com/scuolatoscana.

Learn Italian in Italy. Study Italian in a 16th-century Renaissance palace in the center of Florence, or in a classic Tuscan town just 30 minutes from the sea. Koiné Center's professional language teachers and small class sizes encourage active participation by each student. Cultural program, guided excursions, choice of accommodations including host families.

Dates: Year round; starting dates each month. Cost: Two-week intensive program $290; 3 weeks $390; homestay accommodations from $115 per week. Contact: In Italy: Dr. Andrea Moradei, Koiné Center, Via Pandolfini 27, 50122 Firenze, Italy; (011) 39-055-213881. In North America: (800) 274-6007; homestay@teleport.com. www.koinecenter.com.

Latin America

Language Travel Programs. For all ages and all Spanish levels. Spanish classes, excursions, cultural activities. One week to 6 months. Various settings: beaches, mountains, small towns, large cities, etc. Countries: Mexico, Costa Rica, Guatemala, Honduras, Panamá, El Salvador, Argentina, Chile, Ecuador, Peru, Uruguay, Venezuela, Puerto Rico, Dominican Republic.

Dates: Programs start every week or every month. Cost: Depends on location. Prices start at $175 per week and include classes, homestay, travel insurance, most meals, some cultural activities. Contact: AmeriSpan Unlimited, P.O. Box 40007, Philadelphia, PA 19106; (800) 879-6640, fax (215) 751-1100; info@amerispan.com, www.amerispan.com.

Mexico

Treasures of Colonial Mexico. Deluxe 9-day escorted tours of Guadalajara, Morelia, San Miguel de Allende and Guanajuato. Designed to offer maximum exposure to the people, the culture, the history, the arts, and the medieval charm of Colonial Mexico, our tours feature a relaxed pace, limited motorcoach travel, extended hotel stays, scheduled free time, and small groups.

Dates: Year round. Cost: $1,595 includes accommodations, ground transportation, some meals, guide and escort, entry fees, and airfare from Houston. Contact: Siesta Tours, P.O. Box 90361, Gainesville, FL 32607; (800) 679-2746, fax (352) 371-8368; siesta@ mercury.net, www.mercury.net/~siesta.

Papua New Guinea

Trans Niugini Tours. Nature and culture programs are offered in 3 areas: the Highlands, the Sepik Area, and a marine environment on the North Coast. Each area has its own distinct culture and environment, with comfortable wilderness lodges.

Dates: Weekly departures. Cost: $889-$3,570 per person (land cost). Contact: Bob Bates, Trans Niugini Tours, P.O. Box 371, Mt. Hagen, Papua New Guinea; (800) 521-7242 or (011) 675-542-1438, fax (011) 675-542-2470; travel@pngtours.com, www.pngtours. com.

Spain

CLIC International House Sevilla. CLIC IH, one of Spain's leading language schools, is located in the heart of Seville, the vibrant capital of Andalucia. With year-round intensive Spanish language courses taught by highly qualified and motivated native teachers, CLIC IH combines professionalism with a friendly atmosphere. Accommodations are carefully selected in host families and own apartments. We offer a varied cultural program to places of interest in Seville and the surrounding area.

Dates: Year round. Cost: Approx. $825 for a 4-week course, individual room with a family, and 2 meals per day. Contact: Bernhard Roters, CLIC-International House Seville, Calle Santa Ana 11, 41002 Sevilla, Spain; (011) 34-95-437-4500, fax 1806; clic@arrakis.es, www.clic.es.

Spanish for Seniors. Highly practical language program plus cultural and social activities for seniors. Spanish for the market, for restaurants/bars, renting cars, booking hotels etc. Integrated visits to castles, museums, "Pueblos Blancos" plus activities— cooking lessons, Sevillana dance classes, flamenco parties, etc. Learning and fun in a beautiful Mediterranean setting in a school with students of all ages.

Dates: Starting Feb 2, 16; Mar 2, 16, 30; Apr 13, 27; May 11; Oct 12, 26; Nov 9, 23. Cost: Three lessons per day and cultural activities PTS60,000 (2 weeks); accommodations from PTS33,800 (2 weeks). Contact: Bob Burger, Malaca Instituto, c/Cortada 6, Cerrado de Calderon, 29018 Malaga, Spain; (011) 34-95-229-32-42 or 1896, fax (011) 34-95-229-63-16; espanol@malacainst-ch.es, www. malacainst-ch.es.

United Kingdom and Ireland

Exploring Second Half of Life. With Sheila Ward and Rosemary Ward. Three days for women to explore and celebrate the riches of the second half of life. What is the significance of this period for ourselves and for society?

Dates: Mar, Jul, Sep. Cost: Donations. Contact: Sheila Ward, The Grange, Ellesmere, Shropshire SY12 9DE, U.K.; (011) 44-1691-623495.

Worldwide

American-Int'l Homestays. Stay in English-speaking foreign homes in over 30 countries. Explore foreign cultures responsibly. Learn foreign languages. Perfect for families or seniors. Learn how other people live by living with them in their homes.

Dates: Year round. Cost: From $59 per night. Contact: Joe Kinczel, American-Int'l Homestays, P.O. Box 1754, Nederland, CO 80466; (303) 642-3088 or (800) 876-2048, fax (303) 642-3365; ash@igc.apc.org.

¿?don Quijote In-Country Spanish Language Schools. Intensive Spanish language courses using the communicative method are combined with an intensive immersion in the social and cultural life of some of Spain's most interesting cities (Salamanca, Barçelona, Granada, Malaga). Airport pickup service, study counseling, homestay or student flats, excursions, access to recreational facilities, touring, and sightseeing opportunities. donQuijote now offers intensive Spanish language courses through partner schools in Latin America: Cuernavaca and Mèrida, Mexico; Antigua, Guatemala; Alajuela, Costa Rica; and Quito, Ecuador.

Dates: Year round—Fall, Spring, Winter, and Summer. Cost: Inquire. Contact: ¿?don Quijote, Apartado de Correos 333, 37080 Salamanca, Spain; (011) 34-923-268-860, fax (011) 34-923-268-815; donquijote@offcampus.es, www.teclata.es/donquijote.

Eldertreks. Exotic adventures for travelers 50 and over. Experienced local guides and western escorts. Group size limited to 15 participants. No mandatory single supplement charge.

Dates: Year round. Cost: Vary according to trip. Contact: Gordon Ross, ElderTreks, 597 Markham St., Toronto, ON M6G 2L7, CANADA; (800) 741-7956, fax (416) 588-9839; passages@inforamp.net, www.eldertreks.com.

Exotic Safaris. Small group deluxe educational tours in India, Nepal, and Africa.

Dates: Call for details. Cost: Call for details. Contact: Cindy Harris, VJ's Exotic Safaris, 320 Stevens Ave., Suite 4, Winfield, KS 67156; safaris@southwind.net.

Extraordinary Travel Adventures. Unique combination of adventure, experiential education, and cultural exchange. Trips are to "less known" areas of the world. In-depth immersion into local lifestyles. Some overnights with local families, some travel by native transport, optional language learning components, substantial predeparture literature. A percentage of our profits is donated to communities visited. Trip lengths of 2 to 3 weeks; limited to 16 people maximum.

Dates: Year round. Contact for exact departures. Cost: Land costs range between $2,295-$3,595. Contact: Immersia Travel, 19 North King St., Leesburg, VA 20176; (800) 207-5454 or (703) 443-6939, fax (703) 443-0111; adventure@immersiatravel.com, www.immersiatravel.com.

Travel-Study Seminars. Learn from people of diverse backgrounds about their economic, political, and social realities. Emphasis on the views of the poor and oppressed. Programming in Mexico, Central America, South Africa, and China/Hong Kong. Call for a free listing of upcoming seminars.

Dates: Ongoing. Cost: $1,000-$4,500 depending on destination and length of trip. Contact: Center for Global Education, Augsburg College, 2211 Riverside Ave., Box TR, Minneapolis, MN 55454; (800) 299-8889, fax (612) 330-1695; globaled@augsburg.edu, www.augsburg.edu/global.

Walking The World. We offer outdoor walking trips to people 50 and over. Trips study the local natural and cultural histories of the areas we visit. Trips to Costa Rica, Nepal, Utah, China, Turkey, Peru, Wales, Italy,

France, Ireland, Switzerland, Canada, Colorado, Scotland, Newfoundland, Washington, Maine, Hawaii, India, Mt. Everest, Galapagos, New Zealand, Copper Canyon, Arizona, California, Portugal.

Dates: Year round. Cost: Land cost from $895 to $3,095 includes Walking The World guides, local guides, lodging, most meals, ground transportation, unique and original journal of your trip, t-shirt. Contact: Ward Luthi, Director, Walking The World, P.O. Box 1186, Ft. Collins, CO 80522-1186; (970) 498-0500, fax (970) 498-9100; walktworld@aol.com, www.gorp.com/walkingtheworld.

For more listings of senior travel programs, and for bargains worldwide, travel tips, and all sorts of information on learning, living, working, and traveling abroad, see *Transitions Abroad* magazine. To order a single copy or a subscription, please call 1-800-293-0373 or visit the *Transitions Abroad* web site at www.transabroad.com.

CHAPTER 5

FAMILY
TRAVEL
RESOURCES

Parents approach overseas travel with obvious trepidation. "We're thinking of going to Switzerland with our two-year-old. Are we nuts?" Or, "Our 14-year-old barely speaks to us. Will two weeks in Mexico help or will we end up hating each other?"

Go for it. The experience is well worth it, as long as you know the basic whys and hows of traveling with kids.

Why Travel with Kids

Why shouldn't you just go by yourselves? After all, the children won't appreciate the Louvre or that Tudor inn in England.

You're not the first one to think this way—it's logical. Surprisingly, though, most parents we've talked to said that in retrospect they appreciated the slower pace of traveling with children. The typical adult trip is too often a race from one well-known sight to the next, as you try to cram it all in and become a victim of the 10-countries-in-8-days syndrome.

The best family travel involves staying put, taking it slowly, learning more about everyday life. Leave the kids behind and you're on vacation overseas. Take them along, and you're temporarily living in another land.

Better communication and family cohesion is another reason to travel with kids. A special family trip can, on its own, create a powerful family culture. Years after you return, you'll still hold a solid core of private jokes and common memories that tie your family together.

Many families rediscover the art of conversation. At home, dinner is rushed, with some family members already at play rehearsal or PTA, others not yet back from work or basketball practice. The TV's on and the phone rings at just the wrong times.

On the road, you're all together on a train or in a family room at a youth hostel, and somehow discussions arise. A troop of beggars panhandling on a Paris street leads one kid to ask, "How come some people are rich and other people are poor?" Or a stop at a gilded baroque cathedral prompts another child with little church experience to wonder why religion is so important to some people.

Discussion isn't something you can force. Don't picture yourselves climbing off your transatlantic flight, hopping in your car, and driving away into the sunset discussing politics. Give it time. The longer your trip and the less hectically scheduled it is, the more discussion opportunities will arise. Thrown together in a car for days on end, or sitting around in a TV-less, phone-less rental home, the art of conversation will eventually be reborn.

Traveling with your kids may also be a great way to short-circuit years of adolescent wrangling. When we first traveled overseas our daughter Libby, 13, was just beginning to spend more and more time behind a closed door. But for the duration of our trip, she often had no room of her own, let alone a door. Unable to avoid each other when we had differences, we learned to talk them out in reasonably productive ways, developing communication patterns that lasted for years.

Traveling overseas exposes your family to different points of view. Americans can be very parochial about their lives. So can teenagers. Put them together and you get the American teenager, convinced that there's only one way to dress, speak, or act. Nothing can counteract this tendency quite so well as a trip outside the country. Even on a short trip, it's almost impossible for your kids to avoid noticing that people in different countries eat differently and dress differently than we do, yet still survive.

Traveling also gives your kids valuable coping skills. Travel is not always a day in the park. There's a lot that kids (and adults) can learn from coping with the ups and downs of foreign travel—especially when you plan your trip to make as much contact as possible with the local culture. Take a week's vacation in luxury hotels and your kids won't learn to cope with anything but jet lag. Stay a bit longer and spend a bit less, and they'll learn to eat new foods when there's nothing familiar on the menu, to put on extra sweaters and blankets when there's no central heat, and to use challenging toilets.

Is there anything more important you can teach your children than learning how to communicate, see life from different points of view, and make the most of any situation? Start planning now, and make your dreams happen. What's your excuse for not taking your kids overseas?

How to Travel with Kids

Rule #1 is to stay put for at least part of your trip. This goes counter to all your inclinations. But of the scores of parents who contact us after an overseas trip with kids, none say they wished they'd fit more into the schedule. Most rave about the time they spent "living" instead of "traveling."

This rule is essential if you're traveling with pre-schoolers. Rent a house or apartment and explore the area from home base, with no worries about naps and diaper bags. Renting is not difficult, even for stays of a week, and can save you hundreds of dollars.

With older kids, the benefits of home-stays are different but just as important. Picture it: At home your teens are independent. But on the road they must turn to you for everything from translations to currency rates. This step backwards breeds resentment. A few days in one place, and the kids feel confident and in control again--and family tension levels go way down. One California couple reported that their biggest problem in a two-week home exchange was that their kids preferred hanging around with their new local friends to visiting yet another castle. (Their parents feigned disapproval to keep the kids happy, but were secretly delighted.)

It's hard to control the urge to see the "Big Name Sights" as long as you're traveling, though. So compromise. If you have two weeks, stay put for the first one to get a look at everyday life. Then travel the second week, when jet lag is over and everyone feels rested and in control.

Rule #2 is to explore normal life as much as possible. Spend time in grocery stores picking out foods, or in toy stores comparing the wares with those at home. If your kids are in scouts, visit the local scout troop. Bypass the expensive amusement park for a day at the local school fundraising fête. Hang around playgrounds, and see how quickly your kids join in a pickup soccer game—even when they don't speak a word of the local language.

Rule #3 is to make history and culture digestible to your kids. Buy a disposable camera for each child and encourage them to "collect" gargoyles, roof gables, or church towers. When you visit a museum, start with the gift shop and let each kid choose two postcards, then set out to find the kids' "own" works. Balance each day physically, with a morning cathedral visit, for instance, followed by renting bikes in the afternoon. Let family members take turns choosing the day's itinerary, to avoid a succession of imposed "least-common-denominator" choices that no one hates but no one really likes. Dad's visit to the ball-bearing factory may turn out to be surprisingly interesting, and even the adults may like sliding down that giant sand dune.

Below is a list of some of the best resources to help you travel according to these guidelines. We've also included some organized tours for those who'd like some assistance in planning their overseas family travel.

— *Cynthia Harriman*

Family Travel Organizations

Abercrombie & Kent, 1520 Kensington Rd., Suite 212, Oak Brook, IL 60523, (800) 323-7308. fax (630) 954-3324. A wide range of itineraries tailored to families traveling during summer and school vacation.

AmeriSpan Unlimited, P.O. Box 40007, Philadelphia, PA 19106; (800) 879-6640; info@AmeriSpan.com, www.AmeriSpan.com. Family, teen, senior, and adult language programs in 12 countries in Mexico, Spain, Central and South America. Housing with a host family.

Backroads, 801 Cedar St., Berkeley, CA 94710-1800; (800) 462-2848. Family biking and walking trips in the U.S., Canada, Costa Rica, Czech Republic, France, and Switzerland. Children of all ages welcome.

Butterfield & Robinson, 70 Bond St., Suite 300, Toronto, ON M5B 1X3, Canada; (800) 678-1147. Pricey deluxe family walking and biking trips in Italy, Holland, Morocco, Canada, and Belize for families with teenagers.

Experience Plus, 1925 Wallenberg Dr., Ft. Collins, CO 80526; (800) 685-4565, fax (970) 484-8489; tours@xplus.com, www.xplus.com. Walking and cycling tours in Italy for families with teens.

Family Travel Forum. Membership organization ($48 per year) publishes newsletter and web site on global family travel including destinations, health and parenting tips, travel deals, family tour operators provide customized travel information. FTF Membership Dept., Cathedral Station, P.O. Box 1585, New York, NY 10025-1585; (888) FT-FORUM, fax (212) 665-6136; www.familytravelforum.com.

FAMILYHOSTEL, 6 Garrison Ave., Durham, NH 03824; (800) 733-9753; www.learn.unh.edu. Offers 10-day trips to Austria, Wales, France, Switzerland, and England (destinations vary yearly) to adults traveling with school-age kids 8-15. Trips mix education and recreation plus a chance to meet local families.

Grand Travel, 6900 Wisconsin Ave., Suite 706, Chevy Chase, MD 20815; (800) 247-7651, fax (301) 913-0166; www.grandtrvl.com. Tour company specializing in outings to Europe, Africa, and Australia for grandparents and grandkids.

Family Travel Resources

Hellenic Advantures, 4150 Harriet Ave. S., Minneapolis, MN 55409; (612) 827-0937, fax (612) 827-2444; papag002@tc.umn.edu. Family tours to Greece, with fishing, snorkeling, and even foot races at Olympia.

Hometours International, P.O. Box 11503, Knoxville, TN 37939; (800) 367-4668. Walking tours in England, much cheaper than Backroads or B&R. Also Israeli "Kibbutz Home" program, apartment and villa rentals, plus B and Bs in Britain, France, Italy. Small fee charged for catalogs.

Hospitality Exchange, P.O. Box 561, Lewistown, MT 59457; (406) 566-2500, fax (406) 566-2612. $20 annual membership gets you directory of 250 members in 26 countries. Some can offer overnight accommodations; others could hook you up with local families.

Hostelling International (AYH), 733 15th St. NW, Suite 840, Washington, DC 20005; (202) 783-6161; www.iyhf.org or www.hiayh.org. Plan your own hosteling trip: many hostels have private family rooms. Advance reservations are required.

Idyll, Ltd., P.O. Box 405, Media, PA 19063; (610) 565-5242, fax (610) 565-5142; info@untours.com, www.untours.com. Arranges apartment rentals for families (including one in a German castle) and includes low-key orientation at your destination.

Journeys International, 4011 Jackson Rd., Ann Arbor, MI 48103; (313) 665-4407 or (800) 255-8735; www.journeys-intl.com. Specially-designed socially responsible family trips include Himalayan trekking, African safaris, plus trips to Australia, the Galapagos, Panama, and Costa Rica.

LEX America 68 Leonard St., Belmont, MA 02178; (617) 489-5800, fax (617) 489-5898; exchange@lexlrf.com, www.lexlrf.com. Arranges family homestays in Japan, Korea, Mexico, and France with 25,000 member families. Standard 2-, 4-, or 6-week summer or autumn program or they'll design a custom program—for instance, a homestay to mesh with a business trip.

Overseas Adventure Travel, 625 Mt. Auburn St., Cambridge, MA 02138; (800) 221-0814. Intercultural adventure trips for families and individuals. Families can choose a Galapagos Wildlife Adventure, a Serengeti Safari, or a Costa Rica natural history trip.

SERVAS, 11 John St., Suite 407, New York, NY 10038; (212) 267-0252; usservas@servas.org, http://servas.org. An international co-operative system of hosts and travelers established to help build world peace, goodwill, and understanding. Families and individuals are welcomed as members. $65 annual membership fee for travelers. Please inquire about our new domestic programs for hosts, international students, and lower income families.

Society for the Protection of Nature in Israel, 28 Arrandale Ave., Great Neck, NY 11024; (212) 398-6750, fax (212) 398-1665. Operates 1-14-day hikes and nature explorations—even a camel tour—in different parts of Israel. Expert environmental guides and low costs. Accommodations are in the group's field study centers or hostels. Children age 10 and up welcome.

Special Expeditions, 720 5th Ave., 6th Fl., New York, NY 10019; (800) 762-0003. A variety of itineraries, including the Galapagos, made more interesting with special scavenger hunts and educational puzzles for the kids.

Travelling with Children, Dan and Wendy Hallinan, 2313 Valley St., Berkeley, CA 94702; (510) 848-0929, fax (510) 848-0935; twc87@aol.com. An experienced traveling family arranges home rentals, airfares, and special itineraries for other traveling families, especially in Europe.

Wildland Adventures, 3516 NE 155th St., Seattle, WA 98155; (800) 345-4453, fax (206) 363-6615. Family trips to Costa Rica, Honduras, Belize, Peru, the Galapagos, Turkey, Africa, and Nepal. Some trips include homestays and other intercultural opportunities.

World Pen Pals, P.O. Box 337, Saugerties, NY 12477; Tel./fax (914) 246-7828. Promotes international friendship and cultural understanding through correspondence between young people under age 23. Pen friends offered by gender and continent but for specific countries phone first to verify availability. Send $3 and SASE for each pen pal desired.

Zephyr Press, 13 Robinson St., Somerville, MA 02145; (603) 585-6534. Zephyr publishes a series of "People to People" guides for Russia, Poland, Romania, Czech Republic/Slovak Republic, Hungary/Bulgaria, Baltic Republics. $14 each. While not geared specifically to family travelers, the guides are a good source for family contacts.

Family Travel Publications

Adventuring with Children: An Inspirational Guide to World Travel and the Outdoors by Nan Jeffrey. Excellent overseas and domestic advice for active families who want to backpack, sail, bicycle, or canoe. $14.95 from Menasha Ridge Press, 700 S. 28th St., Suite 206, Birmingham, AL 35233; (800) 247-9437.

Best Places to Go: A Family Destination Guide by Nan Jeffrey. Recommendations and specifics on budget, culturally-aware family visits to Europe and Central and South America. $14.95 from Menasha Ridge Press (above).

Children's Book of London, Children's Book of Britain (Usborne Guides). Available through BritRail, 551 5th Ave., Suite 702, New York, NY 10176; (212) 490-6688. Usborne guides are not widely available in the U.S.

Découvrir Paris est un Jeu d'Enfant by Isabelle Bourdial and Valeri Guidoux. Editions Parigramme/CPL, 28 rue d'Assas, 75006 Paris, France. A great guide in French, to buy on arrival. Covers museums, parks, zoos, markets-even pick-your-own farms near Paris.

Family Travel: Terrific New Vacations for Today's Families by Evelyn Kaye (Blue Panda). Parent-tested trips—where to find them, and what they cost. Includes houseswaps, educational trips with universities, nature trips, and dinosaur digs.

The Family Travel Guides Catalog. Carousel Press, P.O. Box 6038, Berkeley, CA, 94706-0038. (510) 527-5849. Most of the books mentioned in this list-and dozens of others-are available through Carousel Press. Send $1 or 55¢ long SASE for catalog.

The Family Travel Guide by Carole Terwilliger Meyers. A collection of first-person accounts from families who've traveled all over the world, with specific tips. $16.95 from Carousel Press.

Family Travel Times, P.O. Box 14326, Washington, DC 20044-4326; (888) 822-4FTT (4388). $39 per year. Bimonthly newsletter of worldwide family travel news. Lots of tips for traveling with infants to teens.

Guide de la France des Enfants by Marylène Bellenger. Editions Rouge & Or, 11 rue de Javel, 75015 Paris, France. If you can read French, pick this one up in Paris. Exhaustive guide to sites all over France for kids up to 15.

Gutsy Mamas: Travel Tips and Wisdom for Mothers on the Road by Marybeth Bond. Traveler's Tales, San Francisco, CA. Small volume of tips and first-person anecdotes that should help families and single mothers gather the courage to take exotic trips with the kids.

Have Children Will Travel, P.O. Box 152, Lake Oswego, OR 97034; toll-free (877) 699-5869, fax (503) 636-0895. $29 per year. Quarterly family newsletter of travel resources and tips; deb@havechildrenwilltravel.com, http://havechildrenwilltravel.com.

How To Fly—For Kids! (Corkscrew Press). Activities to keep children busy during long, boring plane flights.

How to Take Great Trips with Your Kids by Sanford Portnoy, Joan Flynn Portnoy. $9.95 (Harvard Common Press).

Ireland for Kids by Derek Mackenzie-Hook. $17.95 plus $4 s/h from Mainstream Publishing, distributed by Trafalgar Square, P.O. Box 257, N. Pomfret, VT 05053; (802) 457-1911. Comprehensive guide packed with details on places kids will enjoy.

Japan for Kids: The Ultimate Guide for Parents and their Children by Diane Wiltshire Kanagawa and Jeanne Huey Erickson. Kodansha International, 114 5th Ave., New York, NY 10011. Not just a tour guide: includes everything from playgrounds and museums to how to have a baby in Japan. Comprehensive and well-written.

Kidding Around London, Kidding Around Paris, Kidding Around Spain Guide series written for kids instead of parents, suitable for good readers 8 or older. A solid but unexciting mix of history and sightseeing. $9.95 each. John Muir, Box P.O. Box 613, Sante Fe, NM 87504; (800) 285-4078.

Kids' Britain by Betty Jerman. Pan Macmillan Books, Cavaye Place, London SW10 9PG, England. A comprehensive guidebook available in England but probably unobtainable here. Lists every conceivable site in England, with costs. Buy it when you get to London.

Kids Love Israel; Israel Loves Kids by Barbara Sofer. New 2nd ed. includes lodging, camps, language, food, plus over 300 sightseeing ideas for the whole country. $17.95 from Kar-Ben Copies, 6800 Tildenwood Ln., Rockville, MD 20852; (301) 984-8733.

Kids' Trips in Tokyo: A Family Guide to One-Day Outings by Ivy Maeda, Kitty Kobe, Cynthia Ozeki, and Lyn Sato. Kodansha International. Organized by 1-day itineraries, with info for infants and older kids. Excellent resource.

London for Families by Larry Lain and Michael Lain. Interlink Books, 46 Crosby St., Northampton, MA 01060; (413) 582-7054. Good background logistical information for first-time traveling families and a fairly good selection of sightseeing recommendations.

Take Your Kids to Europe by Cynthia Harriman. 3rd ed. Globe Pequot Press, P.O. Box 833, Old Saybrook, CT 06475; (800) 243-0495. Not simply a list of where to go, but a good intercultural guide for how and why to travel in Europe with children.

Travel with Children by Maureen Wheeler (Lonely Planet). 3rd ed. The definitive guide to third world travel with kids, covering both logistics and cultural interchange; first-person stories from other travelers.

The Traveler's Toolkit: How to Travel Absolutely Anywhere Not specifically for families, but a great "attitude" book to help new travelers feel comfortable taking on the world. Menasha Ridge Press (above).

Inexpensive Rentals

U.S. agencies offer properties starting at about $600 per week. You can rent a house for as little

Paris With Children
Slowing Down to See the World Through Their Eyes

By Sarah Meeker

The same *je ne sais quoi* that sparks romance for adults in Paris can create magic for children. While not a common vacation choice for those with modest incomes and elementary school aged kids, Paris proved to be an affordable and delightful destination for our family. In the darkness of winter, when most people travel in search of sun, we packed up our daughter Quin, six, and son Ian, nine, and headed for two weeks in the city of light.

To feel like we were living in Paris, we rented a one-bedroom apartment at a cost comparable to a hotel. The apartment rental agency, Chez Vous, in Sausalito, California (415-331-5296), has a large selection of rentals in various sizes, locations, and price ranges. We chose a lovely apartment with 12-foot high windows in the Marais quarter. After long days of sightseeing we would stop to pick up supplies for our evening meal, after which we'd watch French TV and read stories about the bloody history of Paris.

Living on a tight budget in Paris is possible. We cut corners by cooking in and limiting shopping to food and postcards. Our consumer needs were gratified by collecting brochures from the various sights we visited. The kids kept journal scrapbooks and filled the pages with their paper souvenirs. Shopping for groceries was a favorite pastime and a means to interact with Parisians.

Since admission into museums and landmarks was our biggest expense, we planned our itinerary around reduced price days. We visited Versailles and the Musée d'Orsay on Sundays. We bought tickets to see the Nutcracker ballet at L'Opéra de Garnier in the "peasant" section for FF30 ($6) each. At a 50 percent savings, we walked half way up the Eiffel Tower and took the elevator from the second level. We hit the Louvre after 3 p.m. and stayed until closing (9:30 p.m.).

We visited parks, gardens, squares, and graveyards at the cost of a metro ticket. While the adults admired the design and identified plants in the formal gardens, the kids let loose in the open spaces. Making our pilgrimage to Jim Morrison's grave, we traipsed through Père Lachaise cemetery on a cold, dark, blustery morning. The kids were fascinated by the elaborate grave markers and thrilled by getting the creeps.

Simply strolling was a favorite pastime, and it never cost more than the price of a few crêpes or ice cream cones for refueling. Watching Parisians living their lives was a source of free entertainment. We stumbled upon a heated game of bocci while wandering through Montemartre, watched school children play in the Arène de Lutèce (remains of a Roman arena near the Jardin des Plantes), and checked out a construction site in Marais where a cobblestone street was being intricately reassembled one stone at a time.

The Metro also provides hours of entertainment. The kids planned our routes and led us through the metro stations like pros. Ian honed his Metro skills to a point where we felt confident that he could find his way home alone. We gave him a spare Metro ticket to carry in his pocket along with his name and address tag. One evening we created a "get to know Paris game" with city and metro maps. We planned a treasure hunt of sorts made up of clues such as: "I had a hunch you'd find me here" (Notre-Dame), or

"It is so cold down here, we're chilled to the bone" (Catacombs). The kids loved solving the riddle and then selected the most efficient metro route to get from site to site.

Besides the zoo (Ménagerie) in the Jardin des Plantes, we skipped typical kid attractions like the Museum of Science (Cité des Sciences) and Euro Disney. The Magic Kingdom's artificial plazas, castles, and main streets could not compare to the bonafide magic of Place des Vosges, Versailles, l'Opéra, Champs Elysées, and Place de la Concorde where real people jousted, danced, marched, and were executed.

We took in all of the major grown-up attractions with kids' eyes. They liked anything that required climbing stairs. The tower at Notre Dame was closed, but we hiked up the Arc de Triomphe, the dome of Sacré-Couer, part of the Eiffel Tower, and down under into the Catacombs Montparnasse—the endless labryinth of dark narrow passageways that became the storage area for millions of human bones in the 1700s and headquarters for the French resistance during World War II. Ian thought it was the coolest spot in Paris.

Oddly, Versailles was a favorite with the kids. They were mesmerized by a life-sized play village built to entertain Marie-Antoinette. Quin had a cottage picked out for each one of her friends.

On the evening at the Louvre we practically had the place to ourselves. Exiting via the I.M. Pei pyramid into the dark courtyard was magical. The Eiffel Tower, Arc de Triomphe, Arc de Carrousel, and the Louvre were all bathed in light.

We prepared the kids for the trip by reading children's books set in or related to France. Quin soaked up *Mirette on the High Wire*, *Liennea's Garden*, and *Madeline*; Ian read *Avion My Uncle Flew* and *The Court of Stone Children*. We gave up on *A Tale of Two Cities*.

Spending two weeks in a social vacuum made for good family bonding. Out of necessity Ian and Quin became buddies. Unbelievably, they were spotted holding hands in the Metro and in the Musée Carnavalet. We had a pleasant plane ride home thanks to this new-found friendship.

In addition to seeing beautiful art and architecture, another reward of foreign travel is the experience of learning to cope with a new and unfamiliar environment. We hope that the experience of being outsiders helped to generate self-confidence (peppered with humility) for our children.

My goal for this trip was to share Paris with our children, not expecting to gain much for myself. I was pleasantly surprised to experience a new perspective that created an even deeper appreciation for the city. My "been there, done that" attitude was quickly squelched as my children helped me to feel the city rather than to just see the famous sights. Our less-frenzied pace and minimized expectations allowed me to slow down and experience the joy of simply being there. Instead of creating a burden, having the kids along added a new richness to my memories of Paris.

as $200 through many local tourist offices in Europe. Or try going directly to some of the following European sources:

Agriturist, Corso Vittorio Emanuele 101, 00186 Rome, Italy; (011) 39-6-685-2342, fax (011) 39-6-685-2424. An agriturismo source for Italian farmstays. Fax and ask for the current price for their catalog.

British Tourist Office, (212) 986-2200. Ask for a free booklet called "City Apartments" for a selection of reasonably-priced family-sized apartments in cities throughout Britain.

Chez Nous, Bridge Mills, Huddersfield Rd., Holmfirth HD7 2TW, England; (011) 44-1484-684-075, fax (011) 44-1484-685-852; http://cheznous.com. Directory of French rentals owned by Brits. They charge only for ads; prices are reasonable ($175 per week plus) because there's no commission. And there's no language gap in making arrangements.

Destination Stockholm, Skårgård AB, Lillström, S-18497 Ljustero, Sweden; (011) 46-8-542-481-00, fax 011) 46-8-542-414-00; dess.skarg@stockholm.mail.telia.com. Cottages in the Stockholm archipelago, starting at about $200 in the off season and $350 in midsummer. Book 7 to 8 months ahead for high season.

Fjordhytter, Lille Markevei 13, P.O. Box 103, 5001 Bergen, Norway; (011) 47-55-23-20-80, fax (011) 47-55-23-24-04. Lovely photo catalog in English with very detailed descriptions. Prices start at $180 off season to $350 high season.

FriFerie Danmark, Liselejevej 60, 3360 Liselejevej, Denmark; (011)-45-42-34-63-34; fax (011)-45-42-34-64-53. Catalog in German and Danish only. Rentals start at about $240 per week off season and $460 midsummer.

German Tourist Offices. Many regional tourist offices publish excellent color-photo guides. Three good ones: Familienferien, Schwarzwald Tourismusverband, Postfach 1660, 79016 Freiburg im Breisgau, Germany; (011) 49-761-31317; fax (011) 49-761-36021. Fränkisches Urlaubskatalog, Tourismusverband Franken, Am Plärrer 14, 90429 Nürnberg, Germany; (011) 49-911-26-42-02, fax (011) 49-911-27-05-47. Urlaub auf Bauern-und Winzerhöfen, Rheinland-Pfalz Tourist Office, Schmittpforte 2, 55437 Ober-Hilbersheim, Germany; (011) 49-6728-1225, fax (011) 49-6728-626.

Irish Cottage Holiday Homes, Cork Kerry Tourism, Tourist House, Grand Parade, Cork, Ireland; (011) 353-21-273-251, fax (011) 353-21-273-504. Good variety of listings from £100 to £500 per week. Also ads for agencies, walking maps of the area, etc.

Maison des Gîtes de France, 59 rue St. Lazare, 75009 Paris, France; (011) 33-1-49-70-75-75, fax (011) 33-1-49-70-75-76. Source for thousands of inexpensive, simple, rural rentals in France. French language may help in arranging terms. Fax for order form for 90 regional guidebooks, which cost about $6 each.

Swiss Farmstays: Enjoy Switzerland's bucolic beauty with a farmhouse vacation. Some lodgings include a kitchen; others offer meals with the inhabitants: Fédération du Tourisme Rural de Suisse Romande, c/o Office du Tourisme, 1530 Payerne, Switzerland; (011) 41-37-61-61-61. Ferien auf dem Bauernhof, Buchungszentrale Verein, Raiffeisenbank, 5644 Auw AG, Switzerland; (011) 41-57-48-17-09. Ferien auf dem Bauernhof, Schweizer Reisekasse (REKA), Neuengasse 15, 3001 Bern, Switzerland; (011) 41-31-329-66-33. Color photo directory with over 150 listings direct from REKA or from Swiss NTO. Text is in German with English key and booking information.

Family Travel Web Sites

A small sample of online family travel resources.

Family Travel Forum, www.familytravelforum.com. The Family Travel Forum

ALTERNATIVE TRAVEL DIRECTORY

(FTF) is dedicated to the ideals, promotion and support of travel with children (see their listing above). Their web site is a full interface to their services. Also includes a selection of family travel titles available through amazon.com.

Federal Travel Service Web Site, www.federaltravel.com. Site for business, family and vacation travel, as well as for those who are traveling to adopt. They are a full service travel agency that has been in operation since 1981, and their web site serves as a 24-hour open door to their services.

Have Children Will Travel, http://havechildrenwilltravel.com. Web site for their newsletter (see their listing above). Not only can you preview and get information about their printed publication, but they'll answer your family travel questions by e-mail.

Quinwell Travel, www.quinwell.com/kidcru1.htm. Information and booking services for traveling with children on cruise ships, and family travel in general.

The Mining Company, http://travelwithkids.miningco.com. The Mining Company hosts a network of comprehensive web sites for over 500 topics. Each site has a "guide," or individual dedicated to keeping the content up-to-date (check www.miningco.com for their homepage). Their family travel site (with Teresa Plowright as the guide) is billed as "a guide to the many ways you can use the Web to plan and even purchase your family holidays: discount airfares, vacation ideas, trip reports, info about destinations, and more."

www.family.com. This Disney-sponsored site offers a large collection of family travel resources in the U.S. and abroad.

www.kidscom.com. A "communication playground" for kids 4-15 in English, French, Spanish, or German. Fill in your specs for a pen pal—say, French, age 14, girl, likes skiing—and find your e-mail soulmate.

www.worldwide.edu. "Travel Planner" accesses scores of pen pals, travel programs, etc. WorldWide Classroom, Box 1166, Milwaukee, WI 53201-1166; (414) 224-3476.

For more listings of family travel resources, and for bargains worldwide, travel tips, and all sorts of information on learning, living, working, and traveling abroad, see *Transitions Abroad* magazine. To order a single copy or a subscription, please call 1-800-293-0373 or visit the *Transitions Abroad* web site at www.transabroad.com.

DISABILITY TRAVEL RESOURCES AND PROGRAMS

More and more people with disabilities are looking to get off the tourist track, get to know the host people and the culture, and still stay within a budget. For travelers with disabilities, these are not always easy to do. Yet more and more of us who use wheelchairs or have other disabilities are becoming independent, nontraditional travelers.

Obviously, access is always an issue, whether it's finding wheelchair accessible accommodations and people who can communicate in sign language or getting information on tape or in Braille.

I've been traveling in my wheelchair for more than 25 years and would like to share some of my best tips:

I use a light-weight manual wheelchair with pop-off tires. I have a net bag under my wheelchair where I store my daypack. A backpack fits on the back of my chair; if I can't carry it myself (since I usually travel alone), I don't take it. I keep a bungee cord with me for when I can't get my chair in a car or to secure it on a train, and I always insist on using my own wheelchair to the airline gate. When I transfer planes I again insist that I get my own chair rather than use the wheelchairs provided by the airlines. Bathrooms are always a hassle, so

I have learned to use creative ways to transfer into narrow bathrooms (or use a belt to narrow my wheelchair width). To be honest, when there are no accessible bathrooms in sight I have found ways to relieve myself discreetly just about anywhere—from outside the Eiffel Tower to a glacier in a national park. You gotta do what you gotta do. Hopefully, one day the access will improve. But in the meantime there is a world out there to be discovered. Bring along an extra pair of pants and a great sense of humor.

I always try to learn some of the local language because it cuts through the barriers when people stare (and they do) and also comes in handy when I need assistance in going up a curb or a flight of steps. Don't accept other people's notions of what is possible—I have climbed Masada in Israel and made it to the top of the Acropolis in Greece. When I go to a museum I'm sure to ask about freight elevators because almost all have them.

I always get information about disability groups where I am going: they will have the best access information and many times they will become your new traveling partners and friends. Remember, you are part of a global family of disabled people.

Don't confuse being flexible and having a positive attitude with settling for less than your rights. I expect equal access and constantly let people know about the possibility of providing access through ramps or other modifications. When I believe my rights have been violated I do whatever is necessary to remedy the situation so the next traveler or disabled person in that country won't have the same frustrations.

For information on your rights regarding airline travel get the free book, **The Air Carriers Act: Make It Work For You.** It's free from the Paralyzed Veterans of America; call toll free: (888) 860-7244. If you feel you have been discriminated against under the Americans with Disabilities Act or Air Carriers Act, contact the Disability Rights Education and Defense Fund: (800) 466-4232 (TDD and voice.)

If you are interested in work, study, research, or volunteering abroad, contact the Clearinghouse on Disability and Exchange at Mobility International USA (below).

The Internet is also improving access to updated accessibility information. Check out the web and do some investigating.

Finally, I hope readers will consider all the incredibly various opportunities listed in *Transitions Abroad* and will inquire of each program that interests them how their needs could be accommodated. In some cases, such as study abroad, you may have rights under the Americans with Disabilities Act.

Since choice is the key, I have included a variety of resources. The specialized group tours tend to be expensive and have the advantages and disadvantages of group travel: they usually have a tourist slant. My favorites are the type of experiences that this magazine highlights: volunteering in a workcamp, doing a community project, taking a language or an art course, or bicycling across the Netherlands on an adapted bicycle (as I have done).

People with disabilities need to venture out. Although obstacles abound, we must pave the way for other travelers and connect with other people with disabilities throughout the world. We need to remind all organizations that organize travel—whether it be ecotourism or study or working abroad—that their planning processes should incorporate including people with all types of disabilities. We are striving for a world where each country adopts laws and policies to make accessibility just the routine way of being. If we are truly traveling to create a better and more just world, then let's be sure that we are including all of its citizens.

— *Susan Sygall*

Disability Organizations

Barrier Free Travel, Ian J. Cooper, 36 Wheatley St., North Bellingen, NSW 2454, Australia; (011) 61-0266551-733. Provides information on travel for persons with disabilities in Australia and the world's major cities. One-time fee of AUS$75. Access Guide to Sydney, $10 plus s/h.

Calvert Trust, Exmoor, Wistlandpound, Kentisbury, Barnstaple, Devon, EX31 4SJ, U.K. Offers holidays for people of all abilities. Both self-catering and catered accommodations. Outdoor activities and indoor pool.

IAMAT, 417 Center St., Lewistown, NY 14092; (716) 754-4883 or (519) 836-0102; iamat@sentex.net, www.sentex.net/~iamat. Lists English-speaking doctors in foreign countries who agree to their standards and fee structure.

Mobility International USA (MIUSA). Available from MIUSA, P.O. Box 10767, Eugene, OR 97440; (541) 343-1284, fax (541) 343-6812; miusa@igc, www.miusa.org. A national, nonprofit organization dedicated to expanding equal opportunities for people with disabilities in international exchange, leadership development, disability rights training, and community service.

Moss Rehab Hospital Referral Service, 1200 W. Tabor Rd., Philadelphia, PA 19144; (215) 456-9600 or 9603. A telephone referral center for international travel accessibility.

National Patient Air Transport Helpline, www.npath.org; (757) 318-9145 or (800) 296-1217. Provides information and referrals for specialized evaluation, diagnosis, treatment, rehabilitation, and/or recovery necessitated by illness or accident. Call or visit their web site for referral information on the availability of charitable long-distance air medical transport.

Society for the Advancement of Travel for the Handicapped, 347 5th Ave., Suite 610, New York, NY 10016; (212) 447-7284; www.sath.org. Publishes newsletter and information booklets on trip planning for persons with disabilities.

Travelin' Talk Network, P.O. Box 3534, Clarksville, TN 37043; (931) 552-6670, fax (931) 552-1182. Membership registration fee is on a sliding scale: $1 for SSI recipients to $50 for businesses. Members (located all over the world) provide specific information and services to disabled travelers.

Disability Publications

Able to Travel: A Rough Guides Special edited by Alison Walsh with Jodi Abbott and Peg L. Smith (Rough Guides). $19.95. Over 100 accounts by and for travelers; includes practical information and resource listings.

Access First News, Access First Travel, 45A Pleasant St., Malden, MA 02148; (800) 557-2047, (781) 322-1610, fax (781) 397-8610.

Newsletter contains destination descriptions, calendar of events, other accessibility information.

Access to the Skies, Paralyzed Veterans Assn., 801 18th St., NW, Washington, DC 20006; (202) 872-1300 ext. 790. Quarterly newsletter provides information on accessible airline travel

Access to the World: A Travel Guide for the Handicapped by Louise Weiss (Books on Demand). $68.20.

Access Travel: Airports. A resource directory of accessibility at 500 major airports. Available free from: Consumer Information Center, Access Travel: Airports, Pueblo, CO 81009.

Accessible Holidays in the British Isles 1997: A Guide for Disabled People by Royal Association for Disability and Rehabilitation (RADAR), 12 City Forum, 250 City Rd., London EC1V 8AF, U.K.; (011) 44-71-250-3222. Over 1,000 places to stay in all parts of the U.K. and Republic of Ireland. £13 postpaid.

Building Bridges edited by Julie Ann Cheshire (Mobility International USA, 3rd ed., 1998). More than 200 pages of suggestions and creative ideas for including, recruiting, and accommodating people with disabilities in international programs. Includes information on volunteer service programs and legal issues for international advisers. Call for pricing information.

The Diabetic Traveler, P.O. Box 8223, Stamford, CT 06905; (203) 327-5832. $18.95 per year. A newsletter with articles and information of particular interest to travelers with diabetes.

Directory of Travel Agencies for the Disabled by Helen Hecker (Twin Peaks Press). $19.95 plus $4 s/h from Twin Peaks Press,

P.O. Box 129, Vancouver, WA 98666-0129; (800) 637-2256 (credit card orders), (360) 694-2462, fax (360) 696-3210; 73743-2634@compuserve.com. Lists more than 370 travel agencies and tour operators in U.S. and worldwide.

Equal Opportunities in the U.S. and Newly Independent States (Mobility International USA). $30 for members, $40 for nonmembers from MIUSA (above). A guide for international exchange organizations on how to effectively recruit, select, and accommodate students with disabilities. Contains more than 50 pages of disability organizations and media contacts in the U.S. and NIS. Also from MIUSA: **You Can Study in the New Independent States (NIS): A Resource Guide for Students with Disabilities.** $20 for members, $30 for nonmembers. Focuses on practical issues for persons with disabilities choosing a site within the NIS; includes detailed accessibility information and survival tips and a resource chapter listing disability organizations in the countries of the NIS.

Guide for the Disabled Traveller by The Automobile Association, Norfolk House, Priestly Road, Basingstoke, Hampshire, RG24 9NY, U.K. Lists places to visit selected from AA publication, **Days Out in Britain and Ireland**. Includes information on accessibility and accommodations at sites of interest, restaurants, and lodgings. £3.99.

Home is in the Heart. Accommodating People with Disabilities in the Homestay Experience. Video provides information and ideas for exchange organizations. Discusses how to recruit homestay families, meet accessibility needs, and accommodate international participants with disabilities. Available in English, open captioned. Order from MIUSA (above).

Hostelling International Directories indicate with a symbol those hostels that are accessible. Available from Hostelling International, P.O. Box 37613, Washington, DC 20013-7613;

(800) 444-6111, fax (202) 783-6171. International guides are $13.95 and North American Guides are free to members, nonmembers $5.

Loud, Proud & Passionate: Including Women with Disabilities in International Development Programs by MIUSA. Contact MIUSA (above) for ordering information, $18 (members), $25 (nonmembers), international orders add $10 s/h. Includes guidelines to ensure inclusion of women with disabilities in the development process, as well as personal experience stories and resources. Alternate formats available upon request.

Mobility International Tourists Guides for European Union Countries offer information for travelers with disabilities. Available from Mobility International, 18, Boulevard Baudoiun, B-1000 Brusscls, Belgium; (011) 32-2-201-5608, fax (011) 32-2-201-5763.

Over the Rainbow. Quarterly newsletter for MIUSA members highlights international opportunities for people with disabilities. Includes resource and scholarship listings as well as updates on the global disability movement. Available in alternate formats. Membership plus newsletter $35 per year,

Ports of Call, 522 E. Broadway, Princeton, IN 47670. Quarterly newsletter covering topics of interest to the disabled traveler, including items on reserving an accessible hotel room, reviews of books and legislation, etc. Subscription: $5 donation suggested.

TDI National Directory and Guide. Annual directory of TTY accessible residences, businesses, government agencies, and interest groups in all 50 states plus special listings of nationwide toll-free numbers and relay services. Resource guide. $25 for 1 year, $45 for 2 years from Telecommunications for the Deaf, Inc., 8630 Fenton St., Suite 604, Silver Springs, MD 20910-3803; (301) 589-3786, TTY (301) 589-3006, fax (301) 589-3797; tdiexdir@aol.com.

Transitions Abroad, Available from Transitions Abroad Publishing, Dept. TRA, Box 3000, Denville, NJ 07834, (800) 293-0373; info@transabroad.com, www.transabroad.com. $24.95/6 issues. Published 6 times a year, this is the only U.S. periodical which gives extensive coverage to all varieties of educational travel abroad. Includes guide to Disability Travel Resources each July.

Travel for the Disabled by Helen Hecker (Twin Peaks Press, address above). $19.95 plus $4 s/h. How and where to find information, travel tips, and access guides for travelers with disabilities.

Travel Resources for the Deaf and Hard of Hearing People. This booklet identifies and lists resources that can help hearing impaired people with travel plans. Available from Loraine DiPietro, Gallaudet Univ., 800 Florida Ave., NE, Washington, DC 20002.

Travel Tips for Hearing Impaired People by American Academy of Otolaryngology; (703) 519-1528.

Vacances Pour Personnes Handicapees by Centre d'Information et de Documentation Jeunesse, CIDJ, 101, quai Branly, 75740 Paris, Cedex 15, France. Forty-one pages of addresses for holidays in France, including information on cultural activities, tourism, and sports. To order send 6 International Reply Coupons.

Wheelchair Through Europe. Graphic Language Press, P.O. Box 270, Cardiff by the Sea, CA 92007; (760) 944-9594. $13. Resources on accessible sites in Europe.

The Wheelchair Traveler, 123 Ball Hill Rd., Milford, NH 03055; (603) 673-4539. Information on hotels, motels, restaurants, and sightseeing for wheelchair users.

A World of Options edited by Christa Bucks (Mobility International USA, 3rd ed., 1997,

658 pp). $30 (members), $35 (individual), $40 (organization member), $45 (organization). International orders add $10 for s/h from MIUSA (above). A comprehensive guide to international exchange, study, and volunteer opportunities for people with disabilities with more than 1,000 resources on exchanges, rights, travel, and financial aid. Includes personal experience stories. Alternate formats available upon request.

Disability Tour Groups

Access/Abilities P.O.Box 458, Mill Valley, CA 94942; (415) 388-3250, fax (415) 383-8718; elieber@accessabil.com, www.accessabil.com. Offers information on travel destinations, including programs, services, accommodations, and transportation.

Accessible Journeys, Howard J. McCoy, 35 W. Sellers Ave., Ridley Park, PA 19078; (800) 846-4537, fax (610) 521-6959; sales@disabilitytravel.com, www.disabilitytravel. com. Slow walkers, wheelchair travelers, friends, and family.

Accessible Kiwi Tours New Zealand, Ltd. Adventure or leisure tours for all, including disabled or elderly. Group or individual tours New Zealand-wide. Accessible Kiwi Tours New Zealand, Ltd., P.O. Box 550, Opotiki, New Zealand; (011) 64-7-315-7867, fax (011) 64-7-315-5056; kiwitour@wave.co.nz.

Accessible Vans of Hawaii, David McKown, 186 Mehani Circle, Kihei, Maui, HI 96753; (800) 303-3750 or (808) 879-5521, fax (808) 879-0649; avavans@maui.net, www.accessiblevans.com. Assists travelers with disabilities in the local area with accessible accommodations, airport arrangements, and transportation.

Alaska Snail Trails, P.O. Box 210894, Anchorage, AK 99521. Ten-day, 5-day, and 1-day Alaskan tours; (800) 348-4532, (907) 337-7517, fax (907) 337-7517.

Disability Travel

Alaska Welcomes You, Paul Sandhofer, P.O. Box 91333, Anchorage, AK 99509; (800) 349-6301; awy@customcpu.com; www.alaska.com/vendors/welcome.html. Accessible Tours in Alaska also publishes quarterly newsletter, "Alaska Update," on accessibilities in Alaska.

Destination World, I Can Tours, Lynette Wilson, P.O. Box 1077, Santa Barbara, CA 93102; (800) 426-3644, fax (805) 569-3795.

Gateway Travel, Linda Abrams, 23A Middle Neck Rd., Great Neck, NY 11021; (516) 466-2242.

The Guided Tour, Inc., 7900 Old York Rd., Suite 114B, Elkins Park, PA 19027-2339; (800) 783-5841 or (215) 782-1370, fax (215) 635-2637. Programs for persons with developmental and physical challenges. Free brochure.

Handicapped Scuba Association International, 1104 El Prado, San Clemente, CA 92692; Tel./fax (714) 498-6128; http://ourworld.compuserve.com/homepages/hsahdq. Offers information on dive trips and where you can learn to dive.

Hidden Treasures Travel, 287 Spendrift Way, Vacaville, CA 95687; (888)-5-HIDDEN, fax (707) 446-5353; treasures@httravel.com, http://httravel.com. This organization specializes in assisting travelers with brain injuries, but serves people of all abilities.

Hospital Audiences, Inc., Tricia Hennesey, 220 W. 42nd St., 13th Floor, New York, NY 10036; (212) 575-7663 or HAI Hotline: (888) 424-4685.

Keli Tours, 19 Hacharoshet St., Keidar-Center, Raanana, Israel; (011) 972-9-740-9490, fax (011) 972-9-740-9408. Offers tours of the Middle East and Israel for people with and without disabilities.

Search Beyond Adventures. Specializes in tours for people with disabilities. Free catalog with 170 tours available. Call (800) 800-9979.

See The World Travel. Agent organizes travel for disabled. See the World Travel, 1903 Brandonview Ave., c/o Summit Travel, Richmond, VA 23231; world2c@bellatlantic.net.

Disability Travel Agencies

Able to Travel/Partnership Travel, Inc., 45A Pleasant, Malden, MA 02148; (800) 559-2047, fax (617) 986-4225).

Associated Travel Service, Ltd. P.O. Box 09027, Milwaukee, WI 53209; (800) 535-2045. Arranges individual and group travel for people with disabilities.

Bare Cove Travel, 16 North St., Hingham, MA 02043; (781) 749-7750, fax (781) 749-1022; apeter6203@aol.com. Arranges travel for people with disabilities.

Brentwood Travel, 300 Chestefield Ctr., Chesterfield, MO 63017; (800) 231-9409 or (314) 532-7477, fax (314) 532-1416. Plans individual and group trips for people with disabilities.

Directions Unlimited, 720 N. Bedford Rd., Bedford Hills, NY 10507; (800) 533-5343 or (914) 241-1700, fax (914) 241-0243; cruiseusa@aol.com. Specializes in arranging vacations and tours for persons with disabilities. Including cruises.

Enable Travel Services, New Frontiers, 7545 S. Univ. Blvd., Littleton, CO 80122. Plans trips for travelers with disabilities, as well as working with groups and individuals.

Flying Wheels Travel, 143 W. Bridge, P.O. Box 382, Owatonna, MN 55060; (800) 535-6790, fax (507) 451-1685; thq@ll.net. A tour operator and travel agency with an international client base.

Full Data Ltd., 808 Malabanas Rd., 2009 Angeles City, The Philippines; (011) 63-2-81-24277, fax (011) 63-2-81-50756. Provides publications and information on travel in Thailand, Taiwan, Macao, China, India, Nepal, Singapore, Vietnam, Laos, and Cambodia.

Hinsdale Travel Service, Janice Perkins, 201 E. Ogden Ave., Suite 100, Hinsdale, IL 60521; (708) 469-7349.

Holiday Care Service, Imperial Buildings, 2nd Floor, Victoria Rd., Horley, Surrey, RH6 7PZ, U.K.; (011) 44-1293-774-535, fax (011) 44-1293-784-647. The U.K.'s central source of holiday information for disabled and disadvantaged persons.

Over The Rainbow Accessible Travel, Inc. David McKown, 186 Mehani Circle, Kihei, HI 96753; (808) 879-5521.

Uniglobe All Points Travel, 175 Olde Half Day Rd., Licolnshire, IL 60069; (847) 913-9786. Offers custom itinerary planning and scuba instruction for people with disabilities.

Wheelchair Travel, Ltd., Trevor Pollitt, 1 Johnston Green, Guildford, Surrey, GU2 6XS, England; (011) 44-1483-233640, fax (011) 44-1483-23772. A self-drive rental, taxi, and tour service specifically for disabled people, especially the wheelchair-user.

Disability Web Sites

The Internet has an ever-growing wealth of resources for people with disabilities who are interested in travel. The following is a sampling of the best resources; for more web sites, try doing an Internet search using keywords such as disabilities, travel, accessibility, etc.

Access-Able Travel Source, (303) 232-2979 (Voice), fax (303) 239-8486; www.access-able.com. A free Internet information service for mature and disabled travelers: accessibility guide for countries, states and provences, and cities; also accommodations, transportation, attractions, adventures, doctors, and equipment rental and repair, specialty travel agents, and a comprehensive list of disability links and publications. Pages include discussion forums and *What's News,* an online newsletter.

Arthur Frommer's Outspoken Encyclopedia of Travel, www.frommers.com/specialpeople/dis. Offers a section on resources for travelers with disabilities.

Canterbury Community Internet Access Project, http://nz.com/webnz/ability/travelindex.html. New Zealand-based site that offers a variety of disability related information, including access information for travelers to New Zealand and Australia.

Channel 4 Travelog, www.channel 4.com/passions/travelog. A guide that includes specific information and advice for disabled travelers, and a new directory containing details of useful organizations, specialized web sites, etc.

Dtour: A Disabled Visitors Guide to Ireland, ireland://ireland.iol.ie/infograf/dtour. Lists facilities in Ireland for travelers who have movement or sensory disabilities.

EWABLEnet, www.dpa.org.sg. The Disabled People's Association of Singapore's web site includes attractions, hotels, and other resources.

Global Access, A Network for Disabled Travelers, www.geocities.com/Paris/1502. Network for disabled travelers to share experiences, with many international contributors. Participants post questions, travel tips, etc., in the Readers Write Section, and receive global input. Also featured are sections on travel books, trip tips, and links to other accessible travel sites.

New Horizons, www.faa.gov/acr/dat.htm. A wealth of information for the disabled air trav-

Disability Travel

eler. Sections include: Planning Your Trip, At the Airport, Getting On and Off the Plane, On the Plane, and Compliance Procedures.

New Mobility, www.newmobility.com. 23815 Stuart Ranch Road, P.O. Box 8987, Malibu, CA 90267; (800) 543-4116 or (310) 317-4522, fax (310) 317-9644. An extension of the print magazine, *New Mobility*. Includes many links to other sites, as well as some information on travel for persons with disabilities.

Tourism for All, http://andi.casaccia.enea.it/hometur.htm. Database information on accessible sites includes Italy, Sweden, Berlin, Germany, Spain, and soon more countries.

Disability Travel Programs

The following listing of programs for people with disabilities was supplied by the organizers in 1998 and is updated in each July/August issue of Transitions Abroad *magazine. Contact the program directors to confirm costs, dates, and other details. Please tell them you read about their programs in this book!*

Costa Rica

Enjoy Learning Spanish Faster. Techniques developed from our ongoing research enable students at Centro Linguistico Latinoamericano to learn more, faster, in a comfortable environment. Classes are 2-5 students plus group learning activities; conversations with middle-class homestay families (1 student per family). Homestays are within walking distance of school in a small town (14,000 population) near the capital, San Jose.

Dates: Year round. Classes begin every Monday, at all levels. Cost: $295 per week for 25 hours of classes. Includes tuition, all meals (7 days a week), homestay, laundry, all materials, Costa Rican dance and cooking classes, and airport transportation. $25 one-time registration. Contact: Susan Shores, Registrar, Latin

American Language Center, 7485 Rush River Dr., Suite 710-123, Sacramento, CA 95831; (916) 447-0938, fax (916) 428-9542; lalc@madre.com.

Mexico

Intensive Language Programs. Intensive Spanish immersion program in groups, 40 class hours per week including Spanish class, lectures, and Hispano-American courses. Executive, semester, and specialized programs for teachers, professionals, nurses, and adults continuing education. Live with Mexican family or in student residence. Excursions to historical and archaeological sites.

Dates: Year round starting every Monday. Cost: Tuition $190 per week; lodging $154 per week. Contact: The Center for Bilingual Multicultural Studies, Javier Espinosa, San Jeronimo #304, Cuernavaca, MOR-62179, Mexico; (011) 52-73-17-10-87, fax (011) 52-73-17-05-33; admin@bilingual-center.com, www.bilingual-center.com.

Worldwide

Services for Handicapped Travelers. Janice Perkins, a wheelchair traveler and professional travel agent, provides a liaison between disabled clients and travel suppliers.

Dates: Year round. Cost: Varies according to services provided. Contact: Janice Perkins, Hinsdale Travel Service, 201 E. Ogden Ave., Hinsdale, IL 60521; (630) 469-7349 or (630) 325-1335 or (630) 325-1342, fax (630) 469-7390.

For more listings of disability travel resources and programs, and for bargains worldwide, travel tips, and all sorts of information on learning, living, working, and traveling abroad, see *Transitions Abroad* magazine. To order a single copy or a subscription, please call 1-800-293-0373 or visit the *Transitions Abroad* web site at www.transabroad.com.

CHAPTER 7

RESPONSIBLE
TRAVEL
RESOURCES

Globalization is often an ugly process. Strip malls in Paris and Peking are as unappealing as those in Peoria. And however "responsible" we may be, as travelers we are all involved. We have so many places to go and so little time. We usually travel by air to reach our destinations. Jet exhaust at high altitudes is one of the greatest threats to the ozone layer protecting our planet. Feeling guilty about it won't help. Becoming active in environmental causes will.

When we travel, most of us love to buy authentic local handicrafts. But do we always ask who is benefitting? Are the goods produced by a local weaver's cooperative or on contract for a middleman who pays a pittance to the artisans? Cooperatives usually produce higher quality goods but charge more. Are we willing to pay the difference?

Experiencing the richness of tropical ecosystems is one of the purest "highs" of traveling. Yet are the tourists and the tour operators giving anything back to preserve the natural beauty that we are traveling to enjoy?

Asking informed questions and then voting with our consumer dollars is one way to be a responsible traveler. Coming back to write and speak about your experiences is another. Supporting your regional ecotour operators and getting involved with environmental tourism groups are still other ways to fulfill our responsibilities.

The following selection of resources is designed to help you in these efforts but it is certainly not exhaustive. Contact *Transitions Abroad* or Deborah McLaren at Rtproject@aol.com to expand it or to comment on the entries.

Responsible travel is more than just a label; it describes a relationship. And, like all healthy relationships, it can't be based on guilt but on equal exchange. So always ask yourself: What am I getting and what am I giving? And then enjoy your trip.

— *By Deborah McLaren & Rob Ramer*

Ecotourism Organizations

Aboriginal Tourism Authority, Inc., P.O. Box 1240, Station "M," Calgary, AB T2P 2L2, Canada; (403) 261-3022, fax (403) 261-5676; tourism@istar.ca, www.aboriginalnet.

com/ata.html. Western Canada's most up-to-date databank, meeting the needs of tour operators and the growing aboriginal tourism market.

Alaska Wilderness Recreation and Tourism Assn. (AWRTA), P.O. Box 22827, Juneau, AK 99802; (907) 463-3038, fax (907) 463-3280; awrta@alaska.net, www.alaska.net/~awrta. Membership organization of small, locally-owned ecotour operators and native-owned ecotourism programs. Promotes the protection of Alaska's wild places.

Alternative Tour Thailand, 14/1 Soi Rajatapan, Rajaprarop Rd., Tayathai, Bangkok 10400, Thailand; (011) 66-2-245-2963. Supports environmental efforts of small communities throughout Thailand by organizing low-impact tours and homestays.

Annapurna Conservation Area Project (ACAP), ACAP Headquarters Ghandruk, Ghandruk Panchayat, Kaski District, Nepal. An international project that uses trekkers' fees to protect the environment and culture of the Gurung people in north central Nepal.

Baikal Reflections, Inc., P.O. Box 310, Mesa, CO 81643-0310; (970) 268-5885, fax (970) 268-5884; baikal@igc.apc.org. Offers programs to Siberia.

Belize Ecotourism Association, 195A Vista Del Mar, Ladyville 025-2806, Belize. Organization of ecotourism groups, provides information.

Bhutan Tourism Authority, Bhutan Tourism Corporation Ltd., P.O. Box 159, Thimphu, Bhutan; (011) 975-2-22854/24045/22647; www.kingdomofbhutan.com/travel.html. The Bhutanese government is implementing a new ecotourism management program in the Jigme Dorji National Park.

Bina Swadaya Tours, JI. Gunung Sahari III/7, Jakarta 10610, P.O. Box 1456, Jakarta, 10014, Indonesia; (011) 62-21-420-44-02, fax (011) 62-21-425-65-40; bst@cbn.net.id. Travelers visit communities and learn about Indonesia's rural and ethnic cultures, lifestyles, and community development efforts, and explore wildlife at national parks and primary forests. The programs are combined with sightseeing trips.

Conservation International, Ecotourism Dept., 2501 M St., NW, Suite 200, Washington, DC 20037; (202) 429-5660, fax (202) 887-0193; www.ecotour.htm. Works with grassroots groups, communities, and environmental NGOs around the world in developing ecotourism programs, such as Eco-escuela in Guatemala.

Eco-Source, P.O. Box 4694, Annapolis, MD 21403-6694; (410) 263-2128, fax (410) 268-0923; hmehta3@aol.com, www.podi.com/ecosource. Connects environmentally responsible individuals and groups worldwide.

Eco-Travel Services, 1212 Broadway, Suite 910, Oakland, CA 94612; (510) 655-4054; ecotravel@wonderlink.com. Nationwide individual and corporate travel arrangements; supports local economies and environmentally conscious operations instead of quick profits; publishes newsletter.

Ecotourism Association of Australia, P.O. Box 3839, Alice Springs, Northern Territory 0871, Australia; (011) 61-89-528-308.

Ecotourism Society, P.O. Box 755, North Bennington, VT 05257; (802) 447-2121, fax (802) 447-2122; ecomail@ecotourism.org, www.ecotourism.org. A membership organization of ecotour operations around the world.

Ecoventure, Ronald Ziegler, Washington State Univ. Libraries, Pullman, WA 99164-5610; fax (509) 335-6721; ziegler@wsu.edu. Ecoventure is helping develop a database, BaseCamp, to provide travelers with information on ecotourism.

European Center for Eco Agro Tourism, P.O. Box 10899, Amsterdam 1001 EW, The Netherlands. Promotes eco-agro tourism, a sustainable tour option for people with green thumbs.

Euroter, 82, rue Francois Rolland, F 94130 Nogent-sur-Marne, France; (011) 331-4514-6421. Publishes principles for developing green tourism in European villages.

Friends of Malae Kahana, P.O. Box 305, Laie, HI 96762; (808) 293-1736. Native Hawaiian civic group operates ecotourism and low-impact tourism along historic beach.

Hawaii Ecotourism Association, P.O. Box 61435, Honolulu, HI 96839; (808) 956-2866, fax (808) 956-2858; tabata@hawaii.edu, www.planet-hawaii.com.hea. Promotes responsible tourism, resource network for Hawaii and the Pacific.

Himalayan High Treks, 241 Dolores St., San Francisco, CA 94103-2211; (800) 455-8735; effie@himalayanhightreks.com, www.himalayanhightreks.com. A small trekking company that specializes in trips to Bhutan, India, Nepal, and Tibet; offers specialized programs for women; publishes newsletter.

Indonesian Ecotourism Network (INDECON), Jalan H. Samali No. 51, Pejaten Barat, Pasar Minggu, Jakarta 12510, Indonesia; (011) 62-21-799-3955; indecon@cbn.net.id. Helps link ecotourists with a wide range of opportunities throughout Indonesia.

International Sonoran Desert Alliance, Box 687, Ajo, AZ 85321-0687; (520) 387-6823; alianzason@aol.com. Involved with ecotourism in Mexico.

Journeys International, 4011 Jackson Rd., Ann Arbor, MI 48103; (313) 665-4407 or (800) 255-8735; www.journeys-intl.com. A well-established ecotour operator; guides are either natives or residents of the countries they visit;

part of their profits support environmental preservation. Destinations include Himalayas, Africa, Australia, the Galapagos, Panama, Belize, and Costa Rica.

Kodukant Ecotourism Initiative, SAARISOO, EE 3482 Joesuu, Parnumaa, Estonia; (011) 372-446-6405. A network of small tour operators living in or nearby protected areas.

Lisle, Inc., 900 CR 269, Leander, TX 78641-9517; (800) 477-1538, fax (512) 259-4404; lisle@utnet.utoledo.edu, www.lisle.utoledo.edu. Pioneer people-to-people program. Destinations include India and Costa Rica (led by *Transitions Abroad* contributing editor Dianne Brause).

Oceanic Society Expeditions, Fort Mason Center, Building E, San Francisco, CA 94123; (415) 441-1106, fax (415) 474-3385; www.oceanic-society.org. Promotes environmental stewardship, education, and research through ecotourism.

Pax World Tours, 1111 16th St., NW, Suite 120, Washington, DC 20036; (202) 293-7290; info@paxworld.org. Works for peace and justice through innovative programs that encourage peacemaking and community-based development. Promotes people-to-people links and responsible tourism.

Samoan Ecotourism Network (SEN), P.O. Box 4606, Matautu-utu, Western Samoa; (011) 685-26-940, fax (011) 685-25-993; ecotour@pactok.peg.apc.org. Concerned about deforestation of primary rainforests, offers ecotours as a form of education and vacation.

Sikkim Biodiversity and Ecotourism, Opp. Krishi Bhawan, c/o G.P. Pant Institute of Himalayan Environment and Development, Sikkim, India; (011) 91-3592-31046, fax (011) 91-3592-31090; sce@gokulnet.com. Developing and implementing regional ecotourism program with local communities in the Sikkim Himalayas.

South American Explorer's Club (SAEC), 126 Indian Creek Rd., Ithaca, NY 14850; (607) 277-0488; explorer@samexplo.org, www.samexplo.org. Promotes ecologically responsible tourism. Has clubhouses in Quito, Ecuador and Lima, Peru. Publishes quarterly magazine and sells books and maps.

Toledo Ecotourism Association (TEA), San Miguel Village, Toledo District, Belize. Contact Pabzo Ack, BTB Information Center, Punta Gorda, P.O. Box 180, Belize; (011) 501-72-2531, fax (011) 501-72-2199; tide@btl.net. Network of indigenous farm cooperatives in pristine Mayan lands.

Top Guides, Treks & Tours, 1825 San Lorenzo Ave., Berkeley, CA 94707-1840; (800) 867-6777 or (510) 527-9884, fax (510) 527-9885; top4advcn@aol.com, http://members.aol.com/top4adven/topguides.

Tour de Cana, P.O. Box 7293, Philadephia, PA 19101; (215) 222-1253, fax (215) 222-1253, ext. 21; tourdecana@igc.apc.org. An outgrowth of the organization Bikes Not Bombs, this group offers bike trekking with a social, cultural, and political emphasis.

Travel Quest, 3250 Barham Blvd., Los Angeles, CA 90068; (213) 876-3250; 74732.3153@compuserve.com. Promotes greater care and understanding of the planet, people, and other beings.

The Travel Specialists, 120 Beacon St., Somerville, MA 02143-4369; (617) 497-8151 or (800) 370-7400, ext. 51; mj@tvlcoll.com. Evaluates travel programs, operators, and the travel industry; arranges alternative trips and programs around the world.

Turismo Ecologico y Cultural del Pueblo Maya, San Cristobal de las Casas, Chiapas, Mexico. An indigenous-owned alternative ecotour group.

Wilderness Travel, 1102 9th St., Berkeley, CA 94710; (510) 558-2488; info@wildernesstravel.com. Promotes cultural preservation and environmental protection; supports conservation, cultural, and development organizations.

Wildland Adventures, Inc., 3516 NE 155th St., Seattle, WA 98155; (800) 345-4453, (206) 365-0686; info@wildland.com, www.wildland.com. Ecotour operator offers group travel, customized trips for independent travelers and families, rainforest workshops, and responsible trips such as trail cleanups and community services. Contributes part of profits to conservation and community development at the local level.

Wildlife Conservation International, P.O. Box 68244, Nairobi, Kenya; (011) 222254-221-699. Information about ecotourism projects in Kenya.

World Wildlife Fund, 1250 24th St., NW, Washington, DC 20037-1175; (202) 293-4800; www.worldwildlife.org. Offers ecotours throughout the world.

Yukon River Tours, 214 2nd Ave., Fairbanks, AK 99701-4811; (907) 452-7162. Alaska native-owned ecotours of the Yukon River educate about local history, environment, wildlife, culture, Athabascan fishcamps.

Responsible Travel Organizations

Airline Ambassadors, 4636 Fairfax Ave., Dallas, TX 75209; (214) 528-9464. Or contact Nancy Larson Rivard at (650) 685-6262, fax (650) 685-6263; airlineamb@aol.com. Group is involved in sustainable tourism discussions at the U.N., and bringing medical supplies abroad.

Asia Tourism Action Network (ANTENNA), 15 Soi Soonvijai 8, New Petchburi

Rd., Bangkok 10310, Thailand. A network in Asia and the Pacific promoting locally controlled tourism; publishes a newsletter.

Badri Dev Pande, Environmental Education and Awareness, P.O. Box 3923, Kathmandu, Nepal. Developing a sustainable tourism master plan of Manaslu region of Nepal.

Broken Bud, 1765-D Le Roy, Berkeley, CA 94709; (510) 843-5506. Formed out of the Center for Responsible Tourism, advocates against prostitution tourism and child trafficking.

Burma Tourism Campaign, The Free Burma Coalition, c/o Dept. of Curriculum and Instruction, Univ. of Wisconsin, 225 N. Mills St., Madison, WI 53706; (608) 827-7734, fax (608) 263-9992; zni@students.wisc.edu, http://danenet.wicip.org/fbc/sites.htm. Before traveling to Burma check out the information from these folks.

Center for Global Education, Augsburg College, 2211 Riverside Ave., Minneapolis, MN 55454; (800) 299-8889; globaled@augsburg.edu, www.augsburg.edu/global. Sponsors travel seminars and semester programs. Participants learn from people of diverse backgrounds about their economic, political, and social realities. Emphasis on those struggling for justice. Programming in Mexico, Central America, and Southern Africa.

Center for Responsible Tourism, P.O. Box 827, San Anselmo, CA 94979; (415) 258 6594. Publishes a monthly newsletter highlighting innovative tourism projects around the world. One of the only responsible travel centers in the U.S., CRT has helped hundreds of travelers, educators, people in other counties. Subscribe—they need your support!

Center for the Advancement of Responsible Travel (CART), 70 Dry Hill Park Rd., Tonbridge, Kent TN10 3BX, U.K. Center of information on responsible tourism in Europe.

Center for Third World Organizing, 1218 East 21st St., Oakland, CA 94606; (510) 533-7583, fax (510) 533-0923; ctwo@igc.org. An excellent resource for information about progressive politics, actions, and organizations in the U.S. and abroad.

COOPRENA (National Eco-Agricultural Cooperative Network of Costa Rica), Apdo. 6939-1000 San Jose, Costa Rica; (011) 506-259-3605/259-3401; cooprena@sol.racsa.co.cr. Consortium of cooperatives developing eco-agro tourism and small farms.

Cousteau Society, Project Ocean Search, 870 Greenbriar Cir., #402, Chesapeake, VA 23320; (757) 523-9335. Good marine guidelines and information about threats to the world's oceans.

Earth Island Institute, 300 Broadway, Suite 28, San Francisco, CA 94133-3312; (415) 788-3666. Publishes "How Green Is Your Tour: Questions to Ask Your Tour Operator." Their sea turtle program offers tours to Mexico where participants learn about and help monitor endangered turtle species.

Earthstewards Network, P.O. Box 10697, Bainbridge Island, WA 98110; (206) 842-7986, fax (206) 842-8918. For Peacetrees projects contact Jerilyn Brusseau or Martha Hathaway at: vizage@aol.com; for Middle East Citizen Diplomacy Projects contact Leah at: (415) 389-6750, fax (415) 389-0324; lgreeninc@aol.com.

Earthwatch, 680 Mt. Auburn St., Watertown, MA 02272; (617) 926-8200, www.earthwatch.org. Offers working vacations with scientists around the world.

Ecumenical Coalition on Third World Tourism (ECTWT), c/o CPDC, P.O. Box

284, Bridgetown, Barbados; contours@ caribnet.net; or ECTWT European office: 19 Chemin des Palettes, CH-1212 Grand Lancy, Switzerland; (011) 41-22-794-49-59, fax (011) 41-22-794-47-50; contours@geneva-link.ch. Only international Third World NGO focusing on impact of tourism, publishes a quarterly magazine called *Contours*.

Elderhostel, 75 Federal St., Boston, MA 02110-1941; (617) 426-8056. For travelers over 50. Environmentally friendly educational travel programs around the world for seniors.

EQUATIONS: Equitable Tourism Options, No. 198, II Cross, Church Rd. (behind old KEB office), New Thippasandra, Bangalore 560 075, India; (011) 9180-528-2313; admin@equation.ilban.ernet.in. Responsible tourism advocate; helps travelers locate environmentally and culturally sensitive projects in India.

Europe Conservation, Via Fusetti, 14-20143 Milano, Italy; (011) 39-2-5810-3135.

Friends of PRONATURA, 240 East Limberlost Dr., Tucson, AZ 85705; (520) 887-1188; closfree@aol.com. Network of ecological groups working in Mexico.

Global Citizens Network, 1931 Iglehart Ave., St. Paul, MN 55104; (612) 644-0960 or (800) 644-9292 (Kim Regnier or Carol North); gcn@mtn.org, www.globalcitizens. org/Color_Home.html. Sends small teams of volunteers on short "alternative vacations" to rural communities worldwide to work on projects and immerse themselves in the daily life of the local culture.

Global Exchange, 2017 Mission St., Suite 303, San Francisco, CA 94110; (415) 255-7296; gx-info@globalexchange.org. Reality tours focus on social, cultural, environmen-tal issues in South Africa, Haiti, Cuba, Mexico, and elsewhere.

Global Family, 210 W. 70th St., #1507, New York, NY 10023. Contact: Margo LaZaro at (212) 877-0992, fax (800) 395-5600 or Patrick MacNamara at patrickUN@aol.com.

Global Service Corps, 300 Broadway, Suite 28, San Francisco, CA 94133; (415) 788-3666 ext. 128, fax (415) 788-7324; gsc@ igc.apc.org, www.earthisland.org/ei/gsc/ gschome.html. Cooperates with grassroots groups in Costa Rica, Kenya, and Thailand to send paid volunteers for 2- to 4-week programs.

Golondrinas Cloudforest Conservation Project, Calle Isabel La Catolica 1559, Quito, Ecuador; (011) 593-2-226-602, fax (011) 593-2-222-390. A conservation organization conserving 25,000 hectares of cloudforests on the northwest slopes of the Andes. They have volunteer and educational programs, including a 4-day trek through the Cerro Golondrinas area.

Indonesia Resources and Information Program (IRIP), P.O. Box 190, Northcote 3070, Australia; (011) 61-3-481-1581. Fosters active links with Indonesians working for change.

Institute for Central American Development Studies (ICADS), Dept. 826, P.O. Box 025216, Miami, FL 33102-5216, or ICADS, Apartado 3-2070, Sabanilla, San Jose, Costa Rica; (011) 506-225-0508, fax (011) 506-234-1337; icads@netbox. com. Field course in resource management and sustainable development and interdisciplinary semester internship programs focusing on development issues from ecological and socio-economic perspectives.

International Bicycle Fund, 4887 Columbia Dr. S, #T-7, Seattle, WA 98108; (206)

767-0848; intlbike@scn.org. Promotes bicycle transport; links with autofree and bicycling organizations around the world; publishes essays on environmentally and culturally friendly traveling; sponsors bicycle tours throughout Africa.

International Institute for Peace Through Tourism, 3680 rue de La Montange, Montreal, PQ, H3G 2AB Canada; (802) 253-8671. Facilitates tourism initiatives that contribute to international peace and cooperation.

ISEC/Ladakh (India) Project, P.O. Box 9475, Berkeley, CA 94709; (510) 527-3873. An educational program that supports innovative grassroots development efforts of the Ladakhi people who live on the western edge of the Tibetan Plateau in India. Good resource materials on counterdevelopment, books, videos. Runs a farm project in Ladakh, providing westerners with an opportunity to work on a Ladakhi farm in the summer months.

Lost Valley Educational Center, 81868 Lost Valley Ln., Dexter, OR 97431; (541) 937-3351; diannebr@aol.com, www.efn.org/~lvec. Dianne G. Brause is a well-known writer and leader in the field of responsible and sustainable travel. She offers opportunities in Central America for participants to live, learn, and work with local people. (See One World Family Travel below.)

Office of Study Abroad, The Univ. of Kansas, 108 Lippincott Hall, Lawrence, KS 66045; (913) 864-3742. Offers a semester at the port town of Golfito on the southern Pacific coast of Costa Rica in anthropology, ecology, biology, and Spanish.

Okologischer Tourismus in Europa (OTE), Bernd Rath, Am Michaelshof 8-10, 53177 Bonn, Germany. Responsible tourism organization; resources in German.

One World Family Travel, 81868 Lost Valley Ln., Dexter, OR 96431; (503) 937-3351; diannebr@aol.com. *Transitions Abroad* contributing editor Dianne Brause publishes a directory of alternative travel resources.

Our Developing World, 13004 Paseo Presada, Saratoga, CA 95070-4125; (408) 379-4431; fax 408-376-0755; vic_@vval. com. Educational project bringing Third World realities to North Americans. Community programs, teacher training materials, resources library. Study tour to South Africa Aug 1-22, 1999.

Partners in Responsible Tourism, P.O. Box 419085-322, San Francisco, CA 94141; (415) 273-1430; bapirt@aol.com, www.pirt.org. Members promote cultural and environmental ethics and practices.

Responsible Tourism Network, RTN Coordinator, P.O. Box 34, Rundle Mall, Adelaide, SA, Australia 5000; (011) 618-232-2727, fax (011) 618-232-2808; bwitty@ozemail. com.au. Responsible tourism by Australians. Works with tourists, travel industry and host communities. Publishes Travel Wise and Travel Smart, practical tips for responsible tourists.

Rethinking Tourism Project, 3831 Upton Ave. N, Minneapolis, MN 55412; (612) 521-0098, Rtproject@aol.com. An educational and networking project for indigenous people. Offers some volunteer opportunities and internships.

School for Field Studies, 16 Broadway, Beverly, MA 01915-4499; (508) 927-7777. Field studies and hands-on opportunities for high school and college students concerned about the environment.

Sierra Club, 85 2nd St., 2nd Fl., San Francisco, CA 94105; (415) 977-5500. Publishes good travel guides, offers conservation focused tours.

Talamanca Association for Ecotourism and Conservation, Puerto Viejo de Talamanca, Limon, Costa Rica. Local environmental organization that offers ecotourism programs.

Tourism Concern, Stapleton House, 277-281 Holloway Rd., London N7 8HN, U.K.; (011) 44-171-753-3330, fax (011) 44-171-753-3331; www.gn.apc.org/tourismconcern, tourconcern@gn.apc.org. Excellent resource on issues related to tourism: land rights, displacement, general responsible tourism information.

Tourism With Insight (Arbeitsgemein-schaft Tourismus mit Einsicht), Hadorter Str. 9B, D-8130 Starnberg, Germany. Responsible tourism study group.

Transitions Abroad, P.O. Box 1300, Amherst, MA 01004-1300; (800) 293-0373, fax (413) 256-0373; trabroad@aol.com, www.transabroad.com. Publications with programs, resources, and first-hand reports on responsible travel throughout the world. Free catalog.

The Travel Specialists, Co-Op America Travel Links, M.J. Kietzke, 120 Beacon St., Somerville, MA 02143; (617) 497-8151; mj@tvlcoll.com. Specializes in responsible travel for individuals and groups, custom designed to suit your special interests.

Tropical Science Center, Apdo. 8-3870, San Jose 1000, Costa Rica; (011) 506-22-6241. Offers open-air classrooms and labs for tropical science students and professionals.

University Research Expeditions Program, Univ. of California, Berkeley, CA 94720-7050; (510) 642-6586. Volunteer programs for travelers of all ages. Director Jean Colvin has developed codes of conduct for researchers working with indigenous peoples and codes for travelers going to the same areas.

Washington Semester Program—International Environment and Development offers 12 weeks in Washington, DC and 3 weeks in Costa Rica studying tourism and development. Contact WSWCP, Tenley Campus, American Univ., Washington, DC 20016-8083; (202) 895-4900; washsem@american.edu.

Publications

Adventures in Nature (Honduras, Mexico, Guatemala, Belize, Costa Rica, Alaska). John Muir Publications, P.O. Box 613, Santa Fe, NM 87504-9738. (Also available from www.greenbuilder.com/bookstore.) Update to the "Natural Destination" series, focusing on environmental travel. The series offers travel info as well as insights on local environmental policy and actors.

Adventuring In... The Sierra Club, 85 2nd St., San Francisco, CA 94105; (415) 977-5500. Adventure travel guide series for many countries. Includes **Adventuring in Central America** by David Rains Wallace. $16. A must-have resource.

All Asia Guide. 1994. $23.95. Charles E. Tuttle Co., 153 Milk St., 5th Fl., Boston, MA 02109. A practical Asia guide.

Asia Through the Backdoor by Rick Steves and Bob Effertz. John Muir Publications (see above). 1995. $17.95. Asia on the cheap and off the beaten path.

Backpacking in Central America. Bradt/Globe Pequot Press, 6 Business Park Rd., P.O. Box 833, Old Saybrook, CT 06475; (203) 395-0440, fax (203) 395-0312. An excellent guide by an experienced Central American hiker.

Beyond Safaris: A Guide to Building People-to-People Ties With Africa by Kevin Danaher. Africa World Press. Global Exchange, 2017 Mission St., Suite 303, San Francisco, CA; (415) 255-7296. 1991. $39.95. A bit old but still one of the best resources for socially conscious travelers in Africa. Lists organizations.

Directory of Environmental Travel Resources. Available for $10 from Dianne Brause, One World Family Travel Network, 81868 Lost Valley Lane, Dexter, OR 97431; (503) 937-3351; diannebr@aol.com.

E Magazine. The Earth Action Network, P.O. Box 5098, Westport, CT 06881; (203) 854-5559. Bimonthly magazine with a focus on the environment.

Earthtrips by Dwight Holing. Living Planet Press, 2940 Newark St., NW, Washington, DC 20008; (202) 686-6262, fax (202) 966-8703. 1991. $12.95.

Eco-Vacations: Enjoy Yourself and Save the Earth by Evelyn Kaye. Blue Panda Publications, 3031 5th St., Boulder, CO 80304; (303) 449-8474, fax (303) 449-7525. 1991. $22.50.

The Ecotraveller's Wildlife Guides by Les Beletsky. Academic Press, 525 B St., Suite 1900, San Diego, CA 92101-4495; (800) 321-5068. Titles include Costa Rica (1998), Belize and Northern Guatemala (1998), Tropical Mexico (1999), Hawaii (1999), Ecuador and the Galapagos Islands (1999). $27.95 each. Each book provides information on natural history, ecology, conservation, and species identification.

Ecotourism and Sustainable Development by Martha Honey. Island Press, 1718 Connecticut Ave., NW, Suite 300, Washington, DC 20009; (202) 232-7933, fax (202) 234-1328. Orders: (800) 828-1302; info@ islandpress. org, www.islandpress.org. $25. Explores the promise and pitfalls of ecotourism.

Ecotourist Guide to the Ecuadorian Amazon by Rolfe Wesche. The Pan-American Center for Geographical Studies and Research, 3er piso, Apdo. 17-01-4273, Quito, Ecuador; (011) 593-245-1200.

Green Travel Sourcebook by Daniel Grotta and Sally Wiener Grotta. John Wiley & Sons, 1 Wiley Dr., Somerset, NJ 08775; (800) 225-5945, fax (732) 302-2300. 1992. $16.95.

Green-Travel Mailing List. For green travel resources on the Internet. To subscribe contact majordomo@igc.apc.org.

Holidays That Don't Cost the Earth by John Elkington and Julia Hailes. Victor Gollancz Ltd., 14 Henrietta St., London, WC2E 8QJ, U.K. 1992. £5.99. A worldwide guide to environmental vacations.

Indigenous Peoples and Global Tourism. Project Report by Deborah McLaren. $6 postpaid. The Rethinking Tourism Project, 3831 Upton Ave. N, Minneapolis, MN 55412; (612) 521-0098.

Last Resorts by Polly Pattullo. Monthly Review Press. $19. (from Amazon.com). Excellent review of the tourism industry in the Caribbean.

Lonely Planet Guides. Lonely Planet Publications, 150 Linden St., Oakland, CA 94607; (800) 275-8555, fax (510) 893-8563; info@lonelyplanet.com. Books on almost every country, emphasizing low-impact travel.

Moon Travel Handbooks. Moon Publications, P.O. Box 3040, Chico, CA 95927; (800) 345-5473, fax (530) 345-6751; travel@ moon.com, www.moon.com. Guides provide thorough cultural, historical, and political coverage, as well as exhaustive practical information.

La Mosquitia: A Guide to the Land of Savannas, Rain Forests and Turtle Hungers by Derek A. Parent. Intrepid Traveler, P.O. Box 438, New York, NY 10034. 1995. $24. The first guidebook to the green jewel of Honduras.

Natour: Special edition on ecotourism. Contact editor Arturo Crosby, Viriato, 20, Madrid, Spain; (011) 91-593-0831.

Nature Tourism: Managing for the Environment edited by Tensie Whelan. Island Press, 1991. $19.95. Orders: (800) 828-1302. Guidelines and essays on nature tourism.

New Frontiers. Anita Pleumarom, Coordinator, Tourism Investigation and Monitoring Team, P.O. Box 51, Chorakhebua, Bangkok 10230, Thailand; fax (011) 66-2-519-2821. A bimonthly newsletter for briefing on tourism, development, and environment issues in the southeast Asian Mekong region.

The New Key to Costa Rica by Beatrice Blake and Anne Becher. Ulysses Press, P.O. Box 3440, Berkeley, CA 94703-3440; (800) 377-2542, fax (510) 601-8307. 1996. $16.95. Good all-around guide to Costa Rica, now in its 11th edition. Blake is a resident of Costa Rica and gives knowledgeable, up to-date advice. Also available: **The New Key to Cancun and the Yucatan** by Richard Harris ($14.95); **The New Key to Ecuador and the Galapagos** by David Pearson and David Middleton ($16.95); and **The New Key to Belize** by Stan Ritz ($14.95).

Rethinking Tourism and Ecotravel: The Paving of Paradise and How You Can Stop It by Deborah McLaren. Kumarian Press, 630 Oakwood Ave., Suite 119, West Hartford, CT 06110-1529; (203) 953-0214, fax (203) 953-8579. 1997. $22. Useful information about the global tourism industry and creative alternatives. Use some of the hundreds of resources listed in this book and you will never travel the same way again.

Structural Adjustment, World Trade and Third World Tourism: An Introduction to the Issues by K.T. Ramesh, Ecumenical Center on Third World Tourism, P.O. Box 35, Senanikhom, Bangkok 10902, Thailand; (011) 662-939-7111; contours@ksc.net.th. Contours, August 1995.

Working With the Environment by Tim Ryder. Vacation Work, 9 Park End St., Oxford OX1 1HJ, England; (011) 44-86-52-41-978. 1996. £10.99. Guide to careers that involve working with the environment. Includes a chapter on environmental tourism.

Responsible Travel and Ecotourism Web Sites

www.bigvolcano.com.au/ercentre/ercpage.htm. The Big Volcano Ecotourism Resource Centre site has a good collection of organizations, web sites, and books of interest.

www.ecomanage.com. The International Society for Eco-Tourism Management is a proactive organization which facilitates positive change in the tourism industry. Their web site is a good place to network and obtain information about the industry in general.

www.ecotour.org/ecotour.htm. The Ecotravel Center site, sponsored by Conservation International, has lists of tour operators, resources, and destinations. Also has a Travel Forum (or chat room) where you can exchange information and ideas with other travelers.

www.ecotourism.org. The Ecotourism Explorer is a well-organized site that will be of interest to ecotravelers and eco-professionals alike.

http://ecotourism.miningco.com. The Mining Company's guide to ecotourism covers a wide range of interests, from destinations to ethics and policies.

www.ecotravel.com. The Ecotravel Directory has an impressive Destinations section offering links to hundreds of culturally, socially, and ecologically responsible tour operators worldwide. Coupled with their Worldwide Hotel Database, this is a very useful site.

www.gn.apc.org/tourismconcern. Tourism Concern is a membership network set up in

1989 to bring together people concerned about tourism's impact on communities and the environment. Their site has a good resource section.

www.gorp.com. The Great Outdoor Recreation Pages (GORP) site is one of the web's most highly regarded travel sites. They have loads of information on a multitude of destinations and adventure travel topics.

www.greentravel.com. The Green Travel Network site was created by travelers rather than tourism professionals. Offers resources, trip planning advice, and discussions for people with active travel on their minds. (Not to be confused with Green-Travel.)

www.green-travel.com/gtdirorg.htm. The Green-Travel Directory of Organizations is a simple list of eco-travel organizations with links to e-mail and web sites.

www.kc3.co.uk/~bicycle/veggie/index.html. The Vegetarian Vacations site has a list of tours, holidays, and courses which offer exclusively vegetarian or vegan cuisine.

www.planeta.com. A synthesis of environmental news and travel information from the Americas. This online journal features articles ranging from practical field guides to academic work on ecotourism. Contact: El Planeta Platica, c/o Ron Mader, Rep. De Cuba 12, #302, Col. Centro 06010, Mexico. To subscribe to the free monthly announcement service, e mail ron@greenbuilder.com.

www.podi.com/ecosource/index.html. Eco-Source's site has provided information and services regarding ecotourism and sustainable development since 1995.

www.travelon.com/adventure. The Travelon Trip Finder is a searchable database of adventure travel programs. Choose from over 80 activities and over 100 destinations, enter your price range and departure time, and get a descriptive list of available tours with links to the operators' contact information.

For more listings of responsible travel resources, and for bargains worldwide, travel tips, and all sorts of information on learning, living, working, and traveling abroad, see *Transitions Abroad* magazine. To order a single copy or a subscription, please call 1-800-293-0373 or visit the *Transitions Abroad* web site at www.transabroad.com.

Responsible Travel Resources

CHAPTER 8

RESPONSIBLE TRAVEL TOURS & PROGRAMS

The following listing of responsible travel tours and programs was supplied by the organizers in 1998 and is updated in each November/ December issue of Transitions Abroad *magazine. Contact the program directors to confirm costs, dates, and other details. Please tell them you read about their programs in this book! Programs based in more than one country or region are listed under "Worldwide."*

Americas

Cemanahuac Community. Trips are highly educational, with college credit (graduate and undergraduate) available. Countries include Mexico, Belize, Costa Rica, and Guatemala. Focus areas include history, anthropology, archaeology, social issues, cooking and cuisine, and popular and folk art. Previous groups include teachers, social workers, artists, senior citizens, chefs, museum members, alumni groups, and other adult participants. Each trip individually planned.

Dates: Field study trips can be held at any time of the year. Cost: Dependent on requirements and length of the field study trips. Contact: Vivian B. Harvey, Educational Programs Coordinator, Cemanahuac Educational Community, Apartado 5-21, Cuernavaca, Morelos, Mexico; (011) 52-73-18-6407, fax (011) 52-73-12-5418; 74052.2570@compuserve.com, www.cemanahuac.com.

Asia

Adventure Tours to Borneo. Personalized walking tours, hiking, scuba diving, mountain biking, bird watching tours to Borneo.

Dates: Year round. Cost: Call for details. Contact: Ken Chung, Foris Adventures, 1300 Clay St., Suite 600, Oakland, CA 94612; (888) GO-FORIS, fax (510) 638-5289; vacation@foris.com, www.foris.com.

Intrepid Small Group Adventures. Intrepid travel in small groups (no more than 12 people), take local transport and stay in small, family-run guest houses that are part of the local environment or community. Intrepid

Adventures is not just a resource efficient and responsible way to travel—it is a highly rewarding way too.

Dates: Year round. Many trips depart weekly. Cost: From $420 for 8 days in Lombok. Includes Western group leader, accommodations, transport, sightseeing, meals. Contact: Adventure Center, 1311 63rd St., Suite 200, Emeryville, CA 94608; (510) 654-1879, fax (510) 654-4200; adventctr@aol.com, www.intrepidtravel.com.au.

Belize

Toledo Ecotourism Association. This Mayan and Garifuna-run organization offers a village guesthouse and cultural activity program nestled in southern Belize's remarkable rainforest habitat. Guests share meals with local families and enjoy rainforest hikes, canoeing, caving, and traditional music and dance. Profits contribute to village health, education, and conservation efforts.

Dates: Ongoing. Cost: Full tour $87.50 (1998). Includes overnight stay, 3 meals, 2 tours, meals, dancing, storytelling. Contact: Toledo Ecotourism Association, Box 75, Punta Gorda, Belize; (011) 501-72-2119, fax (011) 501-72-2199; ttea@btl.net, www.plenty.org/TEA.html.

Canada

Circle VH Enterprises. Located in the middle of the Yukon Territory, Circle VH offers a cozy trapper-style cabin with breakfast or meals in the main house, horses by the hour or day, boat trips down the Pelly River.

Dates: Year round. Cost: Packages range from CAN$525 per person for 3 days to CAN$1,775 for 10 days. Add 7 percent tax. Contact: Circle VH Enterprises, P.O. Box 204, Farc. Yukon, Y0B 1K0, Canada ; Tel./fax (403) 994-2055.

Language Studies Canada Montréal. Using a multi-skill approach students develop effec-

tive communication skills in French. Classes are informative, practical, and enjoyable. Seven levels of 4 weeks each: intensive, 6 hours daily or semi-intensive, 4 hours daily. Maximum of 14 students per class. Audio-visual equipment, multi-media Student Resource Center. Optional activity program. Homestay and alternate accommodations available.

Dates: Year round. Two-week courses begin any Monday. Other programs offered: one-to-one instruction, year round; 2-week. Group 5 executive courses, Jun-Oct; Summer Language Adventure (13- to 17-year-olds), 2-9 weeks in Jul and Aug. Cost: Two weeks intensive program $545 (1998); homestay accommodations $365 (1998). Cost of other services available upon request. Contact: Language Studies Canada Montréal, 1450 City Councillors, Montréal, PQ, H3A 2E6, Canada; (514) 499-9911, fax (514) 499-0332.

Yoga Study and Retreats. Yasodhara Ashram, a vibrant spiritual community founded 35 years ago by Swami Sivanada Radha, offers yoga courses, workshops, spiritual retreats. Situated on Kootenay Lake in the mountains of southeastern British Columbia, the atmosphere is conducive to reflection, meditation, and renewal. The 10 Days of Yoga, an introduction to ashram courses, is offered every quarter. Programs for young adults are also offered at this certified post-secondary institute.

Dates: Year round. Cost: Varies. The 10 Days of Yoga is CAN$825 (CAN$170 deposit). Special youth rates and work programs. Contact: Julie McKay, Yasodhara Ashram, Box 9, Kootenay Bay, BC V0B 1X0, Canada; (604) 227-9224 or (800) 661-8711, fax (604) 227-9494; yashram@netidea.com.

China

Ethnic Minorities of SW China. Culturally sensitive low-impact small group tours explore ethnic minority areas of Guizhou and Yunnan provinces. Emphasis on the vibrant traditional cultures of the Miao (Hmong) and other ethnic people: daily and ceremonial village life, festivals, handcrafts, music, dance, and textile arts.

Dates: Mar 21-Apr 8, Apr 23-May 7, Aug 6-20, Oct 8-22. Cost: From $2,600 depending on itinerary. Includes all air and land costs in China. Contact: Peter Nelson, Minzu Explorations, 18444 Tualata Ave., Lake Oswego, OR 97035; Tel./fax (503) 684-9531; petnels@aol.com.

Costa Rica

Casa Rio Blanco Rainforest Reserve. If adventure and learning is the nature of your journey, then volunteer to work in one of the most complex ecosystems in the world—the rainforest. Meet nice people while participating in rainforest conservation projects and environmental education. The emerald green classroom is right outside your door. Send 3 international reply coupons.

Dates: Four-week sessions throughout the year. Cost: $100 downpayment, $400 upon arrival. Includes meals, cabin and, laundry. Contact: Dee Bocock (new owner), Casa Rio Blanco, Apdo 241-7210, Guapiles Pococi, Costa Rica.

Costa Rican Language Academy. Costa Rican owned and operated language school offers first-rate Spanish instruction in a warm and friendly environment. Teachers with university degrees. Small groups or private classes. Included free in the programs are airport transportation, coffee and natural refreshments, excursions, Latin dance, Costa Rican cooking, music, and conversation classes to provide students with complete cultural immersion.

Dates: Year round (start anytime). Cost: $135 per week or $220 per week for program with homestay. All other activities and services included at no additional cost. Contact: Costa Rican Language Academy, P.O. Box 336-2070, San José, Costa Rica; (011) 506-221-1624/233-8914/233-8938, fax (011) 506-233-8670. In the U.S.: (800) 854-6057; crlang@sol.racsa.co.cr., www.crlang.co.cr/index.html.

Field Course in Sustainable Development. The Institute for Central American Development Studies (ICADS) offers an interdisciplinary semester abroad study program focusing on development issues from ecological, socio-economic perspectives. The 14-week field course includes: 1) 4 weeks of intensive Spanish and urban issues (e.g. waste management, housing, structural adjustment, assembly industry), 2) 5 weeks in the field in different managed and natural ecosystems learning techniques of field research in social and natural sciences (e.g. banana transnationals, traditional agriculture, community cooperatives; cloud forest and watershed management), 3) 5 weeks of independent study—living and working in rural or urban communities. Fall and Spring terms with academic credit.

Dates: Fall and Spring semesters only. Cost: $7,200. Contact: Dr. Karin Gastrich, Ph.D., Field Course Coordinator, ICADS, Dept. 826, P.O. Box 025216, Miami, FL 33102-5216; (011) 506-225-0508, fax (011) 506-234-1337; icads@netbox.com, www.icadscr.com.

Intensive Spanish Immersion. The Institute for Central American Development Studies (ICADS) offers 30-day programs of intensive Spanish languages—4 1/2 hours daily, 5 days a week. Small classes (4 students or less) geared to individual needs. Extra lectures and activities emphasize environmental issues, women's studies, economic development, and human rights. ICADS offers optional afternoon internship placements in grassroots organizations. Supportive informal learning environment. Homestays and field trips.

Dates: Programs begin first day Monday of each month. Cost: One month $1,225. Includes airport pick-up, classes, books, homestay, meals, laundry, lectures, activities, field trips, and internship placements (10% discount after first month). Contact: Sandra Kinghorn, Ph.D., Director, ICADS, Dept. 826,

P.O. Box 025216, Miami, FL 33102-5216; or ICADS, Apartado 3-2070, Sabanilla, San Jose, Costa Rica; (011) 506-225-0508, fax (011) 506-234-1337; icads@netbox.com, www. icadscr.com.

Intensive Spanish Training. The Institute for Central American Development Studies (ICADS) offers 4-week progressive programs in Intensive Spanish Languages—4 1/2 hours daily, 5 days a week. Small classes (4 students or less). Activities and optional afternoon internships emphasize environmental issues, women's issues, development, human rights, and public health. Supportive learning environment. Homestays and field trips. Great alternative for the socially conscious.

Dates: Programs begin first Monday of each month. Cost: $1,325 includes airport pick-up, classes, books, homestay, meals, laundry, lectures, activities, field trips, and internship placements. Contact: ICADS, Dept. 826, P.O. Box 025216, Miami, FL 33102-5216; (011) 506-225-0508, fax (011) 506-234-1337; icads@netbox.com, www. icadscr.com.

Learn Spanish While Volunteering. Assist with the training of Costa Rican public school teachers in ESL and computers. Assist local health clinic, social service agencies, and environmental projects. Enjoy learning Spanish in the morning, volunteer work in the afternoon/evening. Spanish classes of 2-5 students plus group learning activities; conversations with middle-class homestay families (1 student per family). Homestays and most volunteer projects are within walking distance of school in small town near the capital, San Jose. *Note: One participant reported to this publisher that when she arrived in Costa Rica, LALC did not provide any volunteer opportunities for her.* Dates: Year round, all levels. Classes begin every Monday, volunteer program is continuous. Cost: $345 per week for 28 hours of classes and group activities plus Costa

Rican dance and cooking classes. Includes tuition, 3 meals per day, 7 days per week, homestay, laundry, all materials, and airport transportation. $25 one-time registration fee; $100 additional one-time registration fee for volunteer program. Contact: Susan Shores, Registrar, Latin American Language Center, 7485 Rush River Dr., Suite 710-123, Sacramento, CA 95831; (916) 447-0938, fax (916) 428-9542; lalc@madre.com.

Ecuador

Workshops in the Galapagos Islands. Specializing in comprehensive, educationally-oriented, professionally-led 11-day natural history tours of the Galapagos Islands. Special programs include history-oriented trips that follow Darwin's route as well as National Science Teacher Association (NSTA) sponsored tours offering 3 graduate credit hours.

Dates: Monthly departures on 16-passenger yachts. Cost: Approx. $3,000. Airfare not included. Contact: Galapagos Travel, 783 Rio Del Mar Blvd., Suite 47, Aptos, CA 95003; (800) 969-9014, fax (831) 689-9195; galapagos travel@compuserve.com.

El Salvador

Ecotourism in San Carlos Lempa. This area near the Pacific Ocean was repopulated after the recent civil war, and today is an agricultural zone organized for integral socially, economically, and politically sustainable development. Enjoy the beautiful mangrove environment and the beaches while getting to know the people. You will also visit the war museum, organic cashew groves, and the farm school.

Dates: Call for details. Cost: Call for details. Contact: Maryse Brouwer, CORDES San Vicente, apdo 2841, San Salvador, El Salvador; (011) 503-260-8167/8185/8159 (after 3 tones: 123), fax (011) 502-226-4814; cordes.sanvicente@salnet.net.

Europe

Napoleonic Tour to Museums in France. Fifteen-day tour to major French museums and battlefields. Includes air conditioned buses, first-class hotels, 5 dinners, 14 continental breakfasts, English speaking expert guides, 4 cocktail receptions, 2 private collections, limited to 30 guests. Fifteenth anniversary.

Dates: Sep. Cost: $3,295 includes airfare (NY and return), hotels, guides, some meals. Contact: Napoleonic Society of America, 1115 Ponce de Leon Blvd., Clearwater, FL 33756.

France

French and Cookery in a Château. Live and study in 18th-century château with relaxed, convivial atmosphere. Residential French language and Provençal cooking for adults. Comfortable single/twin and shared rooms. Good food and wine at the heart of France's loveliest areas, near Lyon.

Dates: Two weeks in Feb, and every Sunday May-Nov. Cost: From $800 full board and classes in château. Contact: Michael Giammarella in U.S.: (800) 484-1234 ext 0096 or Ecole des Trois Ponts, Château de Matel, 42300 Roanne, France; (011) 33-477-70-80-01, fax (011) 33-477-71-5300; info@3ponts.edu, www.3ponts.edu.

Guatemala

La Paz Spanish School. Spanish language and cultural immersion program. Small, friendly school. Social projects focus on education and women's empowerment. Daily activities (hikes, village visits, speakers, discussions). Five hours of one-on-one daily Spanish instruction. Fun, rewarding experience.

Dates: Year round. Cost: $110 per week ($125 Jun-Aug). Room and board with Guatemalan family. Includes activities, private instruction. Contact: Roy Holman, 5209 19th Ave. NE, Seattle, WA 98105; (206) 729-7664; roymundo@aol.com, www.trafficman.com/xelapages.lapaz.

Indonesia

Ecotourism and Responsible Travel. Programs offer various environmentally friendly journey: watching wildlife at the national park, adventurous trekking in the forest, bamboo rafting, hiking the lip of Mt. Bromo Crater, and snorkeling. The overland trip provides an opportunity to observe and interact with the host people, stay with a family, visit community development project, observe daily life, and enjoy the culture and natural attractions.

Dates: Call for details. Cost: Call for details. Contact: Jarot Sumarwoto, Bina Swadaya Tours, Jln. Gunung Sahari III/7, Jakarta 10610, Indonesia; (011) 62-21-420-44-02, fax (011) 62-21-425-65-40; bst@cbn.net.id.

Italy

Biking and Walking Tours. Specializing in Italy for over 10 years, Ciclismo Classico distills the "Best of Italy," offering more unique Italian destinations than any other active vacation company. Educational, active tours for all abilities in Umbria, Tuscany, Piedmont, the Dolomites, Puglia, Sicily, the Amalfi Coast, Cinque Terre, Sardegna, Abruzzo, Campania, Corsica, and Elba. Ireland, too. Charming accommodations, expert bilingual guides, cooking demonstrations, wine tastings, support vehicle, detailed route instructions, visits to local festivals, countryside picnics—an unforgettable cultural indulgence.

Dates: Apr-Nov (70 departures). Call for specific dates. Cost: $1,500-$3,000. Contact: Lauren Hefferon, Director, Ciclismo

Classico, 13 Marathon St., Arlington, MA 02174; (800) 866-7314 or (781) 646-3377.

Japan

Japan Exchange and Teaching. Sponsored by the Japanese Government, the JET Program invites over 1,000 American college graduates and young professionals to share their language and culture with Japanese youth. One-year positions are available in schools and government offices throughout Japan. Apply by early December for positions beginning in July of the following year.

Dates: One-year contracts renewable by mutual consent not more than 2 times. Cost: Participants receive approx. ¥3,600,000 per year in monthly payments. Contact: JET Program Office, Embassy of Japan, 2520 Massachusetts Ave. NW, Washington, DC 20008; (202) 238-6772, fax (202) 265-9484; eojjet@erols.com, www.jet.org.

Teaching English in Japan. Two-year program to maximize linguistic and cultural integration of participants who work as teachers' assistants. Placements twice yearly in Apr and Aug. Most positions are in junior high schools in urban and rural areas. Bachelor's degree and willingness to learn Japanese required.

Dates: Hiring for positions every Apr and Aug. Applications accepted year round. Cost: Airfare, salary, housing, healthcare provided. No application fees. Contact: Institute for Education on Japan, Earlham College, D-202, Richmond, IN 47374; (888) 685-2726, fax (765) 983-1553; www.earlham.edu/aet/home.htm.

Malta

Prehistory in Mediterranean Malta. Archaeology is adventure in Malta, where 7,000 years of human history continues. New and important discoveries are on the horizon. We'll visit megalithic temples that are the oldest build-

ings still standing on earth and talk with experts who know the sites intimately. Conservation of this remarkable heritage is a global responsibility.

Dates: Varies. Call for availability. Cost: From $1,387 land cost for 8 nights first-class accommodations, nearly all meals, full program of presentations, field trips, and excursions. All program proceeds support historic conservation efforts in Malta and Gozo. Contact: The OTS Foundation Education and Historic Preservation in Malta, P.O. Box 17166, Sarasota, FL 34276; (800) 680-2766, fax (941) 918-0265; otsf@aol.com, www.swift-tourism.com/ots.htm.

Mexico

Intensive Language Programs. Intensive Spanish immersion program in groups, 40 class hours per week including Spanish class, lectures, and Hispano-American courses. Executive, semester, and specialized programs for teachers, professionals, nurses, and adults continuing education. Live with Mexican family or in student residence. Excursions to historical and archaeological sites.

Dates: Year round starting every Monday. Cost: Tuition $190 per week; lodging $154 per week. Contact: The Center for Bilingual Multicultural Studies, Javier Espinosa, San Jeronimo #304, Cuernavaca, MOR-62179, Mexico; (011) 52-73-17-10-87, fax (011) 52-73-17-05-33; admin@bilingual-center.com, www.bilingual-center.com.

Intensive Spanish in Cuernavaca. Cuauhnahuac, founded in 1972, offers a variety of intensive and flexible programs geared to individual needs. Six hours of classes daily with no more than 4 students to a class. Housing with Mexican families who really care about you. Cultural conferences, excursions, and special classes for professionals. College credit available.

Dates: Year round. New classes begin every

Monday. Cost: $70 registration fee; $650 4 weeks tuition; housing $18 per night. Contact: Marcia Snell, 519 Park Dr., Kenilworth, IL 60043; (800) 245-9335, fax (847) 256-9475; lankysam@aol.com.

Language and Culture in Guanajuato. We work with innovative teaching techniques, tailoring instruction to each student's needs. Spanish, Mexican history, politics, culture-cuisine, folk dancing, and Latin American literature.

Dates: Year round. New classes begin every Monday. Cost: $925. Includes 4 weeks of classes and homestay with 3 meals daily. Contact: Director Jorge Barroso, Instituto Falcon, A.C., Guanajuato, Gto. 36000 Mexico; Tel./fax (011) 52-473-1-0745, infalcon@redes. int.com.mx, www.infonet.com.mx/falcon.

Mar de Jade Mexico. Tropical ocean-front responsible tourism center in beautiful unspoiled fishing village near Puerto Vallarta offers unique study options: enjoy great swimming, snorkeling, hiking, and boating; study Spanish in small groups taught by native speakers. Or join the longer work/study program that includes working in development projects such as health clinics, teaching, or working in the community of Mar de Jade itself.

Dates: Year round. Cost: For 21 days, room (shared occupancy), board, Spanish classes (12 hours per week) and 12-15 hours per week of community work), $950. For daily room and board $50. Contact: In Mexico: Mar de Jade, A.P. 81, Las Varas, Nayarit, 63715, Mexico; Tel./ fax (011) 52-327-20184; info@mardejade. com, www.mardejade.com. In U.S.: P.O. Box 1280, Santa Clara, CA 95052; (415) 281-0164.

Mayan Archaeology. Twelve-day river trip on waterways and trade routes the ancient Mayans may themselves have used. Palenque, Bonampak, Yaxchilan, Tikal, Planchon de Las figuras, Altar de Sacrificios, Seibal, Dos Pilas, Aguateca, Arroyo de Piedras, and El Duende are significant sites on this "River of Ruins" itinerary.

Dates: Feb 14 and Mar 11. Cost: $2,150 per person in Mexico. Includes all land transport, lodging, and meals. Contact: CEIBA Adventures, Inc., P.O. Box 2274, Flagstaff, AZ 86003; (520) 527-0171, fax (520) 527-8127; ceiba@primenet.com, www.primenet.com/ ~ceiba.

Travel/Study Seminars. Learn from Mexicans of diverse backgrounds about their economic, political, and social realities. Emphasis on the views of the poor and oppressed. Programming in Cuernavaca, Mexico City, and Chiapas. Call for a free list of upcoming programs.

Dates: Ongoing. Cost: $800-$1,900 depending on package, destination, and length of trip. Contact: Center for Global Education, Augsburg College, 2211 Riverside Ave., Box 307TR, Minneapolis, MN 55454; (800) 299-8889, fax (612) 330-1695; globaled@ augsburg.edu, www.augsburg.edu/global.

New Zealand

New Zealand Pedaltours. New Zealand is a cycling paradise with fantastically beautiful scenery. Cycle as much as you wish each day with a comfortable minibus and trailer to carry your luggage and you at any time. Excellent accommodations and great meals. Experienced local guides knowledgeable about local flora and history.

Dates: Nov-Mar. Cost: $330-$3,245. Contact: Allan Blackman, 522 29th Ave. S., Seattle, WA 98144; (888) 696-2080, fax (206) 727-6597; blackallan@aol.com.

Pacific Region

Hawaii's Kalani Oceanside Retreat. Kalani Educational Retreat, the only coastal lodging facility within Hawaii's largest conservation area, offers traditional culture, healthful cuisine, wellness programs, and extraordinary natural beauty: thermal springs, a naturist dolphin beach, snorkel pools, kayaking, waterfalls, crater lake, and spectacular Volcanoes National Park. Ongoing offerings in yoga, dance, hula, mythology, language, and massage. Or participate in an annual week-long event: men's/women's/couples conferences, dance/music/hula festivals, yoga/meditation/transformation retreats. Applications are also being accepted for our international Volunteer Scholar program.

Dates: Year round. Cost: Lodging $45-$110 per day. Camping $20-$25. $570-$1,120 per week for most programs, including meals and lodging choice. Contact: Richard Koob, Director, Kalani Retreat, RR2, Box 4500, Pahoa-Beach Rd., HI 96778-9724; (800) 800-6886 or (808) 965-7828 (call for fax info); kalani@kalani.com, www.kalani.com.

Papua New Guinca

Trans Niugini Tours. Nature and culture programs are offered in 3 areas: the Highlands, the Sepik Area, and a marine environment on the North Coast. Each area has its own distinct culture and environment, with comfortable wilderness lodges.

Dates: Weekly departures. Cost: $889-$3,570 per person (land cost). Contact: Bob Bates, Trans Niugini Tours, P.O. Box 371, Mt. Hagen, Papua New Guinea; (800) 521-7242 or (011) 675-542-1438, fax (011) 675-542-2470; travel@pngtours.com, www.pngtours.com.

Peru

Manu Biosphere Reserve. Nine-day trip to the isolated Manu Biosphere Reserve in Peru observing wildlife and rainforest in pristine conditions. A combination safari camp and lodge trip.

Dates: Every Sunday from Apr-Dec. Cost: Call for details. Contact: Manu Expeditions, P.O. Box 606, Cusco, Peru; Tel./fax (011) 51-84-226671; adventure@manuexpeditions.com, www.manuexpeditions.com.

Senegal

Crossing Cultures Senegal. In a 3-week program limited to 8 people and custom-tailored to individual interests, participants visit different parts of Senegal and community projects, stay with Senegalese families or in guest houses, use public transportation and experience village life. Extended stays for a field study or volunteer work can be arranged.

Dates: Jan 5-27; Jun 25-Jul 15. Cost: $2,992 includes roundtrip airfare, food, lodging, all transportation in country. Contact: Janet L. Ghattas, Intercultural Dimensions, P.O. Box 391437, Cambridge, MA 02139; (617) 864-8442, fax (617) 868-1273; janetid@aol.com.

South Africa

Travel/Study Seminars. Learn from South Africans of diverse backgrounds about their economic, political, and social realities. Emphasis on the views of those struggling for justice. Special trip planned for the elections. Call for details.

Dates: Apr and Summer 1999. Cost: Approx. $3,900 depending on length of stay. Contact: Center for Global Education, Augsburg College, 2211 Riverside Ave., Box 307TR, Minneapolis, MN 55454; (800) 299-8889, fax (612) 330-1695; globaled@augsburg.edu, www.augsburg.edu/global.

United Kingdom and Ireland

Island Horizons. Specialist in Northwest Scotland highlands and islands (especially Isle of Skye). Guided ecowalks and historical tours. Also audio guides. Share the magic of changing light on water and mountains, the elusive glimpse of wild stag, eagle, otter. Small groups, qualified and insured leaders.

Dates: Apr-Oct. Cost: £545-£695 for 6 days. Includes local travel, accommodations, and meals. Contact: Jean Stewart, Horizons,

Ecotourism Guidelines
Choosing the Organizations and Businesses You Support

By Dianne Brause

I recently compiled a local community publication called "Forever Green: An Ecotourist's Guide to Lane County," bringing ideas I have developed in my work in international travel into the context of my hometown. I found that the same principles apply to traveling to the tropical rainforests of Central America, the African game reserves, or a town in Oregon.

We developed a list of questions that we used to determine which organizations to include within our Ecotourist's Guide. You can use these same criteria to help you assess which types of organizations you would like to support as you travel the world.

For the purposes of the guide we used the following as a working definition of ecotourism: Tourism or visitor-related activities or services that support the local people, culture, and economy in a positive way, while at the same time contributing to ecological protection and sustainability.

An ecotourist supports a business, organization, or service that:

• **Is Locally Owned and Operated.** Local ownership and management means that the money you spend will likely stay within the community and go to the people who are actually doing the work.

• **Supports the Community and is Service Oriented.** Does the business know and care about the local community and is it willing to go the extra mile? For example, our city bus service person recently told me that although the bus from the airport is scheduled to arrive three minutes after the bus that heads out to our rural area leaves, that if we call ahead, the driver will delay his departure until the airport bus has arrived.

• **Supports Local People and the Local Culture.** Does this group use some of its resources to make life better for others in the area? In my community a number of the health food and small grocery stores invite customers to add a $1 or $5 donation to their food purchase to support a program that helps feed many of our poor and homeless.

• **Creates Locally Crafted or Value-Added Items.** Handmade items or products made from the natural resources of an area generally provide "right-livelihood" work and often utilize fewer natural resources than would be the case in a mass production setting.

• **Provides Direct Guest-Host Relationships.** We often travel to learn about people from another area, but do not see any way to actually get to know our hosts and their lives. In the western U.S. a number of working ranches invite guests to take part in the herding of livestock as part of their stay and as a way to learn what ranch life is really about.

• **Is Environmentally Conscious or Focused.** Does the business keep the needs of the environment and ecosystem of the area in mind? Some river-rafting companies teach their customers about the history, ecology, and protection of the river they are floating down and use some of the profits for conservation of the river.

• **Composts, Recycles, and Reduces Pollution.** Does the tour company compost food wastes and recycle all bottles, cans, containers, and paper products?

• **Experiments with Innovative and Alternative Methods.** Does the group take risks with innovative approaches to support sustainability? Our utility company has created a methane generation plant using the escaping gases from the local dump to produce 25 percent of the district's electricity by the year 2000.

• **Offers Hands-on Involvement to Volunteers.** An organization that encourages volunteers to become involved in local projects creates a much deeper connection with the people and culture of an area. Example: A bi-annual beach clean-up day on the Oregon Coast helps visitors and locals get to know one another while helping preserve the environment.

• **Supports Reduction of Resource Usage** (energy, water, transportation). In my area, a bicycle cooperative hires youth to provide "valet parking" of bicycles at all major events in town so that people are encouraged to ride a bike rather than pollute the environment and clog the streets with automobiles.

• **Meets "Green" Criteria or Ecotourism Guidelines.** Is this group serious enough about their interest in protecting the environment to publicly commit to a published standard or guideline for ecotourism? In Costa Rica, one of the hotels we visited committed to designing its buildings and exterior lighting so as not to interfere with the endangered turtles nesting on the adjacent beach.

Most groups won't meet all of the above criteria. Yet at home or abroad these guidelines may help you consider some of the many daily choices you have which impact the health and welfare of people and ecosystems. As a traveler, you can have an important impact on the development of ecotourism and the movement toward sustainability in the 21st century.

Kirkton, Lochcarron, Wester Ross, Scotland IV54 8UF, U.K.; Tel./fax (011) 44-1520-722-238, mobile (011) 44-374-900-151; jeannie@dial.pipex.com, www.glen.co.uk/rc/horizons.

Women's Journey to Ireland. Visit ancient Ireland's pagan and goddess sites, hear traditional music, learn about its culture, history, politics, humor from Irish women. Hosted by Mod O'Donnell, archaeologist, and Lyn O'Donoghue of Mystical Ireland for Women. A relaxed, informal/informed trip open to spontaneity and fun. Plus essay contest: win a trip in Ireland.

Dates: Apr 22-May 6. Cost: $1,250-$1,700, sliding scale (pay what you can afford on this scale). Include 14 nights of accommodations, breakfasts, a welcoming and goodbye dinner, site fees, our own bus and driver, guide, and archaeologist Mod O'Donnell, accompanied by Lyn O'Donoghue. Airfare not included. Contact: Pat Hogan, Sounds & Furies Productions, P.O. Box 21510, 1850 Commerial Dr., Vancouver, BC V5N 4AO, Canada; (604) 253-7189, fax (604) 253-2191; path@lynx.bc.ca.

United States

Alaskan Wilds, Summer and Winter. The premier fly-in wilderness lodge with a stunning Mt. McKinley view. Free flightseeing, 10 guests max, one guide per couple. Fully guided wilderness adventures; fly, canoe, hike, photograph, fish, relax. Winter dog sledding; learn to drive your own dog team into the wilderness of Denali National Park.

Dates: Year round. May 25-Sep 20; Feb 1-Apr 10. Cost: $500 per person per night, guides, cabin, meals, flightseeing. Contact: Jack or Sherri Hayden, Denali West Lodge, P.O. Box 40, Lake Minchumina, AK 99757; Tel./fax (907) 674-3112; minchumina@aol.com, www.alaskan.com/denaliwest.

Worldwide

ActionQuest Sail/Dive Programs. Live-aboard 75-day semester voyages for teens and college students, focusing on experiential education, local history and culture, and college-level academics. Multi-level sailing and scuba certification programs with tropical marine biology, oceanography, community service, conservational research projects, and leadership training. No experience necessary.

Dates: Semester: Jan 9-Mar 25, Sep 25-Dec 9. Summer: Jun 21-Jul 11, Jul 13-Aug 2, Aug 4-21. Cost: $11,250 not including airfare. Summer: From $2,885-$3,885 not including airfare. Contact: James Stoll, Action Quest, P.O. Box 5507, Sarasota, FL 34277; (800) 317-6789, (941) 924-6789, fax (941) 924-6075; actionquest@msn.com, www.actionquest.com.

American-Int'l Homestays. Stay in English-speaking foreign homes in over 30 countries. Explore foreign cultures responsibly. Learn foreign languages. Perfect for families or seniors. Learn how other people live by living with them in their homes.

Dates: Year round. Cost: From $59 per night. Contact: Joe Kinczel, American-Int'l Homestays, P.O. Box 1754, Nederland, CO 80466; (303) 642-3088 or (800) 876-2048, fax (303) 642-3365; ash@igc.apc.org.

College Semester Abroad (SIT). A pioneer in study abroad, the School for International Training (SIT) offers over 57 programs in over 40 countries worldwide. For over 40 years SIT has been a leader in offering field-based study abroad programs to U.S. college and university students.

Dates: Fall and Spring semester. Cost: $8,900-$11,900 depending on location. Includes airfare, tuition, room and board, insurance. Contact: School for International Training, P.O. Box 676, Kipling Rd., Brattleboro, VT 05302; (802) 257-7751, fax (802) 258-3500; csa@sit.edu, www.sit.edu.

Responsible Travel Programs

Coral Cay Conservation Expeditions. Volunteers needed to join major expeditions to help survey and protect coral reefs and tropical forests in the Caribbean, Asia-Pacific, Philippines, Indonesia, Red Sea. No previous experience required. Full accredited training provided (including scuba certification if required). Thousands of CCC volunteers have already helped establish 8 new marine reserves and wildlife sanctuaries worldwide.

Dates: Expeditions depart monthly throughout the year. Cost: From $995 (2 weeks) to $4,415 (12 weeks) excluding flights. Contact: Coral Cay Conservation Ltd., 154 Clapham Park Rd., London SW4 7DE, U.K.; (305) 757-2955 (U.K. office 011-44-171-498-6248, fax 011-44-171-498-8447); ccc@coralcay.demon.co.uk, www.coralcay.org.

The Experiment in International Living. Challenging 3-, 4-, and 5-week summer programs for high school students in 21 countries in Africa, the Americas, Asia, and Oceania. Programs include a cross-cultural orientation and homestay. Community and Ecological Service as well as Language Training programs are available. Also leadership opportunities for experienced college graduates.

Dates: Jun 30-Aug 5. Cost: From $1,800-$4,975. Contact: Anne Thompson, The Experiment in International Living, World Learning, P.O. Box SA, Brattleboro, VT 05302; (800) 345-2929 or (802) 257-7751, fax (802) 258-3428; eil@worldlearning.org, www.world learning.org.

Global Ecology and Cities in the 21st Century. Two different academic programs to be offered by the International Honors Program. "Global Ecology" is a 2-semester program of around-the-world study and travel to England, Tanzania, India, the Philippines, and Mexico with academic coursework in ecology, anthropology, economics, and environmental issues. The "Cities in the 21st Century" program is a 1-semester program of study and travel to South Africa, India, and Brazil with academic coursework in urban studies, anthropology, sociology, economics, and political science.

Dates: "Global Ecology": Sep-May. "Cities in 21st Century": Jan-May. Cost: "Global Ecology": $21,950 plus airfare, includes tuition, room and board. "Cities in the 21st Century": $12,650 plus airfare, includes tuition, room and board. Estimated airfare for each program is $3,900. Contact: Joan Tiffany, Director, International Honors Program, 19 Braddock Pk., Boston, MA 02116; (617) 267-0026, fax (617) 262-9299; info@ihp.edu, www.ihp.edu.

Global Volunteers. "An adventure in service." The nation's premier short-term service programs for people of all ages and backgrounds assist mutual international understanding through ongoing development projects in 19 countries throughout Africa, Asia, the Caribbean, Europe, the South Pacific, North and South America. Programs of 1, 2, and 3 weeks range from natural resource preservation, light construction, and painting to teaching English and assisting with health care. No special skills or foreign languages are required. Ask about the Millennium Service Project.

Dates: Over 130 teams year round. Cost: Tax-deductible program fees range from $400 to $2,095. Airfare not included. Contact: Global Volunteers, 375 E. Little Canada Rd., St. Paul, MN 55117; (800) 487-1074, fax (651) 482-0915; email@globalvolunteers.org, www.globalvolunteers.org.

Natural History and Research Expeditions. Nonprofit founded in 1972 offers the public hands-on opportunities to assist with field research. Also specializes in whale watching and educational natural history excursions.

Dates: Year round. Call for complete listing. Cost: From $1,150-$3,390. Contact: Oceanic Society Expeditions, Ft. Mason Ctr., Bldg. E, San Francisco, CA 94123; (800) 326-

7491 or (415) 441-1106, fax (415) 474-3395; www.oceanic-society.org.

Project Ecotourism. Ecological tourism is promoted through trips to various countries worldwide. Guidelines provided on how to be a responsible and environmentally aware tourist and tour operator. Special emphasis on Suriname's Amazon rainforest.

Dates: Continuous. Cost: Varies. Contact: Nancy Pearlman, Educational Communications, P.O. Box 351419, Los Angeles, CA 90035; (310) 559-9160; ECNP@aol.com.

Reality Tours. Participate in one of our socially responsible, alternative travel experiences to Brazil, Cuba, Chile, Costa Rica, Guatemala, Haiti, India, Iran, Ireland, Palestine/Israel, South Africa, and Vietnam. Gain a first-hand perspective on what communities in these countries are engaged in. Learn from their diverse voices about: peace and conflict, sustainable development, indigenous cultures, arts and religion, health and education, women's issues, and more. Or become a delegate to monitor human rights or observe presidential elections. Special meetings can be arranged to suit your personal interests.

Dates: Monthly throughout the year. Cost: Depending on the destination, trip costs range from $800-$3,000. Costs generally include airfare, but land-only options are available (please call for more details). Contact: Reality Tours Department, Global Exchange, 2017 Mission St., Suite #303, San Francisco, CA 94110; (415) 255-7296 or (800) 497-1994, fax (415) 255-7498; www.globalexchange.org.

University Research Expeditions Program (UREP). Help preserve endangered tropical ecosystems, track elephants in Kenya or pelicans in Baja, excavate archaeological sites in Ireland or Peru, and more. No special experience necessary. Tax deductible contribution. For anyone 16 and older.

Dates: Projects are 2 to 3 weeks. Cost: Var-

ies with project. Call for details. Contact: UREP, Desk MO8, Univ. of California, Berkeley, CA 94720-7050; (510) 642-6586; www.mip.berkeley.edu/urep.

The World for Free. A membership organization for those who want to stay with people, not in hotels. Members all over the world. Write for information and an application.

Dates: Year round. Cost: $25. Contact: The World for Free, c/o Seidboard, P.O. Box 137, Prince St. Sta., New York, NY 10012; fax (212) 979-8167; TWFF@juno.com, www.freeyellow.com/members2/seidboard/twfhome.html.

WorldTeach. WorldTeach is a private nonprofit organization based at Harvard Univ. that contributes to educational development and cultural exchange by placing volunteers as teachers in developing countries. Volunteers teach English, math, science, and environmental education. One-year, 6-month, and summer opportunities. Programs in Costa Rica, Ecuador, Namibia, China, Mexico, and Honduras.

Dates: Year-round departures; deadlines vary depending on program. Cost: $3,600-$5,650. Includes international airfare, health insurance, placement, training, and in-country support. Contact: Admissions Department, WorldTeach, Harvard Institute for International Development, 14 Story St., Cambridge, MA 02138; (800) 4-TEACH-0 or (617) 495-5527, fax (617) 495-1599; info@worldteach.org, www.worldteach.org.

Worldwide Expeditionary Adventures. Zegrahm Expeditions is dedicated to offering an expeditionary adventure to the inquisitive traveler. Our programs are operated with great concern for the environment and sensitivity to fragile wildlife areas and cultures worldwide. Expeditions are accompanied by some of the world's foremost naturalists and expedition leaders.

Dates: Year round. Cost: From $3,690-

$30,000 per person. Contact: Zegrahm Expeditions, 1414 Dexter Ave. N., #327, Seattle, WA 98109; (800) 628-8747 or (206) 285-4000, fax (206) 285-5037; zoe@zeco.com, www.zeco.com.

Youth International. An experiential education program focusing on international travel and intercultural exchange, community service, adventure, and homestays. Teams of 12, aged 18-25, travel together for 1 semester to East Asia and India/Nepal, or East Africa and the Middle East. Assist refugees, hike the Himalayas, build water tanks in Africa, scuba dive, and much more. Also looking for leaders.

Dates: Jan 19-May 30, 1999 (4 1/2 months) and Sep 2-Dec 16, 1999 (3 1/2 months). Cost: Spring $6,900; Fall $5,900 (1998). Prices may change as of Fall '99. Contact: Brad Gillings, Youth International, 1121 Downing St., #2, Denver, CO 80218; Tel./fax (303) 839-5877; youth.international@bigfoot.com, http://home.att.net/~youth-international.

For more listings of responsible travel programs, and for bargains worldwide, travel tips, and all sorts of information on learning, living, working, and traveling abroad, see *Transitions Abroad* magazine. To order a single copy or a subscription, please call 1-800-293-0373 or visit the *Transitions Abroad* web site at www.transabroad.com.

Responsible Travel Programs

CHAPTER 9

VOLUNTEER
PROGRAMS

*Many potential volunteers aspire to serve humanity or are motivated
by some similarly grand ambition. Many past volunteers have discovered that the world is wider and their role smaller than they had
previously thought. While most volunteers return from a project
abroad buzzing with excitement, their lives enriched, others have experienced disillusionment. Either way, they have gained. The process
of shedding illusions, though sometimes uncomfortable, is enlighten-
ing and ultimately rewarding.*

When starting your research for a stint
abroad as a volunteer, it is important to maintain realistic expectations. Think about potential problems and how you would cope.

The best place to begin is with the literature
on volunteering abroad, which can introduce
you to the range of possibilities. Good resources list not only the names and addresses
of relevant organizations, but also their moti-
vating ethos and the costs involved. Ideally,
your research should begin at least a year in
advance of your intended departure, so that
applications can be lodged, sponsorship
money raised, language courses and other preparatory courses attended, and so on.

Much can be discovered from the tone as
well as the content of the literature sent by
placement organizations. For example, the
glossy brochure of a U.K.-based agency that
arranges short stints of volunteer English

teaching reads almost like a tour operator's
hard sell: "Choose your destination—colorful Ghana, exhilarating Mexico, the grandeur
of Ukraine or Siberia, mystic India, lively Brazil or magical China." Sure enough, volunteers
must pay from $1,350 for arrangements in the
Ukraine to more than $2,000 for short place-
ments in Ghana or Mexico, not including
travel to the destination country. These contrast sharply with the printed-on-a-shoestring
directories sent by the main U.S. workcamps
coordinators like Volunteers for Peace. For a
modest contribution of $195 (plus travel
costs), VFP volunteers can join anything from
an environmental project in rural Italy to a
community center for Aboriginal people in the
center of Sydney.

To illustrate further the diversity of cost,
even among projects working towards broadly
similar ends, the new book **Green Volunteers**

includes many conservation organizations looking for volunteers. Of the three operating exclusively in Peru, one runs eco-safaris and charges volunteer naturalists nothing at all; another collects data on marine wildlife and charges volunteers $5 a day for food and a mattress in a shared house; and the last, which monitors the macaw population, charges $50 per day (for a minimum of four weeks). Predictably, the ones charging very little expect their volunteers to have an appropriate background or degree, previous fieldwork experience, and computer skills (in the case of the marine wildlife project). The expensive program requires nothing apart from good health.

For pre-arranged placements, much depends on the efficiency and commitment of the representative or project coordinator on the ground. Promises of expert back-up are easier to make than to keep if the sending organization's local agent is more interested in his or her own prestige than in attending to the day-to-day problems of foreign volunteers. Few steps can be taken to guard against clashes with other individuals. The archaeologist for whom you are cleaning shards of pottery may turn out to be an egomaniacal monster. Fellow participants may not always be your cup of tea either. Voluntary projects attract a diverse range of people of all nationalities and ages, from the wealthy and pampered who complain about every little discomfort to the downright maladjusted. Assuming you fall outside both categories, you may have to call on every ounce of tolerance.

Even when good will predominates, things can go wrong. One young volunteer who arranged a stay with a small grassroots development organization in Sri Lanka felt isolated and miserable when she was billeted with a village family who knew no English. She was given very little to do apart from some menial office tasks. When she asked for something more to do, she was told to visit nursery schools, but she had to refuse on the grounds that her embassy had advised foreigners not

to leave the main roads. Perhaps someone with a little more travel experience might not have felt so daunted by these circumstances, difficult as they were.

A more mainstream example of differing expectations comes from Israel where every year thousands of young people continue to work as volunteers on kibbutzim. In exchange for doing primarily manual work, volunteers are given free room and board, quite a bit of time off, and the chance to make a set of new international friends—all of which are sufficient rewards for most foreign volunteers. But others question the arrangement. In an era when the ideals behind the original communal societies of Israel have been replaced by a more hard-nosed business approach, some young people can't justify working for eight hours a day picking fruit or working on a factory production line for no pay.

In many cases, the longer a volunteer stays the more useful he or she becomes, and the more interesting the jobs assigned. Of those organizations that charge volunteers by the week, some have introduced a progressively decreasing scale of charges. In some cases, long-stay volunteers who have proved their usefulness do not have to contribute toward expenses. However, red tape sometimes gets in the way of this arrangement. Most countries of the world impose a maximum period of stay for foreigners, and it can be very difficult to renew visas in countries like Nepal and Uganda after the original tourist visa has expired. In other cases, there may be a hefty fee for visa renewals and a lot of tiresome form filling by both volunteer and sponsor.

Volunteer vacations are very different from normal vacations, though the difference in cost may be negligible. Restoring historic buildings or teaching classes is just as much work as it would be if you were still at home. Jobs are jobs wherever you do them, and there may be little chance to see the sights or sample the nightlife. Provided you are prepared for such eventualities, you will in all likelihood have a thoroughly interesting and rewarding experience.

Additional Resources. Fabio Ausenda's **Green Volunteers**. Published by Green Volunteers, Via Valebza 5, 20144 Milan, Italy; greenvol@iol.it (in U.S., order from 1-800-525-9379). Lists more than 100 projects and organizations throughout the world for which both short- and long-term volunteers can work with wildlife and habitats in national parks, rainforests, and marine parks.

The Ecovolunteer Network, Central Office, Postbus 800, 7550 Av Hengelo, Netherlands; (011) 31-74-2478-985, fax (011) 31-74-2478-361; info@wolftrail.rottink.com, www.ecovolunteer.org. Umbrella organization offering 25-30 projects on which paying volunteers can obtain hands-on experience of wildlife research and conservation in many countries. Projects last one to four weeks and costs range from $140-$350 per week.

— *By Susan Griffith*

Volunteer Programs

The following listing of volunteer programs was supplied by the organizers in 1998 and is updated in each September/October issue of Transitions Abroad *magazine. Contact the program directors to confirm costs, dates, and other details. Please tell them you read about their programs in this book! Programs based in more than one country or region are listed under "Worldwide."*

Africa

FOCUS in Nigeria. FOCUS recruits certified opthalmologists to provide medical and surgical eye care in an Eye Center established in southeastern Nigeria. Room and board, external transportation, and a house steward are provided. The Center provides the only eye care for a population of 3 to 5 million people.

Dates: Any 3-week period throughout the year. Cost: Approx. $1,700 including airfare to Lagos. Contact: James E. McDonald, FOCUS, Loyola Univ. Chicago, Dept. of Opthamology, 2160 S. 1st Ave., Building 102, Maywood, IL 60153; (708) 216-3408, fax (708) 216-3557.

Project Ghana. Experience the vibrant, colorful culture of West Africa and make a difference at the same time. This unique short-term program enables volunteers to work with local social service organizations in fields as diverse as health care, education, skills training, and arts/recreation. Volunteers receive continual professional support from our U.S. and Ghana-based staff. No skills or experience required.

Dates: Three-week programs run year round. Longer term placements can be arranged. Cost: $1,850 covers all India-based expenses. International airfare, insurance, and visa not included. Program fee is tax deductible. Contact: Cross-Cultural Solutions, 47 Potter Ave., New Rochelle, NY 10801; (800) 380-4777 or (914) 632-0022, fax (914) 632-8494; info@crossculturalsolutions.org, www.crossculturalsolutions.org.

Argentina

Amity Volunteer Teachers Abroad (AVTA). AVTA is a program for volunteer teachers of ESL. Opportunities are currently available in Argentina. Volunteers are placed with a host family, receive a small monthly stipend, and may also take classes at the host institution. Some teaching experience preferred.

Dates: Mar-early Dec. Cost: Roundtrip airfare, health insurance, spending money. Contact: Amity Institute, 10671 Roselle St., Suite 101, San Diego, CA 92121; (619) 455-6364, fax (619) 455-6597; mail@amity.org.

Volunteer Programs

Armenia

Volunteer Exchange. Summer international short-term workcamps undertake restoration and maintenance of medieval buildings and sites, construction and ecological work, social services. In exchange for work, volunteers are provided with free food and accommodations. The program operates on an exchange basis; i.e., each volunteer arrives in exchange for an Armenian volunteer to the given country.

Dates: Summer months; duration varies from 15 days to 1 month. Cost: Free. Contact: Ara Galstian, Assocation for Educational, Work, and Cultural Exchange Programs, 42 Yeznik Coghbatsi St., Apt. 22, Yerevan-375002, Armenia; (011) 374-2-584-733, fax (011) 374-2-505-947; aiep@arminco.com.

Asia

Volunteers in Asia. Private, nonprofit, nonsectarian organization dedicated to increasing understanding between the U.S. and Asia.

Dates: Applications due early Feb. Cost: $1,350 for 1 year, $950 for 2 years, $1,425 Summer. Contact: Amy Tanner, Andrew Lewandowski, or Brad Spielman, P.O. Box 4543, Stanford, CA 94309; (650) 723-3228, fax (650) 725-1805; via@igc.apc.org, www.volasia.org.

Australia

Australian Trust for Conservation Volunteers. ATCV is a national, nonprofit, nonpolitical organization undertaking practical conservation projects including tree planting, seed collection, flora/fauna surveys, endangered species projects, coastal restoration, habitat protection, track construction, and weed eradication. Volunteers work in teams of 6-10; all training is provided.

Dates: Year round in all states and territories; choose any Friday throughout the year as starting date. Cost: Six-week Conservation Experience Package: AUS$840 includes all food, accommodations, and project-related transport within Australia. Contact: ATCV, P.O. Box 423, Ballarat, Victoria 3353, Australia (please include IRC); (011) 61-3-5333-1483, fax (011) 61-3-5333-2290; info@atcv.com.au, www.netconnect. com.au/~atcv.

WWOOF-Australia (Willing Workers on Organic Farms). Learn organic growing while living with host family. Nine hundred hosts in Australia or travel the world with over 600 hosts on all continents.

Dates: Year round. Cost: $30 single, $35 double. Contact: WWOOF Australia, Buchan, Victoria 3885, Australia; (011) 61-3-5155-0218; wwoof@ozemail.com.au.

Bosnia

Neighborhood Facilitators. Citizen-based peacebuilding initiative in Bosnia needs resilient, mature, self-directed people with good communication, problem-solving, and human relations skills. Work on issue of return and reintegration of refugees, housing, jobs and micro enterprises, and democratization through support for local facilitators, information gathering, outreach advocacy, accompaniment, discussion/action groups.

Dates: As needed. Minimum 6-month commitment. Cost: 1998: $500-$700 for training. Once accepted, stipend is available. Contact: Conflict Resolution Catalysts, P.O. Box 836, Montpelier, VT 05601; (800) 445-1165, fax (802) 229-1166; crc@sover.net, www.crcvt.org.

Canada

Lifesharing-Handicapped Adults. Live and work alongside developmentally delayed adults in a rural setting: gardening, woodworking, weaving, baking, forestry; celebrate and socialize together during Christian festivals; art: drama, music, painting, eurythmy. Involve oneself in new social forms. Our life is inspired by Anthroposophy—the work of Rudolf Steiner and Dr. Koenig.

Dates: Year: Apply anytime. Summer: Jun-Aug. Cost: Airfare, Canadian volunteer work visa, 3 months insurance. Contact: Camphill Village Ontario, 7841 4th Line, RR#1, Angus, ON L0M 1B0, Canada; (705) 424-5363, fax (705) 424-1854.

Operation Beaver. Volunteers are recruited from across the world to serve in native and non-native communities in Canada for a variety of community advancement projects in low-income rural areas. Volunteers must be 18.

Dates: Housing construction: Jun, Jul, Aug. Educational: Sep-Jun. Cost: Includes accommodations, food, and travel within Canada. Contact: Marco A. Guzman, Frontiers Foundation, 2615 Danforth Ave., Toronto, ON M4C IL6, Canada; (416) 690-3930, fax (416) 690-3934.

WWOOF-Canada. Organization offers over 300 farm hosts all across Canada and Western U.S., including Hawaii. You help for 4-6 hours a day (animal care, garden work, etc.), receive accommodations, meals, and a wonderful experience. Hundreds of students have done this. Publishes booklet with descriptions of what each farm offers.

Dates: Year round. Cost: Booklet available for $25 and 2 International Postal Coupons; 1999: $30 (single), $40 (couples). Contact: WWOOF-Canada, RR#2, S.18, C.9, Nelson, BC V1L 5P5, Canada; (250) 354-4417.

Central America

Bridges to Community. A nonprofit community development organization which takes groups of volunteers to Central America many times a year. Projects focus on development of infrastructure and empowerment of local people. Trips include education, hands-on work, and critical reflection, with volunteer opportunities in health and construction.

Dates: Call for details. Cost: From $1,200 including airfare (1998). Contact: Carter Via, Executive Director, Bridges to Community, 210 Orchard Ridge Rd., Chappaqua, NY 10514; (914) 238-8354, fax (914) 238-3423; brdgs2comm@aol.com.

Concern America Volunteer Program. Recruits volunteer professionals in the fields of health, adult literacy, sanitation, agroforestry, appropriate technology, and community organizing. Programs emphasize training of community members in impoverished communities to impart skills and knowledge which remain with the community after the volunteer is gone. Volunteer positions only; no employment. Minimum commitment 1 year.

Dates: Year round as available. Cost: Call for details. Concern America provides room and board, roundtrip transportation, health insurance, small monthly stipend, repatriation allowance, support from home office. Contact: Janine Mills, Recruitment Coordinator, Concern America, P.O. Box 1790, Santa Ana, CA 92702; (714) 953-8575, fax (714) 953-1242; concamerinc@earthlink.net, http://home.earthlink.net/concamerinc.

Costa Rica

Intensive Spanish Training. The Institute for Central American Development Studies (ICADS) offers 4-week progressive programs in Intensive Spanish Languages—4 1/2 hours daily, 5 days a week. Small classes (4 students or less). Activities and optional afternoon internships emphasize environmental issues, women's issues, development, human rights, and public health. Supportive learning environment. Homestays and field trips. Great alternative for the socially conscious.

Dates: Programs begin first Monday of each month. Cost: $1,325 includes airport pick-up, classes, books, homestay, meals, laundry, lectures, activities, field trips, and internship placements. Contact: ICADS, Dept. 826, P.O. Box 025216, Miami, FL 33102-5216; (011) 506-225-0508, fax (011) 506-225-234-1337; icads@netbox.com, www.icadscr.com.

Learn Spanish While Volunteering. Assist with the training of Costa Rican public school teachers in ESL and computers. Assist local health clinic, social service agencies, and environmental projects. Enjoy learning Spanish in the morning, volunteer work in the afternoon/evening. Spanish classes of 2-5 students plus group learning activities; conversations with middle-class homestay families (1 student per family). Homestays and most volunteer projects are within walking distance of school in small town near the capital, San Jose.

Dates: Year round, all levels. Classes begin every Monday, volunteer program is continuous. Cost: $345 per week for 28 hours of classes and group activities plus Costa Rican dance and cooking classes. Includes tuition, 3 meals per day, 7 days per week, homestay, laundry, all materials, and airport transportation. $25 one-time registration fee; $100 additional one-time registration fee for volunteer program. Contact: Susan Shores, Registrar, Latin American Language Center, 7485 Rush River Dr., Suite 710-123, Sacramento, CA 95831; (916) 447-0938, fax (916) 428-9542; lalc@madre.com.

A Rainforest Experience. Volunteers needed to work in one of the most complex and biodiverse places in the world. Dissolve barriers and experience a new culture and land while participating in rainforest conservation projects and environmental education. All ages and abilities welcome. Five international reply coupons required.

Dates: Four-week sessions throughout the year. Cost: $500 per month, additional months discounted. Includes a cabin, food, and laundry. Contact: Ms. Di (new owner), Casa Rio Blanco, Apdo. 241-7210, Guapile, Pococi, Costa Rica.

Turtle Tagging in Costa Rica. Travel to Tortuguero on the northern Caribbean coast for 6 nights or 13 nights tagging endangered sea turtles along the secluded black sand beach, the largest nesting site of endangered turtles in the Western hemisphere. Contribute to the efforts of the oldest sea turtle research program in the world, the Caribbean Conservation Corporation (CCC), a U.S.-based nonprofit organization dedicated to the preservation of endangered sea turtles. Participants in this service program check for old tags, measure the shells, watch the egg-laying process, and count the eggs as they drop in the nest.

Dates: Departures each Saturday in Mar, Apr, Jun, Jul, Aug, and Sep. Cost: From $1,585 for 9 days; From $1,985 for 16 days. Contact: Holbrook Travel, Inc., 3540 NW 13th St., Gainesville, FL 32609; Tel./fax (800) 451-7111; www.holbrooktravel.com.

El Salvador

Melida Anaya Montes Language School. Teach small-size English classes, all levels offered. Training provided. Students are adults working in the Salvadoran opposition who need to increase their capacity for their work and/or complete their studies. CIS also seeks volunteers for their human rights work. Volunteers can receive half-price Spanish classes.

Dates: Three-month sessions beginning mid-Jan, Apr, and Aug. Mini-sessions offered Jul and Nov. Cost: No fee. Must pay living costs ($250-$400 per month). Contact: CIS MAM Language School, Boulevard Universitario, Casa #4, San Salvador, El Salvador, Central America; Tel./fax (011) 503-226-2623; cis@netcomsa.com.

France

Restoration of Medieval Buildings. Volunteers restore and maintain medieval buildings and sites, including 2 fortified castles at Ottrott, Alsace, destined as cultural and recreational centers. We provide participants with both cultural enrichment and physical exercise.

Dates: Jul 16-30, Aug 1-15, Aug 16-30. Cost: FF550. Contact: Chantiers d'Études Médiévales, 4 rue du Tonnelet Rouge, 67000 Strasbourg, France; (011) 33-88-37-17-20.

Germany

Work with Children. Help look after mentally handicapped young people (6-16) in a boarding school where houseparents, children, and staff live and work together in family-style house communities. The work includes caring for a small group of children outside of school hours, organizing recreational time, and helping with housework. Knowledge of German is necessary.

Dates: Year round. Cost: Program provides free board and accommodations, social security, and pocket money of DM350 per month. Contact: Mr. Bruno Wegmüller, Heimsonderschule Brachenreuthe, 88662 Überlingen, Germany; (011) 49-7551-8007-0, fax (011) 49-7551-8007-50.

Workcamps, Volunteer Work. We offer the possibility to help on farms working in ecological and anthroposcophic cultivation, working in residential workcamps, and renovating an art school.

Dates: Summer workcamps on biofarms and residentials any time. Cost: DM140 plus health insurance fee. Includes accommodations, food, cultural program (1998). Contact: Nothelfergemeinschaft der Freunde, Postfach 10 15 10, 52349 Düren, Germany; (011) 49-2421-76569, fax (011) 49-2421-76468.

India

Cultural Exchange/Workcamps. CEC-OWOR organizes cultural exchange workcamps. Short-

term, 4 times a year. Participants will be involved in different community projects in villages. Programs will be improvised through discussion with participants. Also possibilities for individual short- and long-term volunteers.

Dates: Cultural/Workcamps Jan 2, Apr 1, Sep 2, and Nov 1. Individual volunteers throughout the year. Cost: $50 registration, $150 food and accommodations. Contact: M. Susairaj, Director, CECOWOR, No. 9 Rajadesing Nagar, Desurpattai Rd., Gingee 604 202, Villupruam Dt., Tamilnadu, India; Tel./fax (011) 91-4145-22747.

Project India. A unique 3-week service program open to people of all ages and backgrounds run by a highly qualified staff of educators, social workers, and cultural advisers. Positions include health care, education, social development, arts/recreation, and more. No skills or experience required.

Dates: Three-week programs run year round. Longer term placements can be arranged. Cost: $1,850 covers all India-based expenses. International airfare, insurance, and visa not included. Program fee is tax deductible. Contact: Cross-Cultural Solutions, 47 Potter Ave., New Rochelle, NY 10801; (914) 632-0022 or (800) 380-4777, fax (914) 632-8494; info@crossculturalsolutions.org, www.crossculturalsolutions.org.

Israel

Interns for Peace. An independent, community-sponsored program dedicated to building trust and respect among the Jewish and Arab citizens of Israel. Develop action-oriented projects in education, sports, health, the arts, community and workplace relations, and adult interest groups. Requirements include: a commitment to furthering Jewish-Arab relations; BA, BS, or equivalent degree; proficiency in Hebrew or Arabic; a previous stay in Israel of at least 6 months; background in sports, business, teaching, health care, youth work, art, music, or com-

Volunteer Programs

munity organizing (professional work experience is a plus).

Dates: Vary. Cost: Must pay own airfare to Israel. Contact: Interns for Peace, 475 Riverside Dr., 16th Fl., New York, NY 10115; (212) 870-2226, fax (212) 870-2119.

Japan

Teaching English in Japan. Two-year program to maximize linguistic and cultural integration of participants who work as teachers' assistants. Placements twice yearly in April and August. Most positions are in junior high schools in urban and rural areas. Bachelor's degree and willingness to learn Japanese required.

Dates: Hiring for positions every Apr and Aug. Applications accepted year round. Cost: Airfare, salary, housing, healthcare provided. No application fees. Contact: Institute for Education on Japan, Earlham College, D-202, Richmond, IN 47374; (888) 685-2726, fax (765) 983-1553; www.earlham.edu/aet/home.htm.

Latin America

Voluntarios Solidarios. Places individual volunteers with grassroots peace and justice groups in Latin America and Caribbean on various projects. Work ranges from translation of documents to teaching homeless children to working in campaigns for demilitarization. Volunteers must be conversationally fluent in Spanish, and pay own expenses.

Dates: Rolling application process, allow 2 plus months from applying and start of service. Serve between 3 months and 2 years. Cost: Travel and living expenses. Contact: John Lindsay-Poland, Fellowship of Reconciliation, 995 Market St., #1414, San Francisco, CA 94103; (415) 495-6334, fax (415) 495-5628; fornatl@igc.apc.org, www.nonviolence.org/for.

Volunteer, Internship Positions. In Costa Rica, Mexico, Guatemala, Ecuador, Argentina, Peru, Dominican Republic. Various positions in the fields of health care, education, tourism, ESL, business, law, marketing, administrative, environmental, and social work. Additional customized options available. Two weeks to 6 months. Inexpensive lodging in homestays or dorms. Some positions provide free room and board.

Dates: Year round. Flexible start dates. Cost: $200 placement and application fee. Travel insurance and pre-departure preparation included. Lodging costs depend on location. Contact: AmeriSpan Unlimited, P.O. Box 40007, Philadelphia, PA 19106; (800) 879-6640, fax (215) 751-1100; info@amerispan.com, www.amerispan.com.

Mexico

Intensive Language Programs. Intensive Spanish immersion program in groups, 40 class hours per week including Spanish class, lectures, and Hispano-American courses. Executive, semester, and specialized programs for teachers, professionals, nurses, and adults continuing education. Live with Mexican family or in student residence. Excursions to historical and archaeological sites.

Dates: Year round starting every Monday. Cost: Tuition $190 per week; lodging $154 per week. Contact: The Center for Bilingual Multicultural Studies, Javier Espinosa, San Jeronimo #304, Cuernavaca, MOR-62179, Mexico; (011) 52-73-17-10-87, fax (011) 52-73-17-05-33; admin@bilingual-center.com, www.bilingual-center.com.

Mar de Jade. Tropical ocean-front retreat center in a beautiful unspoiled fishing village near Puerto Vallarta offers unique volunteer opportunities in a 21-day work/study program. Work in community health program, local construction, cottage industries, and teaching. Study Spanish in small groups with native teachers. Relax and enjoy great swimming, kayaking, hiking, boating, horseback riding, and meditation.

Dates: Year round. Cost: $950 (1998) for 21-day work/study. Includes room (shared occupancy), board, 12 hours per week of Spanish and 15 hours per week of community work. Longer resident program available at lower cost. Vacation/Spanish 1 week minimum: $400 (1998) room, board, 12 hours of Spanish. Vacation only: $50 per night (1998) for any length of time. Contact: Mexico: Mar de Jade/Casa Clinica, A.P. 81, Las Varas, Nayarit, 63715, Mexico; Tel./fax (011) 52-327-20184; U.S.: P.O. Box 1280, Santa Clara, CA 95052; (415) 281-0164; info@mardejade.com, www.mardejade.com.

Stella Maris School of Nursing. Nursing school with 75 students in a small town in the picturesque state of Michoacan seeks volunteers to help at the school in various capacities. Nurses especially needed. Spanish conversational ability necessary to assist students in their studies. Room and some meals provided. Commitment of 6 months required.

Dates: Late Aug-Jun. Cost: None. Contact: Sister Theresa Avila, Stella Maris School of Nursing, Apartado Postal 28, Zacapu, Michoacan CP 58670, Mexico; Tel./fax (011) 52-436-31300.

Strawbale House Building. Third World Opportunities is a 2-pronged program utilizing the border with Mexico as a gigantic classroom. Learn about the realities of poverty, hunger, border issues, and sustainable development. One-week strawbale building projects in Tecate and Las Palmas, Mexico. Applicants must be at least 15 years old.

Dates: Jun-Aug. Cost: $200 plus transportation. Contact: M. Laurel Gray, Coordinator, Third World Opportunities, 1363 Somermont Dr., El Cajon, CA 92021; Tel./fax (619) 449-9381; pgray@ucsd.edu.

Nepal

Volunteer Nepal Himalaya. Participants live near the base of Mt. Everest with a Sherpa family and teach English in a Sherpa school for 3 months. The program also includes a 10-day language and cultural orientation in Kathmandu.

Dates: Feb-May, Sep-Dec. Cost: $2,700. Contact: Scott Dimetrosky, Himalayan Explorers Club, P.O. Box 3665, Boulder, CO 80307; (888) 420-8822, fax (303) 494-8822; himexp@aol.com, www.hec.org.

Volunteer Service Work. This program is designed for those who wish to visit Nepal and contribute their time and skills to benefit the community and its people. The volunteer service work program introduces participants to Nepal's diverse geographical and cultural environment while establishing an awareness and deeper understanding of cultural differences.

Dates: Starting Feb, Apr, Aug or Oct. Other dates upon request. Length: 2-4 months. Cost: $650 includes language instruction, homestay, trekking, rafting, jungle volunteering, food, and accommodations. Contact: Rajesh Shrestha, Director, Cultural Destination Nepal, GPO Box 11535, Kathmandu, Nepal; (011) 977-1-426996, fax (011) 977-1-428925 or (011) 977-1-416417; members@himexp.wlink.com.np or koshi@ccsl.com.np.

Pacific Region

Hawaii's Kalani Oceanside Retreat. Kalani Educational Retreat, the only coastal lodging facility within Hawaii's largest conservation area, offers traditional culture, healthful cuisine, wellness programs, and extraordinary natural beauty: thermal springs, a naturist dolphin beach, snorkel pools, kayaking, waterfalls, crater lake, and spectacular Volcanoes National Park. Ongoing offerings in yoga, dance, hula, mythology, language, and massage. Or participate in an annual week-long event: men's/women's/couples conferences, dance/music/hula festivals, yoga/meditation/transformation retreats. Applications are also being accepted for our international Volunteer Scholar program.

Dates: Year round. Cost: Lodging $45-$110 per day. Camping $20-$25. $570-$1,120 per week for most programs, including meals and lodging choice. Contact: Richard Koob, Director, Kalani Retreat, RR2, Box 4500, Pahoa-Beach Rd., HI 96778-9724; (800) 800-6886 or (808) 965-7828 (call for fax info); kalani@kalani.com, www.kalani.com.

Philippines

Little Children of the Philippines, Inc. LCP is a Christian agency helping to develop caring communities for poor children on Negros Island in central Philippines. LCP has service programs in 7 communities covering health, housing, education, livelihood (agriculture, handicrafts), and value formation. Especially needed: volunteers in marketing, computer technology, journalism, music, carpentry, masonry, and environmental concerns.

Dates: Volunteers negotiate their own period of service. Cost: From East Coast: approx. $1,200 roundtrip airfare, $120 per month for food. Dormitory bed free. Contact: Dr. Douglas Elwood, 361 County Rd. 475, Etowah, TN 37331; Tel./fax (423) 263-2303; lcotw@conc.tds.net.

Senegal

Volunteer Program. Components of this volunteer program include family life education, reproductive health for youth, community development service, skills development in institutional organizations, and administration and management of a youth NGO.

Dates: Jul-Nov. Cost: Call for details. Contact: Cheikh M. Agne, E.E.D.S., P.O. Box 744, Dakar, Senegal, West Africa; Tel./fax (011) 221-821-7367.

Sweden

Working with Mentally Handicapped. Voluntary work with mentally handicapped adults in a camphill village.

Dates: Year round. Cost: None. Contact: Per Iversen, Staffansgården, Box 66, 82060 Delsbo, Sweden; fax (011) 466-531-0968.

Switzerland

Gruppo Volontari. Work on reconstruction projects in the Italian region of Switzerland that has suffered natural disasters. Lodging in a house in the village provided by the municipality. Participate in service projects aimed at helping the populace; e.g., help the aged, cut wood, domestic work, work in the stable and orchard. Volunteers share kitchen, cleaning, shop, and vehicle maintenance duties. Minimum age: 18.

Dates: Jun 1-Sep 30, 7-day minimum, 15-day maximum. Cost: Varies. Contact: Mari Federico, Director, Gruppo Volontari della Svizzera Italiana, CP 12, 6517 Arbedo, Switzerland; (011) 41-071-829-13-37/079-354-01-61.

Taiwan

Overseas Service Corps YMCA (OSCY). Place BAs to PhDs in ESL teaching positions in community-based YMCAs in Taiwan. Degree in teaching, ESL, or general teaching experience preferred. No Chinese language necessary. This conversational English program provides an opportunity for cultural exchange. Must reside in North America and be a citizen of an English-speaking country. Twenty to 30 openings.

Dates: Call any time for a brochure, apply

between Jan 1 and Apr 15 for Sep placement. Cost: $50 application fee. Benefits for successful applicants include: Housing, health insurance, return airfare, paid vacation, bonus, orientation, sponsorship for visa, and monthly stipend. Contact: Janis Sterling, Program Assistant, International Group, YMCA of the USA, 101 N. Wacker Dr., Chicago, IL 60606; (800) 872-9622 ext. 167, fax (312) 977-0884.

Turkey

Workcamps and Study Tours. Gençtur organizes workcamps in small Anatolian villages with manual projects for people over 18. Lasting 2 weeks, camp language English. Enables close contact with locals. Study tour maintains close contact with students, teachers, lawyers, peasants, workers, journalists, etc.

Dates: Workcamps: Jul-Aug-Sep; Study Tours: year round. Cost: Workcamps $45; Study Tours: depends on duration and program. Contact: Gençtur, Mr. Zafer Yilmaz, Istiklal Cad. Zambak Sok. 15/5, 80080 Istanbul, Turkey; (011) 90-212-249-25-15, fax (011) 90-212-249-25-54; workcamps@genctur.com.tr, www.geocities.com/MadisonAvenue/1244.

Uganda

Uganda Rural Development Programs. Volunteers work in rural village development programs including helping in village clinics, teaching in schools, and participating in educational programs for local residents in health and hygiene issues, better farming methods, family finances, and other fields. Volunteers can develop their work programs according to their skills or concerns. Complete program information on the web site.

Dates: Year round. Programs from 1 week to 6 months. Cost: From $820 includes all costs for stay in Uganda. Airfare not included. Contact: Norman McKinney, United Children's Fund, Inc., P.O. Box 20341, Boulder, CO 80308-3341; (303) 464-0137; www.unchildren.org.

United Kingdom and Ireland

Archaeological Excavation. Volunteer and study programs in archaeological excavation techniques based on medieval settlement in mid-Wales. No previous experience necessary, but reasonable fitness required. Must be at least 16 years old.

Dates: Inquire. 7-day minimum. Cost: Volunteers, food and campsite £40 weekly. Tuition, food and campsite £150 (1998). Contact: Dr. C.J. Arnold, Dept. of Continuing Education, Univ. of Wales, 10-11 Laura Pl., Aberystwyth, Ceredigion, SY23 2AU, U.K.; Tel./fax (011) 44-1-970-622742.

Holidays for Disabled People. Residential volunteers required at 2 centers providing holidays for children and adults with learning disabilities and other special needs. Age 18-25 years. Placements up to 6 months. Board and lodging provided, pocket money, travel costs met within U.K.

Dates: Year round. Contact: Glenys Gray, BREAK, 7a Church St., Sheringham, Norfolk NR26 8QR, U.K.; (011) 44-1-263-822717.

Loch Arthur Community. A rural community in the southwest of Scotland where volunteers live and work with adults with learning disabilities. There are 6 households and a large farm, garden, bakery, weavery, and creamery. Volunteers receive board, lodging, and a small amount of pocket money.

Dates: Year round. Cost: Travel to and from community. Contact: Lana Chanarin, Stable Cottage, Loch Arthur, Beeswing, Dumfries DG2 8JQ, Scotland; (011) 44-1-387-760-687, fax (011) 44-1-387-760-618.

Railway Restoration. Didcot Railway Centre is a living museum of the Great Western Rail-

way, with steam locomotives in the original engine shed. Work alongside other volunteers restoring the trains and ancillary equipment.
Dates: Call for details. Cost: Call for details. Contact: Great Western Society, Didcot, Oxfordshire OX11 7NJ, U.K.; (011) 44-1-235-817200, fax (011) 44-1-235-510621.

The Simon Community. Works with the homeless on the streets of London. Runs a night shelter and 3 houses, and does streetwork over London. Promotes a philosophy of acceptance, understanding, and tolerating people.
Dates: Year round. Minimum of 3 months, 6 months preferred. Cost: Full board and lodging provided. Contact: The Simon Community, P.O. Box 1187, London NW5 4HW, England; (011) 44-171-485-6639.

Terrence Higgins Trust. The national voluntary organization leading the fight against AIDS. International volunteers welcome.
Dates: Inquire. Cost: Inquire. Contact: The Terrence Higgins Trust, 52-54 Grays Inn Rd., London WC1X 8JU, U.K.; (011) 44-171-831-0330, fax (011) 44-171-242-0121; www.tht.org.uk.

WWOOF-Ireland. Voluntary work in return for room and board on farms and small holdings throughout Ireland. Learn about organic farming methods, rural Ireland, and its life. Work is varied and you can volunteer from a few days to a few months.
Dates: Year round. Cost: IR £6. Contact: WWOOF, Harpoonstown, Drinagh, Co. Wexford, Ireland.

Working Holidays. Working holidays available throughout the year at peaceful, friendly Buddhist Centre in the beautiful Yorkshire Pennines. Work 35 hours per week in return for food, accommodations, and teachings. Live as part of a Buddhist community and experience a different way of life. Skills not necessary.
Dates: Year round. Cost: Free. Contact:

Losang Dragpa, Buddhist Centre, Dobroyo Castle, Pexwood Rd., Todmorden, W. Yorks 0L 14 7JJ, U.K.; (011) 44-1-706-812247, fax (011) 44-1-706-818901; losangd@aol.com.

United States

Master of International and Intercultural Management. The School for International Training Master of International and Intercultural Management offers concentrations in sustainable development, international education, and training and human resource development in 1 academic year program. This degree is designed for individuals wishing to make a career change or enter the field. A practical training component enables "on-the-job" training and an opportunity to work internationally.
Dates: Call for details. Cost: Call for details. Contact: Kat Eldred, Director of Outreach and Recruitment, Admissions Counselor, School for International Learning, P.O. Box 676, Kipling Rd., Brattleboro, VT 05302; (802) 257-7751, fax (802) 258-3500; admissions@sit.edu, www.sit.edu.

Worldwide

Amizade Volunteer Vacations. Programs offering mix of community service and recreation that provide volunteers with the opportunity to experience firsthand the culture they are working in—Brazilian Amazon, Bolivian Andes, or Greater Yellowstone region. Volunteers do not need any special skills, just a willingness to serve.
Dates: Year round. Cost: Varies. $1,500-$2,600 for Latin America; $150-$600 for Yellowstone. Contact: Amizade, 1334 Dartmouth Ln., Deerfield, IL 60015; (847) 945-9402, fax (847) 945-5676; amizade@worldnet.att.net, http://amizade.org.

College Semester Abroad, SIT. A pioneer in study abroad, The School for International

Training (SIT) offers over 57 programs in over 40 countries worldwide. For over 40 years SIT has been a leader in offering field-based study abroad programs to U.S. college and university students.

Dates: Fall and Spring semester. Cost: $8,900-$11,900 depending on location. Includes airfare, tuition, room and board, insurance. Contact: School for International Training, P.O. Box 676, Kipling Rd., Brattleboro, VT 05302; (802) 257-7751, fax (802) 258-3500; csa@sit.edu, www.sit.edu.

Coral Cay Conservation Expeditions. Volunteers needed to join major expeditions to help survey and protect coral reefs and tropical forests in the Caribbean, Asia-Pacific, Philippines, Indonesia, Red Sea. No previous experience required. Fully accredited, training provided (including scuba certification if required). Thousands of CCC volunteers have already helped establish 8 new marine reserves and wildlife sanctuaries worldwide.

Dates: Expeditions depart monthly throughout the year. Cost: From $995 (2 weeks) to $4,415 (12 weeks) excluding flights. Contact: Coral Cay Conservation Ltd., 154 Clapham Park Rd., London SW4 7DE, U.K.; (305) 757-2955 (U.K. office 011-44-171-498-6248, fax 011-44-171-498-8447); ccc@coralcay.demon.co.uk, www.coralcay.org.

Earthwatch Institute. Unique opportunities to work with leading scientists on 1- to 3-week field research projects worldwide. Earthwatch sponsors 160 expeditions in over 30 U.S. states and in 60 countries. Project disciplines include archaeology, wildlife management, ecology, ornithology and marine mammalogy. No special skills needed—all training is done in the field.

Dates: Year round. Cost: Tax deductible contributions ranging from $695-$2,800 support the research and cover food and lodging expenses. Airfare not included. Contact: Earthwatch, 680 Mt. Auburn St., P.O. Box 9104MA, Watertown, MA 02272; (800) 776-0188, (617) 926-8200; info@earthwatch.org, www.earthwatch.org.

Global Citizens Network. Global Citizens Network provides 1-, 2-, or 3-week cross-cultural volunteer expeditions to rural communities around the world. Current sites include Belize, Guatemala, Kenya, St. Vincent, the Yucatan, New Mexico, and Minnesota. Projects could include building a health clinic, setting up a library, or planting trees to reforest a village.

Dates: Year round. Cost: $500-$1,400 not including airfare. All trip-related expenses are tax-deductible. Limited partial scholarships available. Contact: Global Citizens Network, 130 N. Howell St., St. Paul, MN 55104; (800) 644-9292 or (612) 644-0960; gcn@mtn.org, www.globalcitizens.org.

Global Service Corps. Service-learning opportunities in Costa Rica, Kenya, or Thailand. Live with a village family while assisting grassroots community organizations on development projects. Assist with: rainforest conservation, sustainable agriculture, AIDS/HIV awareness, women's group projects, teaching English. Experience the challenges of developing countries from the inside out. Short- and long-term placements and internship available.

Dates: Year round. Cost: $1,495-$1,795 for 2-4 week project trips. Long-term projects start at $1,445 for 2 months. Includes in-country expenses (room and board, project fees, transportation, orientation, excursions). Airfare not included, discounts available. Contact: Global Service Corps., 300 Broadway, Suite 28, San Francisco, CA 94133-3312; (415) 788-3666 ext. 128, fax (415) 788-7324; gsc@igc.apc.org, www.earthisland.org/ei/gsc/gschome.html.

Global Volunteers. "An adventure in service." The nation's premier short-term service programs for people of all ages and backgrounds. Assist mutual international understanding through ongoing development projects in 19 countries throughout Africa, Asia, the Caribbean, Europe, the South Pacific, North and South America. Programs of 1, 2, and 3 weeks, range from natural resource preservation, light construction, and painting to teaching English and assisting with health care. No special skills or foreign languages are required. Ask about the Millennium Service Project.

Dates: Over 130 teams year round. Cost: Tax-deductible program fees range from $400 to $2,095. Airfare not included. Contact: Global Volunteers, 375 E. Little Canada Rd., St. Paul, MN 55117; (800) 487-1074, fax (651) 482-0915; email@globalvlntrs.org, www. globalvlntrs.org.

Global Works, Inc. Global Works is an environmental and community service-based travel program, with language immersion and homestay options available. A grassroots, not-for-profit organization for students ages 14-18. Experienced leadership. Four-week trips to Ireland, Ecuador, France, the Pacific Northwest, Costa Rica, Puerto Rico, Czech Republic, and the Fiji Islands.

Dates: Late-Jun-mid-Aug, 1998. Cost: $2,550-$3,475. Includes all but airfare. Contact: Global Works, Inc., Pam and Biff Houldin, Directors, RD2, Box 356-B, Huntingdon, PA 16652; (814) 667-2411, fax (814) 667-3853; info@globalworksinc.com, www.globalworksinc.com.

Individual Volunteer Placements. Placements are arranged in Costa Rica, Puerto Rico, Mexico, Ecuador, New Zealand, Australia, and Samoa. Volunteers work in schools, with conservation organizations, on small farms, and with animal rehabs and shelters. Volunteers travel and work on their own, often living with local families.

Dates: Year round. Cost: Placement fees $600-$950 (1998). Contact: John Lee, Explorations in Travel, 275 Jacksonville Stage Rd., Brattleboro, VT 05301; (802) 257-0152 or (802) 257-2784; explore@sover.net, www. exploretravel.com.

International Opportunities Clearinghouse. The Clearinghouse offers: directories of organizations that work in the international development field and offer internships in the U.S. and overseas; information packs (regional or topical) with materials from 15-30 volunteer programs in one's area of interest; and a research and referral service in which ODN researches various options and provides contacts with organizations that best fit an individual's interests.

Dates: Vary by program. Cost: Vary by program. Contact: Wendy Phillips, Overseas Development Network, 333 Valencia St., Suite 101, San Francisco, CA 94103; (415) 431-4204, fax (415) 431-5953; odn@igc.org, www.igc. org/odn.

International Volunteering Network. Involvement Volunteers Association, Inc. (IVI) aims to suit the requirements, abilities, and experiences of individual volunteers in individual or group placements which combine travel with volunteering in: Australia, England, Fiji, Finland, Germany, Ghana, Greece, India, Kenya, Lebanon, Macau and China, Malaysia, Nepal, New Zealand, Pakistan, Poland and Eastern Europe, Spain, South Africa, Thailand, or Vietnam. Placements generally run for a minimum of 2 to 6 weeks to a maximum of 1 year and relate to sustainable environmental conservation or community-based social service, no expertise required. Placements may be on farms, historic gardens, animal reserves, national parks, zoological parks, bird observatories, or research centers. Volunteers can participate in any number of placements, in any number of countries.

Dates: Year round. Cost: Approx. $350 for program, plus $40 per placement. The volunteer meets all travel costs (including insurance). Most hosts provide accommodations and food for free, but some placements in projects or countries with limited resources can cost up to $55 per week for food. Contact: Involvement Volunteers Assn., Inc., P.O. Box 218, Port Melbourne, Victoria 3207, Australia; (011) 61-3-9646-9392, fax (011) 61-3-9646-5504; ivimel@iaccess.com.au, www. iaccess.com.au/ivimel/index.html.

Jesuit Volunteers International. A Catholic/Christian full-time volunteer program for U.S. college grads looking to live simply in a faith community and work for justice. No cost and no pay except room and board, small stipend. Must be interested in faith and justice.

Dates: Call for details. Contact: Vin DeCola, P.O. Box 25478, Washington, DC 20007; (202) 687-1132, fax (202) 687-5082; jvi@gunet.georgetown.edu.

Jewish Volunteer Corps. The Jewish Volunteer Corps sends skilled Jewish men and women to provide technical assistance in the fields of health, agriculture, business, and education to the developing world. JVC volunteers work with local grassroots partner organizations throughout Latin America, Asia, and Africa from 1 to 9 months.

Dates: Year round, minimum 1 month. Cost: JVC covers airfare, NGO's help with housing. Contact: American Jewish World Service, 989 Avenue of the Americas, 10th Fl., New York, NY 10018; (212) 736-2597, fax (212) 736-3463; jvcvol@jws.org.

Mission Service Opportunities. Opportunities are diverse with some positions requiring more experience than others. We need: educators, office workers, RN's, development and community workers, and youth and social service workers. Both national and international.

Dates: Flexible (summer, full year, 2 or more years). Cost: Varies. Depends on service project (assistance for longer-term projects possible). Contact: Mission Service Recruitment Office, Presbytarian Church (U.S.A.), 100 Witherspoon St., Louisville, KY 40202-1396; (800) 779-6779; www.pcusa.org/msr.

Peace Brigades International. PBI provides international human rights observers in areas of extreme conflict. Volunteer teams currently operate in Guatemala, Chiapas, Haiti, Sri Lanka, Colombia, the Balkans, and North American Native communities. PBI is dedicated to the nonviolent resolution of conflicts and works by consensus. Volunteers provide protective accompaniment, peace education, and information.

Dates: Year round (minimum 7 months commitment). Cost: Includes airfare, health insurance, and training costs. Contact: Peace Brigades International, 2642 College Ave., Berkeley, CA 94704; (510) 540-0749, fax (510) 849-1247; pbiusa@igc.apc.org, www.igc.apc.org/pbi.

Peace Corps Opportunities. Since 1961, more than 150,000 Americans have joined the Peace Corps. Assignments are 27 months long. Volunteers must be U.S. citizens at least 18 years old and in good health. Peace Corps has volunteer programs in education, business, agriculture, the environment, and health.

Dates: Apply 9 to 12 months prior to availability. Cost: Volunteers receive transportation to and from assignment, a stipend, complete health care, and $5,400 after 27 months of service. Contact: Peace Corps, 1111 20th St., NW, Washington, DC 20526; (800) 424-8580 (mention code 824); www.peacecorps.gov.

Peacework. Peacework sponsors short-term international volunteer programs in Mexico, Belize, Honduras, the Dominican Republic, Cuba, Costa Rica, Bolivia, Russia, and Vietnam. Projects involve work in housing and building, renovations, childcare, agriculture, and healthcare through indigenous development organizations. Opportunities include travel, community interaction, and examination of regional social, political, cultural, and economic issues.

Dates: Call for details. Cost: Program fee includes all in-country accommodations and arrangements. Fee differs for each trip. Airfare not included. Contact: Ulla Reeves, Program Assistant or Stephen Darr, Director, 305 Washington St., SW, Blacksburg, VA 24060-4745; (540) 953-1376, fax (540) 552-0119; sdarr@compuserve.com, www.peacework.org.

SCI-IVS USA. Promotes cultural exchange and peacemaking through community service projects in the U.S. and abroad. Short-term

Volunteer Programs

work camps as well as longer term (up to 1 year) placements available. Must be 18 to attend international workcamps, 16 within the U.S. A wide variety of workcamp themes and locations possible.

Dates: Jun-Nov (1998). Cost: $65-$250 (1998) includes 1st workcamp ($35 nonrefundable membership) (2nd and 3rd workcamp $40-$120). Contact: Nancy Chappell, SCI-IVS USA., 5474 Walnut Level Rd., Crozet, VA 22932; (804) 823-1826, fax (804) 823-5027; sciivsusa@igc.apc.org, www.wworks.com/~sciivs.

Unique Volunteer and Service Programs. Experience culture in parts of the world that few people ever see. Works with each volunteer to find a project suited to his or her needs. Comparable to the Peace Corps without strenuous application process or long-term commitment. Destinations include Africa, Costa Rica, Ecuador, and Mexico. Wide variety of positions available.

Dates: Ongoing. Cost: Minimum 6 weeks $2,145, 6 months $3,875. Includes tuition, accommodations, full board, insurance, transportation, pick up and return to airport. Contact: Alliances Abroad, 409 Deep Eddy Ave., Austin, TX 78703; (888) 622-7623 or (512) 457-8062, fax (512) 457-8132; www.alliances abroad.com.

Visions in Action. Visions in Action sends volunteers to Africa and to Latin America to work for nonprofit development organizations. Volunteers are placed in diverse fields such as business management, law, health care, journalism, women's issues, democratization, human rights, children's programs, and environmental concerns.

Dates: Jan: Zimbabwe, South Africa, Mexico. Jul: Tanzania, South Africa, Mexico. Sep: Uganda. Oct: Burkina Faso. Cost: $4,000-$6,000. Contact: Shaun Skelton, Visions in Action, 2710 Ontario Rd. NW, Washington, DC 20009; (202) 625-7403, fax (202) 625-2353; visions@igc.apc.org.

Volunteers in World Service. Guardians of the Homeland is an organization offering graduates, skilled, and unskilled youth training for environmental, peace and conflict resolution, voluntary service to the world, skills and crafts to support self and family.

Dates: Write for details. Cost: Write for details. Contact: Prof. Austin Benni Bi, President, Guardians of the Homeland, P.O. Box 7283, Marina, Lagos, Nigeria.

WorldTeach. WorldTeach is a private nonprofit organization based at Harvard Univ. that contributes to educational development and cultural exchange by placing volunteers as teachers in developing countries. Volunteers teach English, math, science, and environmental education. One-year, 6-month, and summer opportunities. Programs in Costa Rica, Ecuador, Namibia, China, Mexico, and Honduras.

Dates: Year-round departures; deadlines vary depending on program. Cost: $3,600-$5,650. Includes international airfare, health insurance, placement, training, and in-country support. Contact: Admissions Department, WorldTeach, Harvard Institute for International Development, 14 Story St., Cambridge, MA 02138; (800) 4-TEACH-0 or (617) 495-5527, fax (617) 495-1599; info@world teach.org, www.worldteach.org.

Youth International. An experiential education program focusing on international travel and intercultural exchange, community service, adventure, and homestays. Teams of 12, aged 18-25, travel together for 1 semester to East Asia and India/Nepal, or East Africa and the Middle East. Assist refugees, hike the Himalayas, build water tanks in Africa, scuba dive, and much more. Also looking for leaders.

Dates: Jan 19-May 30 (4 1/2 months) and Sep 2-Dec 16 (3 1/2 months). Cost: Spring $6,900; Fall $5,900 (1998). Call for details. Contact: Brad Gillings, Youth International, 1121 Downing St., #2, Denver, CO 80218; Tel./

fax (303) 839-5877; youth.international@
bigfoot.com, http://home.att.net/~youth-
international.

**For more listings of volunteer opportunities
and programs**, and for bargains worldwide,
travel tips, and all sorts of information on
learning, living, working, and traveling abroad,
see *Transitions Abroad* magazine. To order a
single copy or a subscription, please call 1-800-
293-0373 or visit the *Transitions Abroad* web
site at www.transabroad.com.

Volunteer Programs

STUDY

Since no two programs or participants are precisely the same, the challenge is to learn enough about the ways in which programs differ from each other to develop a short list of programs which best match individual learning styles, resources, motivations, and interests.

—WILLIAM HOFFA, PAGE 166

Education Abroad

Criteria for Choosing the Right Program

By William Hoffa, Ph.D.

Study abroad today is largely a buyer's bazaar—at least for students who have the financial and academic support of their parents and college and are thus free to shop widely and wisely and for the program which best corresponds to their individual interests and needs. Ending up in the right program demands informed planning.

As the lists below suggest, study abroad is now something that happens virtually across the curriculum as well as the continents of the world. Students at almost all academic levels can now find a range of suitable programs that span the durational spectrum from a full academic year to a few weeks during the summer or winter term.

While admission to selected programs can sometimes be competitive, in point of fact very few programs operate at anything close to full capacity. Most (including all listed in the following pages) welcome applications from any qualified student. Moreover, competition for enrollments between programs is often intense, a situation which can work to the advantage of interested students.

Since no two programs or participants are precisely the same, the challenge is to learn enough about the ways in which programs differ from each other to develop a short list of programs which best match individual learning styles, resources, motivations, and interests. This is best done with the assistance of campus guidance and the resources listed in this chapter. It should also involve the careful reading of program materials and surfing the Internet for program home pages. The final choice depends on being able to successfully balance the following program variables:

Direct Enrollment. At one extreme are programs offering integrated language and cultural immersion via direct enrollment in a foreign educational institution. Integrated programs allow students to experience a foreign culture at first hand through immersion in its educational and social system.

Participants in integrated programs need to be independent, well-prepared, resourceful, adventurous, and adaptive. They usually have to make their own travel and housing arrangements, and they are responsible for making sure that course work can be successfully transferred back to their home campus for credit. This requires considerable preparation and effort.

U.S. College Sponsored. At the other extreme are U.S. campus or agency initiated programs which transfer the American campus to foreign soil. Such stand-alone or "island" programs offer U.S.-standard course work, support services, excursions and social activities, and often living arrangements. Teaching is done fully or in part by U.S. faculty. This insures that equivalent standards are maintained with regard to work load, class time, grading, attendance, calendar, and the like. Island programs often accommodate large numbers of students and offer cultural enrichment activities, such as tours and excursions.

Students who have never been abroad before, and who need at least initial guidance and direction, are likely to be well-served by these more structured programs. In order to find opportunities for additional intellectual and intercultural experience, however, students must use their own initiative to venture forth outside their program setting.

Hybrid Models. Most programs fall between these poles, borrowing features of each. Most attempt to combine the intercultural advantages of more integrated programming with the more pragmatic advantages and conveniences of what are essentially U.S. branch campuses. Some are able to offer several tracks, so that as students become more involved, venturesome, and linguistically able, they can advance along more challenging paths. Courses offered by foreign institutions are often supplemented by American-style course work, discussion groups, or even tutorials.

At their best, hybrid programs offer a pragmatic and often ingenious blend of cultural enrichment and academic challenges.

When to Venture Overseas. Studying abroad is almost always a remarkably broadening and stimulating experience. It is a productively unsettling component of liberal education, leading participants to ask and answer a number of fundamental questions concerning their real long-range interests, skills, and goals. There is thus plenty to be said for thinking about participation earlier rather than later in the college career, somewhere in the sophomore year, so that after return there is ample time to act on redefined directions and goals.

On the other hand, the curricular strengths of current programs make study abroad ideally suited to juniors and seniors who have chosen an academic concentration and are seeking to deepen and diversify it in ways not possible on campus. While studying abroad toward the end of the under-graduate degree is sometimes seen as a last undergraduate fling, it can also function as an important way to broaden career prospects, especially if it includes a workplace internship or other practical experience.

How Long to Stay. While most observers still believe that the longer the experience, the more long-lasting its intellectual and personal impact will be, something is always better than nothing. The huge variety of program models, courses, and geographical locations make study abroad a real pos-sibility for students who hitherto simply could not have considered it, what-ever the program duration. Excellent year, semester, and short-term op-tions abound, each suiting the amount of time students can afford (in an academic and economic sense) to be away from home campus studies. It is important, however, to consider the relative advantages and disadvantages which follow from enrollment in programs of differing lengths.

• The first rule of thumb, affirmed by returned students, is that the longer the program, the greater the intellectual and personal rewards. Academic benefit, crosscultural understanding, career preparation, and maturation all deepen with time. Long-term, fully-integrated programs are thus much more likely to provide students with the crosscultural coping skills favored by global corporations and international service organizations.

• Rule two, however, is that almost any program of any length is likely to offer something of value, and the "right" program can have a tremendous impact, regardless of its length. Short-term programs can be especially valu-able if they are part of a continuum which combines pre-departure and post-return studies and professional interests. The key is that program goals are clear from the start and can indeed be accomplished in the allotted time. Students should avoid over-ambition, and also be suspicious of pro-grams which seem to promise too much.

Program Size. Programs vary tremendously in the number of partici-pants they enroll. Small programs enroll as few as five to 10 students, while larger ones regularly enroll 200 or more. Small programs often are ideal at promoting cultural integration with local students and the culture in gen-eral. The down side is that the program curriculum may be quite limited and fixed. Larger programs can offer a larger range of curricular offerings, excursions, and support services, which, on an economy of scale, become more affordable. This richness, however, sometimes comes at the expense of cultural integration: the group can become an American ghetto. While no program can predict precise enrollments, its sponsor should be able to estimate normal size.

Group size per se may be less important than where the program is located in relation to other programs in the same area. The proximity of many other programs can affect group dynamics and opportunities for cultural integration in the local environment. Also of concern is whether the program itself does the teaching and provides housing, etc., or whether students directly enroll in a foreign university and have opportunities to mingle with its student population. In short, a large program which integrates its students fully or partially in a foreign university represents a quite different educational and social experience than a small program which keeps them together in the same classroom and accommodations. Each has something to be said in its favor.

Language Instruction and Social Discourse. Language study in U.S. high schools and colleges has been slowly on the rise through the 1990s, but most U.S. students still do not possess enough functional proficiency prior to departure to allow them to study or work abroad exclusively in the language they are learning, at least at the start of their program. Even in programs which place a heavy premium on language acquisition overseas, most courses may still be taught in English. Students without a fluency in a foreign language were until recently limited to English-speaking countries and a handful of other programs. Now, virtually wherever they are, it is temptingly easy to resort to English, the leading world language, with other Americans, with foreign counterparts, and even within host families.

Programs in English, in countries where English is a second language, continue to grow. Some such programs are set up by U.S. institutions hoping to expand study abroad participation to students who otherwise might not consider it. Others were recently established by countries themselves interested in internationalizing the higher education of their own students by bringing them into contact with students from other countries, using English as the language of instruction because it is the obvious linguistic medium. Students in such programs are almost always given the opportunity to learn the native language but take other course work in English. Many are amazed at how much language they can learn in a short while and the doors opened by their efforts. Most returnees report no relation between their previous efforts to master a foreign language and what they accomplished overseas.

Indeed, studying a foreign language where it is spoken presents unparalleled opportunities for quantum leaps forward in language proficiency, whatever the starting point. The key question is what, if any, level of foreign language proficiency is required by the program in order to function successfully in the unfamiliar linguistic environment of a foreign setting. Home campus instructors are usually the best judges of this. Acquiring a new cultural consciousness via language study, if not proficiency itself, should remain a goal for all program participants.

Where in the World to Go. Study abroad began as an exclusively Eurocentric venture. Indeed, about two-thirds of all current programming still takes place in Western European countries. There of course remain many sound reasons to choose to live and learn in such "traditional" locations, especially if language and other academic preparations for such study are well underway. But other parts of the global village also beckon and should be considered seriously. A variety of new program options now exist in Eastern Europe, for instance, in Russia and countries formerly part of the Soviet Union, and in the Baltic. In addition, excellent programs are now available throughout Latin America, Asia, Africa, Oceania, and the Middle East.

The arguments for considering programs in non-Western regions are compelling, not the least of which is their growing importance to American interests, world geopolitics, and the global economy and job market. Further, study in a developing country, or in a historically rich culture which is dramatically different from U.S. and Europe, can be especially eye-opening and rewarding. Obviously, somewhat different considerations—cost, transportation, communications, ethnicity, language barriers, safety, security, and health—come into play for students and parents considering programs in less-traditional locations. Program sponsors, however, should have responsible and helpful answers to all such questions.

Where one studies can also be very important to potential employers. A semester in Africa, studying its traditional art and culture, is much less likely to impress the average law school admissions committee than a similar period in Brussels studying the European Union. Of course, the opposite could also be true if an employer or graduate school was looking for evidence of adventurousness in applicants. Similarly, an English-language program which visits numerous countries and gives participants a strong sense of, say, comparative ecological systems and government policies, might appeal to a multinational chemical corporation but seem superficial to a company which valued employees with strong linguistic competencies.

Cost. Apart from the first questions concerning how much in the way of family and institutional resources can be realistically afforded to pay the costs, it is most important to determine what is and is not covered in program fees. No two programs, even in the same location, cost the same, nor are there any guarantees that the same features are covered.

Programs which may seem to be more expensive may offer more features or may just be more honest in leveling with students and parents (or, they may in fact offer less but charge more). Programs which list a lower fee may be in fact hiding costs from potential participants. The key for potential participants therefore is to decide what is essential to ensure the quality, integrity, and affordability of the program experience being sought and what is not. This involves carefully comparing not only sticker price but what one's money actually buys.

In sum, shopping widely and wisely involves taking into account program sponsorship, design, size, language, and location, as well as the ideal time to go overseas and how long to stay in order to achieve the maximum personal, educational, and career benefits. In addition, if receiving academic credit and financial aid to support participation in a given program are matters of importance, as they usually are, it is very important to get institutional approval prior to departure.

CHAPTER 10

STUDY ABROAD RESOURCES

Whether you're a student or an adviser looking for the right international study program, or someone who wants to combine the least expense abroad with the most rewards, you'll find the information you need in the resources described below. Asterisks indicate resources of broadest interest. Best introductory resources are indicated with two asterisks. Resources covering more than one country or region are listed under "Worldwide." Addresses of the publishers are listed starting on page 187.

Africa

Beyond Safaris: A Guide to Building People-to-People Ties with Africa. Kevin Danaher. Africa World Press, Inc. 1991. $14.90 postpaid from Global Exchange. Handbook on how to help build and strengthen links between U.S. citizens and grassroots development efforts in Africa. Annotated list of organizations.

* Study in Africa: New Opportunities for American Students. 1997. $20 postpaid from the National Consortium for Study in Africa, c/o African Studies Center, Michigan State Univ., 100 International Ctr., E. Lansing, MI 48824-1035; (517) 353-1700, fax (517) 432-1209; NCSA@pilot.msu.edu, www.isp.msu. edu/AfricanStudies. Outstanding 27-minute video features onsite in-

terviews with Americans studying in several very different countries in Africa.

Australia

Australia Education 1997. Free from Australian Education Office, Australian Embassy, 1601 Massachusetts Ave. NW, Washington, DC 20036; (800) 245-2575 or (202) 332-8285; aeosec@cais.com, www.austudies. org/aeo. Official information on year, semester, and summer programs; undergraduate, graduate, medical, and law degrees; scholarships and financial aid information (for both U.S. and Canadian citizens); internships. Also available from AEO: **Study Abroad Advisor's Guide** (1997-1998 update) and **Guide to Australian Short Courses**.

Good Universities Guide to Australian Universities, International Education. Dean Ashenden and Sandra Milligan. 1996. Available from DW Thorpe, 18 Salmon St., Port Melbourne VIC 3207, Australia; fax (011) 61-8-9388-2841. Inquire about cost. Profiles and rankings of Australian universities.

Studies in Australia 1997/98. 360 pp. Free (postage is payable) from Magabook Pty Ltd., P.O. Box 444, Rockdale NSW 2216, Australia; (011) 61-2-9567-5300, fax 0399; info@magabook.com.au, www.magabook.com.au. Provides information on over 200 educational institutions throughout Australia, their courses and fees.

Study and Travel in Australia: A Directory of Educational Opportunities in Australia for International Students. 1995. Free from Magabook (above). Overview of Australian education system and profiles of secondary and vocational schools. Also available on CD-ROM.

Austria

Austria: Information for Foreign Students; Summer Language Courses for Foreign Students; Summer Courses in Austria; German Language Courses. Annual. Free from the Austrian Cultural Institute, 950 3rd Ave., 20th Fl., New York, NY 10022; (212) 759-5165. Information for foreign students intending to study at an Austrian institution of higher learning.

Canada

Destination Canada: Information for International Students. Free from Canadian Bureau for International Education (CBIE), 220 Laurier Ave. W., Suite 1100, Ottawa, ON, K1P 5Z9 Canada; (613) 237-4820. General information on Canadian education system and tuition fees.

Directory of Canadian Universities. 1996-97 ed. Annual. $47 U.S., $57 other countries. Association of Universities and Colleges of Canada 350 Albert St., Suite 600, Ottawa ON K1R 1B1, Canada; (613) 563-1236, fax (613) 563-9745. Undergraduate and graduate program listings plus summary information on each university.

China

* China Bound: A Guide to Life in the PRC. Anne Thurston. National Academy of Sciences. 1994. 252 pp. $24.95 plus $4 s/h from National Academy Press, 2101 Constitution Ave. NW, Lockbox 285, Washington, DC 20055; (800) 624-6242, fax (202) 334-2451; www.nap.edu. Invaluable for university students, researchers, and teachers.

* Living in China: A Guide to Teaching and Studying in China, Including Taiwan & Hong Kong. Rebecca Weiner, Margaret Murphy, and Albert Li. China Books. 1997. 300 pp. $19.95 from China Books and Periodicals, Inc., 2929 24th St., San Francisco, CA 94110; (415) 282-2994, fax (415) 282-0944; info@chinabooks.com. Contains directories of universities in China and Taiwan that offer study abroad or teaching placement with contact names and particulars. Good for travel planning as well as teaching and studying.

Yale-China Guide to Living, Studying, and Working in the People's Republic of China, Hong Kong, and Taiwan. 1996. The Yale-China Association, Inc., Box 208223, New Haven, CT 06520-8223; ycaffoc@minerva.cis.yale.edu. Profiles selected study abroad and intensive language programs.

Eastern and Central Europe (See also Russia and NIS)

International Research and Exchanges Board (IREX) Grant. Opportunities for U.S.

Scholars. Annual. Free from International Research and Exchanges Board, 1616 H. St., NW, Washington, DC 20006; (202) 628-8188. Descriptions of academic exchange programs and special projects administered by IREX in the Baltic States, Central and Eastern Europe, Mongolia, and the successor states of the former Soviet Union.

REESWEB: Russian and East European Studies, Univ. of Pittsburgh (home page). Free on the World Wide Web at www.pitt.edu/~cjp/rees.html. Karen Ron-destvedt. Continuously updated. No hard copy version available. Click on "Academic Programs and Centers" for listings of language and study abroad programs. Links to other REES area studies centers and information.

Europe (Western)

The EARLS Guide to Language Schools in Europe 1995. Jeremy J. Garson, ed. 312 pp. $23.95 from Cassell, P.O. Box 605, Herndon, VA 21070; fax (703) 661-1501. Covers the 14 most popular European languages, including Russian. The guide profiles selected schools for each major language and gives details of specialized and general courses for children (ages seven and up), teenagers, adults, and business people.

France

Studies in France. Free from the French Cultural Services, 972 5th Ave., New York, NY 10021; (212) 439-1400, fax (212) 439-1455. Basic document outlining various possibilities for study in France, including direct enrollment at French institutions. Also, distributes **French Courses for Foreign Students** (annual list of French universities and language centers offering summer and year courses for foreigners) and **I Am Going to France** (extensive overview of university degree programs).

Studying and Working in France: A Student Guide. Russell Cousins, Ron Hallmark, and Ian Pickup. 1994. 314 pp. $17.95 from Manchester Univ. Press (distributed in the U.S. by St. Martin's Press). Useful, detailed information on directly enrolling in French universities and language courses; one brief chapter on working.

Germany

CDS International. Free brochures from CDS, 330 7th Ave., New York, NY 10001; (212) 497-3500, fax (212) 497-3535; info@cdsintl.org, www.cdsintl.org. Descriptions of paid study/internship programs offered by CDS for high school and college students and professionals.

Information from the German Academic Exchange Service: Scholarships and Funding for Foreign Students, Graduates, and Academics in Germany; Sommerkürse in Bundesrepublik Deutschland (summer language and culture courses); Postgraduate Courses in Germany, Studying in Germany—Universities Study in Germany—College of Art and Music. Each publication revised annually. Available free from the German Academic Exchange Service (DAAD), 950 3rd Ave., 19th Fl., New York, NY 10022; (212) 758-3223, fax (212) 755-5780; daadny@daad.org, www.daad.org. Complete information about studying in Germany from its official exchange office.

India

Studying in India. Published by Indian Council for Cultural Relations. Free from Indian consulates and embassies. Basic information and advice on studies or research in India's numerous educational and scientific institutions.

Universities Handbook (India). 27th ed. Published biannually. $250 airmail from: As-

Study Abroad Resources

sociation of Indian Universities, AIU House, 16 Kotla Marg, New Delhi 110002, India. Overview of courses of studies, faculty members, degrees, library, and research facilities.

Israel

* Complete Guide to the Israel Experience. 1998. Annual. Available from the World Zionist Organization, 110 E. 59th St., 4th Fl., New York, NY 10022; (800) 274-7723, fax (212) 755-4781; usd@netcom.com, www. usd.org. Information on study and volunteer work opportunities in Israel.

Japan

ABC's of Study in Japan. Association of International Education. Free from the Embassy of Japan, 2520 Massachusetts Ave., NW, Washington, DC 20008. Information on study and research at Japanese universities and graduate schools.

Academic Year in Japan. The Japan-U.S. Educational Commission. 1995. 118 pp. $20 plus $5 s/h from NAFSA. Practical guide distilled from reports from U.S. Fulbright scholars studying in Japan.

Directory of Japan Specialists and Japanese Studies Institutions in the U.S. and Canada. Patricia G. Steinhoff, ed. The Japan Foundation. 1995. $50 plus $8 s/h ($12 non-U.S.) from Association for Asian Studies, 1021 E. Huron St., Ann Arbor, MI 48104; (734) 665-2490, fax (734) 665-3801; postmaster@ aasianst.org, www.aasianst.org.

Japanese Colleges and Universities, 1997-99. Association of International Education, Japan (AIEJ) and Monbusho, Ministry of Education, Science, Sports, and Culture. 1997. Biennial. 395 pp. Available to institutions from the Association of International Education, Infor-

mation Center, 4-5-29 Komaba, Meguro-ku, Tokyo 153, Japan; fax (011) 81-3-5454-5236; www.aiej.or.jp. A directory of degree and short-term programs (latter in English) offered by Japanese institutions and open to foreign students. Producted by AIEJ, a government-sponsored organization that assists with exchanges. Available free from AIEJ: **Index of Majors; Scholarships for International Students in Japan; Student Guide to Japan.**

Survey of Japanese Studies in the United States: The 1990s. $15 plus $4 s/h ($5 outside U.S.) from Association for Asian Studies, 1021 E. Huron St., Ann Arbor, MI 48104; (734) 665-2490, fax (734) 665-3801; postmaster@ aasianst.org, www.aasianst.org.

Latin America/Caribbean

After Latin American Studies. A Guide to Graduate Study and Fellowships, Internships, and Employment. Shirley A. Kregar and Annabelle Conroy. 1995. $10 (check payable to Univ. of Pittsburgh) postpaid from: Center for Latin American Studies, 4E04 Forbes Quad, Univ. of Pittsburgh, Pittsburgh, PA 15260; (412) 648-7392, fax (412) 648-2199; clas+@pitt.edu, www.pit.edu/~clas. Packed with useful information for anyone with career or scholarly interests in this region, though most listings are not overseas. Extensive bibliography. Also available, free: *** A Guide to Financial Assistance for Graduate Study, Dissertation Research and Internships for Students in Latin American Studies,** 1996.

Latin America Study Programs Course Guide. 1995. $35 postpaid from WorldStudy, 9841 SW 73rd Court, Miami, FL 33156; (305) 665-5004, fax (305) 665-7085; worldstudy@compuserve.com. Detailed guide to courses offered at selected universities in Argentina, Chile, Colombia, Costa Rica, and Ecuador.

Self-Arranged Homestays

Consider the Rewards of Doing it Yourself

By Marie Gasper

Both pleasant smells—like fresh lavender picked right from the bushes—and unpleasant smells—like car fumes from the busy sidewalk along the beach—take me back to my homestay in Antibes on the French Riviera. Beyond the smells, I hold images in my mind of light-dazzled Monaco, of Cannes at night from a hilltop, and of the rocky drive between Nice and Monaco and its stunning cliffs. I can still taste the sweet pralines from beach vendors and my lunches of egg and tomato sandwiches on crispy French bread, sweet Italian plums, and lots of cool, refreshing Evian.

From my stay I learned a lot about European culture—in living with my host family, in watching people from all over Europe on the beach in Juan-les-Pins, and in the various excursions we took to the Picasso Museum, to old Antibes, and to the homes of my hosts' extended family.

I also learned a lot about myself. There was homesickness and culture shock, of course. There were also unexpected situations and boredom. Looking back on my experience, I see how some of these problems could have been avoided. Even though I had been to Europe on an organized tour the previous summer, I was not really prepared for a homestay.

Making Connections. With proper preparation, staying with a family for a few weeks during the summer can be a very inexpensive and enjoyable way to experience another culture—especially if you set the homestay up yourself. This type of travel and learning experience has all the rewards of an organized program—including culture and language immersion and the chance to form lifelong friendships. At the same time it frees you from set program dates, requirements and activities, and fees. You decide when you want to go, for how long, and what you do while you are there. You also save a lot of money compared to the costs of an organized homestay program.

There are many ways to find a family abroad to stay with for a few weeks over the summer. You probably have more connections abroad than you think:

• A family member might live abroad or have a close friend who has been or is currently abroad who could host you or help find a family they know to host you.

• You may know foreign students at your high school or college, or their host families in the U.S. Your family might want to host a student themselves. Your parents, grandparents, aunts, and uncles may have hosted students or may have been exchange students. Lifelong friendships often form from exchange programs, and perhaps you could arrange a "second-generation" hosting experience at their house.

• Foreign language teachers often encourage their students to write to students from other countries. Maintaining correspondence with a foreign student frequently results in an invitation abroad. After writing to my French pen pal for several years, she and her family invited me to come visit them in Antibes. You can also make an Internet pen pal.

• Most language teachers have studied abroad and may have connections. They might even be able to suggest a possible host family.

• Talk to your teachers. They have often studied or done research abroad, and could help you with connections.

• Talk to members of your church, synagogue, mosque, etc. for any suggestions they might have. For example, if you are Catholic, talk to priests you know; they often have international contacts. The Society of Friends has a network for Quaker travelers.

• Universities often have visiting scholars who might be delighted to discuss your interest in a homestay and might even issue an invitation.

Making Plans. Let's assume that you've written an introductory letter to a possible host family explaining your interest in staying with them and that their reply has been favorable. Now what?

Decide when you should go, and for how long. If you aren't going to an English-speaking country, a minimum of three weeks is recommended (for those with prior knowledge of the language) to become truly acclimated to the environment and language. When I went to Antibes, my pen pal suggested I come for three weeks, but I only spent two. By the end of the second week, I finally was feeling comfortable; I had been immersed in the language long enough that I was speaking it well and at times I was even dreaming in French. I realized what an advantage it would have been to stay longer.

What will you do there? While a self-arranged homestay may be much cheaper than a program, there will be no prearranged tours and museum visits. It's up to you to make it interesting and rewarding. This involves talking to people who have been there before, looking for information in the library, on the Internet, and at travel agencies, and asking your host and your contact (the family member, teacher, priest, or other person who introduced you to your host family) for any information or brochures that they might have.

Are there places you would like to visit, activities you would like to participate in? Your hosts are not professional tour guides, nor should they be expected to be. Your preparation will help you have a greater appreciation for what you see when you get there. Find out if your host family has activities planned for when you are there—so you will be prepared to participate.

What to Expect. The big cost will be the plane ticket. Incidentals will include transportation costs, museum entrance fees, snacks, and spending money. I spent a total of about $1,300 for my two-week stay in Antibes, about $90 per day. In comparison, for the three-week tour I took the previous summer, I spent a total of approximately $3,200, which works out to about $150 per day.

Discuss the costs of room and board with your host family. Do they expect you to contribute? Would you feel more comfortable doing this? Instead of offering money in exchange for your room and board, you might want to offer your services, such as English tutoring for the family's children, cooking, or a few hours of babysitting each week. One thing to keep in mind is that in many organized homestays of a few weeks, families are not issued a stipend to defray the costs of the student living with them. During my homestay in Antibes, I did not pay my host family a stipend for room and board, but I did bring them many gifts to thank them for their hospitality. In addition to bringing your host family gifts, they might appreciate your asking them if there is anything they would like you to bring from the States.

In addition to learning about them, let your host family know about you: this experience should be a cross-cultural exchange for both student and family.

The research you do beforehand and the communication between you and your host family will help all know what to expect when you arrive at your destination. With a confident attitude, a flexible mindset, and plenty of advance preparation for your adventure, you should have an unforgettable time.

Middle East

Directory of Graduate and Undergraduate Programs and Courses in Middle East Studies in the U.S., Canada, and Abroad. 1995. New ed. in process. $5 for 1995 edition from Middle East Studies Association of North America, Univ. of Arizona, 1643 E. Helen St., P.O. Box 210410, Tuscon, AZ 85721; (520) 621-5850, fax (520) 626-9095; www.mesa.edu.

* **Guide to Study Abroad in The Middle East,** AMIDEAST. Available free from web site: www.amideast.org. Study options throughout the Middle East except Israel.

Netherlands

Study in the Netherlands. Annual. 100 pp. Free from NUFFIC, P.O. Box 29777, 2502 LT The Hague, Netherlands; fax (011) 31-70-426-03-99; mknaapen@nufficcs.nl; www.nufficcs.nl. Official directory of all study abroad and degree courses (most taught in English) open to foreign students in the Netherlands. Also available from NUFFIC: **The Education System of the Netherlands** and materials on living in Holland.

Russia and the NIS

* **The Post-Soviet Handbook: A Guide to Grassroots Organizations and Internet Resources in the Newly Independent States.** M. Holt Ruffin, Joan McCarter, and Richard Upjohn. 1998. 416 pp. Univ. of Washington Press. $19.95 plus $4 s/h from Center for Civil Society International, 2929 N.E. Blakely St., Seattle, WA 98105; (206)-523-4755, fax (206) 523-1974; ccsi@u.washington.edu, http://solar.rtd.utk.edu/~ccsi/ccsihome. html. Comprehensive guide to U.S. and host-country organizations involved in "institution building" in the former Soviet Union; many of these assist with academic, professional, and volunteer exchanges. The CCSI web site provides updates.

Scandinavia

Norden: Higher Education and Research in the Nordic Countries. Overview of higher education systems. Available free from the Nordic Council of Ministers, Store Strandstraede 18, DK-1255 Copenhagen K, Denmark; fax (011) 45-33-96-02-02. **Higher Education in Norway; Studying in Denmark; Study in Finland—University Sector; Swedish in Sweden;** and **Courses in English at Swedish Universities** are available from consulates and embassies of each country.

* **Study in Scandinavia 1997-98.** Annual. Free from the American-Scandinavian Foundation, 725 Park Ave., New York, NY 10021; www.amscan.org. Summer and academic year programs offered to high school and college students and anyone interested in Scandinavia. Available on web site.

Spain

Courses for Foreigners in Spain Sponsored by Spanish Institutions; American Programs in Spain; Study in Spain (entering the Spanish university system). Available from the Education Office of Spain, 150 5th Ave., Suite 918, New York, NY 10011.

United Kingdom and Ireland

* **The BUTEX Guide to Undergraduate Study in the U.K.; The BUTEX Guide to Graduate Study in the U.K.** British Universities Transatlantic Exchange Association (BUTEX). Biennial. Each guide approximately 90 pp. Free from BUTEX Secretariat, Int'l. Office, Univ. of Plymouth, Drake Cir-

Study Abroad Resources

cus, Plymouth, Devon PL4 8AA, U.K.; fax (011) 44-1752-232014; butex@plymouth. ac.uk. Guides from a consortium of 80 U.K. universities, with complete contact information.

Graduate Study and Research in the U.K. The British Council, Education Information Service, 3100 Massachusetts Ave., NW, Washington, DC 20008-3600; fax (202) 898-4612; study.uk@bc-washingtondc.sprint. com. Includes program and funding information.

Study Abroad in Ireland. Annual. Free from Irish Tourist Board, 345 Park Ave., 17th Fl., New York, NY 10154; (800) 223-6470. Academic programs and travel-study tours.

Study in Britain. Guide to undergraduate study and for visiting students. Free from British Information Services, 845 3rd Ave., New York, NY 10022; (212) 752-5747, fax (212) 758-5395; www.britain-info.org. Guide to study abroad and undergraduate degree study.

University Courses in Education Open to Students from Overseas 1998/99. £7.50 surface mail from Universities Council for the Education of Teachers, 58 Gordon Square, London WC1H ONT, England. Postgraduate courses in education open to foreigners at British universities.

Young Britain. Annual. Free from British Tourist Authority, 557 W. 57th St., New York, NY 10176-0799. Information on study, work, and accommodations.

Worldwide

** **Academic Year Abroad 1998/99.** Sara J. Steen, ed. $44.95 postpaid from IIE. Authoritative directory of over 2,400 semester and academic year programs offered by U.S. and foreign universities and private organizations. Indexed for internships, practical training, student teaching, adult courses, volunteer work, as well as fields of study. Companion volume to **Vacation Study Abroad** (below).

* **Advisory List of International Educational Travel & Exchange Programs.** 1997. Annual. Council on Standards for International Educational Travel, 212 Henry St., Alexandria, VA 22314; (703) 739-9050, fax (703) 739-9035. $15 ($20 overseas). Lists programs for high school students which adhere to CSIET's standards. The most valuable single resource for prospective exchange students, host families, and schools.

AIFS Advisors' Guides. Various authors and dates. AIFS. Free. Published quarterly by AIFS; (800) 727-AIFS. Study abroad topics include political advocacy, nontraditional programs, promoting ethnic diversity, and reentry.

* **Alternative Travel Directory: The Complete Guide to work, Study and Travel Overseas.** Clay Hubbs and David Cline, editors. Annual. $23.95 postpaid from Transitions Abroad (below). A compilation of directories of resources and programs for educational travel, study abroad, and working abroad which appeared in the previous year's issues of *Transitions Abroad* magazine; useful for nonsubscribers.

Archaeological Fieldwork Opportunities Bulletin. Annual in January. 144 pp. Archaeological Institute of America. $10 for AIA members, $12 non-members plus $4 s/h from Kendall/Hunt Publishing Co., Order Dept., 4050 Westmark Dr., Dubuque, IA 52002; (800) 228-0810; www.kendallhunt.com (orders can be placed via web site). A comprehensive guide to excavations, field schools, and special programs with openings for volunteers, students, and staff worldwide.

Architecture Schools: Special Programs. Martin Moller, ed. 1996. Annual. 60 pp. $12.95 including shipping from the Association of Collegiate Schools of Architecture, 1735 New York Ave., NW, Washington, DC 20006; (202) 785-2324, fax (202) 628-0448. Lists more than 100 study abroad programs sponsored by U.S. collegiate schools of architecture as well as short-term programs in the U.S.

Back in the USA: Reflecting on Your Study Abroad Experience and Putting It to Work. Dawn Kepets. NAFSA: Association of International Educators, 1995. $10 plus $5 s/h from NAFSA. A 34-page booklet which helps returning students put their cross-cultural experiences into perspective.

* Basic Facts on Study Abroad. CIEE, IIE, NAFSA. 1997. Single copies available free from any of the three joint publishers, bulk orders from NAFSA. Basic information for students interested in an educational experience abroad.

Building Bridges: A Manual on Including People with Disabilities in International Exchange Programs. MIUSA. 1998. $30 members, $40 nonmembers. Information on accessibility, resource lists to recruit people with disabilities, and checklists to identify specific needs of participants with disabilities.

Commonwealth Universities Yearbook. Compiled by the Association of Commonwealth Universities. 73rd ed., 1997. Two-volume set. $250 plus $6 s/h from Stockton Press. Detailed profiles of universities in all 34 of the Commonwealth countries, with comprehensive guide to degree programs and a register of 230,000 academic and administrative staff. Available in major libraries.

** Directory of International Internships: A World of Opportunities. Compiled and edited by Charles A. Gliozzo and Vernieka K. Tyson. 4th ed., 1998. Available for $25 post-paid from Michigan State Univ., Attn: International Placement, Career Services & Placement, 113 Student Services Bldg., East Lansing, MI 48824. Based on a wide survey of organizations, this directory describes a variety of experiential educational opportunities—for academic credit, for pay, or simply for experience. Useful indexes. This is the only directory to internships entirely located abroad.

Directory of Work and Study in Developing Countries. Toby Milner. 1997. 256 pp. Vacation Work. $16.95 from Seven Hills. A comprehensive guide to employment, voluntary work, and academic opportunities in developing countries worldwide. Intended for a British audience, it may omit some organizations of interest to Americans.

Guide to Careers and Graduate Education in Peace Studies. 1996. $4.50 from PAWSS, Hampshire College, Amherst, MA 01002. Includes information on internships, fellowships, and relevant organizations.

A Handbook for Creating Your Own Internship in International Development. Overseas Development Network. Updated 1996. $7.95 plus $1.50 s/h. How to arrange a position with an international development organization; evaluate your skills, motivations, and learning objectives; practical advice on financing an internship, living overseas, and returning home.

Home from Home. Central Bureau for Educational Visits and Exchanges. 3rd ed., 1994. $22.95 postpaid from IIE. Compiled from a comprehensive database used by U.K. government agencies, this guide contains details on homestays, home exchanges, hospitality exchanges, and school exchanges worldwide. Includes profiles of organizations by country.

* How to Read Study Abroad Literature. Lily von Klemperer. Reprinted in IIE's **Academic Year Abroad** and **Vacation Study**

Study Abroad Resources

181

Abroad and in NAFSA's **Guide to Education Abroad.** What to look for in ads for a study abroad program.

InterAct Series. Intercultural Press. (Call for prices.) InterActs analyzes how Americans and nationals of other countries see and do things differently and how these differences affect relationships. Countries/areas covered include Japan, Spain, Mexico, Greece, Israel, Eastern Europe, Russia, Australia, China, Thailand, Arab World, the Philippines, and Sub-Saharan Africa.

International Handbook of Universities. 15th ed. 1998. $245 plus $6 s/h. International Association of Universities. Distributed in U.S. and Canada by Stockton Press. Entries for more than 5,700 universities and other institutions of higher education in 170 countries and territories. Complements **Commonwealth Universities Yearbook.**

* **NAFSA's Guide to Education Abroad.** William Hoffa and John Pearson, eds. NAFSA. 2nd ed., 1997. 494 pp. $45 (non-members), $36 (members) plus $5 s/h. An indispensable reference providing both an overview of principles and practices and detailed information and advice for advisers. Includes bibliography on work, study, and travel; case histories; program evaluation guide.

* **Peace Corps and More: 175 Ways to Work, Study, and Travel at Home and Abroad.** Medea Benjamin and Miya Rodolfo-Sioson. 1997. 107 pp. Global Exchange. $8.95. Describes nearly 200 programs that allow anyone to gain Third World experience while promoting the ideas of social justice and sustainable development.

Planning Guides Catalog. Transitions Abroad Publishing, Inc., P.O. Box 1300, Amherst, MA 01004-1300. Free descriptive listing of planning guides on international work, study, living, educational and socially responsible travel.

Resources for Education Abroad. Bill Nolting and Clay Hubbs. NAFSA: Association of International Educators. 1997. 32 pp. Single copies free, $20 for bundles of 50. "Every conceivable resource on study and work abroad is carefully described and annotated." Also available on NAFSA's web site: www.nafsa.org.

Sojourns. 1998. Canadian Bureau for International Education (CBIE). A searchable computer database of 2,000 work and study opportunities worldwide. Contact CBIE for purchase information.

Student's Guide to the Best Study Abroad Programs: Where to Go from Those Who Know! Greg Tannen and Charley Winkler. 1996. 336 pp. Pocket Books/Simon and Schuster, Inc. $12. Begging the question of what program is best for whom, the authors choose 50 college-level programs they consider "best," and provide excerpts from interviews with participants. While the questions posed are good ones, this selection of programs is highly arbitrary; only disparaging references (no titles) to other resources.

Student Travels Magazine. Fall and spring. Free from Council. Covers rail passes, insurance, work and study opportunities abroad, airfares, car rentals, and other services offered by CIEE and Council Travel.

* **Study Abroad 1998: A Guide to Semester, Summer, and Year Abroad Academic Programs.** Peterson's Guides. 1997. Annual. 956 pages. $29.95 plus $6.75 s/h. Over 1,000 pages of detailed information on over 2,000 programs at more than 500 accredited institutions worldwide.

Peterson's Learning Adventures Around the World: A Guide to Learning Vacations and Summer Study Abroad Programs. Peterson's Guides. 1998. Annual. 873 pp. $26.95 plus $6.75 s/h. Detailed information on over 2,000 short-term and summer study abroad programs, language programs, adventure tours, art tours, volunteer programs, environmental expeditions, archaeological tours, and outdoor adventures. Indexed for program type, location, sponsors, and academic credit.

Studying Abroad/Learning Abroad. J. Daniel Hess. Intercultural Press, 1997. 147 pp. $13.95 plus $3 s/h. This new abridged edition of **The Whole World Guide to Culture Learning** provides a guide to cross-cultural analysis and adaptation.

Study Abroad. UNESCO. Vol. 30, 1998-99. $29.95 plus $5 s/h from Bernan Associates, 4611-F Assembly Dr., Lanham, MD 20706; (800) 867-3457; fax (800) 865-3450. Describes approximately 4,000 international study programs and sources of financial assistance in more than 100 countries.

Survival Kit for Overseas Living: For Americans Planning to Live and Work Abroad. L. Robert Kohls. 3rd ed., 1996. $11.95 plus $3 s/h from Intercultural Press. Practical information and insights into the process of cross-cultural adaptation combined with suggestions for getting the most from an overseas experience.

* **Taking Time Off: Inspiring Stories of Students Who Enjoyed Successful Breaks from College and How You Can Plan Your Own.** Colin Hall and Ron Lieber. 1996. 288 pp. The Noonday Press. $12 from Farrar, Strauss, and Giroux, 19 Union Square West, New York, NY 10003. Thoughtful reports of individuals who studied abroad or interned, worked, volunteered, or traveled both abroad and in the U.S. Contains useful directories to other resources.

** **Vacation Study Abroad 1998/99.** Sara J. Steen, ed. Annual. 1997. $39.95 postpaid from IIE. Authoritative guide to over 2,000 summer and short-term study programs sponsored by U.S. and foreign organizations and language schools in over 60 countries. Indexed for internships, practical training, student teaching, adult courses, volunteer service, as well as

fields of study. Companion volume to **Academic Year Abroad.**

What in the World is Going On? A Guide for Canadians Wishing to Work, Volunteer or Study in Other Countries. Alan Cumyn. 5th ed. 260 pp. 1996. CAN$22 including s/h from Canadian Bureau for International Education, 220 Laurier Ave. W, Suite 1100, Ottawa, Ontario K1P 5Z9, Canada; (613) 237-4820. Includes a lengthy list of study and work abroad possibilities, some restricted to Canadian citizens. Indexed by country and field.

* **World Academic Database CD-ROM.** 1997/98. $435 plus $6 s/h from Stockton Press. Combines information from International Handbook of Universities and World List of Universities with additional information from TRACE. Profiles of each country's educational system plus information on 12,000 institutions in over 170 countries. (This and the two publications following are available in major libraries.)

World List of Universities. 21st ed., 1997. $170 plus $6 s/h from Stockton Press. Addresses of over 9,000 institutions of higher education worldwide.

The World of Learning. 46th ed. 1977. Annual. 2,025 pp. Europa Publications Ltd. $445 plus postage from International Publications Service, c/o Taylor & Francis Group, 1900 Frost Rd., Suite 101, Bristol, PA 19007; (215) 785-5800, fax (215) 785-5515; bkorders@tandf.pa.com. This authoritative guide lists over 26,000 institutions of higher education by country, gives names of staff and faculty, and includes information on international organizations involved in education throughout the world.

A World of Options: A Guide to International Exchange, Community Service and Travel for Persons with Disabilities. Christa Bucks. Mobility International USA. 3rd ed., 1996. 659 pp. $35 individuals, $45

Study Abroad Matters

Top 10 Reasons for African Americans to Study Abroad

By Starlett Craig

Before going abroad, I was an armchair traveler. I sat at my desk semester after semester doing my job as an international student adviser. I was fascinated by all the students I met, but I was most impressed with the commitment of the Jamaican teachers. For the first time in their lives they were a minority in another country. Yet they never stopped pursuing their educational goals. Against the odds, year after year, they came and went, each with that prized possession: a bachelors or masters degree in education.

I wondered what enabled them to be so confident in their ability to succeed in the U.S. Over the years, it became apparent to me that no one had told them that they could not be successful. Study abroad was the ultimate means to achieve the best possible education.

The students I advised became my role models. They are also the model I put before all African American students.

Top 10 Reasons to Study Abroad

1. Expand employment opportunities. According to the Spring 1998 edition of the Black Collegian, which highlights job opportunities for the class of 1998, the job outlook reflects the growing importance of internationalization. The top 10 employers are seeking graduates who can think critically and also have a global perspective.

2. Increase your understanding of the world and our society. We can no longer afford to rely on CNN to tell us what we should know about the world. Changing demographics in the U.S. dictate that we must not only acquire a global competence but we must develop an understanding and an appreciation of diversity in our own country. While study abroad can be a vital link to global competence, it is also an integral part of multicultural competence.

(In *Understanding Diversity* Channing Betes writes: "For centuries, American education, business and government have reflected the culture of the vast majority: white people of European descent. By the year 2000, however, we will see big changes: Out of every 100 children in American classrooms, 33 will be children of color.")

3. Broaden your experience. Travel outside the U.S. is an education in itself.

4. Meet people from different backgrounds and cultures. A period of study outside the U.S. enables you to meet students not only from the host country but other nations as well. It is an opportunity to forge international friendships, understand cultural differences, and get rid of old stereotypes.

5. Increase your income potential. Study abroad on your resume definitely gives you a competitive edge. Black Enterprise recently highlighted the importance of the African American presence in the global marketplace and the numerous career and business options for African Americans who set their sights on the big emerging markets (BEMs).

6. Explore new interests. One student went to Mexico to learn the language and have fun. In addition to a Spanish course, she enrolled in modern dance and ballet. At the end of the day, the professor suggested she remain in Mexico and join his dance troupe. After graduat-

ing, she opted to continue to see the world and signed up for Bunac's Work in Britain program.

7. Learn specific skills that are career related. Learn a second language or do an international internship.

8. Gain new insights and outlooks while enjoying new relationships. By living in the country, you get an insider's perspective on the social and political structure of your host country.

9. Take control of your future. While the debate still continues on the preservation of affirmative action, you will be in a position to compete and fully participate in a global, ethnically diverse workforce.

10. Find out what you want to do in life. While taking a semester off from your regular studies may seem a luxury, it is indeed a wonderful opportunity to redefine your career aspirations in the context of your new self-awareness and newly acquired skills. Many students report that study abroad can be a life-changing experience that can also open many new career choices.

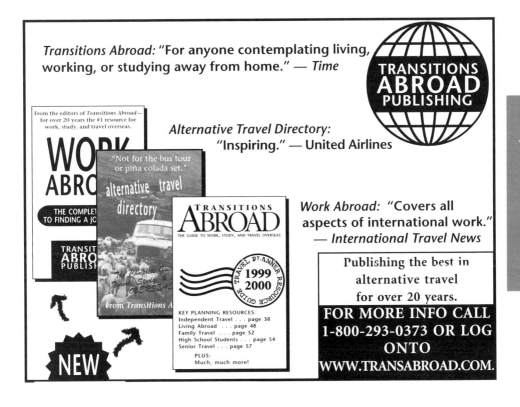

Study Abroad Resources

organizations. A guide to international exchange, study, and volunteer opportunities for people with disabilities.

A Year Between. Central Bureau for Educational Visits and Exchanges. 2nd ed. 1994. $23.95 postpaid from IIE. Designed for young British adults who have a year between high school and college, or during college, and want to explore and learn. Volunteer work, internships service, and study options.

Funding for International Activities

Council Scholarships. Bailey Minority Student Scholarships cover transportation costs for undergraduate students of color to study, work, or volunteer with any Council program. Contact Council at (888) COUNCIL for applications.

* A Student's Guide to Scholarships, Grants, and Funding Publications in International Education and Other Disciplines. Vlada Musayelova, John Harrison, and Charles Gliozzo, eds. 1st ed., April 1997. 79 pp. Published by Michigan State Univ. International Studies and Programs in cooperation with the Michigan State Univ. Library. $5 postpaid ($4 each for 10 copies or more) from: Office of the Dean, International Studies and Programs, Michigan State Univ., East Lansing, MI 48824. Attn: Student Guide. An annotated listing of funding sources with directions on where to go for more information, including web sites.

Fellowships in International Affairs: A Guide to Opportunities in the U.S. and Abroad. Gale Mattox, ed. Women International Security. 1994. 195 pp. $17.95 plus $3.50 s/h from Lynne Rienner Publishers, 1800 30th St., Suite #314, Boulder, CO 80301; (303) 444-6684. Fellowships and grants for students, scholars, and practitioners (most are for graduate and postdoctoral students or professionals).

* Financial Aid for Research and Creative Activities Abroad 1998-2000 Gail Ann Schlachter and R. David Weber. 1997. 345 pp. $30.50 plus $5 s/h from: Reference Service Press, 5000 Windplay Dr., Suite 4, El Dorado Hills, CA 95762; (916) 939-9620, fax (916) 939-9626. Lists over 1,300 funding sources that support research, professional development, teaching assignments, and creative activities (most for graduate students, postdoctorates, professionals).

* Financial Aid for Study Abroad: A Manual for Advisers and Administrators. Stephen Cooper, William W. Cressey, and Nancy K. Stubbs, eds. 1989. $12 (nonmembers) $8 (members) plus $5 s/h from NAFSA. How to use primarily federal sources of financial aid for study abroad programs for undergraduate students and how to utilize this information to help shape institutional policies.

* Financial Aid for Study and Training Abroad 1998-2000 Gail Ann Schlachter and R. David Weber. 1997. 452 pp. $45 plus $5 s/h from Reference Service Press, 5000 Windplay Dr., Suite 4, Eldorado Hills, CA 95762; (916) 939-9620, fax (916) 939-9626. Lists more than 1,000 financial aid opportunities open to Americans at any level. Very useful indexes.

* * Financial Resources for International Study. Sara J. Steen, ed. 1996. IIE. $43.95 postpaid from IIE. Lists funding sources available to support undergraduate, graduate, post-doctorate, and professional learning abroad, from study and research to internships and other work experiences. Very useful indexes, including field of study, internships/work abroad.

Fulbright and Other Grants for Graduate Study Abroad. Annual. Free from IIE, U.S. Student Programs, 809 United Nations Plaza, New York, NY 10017-3580; (212) 984-5330; www.iie.org. Describes grants administered by IIE for study and research abroad.

The International Scholarship Book. Daniel J. Cassidy. 5th ed. 1996. $24.95 paper, $32.95

cloth plus $4 s/h from Prentice-Hall Publishers, 200 Old Tappan Rd., Old Tappan, NJ 07675; (201) 767-5937. Information on private sector funding sources for study abroad compiled by the National Scholarship Research Service.

Money for International Exchange in the Arts. Jane Gullong and Noreen Tomassi, eds. 1992. 126 pp. $16.95 postpaid from IIE. Lists grant sources, exchange programs, and artists residencies and colonies for individuals and organizations in the creative arts.

* **Rotary Foundation Ambassadorial Scholarships.** Information available from The Rotary Foundation of Rotary International, 1 Rotary Center, 1560 Sherman Ave., Evanston, IL 60201-3698; (847) 866-3000, fax (847) 328-8554; www.rotary.org. Information about Rotary scholarships for study abroad, available to undergraduates and graduates who are unrelated to a member of Rotary. Application possible only through local Rotary Clubs.

Key Publishers and Organizations

African-American Institute, 833 U.N. Plaza, New York, NY 10017. Publications on Africa.

American-Scandinavian Foundation Exchange Division, 725 Park Ave., New York, NY 10021; (212) 879-9779, fax (212) 249-3444; asf@amscan.org. Free publications on study, work, and travel in Scandinavia. Offers scholarships.

AMIDEAST, 1730 M St., NW, Washington, DC 20036-4505; (202) 776-9600, (fax (202) 822-6563; inquiries@amideast.org, www. amideast.org. Assists with educational exchanges with Middle East institutions.

British Information Services, 845 3rd Ave., New York, NY 10022; (212) 752-5747, fax

(212) 758-5395; www.britain-info.org. Free fact sheets on study in Britain.

Council on International Education Exchange (CIEE), Publication Dept., 205 E. 42nd St., New York, NY 10017-5706; (888) COUNCIL, fax (212) 822-2699; info@ciee.org, www.ciee.org. Publisher of materials on study, work, and travel abroad.

French Cultural Services, 972 5th Ave., New York, NY 10021; (212) 439-1400, fax (212) 439-1455. Free publications on French higher education and opportunities in France for U.S. students.

German Academic Exchange Service (DAAD), 950 3rd Ave., 19th Fl., New York, NY 10022; (212) 758-3223, fax (212) 755-5780; daad@daad.org, www.daad.org. Information on studying in Germany, including scholarships.

Global Exchange, 2017 Mission St., #303, San Francisco, CA 94110; (800) 497-1994; fax (415) 255-7498; globalexch@igc.org, www. globalexchange.org. Publishes materials on education in and solidarity with developing countries and sponsors fact-finding programs.

Institute of International Education (IIE). IIE Books, Institute of International Education, P.O. Box 371, Annapolis Junction, MD 20701-0371; (800) 445-0443, fax (301) 206-9789; iiebooks@pmds.com. Free catalog. Publisher of authoritative directories for study or teaching abroad and financial aid, and distributor of Central Bureau (U.K.) publications on working abroad. Add $2 s/h per book on orders under $25; $5 per book for orders over $25; or 10 percent for orders over $100 (within the U.S.)

Intercultural Press, P.O. Box 700, Yarmouth, ME 04096; (207) 846-5168, fax (207) 846-5781; interculturalpress@mcimail.com, bookmasters.com/incrt.htm. Leading publisher of books dealing with cross-cultural issues. Free quarterly catalog.

Financing Study Abroad

Rotary Scholarships: One of the Best-Kept Funding Secrets

By Brad Jensen

Although the Rotary Ambassadorial Scholarship Program has sent over 30,000 students overseas since its inception in 1947, it is still one of the best-kept secrets of international educational exchange. True to its motto, "Service Above Self," the Rotary offers a great opportunity for study abroad but seems modest about advertising it.

Rotary's annual expenditure of more than $20 million a year for international exchange programs makes it the largest source of funding for international study. Scholarships are available for high school programs, short-term intensive language study, and academic study abroad. Smaller programs support vocational exchange and university teaching.

The application process is straightforward but it does require some individual initiative. Applications can only be made to local Rotary clubs. It is up to the student to find out when the club meets, who the contact people are, and if the local Rotary has scholarships available for the intended year of application. If you are lucky, your Rotary club will be allowed to select a limited number of applicants, including you, to go on to the district interviews.

It is a good idea to apply to the Rotary in your home town (rather than in your college town) because the first selection occurs at the local level and you will most likely have more competition from other students in a university setting. International students will have to apply from their home country and may not apply for study in their current institution. Each Rotary club sets its own deadline for applications —as early as March and as late as July.

I first learned about the Rotary Scholarships by word of mouth. I was warned ahead of time that I needed to apply far in advance, so I started my search early in the year prior to my intended year of study. The best place to start is with the Rotary's web page (www.rotary. org) to find out where your local club meets and get details about the Rotary Foundation. The web page does not include telephone numbers or contact names, so I called the Chamber of Commerce in my home town and asked for the name of the club's president. Since your local club's president will become your official sponsor, it is a good idea to develop a relationship. Do not show up on the due date and ask for an application without having spoken to the president beforehand.

The main application form is short, straightforward, and easily completed in one or two days. You will also need two recommendations, transcripts, three short essays, and a language competency form. Since I was the first applicant ever from my home town, I had no competition at the local level. My sponsor was satisfied with my application, and she forwarded it on to the district level. In areas where competition is keener, you might be asked to come in for an interview or to give a speech to the local club. In my district, about one in four of the applications receive scholarship awards.

My interviewers seemed most interested in how I would represent Rotary and the U.S. abroad. Rotary is a service organization and my field of study, Information Technology for Development, probably gave me an advantage over other applicants. You are required to name at least five institutions where you would like to study. There seems to be a preference for applicants who are interested in going to universities other than the popular European institutions, particularly those in developing countries.

An important additional advantage of being a Rotary Scholar is the support you receive from the Rotary clubs locally and at your destination country. You are required to give presentations at Rotary clubs, but you should see this more as an opportunity than as a requirement. Many returning scholars that I have talked with mentioned their contacts with Rotary clubs as one of the best experiences of their exchange year. Rotary clubs are found in almost every country, and as a Rotary scholar you have the option of stopping by for a Rotary lunch or dinner almost anywhere in the world.

Rotary Scholarship Options

Ambassadorial Scholarships. The scholarships are generous and cover all expenses. Anyone with at least two years of college or two years of vocational experience may apply for almost any institution in any country. There are no age limits. This is one of the very few scholarships available to undergraduates, so take advantage of it.

The scholarships are for direct enrollment only and may not be used to fund a study abroad program sponsored by a home country institution. The Rotary will not fund unsupervised research, medical internships or residencies, or full-time employment. You can not apply to study in a city, state, or province where you have lived or studied for a period of over six months. You may not be related in any way to any living Rotarian.

Academic Year and Multi-Year. The oldest and largest of the Rotary Scholarship programs, the academic year scholarship, provides up to $23,000 for an academic year abroad. Multi-Year scholarships are available for up to three years—$11,000 per year, $33,000 maximum—and are intended to allow students to complete a degree program at one institution. There are no restrictions on the field of study.

Cultural Ambassadorial Scholarships are available for three or six months of intensive language training and cultural immersion in at an institution assigned by the Rotary Foundation. Scholarships are available for study in the following languages: Arabic, English, French, German, Hebrew, Italian, Japanese, Korean, Mandarin Chinese, Polish, Portuguese, Russian, Spanish, Swahili, and Swedish. Applicants must have competed at least one year of college-level study of their language choice. The awards for 1999-2000 are $10,000 for three months and $17,000 for six months of study.

University Teachers in Developing Countries. Applicant must hold (or have held) a full-time college or university appointment for three or more years but not held any particular title. They must be proficient in the language of the country of choice. Rotarians and non-Rotarians may apply. Candidates must agree to devote at least half of their working time to teaching, but they may also spend time on research or other activities. Awards are available for three to five months ($10,000) or six to 10 months ($20,000).

Vocational Study Scholarship. The vocational scholarship program is a pilot program; only 10-15 scholarships for either $10,000 or $15,000 will be offered per year. Applicants must have at least two years' work experience in their field and be proficient in the language of the country of their choice. Special consideration is given to candidates who plan to study in the fields of food production, literacy, the environment, drug abuse prevention, care for the elderly, or urban peace.

For more information contact your local Rotary club (preferably) or: The Rotary Foundation of Rotary International, 1 Rotary Ctr., 1560 Sherman Ave., Evanston, IL 60201; www.rotary.org.

Mobility International USA (MIUSA), P.O. Box 10767, Eugene, OR 97440; (541) 343-1284 (voice and TDD), fax (541) 343-6812; miusa@igc. Publications and videos on including persons with disabilities in international exchange and travel programs.

NAFSA Publications, P.O. Box 1020, Sewickley, PA 15143; (800) 836-4994, fax (412) 741-0609. Free catalog. Publishers of informational materials, geared toward its professional membership, on study, work, and travel abroad opportunities as well as advising and admissions.

Overseas Development Network, 333 Valencia St., Suite 201, San Francisco, CA 94103; (415) 431-4204, fax (415) 431-5953; odn@igc.org, www.igc.apc.org/odn. Publishes material on work and internships in international development.

Peterson's Guides, 202 Carnegie Center, P.O. Box 2123, Princeton, NJ 08543-2123; (800) 338-3282, fax (609) 243-9150; www.petersons. org. Guides to jobs and careers abroad and study abroad.

Seven Hills Book Distributors, 49 Central Ave., Cincinnati, OH 45202; (800) 545-2005; jenniferb@sevenhillsbooks.com (orders). Carries a wide range of travel books and maps from foreign publishers, including British Tourist Authority and Vacation Work publications.

Stockton Press, 345 Park Ave. S., 10th Fl., New York, NY 10010-1707; (800) 221-2123 or (212) 689-9200, fax (212) 689-9711; grove@ pipeline.com, www.stocktonpress. com. Publishers of directories of universities worldwide.

Superintendent of Documents, U.S. Government Printing Office, Washington, DC 20402; fax (202) 512-2250; gpoaccess@gpo. gov, www.access.gpo.gov. Publishes a wide range of material, including country "Background Notes" series.

Transitions Abroad Publishing, P.O. Box 1300, Amherst, MA 01004-1300; (413) 256-3414; fax (413) 256-0373; info@transabroad. com, www.transabroad.com. The premier publisher of resources for the independent, learning traveler. Publishes the bimonthly magazine *Transitions Abroad*, and the books **The Alternative Travel Directory** and **Work Abroad**.

Vacation Work Publications, 9 Park End St., Oxford OX1 1HJ, England; (011) 44-1865-241978, fax 790885. Publisher of books on work abroad and international careers; distributed in the U.S. by Peterson's Guides and Seven Hills (each has different titles).

Key Web Sites for Education Abroad

Study and Work Abroad Programs

** **www.cie.uci.edu/~cie/iop.** Univ. of California, Irvine. Directories of study, work, research abroad opportunities with links. Concept by Ruth Sylte.

** **www.cie.uci.edu/~cie/world.** "The World at Your Fingertips" by Ruth Sylte. How students and advisers can use the Internet to research options for education abroad.

** **www.iie.org.** Institute of International Education. Online directories of study abroad programs and scholarships. Searchable. Full texts available to IIE members only with password provided by IIE.

** **www.istc.umn.edu.** Univ. of Minnesota ISTC by Richard Warzecha. Searchable directories of study and work abroad and Ann Halpin's volunteer abroad directory. Very comprehensive; excellent search engine.

www.miusa.org. Mobility International's guide to education and travel abroad for people with disabilities.

www.petersons.com. Lacks the detail of Peterson's print study abroad directories.

* www.studyabroad.com is a commercial directory of study and work abroad programs plus good list of language programs.

** www.transabroad.com. Transitions Abroad Publishing's web site features online directories for study, work, and educational travel abroad.

Africa

* www.sas.upenn.edu/African_ Studies/AS.html. African Studies, Univ. of Pennsylvania. Huge number of links. Try a search using phrase "study abroad."

Australia

www.austudies.org/aeo. Australian Education Office: directory and official information on study in Australian universities.

Eastern and Central Europe, NIS

http://clover.slavic.pitt.edu/ ~aatseel. Internships, scholarships, and career information related to Central and E. European studies. Information by the American Association of Teachers of Slavic and East European Languages (AATSEEL).

www.irex.org. IREX: grants and exchanges.

www.pitt.edu/~cjp/rees.html. REESWeb, Univ. of Pittsburg Russian and East European Studies, links and directories (click on "Academic Programs and Centers").

Europe (Western)

www.cdsintl.org. Internship exchanges with Germany.

* www.daad.org. German Academic Exchange Service: comprehensive official information on scholarships and exchanges with Germany.

www.nufficcs.nl. NUFFIC: official information on exchanges with the Netherlands.

Israel

* www.usd.org or www.wzo.org.il. Complete Guide to the Israel Experience (click on "Student Programs"). Study and work opportunities from the World Zionist Organization.

Japan

www.aiej.or.jp. Assn. of International Education (Japan): official information on exchanges with Japan.

www.gwjapan.org/html/jeo.html. Gateway Japan's links to organizations providing study and work opportunities in Japan.

Latin America

www.pitt.edu/~clas. U-Pittsburg Center for Latin American Studies, numerous links with academic area studies centers. Click on "External Financial Assistance" for listings of scholarships and internships.

Middle East

* www.amideast.org. AMIDEAST's Guide to Study Abroad. Click on "Study and Travel in the M.E. and N. Africa" for up-to-date directory.

Russia and the NIS

http://solar.rtd.utk.cdu/~ccsi/ccsihome.html. Center for Civil Society, Univ. of Washington: information on voluntary assistance and NGOs for Russia and Newly Independent States.

United Kingdom and Ireland

www.britain-info.org. British Information Services: official information on study abroad and scholarships for the U.K.

Study Abroad Resources

www.niss.ac.uk/education/butex. BUTEX's directory of graduate study in the U.K. See also www.niss.ac.uk/education/index.html for much more information about higher education in the U.K.

www.thesis.co.uk. Times Higher Education Supplement publishes official rankings of British universities (click on "Statistics" after free registration).

Worldwide

www.edunet.com. The Digital Education Network has a database of international schools in several categories.

www.worldwide.edu. The Worldwide Classroom lists international study programs and has reports from students.

Financial Aid, Grants, Foundations

** www.iie.org. Online and searchable versions of IIE's books **Financial Resources for International Study** and **Funding for United States Study**. Full text available to IIE members only with password provided by IIE.

* www.usia.gov. Information on all Fulbright scholarships (study, research, teaching abroad).

http://arts.endow.gov. National Endowment for the Arts, Guide to International Arts Exchange. Click on "International Partnerships Office."

http://fdncenter.org. Foundation Center: comprehensive information on private-sector grants to institutions, including guides to grants for international programs.

www.finaid.org. National Association of Financial Aid Administrators, includes section on financial aid and scholarships for study abroad.

Sites for International Education Professionals

* BMCPIE-L (a listserv discussion group). Send message "sub BMCPIE-L yourfirstname yourlastname institution" to listserv@uga. cc.uga.edu. NAFSA discussion group for Black and Multicultural Professionals in International Education. Maintained by NAFSA volunteers for advisers interested in promoting greater involvement of minorities in international education.

* www.lexiaintl.org/intled/bookmark.html. An excellent collection of home pages of organizations in international education, ordered by NAFSA categories such as SECUSSA, CAFSS, etc.

* www.uta.fi/FAST. International Education Forum (by John Hopkins): massive information on exchange in Europe, plus worldwide OSEAS advisors database and links to organizations such as the European Association for International Education (EAIE).

** http//listserv.acsu.buffalo.edu/ archives/ secuss-l.html. Searchable archives of SECUSS-L discussions; search possible by topic, author, etc.

** INTER-L (a listserv discussion group). Send message "sub INTER-L yourfirstname yourlastname institution" to listserv@vtvm1. cc.vt.edu. All-NAFSA discussion group maintained by NAFSA-Microsig volunteers. Essential for foreign student advisers. Heavy on immigration regulations.

** SECUSS-L (a listserv discussion group). Send message "sub SECUSS-L yourfirstname yourlastname institution" to listserv@listserv. acsu.buffalo.edu. Discussion group maintained by NAFSA volunteers Art Neisberg, Bill Hoffa, and Katherine Yngve. The best way to plug into the vast knowledge of education abroad professionals.

**TANEWS-L is a free bimonthly electronic newsletter produced by *Transitions Abroad* magazine. TA News provides information about study, work, internship, volunteer, research, and teaching opportunities around the world. Contributions of relevant information are welcome and may be sent to the editor at editor@transabroad.com. To subscribe address an e-mail message to listerv@peach.ease.lsoft.com; in the body of the message, write: SUBSCRIBE TANEWS-L. Do not put anything else in the message body, and send.

** **www.nafsa.org.** NAFSA: Association of International Educators. Homepage of the largest U.S. association for advisers and administrators for education abroad and international students. See the SECUSSA section for a comprehensive annotated bibliography of resources for education abroad.

www.aacrao.com. AACRAO (professional association for credit transfer) home page.

www.cbie.ca. Canadian Bureau for International Education (Canadian counterpart of NAFSA).

For more listings of study abroad resources, and for bargains worldwide, travel tips, and all sorts of information on learning, living, working, and traveling abroad, see *Transitions Abroad* magazine. To order a single copy or a subscription, please call 1-800-293-0373 or visit the *Transitions Abroad* web site at www.transabroad.com.

Study Abroad Resources

ADULT STUDY & TRAVEL PROGRAMS

The following listing of adult study and travel programs was supplied by the organizers in 1998 and is updated in each July/August issue of Transitions Abroad *magazine. Contact the program directors to confirm costs, dates, and other details. Please tell them you read about their programs in this book! Programs based in more than one country or region are listed under "Worldwide."*

Africa

Natural History Safaris. New Horizons offers a variety of educational programs. Wildlife ecology majors study Africa's vast array of wildlife in their natural habitats. Programs for liberal arts students take an in-depth look at the fascinating cultures of various African peoples. Special incentives are offered to professors who lead a group of students from their institution.

Dates: Professor's preference. Cost: Depends on length of program and time of year. Contact: New Horizons Safari Specialists, P.O. Box 5700, Glendale Heights, IL 60139-5700; (630) 893-2545, fax (630) 529-9769; Africa.nh@compuserve.com.

Travel/Study Seminars. Learn from Southern Africans of diverse backgrounds about their economic, political, and social realities. Emphasis on the views of those struggling for justice. Program in South Africa and Namibia. Call for a free listing of upcoming programs.

Dates: Ongoing. Cost: $3,500-$4,400 depending on length of trip. Contact: Center for Global Education, Augsburg College, 2211 Riverside Ave., Box 307TR, Minneapolis, MN 55454; (800) 299-8889, fax (612) 330-1695; globaled@augsburg.edu, www.augsburg.edu/global.

Americas

Cemanahuac Community. Trips are highly educational, with college credit (graduate and undergraduate) available. Countries include Mexico, Belize, Costa Rica, and Guatemala. Focus areas include history, anthropology, archaeology, social issues, cooking and cuisine, and popular and folk art. Previous groups include teachers, social workers, artists, senior citizens, chefs, museum members, alumni groups, and other adult participants. Each trip individually planned.

Dates: Field study trips can be held at any time of the year. Cost: Dependent on requirements and length of the field study trips. Contact: Vivian B. Harvey, Educational Programs Coordinator, Cemanahuac Educational Community, Apartado 5-21, Cuernavaca, Morelos, Mexico; (011) 52-73-18-6407, fax (011) 52-73-12-5418; 74052.2570@compuserve.com, www.cemanahuac.com.

Educational Homestays. Foreign students live with host families and have optional ESL teaching and or excursions. Short- or long-term homestays provided for high school or college students in universities, at language schools, or just visiting America or Canada.

Dates: Any time of year. Cost: $195 and up, depending on program and city. Includes room, meals, airport or bus transfers, plus use of all household amenities and local area supervision. Contact: Connections, John Shephard, 17324 185th Ave. NE, Woodinville, WA 98072; (425) 788-9803, fax (425) 788-2785; www.connections-inc.com.

Argentina

Argentum. Argentum is a Spanish language and culture program for undergraduate, graduate, and high school students. It is part of Universidad Blas Pascal in Córdoba. We offer the total immersion experience. Students can take other classes in literature, Latin American politics, international relations, art, music, economics, and more.

Dates: Semester 1: Mar 16-Jul 4, Semester 2: Aug 4-Nov 27, Intensive: Mid Jun-Jul. Cost: $6,100 for 1 semester, $10,100 for entire year, $2,200 for intensive program, includes tuition and fees, room and board, cultural activities,

and field trips. Contact: Prof. Marta Rosso-O'Laughlin, Argentum, P.O. Box 99, Medford, MA 02153-0099; Tel./fax (781) 488-3552, mrosso@aol.com.

Instituto de Lengua Española (ILEE). Located downtown. Dedicated exclusively to teaching Spanish to foreigners. Small groups and private classes year round. All teachers hold a university degree. Method is intensive, conversation-based. Student body is international, mostly European. Highly recommended worldwide. Ask for individual recommendations in U.S.

Dates: Year round. Cost: Four-week intensive program (20 hours a week) including homestay $1,400; 2 weeks $700. Individual classes: $19 per hour. Registration fee (includes books) $100. Contact: ILEE, Daniel Korman, Director, Lavalle 1619, 7º C, (1048) Buenos Aires, Argentina; Tel./fax (011) 54-1-375-0730. In U.S.: David Babbitz, fax (415) 431-5306; ilee@overnet.com.ar, www.studyabroad.com/ilee.

Australia

Australia—People and Culture. The tour visits Sydney, Canberra, Brisbane, and North Queensland. The program is concerned with how Australians have inscribed meaning onto the oldest of the continents and how they have shaped their worlds. Topics include: Aboriginal dreaming, myths of outlaws and bushrangers, influences of gold rushes, the bush legend, multicultural futures.

Dates: Jul/Aug 1999. Cost: Call for details. Contact: Klaus Grosseholz, Institute of Continuing and TESOL Education, The Univ. of Queensland, Queensland, Australia 4072; (011) 61-7-3365-7575, fax (011) 61-7-3365-7099; klaus@mailbox.uq.edu.au, www.icte.uq.edu.au.

The Adventure Company. The Adventure Company, Australia specializes in top quality adventure and nature tours for individuals and groups. We run a variety of scheduled trips, all of which involve a strong nature element. Many of the tours take place in World Heritage Listed National Parks. Dive with marine researchers, hike the ancient rainforest of far North Queensland, study flora and fauna, or visit Aboriginal art sites dating back 40,000 years.

Dates: Call program for information. Join 1- to 12-day trips. Cost: $50-$1,500, including all trips departing from Cairns. Contact: Gary Hill, The Adventure Company, Australia, P.O. Box 5740, Cairns, Queensland 4870, Australia; (011) 61-7-4051-4777, fax (011) 61-7-4051-4888; adventures@adventures.com.au, www.adventures.com.au. In U.S.: (800) 388-7333.

Belgium

Stavelot Excavation. Excavation of an 11th century Ottonian abbey church in province of Liège destroyed after the French Revolution. Introduction to archaeological methods and fieldwork, including excavation work, drawing, photography, and artifacts registration. Program provides lodging, meals, and insurance. Participants should take a sleeping bag and air mattress. No fares or wages paid.

Dates: TBA. Cost: BEF1,000, no matter how long volunteer stays (1998). Contact: Brigitte Evrard-Neuray, Centre Stavelotain D'Archeologie, Abbaye de Stavelot, 4970 Stavelot, Belgium; Tel./fax (011) 32-80-86-41-13.

Brazil

Fiber Arts/Folk Crafts Tour. Travel/study tour that reflects Brazil's heritage. Attend a hands-on tapestry workshop or special lace program. Learn the registered Brazilian stitch. Rio's 'Folclorico' museum's extensive 'Little Clay People' collection, specialty shops for col-

lectibles, sugar loaf. The baroque magic of Congonhas' soapstone prophets. Amazonas' Marajoara Artifacts, and the Wai Wai tribe's magnificent plumage art.

Dates: 16 days and nights; May 12-29, 1999, Dec 3-19 (1998). Cost: $2,867 per person. Twin '98 tour cost. Contact: Brazilian Views, Inc., 201 E. 66th St., 21G, New York, NY 10021-6480; (212) 472-9530.

Canada

Ecole de français, Montréal. For the last 50 years, the Ecole de français has offered courses in French as a second language to students from around the world. The Ecole is continually improving its programs to meet the changing needs of its students. Choose from Oral and Written Communication French (beginner to advanced), Workshop on Teaching French as a Second Language (for teachers), Contemporary Québec Culture (for advanced students), Business French (intermediate to advanced students).

Dates: Spring: May 18-Jun 10; Summer 1: Jul 5-23; Summer 2: Jul 26-Aug 13; Fall: Sep 13-Dec 10; Winter 2000: Jan 10-Apr 7. Cost: Spring, Summer: (3 weeks, 60 hours) CAN$495; Summer: (3 weeks, 45 hours) CAN$390; Fall/Winter: (12 weeks, 240 hours) CAN$1,495. Prices subject to change. Contact: Serge Bienvenu, Coordinator, Ecole de français, Faculté de l'education permanente, Université de Montréal, C.P. 6128, succursale Centre-ville, Montréal, PQ, H3C 3J7, Canada; (514) 343-6090, fax (514) 343-2430; infolang @fep.umontreal.ca, www.fcp.umontreal.ca/langues/index.html.

English Language Centre, Victoria. The English Language Centre at the Univ. of Victoria is known throughout the world for its high standards of English language instruction. Established in 1970, the ELC offers quality language programs aimed at international and Canadian students wishing to improve their

Adult Travel & Study Programs

English language and cross-cultural skills for personal, professional, and academic purposes. Students from all over the world have attended the ELC. The 12-week Intensive English Language Program is offered 3 times each year, and a series of spring and summer programs are available. UVic is a mid-sized university with 17,000 students and is a friendly and comfortable place to study. It has been rated among the top 3 universities in Canada for the past 5 years.

Dates: Apr 9-Jul 2; Sep 10-Dec 2 (1998); Jan 7-Mar 31 (1999). Cost: Tuition is $2,950 per program. Contact: Ms. Maxine Macgillivray, Co-Director, English Language Centre, Univ. of Victoria, P.O. Box 1700, Victoria, BC V8W 2Y2, Canada; (250) 721-8469, fax (250) 721-6276; mmacgillivray@uvcs.uvic.ca, www.uvcs.uvic.ca/elc.

Intensive English Program. Located in the safe and beautiful city of Vancouver, Canada, we offer a 6-level intensive English program with a wide variety of communication or academic preparation courses. Modern new classrooms, exceptional teachers, organized social activities; homestay, dormitory, and airport welcome available.

Dates: Jan 4-Mar 26, Apr 6-May 25, Jul 5-Aug 27, Sep 20-Dec 10. Cost: Call for details. Contact: Carolyn Foo, the Univ. of British Columbia English Language Institute, 2121 West Mall, Vancouver, BC, V6T 124 Canada; (604) 822-1550, fax (604) 822-1599; eli@cce.ubc.ca, www.eli.cstudies.ubc.ca.

Language and Cultural Studies in Montréal. 1) Semi Intensive French—a theme based program of 3 hours of study a day. 2) Learning Vacations—study the language and culture of Québec while living in Montréal. Take part in French classes in the afternoon with excursions and cultural activities throughout the day.

Dates: 1) Offered from Apr-Nov. Classes begin every 2 weeks (8 students maximum). 2) Available upon request. Groups of 6 or more required. Cost: 1) $435 for 4 weeks, 60 hours, includes access to CD Rom language lab, e-mail and internet; homestay and other accommodations. 2) $3,250 for 9 days all inclusive. Contact: Y&N - Language and Cultural Studies, 404 Saint Pierre, Suite 201, Montréal, PQ, H2Y 2M2 Canada; (514) 840-7228, fax (514) 840-7111; info@languageco.com, www.languageco.com.

Language Studies Canada Montréal. Using a multi-skill approach students develop effective communication skills in French. Classes are informative, practical, and enjoyable. Seven levels of 4 weeks each: intensive, 6 hours daily or semi-intensive, 4 hours daily. Maximum of 14 students per class. Audio-visual equipment, multi-media Student Resource Center. Optional activity program. Homestay and alternate accommodations available.

Dates: Year round. Two-week courses begin any Monday. Other programs offered: one-to-one instruction, year round; 2-week. Group 5 executive courses, Jun-Oct; Summer Language Adventure (13- to 17-year-olds), 2-9 weeks in Jul and Aug. Cost: Two weeks intensive program $545 (1998); homestay accommodations $365 (1998). Cost of other services available upon request. Contact: Language Studies Canada Montréal, 1450 City Councillors, Montréal, PQ, H3A 2E6, Canada; (514) 499-9911, fax (514) 499-0332.

Queen's Univ. School of English. The Queen's Univ. School of English offers 5- and 12-week courses year round at one of Canada's oldest and best-known universities in an almost totally English-speaking community. Students have the option of living in a University residence with monitors, in a homestay, or in University cooperative housing. The English Only Rule is strictly enforced.

Dates: Jan 6-Apr 9, May 5-Aug 6, May 17-Jun 18, July 5-Aug 6, Sep 8-Dec 10. Cost: International students: $2,550 for 12 weeks; $1,275 for 5 weeks, plus mandatory health insurance (price varies). Contact: Mrs. Eleanor

Rogers, Director, The School of English, Queen's Univ., Kingston, ON K7L 3N6, Canada; (613) 533-2472, fax (613) 533-6809; soe@post.queensu.ca, www.queensu.ca/soe.

Whale Research Expeditions. Participate in research with experienced biologists from Minigan Island Study and observe the blue, fin, humpback, and minke whales on 8-meter inflatables. Studying whales involves collection of data and long days at sea.

Dates: Jun 15-Sep 30. Cost: CAN$1,979 per a 7-day session all included. With flight from Montreal. Contact: Louise at (514) 948-3669, fax (514) 948-1131; mieshipolari@videotron. ca (whalenet under affiliates).

Working Landscape Micro-Tours. Short, educational tours that introduce participants to community-based, environmentally sustainable economic models being explored in Cape Breton as alternatives to the traditional resource-based industrial economy. Individuals and/or small groups stay in local bed and breakfast and enjoy the spectacular beauty of Cape Breton.

Dates: Jun-Sep. Cost: CAN$1,259 (3 days); CAN$1,950 (5 days). Contact: Working Landscape Micro-Tours, R.R. #4, Baddeck, NS B0E 1B0, Canada; (902) 929-2063, fax (902) 929-2348; rschneid@sparc.uccb.ns.ca.

Central America

Global Awareness Through Experience (GATE). GATE offers alternative tourism through programs in Central America (Guatemala, El Salvador), Mexico, and Central Europe. Participants connect with Third World people in face-to-face dialogue to explore social, political, economic, religious, and cultural issues. Mutual learning happens between GATE participants and the indigenous people.

Dates: Various open groups. Special groups also welcome. Cost: $700 (Mexico) to $1,600 (Europe) plus airfare. Contact: Beverly

Budelier, GATE, 912 Market St., La Crosse, WI 54601; (608) 791-5283, fax (608) 782-6301; gateusa@juno.com, www.fspa.org (choose Missions, then GATE).

Travel/Study Seminars. Learn from Central Americans of diverse backgrounds about their economic, political, and social realities. Emphasis on the views of those struggling for justice. Programming in El Salvador, Guatemala, and Nicaragua. Call for a free listing of upcoming programs.

Dates: Ongoing. Cost: $1,500-$2,500 depending on length of trip. Contact: Center for Global Education, Augsburg College, 2211 Riverside Ave., Box 307TR, Minneapolis, MN 55454; (800) 299-8889, fax (612) 330-1695; globaled@augsburg.edu, www.augsburg.edu/global.

Costa Rica

COSI (Costa Rica Spanish Institute). COSI offers high quality instruction at reasonable prices. We offer classes in San José and at a beautiful beach. Costa Rican owned and very efficiently operated.

Dates: Year round. Cost: Inquire. Contact: Marvin Lopez, COSI, P.O. Box 1366-2050, San Pedro, San José, Costa Rica; (011) 506-253-9272, fax (011) 506-253-2117. From U.S. (800) 771-5184; cosicr@sol.racsa.co.cr.

Costa Rican Language Academy. Costa Rican-owned and -operated language school offers first-rate Spanish instruction in a warm and friendly environment. Teachers with university degrees. Small groups or private classes. Included free in the programs are airport transportation, coffee and natural refreshments, excursions, Latin dance, Costa Rican cooking, music, and conversation classes to provide students with complete cultural immersion.

Dates: Year round (start anytime). Cost: $135 per week or $220 per week for program with homestay. All other activities and services included at no additional cost. Contact: Costa Rican Language Academy, P.O. Box 336-2070, San José, Costa Rica; (011) 506-221-1624 or 233-8914 or 233-8938, fax (011) 506-233-8670. In the U.S.: (800) 854-6057; crlang@sol.racsa.co.cr., www.crlang. co.cr/index.html.

Intensive Spanish Immersion. The Institute for Central American Development Studies (ICADS) offers 30-day programs of intensive Spanish languages—4 1/2 hours daily, 5 days a week. Small classes (4 students or less) geared to individual needs. Extra lectures and activities emphasize environmental issues, women's studies, economic development, and human rights. ICADS offers optional afternoon internship placements in grassroots organizations. Supportive informal learning environment. Homestays and field trips.

Dates: Programs begin first day Monday of each month. Cost: One month $1,225. Includes airport pick-up, classes, books, homestay, meals, laundry, lectures, activities, field trips, and internship placements (10% discount after first month). Contact: Sandra Kinghorn, Ph.D., Director, ICADS, Dept. 826, P.O. Box 025216, Miami, FL 33102-5216; or ICADS, Apartado 3-2070, Sabanilla, San Jose, Costa Rica; fax (011) 506-234-1337; icads@netbox.com, www.icadscr.com.

Learn Spanish While Volunteering. Assist with the training of Costa Rican public school teachers in ESL and computers. Assist local health clinic, social service agencies, and environmental projects. Enjoy learning Spanish in the morning, volunteer work in the afternoon/evening. Spanish classes of 2-5 students plus group learning activities; conversations with middle-class homestay families (1 student per family). Homestays and most volunteer projects are within walking distance of school in small town near the capital, San Jose.

Dates: Year round, all levels. Classes begin every Monday, volunteer program is continuous. Cost: $345 per week for 28 hours of classes and

group activities plus Costa Rican dance and cooking classes. Includes tuition, 3 meals per day, 7 days per week, homestay, laundry, all materials, and airport transportation. $25 one-time registration fee; $100 additional one-time registration fee for volunteer program. Contact: Susan Shores, Registrar, Latin American Language Center, 7485 Rush River Dr., Suite 710-123, Sacramento, CA 95831; (916) 447-0938, fax (916) 428-9542; lalc@madre.com.

Learn About Tropical Plants. Two-week courses on field identification of trees and shrubs (Dendrology) offered every year in Spanish (March) and in English (June-July). Please ask for opinions by former participants.

Dates: 1999: Mar 8-20 (Spanish); Jun 21-Jul 3 (English); 2000: Mar 13-25 (Spanish); Jun 26-Jul 8, 2000 (English). Cost: Each course is $1,800. Includes fees, material, lodging and meals during 15 days, insurance, course-related local transport, farewell dinner, and certificate of attendance. Contact: Humberto Jiménez Saa, TSC, Apdo. 8-3870-1000, San José, Costa Rica; fax (011) 506-253-4963; hjimenez@sol.racsa.co.cr; www.geocities.com/rainforest/9148.

Monteverde Studios of the Arts. "Where Craft and Culture Meet." Participate in week-long classes in ceramics, painting and drawing, textiles, stained glass, jewelry, basketry, woodworking, dance, photography, storytelling, cooking, also personality studies. Work in teachers' studios and share in the luxuriant surroundings of the rainforest. Classes available in Spanish or English.

Dates: Jan 18-Apr 5. Cost: Room and board, tuition $435-$565. Contact: Sybil Terres Gilmar, Monteverde Studios of the Arts, P.O. Box 766, Narberth, PA 19072; (800) 370-3331; mstudios@sol.racsa.co.cr, www.mvstudios.com.

Rainforest Study Program. Ten-day learning trip includes: Arial Tram, rainforest lodge, guided rainforest hikes (emphasis on natural history), birding, exotic flowers, insect observation, horseback riding, tree climbing, tours

Writing Courses in Britain
Hone Your Skills with Like-Minded Folk
By Chris Grant-Bear

Throughout the British Isles one can find short courses on creative writing where one's creativity and craft can be developed just from being with a group of like-minded folk, all intent on mastering the skills and craftsmanship of writing.

The choice of venue and course content is extensive. Send for full details from the centers below:

Dragon Writer's Courses. 17th-century coaching inn in Wales. Practical grounding in writing skills. The Dragon Hotel, Montgomery, Powys SY15 6AA, Wales; Tel./fax (011) 44-686-668359.

The Univ. of Edinburgh. Courses include introduction, plays, short stories. Alison Wightman, Centre for Continuing Education, 11 Buccleuch Pl., Edinburgh EH 8 9 LW, Scotland; (011) 44-131-650-4400, fax (011) 44-131-667-6097.

Week or weekend courses in Cornwall in a seaside hotel are taught by published writers. Brochure from: Helen Jagger Wood, **Creative Arts Courses**, North Cornwall, Garmoe Cottage, Trefew Rd., Camelford, N. Cornwall PL32 9TP, England; (011) 44-18-4021-2161.

Weekend courses and writers' workshops are held at **Missenden Abbey.** Contact: Elisabeth Cooper, Missenden Abbey, Great Missenden, Bucks, HP 16 OBD, England; Tel. (011) 44-1494- 890295/6.

A rural setting in a converted farm building on 600 acres of Dorset countryside is the perfect setting for creative work. Courses on fiction and playwriting. **The Kingcombe Trust**, Lower Kingcombe, Toller Porcorum, Dorchester, Dorset DT2 OEQ, England; (011) 44-1300-320684.

A six-day writers school is held in Swanwick, Derbyshire each summer. Around 300 writers attend courses at all levels and for all interests. Send SASE to: Brenda Courtie, **The New Vicarage**, Woodford Halse, Daventry NN11 3RE, England.

Fen Farm is a 17th-century farmhouse in Suffolk where residential courses are run year round. Groups of eight or nine writers work with established writers, producers, and/or publishers on the materials they bring along to the course. Full details from: Peter Worboyes, 10 Angel Hill, Bury St. Edmunds, Suffolk IP33 1UZ, England; (011) 44-1284-753110.

Arvon runs five-day residential writing courses at a variety of locations throughout the British Isles for beginning writers and established authors. Small groups work together in workshops and tutorials in a positive environment to share work and take writing seriously. Arvon, England; (011) 44-1422-843714.

The Writing Magazine, published monthly, updates lists of writing centers and workshops throughout the British Isles and Europe. Overseas subscription details from: David St. John Thomas, The Editor, Writers News LTD, P.O. Box 4, Nairn IV 12 4HU, Scotland; (011) 44-1667-454441, fax (011) 44-1667-454401.

Adult Travel & Study Programs

of small and large farms in rainforest ecosystem, beach day, volcano, city tours, lectures, discussions, full-time bilingual guides, and more.

Dates: Apr-Nov. Arranged individually with each group. Cost: $1,170-$1,400. Group reservations only (15-24). One free leader for every 9 enrolled. Includes all expenses and taxes in Costa Rica. Airfare not included. Contact: Karin Stein, Forum International Univ., 850 Juniper Ave., Kellogg, IA 50135; Tel./fax (515) 236-3894 or (925) 671-2900; costari@netins.net, www.selvabananito.com/schools.html.

Sea Turtle Restoration Project. Patrolling tropical beach for nesting female olive ridley turtles, spotting their nests, removing the eggs for relocation to a protected hatchery, releasing hatchlings when they emerge. Also participation in local community education programs and assisting a start-up program in indigenous territory. The location this year is Punta Banco, on the Pacific coast of southern Costa Rica.

Dates: Jul-Dec. Cost: $1,325 includes food, lodging, and transportation. Contact: Jennifer Krill, Sea Turtle Restoration Project, P.O. Box 400, Forest Knolls, CA 94933; www.earthisland.org/projectDirect.cfm.

Spanish Language. Intercultura Language Institute offers intensive Spanish and homestays with selected Costa Rican families. Academic credit available (with prior notice). Additional free cultural activities: Latin-dance, music, theater, cinema, cooking. Weekend excursions to volcanoes, beaches, rainforest. Volunteer opportunities in social, environmental, and political organizations. Beach campus: optional 1 week per month, study on Pacific coast.

Dates: Year round. Cost: $1,045 per month (shorter stays available). Contact: Laura Ellington, Codirector, Intercultura Costa Rica, Apdo. 1952-3000, Heredia, Costa Rica; (011) 506-260-8480, Tel./fax (011) 506-260-9243; intercul@sol.racsa.co.cr, www.alphaluz.com/intercultura.

Cuba

Cuban Organic Farming Delegation. Delegation provides members with a broad view of advances in sustainable agriculture in Cuba. Focus on: research and development, education, production, and policy. Offers access to leaders in the sustainable agriculture movement and high-level policy officials.

Dates: Feb. 20-28. Cost: Approx. $1,350 from Cancun. Includes meals, transportation, interpreters, hotel. Contact: Food First, 398 60th St., Oakland, CA 94618; (510) 654-4400, fax (510) 654-4551; foodfirst@foodfirst.org, www.foodfirst.org.

Ecuador

Academia Latinoamericana. Ecuador's top private Spanish language institute in former diplomat's mansion with gardens, swimming pool, hot tub, in lovely residential area of Quito. Small group classes, executive courses, high school groups, exclusive "SierrAzul Cloud Forest" extension program. Select host family accommodation. Excursions to haciendas, Indian markets, other activities. USA college credit and internships available.

Dates: Year round. Cost: $296 per week. Includes 20 hours of one-on-one lessons, 7 days with host family, 2 meals per day, transfer, services at the school and teaching material. Contact: Suzanne S. Bell, Admissions Director, USA/International, 640 East 3990 South, Suite E, Salt Lake City, UT, 84107; (801) 268-4608, fax (801) 265-9156; academia@juno.com, delco@spanish.com.ec, www.ecua.net.ec/academia.

Spanish in the Middle of the World. Spanish Institute offers the opportunity of learning the language and culture while enjoying the wonderful weather and landscape of 0 degrees latitude. One-on-one and group courses to fit all needs. Accommodation facilities in Ecuadorian homes or dormitories. English teachers may have a job while learning a second language.

Dates: Classes start on Monday year round (except holidays). Cost: $5 per hour includes texts, workbook, language lab, teaching aids, completion diploma. Contact: Benedict Schools of Languages, Edmundo Chiriboga, 713 Y Jorge Paez, Quito, Ecuador; fax (011) 593-2-432729, (011) 593-2-462972; benedict @accessinter.net, www.virtualsystems.com.ec/ benedictq.

Europe

Adult Music Courses. A wide variety of musical activity with classes catering to both practiced and less experienced players. From early music to jazz, from keyboards to vocal and choral work, from chamber music to orchestra.

Dates: Year round. Cost: Call for details. Contact: Helen Marshall, Music Manager, Benslow Music Trust, Little Benslow Hills, Hitchin, Herts SG4 9RB1, U.K; (011) 44-1462-459-446, fax (011) 44-1462-440-171.

Educational Vacations in Florence. Special programs for groups (minimum 5 participants): lectures on art history, Italian music, Italian culture; museum visits; field trips and walking tours; cooking classes and wine appreciation. Available also for individuals.

Dates: Year round. Cost: From $1,200 per week including accommodations and meals. Contact: Dr. Gabriella Ganugi, Lorenzo de'Medici, Via Faenza 43, 50123 Florence, Italy; (011) 39-55-287360, fax (011) 39-55-2398920; ldm@dada.it, www.dada.it/ldm.

Fagottissimo. Bassoon Ensemble and Introduction into maintenance and repair of bassoons with Walter Hermann Sallagar, professional player and teacher, also member Napbirt and Fox team. Participation limited.

Dates: Jul 11-Jul 18. Cost: $700 inclusive price (room and board). Contact: Walter H.

Sallagar, 'Eichendorff's Ruh,' A-2564 Furth, Austria. Fax to Vienna (011) 43-1-71-41710.

ICCE Language and Culture Programs. Learn a language in the country of your host—France, Spain, Italy (also Japan and China). Summer programs and personalized year round sessions. All levels, high school to senior citizens. Academic credit and noncredit. Homestays to deluxe hotels.

Dates: Spring, Summer, Winter sessions; short-term monthly dates. Cost: From $2,549 (2 weeks). Includes roundtrip airfare and transfers, tuition, meals, accommodations, and sightseeing excursions. Contact: Dr. Stanley I. Gochman, Program Coordinator, International Council for Cultural Exchange, 5 Bellport Ln., Bellport, NY 11713; Tel./fax (516) 286-5228.

Impressionist Gardens Tours. Tours of English, French, and Spanish gardens studying the history, design, and plantings with relevant buildings. Groups restricted to 30 people.

Dates: Aug 7-10 (1998). Cost: £334 (1998) includes U.K./France Travel; half-board, fees. Contact: Caroline Holmes, Gardens Millennium to Millennium, Denham Endfarm, Bury St., Edmunds 1P29 5EE, England; Tel./fax (011) 44-1284-810653.

Issue-Specific Travel Courses. Visit 1 to 4 cities. Topics include International Business and Economics, Comparative Education, Historical Literature, Social Service Systems, and other crosscultural studies. Emphasis on personal interaction between students and European professionals and providing a holistic cultural experience. Two- to 5-week programs. Three to 6 credit hours—undergraduate, graduate, or audit basis—through the Univ. of Missouri-Kansas City.

Dates: Early Summer. Cost: Approx. $2,000 (does not include airfare). Contact: People to People International, Collegiate and Professional Studies Abroad, 501 E. Armour Blvd., Kansas City, MO 64109-2200;

Adult Travel & Study Programs

(816) 531-4701, fax (816) 561-7502; collegiate@ptpi.org, www.ptpi.orgstudyabroad.

Language, Arts, and Sports. Active learning vacations. French, Spanish, Italian; cooking, painting, drawing, photography workshops. Combine programs or interests in one vacation. Learn French and sailing or ski; Spanish and golf. Bicycle tours with language lessons. We match individual needs and interests with programs and options: family stay, residence, apartment, hotel; intensive to total immersion (no English); group or one-on-one (including study in and live in your teacher's home).

Dates: Programs run from 1 week to months. Cost: Include room and board, tuition. Contact: Mary Ann Puglisi, eduVacations, 1431 21st St. NW, Suite 302, Washington, DC 20036; (202) 857-8384, fax (202) 835-3756.

Skyros Holistic Holidays. We offer over 200 courses on the beautiful Greek island of Skyros. Courses range from yoga, T'ai Chi, massage, personal development, art, creative writing, dance to drumming, voicework, drama and bodywork. Delicious food and spectacular surroundings.

Dates: Jan.-Dec. Cost: $1,150. Contact: Helen Akif, Skyros, 72 Prince of Wales Rd., London NW5 3NE, U.K.; (011) 171-267-4424; fax (011) 171-284-3063; skyros@easynet.co.uk, www.skyros.com.

France

France Langue Schools in Paris/Nice. Delightful private language institute blocks from the Champs Elysees, Paris, or the sunny beaches of the French Riviera. Year round, all ages and levels. Specialty classes: commerce, cuisine, business, au pair, tourism, DELE, DALF. Custom-designed programs for teachers and high school groups. University credit available. Family stay, residence halls, apartments, or hotel accommodations.

Dates: Contact for information. Cost: Contact for information. Contact: Mr. De Poly, France Langue, 22 ave. Notre Dame, 06000 Nice, France; (011) 33-4-93-13-7888, fax (011) 33-4-93-13-7889; frlang_n@club-internet.fr, www.france_langue.fr.

French and Cookery in a Château. Live and study in 18th-century château with relaxed, convivial atmosphere. Residential French language and Provençal cooking for adults. Comfortable single/twin and shared rooms. Good food and wine at the heart of France's loveliest areas, near Lyon.

Dates: Two weeks in Feb, and every Sunday May-Nov. Cost: From $800 full board and classes in Château. Contact: Michael Giammarella in U.S.: (800) 484-1234 ext 0096 or Ecole des Trois Ponts, Château de Matel, 42300 Roanne, France; (011) 33-477-70-80-01, fax (011) 33-477-71-5300; info@3ponts.edu, www.3ponts.edu.

French Language Immersion. International institute on Mediterranean coast. Short- and long-term French courses. Modern air-conditioned premises in large park. Restaurant with terrace. Top-quality homestay, hotels, apartments. Minimum age 17, maximum unlimited. Students, business people, employees, airline staff, retired people. Charming medieval town linking Provence to Riviera, lively marina, unspoiled beaches.

Dates: Year round. Cost: From FF1,200 per week (tuition). Contact: Institut ELFCA, 66 ave. du Toulon, 83400 Hyeres, France; (011) 33-4-94-65-03-31, fax (011) 33-4-94-65-81-22; elfca@elfca.com, www.elfca.com.

French Language Learning Vacations. Learn French while discovering the châteaux of the Loire Valley, the secrets of Provence, or the sandy beaches of the Mediterranean. Our programs are designed for independent travelers sharing a passion for the French culture and lifestyle. We offer a choice of locations in Tours, Aix-en-Provence, Montpellier, Paris, or Nice.

Dates: Two or more weeks year round. Cost: Two-week packages range from $820-$1,200. Contact: Jim Pondolfino, French-American Exchange, 111 Roberts Court, Box 7, Alexandria, VA 22314; (800) 995-5087, fax (703) 549-2865; faetours@erols.com, www.faetours.com.

French Language Programs in France. Dr. Janice Ovadiah offers a menu of French study programs for many needs, budgets, and durations. Accommodations include homestays, hotels, college campuses, or chateau lodgings. Participants may choose to study in accredited schools in Paris, on the French Riviera, or other attractive French cities. French-language programs and 1-week courses in French cuisine are available during the summer and throughout the year. Programs cater to both general students and business professionals for leisure or intensive study.

Dates: Year round. Cost: Rates vary according to length of program. Contact: Dr. Janice E. Ovadiah, 303 W. 66 St., New York, NY 10023; (212) 724-5823, fax (212) 496-2264; jovadiah@aol.com.

French Study in Château. Study French while staying in a chateau in the Loire Valley with owners' family. Beginners: 25 hours of lessons per week. Very small classes. Advanced: Special Conversation course (22 hours in class) plus introduction to French culture cooking and wine. All excursions guided and transport included. U.S. reference and information available.

Dates: Year round. Every 1st and 3rd week of the month. Cost: $500 per week beginners' course; $800 per week advanced. Full board, lessons, excursions. Contact: Mme. Tartiere, Chateau Bois Minhy, Chemery, France; (011) 33-2-54795101, fax (011) 33-2-57790626.

French Traditional Cuisine Course. One-week course in the rural French village of Anjou (350 kms southwest of Paris) to learn main dishes of French cuisine. Also shopping at outdoor markets, vineyards, and farms.

Dates: One-week program ends Sep 27. Cost: $1,250 (class and full board). Contact: Jacqueline Tilkin, 49310 Les Cerqeux-Sous-Passavant, France; fax (011) 33-2-41-59-55-57.

Horizons Art and Travel. Provence evokes images of grape vines, olives, sun-filled landscapes, and a profusion of antique monuments-it is all this and more. A week in the stunning hilltop village of Venasque, ringed by Roman monuments, sleepy wine villages, red ocher cliffs and mountains. Lodging in a charming bed and breakfast. Workshops include Painting, Photography, Fabric Printing, Faux Finishes.

Dates: Apr 9-16, Sep 25-Oct 1. Cost: $1,425 (lodging, all meals except 1 lunch, tuition, and field trips). Contact: Karen Totman-Gale, Horizons, 108 N. Main St.-T, Sunderland, MA 01375; (413) 665-0300, fax (413) 665-4141; horizons@horizons-art.org, www.horizons-art.org.

L'Ecole de Patisserie Francaise. French pastry shop offers 40 intensive 5-day master workshops per year. Focus is student's choice— from ice creams, sorbets, chocolates, petits fours, celebration cakes, desserts, croissants, brioches, wedding cakes, etc.

Dates: Year round. Cost: FF5,000 per week for tuition. Contact: Mr. D. Richeux, L'Ecole de Patisserie Francaise, 12 rue de la Republique, 30700 Uzes, France; (011) 33-4-66-22-12-09, fax (011) 33-4-66-22-26-36.

Learn French in France (IFG). Whatever the need, whatever the level, IFG Langues has the experience, the skill, and the resources to provide the optimum courses in French. Our team of highly qualified teachers offers individually tailored programs. Courses concentrate first on general language, then on specific professional needs. Host family or hotel on request.

Dates: Courses begin any Monday. Cost: FF470.34 per hour, all taxes included. Contact: Aline Pernot, IFG Languages, 37 quai de

Grenelle, 75015 Paris, France; (011) 33-1-40-59-31-38, fax (011) 33-1-45-75-14-43.

Learning French in Paris. Alliance Française has more than 100 years of experience and a long-established reputation of excellence. We provide general French language courses, French for specific purposes, tailor-made courses, refresher courses and seminars for teachers of French, and services such as homestay service, excursions, free access to the mediatheque and lectures on French literature, theater, and art history.

Dates: Year-round. Monthly sessions. Cost: FF2,960 for 64 hours per month; FF1,480 for 32 hours per month. Contact: Alliance Française, 101 blvd. Raspail, 75270 Paris Cedex 06, France; (011) 33-1-45-44-38-28, fax (011) 33-1-45-44-89-42; afparis_ecole@compuserve.fr, www.paris.alliancefrancaise.fr.

New Year's in Paris. Univ. of Wisconsin-Whitewater alumni and friends trip to Paris. Open to alumni and nonalumni.

Dates: Dec 26-Jan 3 (1998-1999). Departs Chicago O'Hare non-stop to Paris. Cost: $1,300 per person (double). Includes roundtrip airfare, daily breakfast, 7 nights stay in Paris hotel, and tour. Contact: Mark Dorn, Univ. of Wisconsin-Whitewater, Alumni Center, Whitewater, WI 53190; (800) 648-2586; dornm@uwwvax.uww.edu.

Photography and Painting. Atelier Le Bez is a nonprofit organization located in the beautiful Parc Nationale de Haute Langedoc. It brings together small groups to pursue painting, photography, and French culture. The courses are practically based, suitable for all levels, and include field trips and demonstrations. Year round retreats available.

Dates: Jun-Oct, 7- and 10-day courses. Cost: FF3,100 includes tuition, room and board, excursions. Contact: Mabel Odessey, Atelier Le Bez, Le Bez 81260, France; Tel./fax (011) 33-5-63-74-56-22; artlebez@aol.com. English spoken.

Germany

German as a Foreign Language. Various levels of German year round; intensive, crash, and long-term courses, individual tuition. Special feature: German and theater. Special programs: business German for professionals, German for teachers, German in a teacher's home, German for special purposes. Academic year for high school students, international study year, internship, guest studentship, homestays for groups, courses for firms and other institutions (banking, insurance, doctors, lawyers, etc.), residential language camps for juniors, examination preparation. Various types of accommodations. Full range of activities.

Dates: Year round. Cost: Contact school for details. Contact: GLS Sprachenzentrum, Barbara Jaeschke, Managing Director, Kolonnenstrasse 26, 10829 Berlin, Germany; (011) 49-30-787-41-52; fax (011) 49-30-787-41-92; gls.berlin@t-online.de, www.gls-berlin.com.

Summer Study/Travel in Germany. A 4-week study/travel session in Germany and Switzerland. Open to all age groups. Housing in single rooms in college dorm. Included are trips to areas around Lake Constance, Munich, Neuschwanstein, Black Forest, Rhine Falls, Zurich, Lucerne, Strasbourg, Alps. College credit optional.

Dates: Jul 30-Aug 25 (1998). Cost: $1,495 includes room, food allowance, excursions (1998). Contact: Peter Schroeck, Raritan Valley Comm. College; (732) 249-9785; pschroec@rvcc.raritanval.edu.

Greece

Goddess Pilgrimage to Crete. Educational tour for women led by well-known author and feminist thealogian Carol P. Christ. Join us in search of the goddesses of ancient Crete. Academic credit of 1-3 units is available. We are an educational, tax-exempt 501(C)3 organization.

Dates: May 26-Jun 11; Sep 29-Oct 15. Cost: $2,995 includes roundtrip airfare from NYC. All expenses except some meals. Contact: Ariadne Institute, 1306 Crestview Dr., Blacksburg, VA 24060; Tel./fax (540) 951-3070.

Study in Greece. Holiday programs in Greek as a Foreign Language for children (10 plus) and adults; year and semester abroad. Choice of accredited American programs in Greece.

Dates: Vary. Cost: Call for details. Contact: FUTURA, Educational Services, Leof. Kifissias 10-12, 151 25 Marousi, Athens, Greece; (011) 30-1-6855729, fax (011) 30-1-6846335; futura@hellasnet.gr.

Guatemala

Eco-Escuela de Español. The Eco-Escuela de Español offers a unique educational experience by combining intensive Spanish language instruction with volunteer opportunities in conservation and community development projects. Students are immersed in the language, culture, and ecology of Petén, Guatemala—an area renowned for its tropical forests and ancient Mayan ruins. Ecological activities integrate classroom with field-based experiences.

Dates: Every Monday year round. Cost: Classes $65 per week (based on 20 hours of individual instruction per week, Monday-Friday). Room and board with local families $60 per week. Registration fee $10. Contact: Eco-Escuela, GAP Adventures, 266 Dupont St., Toronto, ON, M5R 1V7, Canada; (416) 922-8899, fax (416) 922-0822; adventure@gap.ca.

Escuela de Español "Sakribal." Program provides one-on-one intensive language instruction while giving students the chance to volunteer on student-supported development projects in the surrounding community, working in organic gardens, building houses, and

in the country's only women's shelter. Family stays, guest lecturers, group discussions, and cultural activities round out the immersion program.

Dates: Classes start every Monday year round. Cost: $125 per week (includes classes, family stay, project work, other school activities). Contact: U.S. Office: 550 Ferncroft Ct., Danville, CA 94526; (510) 820-3632, fax (510) 820-6658; sakribal2@aol.com, http://kcyb.com/sakribal.

Israel

Pastor-Parishioner Study Tour. A 2-week program in Israel with daily field trips that concentrate on the geography of Israel and archaeology as they relate to Biblical interpretation. Extensive field trips to Galilee, Dead Sea, Masada, Jerusalem region, including overnights on the Sea of Galilee.

Dates: Apr 12-25 and Oct 25-Nov 7. Cost: $1,325 includes room and board, field trips. Contact: Jerusalem University College, 4249 E. State St., Suite 203, Rockford, IL 61108; (815) 229-5900 or (800) 891-9408, fax (815) 229-5901; 75454.1770@compuserve.com, www.juc.edu.

Saint John's Jerusalem Studies Program. While studying the sacred texts in the Holy Land participants deepen their understanding of sacred scripture from new perspectives. Through encounters with people, culture, and geography, participants come to appreciate the historic and contemporary diversity of Judaism, Christianity, and Islam.

Dates: Feb 1-May 21, Jun 14-Jul 23. Cost: Call for details. Contact: Mary Beth Banken, OSB, Saint John's School of Theology and Seminary, Collegeville, MN 56321-7288; (320) 363-2102, fax (320) 363-2504; mbanken@csbsju.edu, www.ecsbsju.edu/sot.

WUJS Institute in Arad. Year long program for Jewish graduates (21 to 35) combining 7 months of Hebrew ulpan. Jewish and Israel studies, travel, and community volunteer opportunities with 5 months or more of job placement in all fields throughout Israel.

Dates: Sessions begin every Jun, Oct, and Feb. Cost: $2,200. Includes tuition, housing, 1 main meal a day, trips, and seminars. Contact: Ami Blaszkowsky, WUJS Institute, P.O. Box 6177, E. Brunswick, NJ 08816; (888) WUJS-INS, (732) 238-2998; wujsusa@internetmci.com, www.wujs-arad.org.

Italy

Art and Design in Florence. The Accademia Italiana is an international, university-level institute of art and design. The Accademia offers courses in art, fashion, interior, industrial and textile design during the autumn and spring semesters and fashion design, fashion illustration, drawing and painting, window display design and Italian language during the months of June and July.

Dates: Jan 14-May 22, Jun, Jul, Sep 9-Dec 22, 1999. Cost: Depends on course chosen. Contact: Barbara McHugh, Accademia Italiana, Piazza Pitti n. 15, 50125 Florence, Italy; (011) 39-55-284616/211619, fax (011) 39-55-284486;modaita@tin.it, www.gamut.it/accademia.

Biking and Walking Tours. Specializing in Italy for over 10 years, Ciclismo Classico distills the "Best of Italy," offering more unique Italian destinations than any other active vacation company. Educational, active tours for all abilities in Umbria, Tuscany, Piedmont, the Dolomites, Puglia, Sicily, the Amalfi Coast, Cinque Terre, Sardegna, Abruzzo, Campania, Corsica, and Elba. Ireland, too. Charming accommodations, expert bilingual guides, cooking demonstrations, wine tastings, support vehicle, detailed route instructions, visits to local festivals, countryside picnics—an unforgettable cultural indulgence.

Dates: Apr-Nov (70 departures). Call for specific dates. Cost: $1,500-$3,000. Contact:

Lauren Hefferon, Director, Ciclismo Classico, 13 Marathon St., Arlington, MA 02174; (800) 866-7314 or (781) 646-3377.

Humanities Spring on the Road. Students travel from Florence to Pompeii, from Rome to Assisi to see great works of classical, renaissance, and contemporary art and architecture. Students learn to use the great art they see as a springboard for poems, prose, sketches, and their personal development staff includes art historians and painters, poets, and classicists.

Dates: Two weeks around Easter. Cost: $1,950 (1998). Airfare not included. Contact: Jane R. Oliensis, Humanities Spring in Assisi, Santa Maria di Lignano, 2 06081 Assisi (PG), Italy; Tel./fax (011) 39-75-802-400.

Italiaidea. Italiaidea is a center for comprehensive Italian instruction. We offer every level and format of Italian study from intensive short-term "survival Italian courses" to advanced semester-long courses meeting once or twice a week. We offer on-site lectures and visits to historic sites in Italian, conversation, and flexible scheduling. For over 10 years we have been offering college credit courses at numerous U.S. college and university programs in Italy; we now offer both academic assistance and travel/study assistance to our client institutions. Homestays are offered as well as accommodations in shared apartments.

Dates: Year round. Cost: Sixty-hour group course LIT780,000; 25-hour one-on-one program LIT1,200,000; 15 hour-specific purposes or culture LIT1,330,000 (taxes not included). Contact: Carolina Ciampaglia, Co-Director, Piazza della Cancelleria 5, 00186 Roma, Italy; (011) 39-6-68307620, fax (011) 39-6-6892997; italiaidea@italiaidea.com, www.italiaidea.com.

Italian Language Centre G. Leopardi. Sponsored by the Municipality of Belforte all'Isauro, we offer scholarships for Italian language and culture courses. Accommodations in a castle furnished in its original splendid style. All ages, all levels, all year. Friendly atmosphere in a wonderful area among the regions of Tuscany, Umbria, and Emilia Romagna.

Dates: First Monday of each month. Cost: $870 for course, accommodations, extracurricular activities, full board. Contact: Dr. Silvia Ferri, Centro Giacomo Leopardi, Via Castello 61020, Belforte all'Isauro PS, Italy; (011) 39-722-726000, fax (011) 39-722-726010; centroleopardi@wnt.it, www.italian.org.

Italian Language Courses. Two-, 3-, and 4-week courses in the undiscovered heart of Tuscany, in Arezzo (population 100,000). School approved by education ministry. Modern communicative methods, qualified teachers, excellent standards, friendly atmosphere, social and cultural program. A pleasant, satisfying experience. Stay with a family and meet real Italians in historical, artistic Arezzo.

Dates: Courses begin every Monday. Cost: LIT895,000 2 weeks' tuition/accommodations. Contact: Italian Language Courses-ILC, Accademia Toscana, Via Pietro da Cortona 10, 52100 Arezzo, Italy; (011) 39-575-21366, fax (011) 39-575-300426; italcors@ats.it, www.etr.it/accademia_britannica.

Italiano a Modo Mio. Sixth consecutive year: Castiglione della Pescaia/Tuscany; Marzabotto/Bologna; Sulmona. Eight-day customized programs of "breakfast-to-bedtime" full immersion in Italian. Limited to 8 well-motivated adults per class. Studies reinforced by practical application to real-life situations while enjoying Italian food and culture.

Dates: May 9-30; Aug 29-Sep 19; Oct 3-17 (8-day programs). Cost: $2,000-$3,500 includes single occupancy, classes, meals, activities. Airfare not included. Contact: Sergio Stefani, 33 Riverside Dr., 1E, New York, NY 10023; (212) 595-7004; annamaria@italianmyway.com, www.italianmyway.com.

Late Spring/Summer Studies at SACI. Summer studies at Studio Art Centers International (SACI) are open to students enrolled in US institutions who are seeking accredited summer study, independent non-credit students, mature students, and international students interested in studio arts, art history, art conservation and Italian language. The following classes are offered: Drawing, Painting, Printmaking Workshop, Ceramics, Sculpture, Photography, Design Workshop, Batik and Fabric Design, Weaving, Jewelry, Renaissance Art History, Art Conservation, and Italian Language.

Dates: Late Spring: May 13-Jun 21, and Summer: Jun 25-Jul 26. Cost: Tuition: $3,000; housing $950 (5 weeks)/$800 (4 weeks), activity fee $180/$140. Contact: SACI Coordinator, U.S. Student Programs, Institute of International Education, 809 UN Plaza, New York, NY 10017; (800) 344-9186, (212) 984-5548, fax (212) 984-5325; saci@iie.org, www.saci-florence.org.

Learn Italian in Italy. Study Italian in a 16th century Renaissance palace in the center of Florence, or in a classic Tuscan town just 30 minutes from the sea. Koiné Center's professional language teachers and small class sizes encourage active participation by each student. Cultural program, guided excursions, choice of accommodations including host families.

Dates: Year round; starting dates each month. Cost: Two-week intensive program $290; 3 weeks $390; homestay accommodations from $115 per week. Contact: In Italy: Dr. Andrea Moradei, Koiné Center, Via Pandolfini 27, 50122 Firenze, Italy; (011) 39-055-213881. In North America: (800) 274-6007; homestay@teleport.com, www.koinecenter.com.

Myth and Movement. Jeanne Bresciana, renowned dancer, educator, and director of the Isadora Duncan International Institute, combines movement with history, art, music and poetry in a sensory odyssey through locales rich in myth and beauty. Using movement, you will explore the creative forces within yourself and the Tuscan landscape, lush with vineyards awaiting harvest.

Dates: Sep 20-26 (1998). Cost: $2,045 includes meals and local ground transportation. Airfare not included. Contact: Tuscany Institute for Advanced Studies, c/o Ellen Bastio, 4626 Knoy Rd., #7, College Park, MD 20740; (800) 943-8070.

Tech Rome. Tech Rome is a 6-week summer travel-study program of Louisiana Tech Univ. It features hotel housing, 3 meals per day, tours, and traditional classroom courses combined with field travel for college credit. Up to 13 semester hours may be earned in a choice of over 40 courses in diverse subject areas. Courses are taught by American professors.

Dates: May 25-Jul 2. Cost: $4,328 includes tuition, all housing for 6 weeks, 3 meals per day, tours. Group flights are available. Contact: Tech Rome, P.O. Box 3172, Ruston, LA 71272; (318) 257-4854; http://techrome.latech.edu.

Tuscany: Horizons Art and Travel. Tuscany is studded with panoramic landscapes, ancient walled villages, olive groves and vineyards...and capped by the gorgeous cities of Florence and Siena. Lodging in a charming country inn/villa in the heart of Chianti country, perfectly situated to see the sites of the region. Workshops include painting, glass beads, mosaics, book arts, jewelry, photography.

Dates: Apr 17-24, Oct 2-9. Cost: $1,425 (lodging, all meals except 1 lunch, tuition, and field trips). Contact: Karen Totman-Gale, Horizons, 108 N. Main St.-T, Sunderland, MA 01375; (413) 665-0300, fax (413) 665-4141; horizons@ horizons-art.org, www.horizons-art.org.

Japan

Japan Exchange and Teaching (JET) Program. Sponsored by the Japanese Government, the JET Program invites over 1,000 American college graduates and young professionals to share their language and culture with Japanese youth. One-year positions are available in schools and government offices throughout Japan. Apply by early December for positions beginning in July of the following year.

Dates: One-year contracts renewable by mutual consent not more than 2 times. Cost: Participants receive approx. ¥3,600,000 per year in monthly payments. Contact: JET Program Office, Embassy of Japan, 2520 Massachusetts Ave. NW, Washington, DC 20008; (202) 238-6772, fax (202) 265-9484; eojjet@erols.com, www.jet.org.

Malta

Keystone of Mediterranean History. "One of Elderhostel's best, and they've all been good." Seven thousand years of human history are explored with professors and professionals from many disciplines, creating a vivid tapestry of cultural heritage beginning with the oldest buildings still standing on earth. Top quality presentation, abundant inclusion and personal attention create an enriching experience.

Dates: Continuous. Call for availability. Cost: From $2,111 includes airfare from North America, 13 nights accommodations, all meals, full 2-week program or presentations, field trips, and excursions. Contact: The OTS Foundation, P.O. Box 17166, Sarasota, FL 34276; (941) 918-9215, fax (941) 918-0265; otsf@aol.com, www.otsf.org or Elderhostel Registration (617) 426-8056. Catalogs available in U.S. public libraries.

Mexico

Copper Canyon Adventure Travel. Week-long, split-stay trips between a luxurious, yet rustic mountain lodge and an elegant, restored 19th century canyon floor hacienda allow independent travelers to experience, in-depth, the rugged beauty and unique culture of the region. Ancient missions, silver mines, Tarahumara Indians, birds, butterflies, botany. Local guides.

Dates: Year round. Cost: From $1,125, all inclusive; 8 days/7 nights. Contact: Copper Canyon Lodges, 2741 Paldan Dr., Auburn Hills, MI 48326; (800) 776-3942, fax (248) 340-7212; coppercanyon@earthlink.net, www.copper canyonlodges.com.

El Bosque del Caribe, Cancun. Take a professional Spanish course 25 hours per week and enjoy the Caribbean beaches. Relaxed family-like atmosphere. No more than 6 students per class. Special conversation program. Mexican cooking classes and excursions to the Mayan sites. Housing with Mexican families. College credit available.

Dates: Year round. New classes begin every Monday. Group programs arranged at reduced fees. Cost: Enrollment fee $100, $180 per week. One week with a Mexican family $160. Contact: Eduardo Sotelo, Director, Calle Piña 1, S.M. 25, 77500 Cancún, Mexico; (011) 52-98-84-10-38, fax (011) 52-98-84-58-88; bcaribe@mail.cancun-language.com.mx.

Indigenous Learning Adventures. Professional development seminars, accredited master of arts (MA) degree programs and renewal adventures. Yelapa-Puerto Vallarta. Topics: traditional medicine, ethnobotany, nutrition, Mexican cuisine, women's health, energy, medicine, traumatology, environmental studies, Fourth World geopolitics and consciousness studies, Indian and non-Indian faculty. Socially and environmentally responsible. Natural medicine clinic. Service-study programs.

Dates: Year round. Cost: Average $1,375 per week (not including travel). Contact: Center for World Indigenous Studies, 1001 Cooper Pt. Rd. SW, 140-214, Olympia, WA 98502; (781) 643-1918; cwislka@wco.com, www.halcyon.com/FWDP/cwisinfo.html.

Instituto Cultural Oaxaca. Spanish Language and Mexican Culture Immersion Program on lovely Oaxacan estate. Grammar, literature and conversation classes offered at 7 levels. Cultural workshops in cooking, pottery, dancing, weaving, and music. Local conversation partner. Weekly lectures and cultural activities. Seven contact hours daily. Optional tours to archaeological sites and artisan villages. Homestays available. Special group programs.

Dates: Year-round monthly sessions. May begin any Monday. Write, call, or fax for specific dates and informative brochure. Cost: $50 registration fee and $400 per 4-week session or $105 per week. Contact: Lic Lucero Topete, Director, Instituto Cultural Oaxaca, Apartado Postal #340, Oaxaca, Oaxaca, C.P. 68000, Mexico; (011)-52-951-53404, fax (011) 52-951-53728; inscuoax@antequera.com, http://antequera. com/inscuoax.

Intensive Language Programs. Intensive Spanish immersion program in groups, 40 class hours per week including Spanish class, lectures, and Hispano-American courses. Executive, semester, and specialized programs for teachers, professionals, nurses, and adults continuing education. Live with Mexican family or in student residence. Excursions to historical and archaeological sites.

Dates: Year round starting every Monday. Cost: Tuition $190 per week; lodging $154 per week. Contact: The Center for Bilingual Multicultural Studies, Javier Espinosa, San Jeronimo #304, Cuernavaca, MOR-62179, Mexico; (011) 52-73-17-10-87, fax (011) 52-73-17-05-33; admin@bilingual-center.com, www.bilingual-center.com.

Intensive Spanish in Cuernavaca. Cuauhnahuac, founded in 1972, offers a variety of intensive and flexible programs geared to individual needs. Six hours of classes daily with no more than 4 students to a class. Housing with Mexican families who really care about you. Cultural conferences, excursions, and special classes for professionals. College credit available.

Dates: Year round. New classes begin every Monday. Cost: $70 registration fee; $650 for 4 weeks tuition; housing $18 per night. Contact: Marcia Snell, 519 Park Dr., Kenilworth, IL 60043; (800) 245-9335, fax (847) 256-9475; lankysam@aol.com.

Intensive Spanish in Yucatan. Centro de Idiomas del Sureste, A.C. (CIS), founded in 1974, offers 3-5 hours per day of intensive conversational Spanish classes with native-speaking, university-trained professors. Maximum 6 students per group, average 3. Program includes beginner courses to very advanced with related field trips and recommended optional homestay. Also special classes in business, legal, medical vocabulary, or Mayan studies.

Dates: Year round. Starts any Monday, except last 2 weeks in Dec. Cost: Tuition (three hours per day program): $330 first 2 weeks, $115 each additional week, tuition (5 hours per day program): $490 first 2 weeks, $195 each additional week. Contact: Chloe C. Pacheco, Director, Centro de Idiomas del Sureste, A.C., Calle 14 #106 x 25, col. Mexico, CP 97128, Mérida, Yucatán, México; (011) 52-99-26-11-55 or (011) 52-99-26-94-94, 20-28-10, fax 26-90-20; cis@sureste.com.

Language and Culture in Guanajuato. We work with innovative teaching techniques, tailoring instruction to each student's needs. Spanish, Mexican history, politics, culture-cuisine, folk dancing, and Latin American literature.

Dates: Year round. New classes begin every Monday. Cost: $925. Includes 4 weeks of classes and homestay with 3 meals daily. Contact: Director Jorge Barroso, Instituto Falcon, A.C., Guanajuato, Gto. 36000 Mexico; Tel./fax (011) 52-473-1-0745, infalcon@redes.int. com.mx, www.infonet.com.mx/falcon.

Mar de Jade. Tropical ocean-front retreat center in a beautiful unspoiled fishing village near Puerto Vallarta offers unique travel options. Enjoy great swimming, kayaking, hiking, massages, and stress-reduction meditation. Study Spanish in small groups. Gain further insight into local culture by studying and working in a farmers' clinic, local construction, cottage industries, or teaching.

Dates: Year round. Cost: $950 for 21-day work/study. Includes room (shared occupancy), board, 12 hours per week of Spanish and 15 hours per week of work. Longer resident program available at lower cost. Vacation/Spanish 1-week minimum $400 room, board, 12 hours of Spanish. Vacation only $50 per night for any length of time. Contact: In Mexico: Mar de Jade/Casa Clinica, A.P. 81, Las Varas, Nayarit, 63715, Mexico; Tel./fax (011) 52-327-20184; info@mardejade.com, www. mardejade.com. In U.S.: P.O. Box 1280, Santa Clara, CA 95052; (415) 281-0164.

Spanish Training Center. Tutorial: Year round except Christmas week; 4 hours intensive Spanish per day; textbook; city tour; homestay. Summer groups from Jun 15 to Aug 7: 4 hours intensive Spanish per day; city tour; homestay; textbook; weekend trips; extra class workshops.

Dates: Tutorial year round. Summer: Jun 15-Aug 7. Cost: Tutorial $800 (2 weeks), Summer $460 (2 weeks). Contact: Spanish Training Center, c/o Bertha Gómez, 27 Sur 111, La Paz Puebla, México; (011) 52-22-313848, fax (011) 55-22-485365, www.hipermedios.com/etcenter.

Nepal

Explorations in Medicine and Culture. An extraordinary opportunity to learn from experts: a variety of Asian healing systems while you trek through breathtaking vistas of the Himalayas, encounter a variety of cultures and their rituals, visit Chitwan Wildlife Sanctuary, and explore the wondrous city of Kathmandu. Regular and CME tours. Free brochure; (800) 833-2444.

Dates: Mar 14-31; Apr 2-27; Sep 3-21; Oct 4-19; Nov 5- 23. Cost: $2,295-$3,295 plus airfare depending on 16- or 19-day tour and season. Includes breakfast, 3 banquets, lodging, air and land transportation in Nepal, guides and fees. Contact: Explorations, P.O. Box 130465, Ann Arbor, MI 48113; (313) 971-4754, fax (313) 971-0042; emcnepal@worldnet. att.net, www.explorations-alt-med.com.

Sojourn Nepal. Sojourn Nepal is a 12-week program comprised of homestay, language study, lectures, village stay, trekking, and opportunities for apprenticeships in a vast variety of areas. Cultural immersion at its finest.

Dates: Fall and Spring semesters. Cost: $5,000 all inclusive. Airfare not included. Contact: Jennifer Warren, Sojourn Nepal, 2440 N. 56th St., Phoenix, AZ 85008; Tel./fax (602) 840-9197; snepal@aol.com.

Nicaragua

Nicaragua Spanish Schools. The 5 Nicaraguan-run schools in North, Central, and South Nicaragua can be combined into a single Spanish language program in any number or order. Offers small, full-immersion classes, qualified Nica teachers, hospitable family homestays, cultural activities, volunteer opportunities, exciting eco-excursions, y mucho más. Your tuition helps support social/cultural/development programs.

Dates: Year round. Classes start any Monday Cost: Tuition/homestay $185-$210 per week depending on program length. Contact: Nicaragua Spanish Schools, P.O. Box 20042, Santa Barbara, CA 93120; (800) 211-7393; Tel./fax (805) 687-9941; QZGF39A@prodigy.com, http://pages.prodigy.net/nss-pmc.

Papua New Guinea

Trans Niugini Tours. Nature and culture programs are offered in 3 areas: the Highlands, the Sepik Area, and a marine environment on the North Coast. Each area has its own distinct culture and environment, with comfortable wilderness lodges.

Dates: Weekly departures. Cost: $889-$3,570 per person (land cost). Contact: Bob Bates, Trans Niugini Tours, P.O. Box 371, Mt. Hagen, Papua New Guinea; (800) 521-7242 or (011) 675-542-1438, fax (011) 675-542-2470; travel@pngtours.com, www.pngtours.com.

Peru

Drawing From Another World and Time. Peru: Cradle of the Inca Empire featuring Lima, Pisac, Machu Picchu, and Cuzco. A drawing seminar in another world and time with Steve Nocella, Chair of Sculpture Dept. of the Pennsylvania Academy of the Fine Arts. This 10-day class will explore and draw from various ancient ruins and sites.

Dates: Call for details. Cost: Call for details. Contact: Neil di Sabato, PAFA, Continuing Education Programs, 1301 Cherry St., Philadelphia, PA 19107; (215) 972-7632, fax (215) 569-0153; extprogram@pafa.org.

Russia and the NIS

Moscow Study Trips. Since 1980 the program has probed political, economic, and social realities of the USSR, then of Russia's historic transition. Participants, aged 20-70 plus, have come from various backgrounds and countries. No Russian language knowledge needed. University credit may be possible. Sample schedule and anecdotal accounts of past trips on web site.

Dates: Three weeks, mid-May to mid-Jun, late-Jun to late-Jul, or on sufficient demand. Cost: $1,550-$1,750 (estimated 1999), depending on group size, includes full living and program costs for 4 weeks. Air travel arranged in addition. Contact: Eric Fenster, Moscow Study Trips, 27150 Zeman Ave., Euclid, OH 44132; efenster@igc.org, http://ourworld.compuserve.com/homepages/efenster.

South America

Amazon Jungle Safari. An 8-day natural history adventure offering a valuable rainforest experience. Overnights in serene jungle lodges in remote reserves for great bird/wildlife viewing. The small group educational tour is escorted by a qualified U.S. biologist and expert resident guides. Also experience the longest treetop canopy walkway in the Americas, over 1,500 feet long and 115 feet high. Also available are Amazon riverboat cruises and extensions to Cuzco and Machu Picchu.

Dates: Monthly. Cost: $1,995 including air

from Miami, lodging, all meals, excursions. Contact: Charlie Strader, Explorations, Inc., 27655 Kent Road, Bonita Springs, FL 34135; (800) 446-9660, fax (941) 992-7666; cesxplor@aol.com.

Spain

CLIC International House, Sevilla. CLIC IH, one of Spain's leading language schools, is located in the heart of Seville, the vibrant capital of Andalucia. With year-round intensive Spanish language courses, Business Spanish, and official exam preparation taught by highly qualified and motivated native teachers, CLIC IH combines professionalism with a friendly atmosphere. Accommodations are carefully selected and we offer a varied cultural program as well as exchanges with local students.

Dates: Year round. Cost: Approx. $825 for a 4-week course, individual room with a family, and 2 meals per day. Contact: Bernhard Roters, CLIC-International House Seville, Calle Santa Ana 11, 41002 Sevilla, Spain; (011) 34-95-437-4500, fax (011) 34-95-437-1806; clic@arrakis.es, www.clic.es.

=elemadrid= Spanish in Madrid. Our Spanish language school in Madrid, Spain, provides a wide variety of Spanish immersion programs, Spain today classes, leisure activity courses, and weekend excursions in small groups and/or individually tailored private lessons. Accommodations include homestay, apartments, apartment sharing, and hotels.

Dates: Start on the following Mondays: Mar 1, 15, 29; Apr 12, 26; May 10, 24; Jun 6, 21, 28; Jul 5, 19; Aug 2, 16, 30; Sep 13, 27; Oct 11, 25; Nov 8, 22; Dec 7. Cost: Courses $220-$760 per week; accommodations $80-$1,300 per week; leisure activity courses and excursions vary. Contact: =elemadrid= Calle Serrano 4, 28001 Madrid, Spain; Tel./fax (011) 34-91-432-4540/41; hola@elemadrid.com, www.elemadrid.com.

Escuela Internacional. Escuela Internacional offers quality programs in Spanish language and culture with U.S. undergraduate credits in Madrid, Salamanca, and Malaga. Our qualified teachers and small classes (maximum 12 students per class) guarantee you a successful program. Stay with a selected family or in a shared apartment. Enjoy our extensive afternoon activities and weekend excursions. Our professionalism, enthusiasm, and personal touch will make your experience in Spain memorable and fun.

Dates: Year round, 2-48 weeks. Cost: From PTS59,000 for 2 weeks (includes 15 hours per week instruction, room and books) to PTS120,000 (includes 30 hours per week instruction, room and full board, books, activities, and excursion). Contact: Escuela Internacional, Midori Ishizaka, Director of Admissions, c/Talamanca 10, 28807 Alcalá de Henares, Madrid, Spain; (011) 34-91-8831264, fax (011) 34-91-8831301; escuelai@ergos.es, www.ergos.es/escuelai.

Spanish at Malaca Instituto. The quality of Malaca Instituto's Spanish language and cultural program is guaranteed by independent inspection (see www.eaquals.org). Our students come from all over the world. Full accommodations and activity/excursion program. Qualifying students can apply for college academic credit. For all ages 16-90.

Dates: Every 2 weeks from Jan 4 (min. 2 weeks, max. academic year). Cost: Four lessons per day plus materials PST43,700 (2 weeks). Accommodations from PTS33,800 (2 weeks). Contact: Bob Burger, Malaca Instituto, c/Cortada 6, Cerrado de Calderon, 29018 Malaga, Spain; (011) 34-95-229-32-42 or 1896, fax (011) 34-95-229-63-16; espanol@malacainst-ch.es, www. malacainst-ch.es.

Spanish Courses in Malaga. Spanish courses in Malaga, Spain. All grades, small groups, 4 hours daily, courses commencing each month. Living with Spanish families (or in small apartment in town center).

Contact: F. Marin Fernandez, Director,

Cooking in Tuscany

Hands-On Lessons in La Cucina Tradizionale

By Clay and Joanna Hubbs

In 1976 we worked for the year in the south of France. While our children attended French schools, we took frequent trips across the Italian border to Liguria and Tuscany, stopping in village trattoria to sample for the first time "la cucina tradizionale," the regional cooking of Italian housewives.

From village to village and region to region the variety of the dishes—in the ingredients but particularly in the preparation—was astonishing. Then of course the villages were much more isolated from one another and Italian housewives had access only to ingredients found within a small radius of their kitchens. They combined these local ingredients in special ways handed down for generations.

In **Eating in Italy**, Faith Heller Willinger's authoritative guide to the gastronomic pleasures of northern Italy, the author points out that the variety in Italian cooking from one town or region to the next is due to the combination of geography, climate, and conquest. Over centuries hordes of invaders made Italy what Willinger calls a "Mediterranean melting pot" stretching from the mountains bordering Austria and Germany in the north to the sunny African islands of the south.

The overall extent to which traditional Italian cooking has suffered with the coming of rapid transportation and communication is a matter of debate. But thanks to the efforts of Willinger and others—most notably the "Slow Food" association with headquarters in the northern province of Piedmonte—who are tenaciously tracking down those who have clung to (and rediscovered) the old ways of producing and preparing food and wine, it's now possible for even the short-time visitor not only to taste the various foods of the past but learn to prepare them.

To locate the schools that specialize in teaching the art of traditional Tuscan cooking we consulted Willinger, a New Yorker who has lived in Florence for more than 20 years and whose cookbook, **Red, White, and Greens**, gets almost daily use in our own kitchen.

From Willinger's recommendations we chose three schools to visit: the Capezzana Wine and Culinary Center, on the estate of Count Ugo Contini Bonaccossi in the Carmignano, a wine area west of Florence; Judy Witts' Mangia Firenze program, run since 1988 from her apartment overlooking the central food market in Florence, and La Bottega del 30 Cooking School, associated with the famous restaurant of the same name, located in the heart of the Chianti east of Siena.

The three schools and the teachers are very different, but their goals are the same: to impart the ancient culinary techniques of the women cooks of Tuscany following local recipes. The cooking is done by the students themselves in traditional Tuscan kitchens using fresh local ingredients which the students have helped to select.

Tenuta di Capezzana

The Capezzana Wine and Culinary Center is located in an imposing Medici villa on an estate that has been famous for its wine and olives since the ninth century. Countess Lisa, known as one of the best home cooks in Tuscany, has for the past five years used the estate's kitchen and facilities to offer a series of programs designed especially for food professionals, skilled

Adult Travel & Study Programs

cooks, and those involved with food and wine.

More than a cooking school, the Center, in which all the family participates, offers an introduction to Tuscan life. After a first night at the Hotel Principe in Florence, the five-day program begins in the traditional kitchens of the estate with a morning cooking class, lunch, and hands-on pizza and focaccia cooking using a wood oven.

The second day is devoted to tasting and pairing wines with food under the guidance of winemaster Nicholas Belfrage. Dinner is at a local restaurant. The third day starts with a shopping trip to Florence's Sant' Ambrosio market where students select for themselves what they will prepare for dinner. Lunch is at Florence's top restaurant for traditional cooking, Cibreo. On day four students visit local artisans— bakers, butchers, chocolate makers, etc.— before another hands-on cooking session in the Capezzana kitchen.

Day five is taken up with an exploration of the Chianti and its wines, tasting local cheeses and salamis at wineries, and buying meats, fruits, and vegetables for the farewell dinner with the Contini Bonaccossi family. The elaborate farewell banquet is prepared by a guest chef.

In addition to the cooking school, the Center also offers weekend wine tasting courses under the guidance of a master of wine. (The Institute of Masters of Wine is an internationally recognized body of experts on wine production and assessment.) The estate sells its own famous collection of wines and olive oil. Benedetta Contini Bonaccossi, who is in charge of sales, also can arrange stays at local farms.

A stay at Capezzana is most remarkable for the brief sense of the "Tuscan experience." Guests stay in a wing of the villa and join the warmly hospitable Bonaccossi family at meals. The lively talk is mostly of food and wines—while you enjoy "your" food and the best wines of the region.

Mangia Firenze

A Tuscan experience of a different nature is to be had in Florence with the transplanted American, and Tuscan food fanatic, Judy Witts Francini. The key to Tuscan cooking is using the very best and freshest ingredients and doing as little as possible to alter their natural tastes. Judy's "From the Market to the Table" classes consist of shopping at the Central Market, just outside her window, and bringing the ingredients directly to her kitchen for preparation and consumption.

"The problem with living in the country," says Judy, "is that everything you want may not be in perfect readiness when you want it. At the market you have a wide selection of the best."

On Mondays, Judy takes students on a walking tour of the market. They get acquainted with the raw ingredients on display at the stalls while being instructed by Judy and the vendors on what to look for to find the best quality produce. Lunch is at a local trattoria where students taste what a master cook does with the produce the students have just examined. After lunch, the walk continues—to specialty food and kitchen stores in the center of Florence.

The hands-on cooking portion of the program comes on Tuesday, Wednesday, and Thursday. With Judy as their guide, students select the best the market has to offer in planning their menu. At a local wine bar an experienced expert helps them select the wines for their meal. The pace is relaxed, with plenty of time for tasting and expert advice from the growers and vendors on the best ways to prepare their products. Then it's on to the kitchen.

On Fridays, Judy, like the Bonaccossi family, takes her students to the Chianti Classico wine region between Florence and Siena for visits to local food purveyors, artisans, and wineries.

Lunch is at a trattoria that's part of a 250-year-old winery.
La Bottega del 30

Tucked away in a tiny medieval borgo dominated by a winery is one of the Chianti's finest restaurants, La Bottega del 30. Several years ago, the charming young chef, Hélène Stoquelet, married a Tuscan, Franco Camelia, and began to study the ways of traditional Tuscan country cooking—which she has adapted and refined to such a point that the restaurant has recently received a Michelin star.

Cooking classes are held in a specially-designed kitchen apart from the restaurant. Each student has his or her own stove, work space, utensils, and ingredients. (Students keep their utensils after finishing the course.) The emphasis each day is on a separate part of the meal: Monday, antipasti; Tuesday, soups and sauces; Wednesday, fresh pastas; Thursday, meats; Friday, dessert.

After each lesson, which lasts from 10 a.m. to approximately 2 p.m., students lunch in the dining room, eating the dishes they have prepared accompanied by appropriate wines.

The ancient culinary techniques of the women of Chianti are taught in an adjoining room which reproduces exactly a traditional kitchen, complete with a wood oven for baking, a brazier, and a huge country fireplace. In the same building is a well-stocked library and videocassette collection, a wine cellar, and a museum of old farm implements and utensils used for preparing traditional Tuscan meals.

One-day lessons Monday through Friday cost LIT260,000 ($160) per person with lunch and wine tasting. On Thursdays and Fridays there is the option of a one-day lesson plus dinner at the restaurant; on Mondays and Wednesdays the one-day option is a cooking class, lunch, and wine tasting followed by an excursions to the castles of the Chianti and dinner at a typical restaurant.

Having participated in sessions at all three schools, we came to two conclusions. The first is that there surely is no better way to get a sense of Tuscany, one of the most beautiful areas of Italy and richest in artistic and crafts heritage, than to immerse oneself in its culinary traditions. At the schools we attended you can almost "taste" the countryside—and meet some of the people who have maintained its traditional ways of growing and preparing food.

The second is that this brief immersion in the Tuscan experience is likely to have lasting effects. We came home with our bags packed with the olive oil from Capezzana and aged cheese from the Central Market in Florence to combine with fresh vegetables from our garden. (And of course with recipes for our favorite dishes.) When the supply runs out—and it all too quickly will—we'll find a way to replace it.

Tuscan Cooking Schools

Tenuata di Capezzana, via Capezzana 100, Carmignano 50042, Italy; (011) 39-55-870-6004, fax (011) 39-55-870-6673; capezzana@dada.it. In the U.S. contact: Marlene Levinson, 55 Rayclilff Terr., San Francisco, CA 94115; (415) 928-7711, fax (415) 928-7789; mlcooker@pacbell.net. Courses: Spring and Fall (April-May, September-November). One-day sessions: $120-$200 per person depending upon number (includes recipes, apron, and a bottle of Capezzana olive oil). Six-day school (including one night in Hotel Principe in Florence): $2,350. Accommodations are in a wing of the Capezzana villa. The estate has a swimming pool, tennis courts, and pathways for walking and jogging.

Mangia Firenze, via Taddea, 31, Firenze 50123, Italy; Tel./fax (011) 39-55-29-25-78. In the U.S. contact: 2130 Comistas Dr., Walnut Creek, CA 94598; Tel./fax (925) 939-6346; www.mangiafirenze.com (online class registration and sample recipes). Courses: Weekdays year round. Florence walking tour (Monday): $100 per person includes wine tasting and lunch. "From the Market to the Table" cooking classes (Tuesday, Wednesday, Thursday): $200 per person includes single class with printed recipes. Chianti tour (Friday): $200 per person includes transportation, wine tasting, lunch. Three-day session (choice of days above): $650 per person includes copy of Judy's cookbook, an apron, and certificate of attendance. Week-long or one-day custom culinary programs can be designed for groups of six to eight. Accommodations can be arranged in Florence or the Chianti.

   La Bottega del 30, Scuola di Cucina, via Nuova 6, Localitá Villa a Sesta, Castelnuova Berardenga 53019, Siena, Italy; Tel./fax (011) 39-577-359226; labottegadel30@ novamedia.it, www.nettuno.it/fiera/labottegadel30. Courses: Spring and Fall (April-June, September-November). Five-day course including daily lunch and wine tasting, two dinners at Bottega del 30 restaurant, two dinners at other restaurants in the Chianti and light dinner on arrival day, two tours to castles and wineries, accommodations for seven nights, daily breakfast, personal set of cooking equipment and recipes: $4,350-$4,700 for two people. Five-day course for two people including lunch, cooking equipment, and recipes: $1,600. One-day lessons Monday-Friday: $160 per person. (Prices are for 1998.)

Books and Organizations

Arcigola Slow Food, via della Mendicita Istruita 14, Bra CN 12042, Italy; (011) 39-172-411-273, fax (011) 39-172-421-293. Arcigola or "Big Gluttony," is a nationwide (and becoming international) organization of Italians fighting the invasion of fast food and supporting local, traditional cooking. Local chapters sponsor food and wine events and publish books and magazines, including **Osteria d'Italia**, a guide to restaurants offering reasonably priced traditional regional cooking.

   Giuliano Bugialli's Food of Tuscany (Stewart Tabori and Chang, $50). Stunning photographs but somewhat complicated recipes.

   Eating in Italy: A Traveler's Guide to the Gastronomic Pleasures of Northern Italy by Faith Heller Willinger (William Morrow, 1998, $20). An in-depth guide to the food and wine of northern Italy. Detailed information on where to find traditional cooking, by region.

   Essentials of Classic Italian Cooking by Marcella Hazan (Knopf, $30). Widely considered the finest single-volume Italian cookbook. Covers the basics of traditional Italian cooking.

   A Food Lover's Companion to Tuscany by Carla Capalbo (Chronicle Books, $14.95). A town-by-town taster's guide to Tuscany. Useful appendices include market days, wine varietals, etc.

   The Guide to Cooking Schools by Margery Shaw (Shaw Guides, 1999, $19.95). Lists vacation cooking courses worldwide. Updates on web at www.shawguides.com.

   Italy for the Gourmet Traveler by Fred Plotkin (Little Brown, $19.95). Largest single guide to eating in Italy. Includes regional recipes.

   Red, White, and Greens: The Italian Way with Vegetables by Faith Heller Willinger (Harper Collins, $25). The Italian approach to vegetables by knowledgeable author of **Eating in Italy** (above).

Centro de Estudios de Castellano, Ave. Juan Sebastian Elcano, 120, Málaga, 29017 Spain; Tel./fax (011) 34-95-2290-551; ryoga@arrakis. es, www.arrakis.es/~ryoga.

Spanish for Seniors. Highly practical language program plus cultural and social activities for seniors. Spanish for the market, for restaurants/bars, renting cars, booking hotels etc. Integrated visits to castles, museums, "Pueblos Blancos," plus activities—cooking lessons, Sevillana dance classes, flamenco parties, etc. Learning and fun in a beautiful Mediterranean setting in a school with students of all ages.

Dates: Starting Feb 2, 16; Mar 2, 16, 30; Apr 13, 27; May 11; Oct 12, 26; Nov 9, 23. Cost: Three lessons per day and cultural activities PTS60,000 (2 weeks); accommodations from PTS33,800 (2 weeks). Contact: Bob Burger, Malaca Instituto, c/Cortada 6, Cerrado de Calderon, 29018 Malaga, Spain; (011) 34-95-229-32 42 or 1896, fax 229-63-16; espanol@ malacainst-ch.es, www.malacainst-ch.es.

Spanish in Northern Spain. All levels: Oral exercises in grammar and vocabulary, guided conversation according to the student's level. From intermediate level: Commentaries on newspaper articles and literary or other texts, prepared discussions on current affairs, history, literature, art, videos, etc. In all cases, the emphasis in class is on the spoken language.

Dates: Year round. Cost: PTAS49,600 per week, including course fees and half-board family accommodations. Contact: Ingrid Antons, inlingua Santander, Avda. De Pontejos, 5 E-39005 Santander, Spain; (011) 34-942-278465, fax (011) 34-942-274402; inlingua-sdr@nexo.es, www.inlingua.com/ Santander.htm.

Summer Study in Salamanca. Spend over 4 weeks in Spain studying Spanish language, literature, and culture at the prestigious Colegio de España in Salamanca. The program is designed for college students, graduates, and teachers, as well as for college-bound high school students. Program options: A) Intensive undergraduate language and culture; up to 9 credits. B) Literature, language and culture, and business Spanish; 6 graduate or advanced undergraduate credits.

Dates: Jul 1-30, 1999. Cost: Program A: $1,850. Program B: $2,050. Contact: Prof. Mario F. Trubiano, Director, URI Summer Program in Spain, Dept. of Languages, Univ. of Rhode Island, Kingston, RI 02881-0812; (401) 874-4717 or (401) 874-5911; fax (401) 874-4694.

United Kingdom and Ireland

Central Saint Martins Short Courses. Short practical courses in all aspects of art and design suitable for professional and student artists and designers. Includes fashion, graphics, fine art, theater design, textiles, product design, computer graphics, and multimedia. All courses held in heart of London in the U.K.'s largest college of art and design.

Dates: Courses run year round in evenings and on Saturdays. Intensive week long courses in Summer, Christmas, and Easter. Cost: Costs from £150 ($250) per week for tuition. Accommodations from £22 ($35) per night. Contact: Developments at Central Saint Martins, Southampton Row, London WC1B 4AP, U.K.; (011) 44-171-514-7015, fax (011) 44-171-514-7016; shortcourse@cstm.co.uk, www.csm. linst.ac.uk.

Edinburgh Univ. Summer Courses. Scotland past and present: Art, Architecture, History, Literature, Archaeology, Presentation skill, Ethnology, Gaelic, Music, Drama, Creative Writing, Film, Ecology, the Edinburgh Festival. Courses last 1-4 weeks each. Instruction by University professors: highest academic standards. Integral field trips; theatre/concert/ cinema tickets provided. Social program. Choice of accommodations.

Dates: Jun-Sep. Cost: Inquire. Contact:

Elaine Mowat, Univ. of Edinburgh, Centre for Continuing Education, 11 Buccleuch Pl., Edinburgh EH8 9LW, U.K.; (011) 44-131-650-4400, fax (011) 44-131-667-6097; CCE@ed.ac.uk, www.cce.ed.ac.uk/summer.

Ireland: Culture and Politics. Comprehensive academic program on all aspects of Irish heritage and culture. Day trips to historical and archaeological sites. Theater, musical events, poetry readings; full social program. Accommodations on campus or with families.

Dates: Jun 30-Jul 16. Cost: $700 ($1,100 with bed and breakfast). Contact: UCD International Summer School, Belfield, Dublin 4, Ireland; (011) 353-1-475004, fax (011) 353-1-7067211; summer.school@ucd.ie, www.ucd.ie/summerschool.

An Irish Idyll. From historic Dublin to mountain landscapes, fields of green to quaint villages and dramatic ocean views...this evocative country has a beauty all its own. Lodging in a charming bed and breakfast in the gorgeous seaside village of Kinsale—perfectly situated to see the diversity of the Irish panorama. Workshops include painting, jewlery, hats and bags, fiber arts and felting, photography.

Dates: Jun 12-19, Oct 2-9. Cost: $1,425 (lodging, meals, tuition, and field trips). Contact: Karen Totman-Gale, Horizons, 108 N. Main St.-T, Sunderland, MA 01375; (413) 665-0300, fax (413) 665-4141; horizons@horizons-art.org, www.horizons-art.org.

Irish Language and Culture. Irish language programs at all learning levels for adults are offered by Oideas Gael, which also offers cultural activities, learning programs in hillwalking, dances of Ireland, painting, tapestry weaving, Raku-Celtic pottery, and archaeology.

Dates: Weekly, Apr-Sep. Cost: $150 plus accommodations (from $90 per week). Contact: Liam O'Cuinneagain, Director, Oideas Gael, Gleann Cholm Cille, County Donegal, Ireland; (011) 353-73-30248, fax (011) 353-73-30348; oidsgael@iol.ie.

Oxford Advanced Studies Program. The program is an academic and cultural summer course held at Magdalen College, one of Oxford's oldest and most famous colleges. Students select 2 or 3 subjects from a wide choice; teaching is in a combination of small seminar groups and individual tutorials. The social and cultural program is packed with a variety of exciting experiences.

Dates: Jul 5-30, 1999. Cost: $5,150. Contact: Mrs. J. Ives, U.S. Registrar, Oxford Advanced Studies Program, P.O. Box 2043, Darien, CT 06820; (203) 966-2886, fax (203) 972-3083; oxedge@aol.com.

Summer Academic Program. Save time and money by studying in the Summer Academic Program at the Univ. of Stirling in the heart of Scotland. This program includes units in adult education, business studies, East Asian studies, English literature, environmental education, film and media studies, French, history, politics; each unit represents 5 U.S. course credits.

Dates: Jun 28-Aug 21. Cost: Each semester unit costs £460 (overseas rate), and half-unit costs £230. Lodging in single-study bedroom in self-catering apartment is approximately £45 per week. Contact: Dorothy Kelso, Administrator, Univ. of Stirling, Summer Academic Program, Stirling FK9 4LA, U.K.; (011) 44-1786-467955; fax (011) 44-1786-463398; pt-degree@stir.ac.uk, www.stir.ac.uk/theuni/suinfo/courses/sap.

Summer Academy. Summer Academy offers study holidays at 15 British and Irish universities. The course fee includes full board accommodations for 6 to 7 nights, tuition fees, and course-related excursions. Study topics include: heritage, the arts, countryside, and creative writing. Accommodations are in single rooms in university residence halls. Locations include: Aberystwyth, Canterbury,

Cork (Ireland), Durham, Exeter, Glasgow, Maynooth (Ireland), Norwich, Oxford, Sheffield, Southampton, Stirling, Swansea, and York.

Dates: Call for details. Cost: Call for details. Contact: Andrea McDonnell, Marketing and Reservations Coordinator, Summer Academy, Keynes College, The Univ., Canterbury, Kent CT2 7NP, U.K.; (011) 44-1227-470402/ 823473, fax (011) 44-1227-784338; summeracademy@ukc.ac.uk.

TESOL/CELTA Programs. Part-time, 7.5 hours per week for 20 weeks, to gain the widely recognized Trinity College validated Certificate in TESOL to teach EFL. Also offer a 5-week intensive full-time course to gain the internationally recognized Cambridge CELTA qualification to teach EFL.

Dates: TESOL program: Jan 11-Jun 25. CELTA program: Jan and Apr. Cost: TESOL program £685; CELTA program £695. Contact: David Kimmins, Southwark College, The Cut, London SE1 8LE, U.K.; (011) 44-171-815-1682.

Yeats International Summer School. Focus on Yeats' poetry, plays, and prose—the school presents the author in the widest of contexts, offering lectures and seminars that consider Yeats in relation to Dante, Swift, Goethe, Beckett, and contemporary poetry and prose.

Dates: Aug 1-15 (1998). Cost: £300 or $500 includes lectures, seminars, and readings (1998). Contact: Secretary, Yeats Society, Hyde Bridge, Sligo, Ireland; (011) 353-71-42673, fax (011) 353-71-42780.

United States

Masters of International and Intercultural Management. The School for International Training Masters of International and Intercultural Management offers concentrations in sustainable development, international education, and training and human resource de-

velopment in 1 academic year program. This degree is designed for individuals wishing to make a career change or enter the field. A practical training component enables "on-the-job" training and an opportunity to work internationally.

Dates: Call for details. Cost: Call for details. Contact: Kat Eldred, Director of Outreach and Recruitment, Admissions Counselor, School for International Learning, P.O. Box 676, Kipling Rd., Brattleboro, VT 05302; (802) 257-7751, fax (802) 258-3500; admissions@sit.edu, www.sit.edu.

St Giles Language Teaching Center. Earn the Certificate in English Language Teaching to Adults (CELTA) in San Francisco, approved by the Royal Society of Arts/Univ. of Cambridge Examination Syndicate and the California Bureau for Private Postsecondary and Vocational Education. The course on practical training and teaching methodology includes access to international job postings, graduate contacts, and teaching opportunities abroad. EFL school on site for observation and practice teaching. Part of a group of schools in England, Switzerland, and the U.S. with over 40 years of teaching and training experience, led by highly-qualified instructors with extensive overseas teaching experience. CELTA courses also offered in Brighton and London, England.

Dates: Jan 11-Feb 5, Apr 5-30, Jun 7-Jul 2, Sep 13-Oct 8, Oct 25-Nov 19. Cost: $2,550. Contact: St Giles Language Teaching Center, 1 Hallidie Plaza, Suite 350, San Francisco, CA 94102; (415) 788-3552, fax (415) 788-1923; sfstgile@slip.net, www.stgiles-usa.com.

Worldwide

'SD 20' Small Groups Intensive. Small groups (3-8 participants) on all levels offered year round. Lessons taught exclusively by native speakers trained constantly. Follow-up courses available at 280 inlingua schools worldwide.

Accommodations, transfer, special free time activities (festival of music, rafting, skisafari, etc.). Tailor-made packages for agencies, schools, companies, etc. on request.

Dates: Beginners: Jan 11, Feb 1, Mar 1, Mar 29, May 3, Jun 7, Jul 5, Aug 2, Aug 16, Sep 6, Oct 4, Nov 8, Dec 6. With knowledge (assessment test before start): every Monday year round. Cost: Two weeks AS5,700, 3 weeks AS7,700, 4 weeks AS9,450; 1 additional week AS2,250 (1998). Includes 20 lessons per week plus 3 hours free time activities per week, inlingua book, registration fees, assessment test, exempt from VAT. Contact: Inlingua Salzburg, Linzer Gasse 17/t, A-5020, Salzburg, Austria; (011) 43-662-87-11-01, fax (011) 43-662-87-11-01-85; inlinguiasbg@fc.alpin.or.at.

ActionQuest Sail/Dive Programs. Live-aboard 75-day semester voyages for teens and college students, focusing on experiential education, local history and culture, and college-level academics. Multi-level sailing and scuba certification programs with tropical marine biology, oceanography, community service, conservational research projects, and leadership training. No experience necessary.

Dates: Semester: Jan 9-Mar 25, Sep 25-Dec 9. Cost: $11,250 not including airfare. Contact: ActionQuest, P.O. Box 5507, Sarasota, FL 34277; (800) 317-6789, (941) 924-6789, fax (941) 924-6075; actionquest@msn.com, www.actionquest.com.

CCI Adult Homestays Abroad. CCI offers a variety of educational homestay programs to the adult traveler. Independent homestay, language-travel, and internship programs available throughout Europe, Asia, Africa, South America, and Mexico.

Dates: Open. Cost: $515 and up. Contact: Kathleen Baader, CCI, 17 North 2nd Ave., St. Charles, IL 60714; (888) ABROAD1, fax (630) 377-2307; info@cci-exchange.com, www.cci-exchange.com.

College Semester Abroad (SIT). A pioneer in study abroad, The School for International Training (SIT) offers over 57 programs in over 40 countries worldwide. For over 40 years SIT has been a leader in offering field-based study abroad programs to U.S. college and university students.

Dates: Fall and Spring semester. Cost: $8,900-$11,900 depending on location. Includes airfare, tuition, room and board, insurance. Contact: School for International Training, P.O. Box 676, Kipling Rd., Brattleboro, VT 05302; (802) 257-7751, fax (802) 258-3500; csa@sit.edu, www.sit.edu.

¿?don Quijote In-Country Spanish Language Schools. Intensive Spanish language courses using the communicative method are combined with an intensive immersion in the social and cultural life of some of Spain's most interesting cities (Salamanca, Barçelona, Granada, Malaga). Airport pick-up service, study counseling, homestay or student flats, excursions, access to recreational facilities, touring, and sightseeing opportunities. donQuijote now offers intensive Spanish language courses through partner schools in Latin America: Cuernavaca and Mèrida, Mexico; Antigua, Guatemala; Alajuela, Costa Rica; and Quito, Ecuador.

Dates: Year round—Fall, Spring, Winter, and Summer. Cost: Inquire. Contact: ¿?don Quijote, Apartado de Correos 333, 37080 Salamanca, Spain; (011) 34-923-268-860, fax (011) 34-923-268-815; donquijote@offcampus.es, www.teclata.es/donquijote.

Earthwatch Institute. Unique opportunities to work with leading scientists on 1- to 3-week field research projects worldwide. Earthwatch sponsors 160 expeditions in over 30 U.S. states and in 60 countries. Project disciplines include archaeology, wildlife management, ecology, ornithology, and marine mammalogy. No special skills needed—all training is done in the field.

Dates: Year round. Cost: Tax deductible contributions ranging from $695-$2,800 support the research and cover food and lodging expenses. Airfare not included. Contact:

Earthwatch, 680 Mt. Auburn St., P.O. Box 9104MA, Watertown, MA 02272; (800) 776-0188, (617) 926-8200; info@earthwatch.org, www.earthwatch.org.

Field Studies Council Overseas. Special interest natural history and environmental study courses, 1 to 4 weeks' duration. Groups of 10 to 15 people, accompanied by 2 tutors.

Dates: Ongoing. Cost: Range from £540 to £4,400. Contact: Field Studies Council Overseas, Montford Bridge, Shrewsbury SY4 1HW, England; (011) 44-1743-850164/850522, fax (011) 44-1743-850599; fsaoverseas@compuserve.com, www.fscOverseas.mcmail.com.

Global Ecology and Cities in the 21st Century. Two different academic programs to be offered by the International Honors Program. "Global Ecology" is a 2-semester program of around-the-world study and travel to England, Tanzania, India, the Philippines, and Mexico with academic coursework in ecology, anthropology, economics, and environmental issues. The "Cities in the 21st Century" program is a 1-semester program of study and travel to South Africa, India, and Brazil with academic coursework in urban studies, anthropology, sociology, economics, and political science.

Dates: "Global Ecology": Sep-May. "Cities in 21st Century": Jan-May. Cost: "Global Ecology": $21,950 plus airfare, includes tuition, room and board. "Cities in the 21st Century": $12,650 plus airfare, includes tuition, room and board. Estimated airfare for each program is $3,900. Contact: Joan Tiffany, Director, International Honors Program, 19 Braddock Pk., Boston, MA 02116; (617) 267-0026, fax (617) 262-9299; info@ihp.edu, www.ihp.edu.

Global Volunteers. "An adventure in service." The nation's premier short-term service programs for people of all ages and backgrounds. Assist mutual international understanding through ongoing development projects in 19 countries throughout Africa, Asia, the Caribbean, Europe, the South Pacific, North and South America. Programs of 1, 2, and 3 weeks range from natural resource preservation, light construction, and painting, to teaching English and assisting with health care. No special skills or foreign languages are required. Ask about the Millennium Service Project.

Dates: Over 130 teams year round. Cost: Tax-deductible program fees range from $400 to $2,095. Airfare not included. Contact: Global Volunteers, 375 E. Little Canada Rd., St. Paul, MN 55117; (800) 487-1074, fax (651) 482-0915; email@globalvlntrs.org, www.globalvolunteers.org.

Homestay and School Placements. Learn about Canadian culture while living with a family. An affordable alternative for visitors of all ages.

Dates: At least 4 weeks prior to arrival. Cost: $840 for 4 weeks, including private room and 2 meals daily. Contact: Bowers Homestay and Educational Services of Canada, 1 Holswade Rd., Toronto, ON M1L 2G1, Canada; (416) 751-0698, fax (416) 751-3670; rbowers@acros.org.

International Travel Study. Educational faculty-led programs each year range from 1 to 4 weeks in length and offer university credit. Locations include France, Italy, Greece, Turkey, Mexico, Africa, South America, Great Britain, and more. Travel programs focus on art, language, or geography, among a variety of specialties.

Dates: Summer programs May 30-Aug 30; programs in spring and fall. Cost: From $2,300-$4,000. Contact: Mary Pieratt, Director, Travel Study Programs, San Francisco State Univ., College of Extended Learning, 22 Tapia Dr., San Francisco, CA 94132; (415) 338-1533, fax (415) 585-7345; travel@sfsu.edu; www.cel.sfsu.edu.

Language and Culture Immersion. Learn a language and enjoy an exciting variety of cultural and social experiences. Short-term and long-term programs year round for all ages and levels throughout Europe, Asia, Central and South America. Homestays available. Special programs for families, teens, seniors, executives, teachers, professionals. College credit available.

Dates: Year round. Cost: Varies with program. Contact: Nancy Forman, Language Liaison Inc., 20533 Biscayne Blvd., Suite. 4-162, Miami, FL 33180; (800) 284-4448 or (954) 455-3411, fax (954) 455-3413, learn@languageliaison.com, www.languageliaison.com.

Marine Biology Field Courses and Research. The Huntsman Marine Science Centre has a number of different field courses with academic credit such as aquaculture, marine biology, marine mammals, environment studies, etc. and various offerings tailored to the needs of high school students or seniors in our Public Education Program. Also: research facilities for marine scientists and graduate students with well-equipped laboratories and year-round occupation.

Dates: May 2-Oct 31 (field courses, year round for research). Cost: Courses with academic credit (all-inclusive): $915. Research costs available on demand. Contact: M.D.B. Burt, Director, Academic Programs, Huntsman Marine Science Centre, St. Andrews, NB E0G 2X0, Canada.

Sivananda Yoga Teachers Training Course. An intensive 4-week residential program developed by Swami Vishnu-devananda is offered several times a year at Sivananda ashrams worldwide. The course involves theory and practice of all aspects of classical yoga: postures, breathing, relaxation, diet, philosophy, and meditation.

Dates: India: Jan and Nov; Nassua: Feb; California: May; Canada: Jul; New York: Sep; Spain: Sep; Uruguay: Oct. Cost: $1,450 tent, $1,800 dormitory. Contact: The Secretary, Sivananda Ashram Yoga Camp, 673 8th Ave., Val Morin, PQ J0T 2R0, CANADA; (819) 322-3226 or (800) 263-9642 (in Canada), fax (819) 322-5876; h.q.@sivananda.org; www.sivananda.org/camp.html.

Unique Volunteer and Service Programs. Experience culture in parts of the world that few people ever see. Works with each volunteer to find a project suited to his or her needs. Comparable to the Peace Corps without strenuous application process or long-term commitment. Destinations include Africa, Costa Rica, Ecuador, and Mexico. Wide variety of positions available.

Dates: Ongoing. Cost: Minimum 6 weeks $2,145, 6 months $3,875. Includes tuition, accommodations, full board, insurance, transportation, pick up and return to airport. Contact: Alliances Abroad, 409 Deep Eddy Ave., Austin, TX 78703; (888) 622-7623 or (512) 457-8062, fax (512) 457-8132; www.alliancesabroad.com.

Univ. of California Research Expeditions Program-UREP. Adventure with a purpose. Join research expeditions in archaeology, anthropology, environmental studies and more. Get off the beaten track, help in research that benefits local communities. No special experience necessary. Free brochure.

Dates: May-Sep (2 weeks). Cost: From $700-$1,700 (tax deductible). Contact: Univ. of California Research Expeditions Program (UREP); (530) 752-0692, fax (530) 752-0681; urep@ucdavis, www.mip.berkeley.edu/ure.

Various Educational Tours. Voyageur is a group travel company specializing in fully-escorted cultural and educational travel programs to Europe and other overseas destinations. We offer an exciting world of travel opportunities for groups of all ages and interests: high school students, college students, senior citizens, church and social organizations, etc.

Dates: Various. Cost: Call for free brochure. Contact: Voyageur, 120 Stafford St., Worcester, MA 01603-1435; (800) 767-7667; info@govoyageur.com, www.govoyageur.com.

For more listings of adult study and travel programs, and for bargains worldwide, travel tips, and all sorts of information on learning, living, working, and traveling abroad, see *Transitions Abroad* magazine. To order a single copy or a subscription, please call 1-800-293-0373 or visit the *Transitions Abroad* web site at www.transabroad.com.

Adult Travel & Study Programs

CHAPTER 12

LANGUAGE SCHOOLS

The following listing of language schools was supplied by the organizers in 1998 and is updated in each May/June issue of Transitions Abroad *magazine. Contact the program directors to confirm costs, dates, and other details. Please tell them you read about their programs in this book! Programs based in more than one country or region are listed under "Worldwide."*

Africa

Culture and the Arts. An introduction to the rich history, culture, and the arts of the very diverse and ancient people of Senegal and The Gambia. The focus will be on the visual and performing arts. Meet new people, learn new artistic techniques, attend ceremonies and performances, and expand your understanding of West African art and culture.

Dates: Approx. May-Jun. Cost: $2,690. Includes airfare, hotel accommodations, 2 meals per day, tuition for 3 credits. Contact: Rockland Community College, Center for International Studies, 145 College Rd., Suffern, NY 10901; (914) 574-4205, fax (914) 574-4423; study-abroad@sunyrockland.edu.

Argentina

Argentine Universities Program. COPA offers an integrated study opportunity in which undergraduate students live with families and study with degree-seeking Argentine students. Three partner universities offer unique blends of location, academics, and student population. Academic program includes optional program classes and a required Spanish course. A 6-week, non-integrated summer program is also available.

Dates: Spring: Mar-Jul, fall: Jul-Dec, Summer: Jun-Jul. Cost: $7,985 per semester includes tuition, housing, 2 meals daily, orientation, excursions, support services. Contact: Cooperating Programs in the Americas, Butler Univ., 4600 Sunset Ave., Indianapolis, IN 46208; (888) 344-9299, fax (317) 940-9704; COPA@butler.edu.

Argentum. Argentum is a Spanish language and culture program for undergraduate, graduate, and high school students. It is part of Universidad Blas Pascal in Córdoba. We offer the total immersion experience. Students can take other classes in literature, Latin American politics, international relations, art, music, economics, and more.

Dates: Semester 1: Mar 16-Jul 4, Semester 2: Aug 4-Nov 27, Intensive: Mid Jun-Jul. Cost: $6,100 for 1 semester, $10,100 for entire year, $2,200 for intensive program, includes tuition and fees, room and board, cultural activities, and field trips. Contact: Prof. Marta Rosso-O'Laughlin, Argentum, P.O. Box 99, Medford, MA 02153-0099; Tel./fax (781) 488-3552, mrosso@aol.com.

Instituto de Lengua Española (ILEE). Located downtown in the most European-like city in Latin America, Buenos Aires. Dedicated exclusively to teaching Spanish to foreigners. Small groups and private classes year round. All teachers hold Master's degrees in Education or Literature and have been full-time Spanish professors for years. Method is intensive, conversation-based. Student body is international. Highly recommended worldwide. Ask for individual references in U.S.

Dates: Year round. Cost: Four-week intensive program (20 hours per week) including homestay $1,400; 2 weeks $700. Private classes $19 per hour. Registration fee (includes books) $100. Contact: Daniel Korman, I.L.E.E., Director, Lavalle 1619 7º C (1048), Buenos Aires, Argentina; Tel./fax (011) 54-1-375-0730. In U.S.: David Babbitz; (415) 431-8219, fax (415) 431-5306; ilee@overnet.com.ar, www.study abroad.com/ilee.

Austria

Deutsch in Graz. "The whole city is our classroom." German language courses for all age groups; 7 different levels; team-teaching and related activities in the afternoon with groups of 8 or more (12 students max.). By setting interactive tasks and providing individual help we ensure that knowledge is quickly put into practice. Various leisure activities. Accommodations arranged.

Dates: Year round. Cost: Example: 3-week intensive course (81 units) from AS9,900. Contact: Dr. Monika Schneeberger, Deutsch in Graz, Kalchberggasse 10, A-8010 Graz, Austria; (011) 43-316-833900, fax (011) 43-316-833900-6; dig@styria.com, www.dig.co.at.

Deutsch in Graz: In-Service Training. Special programs: in-service training for teachers of German (methodology)*; Austrian civilization and literature*, German for business; courses for children and young people with sport and activities program*; one-to-one tuition; tailor-made courses for school classes and student groups; examination center for the Austrian Language Certificate, and diploma business German (*in summer).

Dates: Year round. Cost: Example: 1-week in-service training (28 units), AS5,100. Contact: Dr. Monika Schneeberger, Deutsch in Graz, Kalchberggasse 10, A-8010 Graz, Austria; (011) 43-316-833900, fax (011) 43-316-833900-6; dig@styria.com, www.dig.co.at.

Deutsch-Institut Tirol. German language courses for foreigners above age 16. Any level from beginner to far advanced. Schedule for the typical day: a) mornings: half-day intensive course in classes of 6 students maximum; conversation, TV, newspapers, tapes, books, grammar, pronunciation; b) afternoons: 3 times at least per week diverse recreational programs in company of a teacher: skiing, hiking, swimming, excursions; c) evenings: 3 times per week 2 lessons, 3 times per week social programs with teacher.

Dates: Year round. Start at any time. Course length optional. Cost: Course and programs: ATS5,000 per week. Room and breakfast: from ATS200 per day. Evening meal at ATS770 per week possible. Contact: Hans Ebenhöh, Director, Am Sandhügel 2, A-6370 Kitzbühel, Austria; (011) 43-5356-71274, fax (011) 43-5356-72363; dit@kitz.netwing.at, www.netwing.at/tirol/kitz/ats/dit.

German Courses at the University. German for beginners and advanced students, perfectionist courses, courses for students of the German language and teachers of German in foreign countries (6 levels). Lectures on German and Austrian literature, music, Austria—the country, people, and language. Special courses: translation, commercial German, commercial correspondence, phonetics. Excursions.

Dates: Three sessions: Jul 4-31, Aug 1-28, Aug 31-Sep 18. Cost: Course fee (4 weeks): approx. ATS4,500. Accommodations: approx. ATS5,800. Contact: Magister Sigrun Inmann-Trojer, Wiener Internationale Hochschulkurse, Universität, Dr. Karl Lueger-Ring 1, A1010 Wien; (011) 43-1-405-12-54-0, fax (011) 43-1-405-12-54/10.

German Intensive Courses. Qualified teachers who work full-time at IKI train you in all language skills (listening, speaking, reading, writing). You learn German in a friendly and communicative atmosphere using audiovisual and up-to-date course material.

Dates: First of each month. Cost: ATS4,400 for 4 weeks (course material included) (1998). Contact: Internationales Kulturinstitut, Opernring 7, A-1010 Wien, Austria; (011) 431-5867321, fax (011) 431-5862993; iki@friends. at.

International German Language Courses. German language classes at all levels and for all ages. Phonetics, cultural and touristic events, all kinds of sports.

Dates: One-month summer courses. Cost: ATS5,700. Includes daily lessons and lodging, and half board with host family. Contact: Helmut Lerch, Director, Interschool, Deutsch in Innsbruck, A-6020 Innsbruck, Kohlstattgasse 3, Austria; (011) 43-0512-58-89-57.

Internationale Hochschulkurse. German courses at the University for beginners and advanced students, perfectionist courses (6 levels). Lectures on German and Austrian literature, music, linguistics, introduction to Austria. Special courses: translation into German, commercial correspondence, business German, medical terminology, communication, phonetics, Vienna waltz. Excursions.

Dates: Jul 4-31, Aug 1-28, Aug 31-Sep 18. Cost: Course fee (4 weeks): approx. ATS4,500. Accommodations: approx. ATS5,800. Contact: Magister Sigrun Inmann-Trojer, Wiener Internationale Hochschulkurse, Universität, Dr. Karl Lueger-Ring 1, A1010 Wien, Austria; (011) 43-1-405-12-54, fax (011) 43-1-405-5410.

Intl. Summer—Univ. of Vienna. European studies focusing on political, economic, legal, and cultural aspects of the New Europe (taught in English) plus German language instruction. Outstanding academic reputation. Most conducive conditions for intercultural and social exchange. Beautifully located on the shore of Wolfgangsee/Salzburg. Excellent sports facilities. Excursions to Salzburg and Vienna.

Dates: Jul 18-Aug 17 (1998). Application deadline: May 31. Cost: ATS29,000 shillings (approx. $2,300). Includes registration, full board and tuition for 4-week session, use of all sports facilities (tennis, sailing and wind surfing lessons), a ticket to the Salzburg Festi-

Language Schools

val, all planned excursions, and a trip to Vienna (half-board). Contact: Univ. of Vienna, International Summer Program Office, Dr. Karl Lueger-Ring 1, A1010 Vienna, Austria; Tel./fax (011) 43-1-40-34-988; sommerhochschule@univie.ac.at, www.univie.ac.at/sommerhochschule.

Benelux

ISOK Voor. Study of the Dutch language, contact with Dutch culture. Group lessons or one-to-one. Homestay with carefully chosen Dutch families.

Dates: No time limit. Cost: Homestay DFL350 per week; group lessons DFL15 per session; private lessons DFL25 per hour. Contact: Mr. J.F.H. de Zeeuw, Principal, Jan-Tooropastraat 4, 2225 XT, Katwijk AAN ZEE, Holland; (011) 31-71-4013533.

Canada

Ecole de français, Montréal. For the last 50 years, the Ecole de français has offered courses in French as a second language to students from around the world. The Ecole is continually improving its programs to meet the changing needs of its students. Choose from Oral and Written Communication French (beginner to advanced), Workshop on Teaching French as a Second Language (for teachers), Contemporary Québec Culture (for advanced students), Business French (intermediate to advanced students).

Dates: Spring: May 18-Jun 10; Summer 1: Jul 5-23; Summer 2: Jul 26-Aug 13; Fall: Sep 13-Dec 10; Winter 2000: Jan 10-Apr 7. Cost: Spring, Summer: (3 weeks, 60 hours) CAN$495; Summer: (3 weeks, 45 hours) CAN$390; Fall/Winter: (12 weeks, 240 hours) CAN$1,495. Prices subject to change. Contact: Serge Bienvenu, Coordinator, Ecole de français, Faculté de l'education permanente, Université de Montréal, C.P. 6128, succursale Centre-ville, Montréal, PQ, H3C 3J7, Canada; (514) 343-6090, fax (514) 343-2430; infolang@fep.umontreal.ca, www.fep.umontreal.ca/langues/index.html.

English Language, Univ. of Victoria. The English Language Centre is known throughout the world for its high standards of English language instruction. Established in 1970, the ELC offers quality language programs aimed at international and Canadian students wishing to improve their English language and cross-cultural skills for personal, professional, and academic purposes. Students from all over the world have attended the ELC. The 12-week Intensive English Language Program is offered 3 times each year, and a series of spring and summer programs are available.

Dates: Mar 31-May 8; May 25-Jun 26; Jul 6-31; Jul 6-Aug 14; Aug 3-28. Cost: Mar 31-May 8: tuition only $1,925; May 25-Jun 26: tuition only $1,585; Jul 6-31: tuition only $1,295; Jul 6-Aug 14; tuition only $1,925; Aug 3-28: tuition only $1,295. Contact: Ms. Bronwyn Jenkins, Co-Director, English Language Centre, Univ. of Victoria, P.O. Box 1700, Victoria, BC V8W 2Y2, Canada; (250) 721-8469, fax (250) 721-6276; bjenkins@uvcs.uvic.ca, www.uvcs.uvic.ca/elc.

General English and French. Intensive (6 hours per day) and semi intensive (4 hours per day) program; 10 levels of English, 6 levels of French. Thirteen major start dates.

Dates: Call for details. Cost: Intensive: 4 weeks CAN$1,140; semi intensive: 4 weeks CAN$900. Contact: LSC Language Studies Canada, 124 Eglinton Ave. W., 4th Fl., Toronto, ON, M4R 2G8, Canada; (416) 488-2200, fax (416) 488-2225.

Intensive English Second Language. Intensive training in speaking, listening, writing, and reading. Advanced level. Students may combine postsecondary courses and language study. Program open to students at basic, intermediate, and advanced language levels. Students may enhance their language studies through participation in extracurricular activities and homestay with Canadian families.

Dates: Sep-Dec, Jan-Apr. Cost: CAN$3,750 tuition only (for 1 semester). Contact: Ms. Suzanne Woods, International Project Officer/Adviser, Sir Sandford Fleming College, Brealey Dr., Peterborough, ON, Canada; (705) 749-

5530 ext. 1262, fax (705) 749-5526; swoods@flemingc.on.ca.

Language and Cultural Studies in Montréal. 1) Semi-intensive French—a theme based program of 3 hours of study a day. 2) Learning Vacations—study the language and culture of Québec while living in Montréal. Take part in French classes in the afternoon with excursions and cultural activities throughout the day.

Dates: 1) Offered from Apr-Nov. Classes begin every 2 weeks (8 students maximum). 2) Available upon request. Groups of 6 or more required. Cost: 1) $435 for 4 weeks, 60 hours, includes access to CD Rom language lab, e-mail and Internet; homestay and other accommodations. 2) $3,250 for 9 days all inclusive. Contact: Y&N - Language and Cultural Studies, 404 Saint Pierre, Suite 201, Montréal, PQ, H2Y 2M2, Canada; (514) 840-7228, fax (514) 840-7111; info@languageco.com, www.languageco.com.

Language Course. Courses in 28 languages, language labs, computer labs, in-house cafeteria, Microsoft certification, homestays available.

Dates: First Monday of every month. Cost: $675 includes books, registration, full-time course. Contact: (514) 281-1016, fax (514) 281-6275; www.platocollege.com.

Language Studies Canada Montréal. Using a multi-skill approach students develop effective communication skills in French. Classes are informative, practical, and enjoyable. Seven levels of 4 weeks each: intensive, 6 hours daily or semi-intensive, 4 hours daily. Maximum of 14 students per class. Audio-visual equipment, multi-media Student Resource Center. Optional activity program. Homestay and alternate accommodations available.

Dates: Year round. Two-week courses begin any Monday. Other programs offered: one-to-one instruction, year round; 2-week. Group 5 executive courses, Jun-Oct; Summer Language Adventure (13- to 17-year-olds), 2-9 weeks in Jul and Aug. Cost: Two weeks intensive program $545 (1998); homestay accommodations $365 (1998). Cost of other services available upon request. Contact: Language Studies Canada Montréal, 1450 City Councillors, Montréal, PQ, H3A 2E6, Canada; (514) 499-9911, fax (514) 499-0332.

Queen's Univ. School of English. The Queen's Univ. School of English offers 5- and 12-week courses year round at one of Canada's oldest and best-known universities in an almost totally English-speaking community. Students have the option of living in a University residence with monitors, in a homestay, or in University cooperative housing. The English Only Rule is strictly enforced.

Dates: Jan 6-Apr 9, May 5-Aug 6, May 17-Jun 18, July 5-Aug 6, Sep 8-Dec 10. Cost: International students: $2,550 for 12 weeks; $1,275 for 5 weeks, plus mandatory health insurance (price varies). Contact: Mrs. Eleanor Rogers, Director, The School of English, Queen's Univ., Kingston, ON K7L 3N6, Canada; (613) 533-2472, fax (613) 533-6809; soe@post.queensu.ca, www.queensu.ca/soe.

Special Intensive French Program. McGill Univ. was founded in 1821 and is internationally renowned for its high academic standards. The Special Intensive French courses are offered at 5 levels and run for 9 weeks. Classes are limited to about 15 students per class. There are 4 sessions a year. Instructional methods include the use of a modern language laboratory, audio-visual equipment, and a wide range of activities stressing the communicative approach.

Dates: Spring: Apr-Jun; Summer: Jun-Aug ; Fall Sep-Nov 20; Winter: Jan-Mar 20. Contact program director for exact dates. Cost: CAN$1,795 for international students, CAN$1,450 for Canadian citizens and permanent residents. Contact: Ms. M. Brettler, 770 Sherbrooke St. W., Montreal PQ, H3A 1G1 Canada; (514) 398-6160, fax (514) 398-2650; lang@conted.lan.mcgill.ca.

Univ. of New Brunswick ELP. Established in 1954 in eastern Canada, tradition of expertise with international clientele. Language contract base; courses designed for client needs; experienced staff; residential approach. Participants live and learn English nonstop weekdays and weekends. Classes extend into the community. Extensive diagnosis, ongoing assessment, constant quality control.

Dates: Three-week format (monthly Sep-Apr) in homestay; 5-week format (May-Jun, Jul-Aug) in university residence. Cost: Three weeks CAN$3,509; 5 weeks CAN$1,850. Includes tuition, materials, meals, accommodations, and weekend socio-cultural activities. Contact: Mrs. Mary E. Murray, Director, Univ. of New Brunswick, English Language Programme, P.O. Box 4400, Fredericton, NB E3B 5A3, Canada; (506) 453-3564, fax (506) 453-3578; elp@unb.ca.

Chile

Chilean Universities Program: Santiago. COPA's program in Santiago, Chile, is designed for advanced undergraduate and graduate students. The interdisciplinary program focuses on issues of national and international development using the case of Chile as special focus. Optional directed research project. Unique out-of-classroom opportunities provide contact with Chilean legislators and policy-makers.

Dates: Spring semester: Mar-Jul, Fall semester: Jul-Dec. Cost: $7,500 includes tuition, housing, and 2 meals daily, orientation, excursions, support services. Contact: Cooperating Programs in the Americas, Butler Univ., 4600 Sunset Ave., Indianapolis, IN 46208; (888) 344-9299, fax (317) 940-9704; COPA@butler.edu.

Chilean Universities Program: Valparaíso. In the twin coastal cities of Valparaíso and Viña del Mar, the home to our program, students take integrated classes with Chilean students and live with a host family. Two program classes are available to complement UCV's course offerings.

Dates: Spring semester: Mar-Jul, Fall semester: Jul-Dec, Summer: Jun-Jul. Cost: Semester $6,900. Includes tuition, housing and 2 meals daily, orientation, excursions, support services. Contact: Cooperating Programs in the Americas, Butler Univ., 4600 Sunset Ave., Indianapolis, IN 46208; (888) 344-9299, fax (317) 940-9704; COPA@butler.edu.

Spanish and Latin American Studies. Santiago offers intensive language studies fulfilling up to 2 years of university Spanish requirements in 1 semester, with additional courses in literature, business, teacher ed., history, political science. Week-long, program-oriented field trips to the south and north of Chile, homestays, and many university activities at Chilean university.

Dates: Spring semester Jan-May; Fall semester Aug-Dec. Cost: One semester $3,790; Fall and Spring $6,340. Contact: University Studies Abroad Consortium (USAC), Univ. of Nevada, Reno #323, Reno, NV 89557-0093; (702) 784-6569, fax (702) 784-6010; usac@admin.unr.edu, www.scs.unr.edu/~usac.

Spanish in Chile. Linguatec offers intensive Spanish language training for executives, visitors and international students. Our highly educated and experienced instructors use Linguatec's easy conversational approach to language instruction, complemented by our video laserdiscs that offer an exciting, stop-action and instant replay teaching support system.

Dates: Classes begin every Monday. Cost: $300 per week for 20 hours of group classes. Contact: Bill Arnold, Linguatec Language Center, Los Leones 439, Providencia, Santiago, Chile; (011) 56-2-233-4356, fax (011) 56-2-234-1380; barnold@ruena.cl, www.linguatec.cl.

China

Chinese Studies (Chengdu). The Chinese Studies Program offers intensive language study fulfilling up to 2 years of university language requirements in 1 semester. Additional courses in art history, economics, anthropology, political science, physics, chemistry, literature, history, and calligraphy are taught in English and offer a multidisciplinary approach to understanding the complexities of China and Asia.

Dates: Spring: Jan-May; Summer: Jun-Aug 2; Fall: Aug-Dec. Cost: Fall or Spring $4,260; Summer $1,680; year $6,860. Contact: University Studies Abroad Consortium (USAC), Univ. of Nevada, Reno #323, Reno, NV 89557-0093; (702) 784-6569, fax (702) 784-6010; usac@admin.unr.edu, www.scs.unr.edu/~usac.

Mandarin Language Study. Study intensive Mandarin Chinese at Beijing Language and Culture Univ., the only university in China specializing in teaching Mandarin to foreigners. Classes are intensive with 20 hours of classroom instruction per week. Fees include tuition, textbooks, double-occupancy accommodations, sightseeing in Beijing, cultural activities, orientation, visa processing, and roundtrip airfare from San Francisco.

Dates: Spring, Summer, Fall programs, and 1-year program. Cost: Six weeks $3,250, 20 weeks $4,990, 12 weeks $4,190, 1 year $7,190. Contact: China Advocates, 1635 Irving St., San Francisco, CA 94122; (800) 333-6474, fax (415) 753-0412; chinaadv@aol.com.

Costa Rica

Costa Rican Language Academy. Costa Rican-owned and-operated language school offers first-rate Spanish instruction in a warm and friendly environment. Teachers with university degrees. Small groups or private classes. Included free in the programs are airport transportation, coffee and natural refreshments, excursions, Latin dance, Costa Rican cooking, music, and conversation classes to provide students with complete cultural immersion.

Dates: Year round (start anytime). Cost: $135 per week or $220 per week for program with homestay. All other activities and services included at no additional cost. Contact: Costa Rican Language Academy, P.O. Box 336-2070, San José, Costa Rica; (011) 506-221-1624 or 233-8914 or 233-8938, fax (011) 506-233-8670. In the U.S.: (800) 854-6057; crlang@sol.racsa.co.cr., www.crlang.co.cr/index.html.

Enjoy Learning Spanish Faster. Techniques developed from our ongoing research enable students at Centro Linguistico Latinoamericano to learn more, faster, in a comfortable environment. Classes are 2-5 students plus group learning activities; conversations with middle-class homestay families (1 student per family). Homestays are within walking distance of school in small town (14,000 population) near the capital, San Jose.

Dates: Year round. Classes begin every Monday, at all levels. Cost: $295 per week for 25 hours of classes. Includes tuition, all meals (7 days a week), homestay, laundry, all materials, Costa Rican dance and cooking classes, and airport transportation. $25 one-time registration. Contact: Susan Shores, Registrar, Latin American Language Center, 7485 Rush River Dr., Suite 710-123, Sacramento, CA 95831; (916) 447-0938, fax (916) 428-9542; lalc@madre.com.

ILISA and Language Link. ILISA offers intensive Spanish language programs with a professional emphasis in the quiet university area of San Pedro, a suburb of San Jose, Costa Rica. Your choice of either 4 hours daily of small classes (never more than 4 students), a combination of 4 hours group and 2 hours private, or completely private. Professional adults, college students, and all Spanish levels. Academic credit through accredited university. Caring homestays and 3 additional weekly activities included. Excursion program. A well-developed program is available for families, with nanny care.

Dates: Year round, 2-12 weeks, start any Monday. Summer months fill very early. Cost: Four hours daily of group classes and homestay: 2 weeks $835. Includes registration, insurance, tuition, materials, airport pickup, private room, and 2 meals daily. Contact: Kay G. Rafool, Language Link Inc., P.O. Box 3006, Peoria, IL 61612; (800) 552-2051, fax (309)

672-2926; info@langlink.com, www.langlink. com.

Institute for Progressive Communications. IPC offers summer courses at Radio for Peace International, which transmits from the Univ. for Peace. Learn hands-on radio production at RFPI and receive intensive Spanish instruction near a beautiful rainforest preserve.

Dates: Jun 29-Jul 24, Aug 3-28. Cost: $1,170 includes room and board, coursework, and transportation. Contact: IPC, SBO #66, P.O. Box 025292, Miami, FL 33102-5292; (011) 506-249-1821, fax (011) 506-249-1095; rfpicr@sol.racsa.co.cr, www.clark.net/pub/cwilkins/rfpi.

Instituto de Lenguaje "Pura Vida." Only minutes from the capital in the fresh mountain air of Heredia. Intense total immersion methods of teaching. Morning classes and daily cultural activities all conducted in Spanish, maximum 5 students per class. Teachers hold university degrees. Latin music and dance lessons, tours, trips, parties. Learn Spanish fast.

Dates: Classes for all levels start every Monday year round. Cost: Language only, 20 hours per week $230; total immersion, 35 hours per week with homestay $370; children's classes with homestay $370 per week, daycare available. Contact: Instituto de Lenguaje "Pura Vida," P.O. Box 730, Garden Grove, CA 92842; (714) 534-0125, fax (714) 534-1201; BS7324@aol.com, www.arweb.com/puravida.

Intensive Spanish Training. The Institute for Central American Development Studies (ICADS) offers 4-week progressive programs in Intensive Spanish Languages—4 1/2 hours daily, 5 days a week. Small classes (4 students or less). Activities and optional afternoon internships emphasize environmental issues, women's issues, development, human rights, and public health. Supportive learning environment. Homestays and field trips. Great alternative for the socially conscious.

Dates: Programs begin first Monday of each

month. Cost: $1,325 includes airport pick-up, classes, books, homestay, meals, laundry, lectures, activities, field trips, and internship placements. Contact: ICADS, Dept. 826, P.O. Box 025216, Miami, FL 33102-5216; (011) 506-225-0508, fax (011) 506-225-234-1337; icads@netbox.com, www.icadscr.com.

IPEE Spanish Language School. IPEE is a premier Spanish language school. Seven levels (standard and intensive courses), excursions, excellent homestays. Credit available. Our professors are co-owners and take a personal interest in aspects of our students' stay.

Dates: Year round programs. New classes start every Monday. One week to 6 months. Cost: One week $374, 2 weeks $679, 3 weeks $1,002, 4 weeks $1,229, 5 weeks $1,229, 6 weeks $1,779, 7 weeks $2,079, 8 weeks plus $275 per week. Includes homestay, 2 meals per day, laundry service, private room, all text and work books, airport pickup service, Latin dance class, exotic food class, other cultural classes. Contact: Robert Levy, Director, IPEE, 16057 Tampa Palms Blvd., Suite 158, Tampa, FL 33647; Tel./fax (813) 988-3916; ipee@gate.net, www.gate.net/~ipee/.

Spanish and More in Heredia. Heredia offers intensive language studies which fulfills up to 2-year university Spanish requirements in a semester or 1 year in the 8-week summer program. Additional courses offered in political science, history, biology, teacher ed., business, literature, etc. Program organized week-long and weekend field trips, homestays, and many local university activities.

Dates: Spring term: Jan-May; Summer sessions: May-Jul, Jun-Aug, Jul-Aug; Fall term: Aug-Dec. Contact for exact dates. Cost: Fall or Spring semester $4,390; year $7,190; Jun or Jul $1,980; Aug $1,610; Jun and Jul $3,680; June, July, and Aug $3,190; Jun, Jul, and Aug $4,680. Contact: University Studies Abroad Consortium (USAC), Univ. of Nevada, Reno #323, Reno, NV 89557-0093; (702) 784-6569, fax (702) 784-6010; usac@admin.unr.edu, www.scs.unr.edu/~usac.

Benefits of a Language Study Vacation

Combining Three Different Travel Experiences in One

By Roger L. Edwards, Jr.

A vacation that combines travel with foreign language study offers several advantages over typical "tourist" vacations: A richer vacation experience, peace of mind, savings, and a point of departure for additional travel. A language study vacation combines three different travel experiences into one:

Educational Experience. The best way to acquire a foreign language is to be immersed—to see it, hear it, and *have* to speak it every day.

Tourist Experience. Just because you're taking classes and studying doesn't mean you have to sacrifice fun. Many immersion schools are situated in or near interesting locations and provide tours of the cities in which they're located. Moreover, excursions to more distant locations are often available.

Cultural Experience. Many schools offer activities (classes in arts, crafts, dance, cooking, etc.) that allow you to gain valuable insight into the culture. If you choose the homestay option, you'll get a first-hand glimpse into the culture and how the locals actually live. You sit at their dinner table, interact with them, and share in their activities. It's in this way that lasting friendships develop.

Peace of mind. If you've never traveled abroad before, this kind of vacation lessens the "first-time-abroad" jitters. Why? Because of the structure provided by such programs. Although you may arrive in the country alone, you won't be alone. You may be greeted and picked up at the airport and taken to your host family. Once you're at the school, you'll meet other students and either plan independent activities and excursions with them or join in those sponsored by the school.

Savings. Food and lodging are often the most expensive part of traveling. A homestay will cost you far less than a hotel stay for the same duration, and two meals are usually included with each homestay. Moreover, some merchants, restaurants, touring companies, etc. offer discounts to language school students.

A point of departure. Language programs are great starting points for more extensive vacations. The structured school setting gives you a chance to get acclimated to your new surroundings and to gather suggestions from locals about what to do and see before you branch out to more distant locations for sightseeing, eco-tours, volunteer projects, etc.

Spanish Immersion Program. Nestled in colonial Barva, equidistant from Heredia's National Univ. and surrounding mountains, Escuela Latina offers an intensive, experience-based Spanish language and culture program. Students live in nearby homestays. Classes (max. 6 students) are taught entirely in Spanish. Dance, music, and cooking classes included in tuition. Volunteer opportunities offered.

Dates: Classes begin every Monday. Cost: $995 for 4 weeks including homestay. Contact: Jill Dewey, Apdo 203-3000, Heredia, Costa Rica; (011) 506-237-5709, fax (011) 506-261-5233; eslatina@amerisol.cr. In the U.S.: Roger Dewey, (970) 242-6960, fax (970) 242-6967.

Spanish Language. Intercultura Language Institute offers intensive Spanish and homestays with selected Costa Rican families. Academic credit available (with prior notice). Additional free cultural activities: Latin-dance, music, theater, cinema, cooking. Weekend excursions to volcanoes, beaches, rainforest. Volunteer opportunities in social, environmental, and political organizations. Beach campus: optional 1 week per month, study on Pacific coast.

Dates: Year round. Cost: $1,045 per month (shorter stays available). Contact: Laura Ellington, Codirector, Intercultura Costa Rica, Apdo. 1952-3000, Heredia, Costa Rica; (011) 506-260-8480, Tel./fax (011) 506-260-9243; intercul@sol.racsa.co.cr, www.alphaluz.com/intercultura.

Spanish Language Program. Twenty hours of small group instruction, maximum 4 students per class, Monday-Friday. All ages and all levels. Each student takes an oral and written exam and is placed at a level that matches his/her knowledge. Students live with a Costa Rican family. Organized activities are part of the program.

Dates: Courses start every Monday of the year. Cost: Four-week program $1,090: host family stay, language classes 4 hours per day, 5 days a week. (Also 1-week, 2-week, or 3-week program.) Contact: Guiselle Ballestero, Sonia Rojas, Ronny Garcia; (011) 506-458-3157, fax (011) 506-458-3214; www.institutodecultura.com.

Univ. Nacional Autónoma de Heredia. Costa Rica is exceptional for its political stability and environmental sensitivity. Our undergraduate program at Universidad Nacional Autonoma allows participants to enroll in both program classes and regular university courses while living with local host families. Many extracurricular activities are available through the University.

Dates: Spring semester: Feb-Jun, Fall semester: Jul-Dec. Cost: $6,695 per semester includes tuition, housing, 2 meals daily, orientation, excursions, support services. Contact: Cooperating Programs in the Americas, Butler Univ., 4600 Sunset Ave., Indianapolis, IN 46208; (888) 344-9299, fax (317) 940-9704; COPA@butler.edu.

Ecuador

Academia de Español Quito. Specially designed programs for foreign students. One-on-one instruction up to 7 hours daily. Courses based on conversation, vocabulary, and grammar at all levels. Cultural and social activities provided weekly. The system is self-paced, and it is possible to start at any time. Earn academic credits. Live with an Ecuadorian family, 1 student per family, full board.

Dates: Year round. Cost: $1,600 for 4 weeks includes tuition, meals, housing, fees, airport transfer. Contact: Edgar J. Alvarez, Director, 130 Marchena St. and 10 de Agosto Ave., P.O. Box 17-15-0039-C, Quito, Ecuador; (011) 593-2-553647/554811, fax (011) 593-2-506474/504330; edalvare@pi.pro.ec, www.academiaquito.com.ec.

Academia Latinoamericana. Ecuador's top private Spanish language institute in former diplomat's mansion with gardens, swimming pool, hot tub, in lovely residential area of Quito. Small group classes, executive courses, high school groups, exclusive "SierrAzul Cloud Forest" extension program. Select host family accommodation. Excursions to haciendas, Indian markets, other activities. USA college credit and internships available.

Dates: Year round. Cost: $296 per week. Includes 20 hours of one-on-one lessons, 7 days with host family, 2 meals per day, transfer, services at the school and teaching material. Contact: Suzanne S. Bell, Admissions Director, USA/International, 640 East 3990 South, Suite E, Salt Lake City, UT, 84107; (801) 268-4608, fax (801) 265-9156; academia@juno.com or delco@spanish.com. ec, www.ecua.net.ec/academia.

Language Schools. A simple, modern, and efficient teaching method in which students are encouraged to use commonly used written and spoken expressions. We cater both for a broad range of interests—including society, culture, politics, history, and the economy—as well as particular specializations for all ages and all levels.

Dates: Year round. Cost: One-to-one classes: $6 per hour. Accommodations with families: $16 per day. Incription: $40. Contact: Sylvia Paucar, Academia de Español, "Mitad del Mundo," Gustavo Darquea Terán 0e2-58 y Versalles, Ecuador; (011) 593 2-567875/546827/567875; mitmundl@mitadmundo.com.ec, www.pub.ecua.net.ec/mitadmundo.

Spanish in the Middle of the World. Spanish Institute offers the opportunity of learning the language and culture while enjoying the wonderful weather and landscape of 0 degrees latitude. One-on-one and group courses to fit all needs. Accommodation facilities in Ecuadorian homes or dormitories. English teachers may have a job while learning a second language.

Dates: Classes start on Monday year round

(except holidays). Cost: $5 per hour includes texts, workbook, language lab, teaching aids, completion diploma. Contact: Benedict Schools of Languages, Edmundo Chiriboga, 713 Y Jorge Paez, Quito, Ecuador; fax (011) 593-2-432729, 462972; benedict@access inter.net, www.virtual systems.com.ec. benedictq.

Egypt

The American Univ. in Cairo. Intensive Arabic language training in Modern Standard, Egyptian Colloquial, and Fusha at the elementary, intermediate, and advanced levels is given by the Arabic Language Institute of The American Univ. in Cairo. Full use is made of the Arabic speaking environment of Cairo and classes are enhanced by field trips.

Dates: Sep-Jan; Feb-Jun; Jun-Jul. Cost: Approx. $5,150 per semester for tuition plus room and board. Contact: Matrans Davidson, Office of Student Affairs, American Univ. in Cairo, 420 5th Ave., 3rd Fl., New York, NY 10018; aucegypt@aucnyo.edu.

El Salvador

Melida Anaya Montes Language School. The Melida Anaya Montes Language School offers intensive Spanish courses at all levels utilizing popular education methodology and participatory techniques. Students can lodge at nearby inexpensive guest houses or will be placed with Salvadoran families. Program includes meetings and activities with popular organizations, weekend excursions to developing communities, archaeological ruins, other places of interest.

Dates: Two- and 4-week sessions taught year round. Cost: $95 per week for classes; room and board $50 per week. Contact: CISPES c/o School, 19 W. 21st St., Suite 502, New York, NY 10010; (212) 229-1290; cis@nicarao.apc.org.

Language Schools

Melida Anaya Montes Spanish School. The MAM Spanish School offers intensive courses at all levels, utilizing popular education techniques and participatory methodology. An integral part of the program includes participation in afternoon meetings with popular organizations, excursions to developing communities and other places of interest, and housing with Salvadoran families with diverse interests.

Dates: Classes begin the 1st and 3rd Monday of every month, except on national holidays (Easter week, May 1, Jun 22, 1st week of Aug, Sep 15, Nov 2, and Christmas and New Year's week). Cost: Weekly costs: Spanish classes $100, administrative fee $12.50, cultural program $25, room and board $60. Contact: CIS MAM Language School, Boulevard Universitario, Casa #4, San Salvador, El Salvador, Centro America; Tel./fax (011) 503-226-2623; cis@nicarao.org.ni.

Europe

German Language Courses. German courses for adults with culture program in Vienna (age 16 and over).

Dates: Jul and Aug. Cost: Call for details. Contact: Oekista, Tuerkenstrasse 8\1, 1090 Vienna, Austria; fax (011) 43-1-401-488800; german.course@oekista.co.at, www.oekista.co.at.

Italian Language, Art, and Culture. We offer year round courses in Italian language, art, culture, and cookery for groups or individuals. Each lessons lasts 60 minutes and is taught in Italian by a fully qualified native speaker. We have a free accommodations service and busy social program.

Dates: Courses start every second Monday. Cost: Call for details. Contact: Sonia di Centa, Centro Internationale Dante Alighieri, Piazza la Lizza 10, 53100 Siena, Italy; (011) 39-577-49533, fax (011) 39-577-270646; dantesi@iol.it, http://web.tin.it/sienaol/cida.htm.

Italian Language for Foreigners. Our school was founded in 1889 and has more than a century of experience in teaching Italian to foreign students from all over the world. The aim of the Dante Alighieri Society, with over 500 committees both in Italy and abroad, is to favor and promote Italian language and culture.

Dates: Contact for details. Cost: Contact for details. Contact: Paoletti Varia, Societa Dante Alighieri, via Gimo Capponi, 4, Firenze 50121, Italy; segretaria@cantealighieri.it.

Language, Arts, and Sports. Active learning vacations. French, Spanish, Italian; cooking, painting, drawing, photography workshops. Combine programs or interests in one vacation. Learn French and sailing or ski; Spanish and golf. Bicycle tours with language lessons. We match individual needs and interests with programs and options: family stay, residence, apartment, hotel; intensive to total immersion (no English); group or one-on-one (including study in and live in your teacher's home).

Dates: Programs run from 1 week to months. Cost: Include room and board, tuition. Contact: Mary Ann Puglisi, eduVacations, 1431 21st St. NW, Suite 302, Washington, DC 20036; (202) 857-8384, fax (202) 835-3756.

France

Bilingual Summer Courses. Courses in French or in French and English in the morning, 20 hours per week. Activities in the afternoon: sports, visits to chateaux de la Loire, 1 excursion on Saturdays (Paris, Mont St. Michel, etc.)

Dates: Jul 5-Aug 20. Cost: $1,500 for 4 weeks' tuition, homestay, activities. Contact: Ph. Minereau, St. Denis, European School, BP 146-37600, Loches, France; (011) 33-247-5904-26, fax (011) 33-247-94050; saint-denis@touraine.com, www.touraine.com/saint-denis.

Francais Gènèral et de Spècialitè. Courses for adults who need to express themselves with the greatest possible fluency, whether for leisure or professional purposes. Courses may be coupled with commercial or business French. One to 8 weeks, 4 lessons per day or more, 5-10 participants per group (2-4 in business French). Extracurricular activities outside class: golf, painting, cooking, excursions.

Dates: Every second Monday. Cost: From FF3,500 for 2 weeks. Contact: IS, Aix-en-Provence, 9 Cours des Arts et Mètiers, Aix-en-Provence 13100, France; (011) 33-4-42-93-47-90, fax (011) 33-4-42-26-31-80; aix@aix.pacwan.net.

France Langue Schools in Paris/Nice. Delightful private language institute blocks from the Champs Elysees, Paris, or the sunny beaches of the French Riviera. Year round, all ages and levels. Specialty classes: commerce, cuisine, business, au pair, tourism, DELE, DALF. Custom-designed programs for teachers and high school groups. University credit available. Family stay, residence halls, apartments, or hotel accommodations.

Dates: Contact for information. Cost: Contact for information. Contact: Mr. De Poly, France Langue, 22 ave. Notre Dame, 06000 Nice, France; (011) 33-4-93-13-7888, fax (011) 33-4-93-13-7889; frlang_n@club-internet.fr, www.france.langue.fr.

French-American Exchange. FAE offers language programs in Montpellier, Tours, and Aix-en-Provence from 2 weeks to a full academic year. Housing is arranged with families, in apartments, student residences, or hotels. All programs begin with a weekend in Paris and include tuition, fees, housing, and meals (transportation may also be arranged at additional charge). Ideal for the independent traveler.

Dates: Summer: Jun, Jul, Aug, Sep; trimester: Oct-Dec, Jan-Mar, Apr-Jun; semester: Sep/Oct-Jan, Jan-May, Feb-Jun; year: Sep-Jun, Oct-May; 2 or more weeks year round. Cost: Summer $1,742 (4 weeks); trimester $3,020; semester $5,330-$5,502; year $9,795-$14,050; 2 weeks starting from $775. Contact: Jim Pondolfino, Director, 111 Roberts Ct., Box 7, Alexandria, VA 22314; (800) 995-5087, fax (703) 549-2865; faetours@erols.com, www.faetours.com.

French and Cookery in a Château. Live and study in 18th-century château with relaxed, convivial atmosphere. Residential French language and Provençal cooking for adults. Comfortable single/twin and shared rooms. Good food and wine at the heart of one of France's loveliest areas, near Lyon.

Dates: Two weeks in Feb, and every Sunday May-Nov. Cost: From $800 full board and classes in château. Contact: Michael Giammarella in U.S.: (800) 484-1234 ext 0096 or Ecole des Trois Ponts, Château de Matel, 42300 Roanne, France; (011) 33-477-70-80-01, fax (011) 33-477-71-5300; info@3ponts. edu, www.3ponts.edu.

French Courses in Bordeaux. International school that offers intensive French programs for adults in Bordeaux—one of Europe's most exciting cities. Mini groups of 4-8 participants max. per class and level allowing personalized attention and fast results. Wide range of courses: Central French, Specialized Business, Bordeaux Wine Course, course at the teacher's home.

Dates: Bordeaux Wine Course. Beginners—first Monday of each month. Cost: Two weeks, 15 hours per week, FF2,700. Contact: Anastasia-BLS, 1 Cours Georges Clemenceau, 33000 Bordeaux, France; (011) 33-556-51-0076, fax (011) 33-556-51-7615; bls@imaginet.fr, www.bls-bordeaux.com.

French Language Immersion. International institute on Mediterranean coast. Short- and long-term French courses. Modern air-conditioned premises in large park. Restaurant with terrace. Top-quality homestay, hotels, apartments. Minimum age 17, maximum unlimited. Students, business people, employees, airline staff, retired people. Charming medieval town linking Provence to Riviera, lively marina, unspoiled beaches.

Dates: Year round. Cost: From FF1,200 per week (tuition). Contact: Institut ELFCA, 66 ave. du Toulon, 83400 Hyeres, France; (011) 33-4-94-65-03-31, fax (011) 33-4-94-65-81-22; elfca@elfca.com, www.elfca.com.

French Language Learning Vacations. Learn French while discovering the Chateaux of the Loire Valley, the secrets of Provence, or the sandy beaches of the Mediterranean. Our programs are designed for independent travelers sharing a passion for the French culture and lifestyle. We offer a choice of locations in Tours, Aix-en-Provence, Montpellier, Paris, or Nice.

Dates: Two or more weeks year round. Cost: Two-week packages range from $820-$1,200. Contact: Jim Pondolfino, French-American Exchange, 111 Roberts Court, Box 7, Alexandria, VA 22314; (800) 995-5087, fax (703) 549-2865; faetours@erols.com, www.faetours.com.

French Studies (Pau). Pau offers intensive language studies—up to 4 semesters of university language courses in 1 semester, 1 year in the 8-week summer program, in addition to art, political science, history, literature, second language teaching methods, etc. Week-long field trips to Paris, homestay or student residence, and many activities at the French university.

Dates: Spring semester: Jan-Apr; Summer sessions: May-Jun; Jun-Aug; Jul-Aug; Fall semester: Sep-Dec. Contact for exact dates. Cost: Fall or Spring semester $4,280; Jun $1,700; Jul $1,880; Aug $1,380; Jun and Jul $3,480; Jun and Aug $2,870; Jul and Aug $2,970; Jun, Jul, and Aug $4,580; year $6,980. Contact: University Studies Abroad Consortium (USAC), Univ. of Nevada, Reno #323, Reno, NV 89557-0093; (702) 784-6569, fax (702) 784-6010; usac@admin.unr.edu, www.scs.unr.edu/~usac.

Learn French in France (CES). Language immersion courses in France (Paris, Nice, Antibes, Bordeaux, Cannes, Monaco, Montpellier, Aix-en-Provence, Tours). Private language schools centrally located, convenient to interesting places, cultural events, sports activities. Programs feature qualified teachers, small classes, attractive surroundings and facilities. Affordable prices for instruction. Accommodations with French families with meals, student residences, apartments, and nearby hotels.

Dates: Year round. Two weeks or more. Cost: Two-week courses with or without accommodations range from $605 to $2,260. Contact: Ms. Lorraine Haber, Study Abroad Coordinator, CES Study Abroad Program, The Center for English Studies, 330 7th Ave., 6th Fl., New York, NY 10001; (212) 629-7300, fax (212) 736-7950.

Learn French in France (IFG). Whatever the need, whatever the level, IFG Langues has the experience, the skill, and the resources to provide the optimum courses in French. Our team of highly qualified teachers offers individually tailored programs. Courses concentrate first on general language, then on specific professional needs. Host family or hotel on request.

Dates: Courses begin any Monday. Cost: FF470.34 per hour, all taxes included. Contact: Aline Pernot, IFG Languages, 37, quai de Grenelle, 75015 Paris, France; (011) 33-1-40-59-31-38, fax (011) 33-1-45-75-14-43.

Learn French in the "Pink City." Discover Toulouse in between the Mediterranean Sea, the Atlantic Ocean, and the Pyrenees. Year-round intensive courses and workshops. All levels of proficiency. Free placement test. Special for summer: linguistic training for higher education; training session for foreign teachers of French. Affordable accommodations (in dormitories) available Jul-Sep.

Dates: Sessions start in Jul, Aug, Sep, Oct, and Mar. Cost: From FF1,700 per session up. Contact: Mr. Christian Depierre, C.E.F.L.E., Université de Toulouse II - Le Mirail, 5, allées

Antonio Machado, 31058 Toulouse Cedex 1, France; (011) 33-5-61-50-42-38, fax (011) 33-5-61-50-41-35; cefle@cict.fr, www.univ-tlse2.fr/cefle.

Live and Learn French. Live with a carefully selected, welcoming French family in the Paris region. Learn from a family member/teacher who has a university degree and will tailor a private course to suit your needs. Share in a cultural and learning experience that will develop both your understanding of the language and the people who speak it. Minimum of 1 week stay. We also offer touristic stays in English or French.

Dates: Year round. Cost: Fifteen hours of study per week $1,150; 20 hours of study per week $1,310. Two people $1,675 per week. Prices include room, 3 meals a day, and instruction. Contact: Sara S. Monick, Live & Learn, 4215 Poplar Dr., Minneapolis, MN 55422; (612) 374-2444, fax (612) 333-3554; DHILLI608@aol.com.

Summer Studies on Riviera. For the 22nd consecutive year, summer language courses open to an international public of all ages and levels. Instruction: 4, 6, or 8 hours per day. Accommodations: French families, hotels, apartments. Social and cultural activities, tennis, golf, and windsurfing. Skilled and devoted French-born teachers. In Jun/Jul, cadets from the Military Academy of West Point.

Dates: Jun 14-Aug 16 in 2-, 3-, and 4-week sessions. Cost: Two weeks: FF5,300, 3 weeks: FF7,000 for tuition and family stay. Contact: France Langue & Culture, 37 bis av. Brancolar, 06100 Nice, France; Tél./fax (011) 33-93-46-8-35-06-98; www.algonet.se/~t-i.

Where Finest French Is Spoken. Study and live in the Loire Valley, at CLE, a leading private institute for French studies since 1985. Short- and long-term intensive courses in a restored 18th century building in historic Tours. Maximum of 7 students per class. Professionally trained teachers. Top-quality homestay, hotels, apartments. Minimum age 18.

Dates: Year round. Cost: Tuition FF1,680 per week. Family stay FF950 per week. Contact: Isabelle or Hervé Aubert, Owners and Managers, CLE, 7-9 place de Châtcauneuf, 37000 Tours, France; (011) 33-247-64-06-19, fax (011) 33-247-64-05-84-61; herve@cle.fr, www.cle.fr.

Germany

Collegium Palatinum Heidelberg. A German language institute, located in downtown Heidelberg, offering German at all levels from beginner to advanced. Two-, 4- and 8-week courses year round. Combination courses, one-on-one tuition and customized courses for groups. Recreational and cultural program. Accommodations: residential, guest family, private arrangement, or hotel.

Dates: Year round. Cost: Four weeks DM2,370; 8 weeks DM1,730. Activity program extra. Contact: Mrs. Martine Berthet-Richter, PR Director, Adenauerplatz 8, D-69115 Heidelberg, Germany; (011) 49-6221-46289, fax (011) 49-6221-182023; SchillerUS@aol.com.

Deutsch als Fremdsprache und Wirtschaftsdeutsch. 1) Intensive Course Standard German on 5 levels (beginner to advanced), 10 weeks with 200 lessons; 2) Summer Class Standard German for advanced students; 3) Summer Class Business German for advanced students. 2) and 3) 4 weeks, 120 lessons. Institute located on university campus. Accommodations in selected host families, leisure-time program.

Dates: 1) Apr 15-Jun 26, Jul 20-Sep 25, Oct 12-Dec 18; 2) Aug 3-Aug 28; 3) Sep 1-Sep 25. Cost: Without accommodations: 1) DM1,198, 2) DM700, 3) DM995; with accommodations 1) DM1,600, 2) DM1,100, 3) DM1,465. Contact: Maria Yendell, Institute für Internationale Kommunikation in Zusammenarbeit mit der Heinrich-Heine-Universität e.V., Universitätsstr. 1, Geb. 23.31/U1.73, D-40225 Düsseldorf, Germany; (011) 49-211-81-15182, fax (011) 49-211-81-12537; iik@phil-fak.uni-duesseldorf.de, www.iik-duesseldorf.de.

German as a Foreign Language. Various levels of German year round; intensive, crash, and long-term courses, individual tuition. Special feature: German and theater. Special programs: business German for professionals, German for teachers, German in a teacher's home, German for special purposes. Academic year for high school students, international study year, internship, guest studentship, homestays for groups, courses for firms and other institutions (banking, insurance, doctors, lawyers, etc.), residential language camps for juniors, examination preparation. Various types of accommodations. Full range of activities.

Dates: Year round. Cost: Contact school for details. Contact: GLS Sprachenzentrum, Barbara Jaeschke, Managing Director, Kolonnenstrasse 26, 10829 Berlin, Germany; (011) 49-30-787 41-52; fax (011) 49-30-787-41-92; gls.berlin@t-online.de, www.gls-berlin.com.

German as a Foreign Language. Students from all over the world are taught in small groups or on an individual basis. The school accepts all levels from total beginner to advanced, prepares for official examinations, offers courses for specific purposes, etc. Part of all courses: transmission of German culture, history, and news. The variety of art, culture and leisure activities in and around Munich provides each student endless possibilities. Baviera even has a Travel Service offering flights, tours, etc. Academic credit available.

Dates: Year round except Christmas. Courses start every Monday. Cost: Small group: DM506 (inc. VAT) per week. Accommodations extra. Contact: Baviera, Nymphenburger Str. 154, 80634 Munich, Germany; (011) 49-89-1665599, fax (011) 49-89-1665530; baviera@t-online.de.

German as a Foreign Language. Intensive language courses (18 and over) for people who wish to prepare themselves for entrance examinations required by German universities or for persons who need a good working knowledge of German for profession.

Dates: Year round. Cost: DM2,900. Includes accommodations and full board for 2 months (1998). Contact: Claudia Schöttler, Akademie Klausenhof, Klausenhofstr, 100 D-46499 Hamminkeln-Dingden; (011) 49-2852-89329, fax (011) 49-2852-89300; akademie.klausenhof @t-online.de.

German Language Courses. International House Freiburg offers 3 types of courses for: adults and business people: intensive group courses, one-to-one; university students: trimester and summer intensive courses; juniors: summer holiday courses.

Dates: Vary. Cost: TBA. Contact: International House, Dieter Löffner, Werderring 18, Freiburg, D-79098, Germany; (011) 49-761-34751, fax (011) 49-761-382476; ihfreiburg@ihfreiburg. toplink.de.

German Language Courses. 1. Group tuition available at all levels. 2. One-on-one tuition, tailor made. 3. Summer school in Aug for ages 11-16. 4. Cultural program.

Dates: Any Monday, year round. Cost: Two week group tuition, 10 lessons a week DM720; half board, single room DM410. Contact: Inlingua, Senalinger-Tor-Platz 6, D-80336 Munich, Germany; (011) 49-89-2311530, fax (011) 49-89-2609920; info@inlingua.de, www.inlingua.de.

German Language Courses in Berlin. Intensive German courses throughout the entire year and special summer courses. International, friendly atmosphere, all levels, beginners' courses monthly; start for other levels any Monday after a placement test; min. age: 16. Accommodations with German families include half board and breakfast.

Dates: Jan 11, Feb 8, Mar 8, Apr 5, May 3, May 31, Jun 28, Jul 26, Aug 23, Sep 20, Oct 18, Nov 15. Cost: DM1,460 includes 4-week course (20 hours per week), accommodations, breakfast. Contact: Die Neue Schule, Gieselerstr. 30A,

10713 Berlin, Germany; (011) 49-30-873-0373, fax (011) 49-30-873-8613; neue.schule@t-online.de, www.netlounge.com/Neue-Schule.

German Language in Munich. Group tuition available at all levels. Choose 20, 26, or 30 lessons a week or preparation for officially recognized exams. One-to-one tuition with 10, 20, 30, 40, or 50 lessons a week.

Dates: Every Monday, year round. Cost: Twenty lessons a week (group): DM740 (tuition only, 2 weeks); half board, single room DM420 per week. Contact: Inlingua School, Sendlinger-Tor-Ph. 6, D-80336 Muenchen, Germany; (011) 49-89-2311530, fax (011) 49-89-2609920; muenchen@inlingua.de, www.inlingua.de/muenchen.

German Studies. Intensive language study—up to 2 years of university language requirements in 1 semester. Additional courses in history, political science, culture, literature, etc. Program-organized field trips and housing. Beautiful city only 30 minutes from Hamburg.

Dates: Spring semester: Jan-May; Summer: May-Jun and Jun-Jul ; Fall semester: Aug-Dec. Contact program director for exact dates. Cost: One semester: $3,760; Fall and Spring: $5,860; Summer: $1,460 per session, $2,480 both sessions. Contact: University Studies Abroad Consortium (USAC), Univ. of Nevada, Reno #323, Reno, NV 89557-0093; (702) 784-6569, fax (702) 784-6010; usac@admin.unr.edu, www.scs.unr.edu/~usac.

Learn German in Germany or Austria. Language immersion courses in Germany (Berlin, Freiburg, Stuttgart, Munich, Hamburg, Frankfurt) or Austria (Vienna). Private language schools centrally located, convenient to interesting places, cultural events, sports activities. Programs feature qualified teachers, small classes, attractive surroundings and facilities. Affordable prices for instruction. Accommodations with German or Austrian families with meals, student residences, apartments, and nearby hotels.

Dates: Year round. Two weeks or more. Cost:

Two-week courses with or without accommodations range from $465-$1,355. Contact: Ms. Lorraine Haber, Study Abroad Coordinator, CES Study Abroad Program, The Center for English Studies, 330 7th Ave., 6th Fl., New York, NY 10001; (212) 629-7300, fax (212) 736-7950.

Greece

Intensive Modern Greek Language. Beginning, intermediate, and advanced levels of modern Greek classes meet for a total of 60 hours of intensive exercises and instruction in speaking, vocabulary, role-playing, grammar, reading, and writing. Held on the island of Paros.

Dates: Jun-Jul. Cost: $1,750. Includes tuition, course materials, housing. Contact: College Year in Athens, North American Office, Dept. T, P.O. Box 390890, Cambridge, MA 02139-0010; (617) 494-1008, fax (617) 494-1662; cyathens@aol.com.

Modern Greek Language. The modern Greek language program is a comprehensive, integrated approach to learning modern Greek. Courses are year round, and include beginning through advanced proficiency levels. The syllabus has been created to teach the language to adults of all nationalities, using textbooks developed at the Center. Classes are small, with an average of 8-12 participants in each course. Three-week summer courses in July on the island of Spetses.

Dates: Year round, new courses begin every month. Cost: $600 per 60-hour course. Contact: Rosemary Donnelly, Program Director, 48 Archimidous St., Athens 116 36, Greece; (011) 301 701 5242, fax (011) 30 1701 8603.

Guatemala

Casa Xelajú. Casa Xelajú, a socially responsible institute in Quetzaltenango, offers Spanish and Quiché language instruction, internships, voluntary work, semester abroad, and educational tours. One-on-one instruction 5 hours a day. Graduate/undergraduate credit in Spanish available, transferable nationwide. Homestay, daily activities, excursions, reforestation/community projects, and lectures on women, development, cultural issues.

Dates: Year round. Classes begin every Monday. Cost: Spanish program and homestay: $150 per week from Sep-May; $180 per week Jun-Aug. Internships: $55 per week including homestay, 3 meals a day, 7 days a week and one-on-one instruction. $40 registration for both programs. For other programs, please contact us. Contact: Julio E. Batres, Director General, Casa Xelaju, P.O. Box 3275, Austin, TX 78764; (512) 416-6991, fax (512) 416-8965; info@casaxelaju.com, www. casaxelaju.com. In Guatemala: Casa Xelaju Quetzaltenango, 9a. calle 11-26 Zona 1, Quetzaltenango, Guatemala; Tel./fax (011) 502-761-2628; office@casaxelaju.com.

Centro Linguistico Maya (CLM). One-on-one Spanish instruction at one of Antigua's most respected institutions. Flexible programs from 4 to 7 hours of instruction per day include local excursions twice a week. Airport reception any time and homestay placement upon arrival. Wide range of hotels are also available.

Dates: Ongoing. Cost: $135 per week includes 4 hours of instruction per day and room and board with a local family. $25 for airport reception. $50 inscription fee. Contact: Guatemala Unlimited, P.O. Box 786, Berkeley, CA 94701; (800) 733-3350, fax (415) 661-6149; guatemala1 @aol.com.

Eco-Escuela de Español. The Eco-Escuela de Español offers a unique educational experience by combining intensive Spanish language instruction with volunteer opportunities in conservation and community development projects. Students are immersed in the language, culture, and ecology of Petén, Guatemala—an area renowned for its tropical forests and ancient Mayan ruins. Ecological activities integrate classroom with field-based experiences.

Dates: Every Monday year round. Cost: Classes $65 per week (based on 20 hours of individual instruction per week, Monday-Friday). Room and board with local families $60 per week. Registration fee $10. Contact: Eco-Escuela, GAP Adventures, 266 Dupont St., Toronto, ON, M5R 1V7, Canada; (416) 922-8899, fax (416) 922-0822; adventure@gap.ca.

ICA Spanish/Guatemalan Culture. Our complete immersion program consists of one-on-one personalized language instruction 5 hours per day, 5 days per week, living with a Guatemalan family, and daily cultural activities include visits to surrounding villages, markets, cultural conferences, etc. It is also possible to do volunteer work for projects that help benefit the community.

Dates: Year round, 1-week classes. Cost: $120 per week Sep-May, $130 per week Jun-Aug. Contact: Bonnie and Dale Barth, U.S. Contacts, RR #2, Box 101, Stanton, NE 68779; Tel./fax (402) 439-2943. Or: Enrique Diaz, Director, la Calle 16-93, Zona 1, Quetzaltenango, Guatemala, C.A.; Tel./fax (011) 502-763-1871; icaxela@c.net.gt, www.jps.net/freedom4u/ica.

Kie-Balam Spanish Language School. The school features one-on-one instruction with university-degreed teachers. Special group rate program for teachers, social workers and medical personnel. Course work transfers to degree programs. School starts rural lending libraries, helps at a battered women's shelter, and works with a special education school.

Dates: Year round, classes start Mondays. Cost: Application fee $50; tuition $125 per week (includes room and board). Contact: Martha Weese, 1007 Duncan Ave., Elgin, IL 60120; (847) 888-2514 (U.S.), (011) 502-7-611636; fax (011) 502-7-610391(Guatemala from U.S.); moebius@ super-highway.net, http://super-highway.net/ ~moebius.

P.L.F.M. of Antigua. Proyecto Linguistico Francisco Marroquin of Antigua offers intensive Spanish language programs in the charming colonial city of Antigua, Guatemala. Includes 7 hours daily of one-on-one instruction. Professional adults, students, retirees, and families at all Spanish levels are accommodated in this non-profit school, dedicated to the preservation of the Mayan languages, as well as to teaching Spanish. P.L.F.M. is authorized to administer the Foreign Service Institute exam to evaluate Spanish competency. Homestays in private rooms with local families are available. Programs of 1 to 12 weeks. Registration and airport pickups can be easily arranged through our toll-free phone.

Dates: Year round. New classes begin every Monday. (Summer months fill very early.) Cost: Registration fee $40, $135 per week tuition, $65 per week homestay. Includes all meals (except Sundays). Contact: Kay G. Rafool, Language Link Inc. (U.S. Office for P.L.F.M.), P.O. Box 3006, Peoria, IL 61612; (800) 552-2051, fax (309) 692-2926; info@langlink.com, www.plfm-antigua.org.

Spanish Immersion Program. Probigua is dedicated to two goals: 1) providing the beginning, intermediate, and advanced Spanish student with an intensive, total immersion experience with one-one-one instruction, trips, daily group activities and homestays; 2) helping the children of Guatemala by donating the school's profits to establish and maintain libraries in many rural villages.

Dates: Year round. Cost: Homestay $50 per week; 4 hours of daily classes $70 per week; 5 hours $80 per week; 6 hours $90 per week; 7 hours $100 per week. (Prices subject to change without notice in 1999.) Contact: Rigoberto Zamora Charuc, General Manager, Academia de Español Probigua, 6a. Avenida Norte #41-B, La Antigua 03001, Guatemala; Tel./fax (011) 502-8320-860, fax (011) 502-8320-082; probigua@conexion.com.gt, http://probigua.conexion.com.

Honduras

Centro Internacional de Idiomas. Spanish in the Caribbean in beautiful La Ceiba. International airport, gateway to great diving in the Bay

Islands. Learn surrounded by natural rainforests, wild life reserves. One-on-one student-teacher ratio. Intensive survival skills, conversation, grammar, and vocabulary. All certified teachers, some bilingual. The school is completely air conditioned.

Dates: Year round. Cost: $200 for 4-hour classes, 5 days per week, 7-day homestay. Contact: Belinda Linton, Director, Centro Internacional de Idiomas, IMC-TGU, Dept. 277, P.O. Box 025320, Miami, FL 33102-5320; Tel./fax (011) 504-440-0547; cii@tropicohn.com, www.worldwide.edu/honduras/cici.

Ixbalanque Escuela de Español. Study just 1 km from the ruins or 2 km from the beach. We now have 2 campuses, one next to the Mayan Ruins of Copan and the other in Trujillo, located on the north coast of Honduras. We offer one-to-one student to teacher ratio, a library with games, and study areas. All teachers are Honduran and are trained and certified to teach.

Dates: Closed during Easter week. Cost: $185 per week for 4 hours of class, 5 days per week, 7 nights of room and board with local family; $125 for classes only. Contact: Darla Brown de Hernández, Ixbalanque Escuela de Español, Copán Ruinas, Honduras, C.A.; Tel./fax (011) 504-61-4432. In Trujillo: (011) 504-44-4461; ixbalan@gbm.hn.

Israel

Master of Arts Degree. Ancient History of Syro-Palestine, Middle Eastern Studies, New Testament Backgrounds, Hebrew Language, Hebrew Bible Translation. Two-year MA degrees. Extensive fieldwork and study in the languages, geography, history, culture, social, and religious aspects of Israel and the Middle East.

Dates: Sep-May every year. Cost: Approx. $7,700 per semester. Includes tuition, room and board, fees. Contact: Jerusalem Univ. College, Amelia Nakai, Program Coordinator, 4249 E. State St., Suite 203, Rockford, IL 61108; (815) 229-5900 or (800) 891-9408, fax (815) 229-

5901; 75454.1770@compuserve.com, www. juc.edu.

Italy

Aolmaia Country School. Learning vacation in Tuscany: Aolmaia is an Italian language and culture school that offers intensive 2-week courses for foreigners.

Dates: Apr-Oct. Cost: $590 for 2-week courses. Contact: Pierpaolo Chiartosini, Aolmaia Country School, via cafaggio 12, 56027 San Miniato (PI) Italy; (011) 39-571-408038; pi.chiartosini@leonet.it.

Business, Economics, Italian Studies. Turin offers a diversified curriculum in English and in business and economics, plus intensive courses in Italian language and culture, literature, etc., at the foot of the majestic Alps. Program-organized housing and field trips and many Italian university activities.

Dates: Spring semester: Jan-Apr. Summer session: Jun-Jul and Jun-Jul 24; Fall semester: Aug-Dec. Contact program director for exact dates. Cost: $6,980 Fall and Spring semesters; Summer: $1,580 per session $2,880 both sessions. Fall: $3,980, Spring: $4,280, year: $6,980. Contact: University Studies Abroad Consortium (USAC), Univ. of Nevada, Reno #323, Reno, NV 89557-0093; (702) 784-6569, fax (702) 784-6010; usac@admin.unr.edu, www.scs.unr.edu/~usac.

Italiaidea. Italiaidea is a center for comprehensive Italian instruction. We offer every level and format of Italian study from intensive short-term "survival Italian courses" to advanced semester-long courses meeting once or twice a week. We offer on-site lectures and visits to historic sites in Italian, conversation, and flexible scheduling. For over 10 years we have been offering college credit courses at numerous U.S. college and university programs in Italy; we now offer both academic assistance and travel/study assistance to our client institutions. Homestays are offered as well as accommodations in shared apartments.

Dates: Year round. Cost: Sixty-hour group course LIT780,000; 25-hour one-on-one program LIT1,200,000; 15 hour-specific purposes or culture LIT1,330,000 (taxes not included). Contact: Carolina Ciampaglia, Co-Director, Piazza della Cancelleria 5, 00186 Roma, Italy; (011) 39-6-68307620, fax (011) 39-6-6892997; italiaidea@italiaidea.com, www.italiaidea.com.

Italian at the Seaside. Italian language and culture courses in Viareggio, one of Tuscany's most beautiful beach towns. Stay in small hotels or shared apartments with use of kitchen. Enjoy the language, enjoy the beach, enjoy life.

Dates: Jun-Sep, every 2 weeks. Cost: LIT870,000 (1998) includes 2-week course and accommodations. Contact: Mr. Giovanni Poggi, Centro Culturale Giacomo Puccini, Via Ugo Foscolo, 36-55049 Viareggio, Italy; (011) 39-55-290305, fax (011) 39-55-290396; puccini@ats.it, www.bwline.com/itschools/puccini.

Italian for Foreigners. The Univ. of Bergamo offers 3 courses: non-intensive course with 4 hours of lessons a week in autumn and spring, and summer intensive course with 5 hours of lessons a day. From beginner to advanced. Includes cultural trips and some lessons on contemporary Italian culture.

Dates: Feb 23-Jun 5, Jul 6-Jul 31, Dec 12-Jan 22. Cost: LIT700,000 Spring and Autumn, LIT850,000 Summer (lessons, materials). Contact: Segreteria dei Corsi di Lingua e Cultura Italiana per Stranieri, Universita di Bergamo, Piazza Vecchia, 8, 24129 Bergamo, Italy; Tel./fax (011) 39-35-277407; citastra@ibguniv.unibg.it, www.unibg.it/cis.html.

Italian for Foreigners. Intensive courses 15 hours, 20 hours, 30 hours per week. Individual courses. Accommodations: family or flat.

Dates: Call for details. Cost: Call for details. Contact: Ursula Boess; fax (011) 396-440-888;

dilit@tin.it, http://web.tin.it/percorsi/perdeli.htm.

Italian in Florence. Two-week program: Italian language course, 4 hours per day and accommodations in single room with Italian family and activities.

Dates: Every 2 weeks. Cost: $450 includes course, accommodations, activities for 2 weeks. Contact: Alberto Delmelia, Scuola Toscana, Via Benci 23, 50122 Florence, Italy; Tel./fax (011) 39-55-24-4583; scuola.toscana@firenze.net, www.waf.com/scuola toscana.

Italian in Sunny Sicily. Learn Italian in sunny Sicily. All levels. Accommodations in flats or hotels at the sea. Two weeks with accommodations in flats and 40 lessons. LIT700,000 (about $400).

Dates: Course starts every Sunday Mar-Nov. Cost: Course only 2 weeks, 40 lessons: LIT300,000. Accommodations in triple room: LIT370,000. Single room in a family with breakfast: LIT630,000. Single room in a flat by the sea: LIT690,000. Contact: Thomas Gruessner, Solemar-Sicilia, Via F. Perez 85a I 90010, Aspara (PA), Italy; (011) 39-338-7372833; solemar-sicilia@datastudio.it, www.solemar-sicilia.it.

Italian Language and Culture. Intensive language courses, schedules ranging from 10 to 30 lessons per week, small groups of different age and nationalities, art history, modern history, Italian literature, Italian cinema, technical language courses, art courses, extra-curricular activities.

Dates: Three week courses Jan-Nov. Cost: From LIT440,000-LIT1,090,000. Contact: Europass, Enzo Boddi, Director of Studies, via S. Egidio 12, 50122 Florence, Italy; (011) 39-55-2345802, fax (011) 39-55-2479995; fpeuropass@fi.flashnet.it.

Italian Language and Culture. Courses in Italian Language and Culture at all levels. Twenty-five hours tuition per week. Small classes. Special courses in Italian for business and Italian musical culture for opera singers. Housing provided with host families or furnished apartments. Situated in small town in central Italy where you can live "Al Italiana" with Italians.

Dates: Mar 14-Oct 23. Courses begin every 4 weeks. Cost: LIT890,000 for a 4-week course, shorter periods possible. Contact: Anna Bernard, Paola Colzani, Centro Studi Italiani, V. Boscarini, 1-60149, Urbania (PS), Italy; (011) 39-722-318950, fax (011) 39-722-317286; urbania1@pesaro.com, www.pesaro.com/urbaniastudy.

Italian Language and Culture. Italian language courses (up to 8 hours per day), small classes, 6 levels of ability, credits available, cooking, wine, art history, fashion and design classes, experienced teachers, location in the city centers (Florence, Rome, and Siena).

Dates: Year round, starts every 2 weeks. Cost: Language course $215 (2 weeks). Contact: Mr. Giambattista Pace, Central Marketing Office, Scuolo Leonardo da Vinci, via Brunelleschi 4, 50123, Firenze, Italy; (011) 39-55-29-03-05, fax (011) 39-55-29-03-96; scuolaleonardo@scuolaleonardo.com, www.scuolaleonardo.com.

Italian Language Courses. Institute Galilei specializes in individually tailored one-to-one courses in Florence, in the countryside, and on the island of Elba. Training in specific vocabularies (economics, law, art history, etc.). All courses are divided into 10 levels. The Institute also organizes small group courses in 3 levels lasting from 2 weeks on.

Dates: One-to-one courses start and end on any day requested; small group courses start every 2 weeks. Cost: Starting from $365 per week. Includes textbooks and notebooks, use of videotapes; nonspecialized medical assistance, housing service, certificates and diplomas, weekly tours with a guide to the museums and churches of Florence, school tax, examination fee. Contact: Alexandra Schmitz, Istituto Galilei, via degli Alfani 68, 50121 Florence, Italy; (011) 39-55-294680, fax (011) 39-55-283481; info.galilei.it, www.galilei.it.

Italian Language Courses. Two-, 3-, and 4-week courses in the undiscovered heart of Tuscany, in Arezzo (population 100,000). School approved by education ministry. Modern communicative methods, qualified teachers, excellent standards, friendly atmosphere, social and cultural program. A pleasant, satisfying experience. Stay with a family and meet real Italians in historical, artistic Arezzo.

Dates: Courses begin every Monday. Cost: LIT895,000 2 weeks' tuition/accommodations. Contact: Italian Language Courses-ILC, Accademia Toscana, Via Pietro da Cortona 10, 52100 Arezzo, Italy; (011) 39-575-21366, fax (011) 39-575-300426; italcors@ats.it, www.etr.it/accademia_britannica.

Italian Language for Foreigners. Small courses: (2 hours a day); main mini-groups (4 hours a day); intensive (main course plus 6 private lessons); two-on-one (1 teacher plus 2 students); individual tuition. Special courses: Tourist Industry, Business Italian. Small groups (max. 6 students). Sports (sailing, catamaran, surfing), excursions (Calabria, Sicily). Accommodations in apartments.

Dates: Mar 1-Nov 26. Cost: Two-week course includes single room LIT885,000. Contact: Caffé Italiano Club, Largo A. Pandullo 5, 89861 Tropea (VV), Italy; (011) 390-963-60-32-84, fax (011) 390-963-61-786; caffeitaliano@tin.it, www.paginegialle.it/caffeital.

Italiano a Modo Mio. Sixth consecutive year: Castiglione della Pescaia/Tuscany; Marzabotto/Bologna; Sulmona. Eight-day customized programs of "breakfast-to-bedtime" full immersion in Italian. Limited to 8 well-motivated adults per class. Studies reinforced by practical application to real-life situations while enjoying Italian food and culture.

Dates: May 9-30; Aug 29-Sep 19; Oct 3-17 (8-day programs). Cost: $2,000-$3,500 includes single occupancy, classes, meals, activities. Airfare not included. Contact: Sergio Stefani, 33 Riverside Dr., 1E, New York, NY 10023; (212) 595-7004; annamaria@italianmyway.com, www.italianmyway.com.

Learn Italian in Florence. Italian language courses available 12 months a year, from 1 week to 7 months. Seven different levels available—2, 4, or 6 hours a day; possibility of combining group courses with 1 hour individual tutoring a day; combine Italian with cooking and wine appreciation.

Dates: Any Monday (except beginners). Cost: From LIT260,000. Contact: Dr. Gabriella Ganugi, Lorenzo de'Medici, Via Faenza 43, 50123 Florence, Italy; (011) 39-55-287143, fax (011) 39-55-2398920; ldm@dada.it, www.dada.it/ldm.

Learn Italian in Italy. Language immersion courses in Italy (Rome, Florence, Siena, Viareggio, Rimini, Bologna, Venice, Portico, Milan). Private language schools centrally located, convenient to interesting places, cultural events, sports activities. Programs feature qualified teachers, small classes, attractive surroundings and facilities. Affordable prices for instruction. Accommodations with Italian families with meals, student residences, apartments, and nearby hotels.

Dates: Year round. Two weeks or more. Cost: Two-week courses with or without accommodations range from $295-$905. Contact: Ms. Lorraine Haber, Study Abroad Coordinator, CES Study Abroad Program, The Center for English Studies, 330 7th Ave., 6th Fl., New York, NY 10001; (212) 629-7300, fax (212) 736-7950.

Learn Italian in Italy. Study Italian in a 16th century Renaissance palace in the center of Florence, or in a classic Tuscan town just 30 minutes from the sea. Koiné Center's professional language teachers and small class sizes encourage active participation by each student. Cultural program, guided excursions, choice of accommodations including host families.

Dates: Year round; starting dates each month. Cost: Two-week intensive program $290; 3 weeks $390; homestay accommodations from $115 per week. Contact: In Italy: Dr. Andrea Moradei, Koiné Center, Via Pandolfini 27, 50122 Firenze, Italy; (011) 39-55-213881. In North America: (800) 274-6007; homestay@teleport.com. www.koinecenter.com.

Learn Real Italian in Florence. We offer intensive (and not so intensive) group, individual, and combined lessons in Italian language and culture designed to fit any schedule here in Florence, Italy's cultural capital. Come visit and find out more about us at our web site, www.istitutodonatello.com. We also assist with finding accommodations, including homestays, while studying here.

Dates: Courses every month, year round. Cost: Beginning at LIT850,000 for 20 hours per week for 4-week group courses (total 80 hours). Contact: Gianluca Mugnai, Director, Istituto di Lingua e Cultura Italiana Donatello, Via Galliano 1, 50144 Firenze, Italy; (011) 39-55-354112, fax (011) 39-55-355686; donatello@istitutodonatello.com, www.istitutodonatello.com.

Linguanova—Culture and Language. Come learn Italian language and also Italian cooking, music, art, and cinema in Livorno, a pleasant Tuscan town overlooking the sea. Maximum 6 students per group.

Dates: Courses begin: May 4, 18; Jun 1, 15, 29; Jul 13, 27; Aug 10, 24; Sep 7, 21; Oct 5, 19; Nov 2, 16, 30; Dec 7, 21. Cost: Standard course LIT350,000 (2 weeks), LIT600,000 (4 weeks), Intensive course LIT500,000 (2 weeks), LIT900,000 (4 weeks). Contact: Massimo Maggini, Linguanova, via Borra 35, 57123 Livorno, Italy; Tel./fax (011) 39-586-88-3453; lingua@hardlink.com, www.hardlink.com/linguanova.

Studio Art Centers International. Combine beginning, intermediate or advanced Italian language studies with courses in studio arts, art history, art conversation or cultural studies at SACI's central Florence location. Outside the classroom, students are partnered with Italian university students for language and cultural exchange. Programs include year/semester abroad, late spring and summer studies.

Dates: Sep-Dec; Jan-Apr; May-Jun; Jun-Jul. Cost: Fall/Spring tuition $7,725 per term (1998/99); late Spring/Summer $3,000 (1998). Contact: SACI Coordinator, U.S. Student Programs, Institute of International Education, 809 UN Plaza, New York, NY 10017-3580; (800) 344-9186, (212) 984-5548, fax (212) 984-5325; saci@iie.org, www.saci-florence.org.

Japan

College of Business and Communication. This is the college for beginners to advanced in Japanese to study the language, life, and culture of Japan.

Dates: Regular course Apr-Oct; short course any time. Cost: Regular course ¥790,000 for 1 year; short course ¥90,000 for 4 weeks, ¥140,000 for 8 weeks, ¥190,000 for 12 weeks. Contact: Ms. Mutsumi Harada, Dept. of Japanese, College of Business and Communication, Kawasaki 20-7 Ekimae-honcho, Kawasaki-ku, Kanagawa ken 210-0007, Japan; (011) 81-44-244 3959, fax (011) 81-44-244-2499; cbc@kw.NetLaputa.ne.jp, www.NetLaputa.ne.jp/~cbc.

Communicative Japanese Courses. Intensive program designed to develop conversational skills including reading and writing. University Entrance Preparatory program, part-time and evening program. Special lectures on

Language Schools

Japanese traditions. A teaching method proven by the U.S. Department State's Foreign Service Institute.

Dates: Every 3 months (from Jul, Oct, Jan, and Apr). Cost: ¥155,400 for 3 months (4 hours per day, 5 days per week). Contact: Academy of Language Arts, No. 2 Tobundo Bldg., 5F 2-16 Ageba-cho, Shinjuku-ku, Tokyo 162, Japan; (011) 81-3-3235-0071, fax (011) 81-3-3235-0004; ala@a2.mbn.or.jp, http://kbic.ardour.co.jp/~newgensi/ala.

Japanese Language School. General course and intensive courses. General course: Apr and Oct admission; Intensive course: 3 months; junior, middle, and upper-level classes.

Dates: Deadline for Apr is Nov 15. For October, May 15. Cost: ¥600,000 per year. Contact: Samu Language School, 2-3-20, Hyakunin-cho, Shinjuku-ku, Tokyo, Japan; (011) 81-3-3205-2020, fax (011) 81-3-3205-2022; http://plaza5.mbn.or.jp/~aiueo/index.html.

Latin America

Spanish Immersion Programs. Study with small groups or private tutor. Live with local host families or in hotels. One-week to 6 months. All ages and levels. Various settings: beaches, mountains, small towns, large cities, etc. Country options: Costa Rica, Guatemala, Honduras, Panamá, El Salvador, Argentina, Chile, Ecuador, Peru, Uruguay, Venezuela, Puerto Rico, Dominican Republic.

Dates: Rolling admission. Programs start every week or every month. Cost: Depends on location. Prices start at $175 per week and include classes, homestay, travel insurance, most meals, some cultural activities. Contact: AmeriSpan Unlimited, P.O. Box 40007, Philadelphia, PA 19106; (800) 879-6640, fax (215) 751-1100; info@amerispan.com, www.amerispan.com.

Mexico

El Bosque del Caribe, Cancun. Take a professional Spanish course 25 hours per week and enjoy the Caribbean beaches. Relaxed family-like atmosphere. No more than 6 students per class. Special conversation program. Mexican cooking classes and excursions to the Mayan sites. Housing with Mexican families. College credit available.

Dates: Year round. New classes begin every Monday. Group programs arranged at reduced fees. Cost: Enrollment fee $100, $180 per week. One week with a Mexican family $160. Contact: Eduardo Sotelo, Director, Calle Piña 1, S.M. 25, 77500 Cancún, Mexico; (011) 52-98-84-10-38, fax (011) 52-98-84-58-88; bcaribe@mail.cancun-language.com.mx.

Experiencia: Cuernavaca, Mexico. Experiencia has offered intensive Spanish language courses and homestay programs since 1977. Groups of no more than 5 students, study for as short as 1 week. Extracurricular activities, such as bilingual exchanges, lectures, cultural events, and Saturday excursions are included. Sunday and 3-day excursions offered for a small fee.

Dates: Year round. Group classes begin every Monday. Cost: Group studies: 1 week $135, 4 weeks $500, 8 weeks $900. Further discounts for extended study. (Double the amounts for one-on-one instruction.) Plus $100 one-time registration fee. Books $16. Accommodations with a Mexican family or in dorm begin at $9 per night. Contact: Sherry Howell, Experiencia Representative, 1303 Candelero Court, Placerville, CA 95667; (888) 397-8363 or (530) 622-4262, fax (530) 626-4272; study@experiencia.com, www.experiencia.com.

Guadalajara Summer School. For the 47th year, the Univ. of Arizona Guadalajara Summer School will offer intensive Spanish in the 6-week session, intensive Spanish in the

3-week session, and upper-division Spanish and Mexico-related courses in the 5-week session. Courses may be taken for credit or audit.

Dates: Jul 5-Aug 19. Cost: $1,057-$2,000 includes tuition and host family housing with meals. Contact: Dr. Macario Saldate IV, Director, Guadalajara Summer School, The Univ. of Arizona, P.O. Box 40966, Tucson, AZ 85717; (520) 621-5137; janeg@u.arizona.edu, www.coh.arizona.edu/gss.

IMAC (Spanish in Guadalajara). Instituto Mexico Americano de Cultura was established in 1977 and has been accredited by the Ministry of Education since. All levels in groups (max 5) or individual tutoring. One- to 12-week courses. Other services include: Multimedia center, e-mail, fax, and free homestay family location.

Dates: Year round. Begin any Monday. Cost: Check web site for detailed information. Contact: Mr. Osmar Canul, Instituto México Americano de Cultura, Donato Guerro 180 (Historic Downtown), Guadalajara 44100, Mexico; (011) 52-3-613-1080, fax (011) 52-3-613-4621; spanish-imac@ram.com.mx, http://imac.ram.com. mx/imac/spanish/spanish.html.mx.

Instituto Allende. Arts and crafts, Spanish at all levels, Mexican studies, field trips, lectures. BFA, MFA programs. College transfer credit. Incorporated with the Univ. of Guanajuato since 1953. Noncredit students of all ages also welcome. Campus is the 18th century hacienda of the Counts of Canal.

Dates: Year round. Cost: Tuition, Spanish $150-$420 per 4 weeks, depending on hours. Contact: Rodolfo Fernandez, Executive Director, Instituto Allende, San Miguel de Allende, Guanajuato, Mexico 37700; (011) 52-415-2-01-90, fax (011) 52-415-2-45-38; allende1@celaya.ugto.mx.

Instituto Cultural Oaxaca. Spanish Language and Mexican Culture Immersion Program on lovely Oaxacan estate. Grammar, literature, and conversation classes offered at 7 levels. Cultural workshops in cooking, pottery, dancing, weaving, and music. Local conversation partner. Weekly lectures and cultural activities. Seven contact hours daily. Optional tours to archaeological sites and artisan villages. Homestays available. Special group programs.

Dates: Year-round monthly sessions. May begin any Monday. Write, call, or fax for specific dates and informative brochure. Cost: $50 registration fee and $400 per 4-week session or $105 per week. Contact: Lic Lucero Topete, Director, Instituto Cultural Oaxaca, Apartado Postal #340, Oaxaca, Oaxaca, C.P. 68000, Mexico; (011)-52-951-53404, fax (011) 52-951-53728; inscuoax@antequera.com, http://antequera.com/inscuoax.

Instituto Habla Hispaña. Our team of highly qualified professors has designed a practical, dynamic, and communicative method to learn Spanish in a spontaneous and natural way: 20 hours per week of intensive Spanish in a classroom with a maximum of 10 students. Ten hours per week of seminars, working groups, and guided walking tours.

Dates: A 4-week session begins each month. Cost: One week $100, 2 weeks $190, 3 weeks $280, 4 weeks $360. Minimum enrollment 1 week. Lessons and books included. One-on-one personalized instruction (businesses, teachers, etc.) $10 per hour upon request. Contact: Instituto Habla Hispaña, c/o Kima Cargill, 814 E. 45th St., Austin, TX 78751; (512) 452-2405; kcargill@mail.utexas.edu, wwwvms.utexas.edu/~kcargill/index.html.

Intensive Language Programs. Intensive Spanish immersion program in groups, 40 class hours per week including Spanish class, lectures, and Hispano-American courses. Executive, semester, and specialized pro-

Language Schools

grams for teachers, professionals, nurses, and adults continuing education. Live with Mexican family or in student residence. Excursions to historical and archaeological sites.

Dates: Year round starting every Monday. Cost: Tuition $190 per week; lodging $154 per week. Contact: The Center for Bilingual Multicultural Studies, Javier Espinosa, San Jeronimo #304, Cuernavaca, MOR-62179, Mexico; (011) 52-73-17-10-87, fax (011) 52-73-17-05-33; admin@bilingual-center.com, www.bilingual-center.com.

Intensive Spanish Classes. One-on-one Spanish instruction, accommodating individual styles, personal interests, and preferences. Special classes for "survival" travel Spanish, teachers, physicians, other professions. Specially trained, bilingual teachers. Homestay available with Mexican families, private room within walking distance. Additionally: cooking, weaving and jewelry making classes, talks and language interchanges.

Dates: Year round. Cost: $150 per week including 7 days homestay and 15 hours individual classes. Contact: Instituto Jovel, Maria Adelin a Flores #21, San Cristobal de las Casas, Chiapas, Mexico 29200; Tel./fax (011) 52-967-84069; jovel@sancristobal.podernet.com.mx, www.interlog.com/jovel.

Intensive Spanish Course. The Academia Hispano Americana, the oldest full-time specialized Spanish language program in Mexico, offers students 35 hours per week of activities in the Spanish language. Courses are held year round and start almost every 4 weeks. San Miguel is a pleasant mountain community with clear air and many cultural opportunities.

Dates: Jan 4, Feb 1, Mar 1, Mar 29, Apr 5, May 3 and 31, Jun 28, Jul 26, Aug 23, Sep 20, Oct 18, Nov 15. Cost: Tuition $400 per session, discounts after first full session. Room and board from $15 per day. Contact: Gary De Mirjyn, Director, Academia Hispano Americana, Mesones 4, San Miguel de Allende, Gto., Mexico; (011) 52-415-2-0349 or 2-4349, fax (011) 52-415-2-2333; academia@unisono.net.mx.

Intensive Spanish in Cuernavaca. Cuauhnahuac, founded in 1972, offers a variety of intensive and flexible programs geared to individual needs. Six hours of classes daily with no more than 4 students to a class. Housing with Mexican families who really care about you. Cultural conferences, excursions, and special classes for professionals. College credit available.

Dates: Year round. New classes begin every Monday. Cost: $70 registration fee; $650 4 weeks tuition; housing $18 per night. Contact: Marcia Snell, 519 Park Dr., Kenilworth, IL 60043; (800) 245-9335, fax (847) 256-9475; lankysam@aol.com.

Intensive Spanish in Yucatan. Centro de Idiomas del Sureste, A.C. (CIS), founded in 1974, offers 3-5 hours per day of intensive conversational Spanish classes with native-speaking, university-trained professors. Maximum 6 students per group, average 3. Program includes beginner courses to very advanced with related field trips and recommended optional homestay. Also special classes in business, legal, medical vocabulary, or Mayan studies.

Dates: Year round. Starts any Monday, except last 2 weeks in Dec. Cost: Tuition (3 hours per day program: $330 first 2 weeks, $115 each additional week); tuition 5 hours per day programs $490 first 2 weeks, $195 each additional week. Contact: Chloe C. Pacheco, Director, Centro de Idiomas del Sureste, A.C., Calle 14 #106 X25, col. Mexico, CP 97128, Mérida, Yucatán, Mexico; (011) 52-99-26-11-55 or (011) 52-99-26-94-94, 20-28-10, fax (011) 52-99-26-90-20.

Language and Culture in Guanajuato. We work with innovative teaching techniques, tailoring instruction to each student's needs. Spanish, Mexican history, politics, culture-cuisine, folk dancing, and Latin American literature.

Dates: Year round. New classes begin every

Monday. Cost: $925. Includes 4 weeks of classes and homestay with 3 meals daily. Contact: Director Jorge Barroso, Instituto Falcon, A.C., Guanajuato, Gto. 36000 Mexico; Tel./fax (011) 52-473-1-0745, infalcon@redes.int. com.mx, www.infonet.com.mx/falcon.

Language Institute of Colima. Total immersion with classes throughout the year Monday-Friday. Students live with local host families and attend 5 hours of instruction daily, no more than 5 students per class. Academic and continuing education credit available. Customized courses for law enforcement, medical, and other professionals. Many extras, including beach excursions.

Dates: Year round. Cost: Registration $80; tuition $415 1st week, $345 each successive week. Tuition private room: $445 1st week, $375 each successive week. Ten percent discount for group of 3 or more or stay of 4 weeks or longer. Contact: Dennis Bourassa, Language Institute of Colima, P.O. Box 459, Garberville, CA 95542-0459; (800) 604-6579, fax (707) 923-4232; colima@northcoast.com, www. northcoast.com/~licolima.

Latin American Studies, Spanish. Intensive Spanish language study in small groups at all language levels, taught by native speakers. Latin American studies courses in history, literature, Mexican arts and crafts, current events, Mexican cuisine, anthropology of Mexico, extensive program of field study excursions led by Cemanahuac anthropologists. Academic credit available; professional seminars arranged; family homestay highly recommended.

Dates: Classes begin each Monday year round. Cost: Registration, tuition, room and board with Mexican family for 2 weeks: $756. Contact: Vivian B. Harvey, Educational Programs Coordinator, Cemanahuac Educational Community, Apartado 5-21, Cuernavaca, Morelos, Mexico; (011) 52-73-18-6407, fax (011)52-73-12-5418; 74052.2570@compuserve. com, www.cemanahuac.com. Call (800) 247-6641 for a brochure.

Mar de Jade, Mexico. Tropical ocean-front responsible tourism center in a beautiful unspoiled fishing village near Puerto Vallarta offers unique study options. Learn Spanish in small groups and enjoy great swimming, kayaking, hiking, horseback riding, and meditation. Gain insight into rural culture by studying and working in a farmers' clinic, local construction, cottage industries, or teaching.

Dates: Year round. Cost: $950 for 21-day work/study. Includes room (shared occupancy), board, 12 hours per week of Spanish and 15 hours per week of work. Longer resident program available at lower cost. Vacation/Spanish 1-week $400 (includes room, board, and 12 hours of Spanish) 1 week minimum; 21-day Vacation/Spanish $950. Vacation only $50 per night for any length of time. Contact: In Mexico: Mar de Jade/Casa Clinica, A.P. 81, Las Varas, Nayarit, 63715, Mexico; Tel./fax (011) 52-327-20184. In U.S.: P.O. Box 1280, Santa Clara, CA 95052; voice mail (415) 281-0164; info@mardejade.com, www.mardejade.com.

Spanish Courses in Oaxaca. We offer different programs according to the student's individual needs making it possible to advance more rapidly in one's knowledge and practice of Spanish. To study at Becari is not only to learn a new language but also to enter another culture.

Dates: Starting every Monday. Cost: Regular $75; intensive $100; super-intensive $150-$170. Contact: Becari Language School, M. Bravo 210, Int. Plaza San Cristóbal, 68000 Oaxaca, Mexico; Tel./fax (011) 52-951-4-6076; becari@antequera.com, http://antequera.com/becari.

Spanish in Guadalajara. Vancouver Language Centre offers various Spanish language courses in Guadalajara, Mexico. Part-time and full-time courses range from 1 week to 1 year. The curriculum is sophisticated and well-organized, with 8 levels. Teachers are native Spanish speakers with formal training in teaching Spanish as a Foreign Language. VLC

Language Schools

also offers homestay accommodations and a variety of leisure and sightseeing activities.

Dates: Monthly. Cost: $150 per week (tuition only). Contact: Vancouver Language Centre, Avenida Vallarda 1151, Col. Americana, CP 44100, Guadalajara, Jalisco, Mexico; (011) 52-3-826-0944, fax (011) 52-3-825-2051; vic@vec.bc.ca, www.vec.bc.ca.

Spanish in the Land of the Maya. Learn, live, and love Spanish in the land of the Maya. Discover Mayan ruins and visit living Mayan Villages. Enjoy the relaxed atmosphere of colonial San Cristóbal de las Casas, Chiapas and experience the lush vegetation of the Chiapas' Highlands and the only tropical forest in North America.

Dates: Year round starting lessons every Monday and homestays any day of the week. Cost: $170 per week (group lessons, double occupancy). For upper scale lodging, single room and private instruction please inquire. Includes stay with a local family, 3 meals per day, 15 hours of Spanish instruction per week, workbooks, participation in cultural activities, access to dark room and screen printing shop, certificate. Contact: Centro Bilingüe Roberto Rivas-Bastidas or Israel Rivas-Bastidas, rrivas@sancristobal.podernet.com.mx, www.mexonline.com/centro1.htm. Centro Bilingüe Calle Real de Guadalupe 55, Centro Cultural "El Puente," San Cristóbal de las Casas, Chiapas, Mexico, 29230; Tel./fax (011) 52-967-8-37-23, fax/voice mail (011) 52-967-8-41-57; spanish@sancristobal.podernet.com.mx.

Universal Centro de Lengua. Universal offers Spanish language programs specifically tailored to meet the needs of each student. Spanish courses are offered at all levels, individually or in groups, and are complemented by diverse lectures. Classes range from 2 to 5 students and meet 5 hours daily with hourly breaks of 10 minutes.

Dates: Year round. Cost: Normal $140 per week, advanced $180 per week, professional $200 per week. Contact: Ramiro Cuellar

Hernandez, Universal Centro de Lengua, J.H. Preciado #171, Col. San Anton, Cuernavaca, Morelos, Mexico; (011) 52-73-18-29-04/12-49-02, fax (011) 52-73-18-29-10; students@universal-spanish.com, universa@laneta.apc.org.

New Zealand

English Language Courses. English courses plus a New Zealand experience.

Dates: TBA Cost: TBA Contact: John Lanedon, Dominion English Schools, Box 447, Auckland, New Zealand; (011) 648-3773280, fax (011) 648-3773473; english@dominion.school.nz.

General Studies in New Zealand. Located in the City of Hamilton at the Univ. of Waikato, students are able to take a variety of courses in several disciplines. The courses concerning New Zealand/Pacific Society and Culture are especially popular with international students. Students are able to enjoy excellent study facilities and participate in organized university activities.

Dates: Semester 1: Jul-Oct; Semester 2: Feb-Jun. Contact program director for exact dates. Cost: Semester 1 or 2 $4,315; year $7,775. Contact: University Studies Abroad Consortium (USAC), Univ. of Nevada, Reno #323, Reno, NV 89557-0093; (702) 784-6569, fax (702) 784-6010; usac@admin.unr.edu, www.scs.unr.edu/~usac.

Nicaragua

Casa Xalteva Language Center. Casa Xalteva offers high quality intensive Spanish language courses at beginning, intermediate, and advanced levels with Nicaraguan teachers. Classes have a maximum of 4 students and meet 4 hours per day Monday-Friday. We also offer homestays with families, volunteer work opportunities, and cultural programs.

Dates: Classes begin each Monday year round.

Cost: Instruction - $125 per week; homestays $60 per week. Contact: Casa Xalteva, Calle Real Xalteva #103, Granada, Nicaragua; (011) 505-552-2436. In U.S. (505) 254-7535; casaxal@ibw.com.ni, www.ibw.com. ni/~casaxal.

Los Pipitos Sacuanjoche. Full immersion program in Esteli, Nicaragua (max. 5 students), qualified native teachers, Spanish only methodology, visits to places of your interest, family stay, weekend excursions, study on the beach, volunteer work, internships. Non-profit school benefitting the Association of Parents With Handicapped Children. Flexibility is part of our program.

Dates: Classes start on Monday. Cost: $120 (class, visits, family, meals) per week. Discounts for groups. Contact: Katharina Pfotner, Los Pipitos Sacuanjoche, Apdo. Post #80, Esteli, Nicaragua; (011) 505-713-2154, fax (011) 505-713-2240; kathrin@ibw.com.ni.

Portugal

Portuguese in Portugal. Year round Portuguese courses for groups and individuals. Full range of services offered—accommodations, extracurricular activities. Credit available through some U.S. universities. Teacher training also available.

Dates: Call for details. Cost: Call for details. Contact: Cial - Centro de Linguas; (011) 351-1-794-04-48, fax (011) 351-796-07-83; cialis@mail.telepac.pt.

Puerto Rico

Instituto Internacional Euskalduna. Spanish language and culture program on a beautiful Caribbean island. Travel with 2 weeks notice, no passport or visa needed. We offer: communicative, learner-centered classes with a maximum of 6 students. U.S. university credit; monthly calendar of events; classes at all levels; and an optional homestay program, with or without meals.

Dates: Classes begin second and fourth Monday of every month. Cost: Programs starting at $560. Contact: Director of Study Abroad, NESOL/IIE, Edif. Euskalduna, Calle Navarro #56, Hato Rey, PR 00918; (787) 281-8013, fax (787) 767-1494; nesol@coqui.net.

Russia

Russian as a Foreign Language. General Russian, Business Russian, TORFL (Teaching of Russian as a Foreign Language), individual and group courses, semester and part-time courses, crash courses for businessmen, labor service, unique cultural program. Accommodations with a Russian host-family, a hotel, or student hostel included in the total course fee.

Dates: Courses start any Monday throughout the year. Cost: From $1,220 per month, all but airfare. Contact: Vyatcheslav Oguretchnikov, ProBa Language Centre, street address: Russia, 197376, St. Petersburg, Professora Popova str. 5; mailing address: P.O. Box 109, Lappeenranta, Fin-53101, Finland; (011) 7-812-325618, fax (011) 7-812-3462758; sp@mail.nevalink.ru, www.studyrussian.spb.ru.

Russian as a Foreign Language. The Moscow Linguistic Center offers Intensive Russian courses for beginning, intermediate, and advanced students, business Russian, and Russian for special purposes. Group and one-on-one lessons. "Russian Express" program is under UNESCO auspices. Stay with host family (half-board, single room) or in residential accommodations. Moscow Linguistic Center is a member of IALC.

Dates: Year round. Enrollment every Monday. Cost: Tuition fees: group lessons (20 hours per week) $200 per week; one-on-one lessons $15 per academic hour. Family accommodations $210 per week (half-board); residential accommodations $15 per night (no meal). Contact: Mrs. Svetlana Khatchatourova, Director, or Mrs. Galina Kriusheva, Deputy Director, Moscow Linguistic Center 17, Presnensky val, 123557, Moscow, Russia; (011) 7-95-737-0183, fax (011) 7-95-737-0193;

mlc@mail.infotel.ru, www.geocities.com/ Athens/Forum/4143.

Russian in Russia. We offer our programs of the Russian language for international students in St. Petersburg, Russia. Our goal is to provide high quality language programs for all ages and types of participants. All of our teachers are university graduates who have qualifications in teaching Russian as a foreign language. We provide host family and hotel accommodations for all of our students.

Dates: General Russian course starts first Monday of every month. Intensive Russian (12-week course) starts on: Jun 1, Sep 7, Dec 7 (1998). Business Russian course starts 4 times a year: Jan, Apr, Jul, Oct. Summer courses start every Monday. Cost: General Russian course: $380 for 4 weeks (20 hours per week). Intensive Russian course: $1,710 for 12 weeks (30 hours per week). Business Russian course: $570 for 4 weeks (30 hours per week). Summer courses: $142.50 for 1 week (30 hours per week). Contact: In Russia: Meridian-37, Valentina Pavlovskaya, P.O. Box 223, St. Petersburg, 193015 Russia; Tel./fax (011) 7-812-110-0464; meridian@neva.spb.ru. In U.S.: Meridian-37, P.O. Box 465, Rindge, NH 03461; (603) 381-8146; info@meridian-37.com, www.meridian-37.com.

Spain

Academia Eurolink. Our courses combine writing, reading, listening and speaking for all levels including preparation for D.E.L.E. examinations.

Dates: Year round. Cost: TBA. Contact: Academia Eurolink, Calle Cantarranas 23, Almaurin El Grande, Malaga 29120, Spain.

Advisers for Int'l. Programs in Spain. If you want to have fun in Spain and learn Spanish at Univ. of Valencia in the Mediterranean coast, consult us.

Dates: Univ. of North Texas Program: Sep 1-Sep 29, early Sep-middle Dec, middle Jan-early May, early Sep-early May. Cost: Univ. of North Texas Program, $1,700 Sep program. For semester and academic year program please consult with Univ. of Albany-SUNY. Contact: Fernando Ribas, Marketing Area VIP, Advisers for Int'l. Programs in Spain, S.L C/ Fernando el Catolico 73, pta. 9 46008 Valencia, Spain; Tel./fax (011) 34-6-382-22-78; aip@xpress.es, www.xpress.es/aip.

CLIC International House Sevilla. CLIC IH, one of Spain's leading language schools, is located in the heart of Seville, the vibrant capital of Andalucia. With year-round intensive Spanish language courses, business Spanish, and official exam preparation taught by highly qualified and motivated native teachers, CLIC IH combines professionalism with a friendly atmosphere. Accommodations are carefully selected. We offer a varied cultural program as well as exchanges with local students.

Dates: Year round. Cost: Approx. $825 for 4-week course plus individual room with a family, 2 meals per day. Contact: Bernhard Roters, CLIC-Intenational House Seville, Calle Santa Ana 11, 41002 Sevilla, Spain; (011) 34-954-374-500, fax (011) 34-954-374-1806; clic@arrakis.es, www.clic.es.

CP Language Institutes. A Spanish language institute located in the town center of Madrid. Two- to 8-week standard and intensive courses, 4 hours per day. One-on-one instruction, customized courses for groups and combination courses. All levels available. Classes are small and thus offer a great deal of attention to the student. Cultural activities are an integral part of the program. Accommodations in selected guest families.

Dates: Year round (except for the month of Aug). Cost: PTS22,500 per week, 20 hours tuition; PTS23,000 (approx.) half-board accommodations in guest family. Contact: Mrs. Maria Dolores Romero, CP Language Institute, c/o Schiller International Univ., Calle San Bernardo 97/99, 28015 Madrid, Spain; SchillerUS@aol.com.

=elemadrid= Spanish in Madrid. Our Spanish language school in Madrid, Spain, provides a wide variety of Spanish immersion programs, Spain today classes, leisure activity courses, and weekend excursions in small groups and/or individually tailored private lessons. Accommodations include homestay, apartments, apartment sharing, and hotels.

Dates: Start on the following Mondays: Mar 1, 15, 29; Apr 12, 26; May 10, 24; Jun 6, 21, 28; Jul 5, 19; Aug 2, 16, 30; Sep 13, 27; Oct 11, 25; Nov 8, 22; Dec 7. Cost: Courses $220-$760 per week; accommodations $80-$1,300 per week; leisure activity courses and excursions vary. Contact: =elemadrid= Calle Serrano 4, 28001 Madrid, Spain; Tel./fax (011) 34-91-432-4540/41; hola@elemadrid.com, www.elemadrid.com.

"El Pueblo" School of Languages. Innovative language program ideally situated in a small village in the heart of Castile Spain offers true immersion in both language and culture. Courses designed to meet each new group's (or individual's) particular interests. Emphasis on communicative interaction with the community reinforced with classroom study and field trips. Prescreened host family accommodations.

Dates: Year round. Cost: $459 (1 week), $795 (2 weeks), $1,175 (3 weeks), $1,565 (1 month); includes 25 hours instruction per week, all materials, housing (private rooms), 2 meals per day, plus daily excursions to local points of interest. Contact: Juan Miguel Velasco, Director, Plaza Mayor 1, 40430 Bernardos (Segovia), Spain; Tel./fax (011) 34-21-56 65 14. In U.S.: Lynda Denman, 954 W. Leadora Ave., Glendora, CA 91741; Tel./fax (626) 914-0494. Portfolio of information available on request.

Escuela Internacional. Escuela Internacional offers quality programs in Spanish language and culture with U.S. undergraduate credits in Madrid, Salamanca, and Malaga. Our qualified teachers and small classes (maximum 12 students per class) guarantee you a successful program. Stay with a selected family or in a shared apartment. Enjoy our extensive afternoon activities and weekend excursions. Our professionalism, enthusiasm, and personal touch will make your experience in Spain memorable and fun.

Dates: Year round, 2-48 weeks. Cost: From PTS59,000 for 2 weeks (includes 15 hours per week instruction, room and books) to PTS120,000 (includes 30 hours per week instruction, room and full board, books, activities, and excursion). Contact: Escuela Internacional, Midori Ishizaka, Director of Admissions, c/Talamanca 10, 28807 Alcalá de Henares, Madrid, Spain; (011) 34-91-8831264, fax (011) 34-91-8831301; escuelai@ergos.es, www.ergos.es/escuelai.

Euroschools, Vigo. Prestigious school located on beautiful northwest coast in dynamic seaside city with Spain's finest beaches. Year-round program for students, professionals, and business people at all levels: Intensive group courses, Prep. for DELE examinations, Spanish culture, private classes. Accommodations with Spanish families or in student residence. Special summer program for young people aged 12-20.

Dates: Courses start every other Monday from Jan 7. Duration: 2 weeks or more. All inclusive 4-week summer program for young people begins Jul 6, Aug 3, Aug 31. Cost: Per week: Summer Intensive Program PTAS22,500 (20 hours); Jan-Jun Intensive PTAS20,500 (20 hours); DELE Examination Preparation PTAS22,000 (20 hours); Spanish Culture PTAS 6,200 (6 hours); private classes PTAS15,500 (5 hours); 4-week summer program PTAS163,500. Accommodations cost per week, half board: Spanish family (single room) PTAS21,700; student residence PTAS17,500 (shared room). Contact: John Moriarty, Director, European Language Schools, S.L., Regueiro, 2, 36211 Vigo, Spain; Tel./fax (011) 34-86-291748; euroschools@moriartys.com.

IMSOL School of Languages. Intensive language program with the opportunity to study Spanish language, civilization, and culture in one of the most beautiful regions in Spain (Andalucía). We offer courses in small groups year round at all levels in Granada and Almunecac, a little village in Costa del Sol. Stay with a selected family or in a shared apartment. Enjoy our extensive afternoon activities and weekend excursions.

Dates: Year round. Classes begin every Monday. Cost: From $343. Contact: Concha Saez, IMSOL, Calle Cueste de la Alhacaba 31, 18010 Granada, Spain; Tel./fax (011) 34-9-58-293732; imsol@nsi.es, www.bd-andalucia.es/imsol.html.

Intensive Language Courses. I.H.C., a Spanish language school in Madrid, has developed its own methodology and is assisted by a team of highly qualified teachers. Offering a wide variety of courses and social activities, we can also provide accommodations.

Dates: Begin any Monday. Cost: 1998: Twenty hours group tuition plus family half board: $325 per week. Contact: Ms. Eva Hernandez, Instituto Hernan Cortes, Diego de Leon 16, 28006 Madrid, Spain; (011) 34-91-563-4601, fax (011) 34-91-563-4526; hernancortes@rauta.es, www.nauta.es@hernancortes.

Lacunza-Escuela Internacional. In Lacunza you will learn to communicate in Spanish. In a recognized school with a well-studied method, teachers who like their profession, and a dedication that goes beyond the courses, accommodations, and activities. San Sebastian, beach, mountains, woods, hospitable people, appreciated gastronomy. Come to learn Spanish, you will never forget.

Dates: Jan 4 and then every 2 weeks. Cost: 4-week course is PTS86,000, course and shared apartment is PTS141,000 (1998). Contact: Itxiar Gorostidi, Lacunza-Escuela Internacional, Moraza 5, 20006 San Sebastian, Spain; (011) 34-943-471-487, fax (011) 34-943-463061; lacunzae@sarenet.es.

Learn Spanish in Spain. Language immersion courses in Spain (Barcelona, Canary Islands, Granada, Madrid, Malaga, San Sebastian, Seville, and Valencia). Private language schools centrally located, convenient to interesting places, cultural events, and sports activities. Programs feature qualified teachers, small classes, attractive surroundings and facilities. Affordable prices for instruction. Accommodations with Spanish families with meals; student residences; apartments; and nearby hotels.

Dates: Year round. Two weeks or more. Cost: Two-week courses with or without accommodations range from $245-$865. Contact: Ms. Lorraine Haber, Study Abroad Coordinator, CES Study Abroad Program, The Center for English Studies, 330 7th Ave., 6th Fl., New York, NY 10001; (212) 629-7300, fax (212) 736-7950.

One-to-One Residential Spanish. Dialogue specializes in language programs that adapt to your learning style and pace. Whether you are a beginner or an advanced student, you will improve your understanding of Spanish culture, as well as your communication skills. Meals, breaks, and evening activities take place in the company of tutors.

Dates: Any week except Christmas. Cost: $1,217-$1,928 per week. Includes room, meals, teaching materials, tuition, evening activities. Contact: Mr. Julian Melbourne, Dialogue Idiomas Ltd., Bonavista 795, 08635 Sant Esteve Sesrovires, Barcelona, Spain; (011) 34-93-771-43-06, fax (011) 34-93-771-50-22; dialogue@bcn.servicom.es, www.sogid.be/dialogue.

Semester in Spain. Semester, year, summer, and January terms for high school graduates, college students, and adult learners. Beginning, intermediate, and advanced Spanish language studies along with Spanish literature, culture, history, and art. All courses taught in Spanish by native Spaniards. Four courses per semester, 4 credits each. Homestays are arranged for all students. January term and summer terms also.

Dates: Winter: Jan 4-23; Spring: Jan 27-May

21; Summer: May 31-Jun 25 and/or Jun 28-Jul 21; Fall: Aug 26-Dec 18. Cost: Fall or Spring $7,950; year approx. $15,900; Summer and Jan term approx. $2,000 each term. Includes tuition, books, room and board. Contact: Debra Veenstra, U.S. Coordinator, Semester in Spain, Dept. TA, 6601 W. College Dr., Palos Heights, IL 60463; (800) 748-0087 or (708) 239-4766, fax (708) 239-3986.

Spanish and Basque Studies (Bilbao). The Getxo-Bilbao area offers intensive language studies (Spanish or Basque) that fulfill up to 2 years of university language requirements in 1 semester, plus courses in history, political science, art, culture, economics, teacher education, literature, etc. Program organized field trips, housing, and many local university activities at this seaside city.

Dates: Spring semester: Jan-May; Fall semester: Aug-Dec 16. Cost: Fall or Spring semester $4,390; year $7,190. Contact: University Studies Abroad Consortium (USAC), Univ. of Nevada, Reno #323, Reno, NV 89557-0093; (702) 784-6569, fax (702) 784-6010; usac@admin.unr.edu, www.scs.unr. edu/~usac.

Spanish and Basque Studies (San Sebastian). San Sebastian offers intensive language (Spanish or Basque) that fulfill up to 2 years of university language requirements in 1 semester, plus courses in history, literature, political science, economics, art, teacher education, etc. Program organized field trips to Madrid and elsewhere, housing, and many local university activities in this beautiful seaside resort.

Dates: Spring semester: Jan-May; Summer sessions: Jul, Jun, Aug; Fall semester: Aug-Dec. Contact program director for exact dates of each semester. Cost: Fall or Spring semester $6,290; year $9,880; Jun or Jul $1,980; Aug $1,610; Jun and Jul $3,680; Jun, July or Aug $3,190; Jun, Jul, and Aug $4,680. Contact: University Studies Abroad Consortium (USAC), Univ. of Nevada, Reno #323, Reno, NV 89557-0093; (702) 784-6569, fax (702) 784-6010; usac@admin.unr.edu, www.scs. unr.edu/~usac.

Spanish at Malaca Instituto. The quality of Malaca Instituto's Spanish language and cultural programs is guaranteed by independent inspection (see www.eaquals.org). For all ages 16-90. Our students come from all over the world. Full accommodations, activity and excursion program. A 10-minute walk from Mediterranean beaches.

Dates: Every 2 weeks. (Min. 2 weeks, max. 1 academic year.) Cost: Call for information. Contact: Bob Burger, Malaca Instituto, c/o Cortada 6, Cerrado de Calderon, 29018 Malaga, Spain; (011) 34-95-229-32-42 or 1896, fax (011) 34-95-229-63-16; espanol@malacainst-ch.es, www.malacainst-ch.es.

Spanish Courses in Malaga. Spanish courses in Malaga, Spain. All grades, small groups, 4 hours daily, courses commencing each month. Living with Spanish families (or in small apartment in town center).

Contact: F. Marin Fernandez, Director, Centro de Estudios de Castellano, Ave. Juan Sebastian Elcano, 120, Malaga, 29017 Spain; Tel./fax (011) 34-95-2290-551; ryoga@arrakis.es, www.arrakis.es/~ryoga.

Spanish for Foreigners. Intensive courses (45 hours of classes), 2-8 students per class; sociocultural program. Accommodations: choice of homestays, apartments, and hotels.

Dates: First Monday of each month. Cost: Tuition $4,300 (1998). Contact: Eduardo Vila, Hola! Idiomas, Francesc Gumá 25, 08870 Sitges, Barcelona, Spain; (011) 34-93-894-1333, fax (011) 34-93-894-9621; www. holasitges.com.

Spanish in Southern Spain. Learn Spanish in the beautiful south of Spain. Enjoy the weather and 22 kms of sandy beaches while you study. This is a coastal town with little international tourism that guarantees you will only meet Spanish people and hear Spanish spoken.

Dates: Winter courses: Oct-May, summer courses: Jun-Sep. Cost: Two weeks PTS 35,000—30 hours of class. Contact: Mr. Ian

Walsh, Academia de Idiomas Trinity School, Calle Ave del Paraiso No. º6, 11500 el Puerto de Santa Maria, Cadiz, Spain; (011) 34-956-871926, fax (011) 34-956-541918; trinity@spa.es, www.spa.es/~trinity.

Spanish Language and Culture. Offered by a Spanish higher education institution. All grades. Small groups (about 15 students). Three different accommodations options: halls of residence, host family, and shared flats (self-catering). Summer courses (Jul-Aug) and permanent. An attractive cultural-touristic program is also available. Special rates for shorter periods (minimum 1 month).

Dates: Permanent course: Oct-Jun. Summer courses: Jul, Aug. Contact program director for exact dates. Cost: Summer course: 1 month PTS70,000; 2 months PTS100,000; full academic year PTS190,000; 4 month-session PTS100,000. Contact: Cursos de Español, Lengua Extranjera, Universidad de León, Avda. Facultad 25, 24071, León, Spain; (011) 34-87-291646 or 291650, fax (011) 34-87-291693; neggeuri@isidoro.unileon.es.

Summer in Madrid. Students study Spanish language and/or culture: Spanish 2 (Beginning Spanish 2); Spanish 3 (intermediate Spanish 1); Spanish 9 (civilization of Spain); Spanish 4 (intermediate Spanish 2).

Dates: Jun-Jul. Cost: Call for details. Contact: Nancy Nieman, Santa Monica College, 1900 Pico Blvd., Santa Monica, CA 90405; (310) 452-9270, fax (310) 581-8618; nnieman@smc.edu.

URI Summer Study in Salamanca. Spend over 4 weeks in Spain studying Spanish language, literature, and culture at the prestigious Colegio de España in Salamanca. The program is designed for college students, graduates, and teachers, as well as for college-bound high school students. Program A: Intensive Undergraduate Language and Culture. Up to 9 credits. Program B: Literature, Language and Culture, and Business

Spanish. Six graduate or advanced undergraduate credits.

Dates: Jul. Cost: Program A $1,850; Program B $2,050. Contact: Mario F. Trubiano, Director, Summer Program in Spain, Dept. of Languages, Univ. of Rhode Island, Kingston, RI 02881-0812; (401) 874-4717 or (401) 874-5911 or (after 5 p.m.) (401) 789-9501, fax (401) 874-4694.

Sweden

Intensive Summer Courses in Sweden. Swedish language in Uppsala. Beginners, intermediate, and higher intermediate. Tuition, study visits, language laboratory, sightseeing, welcoming lunch. Small groups.

Dates: Jul, Aug. Cost: Approx. $973. Includes tuition and material. Contact: Marlene Wälivara, Folkuniversitet-et, Box 386, S-75106 Uppsala, Sweden; (011) 46-18-680010, fax (011) 46-18-693484; marlene.walivara@folkuni.se, www.folkuni.se/uppsala.

Uppsala Univ. Int'l. Summer Session. Sweden's oldest academic summer program focuses on learning the Swedish language. All levels from beginners to advanced. Additional courses in Swedish history, social institutions, arts in Sweden, Swedish film. Excursions every Friday. Extensive evening program includes both lectures and entertainment. Single rooms in dormitories or apartments. Open to both students and adults. Credit possible.

Dates: Jun-Aug; Jun-Jul; Jul-Aug. Contact for exact dates. Cost: SEK22,200 (approx. $2,775) for the 8-week session, SEK12,000 (approx. $1,500) for the 4-week session. Includes room, some meals, all classes, evening and excursion program. Contact: Dr. Nelleke Dorrestÿn, Uppsala Univ. Int. Summer Session, Box 513, 751 20 Uppsala, Sweden; (011) 31-71-541-4955, fax (011) 31-71-541-7705 or mobile phone (011) 31-6-22439491; nduiss@wxs.nl, www.uuiss.uu.se.

Switzerland

CP Language Institute. The language school is located in Leysin, a beautiful mountain resort above Lake Geneva in a former Grand Hotel. CP offers 2- to 32-week intensive French language courses at all levels. International student body, highly experienced teachers, and a unique atmosphere. Classes are small and thus offer a great deal of personal attention. Activity and recreational programs offered. Courses can be taken in conjunction with university courses at the American College of Switzerland.

Dates: Year round. Cost: Per week: Tuition SFR775 including 24 hours tuition and full board accommodations. Contact: Mrs. Françoise Bailey, CP Language Institutes, c/o American College of Switzerland, CH 1854 Leysin, Switzerland; (011) 41-24-494-22-23, fax (011) 41-24-494-13-46.

Intensive French. Founded in 1908, Lemania College is located in the city of Lausanne in a peaceful setting on the shore of Lake Geneva. The professional team of experienced teachers, the individual syllabuses, the computer-assisted language learning method, and the French-speaking area will bring students up to their expected level for official examinations. Leisure activities, sports, and excursions available.

Dates: Year round. Cost: Per week: tuition $450; lodging in boarding house $800, with family: $400; in apartment $170. Contact: Lemania College, Miss E. Perni, International Admissions Office, Chemin de Préville 3, 1001 Lausanne, Switzerland; (011) 41-21-320-15-01, fax (011) 41-21-312-67-00; hirtlemania@fasnet.ch.

Univ. of Geneva Summer Courses. French language and civilization at all levels, beginners to advanced. All instructors have a university diploma. Excursions and visits to Geneva and its surroundings. Class of 15-20 students. Minimum age 17.

Dates: Jul 12-30, Aug 2-20, Aug 23-Sep 10, Sep 13-Oct 1. Cost: SFR470 for 3 weeks (tuition). Contact: Mr. Gérard Benz, Univ. of Geneva, Summer Courses, rue de Candolle 3, CH-1211 Geneva 4, Switzerland; (011) 41-22-705-74-34, fax (011) 41-22-705-74-39; elcfete@uni2a.unige. ch, www.unige.ch/lettres/elcf/coursete/cournet.html.

Thailand

Southeast Asian Studies (Bangkok). Diverse courses in culture, language, economics, business, society, and religions provide a fascinating, well-balanced approach to Southeast Asia. Program-organized field trips, student residence halls, and many university activities at one of Thailand's most modern universities.

Dates: Spring semester: Jan-May; Summer session: Jun-Aug 4; Fall semester: Aug-Dec. Contact program director for exact dates. Cost: One semester: $2,680; year: $4,380; Summer session: $1,480. Contact: University Studies Abroad Consortium (USAC), Univ. of Nevada, Reno #323, Reno, NV 89557-0093; (702) 784-6569, fax (702) 784-6010; usac@adminunr.edu, www.scs.unr.edu/~usac.

United Kingdom and Ireland

Teach English as a Foreign Language. Courses in central London leading to the Cambridge/RSA Certificate (CELTA), regarded internationally as the ideal qualification in TEFL. International House has 40 years experience in training teachers and can offer jobs to those recently qualified in its 110 schools in 27 countries.

Dates: Four-week (110 hours) intensive courses. Contact program director for starting dates of each 4-week session. Cost: £944 includes Cambridge/RSA registration. Contact: Teacher Training Development, International House, 106 Piccadilly, London

W1V 9FL, England; (011) 44-171-491-2598, fax (011) 44-171-499-0174; teacher@dial. pipex.com.

United States

Boston TEFL Course. International TEFL Certificate, limited enrollment, no second language necessary, second career persons welcome, global placement guidance, humanistic orientation to cross-cultural education, teacher training at American English Language Foundation, Harvard Univ. Club, or other accommodations, PDP eligible by Massachusetts Department of Education. Also offers the Certificate in Teaching Business-English (Cert. TBE), Executive English, and Accent reduction program.

Dates: Full-time intensive course monthly; part-time courses offered periodically throughout the year. Cert.TBE Course - Intensive 1-week course offered monthly. Cost: $2,300 includes tuition, nonrefundable $95 application fee, internship, international resume, job placement guidance, video lab, all books and materials. Contact: Thomas A. Kane, PhD, Worldwide Teachers Development Institute, 266 Beacon St., Boston, MA 02116; (800) 875-5564, fax (617) 262-0308; bostontefl@aol.com; www.to-get.com/BostonTEFL.

Career English Language Center. Established in 1975, the Career English Language Center for International Students (CELCIS) is an intensive English program designed to prepare second-language learners to study in higher education in the U.S. It is also useful for those needing English for their professions.

Dates: Jan 4-Apr 23, May 3-Jun 24, Jun 28-Aug 13, Aug 30-Dec 10. Cost: Spring/Summer sessions: $3,128 includes tuition, books, housing, food, hospital insurance. Fall and Winter semesters: $5,664. Contact: Laura Latulippe, CELCIS, Western Michigan Univ., 22-B Ellsworth Hall, WMU, Kalamazoo, MI 49008;

fax (616) 387-4806; www.wmich.edu/oia/celcis.

English Language Program. A quality intensive English Program on the campus of a major state university, offering small classes, classmates from many countries, teachers with graduate degrees, and a friendly, safe community to live in.

Dates: Jun-Jul, mid-Aug to mid-Dec, mid-Jan to mid-May. Cost: $3,550 semester, $2,300 Summer session (tuition, campus and health fees). Contact: Enid Cocke, English Language Program, Kansas State Univ., Fairchild Hall, Manhattan, KS 66506; elp@ksu.edu, www.ksu.edu/elp.

Executive Spanish Camp. Nine-day intensive program in a complete immersion setting for beginners to high intermediate. Two locations: Cd Juarez, Mexico (El Paso, TX) or mountain retreat in southern New Mexico. Includes cultural training and emphasizes oral skills. Over 1,000 past campers have called it a valuable and enjoyable experience.

Dates: Jan 29-Feb 7, Apr 23-May 2, July 16-25, Oct 8-17. Cost: $1,595-$1,995 all inclusive, double occupancy. Contact: Language Plus, 4110 Rio Bravo, El Paso, TX 79902; (915) 544-8600, fax (915) 544-8640; langplus@aol.com, www.languageplus.com.

St Giles Language Teaching Center. Earn the Certificate in English Language Teaching to Adults (CELTA) in San Francisco, approved by the Royal Society of Arts/Univ. of Cambridge Examination Syndicate and the California Bureau for Private Postsecondary and Vocational Education. The course on practical training and teaching methodology, includes access to international job postings, graduate contacts, and teaching opportunities abroad. EFL school on site for observation and practice teaching. Part of a group of schools in England, Switzerland, and the U.S. with over 40 years of teaching and training experience, led by highly-qualified instructors with extensive overseas teaching experience. CELTA courses also offered in Brighton and London, England.

Dates: Jan 11-Feb 5, Apr 5-30, Jun 7-Jul 2, Sep 13-Oct 8, Oct 25-Nov 19. Cost: $2,550. Contact: St Giles Language Teaching Center, 1 Hallidie Plaza, Suite 350, San Francisco, CA 94102; (415) 788-3552, fax (415) 788-1923; sfstgile@slip.net, www.stgiles-usa.com.

Worldwide

Academic Credit for Travel. Language immersion programs, work-intern-volunteer experiences worldwide. Independent study courses that provide academic credit for travel undertaken anywhere/anytime in the world. Open to high school, college students, and teachers. Undergraduate and post graduate. Language (Spanish, Italian, French) credit available. Suitable for study abroad, language immersion, short trips, and sabbaticals.

Dates: Year round. Cost: Approx. $65 per credit. Contact: Professor Steve Tash, Language and Travel Study Programs, P.O. Box 16501, Irvine, CA 92623-6501; (800) 484-1081, ext. 7775 (9 a.m.-9 p.m. PST), fax (949) 552-0740; travelstudy@yahoo.com, www.studyabroadandwork.com.

¿?don Quijote In-Country Spanish Language Schools. Intensive Spanish language courses using the communicative method are combined with an intensive immersion in the social and cultural life of some of Spain's most interesting cities (Salamanca, Barçelona, Granada, Malaga). Airport pick-up service, study counseling, homestay or student flats, excursions, access to recreational facilities, touring, and sightseeing opportunities. ¿?don Quijote now offers intensive Spanish language courses through partner schools in Latin America: Cuernavaca and Mèrida, Mexico; Antigua, Guatemala; Alajuela, Costa Rica; and Quito, Ecuador.

Dates: Year round—Fall, Spring, Winter, and Summer. Cost: Inquire. Contact: ¿?don Quijote, Apartado de Correos 333, 37080 Salamanca, Spain; (011) 34-923-268-860, fax (011) 34-923-268-815; donquijote@offcampus.es, www.teclata.es/donquijote.

English Tuition. General English in U.K. (London, Brighton, and Eastbourne), U.S. (San Francisco and Boston), and Switzerland (St. Gallen). Year round. Recognized by British Council. Examination English. English for business.

Dates: Every 2 weeks. Cost: From £193 (1998). Contact: St Giles College, Head Office, 154 Southampton Row, London WC1B 5AX, U.K.; (011) 44-171-837-0404, fax (011) 44-171-837-4099.

Global Volunteers. "An adventure in service." The nation's premier short-term service programs for people of all ages and backgrounds. Assist mutual international understanding through ongoing development projects in 19 countries throughout Africa, Asia, the Caribbean, Europe, the South Pacific, North and South America. Programs of 1, 2, and 3 weeks, range from natural resource preservation, light construction, and painting to teaching English and assisting with health care. No special skills or foreign languages are required. Ask about the Millennium Service Project.

Dates: Over 130 teams year round. Cost: Tax-deductible program fees range from $400 to $2,095. Airfare not included. Contact: Global Volunteers, 375 E. Little Canada Rd., St. Paul, MN 55117; (800) 487-1074, fax (651) 482-0915; email@globalvolunteers.org, www.globalvolunteers.org.

Home Language International. Live in your teacher's home. Learn the language of your choice in the country of your choice. Individual lessons with your own private teacher ensures a program tailor-made to your requirements and isolation from the English language. Countries include France, Germany, Spain, Italy, Russia, Taiwan, etc.

Dates: Year-round courses in weekly units,

Sunday to Sunday. Cost: From $1,050 per week: full board with teacher and 15 hours lessons. Contact: Sarah Amerena, Home Language International, Reservations Office, 17 Royal Crescent, Ramsgate, Kent CT11 9PE, U.K.; (011) 44-1843-851116; fax (011) 44-1843-590300; hli@btinternet.com, www.hli.co.uk.

Language and Culture Immersion. Learn a language and enjoy an exciting variety of cultural and social experiences. Short-term and long-term programs year round for all ages and levels throughout Europe, Asia, Central and South America. Homestays available. Special programs for families, teens, seniors, executives, teachers, professionals. College credit available.

Dates: Year round. Cost: Varies with program. Contact: Nancy Forman, Language Liaison Inc., 20533 Biscayne Blvd., Suite. 4-162, Miami, FL 33180; (800) 284-4448 or (954) 455-3411, fax (954) 455-3413, learn@languageliaison.com, www.languageliaison. com.

Language Immersion Programs. Learn a language in the country where it's spoken. Intensive foreign language training offered in Costa Rica, Russia, Spain, France, Italy, Germany, and Ecuador for students aged 16 and older. Classes are taught in up to 8 different proficiency levels and are suitable for beginners as well as people with advanced linguistic skills. All courses include accommodations and meals. Lots of extracurricular activities available. Students can earn college credit through Providence College.

Dates: Courses start every second Monday year round. Year programs commence in Sep, semester programs in Jan, May, and Sep. Cost: Varies with program, approx. $950 per 2-week course. Contact: Stephanie Greco, Director of, Admissions, EF International Language Schools, EF Center, 1 Education St., Cambridge, MA 02142; (800) 992-1892, fax (617) 619-1701; ils@ef.com.

Middlebury College Summer Language Courses. Middlebury College's Summer Language Schools in Vermont offer language immersion in a unique, controlled linguistic environment. Since 1915, Middlebury has provided students with unlimited opportunities to speak in their target language with native and near-native language professionals and with each other (Arabic, Chinese, French, German, Italian, Japanese, Russian, and Spanish). Undergraduate and graduate credit available. Programs range from beginner to advanced. MA and DML (Doctor of Modern Languages) degree programs also available. Linkage with Middlebury's Schools Abroad. Summer sessions range from 3 to 9 weeks in duration, depending upon the school. Student to faculty ratio is less than 6 to 1.

Dates: Nine-week sessions (Arabic, Chinese, Japanese, and Russian) Jun 11-Aug 13, 1999; 7-week sessions (French, German, Italian, and Spanish) Jun 25 Aug 13, 1999; 6-week graduate sessions (French, German, Italian, Russian, and Spanish) Jun 28-Aug 13, 1999. Cost: Tuition varies from $975 for a 3-week session to $3,800 for 9 weeks. Room and board additional. Contact: The Language Schools, Middlebury College, Middlebury, VT 05753; (802) 443-5510, fax (802) 443-2075; languages@middlebury.edu, www.middlebury.edu/~ls.

Peace Corps. Since 1961, more than 150,000 Americans have joined the Peace Corps. Assignments are 27 months long. Volunteers must be U.S. citizens, at least 18 years old, and in good health. Peace Corps has volunteer programs in education, business, agriculture, the environment, and health.

Dates: Apply 9-12 months prior to availability. Cost: Volunteers receive transportation to and from assignment, a stipend, complete health care, and $5,400 after 27 months of service. Contact: Peace Corps, Room 8506, 1990 K St. W., Washington, DC 20526; (800) 424-8580 (mention code 824); www.peacecorps.gov.

Spanish for Foreigners. Standard courses (20 lessons a week). Summer courses (15 lessons a week). One-to-one. Full and varied social program. Exams "Cervantes Institute." Accommodations with family or hotel. Highly qualified, caring, and experienced staff located in the center of northern green Spain.

Dates: Year round. Cost: From PTS50,000 all inclusive (family stays). Contact: Mrs. S. Valles, Escuela de Idiomas Alce, c/Nogales 2, Oviedo 33006, Spain; Tel./fax (011) 34-8-525-4543; alce.idiomas@fade.es.

TEFL and On-the-Job Tuition. Student exchange, business and language tuition, computer training, multimedia courses, translations on and offline, interpreting, hostess training, secretarial courses.

Dates: Call for details. Cost: Call for details. Contact: International Benedict Schools, P.O. Box 270, CH 1000, Lausanne 9, Switzerland; (011) 21-323-66-55, fax (011) 21-311-02-29; benedict@worlcom.ch, www.benedictschools.

For more listings of language schools, and for bargains worldwide, travel tips, and all sorts of information on learning, living, working, and traveling abroad, see *Transitions Abroad* magazine. To order a single copy or a subscription, please call 1-800-293-0373 or visit the *Transitions Abroad* web site at www.transabroad.com.

CHAPTER 13

STUDY PROGRAMS

The following listing of study programs was supplied by the organizers in 1998 and is updated in each March/April issue of Transitions Abroad *magazine. To subscribe to* Transitions Abroad, *call 1-800-293-0373 or visit www.transabroad.com. Contact the program directors to confirm costs, dates, and other details. Please tell them you read about their programs in this book! Programs based in more than one country or region are listed under "Worldwide."*

Africa

Culture and the Arts. An introduction to the rich history, culture, and the arts of the very diverse and ancient people of Senegal and The Gambia. The focus will be on the visual and performing arts. Meet new people, learn new artistic techniques, attend ceremonies and performances, and expand your understanding of West African art and culture.

Dates: Jun. Cost: $2,690. Includes airfare, hotel accommodations, 2 meals per day, tuition for 3 credits. Contact: Rockland Community College, Center for International Studies, 145 College Rd., Suffern, NY 10901; (914) 574-4205, fax (914) 574-4423; study-abroad@sunyrockland.edu.

Kalamazoo in Africa. Programs combine academics and experiential learning. Course work in a host-country setting (with local students in university courses) gives participants a broad overview of the host country. Instruction in the local language as well as internships or independent projects provide opportunities for greater understanding of the host culture.

Dates: Senegal and Kenya: Sep-Jun. Cost: $24,249 (1998-99). Includes roundtrip international transportation, tuition and fees, room and board, and some excursions. Contact: Center for International Programs, Kalamazoo College, 1200 Academy, Kalamazoo, MI 49006; (616) 337-7133, fax (616) 337-7400; cip@kzoo.edu.

Natural History Safaris. New Horizons offers a variety of educational programs. Wildlife ecology majors study Africa's vast array of wildlife in their natural habitats. Programs for liberal arts students take an in-depth look at the fascinating cultures of various African peoples. Special incentives are offered to professors who lead a group of students from their institution.

Dates: Professor's preference. Cost: Depends on length of program and time of year. Contact: New Horizons Safari Specialists, P.O. Box 5700, Glendale Heights, IL 60139-5700; (630) 893-2545, fax (630) 529-9769; Africa.nh@compuserve.com.

Univ. of Wisconsin in West Africa. Study abroad in Francophone Africa at the Université Gaston Berger in Saint Louis, Senegal. Students experience a blend of Africa, French, and Muslim traditions while they live in dorms with Senegalese roommates. Classes taught in French in a variety of humanities and social sciences. Includes a year-long course in Wolof and an independent fieldwork project. Orientation includes several days in Madison and 2 weeks in Dakar, Senegal. Four semesters of French or equivalent required. Application deadline: first Friday in Feb. Late applications considered on a space-available basis.

Dates: Mid-Sep-mid-Jun. Cost: Call for current information. Contact: Office of International Studies and Programs, 261 Bascom Hall, Univ. of Wisconsin, 500 Lincoln Dr., Madison, WI 53706; (608) 262-2851, fax (608) 262-6998; peeradv@macc.wisc.edu.

Argentina

Instituto de Lengua Española (ILEE). Located downtown in the most European-like city in Latin America, Buenos Aires. Dedicated exclusively to teaching Spanish to foreigners. Small groups and private classes year round. All teachers hold Master's degrees in Education or Literature and have been full-time Spanish professors for years. Method is intensive, conversation-based. Student body is international. Highly recommended worldwide. Ask for individual references in U.S.

Dates: Year round. Cost: Four-week intensive program (20 hours per week) including homestay $1,400; 2 weeks $700. Private classes $19 per hour. Registration fee (includes books) $100. Contact: Daniel Korman, I.L.E.E., Director, Lavalle 1619 7° C (1048), Buenos Aires, Argentina; Tel./fax (011) 54-1-375-0730. In U.S.: David Babbitz; (415) 431-8219, fax (415) 431-5306; ilee@overnet.com.ar, www.study abroad.com/ilee.

Spanish and More. Study Spanish language in Buenos Aires, take credit-transferred curricular courses in all disciplines, South American culture courses, and Tango dance classes at Universidad de Belgrano. Homestays or private student residences.

Dates: Mar-Jul; Aug-Dec. Cost: Inquire. Contact: Julia Capurro, Director, Office of International Programs, Universidad de Belgrano, Zabala 1837 (1426) Buenos Aires, Argentina; (011) 54-1-788-5400, fax (011) 54-1-784-9894; jc@ub.edu.ar, www.edu.ar.

Australia

AustraLearn: Study in Australia. AustraLearn is the most comprehensive Australian study abroad program for U.S. students. You can choose from universities throughout Australia (Queensland, Victoria, Western Australia, New South Wales, Australian capital Territory, South Australia, Tasmania, and the Northern Territory). Semester, year, graduate, short-term experiential, and internship programs are available. Pre-trip orientation.

Dates: Semester/Year (Feb or Jul admit), Summer or Winter abroad short courses. Cost: Semester: $6,500-$9,500, short-term internship: $3,500-$4,200. Contact: Ms. Cynthia Flannery-Banks, Director, AustraLearn, 110 16th St., CSU Denver Center, Denver, CO 80202; (800) 980-0033, fax (303) 446-5955; studyabroad@australearn.org.

Certificate in Baking. This 6-month course provides basic skills in breadmaking, pastrycooking, and baking. Graduates are eligible to apply for employment in the baking/pastrycooking industry.

Dates: Feb 8, Jul 19. Cost: $5,270 plus living expenses (approx. $211 per week). Contact: Mr. Vernon Bruce, Manager, International Education, William Angliss Institute of TAFE, 555 La Trobe St., Melbourne, 3000 Australia; (011) 61-3-9606-2139, fax (011) 61-3-9670-9348; vern@angliss.vic.edu.au, www.angliss.vic.edu.au.

Certificate in Cookery (Western) or (Asian). These 26-week courses provide students with industry-recognized qualifications in Western or Asian cuisines. The Asian program covers the cuisines of regional China and Southeast Asia including Cantonese, Sichuan, Chui Chow, Northern Chinese, Thai, Vietnamese, Malaysian, Indonesian, and Nonya. Graduates are eligible to seek employment as cooks.

Dates: Feb 8, Jul 19. Cost: $3,800 tuition plus living expenses (approx. $143 per week). Contact: Mr. Vernon Bruce, Manager, International Education, William Angliss Institute of TAFE, 555 La Trobe St., Melbourne, 3000 Australia; (011) 61-3-9606-2139, fax (011) 61-3-9670-9348; vernb@angliss.vic.edu.au, www.angliss.edu.au.

Education Australia. Study abroad for a semester or a year at Australian National Univ. (Canberra), Deakin Univ. (Victoria), Univ. of Ballarat (Victoria), Univ. of Tasmania (Tasmania), Univ. of Wollongong (New South Wales), or the Australian Catholic Univ. (several states). In New Zealand courses are offered at the Univ. of Canterbury and Lincoln Univ. (Christchurch). Liberal arts, science, business, biology, psychology, education, Australian studies, etc. Customized internships in all fields are also available.

Dates: Mid-Jul-mid-Nov, mid-Feb-late Jun. Cost: Tuition approx. $4,400, accommodations approx. $2,250. Airfare. Contact: Dr. Maurice A. Howe, Executive Director, Education Australia, P.O. Box 2233, Amherst, MA 01004; (800) 344-

6741, fax (413) 549-0741; edaust@javanet.com, www.javanet.com/~edaust.

General Studies in Australia. Victoria offers nearly every discipline in undergraduate/graduate levels at 5 different university campus sites: Australian studies, art, journalism, performing arts, women's studies, biology, chemistry, math, business, computing, etc. Known as the Garden State, Victoria has some of the country's most beautiful mountain and coastal areas.

Dates: First semester: Jul 12-Nov 13 (1998); second semester: Feb 21-Jun 25 (1999). Cost: $4,315 per semester, $7,775 for 1 year. Contact: University Studies Abroad Consortium (USAC), Univ. of Nevada, Reno #323, Reno, NV 89557-0093; (702) 784-6569, fax (702) 784-6010; usac@admin.unr.edu, www.scs.unr.edu/~usac.

Semester in Australia. The Australian International Hotel School in Canberra offers semester and shorter summer programs focusing on international hospitality management. Students earn 12-15 credits; courses include Pacific Tourism, Multicultural Management, International Cuisine, Global Hotel Operations, and Resort Development. Students live at AIHS and participate in many travel and cultural activities.

Dates: Semester: Feb 1-May 7. Summer: May 24-Jul 9. Cost: Semester: $8,500 includes tuition, room and board, and course-related trips. Summer: $4,950. Contact: Prof. Richard H. Penner, AIHS Semester in Australia, Cornell Univ., 182 Statler Hall, Ithaca, NY 14853-6902; (607) 255-1842, (800) 235-8220, fax (607) 255-4179; aihs@cornell.edu, http://hotelschool.cornell.edu/aihs.

Study in Australia. Nine programs available in Sydney, Melbourne, Brisbane and Gold Coast, including summer opportunities in cooperation with the National Institute of Dramatic Art and the Univ. of New South Wales. Full range of program services. Need-based scholarships available.

Dates: Fall, Spring, Academic year, Summer. Cost: Varies. Call for current fees. Contact:

Study Programs

Christopher Hennessy, Beaver College CEA, 450 S. Easton Rd., Glenside, PA 19038-3295; (888) BEAVER-9, fax (215) 572-2174; cea@beaver.edu, www.beaver.edu/cea.

Univ. of Melbourne. Study abroad at Australia's premier university, located in the World's Most Liveable City. Program includes top-notch academic departments, guaranteed housing and unique educational excursions. Campus is a quick tram ride to the beach and a 5-minute walk to the city center. Select from thousands of courses in 11 faculties.

Dates: Semester 1: Feb-Jun; Semester 2: Jul-Nov. Cost: Tuition fees: AUS$6,250 per semester; AUS$12,500 per year. Health cover AUS$148 for 6 months; AUS$274 for 12 months. Contact: Study Abroad Manager, International Centre, Univ. of Melbourne, Parkville, Victoria, 3052 Australia; (011) 61-3-9344-4505, fax (011) 61-3-9349-3204; m.riordan@international.unimelb.edu.au, www.unimelb.edu.au/international/sabroad.html.

Univ. of South Australia. The Univ. of South Australia hosts study abroad programs for university students wishing to undertake a semester (or 2) of their studies overseas and have the credits transferred to their home institution. USA offers many field-based units, giving the students the opportunity to study in different environments and to learn about something unavailable at home: Aboriginal culture, Australia's environmental settings, South Australian history.

Dates: Semester 1: Feb 22-Jul 4; Semester 2: Jul 19-Nov 30. Cost: Call for details. Contact: Study Abroad Adviser, Int'l. Office, Univ. of South Australia, GPO Box 2471, Adelaide, South Australia 5001; (011) 61-8-302-0169, fax (011) 61-8-302-0233; chris.haas@unisa.edu.au. For students in the U.S. and Canada: American Univ. Int'l. Program (AUISP); auip@peak.peak.com; (970) 495-0869, fax (970) 484-6997; or Australearn, (800) 980-0033 or (303) 446-2214, fax (303) 446-5595; sackroyal@austrlearn.org.

Austria

European Studies in Vienna. Semester program with 3 distinct tracks of study: Central European Studies (fall), European Integration: European Union (spring), and Hungary, Romania, Bulgaria, and Former Yugoslavia Studies (spring). No knowledge of German required, study of German during program. Extensive field study trips.

Dates: Fall, Spring, Academic year, and Summer. pre-sessions in Intensive German Language. Cost: Summer: psychology or art nouveau $2,800; both courses $3,900, Fall or Spring semester $10,395, Pre-session $2,200 alone or $1,575 with semester, full year $19,425 (1998-99), Contact: Stacy Johnson, Program Coordinator, Beaver College Center for Education Abroad, 450 S. Easton Rd., Glenside, PA 19038-3295; (888) BEAVER-9, fax (215) 572-2174; cea@beaver.edu, www.beaver.edu/cea.

Vienna Master Courses for Music. Master classes (2 weeks) in: singing, opera, lied, piano, violin, cello, guitar, chamber music, conducting, flute. Diploma for active participation, certificate for listeners, final concerts. Twenty lessons per week. Instructors are leading artists or renowned teachers.

Dates: Jul 5-Aug 15. Cost: Registration fee: AS1,500; course fee active: AS5,200; listen AS2,700. Contact: Vienna Master Courses, A-1030 Vienna, Reisnerstr. 3, Austria; (011) 43-1-714-88-22, fax (011) 43-1-714-88-21 (Elisabeth Keschmann or Monika Wiladauer).

Belgium

MA in Business. The MA program combines several key courses from the MBA program with subjects concerning the theory and implementation of communication and public relations. European Univ. graduates are prepared for careers in public relations, human resources, and training development and organizational consulting. A full-time student can complete the program in 1 academic year.

Dates: Early Oct through Dec, early Jan through mid-Mar, and mid-Mar through mid-Jun. Cost: Tuition BEF360,000 per program (full-time or part-time). Contact: Mr. Luc Van Mele, Dean, Jacob Jordaenstraat 77, 2018 Antwerp, Belgium; (011) 32-3-218-54-31, fax (011) 32-3-218-58-68; info@euruni. be.

MBA. The MBA program covers many aspects of international operations. The emphasis is on international finance and marketing as well as strategic management; it includes a solid foundation in the traditional management disciplines. A full-time student can complete the program in 1 academic year.

Dates: Early Oct to Dec, early Jan to mid-Mar, and mid-Mar to mid-Jun. Cost: Tuition BEF360,000 per program (full-time or part-time). Contact: Mr. Luc Van Mele, Dean, Jacob Jordaenstraat 77, 2018 Antwerp, Belgium; (011) 32-3-218-54-31, fax (011) 32-3-218-58-68; info@euruni.be.

Vesalius College. Vesalius College is the international undergraduate English language college of the Vrije Univ. Brussel-VUB. It offers American-style, liberal arts and sciences programs in coordination with Boston Univ. BA and BS in business economics, international affairs, political studies, literature, communications and computing. About 400 students representing over 60 nationalities have access to excellent research and sports facilities. Over 90 percent of faculty hold PhDs.

Dates: Aug-Dec (Fall), Jan-May (Spring), Jun-Jul (Summer). Cost: $4,500 per semester (tuition and fees) Contact: Admissions Dept. 64/9, Vesalius College-VUB, Pleinlaan

2, B-1050 Brussels, Belgium; (011) 32-2-629-36-26, fax (011) 32-2-629-36-37; vesalius@vub. ac.be, www.vub.ac.be/VECO.

Brazil

Brazil's Economy and Business Environment. Study and observe the business and process of economic development in Brazil. Open to students of all majors. Lasts 6 weeks—early Jun to mid-Jul. Seminars taught in English by faculty from the Univ. of São Paulo. A series of field trips allow students to observe first-hand the process of economic development in an emerging market. All students take intensive language course. No knowledge of Portuguese necessary. Housing with local hosts.

Dates: Early Jun-mid-Jul. Cost: $3,200 (1998) includes tuition, registration fees, room and partial board, field trips, and medical emergency evacuation insurance. Contact: Illinois Programs Abroad, Univ. of Illinois, 115 International Studies Bldg., 910 S. 5th St., Champaign, IL 61820; (800) 531-4404, fax (217) 244-0249; ipa@uiuc.edu, www.uiuc.edu/providers/ips/sao.

Canada

Ecole de français, Montréal. For the last 50 years, the Ecole de français has offered courses in French as a second language to students from around the world. The Ecole is continually improving its programs to meet the changing needs of its students. Choose from Oral and Written Communication French (beginner to advanced), Workshop on Teaching French as a Second Language (for teachers), Contemporary Québec Culture (for advanced students), Business French (intermediate to advanced students).

Dates: Spring: May 18-Jun 10; Summer 1: Jul 5-23; Summer 2: Jul 26-Aug 13; Fall: Sep 13-Dec 10; Winter 2000: Jan 10-Apr 7. Cost:

Spring/Summer: (3 weeks, 60 hours) CAN$495; Summer: (3 weeks, 45 hours) CAN$390; Fall/Winter: (12 weeks, 240 hours) CAN$1,495. Prices subject to change. Contact: Serge Bienvenu, Coordinator, Ecole de français, Faculté de l'education permanente, Université de Montréal, C.P. 6128, succursale Centre-ville, Montréal, PQ, H3C 3J7, Canada; (514) 343-6090, fax (514) 343-2430; infolang@fep.umontreal.ca, www.fep. umontreal.ca/langues/index.html.

École de langue française de Trois-Pistoles. The oldest university-sponsored French immersion school in Canada, our school offers two 5-week sessions each year. Courses are offered in the areas of French language, culture, theater, and political science. Guided by dynamic monitors, students participate in an afternoon workshop and a varied sociocultural program. Accommodations and meals, as well as an opportunity to practice French in an informal setting, provided by families in Trois-Pistoles.

Dates: May 10-Jun 11; Jul 5-Aug 6. Cost: CAN$1,700 plus CAN$300 program deposit ($150 refundable). Contact: Maryanne Giangregorio, Administrative Assistant, The Univ. of Western Ontario, École de langue française de Trois-Pistoles, Univ. College 219, London, ON, N6A 3K7, Canada; (519) 661-3637, fax (519) 661-3799; tpistole@julian.uwo.ca, www.cstudies.uwo.ca/trp.

English Language Centre, Victoria. The English Language Centre at the Univ. of Victoria is known throughout the world for its high standards of English language instruction. Established in 1970, the ELC offers quality language programs aimed at international and Canadian students wishing to improve their English language and cross-cultural skills for personal, professional, and academic purposes. Students from all over the world have attended the ELC. The 12-week Intensive English Language Program is offered 3 times each year, and a series of spring and summer pro-

grams are available. UVic is a mid-sized university with 17,000 students and is a friendly and comfortable place to study. It has been rated among the top 3 universities in Canada for the past 5 years.

Dates: Jan-Mar, Apr-Jul, Sep-Dec. Cost: Tuition is $2,950 per program. Contact: Ms. Maxine Macgillivray, Co-Director, English Language Centre, Univ. of Victoria, P.O. Box 1700, Victoria, BC V8W 2Y2, Canada; (250) 721-8469, fax (250) 721-6276; mmacgillivray @uvcs.uvic.ca, www.uvcs. uvic.ca/elc.

Chile

CWU Semester Program in Chile. Semester abroad program hosted by the Universidad Autral de Chile (Valdivia) that combines intensive language training, core electives in Latin American politics, history and literature, direct enrollment courses, and field research/independent study. Participants enjoy cross-cultural learning experience in the beautiful lake region of southern Chile.

Dates: Spring semester Mar 15-Jul 6 (approx.); Fall Aug 15-Dec 15. Cost: Approx. $4,000 (tuition, housing and meals). Contact: Study Abroad Advisor, Central Washington Univ., Office of International Studies and Programs, 400 E. 8th Ave., Ellensburg, WA 98926-7408; (509) 963-3612, fax (509) 963-1558; goabroad@cwu.edu.

Rice Univ. Fall Semester in Chile. This program provides an opportunity for students to study at the Universidad de Chile in Santiago, under the direction of a Rice Univ. professor. Participants live with Chilean families and attend classes with Chilean students. All credits earned in the program will be granted by Rice Univ.

Dates: Approx. Aug 2-Dec 13. Cost: $9,770 (1998). Includes tuition at Rice Univ., room and board, receptions, excursions and tickets to shows and museums. Contact: Beverly

Konzem, Dept. Coordinator, Rice Univ., Dept. of Hispanic and Classical Studies, MS34, Box 1892, Houston, TX 77251-1892; (713) 285-5451, fax (713) 527-4863; span@rice.edu, www.ruf.rice.edu/~span/cl.

Spanish and Latin American Studies. Santiago offers intensive language studies fulfilling up to 2 years of university Spanish requirements in 1 semester, with additional courses in literature, business, teacher ed., history, political science. Week-long program-oriented field trips to the south and north of Chile, homestays, and many university activities at Chilean university.

Dates: Spring semester Jan-May; Fall semester Aug-Dec. Cost: One semester $3,790; Fall and Spring $6,340. Contact: University Studies Abroad Consortium (USAC), Univ. of Nevada, Reno #323, Reno, NV 89557-0093; (702) 784-6569, fax (702) 784-6010; usac@admin.unr.edu, www.scs.unr.edu/~usac.

China

BCA Program in Dalian. Earn 16-20 credits per semester at the Dalian Univ. of Foreign Languages in China, with a 1-week orientation period, field trips, and extended study tours through Beijing and northern or southern China. Advanced Chinese program requires college intermediate level language; beginning program has no language prerequisite. Students from all U.S. colleges and universities accepted. All levels of Chinese language available plus Russian and Japanese, Chinese History and Culture, internships.

Dates: Fall: Sep-Dec or Jan; Spring: Feb-Jun or Jul; Year: Sep-Jun or Jul. Cost: $13,545 (academic year); $7,945 (semester) includes international transportation, tuition, room and board, insurance, group in-country travel. Contact: Beverly S. Eikenberry, 605 E. College Ave., North Manchester, IN 46962; (219) 982-5238, fax (219) 982-7755; bca@manchester.edu, www.studyabroad.com/bca.

Chinese Studies (Chengdu). The Chinese Studies Program offers intensive language study fulfilling up to 2 years of university language requirements in 1 semester. Additional courses in art history, economics, anthropology, political science, physics, chemistry, literature, history, and calligraphy are taught in English and offer a multidisciplinary approach to understanding the complexities of China and Asia.

Dates: Spring: Jan-May; Summer: Jun-Aug; Fall: Aug-Dec. Cost: Fall or Spring $4,260; Summer $1,680; year $6,860. Contact: University Studies Abroad Consortium (USAC), Univ. of Nevada, Reno #323, Reno, NV 89557-0093; (702) 784-6569, fax (702) 784-6010; usac@admin.unr.edu, www.scs.unr.edu/~usac.

College of William and Mary. Summer/fall in China. Six-month intensive 3rd year language program offers study tour, 2 terms of instruction (Chinese, history, anthropology, optional calligraphy, Tai Chi) at Beijing Normal Univ. University lodging. Resident director.

Dates: Jun 1-mid-Dec. Cost: $9,995 (1998) includes international travel, study tour with lodging and meals, lodging and instruction in Beijing, excursions, resident director. Contact: Ann M. Moore, College of William and Mary, Programs Abroad, Dept. TA, P.O. Box 8795, Williamsburg, VA 23187-8795; (757) 221-3594, fax (757) 221-3597; ammoo2@facstaff.wm.edu, www.wm.edu/academics/reves/beijing.html.

Friends World Program. A semester or year program at Zhejiang Univ. in Hangzhou, including Chinese language instruction, field trips, and an extensive stay in Yunnan Province spring semester. Classes include Chinese culture, customs, Chinese arts or calligraphy. Students also have their own research projects which may include the study of Chinese medicine, gender issues, religion, or environmental issues. Students may earn 12-18 credits per semester.

Dates: Fall: early Sep to end of Dec; or, for year to mid-May; Spring semester is limited to year-long participants. Cost: $11,090 per semester in 1998/1999. Includes tuition, travel, room and board, fees, and books. Contact: Stephanie Pollack, Friends World Program, 239 Montauk Highway, Southampton, NY 11968; (516) 287-8475; fw@southampton. liunet.edu.

Pitzer College in China. Traditional Chinese medicine (TCM), a 3,-000-year-old practice, is the focus of Pitzer's China program. Students live in Shanghai, study with renowned TCM practitioners, live with Chinese roommates, and study language and culture at East China Normal Univ.

Dates: Mid-Aug-mid-Dec; early Feb-mid-Jun. Cost: 1998-99: $14,720 tuition, room and board, roundtrip airfare, field trips, evacuation insurance. Contact: External Studies, Pitzer College, 1050 N. Mills Ave., Claremont, CA 91711; (909) 621-8104, fax (909) 621-0518; external_studies@pitzer.edu, www. pitzer.edu/academics/ilcenter/external_studies/ index.html.

Colombia

Community Internships in Latin America. Emphasis on community participation for social change. Students work 3 days a week in an internship, meet together for core seminar and internship seminar, and carry out independent study project. Wide range of internship opportunities in community development and related activities. Based in Bogotá. Family homestay. Latin American faculty. Full semester's credit, U.S. transcript provided. All majors, 2 years Spanish language required.

Dates: Early Feb-mid-May. Cost: $9,000 (1998-99). Includes tuition, room and board,

field trips. Contact: Rebecca Rassier, Director of Student Services, HECUA, Mail #36, Hamline Univ., 1536 Hewitt Ave., St. Paul, MN 55104-1284; (612) 646-8832 or (800) 554-9421, fax (612) 659-9421; hecua@hamline. edu, www.hamline.edu/~hecua.

Culture and Society in Latin America. Innovative approach combines classroom experience with extensive field work. Courses include ideologies of social change, Latin American arts and society, Latin American literature's perspectives on social change, and independent study. Based in Bogotá, with field study and travel in Colombia, Guatemala, and the Caribbean. Family homestay. Latin American faculty. Full semester's credit, U.S. transcript provided. All majors, 2 years Spanish language required.

Dates: Early Feb-mid-May. Cost: $9,000 (1998-99). Includes tuition, room and board, field trips. Contact: Rebecca Rassier, Director of Student Services, HECUA, Mail #36, Hamline Univ., 1536 Hewitt Ave., St. Paul, MN 55104-1284; (612) 646-8832 or (800) 554-1089), fax (612) 659-9421; hecua@hamline. edu, www.hamline.edu/~hecua.

South American Urban Semester. Innovative approach combines classroom experience with extensive field work. Courses include introduction to Latin America, urbanization and development in Latin America, Spanish language, and independent study. Based in Bogotá, with field study and travel in Colombia, Guatemala, and Ecuador. Family homestay. Latin American faculty. Full semester's credit, U.S. transcript provided. All majors, 2 years Spanish language required.

Dates: Late Aug-early Dec. Cost: $9,000 (1998-99). Includes tuition, room and board, field trips. Contact: Rebecca Rassier, Director of Student Services, HECUA, Mail #36, Hamline Univ., 1536 Hewitt Ave., St. Paul, MN 55104-1284; (612) 646-8832 or (800) 554-1089, fax (612) 659-9421; hecua@hamline. edu; www.hamline.edu/~hecua.

Costa Rica

Enjoy Learning Spanish Faster. Techniques developed from our ongoing research enable students to learn more, faster, in a comfortable environment. Classes of 2-5 students plus group learning activities; conversations with middle-class homestay families (1 student per family). Homestays are within walking distance of school in small town near the capital, San Jose.

Dates: Year round. Classes begin every Monday at all levels. Cost: $345 per week for 28 hours of classes and group activities plus Costa Rican dance and cooking classes. Includes tuition, 3 meals per day, 7 days per week, homestay, laundry, all materials, and airport transportation. $25 one-time registration fee. Contact: Susan Shores, Registrar, Latin American Language Center, 7485 Rush River Dr., Suite 710-123, Sacramento, CA 95831; (916) 447-0938, fax (916) 428-9542; lalc@madre.com.

Friends World Program. A semester or year in Latin America at Friends World Center in San José, Costa Rica, incorporates seminars, field study, travel, and independent projects. Seminars to introduce students into Latin America and its culture include Central American realities today, intensive Spanish for any level student, ecology and development, women's studies in Latin America. Independent work has included: ecology, community development, peace studies, health and refugee studies. Students may earn 12-18 credits per semester.

Dates: Fall: mid-Sep-mid-Dec; Spring: mid-Jan-mid-May. Cost: $11,690 per semester in 1998/1999. Includes tuition, travel, room and board, fees and books. Contact: Stephanie Pollack, Friends World Program, 239 Montauk Hwy., Southampton, NY 11968; (516) 287-8475; fw@southampton.liunet.edu.

Intercultura and Language Link. Intensive Spanish language programs in peaceful Costa Rica. Your choice of either 4 hours daily of small classes, a combination of 4 hours group and 2 hours private, or completely private. Professional adults, college students, and all Spanish levels accommodated. Programs of 1 to 12 weeks starting on any Monday. U.S. graduate and undergraduate credit through accredited university. Free weekly activities, caring homestays, and excursions to rainforests, volcano parks of great natural beauty. Intercultura is located in Heredia, a small university town, located 30 minutes outside the busy capital city. Option of a week's stay at our beach campus.

Dates: Year round. New classes begin every Monday. (Summer months fill very early.) Cost: Four hours daily of group classes and homestay: 2 weeks $595, 4 weeks $1,045. Includes registration, insurance, tuition, airport pickup, private room, and 2 meals daily. Contact: Kay G. Rafool, Language Link Inc., P.O. Box 3006, Peoria, IL 61612; (800) 552-2051, fax (309) 692-2926; info@langlink.com; www.langlink.com.

Learn About Tropical Plants. Two-week courses on field identification of trees and shrubs (Dendrology) offered every year in Spanish (March) and in English (June-July). Please ask for opinions by former participants. Dates: 1999: Mar 8-20 (Spanish); Jun 21-Jul 3 (English); 2000: Mar 13-25 (Spanish); Jun 26-Jul 8, 2000 (English). Cost: Each course is $1,800. Includes fees, material, lodging and meals during 15 days, insurance, course-related local transport, farewell dinner, and certificate of attendance. Contact: Humberto Jiménez Saa, TSC, Apdo. 8-3870-1000, San José, Costa Rica; (506) 253 3267, fax (011) 506-253-4963; hjimenez@sol.racsa.co.cr; www.geocities.com/rainforest/9148.

Learn Spanish While Volunteering. Assist with the training of Costa Rican public school teachers in ESL and computers. Assist local health clinic, social service agencies, and environmental projects. Enjoy learning Spanish in the morning, volunteer work in the afternoon/evening. Spanish classes of 2-5 students plus group learning activities; conversations with middle-class homestay families (1 student per family). Homestays and most volunteer projects are within walking distance of school in small town near the capital, San Jose.

Dates: Year round, all levels. Classes begin every Monday, volunteer program is continuous. Cost: $345 per week for 28 hours of classes and group activities plus Costa Rican dance and cooking classes. Includes tuition, 3 meals per day, 7 days per week, homestay, laundry, all materials, and airport transportation. $25 one-time registration fee; $100 additional one-time registration fee for volunteer program. Contact: Susan Shores, Registrar, Latin American Language Center, 7485 Rush River Dr., Suite 710-123, Sacramento, CA 95831; (916) 447-0938, fax (916) 428-9542; lalc@madre.com.

Spanish and More in Heredia. Heredia offers intensive language studies which fulfills up to 2-year university Spanish requirements in a semester or 1 year in the 8-week summer program. Additional courses offered in political science, history, biology, teacher ed., business, literature, etc. Program organized week-long and weekend field trips, homestays, and many local university activities.

Dates: Spring term: Jan-May; Summer sessions: May-Jul, Jun-Aug, Jul-Aug 30; Fall term: Aug-Dec. Cost: Fall or Spring semester $4,390; year $7,190; Jun or Jul $1,980; Aug $1,610; Jun and Jul $3,680; June, July, and Aug $3,190; Jun, Jul, and Aug $4,680. Contact: University Studies Abroad Consortium (USAC), Univ. of Nevada, Reno #323, Reno, NV 89557-0093; (702) 784-6569, fax (702) 784-6010; usac@admin.unr.edu, www.scs.unr.edu/~usac.

Spanish Language. Intercultura Language Institute offers intensive Spanish and homestays with selected Costa Rican families. Academic credit available (with prior notice). Additional free cultural activities: Latin-dance, music, theater, cinema, cooking. Weekend excursions to volcanoes, beaches, rainforest. Volunteer opportunities in social, environmental, and political organizations. Beach campus: optional 1 week per month, study on Pacific coast.

Dates: Year round. Cost: $1,045 per month (shorter stays available). Contact: Laura Ellington, Codirector, Intercultura Costa Rica, Apdo. 1952-3000, Heredia, Costa Rica; (011) 506-260-8480, Tel./fax (011) 506-260-9243; intercul@sol.racsa.co.cr, www.alphaluz.com/intercultura.

Spanish Language Program. Twenty hours of small group instruction, maximum 4 students per class, Monday-Friday. All ages and all levels. Each student takes an oral and written exam and is placed at a level that matches his/her knowledge. Students live with a Costa Rican family. Organized activities are part of the program.

Dates: Courses start every Monday of the year. Cost: Four-week program $1,090: host family stay, language classes 4 hours per day, 5 days a week. (Also 1-week, 2-week, or 3-week program.) Contact: Guiselle Ballestero, Sonia Rojas, Ronny Garcia; (011) 506-458-3157, fax (011) 506-458-3214; www. institutodecultura. com.

Universidad de Costa Rica. A graduate and undergraduate program at the Universidad de Costa Rica for students interested in studying courses in language, literature, culture and civilization, composition, and history of Costa Rica. All courses are taught by full-time faculty members from the Univ. of Costa Rica, the most prestigious university in Costa Rica. A lot of extra activities and excursions are organized for students. Students stay with Costa Rican families.

Dates: Summer: Jun-Jul; semester: Fall and Winter. Cost: Total cost $1,885 including airfare. Contact: Modern Language Studies

Abroad, P.O. Box 623, Griffith, IN 46319; Tel./ fax (219) 838-9460.

Cuba

Introduction to Contemporary Cuba. Four-credit, 3 1/2-week summer and winter program taught at the Univ. of Havana by Cuban faculty. A unique opportunity to experience the blend of African, European, and American cultures that form Cuba. Study trips to Pinar del Rio, Matanzas provinces, Varadero beach, Regla, Ernest Hemingway's home, and other sites. Orientation in Cancún.

Dates: Summer: Jun 3-26. Winter: Call for details. Cost: $2,510 includes tuition, lodging with 2 meals per day, study/visits and tours, orientation meeting and night in Cancún, Mexico; hotel-airport transfers, roundtrip flight between Cancún and Havana, transcript from The Center for Cross-Cultural Study. Contact: Dr. Judith Ortiz, Director U.S., Center for Cross-Cultural Study, 446 Main St., Amherst, MA 01002; (800) 377-2621, fax (413) 256-1968; cccs@crocker.com, www.cccs.com.

Czech Republic

Penn-in-Prague. For students interested in Jewish studies and Czech culture, this program, located amidst the fairy tale beauty of Prague and affiliated with Charles Univ. and the Jewish Museum of Prague, offers an insight into the rich history and urgent contemporary problems of this important region, as well as an opportunity to learn beginning and intermediate Czech. Some internships can be arranged with the Jewish Museum.

Dates: Jul 6-Aug 14. Cost: Tuition $2,968; housing and excursion $850. Contact: Penn Summer Abroad, College of General Studies, Univ. of Pennsylvania, 3440 Market St., Suite 100, Philadelphia, PA 19104-3335; (215) 898-5738, fax (215) 573-2053.

Ecuador

Academia de Español Quito. The Academia de Español Quito offers intensive Spanish language programs in the exciting capital of Ecuador. Choose from 4 to 7 hours daily of completely private classes, one-on-one instruction. Professional adults, college students, and all Spanish levels accommodated in a very well-organized school. Programs of 1 to 12 weeks starting on any Monday. U.S. graduate and undergraduate credit. Caring homestays and many additional weekly activities included. In the Activa program students study 4 hours in the morning in the classroom and in the afternoon explore Quito and surrounding area with their teacher. The Anaconda is a 1-week program located on an island in an Amazon River tributary. Group classes in the morning; explore the jungle and rainforest in the afternoon. Also discounted Galapagos trips.

Dates: Year round. New classes begin every Monday. (Summer months fill very early.) Cost: Four hours daily private classes and homestay: $260 per week; 7 hours daily Activa program (includes all transportation, entry fees, etc.): $385 per week; Anaconda program $470. Includes tuition, insurance, materials, airport pickup, private room, 3 meals daily, and laundry. Contact: Kay G. Rafool, Language Link Inc., P.O. Box 3006, Peoria, IL 61612; (800) 552-2051, fax (309) 692-2926; info@langlink.com; www.langlink.com.

BCA Program in Quito. Earn 13-18 credits per semester at Universidad San Francisco de Quito, with a fall 4-week intensive language and orientation, homestay with Ecuadoran families, field trips, extended study tour to Amazon headwaters and Galápagos islands. Students from all U.S. colleges and universities accepted. Intermediate level college Spanish required. Full liberal arts curriculum available. Ecology field studies and internships.

Dates: Fall: Aug-Dec; Spring: Jan-May; Year: Aug-May. Cost: $18,845 (academic year);

$10,545 (semester). Includes international transportation, room and board, tuition, insurance, group travel in country. Contact: Beverly S. Eikenberry, 605 E. College Ave., North Manchester, IN 46962; (219) 982-5238, fax (219) 982-7755; bca@manchester.edu, www.studyabroad.com/bca.

Environmental Studies in Ecuador. The program focuses on the growing conflict between the development of Ecuador's economy and the preservation of its ecological resources. Program includes course work in Spanish with Ecuadoran students at the Universidad San Francisco de Quito, field study trips to several regions of the country, and an independent research project. Minimum 2 years college Spanish and strong background in biology required.

Dates: Jan-mid-Jun. Cost: (1998-99) $16,166 includes roundtrip international transportation, tuition and fees, field study trips, room and board, and some excursions. Contact: Center for International Programs, Kalamazoo College, 1200 Academy, Kalamazoo, MI 49006; (616) 337-7133, fax (616) 337-7400; cip@kzoo.edu.

Universidad San Francisco de Quito. Students take courses with Ecuadoran students in a variety of subjects areas for semester or year. Housing arranged in local homes. Resident director conducts orientation and excursions. Courses taught in Spanish; 4 semesters of college-level Spanish required.

Dates: Spring semester: Jan-May; Fall semester: Aug-Dec; Year: Aug-May. Cost: $6,500/$11,900 (1998-1999 fees) includes: tuition, registration, excursions, orientation, room and board, support services, on-site director, medical emergency evacuation insurance. Contact: Illinois Programs Abroad, Univ. of Illinois, 115 International Studies Bldg., 910 S. 5th St., Champaign, IL 61820; (800) 531-4404, fax (217) 244-0249; ipa@uiuc.edu, www.uiuc.edu/providers/ips/sao.

Egypt

The American Univ. in Cairo. Study for 1 or 2 semesters with Egyptian students at an American-style liberal arts university in the heart of Cairo. Study abroad students may elect courses from the general course offerings; most popular are those dealing with Middle East, Egyptian, and Arab history, politics, culture, Egyptology, Islamic studies, Arabic language. Language of instruction is English.

Dates: Sep-Jan, Feb-Jun, Jun-Jul. Cost: Approx. $5,150 per semester for tuition fees plus room and board. Contact: Matrans Davidson, Office of Student Affairs, American Univ. in Cairo, 420 5th Ave., 3rd Fl., New York, NY 10018; aucegypt@aucnyo.edu.

Estonia

Baltic Studies Program in Tartu. Students take courses at the Univ. of Tartu—3 focus on the changing economy and society, 2 electives (all in English), and an Estonian language course (all levels). Housing includes dormitories, host families, or local apartments. Scheduled excursions to historical sites and cultural institutions in Estonia and the former USSR enhance classroom experience.

Dates: Fall: Aug-Dec; Spring: Feb-Jun. Cost: Call for cost. Contact: Jill A. Perry Redin, Coordinator of Study Abroad Programs, Bentley College, International Center, 175 Forest St., Waltham, MA 02154; (781) 891-3474, fax (781) 891-2819; inprinfo@bentley.edu, www.bentley.edu/resource/international.

Europe

Archaeology Summer School. Introduces participants to the theory and practice of archaeology in general and to Mediterranean and Maltese archaeology in particular. Two-week course is followed by 4 weeks of excavation and finds processing experience. Participants may register for a range of 2-6 week options.

Dates: Jun 15-Jul 24. Cost: From $700-$2,100 includes accommodations. Contact: Jean P. Killick, International Office, Foundation for International Studies, Old Univ. Bldg., St. Paul St., Valletta, Malta; (011) 356-234121/2, fax (011) 356-230538; jkil@cis. um.edu.mt.

Art Under One Roof. Applied Arts Institute-Europe. Study for a semester or academic year with us in Florence or Paris, learn a language and live the arts. Painting, sculpture, restoration, fresco painting, jewelry making, furniture and interior design, boutique design, shoe and handbag design, furniture restoration, tiffany arts, and many more.

Dates: Jan-Apr, May-Jul, Sep-Dec. Cost: $2,500 per semester. Includes tuition only. Contact: Art Under One Roof (Arte Sotto un Tetto), Via Pandolfini, 46-R - 50122 Florence, Italy; Tel./fax (011) 39-55-247-8867; berarducci@iol.it.

Baroque Art. This course, a general overview of the 16th-18th century art in Malta which focuses on the rich heritage of works in the Cathedral of St. John (Valletta), is primarily aimed at history of art students at both under- and post-graduate levels and others with an informed interest in art history.

Dates: Jul 6-Jul 24. Cost: $950 includes accommodations. Contact: Jean P. Killick, International Office, Foundation for International Studies, Old Univ. Bldg., St. Paul St., Valletta, Malta; (011) 356-234121/2, fax (011) 356-230538; jkil@cis.um.edu.mt.

Bio-Architecture. International Workshop or Bio-Tech Architecture offers an introduction to the basic principles of Bio-Tech design and related technologies, followed by a series of in-depth sessions on the approach and working methods of each of the main speakers. Main program supplemented by evening lectures and site visits (AIA, Continuing Education Program).

Dates: Jun 8-13. Cost: Contact coordinator. Contact: Jean P. Killick, International Office, Foundation for International Studies, Old Univ. Bldg., St. Paul St., Valletta, Malta; (011) 356-234121/2, fax (011) 356-230538; jkil@cis. um.edu.mt.

Bowling Green in Salzburg. The Bowling Green State Univ. Academic Year Abroad in Salzburg program, presently in its 30th year (on the web site at www.bgsu/department/greal/AYA-Salzburg.html), is designed to help American students perfect their German skills. Participants gain first-hand knowledge of German-speaking countries while earning credit toward undergraduate and master's degrees in a variety of subjects.

Dates: Full year program. Cost: $12,389 (non-res.). Contact: Bowling Green State Univ., Dept. of German, Russian, and EAL; (419) 372-6815, fax (419) 372-2571; sidors@bgnet.bgsu.edu.

Budapest Semesters in Mathematics. A rigorous mathematics program for students attending colleges and universities in North America majoring in mathematics or computer science. Classes taught in English by eminent Hungarian professors. Unlike any other program you will ever encounter. Mix it all in a world as warm and friendly as Budapest, and it's paradise.

Dates: Spring: Feb-May; Fall: Sep-Dec. Cost: Tuition: $3,500 plus $300 refundable housing deposit. Contact: Prof. Paul D. Humke, Director, Budapest Semesters in Mathematics, St. Olaf College, 1520 St. Olaf Ave., Northfield, MN 55057; (800) 277-0434; budapest@stolaf.edu, www.stolaf.edu/depts/math/budapest.

Central European University. Central European Univ. is an internationally recognized institution of postgraduate education in the social sciences and humanities. Based in Budapest, Hungary with a branch teaching site in Warsaw, Poland, CEU offers Masters and PhD programs accredited by U.S., U.K., or

Polish accrediting agencies. CEU is chartered by the Board of Regents of the State of New York.

Dates: Year round. Cost: Tuition $11,000; living expenses $5,000 (approx.). A wide variety of financial aid is available, including 625 full fellowships for students from Central and Eastern Europe and the former Soviet Union. Contact: Admissions Office, Central European Univ., Nador u. 9 1051, Budapest, Hungary; (011) 36-1-327-3009, fax (011) 36-1-327-3211; external@ceu.hu, www.ceu.hu.

The European Union Today and Tomorrow. This multidisciplinary 7-week program in English integrates political, managerial, and technological perspectives which enable graduate students in business, engineering, law, political science, and international affairs to understand the impact and complexity of European integration. Paid internship or long-term employment opportunities with sponsoring companies available.

Dates: Jun-Jul. Cost: $5,200 tuition includes: field trips, housing in single rooms, a meal plan covering breakfast daily and lunch weekdays, plus dinner week nights at the French Univ. restaurant. Contact: Ms. Karen Weisblatt, EU/SP-SCIENCES PO, 27 rue Saint Guillaume, 75337 Paris Cedex 07, France; (011) 33-1-45-49-50-67, fax (011) 33-1-45-49-51-42; eusp@sciences-po.fr, www.europaris.edu.

Friends World Program. A semester or year program in Europe beginning at Friends World Center in London includes an intensive introduction into European culture and history. The program offers seminars, field study, travel, and independent work anywhere in Europe. The center serves as a base to explore all regions and cultures in the European continent. Field studies in literature, politics, arts, history, peace studies, theater, education, and community development are all available. Students may earn 12-18 credits per semester.

Dates: Fall: early Sep-mid-Dec; Spring: mid-Jan-mid-May. Cost: $12,990 per semester in 1998/1999. Includes tuition, travel, room and board, fees and books. Contact: Stephanie Pollack, Friends World Program, 239 Montauk Hwy., Southampton, NY 11968; (516) 287-8475; fw@southampton.liunet.edu.

International Business Studies. IBS is a 4-year undergraduate program leading to a Bachelor's degree. The program offers a wide range of modules on subjects like International Marketing, Management, and Communication. In the third year students will go abroad for study and for an industrial placement.

Dates: Entry end of Aug or Jan, deadlines 15 of May or Nov. Cost: For non-EU students: approx. $5,000 (including accommodations). Contact: Arnhem Business School, P.O. Box 5171, NL-6803 Ed Arnhem, The Netherlands. International Office: (011) 31-26-369-1333, fax (011) 31-26-369-1367; international@heao.han.nl, www.heao-arnhem.nl.

Issue-Specific Travel Courses. Visit 1 to 4 cities. Topics include International Business and Economics, Comparative Education, Historical Literature, Social Service Systems, and other crosscultural studies. Emphasis on personal interaction between students and European professionals and providing a holistic cultural experience. Two- to 5-week programs. Three to 6 credit hours—undergraduate, graduate, or audit basis—through the Univ. of Missouri-Kansas City.

Dates: Early Summer. Cost: Approx. $2,000 (does not include airfare). Contact: People to People International, Collegiate and Professional Studies Abroad, 501 E. Armour Blvd., Kansas City, MO 64109-2200; (816) 531-4701, fax (816) 561-7502; collegiate@ptpi.org, www.ptpi.org/studyabroad.

The Mediterranean: An Environmental Overview. The interdisciplinary course gives an overview of the most important aspects of the Mediterranean environment, both natural and human. A wide range of topics is covered during 8 lecture sessions and 3 site visits.

Dates: Jun 22-26. Cost: Contact coordinator. Contact: Jean P. Killick, International Office, Foundation for International Studies, Old Univ. Bldg., St. Paul St., Valletta, Malta; (011) 356-234121/2, fax (011) 356-230538; jkil@cis.um.edu.mt.

Middlebury College Schools Abroad.

Middlebury College operates Schools Abroad in Florence, Madrid, Mainz, Paris, Segovia, and 3 cities in Russia (Moscow, Voronezh, and Yaroslavl) for its own students and students from other colleges who meet the language requirements. Middlebury's Schools Abroad are renowned to be intellectually challenging and culturally stimulating. Undergraduate and graduate programs offered.

Dates: Most schools are Sep-Dec, and Jan-May, except Mainz that is Oct-Feb and Mar-Jul. Cost: 1999-2000 fees: Florence, Getafe, Logroño, Madrid, Mainz, Paris, Segovia Year: $11,485 (tuition only); semester: $6,000 (tuition only). Irkutsk, Moscow year: $17,770 (tuition, room, visas, and roundtrip airfare from NYC); semester: $11,000 (tuition, room, visas, and roundtrip airfare from NYC). Voronezh, Yaroslavl Year: $16,470 (tuition, room, partial board, visas, and roundtrip airfare from NYC); semester: $8,235 (tuition, room, partial board, visas, and roundtrip airfare from NYC). Contact: Schools Abroad, Middlebury College, Middlebury, VT 05753; (802) 443-5745, fax (802) 443-3157; schoolsabroad@middlebury.edu, www.middlebury.edu/~ls.

MPHIL./Diploma in Publishing Studies.

Wide-ranging course on print (book and magazine) and electronic publishing, business, legal aspects, marketing, tuition in editorial; projects develop teamworking, design, desktop publishing skills; strong international component; experienced professional staff; modern library, excellent facilities for comput-

ing; hand-printing; individual dissertation; excellent employment record. Beautiful campus close to Edinburgh and Glasgow.

Dates: Sep 1999-May 2000. Cost: Varies. Contact: Centre for Publishing Studies, Univ. of Stirling, Stirling FK9 4LA, U.K. (011) 44-1786-46796, fax (011) 44-1786-466210; engll@stir.ac.uk, ww.stir.ac.uk/publishing.

Rock Art in the Alps. Project consists of surveying, recording, and tracing engraved rocks—from Neolithic to Middle Age. During the summer school there will be visits to other rock-art sites and museums. Other activities include lectures about archaeology and rock art of the world and night photographing experiences.

Dates: Jul-Aug. Cost: LIT65,000. Contact: Cooperativa Archeologica "Le Orme Dell'Umo," Piazzale Donatori di Sangue, No. 1, 25040 Cerveno (BS), Italy; (011) 39 364-433983, fax (011) 39-364-434351; rupestre@10mb.com.

Summer School-Shakespearean Acting. One of U.K.'s top drama schools offers an intensive Shakespeare course, full-time, over 4 weeks.

Dates: Jul 12-Aug 6. Cost: £850 (subject to increase). Contact: Administrations, London Academy of Performing Arts, St. Matthew's Church, St. Petersburgh Pl., London W2 4LA, U.K.; (011) 44-171-727-0220; londonacademy.performingarts@btinternet.com.

France

Academic Year Abroad Paris. Direct registration at the Sorbonne in liberal arts, fine arts, social sciences, and AYA-sponsored orientation and tutorials. Political science possible at Sciences Po. Supplementary courses at Institut Catholique, intensive language at the Cours de Civilisation of the Sorbonne. Optional room and board with Parisian families and cultural activities.

Dates: Late Sep-mid-Jan; late Jan-end May.

Cost: Term $7,700; year $13,200. Includes tuition, tutorials, room and board, and cultural activities. Contact: Dr. A.M. Cinquemani, Academic Year Abroad, P.O. 733, Stone Ridge, NY 12484-0733; Fax (914) 687-2470; aya@ulster.net, www.studyabroad.com/aya.

BCA in Strasbourg or Nancy. Earn 14-16 credits per semester at either the Université de Nancy or the Université de Strasbourg, with a fall 4-week intensive language training and orientation plus field trips and extended study tour to Paris. Selective Honors Program offered in both universities. Internships available. Students accepted from all U.S. colleges and universities. Intermediate level college French required.

Dates: Fall: Sep-Dec or Jan; Spring: Jan-May or Jun; Year: Sep-May or Jun (year). Cost: $18,845 (academic year), $10,545 (semester). Includes international transportation, room and board, tuition, insurance, group travel in country. Contact: Beverly S. Eikenberry, 605 E. College Ave., North Manchester, IN 46962; (219) 982-5238, fax (219) 982-7755; bca@manchester. edu, www.studyabroad.com/bca.

College of William and Mary. Junior Year in Montepellier. One-year direct enrollment program for advanced students of French including Paris stay with tours, 1-month intensive pre-session with excursions, full academic year direct enrollment at French university, services of a faculty resident director, housing coordinator, and friendship family coordinator.

Dates: Aug 28, 1999-Jun 20, 2000. Cost: $12,190 (1998) includes international airfare; Paris stay with tours, hotel and some meals; transportation to Montpellier; 1 month pre-session with excursions, lodging and meals; instruction at Université Paul Valéry; lodging in dormitories or apartments; services of a housing coordinator; friendship family cultural program; services of a faculty director, and credit through William and Mary. Additional costs include meals during academic year, personal travel, books, and incidental

expenses. Contact: Ann M. Moore, College of William and Mary, Programs Abroad, Dept. TA, P.O. Box 8795, Williamsburg, VA 23187-8795; (757) 221-3594, fax (757) 221-3597; ammoo2@facstaff.wm.edu, www.wm.edu/ academics/reves/montpellier2.html.

College of William and Mary. Summer in Montepellier. One-month intensive intermediate oral and written French program with Paris stay, homestays, excursions, William and Mary faculty director.

Dates: Jul 1-31. Cost: $3,840 (1998) includes international airfare; transportation Paris stay with tours, hotel, breakfast, one lunch; transportation to Montpellier; instruction with excursions; lodging and some meals with French families; services of a faculty resident director. Contact: Ann M. Moore, College of William and Mary, Programs Abroad, Dept. TA, P.O. Box 8795, Williamsburg, VA 23187-8795; (757) 221-3594, fax (757) 221-3597; ammoo2@facstaff.wm.edu, www.wm.edu/ academics/reves/montpellier.html.

Cornell in Paris (EDUCO). Spend a semester or year studying at leading universities of Paris: Paris I (Pantheon-Sorbonne), Paris VII, and Institut d'Etudes Politiques (Sciences Po). Extensive orientation, language preparation, and special coursework at the Cornell-Duke (EDUCO) Center on rue Montparnasse. Housing arranged in private residences or apartments. Four semesters of university-level French required.

Dates: Mid-Sep-late Jan and late Jan-mid-Jun. Cost: $13,300 per semester (1996-1997). Includes tuition and fees, housing, some meals, orientation, language instruction, field trips, and excursions. Contact: Cornell Abroad, 474 Uris Hall, Ithaca, NY 14853-7601; (607) 255-6224, fax (607) 255-8700; CUAbroad@cornell.edu.

Davidson in Tours. Academic year at Univ. of Tours or semester at the Institute of Touraine in Tours. Earn 8 course credits for the year or

4 per semester. Live with families in Tours. A 2- to 4-week stay in Paris as well as numerous group activities and excursions is included. A Davidson faculty member serves as resident director and teaches one course each semester.

Dates: Sep-Jun (may attend for semester or year). Cost: $13,500 per semester includes all academic expenses, room, board, international airfare, excursions, international student identity card. Contact: Carolyn Ortmayer, Office of Study Abroad, Davidson College, P.O. Box 1719, Davidson, NC 28036; (704) 892-2250, fax (704) 892-2005; abroad@davidson.edu, www.davidson.edu/administrative/study_abroad/abroad.html.

French in France. Among the ways to learn French, total immersion is the most enjoyable and the most effective. We have been doing it for 20 years in a small historical city located in Normandy (west of Paris, close to the seaside). We welcome people at any age and any level in 1- to 10-week programs, intensive or vacation type, from mid-March to mid-November.

Dates: Spring: Mar-May; Summer: Jun-Aug; Fall: Sep-Nov. Cost: From $525 per week (tuition, room and board, and excursions). Contact: Dr. Almeras, Chairman, French American Study Center, 12, 14, Blvd. Carnot, B.P. 176, 14104 Lisieux Cedex, France (011) 33-2-31-31-22-01, fax (011) 33-2-31-31-22-21; centre.normandie@wanadoo.fr.

French Language and Culture. Intensive French program. Classes at all levels from beginning to advanced. Placement tests determine language ability. A wide choice of cultural courses plus business French. Progress monitored with graded exercises, assignments, midterm and final examinations. Credits transferred. Cultural activities and excursions, board and lodging (several alternatives), sessions for teachers of French.

Dates: Jul 5-31, Aug 3-28, Sep 1-29 and academic year: Sep-Dec, Oct-Jan, Feb-Jun. Cost: Tuition and fees: Jul FF3,980, Aug FF3,980, Sep

FF4,480, 1 semester FF8,500. Contact: Marc Melin, Directeur, 3, place André Leroy, BP 808, 49008 Angers Cedex 01, France; (011) 33-2-41-88-30-15, fax (011) 33-2-41-87-71-67; cidef@uco.fr.

French Language Learning Vacations. Learn French while discovering the chateaux of the Loire Valley, the secrets of Provence, or the sandy beaches of the Mediterranean. Our programs are designed for independent travelers sharing a passion for the French culture and lifestyle. We offer a choice of locations in Tours, Aix-en-Provence, Montpellier, Paris, or Nice.

Dates: Two or more weeks year round. Cost: Two-week packages range from $820-$1,200. Contact: Jim Pondolfino, French-American Exchange, 111 Roberts Court, Box 7, Alexandria, VA 22314; (800) 995-5087, fax (703) 549-2865; faetours@erols.com, www.faetours.com.

French Studies (Pau). Pau offers intensive language studies—up to 4 semesters of university language courses in 1 semester, 1 year in the 8-week summer program, in addition to art, political science, history, literature, second language teaching methods, etc. Week-long field trips to Paris, homestay or student residence, and many activities at the French university.

Dates: Spring semester: Jan-Apr; Summer sessions: May-Jun; Jun-Aug; Jul-Aug 23; Fall semester: Sep-Dec. Cost: Fall or Spring semester $4,280; Jun $1,700; Jul $1,880; Aug $1,380; Jun and Jul $3,480; Jun and Aug $2,870; Jul and Aug $2,970; Jun, Jul, and Aug $4,580; year $6,980. Contact: University Studies Abroad Consortium (USAC), Univ. of Nevada, Reno #323, Reno, NV 89557-0093; (702) 784-6569, fax (702) 784-6010; usac@admin.unr.edu, www.scs.unr.edu/~usac.

Institute for American Universities. Founded in 1957 under the auspices of l'Université d'Aix-Marseille, the Institute offers full-year, semester, and summer programs in Aix-en-Provence. Instruction in French and English: Archaeology and Art History; French Language and Culture Studies, and International Studies and Social Sciences; The Marchutz School of Painting and Drawing: Studio Art and Art Criticism in Avignon. Instruction exclusively in French: Advanced French Studies: art history, culture, history and literature. Students are generally housed in French homes.

Dates: Jun 14-Jul 23; Sep 7-Dec 20; Jan 11-May 18. Cost: Summer 1999: $3,305. Includes tuition, books, field trips, room and daily breakfast and dinner; 1998-1999: semester $9,145, year $18,190. Includes tuition, books, insurance (optional), room and daily breakfast and dinner, activity deposit, damage deposit. Contact: Institute for American Universities, U.S. Office, P.O. Box 592, Evanston, IL 60204; (800) 221-2051, fax (847) 864-6897; iauusa@univ-aix.fr, www.iau-univ.org.

Intensive Professional Culinary Program. Over 24 weeks this new Lenotre program alternates intensive culinary training in small classes at Ecole Lenotre with hands-on experience in Lenotre kitchens, restaurants, and gourmet boutiques. By the end of the program, students earn qualification as a professional maker of fine French cuisine and pastry.

Dates: Year round, except Aug and 2 weeks during Christmas and New Year's Eve. Cost: FF120,000 (approx. $20,000) includes breakfast and lunch. Contact: Marie-Anne Dufeu, Ecole Lenotre, 40 rue Pierre Curie, B.P. 6, 78375 Plaisir Cedex, France; (011) 33-1-30-81-46-34/35, fax (011) 33-1-30-54-73-70.

Internships in Francophone Europe. IFE is an academic internship program—accredited at a number of schools—that places student interns in mid to high levels of French public life including government, politics, the press, social institutions, NGOs, etc. IFE is a selective admissions program for motivated students, proficient in French, who are interested in immersion in the working life of a French

institution and in today's France. The program includes intensive preparatory course work in French history, sociology, politics, language training, and the completion of a research project related to the internship. Open to undergraduates and recent graduates.

Dates: May 1 deadline for Fall semester (Aug-Dec); Nov 1 deadline for Spring semester (Jan-May). Cost: $5,950 (tuition only); tuition plus housing (approx.) $7,660. Need-based scholarships available, especially for post BA's. Contact: Bernard Riviere Platt, Director, Internships in Francophone Europe, 26, rue Cmdt. Mouchotte J108, 75014 Paris, France; (011) 33-1-43-21-78-07, fax (011) 33-1-42-79-94-13; ifeparis@compuserve.com.

Kalamazoo in Clermont-Ferrand. This university-integrated program begins with an intensive French course and an orientation. Participants enroll in regular courses at the Ecole Supérieure Normale de Commerce. All participants complete a local business project working with French students in small groups. Minimum of 2 years of college French is required.

Dates: Late Aug-late May (academic year); late Aug-late Feb (Fall). Cost: Academic year: (1998-99) $24,249; Fall: $16,166. Both fees include roundtrip international transportation, tuition and fees, room and board, and some excursions. Contact: Center for International Programs, Kalamazoo College, 1200 Academy, Kalamazoo, MI 49006; (616) 337-7133, fax (616) 337-7400; cip@kzoo.edu.

Penn-in-Bordeaux. For students interested in anthropology, archaeology, and the origins of humankind. This program is located near Lascaux and Cro-Magnon, areas where anthropologists have unearthed much of our knowledge about the beginnings of modern humankind. It will center on the issue of what makes us human and how this quality evolved. Lectures will be augmented with the examination of artifacts and fossils as well as visits to important sites.

Dates: Jul 5-Jul 23. Cost: Tuition $1,484;

housing and excursions $400. Contact: Penn Summer Abroad, College of General Studies, Univ. of Pennsylvania, 3440 Market St., Suite 100, Philadelphia, PA 19104-3335; (215) 898-5738, fax (215) 573-2053.

Penn-in-Compiegne. For students with some proficiency in French who are interested in international relations, economics, or business. The program, affiliated with The Université de Technologie de Compiegne, also offers a 2-week internship in a French enterprise. Students live with local families.

Dates: May 23-Jul 2; with internship: May 23-Jul 18. Cost: Tuition $2,968; room and board, and activities $960 (study only) or $1,280 (full program). Contact: Penn Summer Abroad, College of General Studies, Univ. of Pennsylvania, 3440 Market St., Suite 100, Philadelphia, PA 19104-3335; (215) 898-5738, fax (215) 573-2053.

Penn-in-Tours. For students interested in French language, literature, art, and civilization. Penn-in-Tours also offers various cultural opportunities and excursions in the beautiful Loire Valley. Students live with local families.

Dates: May 25-Jul 8. Cost: Tuition $2,968; family lodging $1,300; excursion and activity fee $200. Contact: Penn Summer Abroad, College of General Studies, Univ. of Pennsylvania, 3440 Market St., Suite 100, Philadelphia, PA 19104-3335; (215) 898-5738, fax (215) 573-2053.

Sarah Lawrence College in Paris. Combines individually crafted programs of study with total immersion in the academic and social life of Paris. Options include enrollment in the great French institutions of learning, with access to a full range of courses usually open only to French students, small seminars, and the creative arts. Private tutorials with French faculty, focusing on student's interests.

Dates: Sep-May (may attend for semester or year). Cost: $11, 820 (1 semester) includes all academic expenses, field trips, and cultural activities. Merit scholarships are available. Contact: Prema Samuel, Sarah Lawrence College in Paris, Box CR, Bronxville, NY 10708; (800) 873-4752.

Germany

BCA Program in Marburg. Earn 14-16 credits per semester at Phillipps-Universität in Marburg, with a 4-week intensive language training and orientation, field trips, and an extended study tour to Eastern Germany or Prague. Internships available. Students accepted from all U.S. colleges and universities. Intermediate level college German required.

Dates: Fall: Sep-Feb; Spring: Feb-Jul; Year: Sep-Jul. Cost: $18,845 (academic year), $10,545 (semester). Includes international transportation, room and board, tuition, insurance, group travel in country. Contact: Beverly S. Eikenberry, 605 E. College Ave., North Manchester, IN 46962; (219) 982-5238, fax (219) 982-7755; bca@manchester.edu, www.studyabroad.com/bca.

Davidson in Würzburg. This program starts with a month-long family stay in northern Germany followed by an intensive language course in Würzburg after which students enroll at the university. Students earn 8 course credits for the year. A Davidson faculty member serves as resident director and teaches 1 course in the fall. Students live in dormitories. Numerous group activities and excursions are included.

Dates: Sep 1-late Jul. Cost: $24,000 includes all academic expenses, room, international airfare, insurance, excursions. Contact: Carolyn Ortmayer, Office of Study Abroad, Davidson College, P.O. Box 1719, Davidson, NC 28036; (704) 892-2250, fax (704) 892-2005; abroad@davidson.edu, www.davidson.edu/administrative/study_abroad/abroad.html.

German as a Foreign Language. Various levels of German year round; intensive, crash, and long-term courses, individual tuition. Special feature: German and theater. Special programs: business German for professionals, German for teachers, German in a teacher's home, German for special purposes. Academic year for high school students, international study year, internship, guest studentship, homestays for groups, courses for firms and other institutions (banking, insurance, doctors, lawyers, etc.), residential language camps for juniors, examination preparation. Various types of accommodations. Full range of activities.

Dates: Year round. Cost: Contact school for details. Contact: GLS Sprachenzentrum, Barbara Jaeschke, Managing Director, Kolonnenstrasse 26, 10829 Berlin, Germany; (011) 49-30-787-41-52; fax (011) 49-30-787-41-92; gls.berlin@t-online.de, www.gls-berlin.com.

German Studies. Intensive language study—up to 2 years of university language requirements in 1 semester. Additional courses in history, political science, culture, literature, etc. Program-organized field trips and housing. Beautiful city only 30 minutes from Hamburg.

Dates: Spring semester: Jan-May; Summer: May-Jun and Jun-Jul; Fall semester: Aug-Dec. Cost: One semester: $3,760; Fall and Spring: $5,860; Summer: $1,460 per session, $2,480 both sessions. Contact: University Studies Abroad Consortium (USAC), Univ. of Nevada, Reno #323, Reno, NV 89557-0093; (702) 784-6569, fax (702) 784-6010; usac@admin.unr.edu, www.scs.unr.edu/~usac.

Kalamazoo in Erlangen. This university-integrated program begins with a 5- to 6-week intensive German course. Participants then enroll in regular courses at the Univ. of Erlangen-Nuernberg. All participants complete an individualized cultural research project or internship of personal interest un-der the guidance of a local mentor. Minimum of 2 years of college German required.

Dates: Late Sep-late Jul (academic year); late Sep-late Feb (Fall); Apr-late-Jul (Spring). Cost: (1998-99) Academic year: $24,249; one semester $16,166 includes roundtrip international transportation, tuition and fees, room and board, and some excursions. Contact: Center for International Programs, Kalamazoo College, 1200 Academy, Kalamazoo, MI 49006; (616) 337-7133, fax (616) 337-7400; cip@kzoo.edu.

Mannheim Program for Bilingual Careers. A professional program abroad for young Americans who wish additional language training, university study in Germany, and option of a paid internship under the auspices of AGABUR Foundation, Inc. Designed for undergrads, graduating seniors, and young professionals. See web site for application form and information.

Dates: Spring: Mar-Aug; Summer: Jun-Aug; Fall: Sep-Feb. Cost: Six months $7,935 (plus $500), 3 months $4,500 (plus $500). Contact: Prof. Gerhard Austin, AGABUR Foundation, Inc., 9 Eastwood Rd., Storrs, CT 06268-2401; (860) 429-1279, fax (860) 487-7709; austin@uconnvm.uconn.edu, www.mannheim-program.necaweb.com.

Penn-in-Freiburg. For students interested in coursework in intensive intermediate German. This program offers German language students an opportunity to gain proficiency skills and cultural insight while studying in the center of Renaissance Germany.

Dates: Jul 20-Aug 28. Cost: Tuition $2,968; housing and activities $600. Contact: Penn Summer Abroad, College of General Studies, Univ. of Pennsylvania, 3440 Market St., Suite 100, Philadelphia, PA 19104-3335; (215) 898-5738, fax (215) 573-2053.

Schiller International Univ. at Heidelberg. Schiller Univ. is an American-style university with all courses except language classes taught in English. Schiller's particular strengths are in international business and international relations but it offers courses in the humanities and social sciences as well. Students may take German at Schiller or intensive German at the Collegium Palatinum, a specialized language division. One semester college German or equivalent is required.

Dates: Fall: late Aug-mid-Dec; Spring: mid-Jan-mid-May. Cost estimate: $7,425 per semester. Estimates include full-day orientation before departure, application fee, room and food allowance in residence hall, mandatory German insurance, airfare, books and supplies, health and accident insurance, German Residence Permit, administrative fees. SUNY tuition not included. Contact: Office of International Programs, Box 2000, SUNY Cortland, Cortland, NY 13045; (607) 753-2209, fax (607) 753-5989; studyabroad@cortland.edu, www.study abroad.com/suny/cortland.

Semester in Regensburg. This program combines German language courses at the beginning and intermediate levels with a range of courses in humanities, German culture, business law, and international business taught in English. Language courses are taught by Univ. of Regensburg faculty and others by Murray State Univ. faculty. No prior knowledge of German is required.

Dates: Aug-Dec. Cost: $2,895 program fee, MSU tuition ($1,060 for KY residents, $2,860 others), airfare. Contact: Dr. Fred Miller, Regensburg Program Director, Murray State Univ., P.O. Box 9, Murray, KY 42071; (502) 762-6206, fax (502) 762-3740; Fred.Miller@ murraystate.edu, or Ms. Linda Bartnik, Center for International Programs, P.O. Box 9, Murray State Univ., Murray, KY 42071; (502) 752-4152, fax (502) 762-3237; linda.bartnik@murray state.edu, www.mursuky.edu/qacd/cip/sirprog. htm

Univ. of Maryland Univ. College at Schwäbisch Gmünd. UMUC at Schwäbisch Gmünd is a 4-year residential campus located 33 km from Stuttgart in scenic southern Germany. Through classes taught in English, individualized attention, and an international student body, UMUC provides an ideal environment for academic achievement and cultural enrichment. Applications are invited from potential freshman, transfer, and semester or academic year abroad students.

Dates: Semesters run from Aug-Dec and Jan-May. Cost: Approx. $11,500 per year for tuition, approx. $4,700 for double room with full board. For Maryland residents, tuition is $6,200 per year. Contact: Jennifer Kist, International Admissions Counselor, UMUC-International Programs, University Blvd. at Adelphi Rd., College Park, MD 20742-1644; (301) 985-7442, fax (301) 985-7959; sginfo@polaris.umuc.edu or Admissions Office, UMUC, Universitätspark, 73525 Schwäbisch Gmünd, Germany; (011) 49-7171-18070, fax (011) 49-7171-180732; enroll@ admin.sg.umuc.edu.

Wayne State Univ.'s Junior Year in Munich. The full university curriculum in arts and sciences at the Univ. of Munich will be open to you, plus German studies courses through the program itself. All instruction is in German, taught by German faculty. A 6-week orientation period of intensive language preparation precedes the beginning of university classes. Juniors, seniors, and graduate students with 2 years of college German and an overall "B" average are eligible.

Dates: Sep 21-Jul 31. Includes a 2-month semester break. Cost: $7,300 for tuition and fees. Scholarships and financial aid available. Contact: Junior Year in Germany, Wayne State Univ., Detroit, MI 48202; (313) 577-4605, fax (313) 577-3266; jym@wayne.edu.

Greece

An Archaeological Tour of Greece. Obtain first-hand knowledge of the art and architecture of ancient Greece through on-site archaeological visits and museum tours. This is the only course of its kind in which students are invited to have one of their lectures inside the Parthenon. Other highlights include visits to Sparta, Corinth, Mycenae, the Olympia Grounds, Delphi, Thermopylae, and Mystra, the world's best-preserved medieval city. The trip ends with 4 days on the island of Mykonos and a visit to the "birthplace" of Apollo.

Dates: Jun 7-Jun 29 (1998). Cost: $2,800 (3 credits) includes roundtrip airfare, double occupancy rooms, breakfast daily, bus, ship, and airport transfers. Contact: Dora Riomayor, Director of International Studies, School of Visual Arts, 209 E. 23rd St., New York, NY 10010-3994; (212) 592-2543, fax (212) 592-2545.

BCA Program in Athens. Earn 15-16 credits per semester at the Univ. of La Verne Athens, with a 1-week orientation and survival Greek training. Field trips and an extended study tour. All classes taught in English by international faculty. No foreign language prerequisite. Graduate courses in business and education. Students from all U.S. colleges and universities accepted. Full liberal arts curriculum for undergraduates.

Dates: Fall: Sep-Nov; Spring: Mar-Jun: Year: Sep-Jun. Cost: $18,845 (academic year), $10,545 (semester). Includes international transportation, room and board, tuition, insurance, group travel in country, and 1 travel tour. Contact: Beverly S. Eikenberry, 605 E. College Ave., North Manchester, IN 46962; (219) 982-5238, fax (219) 982-7755; bca@manchester.edu, www.studyabroad.com/bca.

Beaver College Study in Greece. An individualized opportunity to learn about Greece, its people and its heritage. Courses available in classical, Byzantine, and modern Greek studies, with required study of modern Greek language (no prior knowledge of Greek required). On-site resident director and expert specialist faculty. Field trips. Full range of program services. Scholarships available.

Dates: Fall, Spring, full year, and Summer. Cost: Summer: $3,300 (1998); full year:

$16,950 (1998-99); Fall or Spring semester: $8,800. Contact: Susan Plummer, Beaver College CEA, 450 S. Easton Rd., Glenside, PA 19038-3295; (888) BEAVER-9, fax (215) 572-2174; cea@beaver.edu, www.beaver.edu/cea.

College Year in Athens (CYA). One- or 2-semester programs during the academic year. The 2-track curriculum offers a focus on either Ancient Greek Civilization or Mediterranean Studies and is supplemented by at least 10 days each semester of study and travel within Greece. Instruction is in English. Credit is granted by prearrangement with the home institution.

Dates: Aug 30-Dec 17, 1999; Jan 17-May 12, 2000. Cost: Semester fee of $9,900 includes tuition, housing, partial board, study, travel, most course materials, $100 refundable damage deposit. Contact: College Year in Athens, North American Office, Dept. T, P.O. Box 390890, Cambridge, MA 02139-0010; (617) 494-1008, fax (617) 494-1662; cyathens@aol.com.

CYA Summer 1998. Three- and 6-week programs on Ancient Greek Civilization, Modern Greek Language (4 levels).

Dates: Jun-Jul. Cost: $3,450 (Jun 9-Jul 17, including study-travel); $1,750 (Jun 29-Jul 17 on island of Paros); $1,550 (Jun 9-Jun 26 in Athens). Covers tuition, housing, and course materials. Contact: College Year in Athens, North American Office, Dept. T, P.O. Box 390890, Cambridge, MA 02139-0010; (617) 494-1008, fax (617) 494-1662; cyathens@aol.com.

Odyssey in Athens. Odyssey in Athens is a semester or full year program for mature and resourceful college-age students eager to explore the rich cultural and historical landscape of Greece. Sponsored by the University of Indianapolis at Athens, we offer courses in language, culture, art, business and international affairs. Accredited by the Midwest Association of Schools and Colleges.

Dates: First semester: Mid-Sep-mid-Dec, 2nd semester: Mid-Feb-mid-Jun. Cost: $6,800 for 1 semester, $12,824 for full year. Includes tuition, fees, housing, and excursions. Contact: Barbara Tsairis, U.S. Director, P.O. Box 5666, Portsmouth, NH 03802-5666; odyssey@star.net, www.star.net/People/~odyssey.

Guatemala

Eco-Escuela de Español. The Eco-Escuela de Español offers a unique educational experience by combining intensive Spanish language instruction with volunteer opportunities in conservation and community development projects. Students are immersed in the language, culture, and ecology of Petén, Guatemala—an area renowned for its tropical forests and ancient Mayan ruins. Ecological activities integrate classroom with field-based experiences.

Dates: Every Monday year round. Cost: Classes $65 per week (based on 20 hours of individual instruction per week, Monday-Friday). Room and board with local families $60 per week. Registration fee $10. Contact: Eco-Escuela, GAP Adventures, 266 Dupont St., Toronto, ON, M5R 1V7, Canada; (416) 922-8899, fax (416) 922-0822; adventure@gap.ca.

Honduras

Centro Internacional de Idiomas. Spanish in the Caribbean in beautiful La Cciba. International airport, gateway to great diving in the Bay Islands. Learn surrounded by natural rainforests, wild life reserves. One-on-one student-teacher ratio. Intensive survival skills, conversation, grammar, and vocabulary. All certified teachers, some bilingual. The school is completely air conditioned.

Dates: Year round. Cost: $200 for 4-hour classes, 5 days per week, 7-day homestay. Contact: Belinda Linton, Director, Centro Internacional de Idiomas, IMC-TGU, Dept. 277, P.O. Box 025320, Miami, FL 33102-5320; Tel./fax (011) 504-440-0547; cii@tropicohn.com, www.worldwide.edu/honduras/cici.

Hong Kong

Cantonese and Putonghua. Intensive Cantonese and Putonghua courses from beginning through advanced levels for foreigners, optimum 15 classroom hours per week. At advanced levels, part-time or private tutorials available. Students at any level may register for admission to any term. Center study recognized by major international universities for degree credit.

Dates: Fall term (Sep); Spring term (Jan); Summer term (Jun). Cost: HK$23,250 (Fall); HK$23,250 (Spring); HK$16,950 (Summer). Contact: Director, New Asia—Yale-in-China Chinese Language Ctr., Shatin, NT, Hong Kong; (011) 852-2609-6727, fax (011) 852-2603-5004; chilangctr@cuhk.edu.hk, www.cuhk.edu.hk/lac.

International Asian Studies Programme (IASP). IASP is a nondegree program for international students for 1 semester or 1 year at The Chinese Univ. of Hong Kong. It offers an Asian Studies curriculum, intensive Chinese language program, independent research under faculty supervision, Teaching-in-China, and other cultural activities. Students may take other university courses.

Dates: Sep-May (academic year); Sep-Dec (1st term); Jan-May (2nd term). Application deadline for academic year or 1st term: March 15 (for North American applicants), Apr 1 (applicants outside North America). Application deadline for 2nd term: Oct 1 (for all applicants). Cost: 1998-99 rates in U.S.: $18,100 per year, $11,665 per term (undergraduate/postgraduate student); $13,310 per year, $8,535 per term (research student). Includes tuition, Chinese language instruction, dormitory accommodations, basic medical care, orientation program, University student union membership, 1 copy of official transcript. Contact: North America: Ms. Shelley Stonecipher, c/o Yale-China Association, P.O. Box 208223, New Haven, CT 06520-8223; (203) 432-0850, fax (203) 432-7246; iasp@yale.edu. Outside North America: Office of International Studies Programmes, The Chinese Univ. of Hong Kong Shatin, New Territories Hong Kong SAR; (011) 852-2609-7597, fax (011) 852-2603-5045; oisp@cuhk.edu.hk, www.cuhk.edu.hk/oisp.

Syracuse Univ. in Hong Kong. Focus on international business and economy in Asia. Courses on business, economics, political science, history, Chinese language, sociology. Internships in Hong Kong, field trips to Beijing, Shanghai, elsewhere. Based at City Univ. of Hong Kong. Housing in residence halls, apartments.

Dates: Jan-May. Cost: $8,755 tuition (1998); $6,450 includes housing, excursions, roundtrip travel. Contact: James Buschman, Associate Director, Syracuse Univ., 119 Euclid Ave., Syracuse, NY 13244-4170; (800) 235-3472, fax (315) 443-4593; suabroad@syr.edu.

India

BCA Program in Cochin. Earn 16-18 credits per semester at Cochin Univ. of Science and Technology with a 2-week orientation in country, field trips, and extended study tour to Madras, Bombay, Madurai, and Mysore. Courses in all academic disciplines taught in English. Students accepted from all U.S. colleges and universities.

Dates: Sep-Dec or Jan-May. Cost: $13,545 (academic year), $7,945 (semester). Includes international transportation, room and board, tuition, insurance, group travel in country. Contact: Beverly S. Eikenberry, 605 E. College Ave., North Manchester, IN 46962; (219) 982-5238, fax (219) 982-7755; bca@manchester.edu, www.studyabroad.com/bca.

Community Development. This study/travel course based in rural India offers intensive study of 3 connected issues: community development at the village and city street level, the environment, and the roles of women in balancing the demands of the community. Each of the 4 sequential courses begins with an orientation; students then visit development projects where they observe and are taught by development professionals. Appropriate for students from many majors. While the program introduces the religions and cultures of India to students as essential to understanding and learning, the focus of the course is on current issues of development in India.

Dates: Sep-Dec. Contact: Ruth S. Mason, Director of International Education, Gustavus Adolphus College, St. Peter, MN 56082; (507) 933-7545, fax (507) 933-6277.

Friends World Program. A semester or year program in India at the Friends World Center in Bangalore includes orientation, intensive seminars, field studies, travel, and independent work. The core curriculum serves as an introduction to India's complex cultures. Independent study sample topics include: Gandhian studies, sustainable development, Buddhist studies in Nepal, dance, women's studies, philosophy, and traditional medicine. Students may earn 12-18 credits per semester.

Dates: Fall: mid-Sep-mid-Dec; Spring: mid-Jan-mid-May. Cost: $12,290 per semester in 1998/1999. Includes tuition, travel, room and board, fees, and books. Contact: Stephanie Pollack, Friends World Program, 239 Montauk Hwy., Southampton, NY 11968; (516) 287-8475; fw@southampton.liunet.edu.

Penn-in-India. For students interested in South Asian studies, performing arts, religion, economics, and traditional medicine, PSA's newest program offers students a survey of both India's rich cultural history and its burgeoning industrial life. The program is located in Pune, a cosmopolitan city of 4,000,000 which is a thriving arts center, a hub of scholarship, and a growing economic presence. Students will live with Indian families in the area and be involved in community projects.

Dates: Jun 25-Aug 7. Cost: Tuition $2,968; program cost $1,790. Contact: Penn Summer Abroad, College of General Studies, Univ. of Pennsylvania, 3440 Market St., Suite 100, Philadelphia, PA 19104-3335; (215) 898-5738, fax (215) 573-2053.

Sustainable Communities Semester. A Geocommons College program in ecological awareness, cooperative community, and mindful living. Participants spend 3 months in Auroville, an international community of 1,300 people working toward sustainability and "human unity," 3 weeks traveling in India, and 1 week at Plum Village, a Buddhist community in France. College credit through Univ. of New Hampshire.

Dates: Spring semester: approx. Jan 9-Apr 28; Fall semester: approx. Aug 24-Dec 8. Cost: Approx. $9,400 for tuition, room and board, and travel. Current financial aid accepted, some grants. Contact: Lily Fessenden, Executive Director, Geocommons College Program, Derbyshire Farm, Temple, NH 03084; Tel./fax (603) 654-6705; geo@ic.org, www.ic.org/geo.

Wisconsin College Year in India. The program provides integrated language training, tutorial instruction, and independent fieldwork projects, beginning with summer school in the U.S. The 4 program sites are at Banaras Hindu Univ. (for Hindu-Urdu students); Hyderabad Univ., Hyderabad, A.P. (for Telugu students); Madurai Kamaraj Univ. (for Tamil students), and Kerala Univ., Thiruvanan-thapuram, Kerala (for Malayalam students).

Dates: Summer in Madison: early Jun-mid-Aug; academic program abroad: late

Aug-Apr. Cost: Call for current information. Contact: Office of International Studies and Programs, 261 Bascom Hall, 500 Lincoln Dr., Madison, WI 53706; (608) 262-2851, fax (608) 262-6998; peeradv@macc.wisc.edu.

Indonesia

Study in Bali. Join the Naropa Institute (NCA accredited) program in Bali, Indonesia. Bali, often called the Island of the Gods, is the ideal setting for exploring art in everyday life. The Naropa Institute Program in Bali offers courses in culture, language, gamelan music, dance, painting, mask making, batik, and meditation. All classes are taught by master Balinese artists and scholars, as well as Naropa faculty.

Dates: Mid-Feb-mid-Apr. Cost: $5,600 (1998). Includes tuition (9 semester credits), room and partial board, program expenses. Airfare not included. Three credits extra available for independent study. Contact: Study Abroad Office, The Naropa Institute, 2130 Arapahoe Ave., Boulder, CO 80302; (303) 546-3594, fax (303) 444-0410; peter@naropa.edu.

Israel

Bar-Ilan Univ. Junior Year. Eligible students must have completed at least 1 year of university study. Bar-Ilan Univ., a 100-acre campus, is located in Ramat Gan, a beautiful suburb of Tel Aviv. Courses offered in humanities, international relations, Israeli studies, Judaic studies, Middle Eastern studies, natural and social sciences. All courses taught in English. The only program in Israel providing university study with an emphasis on Jewish culture and heritage as a key component. Option of 1 year or semester. Program includes optional touring throughout Israel, volunteer work, and intensive Hebrew language study. Students may live in campus dorms or off-campus apartments. Financial aid available.

Dates: Sep-Jan, Feb-Jun. Cost: Approx. $10,000 per year ($5,000 per semester). Includes tuition, housing, and trips throughout Israel. Contact: Bar-Ilan Univ., Office of Academic Affairs, 91 5th Ave., New York, NY 10003; (212) 337-1286 or (888) BIU-YEAR, fax (212) 337-1274; tobiu@idt.net, www.roxcorp.com/barilan.

Friends World Program. A semester or year program in the Middle East at Friends World Center in Jerusalem consists of intensive seminars that introduce students to the culture of the Middle East. Field work, travel, and independent research are also offered. Sample topics include: desert agriculture, archaeology, anthropology, journalism, public health, conflict resolution, religious studies. Fieldwork can be conducted in Israel, Jordan, and other countries and may earn 12-18 credits per semester.

Dates: Fall: mid-Sep-mid-Dec; Spring: mid-Jan-mid-May. Cost: $12,090 per semester in 1998/1999. Includes tuition, travel, room and board, fees and books. Contact: Stephanie Pollack, Friends World Program, 239 Montauk Hwy., Southampton, NY 11968; (516) 287-8475; fw@southampton.liunet.edu.

Geography, History, Archaeology. A 3-week program (4 semester hours of graduate/undergraduate credit) with extensive field trips throughout the region. Introduces the student to the geography, history, and archaeology of Israel and Trans-Jordan as they relate to Biblical studies.

Dates: Call for dates, programs run year round. Cost: $1,695 on-campus dorm; $1,865 off-campus hotel. Contact: Jerusalem University College, 4249 E. State St., Suite 203, Rockford, IL 61108; (815) 229-5900 or (800) 891-9408, fax (815) 229-5901; 75454.1770@compuserve.com, www.juc.edu.

Jesus and His Times. A 2-week (2-semester hour) program of studies related to the geog-

raphy, history, culture, and archaeology of the Second Temple period (time of Christ). Concentrations in the Jerusalem and Galilee regions.

Dates: Jun 28-Jul 11. Cost: $1,100 on campus; $1,325 off-campus hotel. Contact: Jerusalem University College, 4249 E. State St., Suite 203, Rockford, IL 61108; (815) 229-5900 or (800) 891-9408, fax (815) 229-5901; 75454.1770@compuserve.com, www.juc.edu.

Master of Arts Degree. Ancient History of Syro-Palestine, Middle Eastern Studies, New Testament Backgrounds, Hebrew Language, Hebrew Bible Translation. Two-year MA degrees. Extensive fieldwork and study in the languages, geography, history, culture, social, and religious aspects of Israel and the Middle East.

Dates: Sep-May every year. Cost: Approx. $7,700 per semester. Includes tuition, room and board, fees. Contact: Jerusalem Univ. College, Amelia Nakai, Program Coordinator, 4249 E. State St., Suite 203, Rockford, IL 61108; (815) 229-5900 or (800) 891-9408, fax (815) 229-5901; 75454.1770@compuserve.com, www.juc.edu.

Pardes Institute of Jewish Studies. Since 1972, Pardes has been the standard of excellence in the teaching of classic Jewish texts in an open environment.

Dates: TBA. Cost: TBA. Contact: American Pardes Foundation, 165 E. 56th St., New York, NY 10022; (212) 230-1316, fax (212) 230-1265; pardesusa@aol.com, www.pardes.org.il.

Semester on Green Kibbutzim. A Geo-commons College Year program exploring ecology, community, and sustainable living. Spend 10 weeks studying and working in sustainable community design at Kibbutz Gezer, 2 weeks studying solar energy and desert ecology at Kibbutzim in the Arava Valley, and 3 weeks visiting ecological projects and kibbutzim in the Galilee. College credit available through Univ. of New Hampshire.

Dates: Spring semester: Jan-Apr; Fall semester: Sep-Dec. Cost: Approx. $9,400 for tuition, room and board, and travel. Current financial aid usually applies. Some grants. Contact: Lily Fessenden, Executive Director, Geocommons College Program, Derbyshire Farm, Temple, NH 03084; Tel./fax (603) 654-6705; geo@ic.org, www.ic.org/geo.

Italy

Academic Programs in Florence. Spend a semester/year/summer session in the heart of the Renaissance. More than 250 courses available: Studio Art (painting, drawing, etc.), Art History, Communications, Liberal Arts, Italian Language, Sociology, International Business, etc. in an international atmosphere.

Dates: Semesters: mid-Jan-end of Apr; Summer: May-Jun-Jul-Aug. Beginning Sep-mid-Dec. Cost: From LIT1,200,000. Contact: Dr. Gabriella Ganugi, The Art Institute of Florence, Lorenzo de'Medici, Via Faenza 43, 50123 Florence, Italy; (011) 39-55-287360, fax (011) 39-55-23989 20/287203; ldm@dada.it, www.dada.it/ldm.

Academic Year Abroad Milano. Direct registration at the Università Bocconi in business and economics, at the Università Cattolica in liberal arts, fine arts, and social sciences. AYA-sponsored intensive language tutorials at the Istituto Dante Alighieri. Optional cultural activities. Direttrice assists students in finding apartments in Milano.

Dates: Bocconi: late Sep-late Jan; late Feb-end Jun; Cattolica: late Oct-end Jun. Cost: Term $3,800; year $5,900. Includes tuition, tutorials, and cultural activities. Contact: Dr. A.M. Cinquemani, Academic Year Abroad, P.O. 733, Stone Ridge, NY 12484-0733; Fax (914) 687-2470; aya@ulster.net, www.studyabroad.com/aya/.

American Univ. of Rome. Programs for students of international business, international relations, Italian civilization and culture, Italian studies and communications. Credits fully transferable through affiliations with U.S. institutions. Housing in studio apartments. All courses (except language classes) in English. All programs are designed to provide students with studies of immediate relevance in a highly competitive job market.

Dates: Fall and Spring semesters plus May/Jun summer sessions. Cost: $4,634 per semester, tuition/housing $2,500. Contact: Mary B. Handley, Director of Administration, American Univ. of Rome, Via Pietro Roselli 4, Rome 00153, Italy; (011) 39-6-58330919, fax (011) 39-6-58330992.

Art and Design in Florence. The Accademia Italiana is an international, university-level institute of art and design. The Accademia offers courses in art, fashion, interior, industrial and textile design during the autumn and spring semesters and fashion design, fashion illustration, drawing and painting, window display design and Italian language during the months of June and July.

Dates: Jan-May, Jun, Jul, Sep-Dec. Cost: Depends on course chosen. Contact: Barbara McHugh, Accademia Italiana, Piazza Pitti n. 15, 50125 Florence, Italy; (011) 39-55-284616/211619, fax (011) 39-55-284486; modaita@tin.it, www.gamut.it/accademia.

Art Under One Roof (Arte Sotto un Tetto). One of Europe's most complete art studio programs. Over 40 monthly courses and academic semester programs. Studies include Euro programs, split between our Paris and Florence Center. Academic studies include jewelry making, interior and boutique design, furniture and industrial design, painting restoration, painting and drawing, figurative sculpture, mural and fresco painting, photography, wood decoration, and many more.

Dates: Academic studies: Jan, May, Sep. Many courses offered monthly. Deadlines: 90 days prior. Cost: Academic Semester Studies $3,000; month courses: from $450. Contact: Arte Sotto un Tetto Admissions, Paris and Florence Programs, Via Pandolfini, 46/R 50122

Florence, Italy; Tel./fax (011) 39-55-247-8867; berarducci@iol.it.

Buffalo State Siena Program. Experience a medieval city as your neighborhood through placement with a family and access to university facilities. Enjoy a unique, economical program revolving around art, Italian language, and civilization. Participate in classroom work complemented by excursions, workshops, and frequent informal gatherings. Learn from bilingual instructors in a user-friendly atmosphere (average student-teacher ratio 8:1).

Dates: Early Sep to mid-Dec; late Jan-early May. Cost: $7,262 per semester (1998) for New York state residents, nonresidents add $2,450. Includes tuition fees, room, board, required field trips, insurance, airfare. Contact: Dr. Lee Ann Grace, Director, Buffalo State College, 1300 Elmwood Ave., Buffalo, NY 14222-1095; (716) 878-4620, fax (716) 878-3054; gracela@buffalotstate.edu, www.buffalostate.edu/~intnated.

Business, Economics, Italian Studies. Turin offers a diversified curriculum in English and in business and economics, plus intensive courses in Italian language and culture, literature, etc., at the foot of the majestic Alps. Program-organized housing and field trips and many Italian university activities.

Dates: Spring semester: Jan-Apr. Summer sessions: Jun and Jul; Fall semester: Aug-Dec. Cost: $6,980 Fall and Spring semesters; Summer: $1,580 per session $2,880 both sessions. Fall: $3,980, Spring: $4,280, year: $6,980 (all prices are for 1998). Contact: University Studies Abroad Consortium (USAC), Univ. of Nevada, Reno #323, Reno, NV 89557-0093; (702) 784-6569, fax (702) 784-6010; usac@admin.unr.edu, www.scs.unr.edu/~usac.

Ceramics or Sculpture in Urbino. Five-week studio art program offering William and Mary instruction and credit, optional additional art courses (at additional cost), homestays in Urbino, excursions to major artistic and cultural sites.

Dates: End of Jun-Aug 7 (1998). Cost: $4,240 includes William and Mary instruction, credit and materials; international airfare; homestay with 2 meals per day in Urbino; excursions with lodging. Additional costs include breakfasts in Urbino, meals on excursions, tuition for optional additional course (approx. $500), incidentals, personal travel. Contact: Ann M. Moore, College of William and Mary, Programs Abroad, Dept. TA, P.O. Box 8795, Williamsburg, VA 23187-8795; (757) 221-3594, fax (757) 221-3597; Ann@reves.is.wm.edu, www.wm.edu/academics/reves/urbino.

College of William and Mary. Summer in Florence. One-month program in Italian language (beginning to advanced) including art history course taught in English, with William and Mary credit, homestays with 2 meals per day, excursions include lodging and meals for weekend trip to Venice.

Dates: May 29-Jun 26. Cost: $3,350 (1998) includes instruction and credit, books, lodging including 2 meals per day with Italian family (2 students per family), excursions include weekend trip to Venice with lodging and meals. Additional costs include international airfare, lunches in Florence, incidentals, and personal travel. Contact: Ann M. Moore, College of William and Mary, Programs Abroad, Dept. TA, P.O. Box 8795, Williamsburg, VA 23187-8795; (757) 221-3594, fax (757) 221-3597; ammoo2@facstaff.wm.edu, www.wm. edu/academics/reves/florence.html.

The Florence Academy of Art. Summer workshops: Drawing the Figure in Three Renaissance Techniques, Figure Painting in Oil and Trompe l'Oeil. Private studio rentals available. Evening history and art history lectures and field trips. Studio access 9 a.m.-9 p.m. The Academy is located in the center of Florence, near the Accademia and the Uffizi Gallery.

Dates: Jul 6-31 (1998). Cost: $1,050 includes instruction, field trips, lectures, student assistance. Contact: Susan Tintori, The Florence Academy of Art, Via delle Casine 21R, 50122 Florence, Italy; (011) 39-55-245444, fax (011) 39-55-2343701.

Intensive Italian Program-Perugia. The Univ. of Oregon 6-week summer session in Perugia offers an Italian immersion experience combined with an intensive-experience of language study. Courses are also available in Italian culture, literature, art history, music, history, and other subjects. The primary goal of this program is the study of the Italian language.

Dates: Jul 1-Aug 13. Cost: $1,275 Univ. of Oregon study abroad fee, includes tuition. Contact: Regina Psaki, Romance Languages, Univ. of Oregon, Eugene, OR 97403-1233; (541) 346-4042, fax (541) 346-4030; rpsaki@oregon.uoregon.edu or Melanie Wiliams, OIEE, Univ. of Oregon, Eugene, OR 97403-5209; (541) 346-3207, fax (541) 346-1232; melaniew@oregon.uoregon.edu, http://darkwing.uoregon.edu/~oieehome/os.

Italian Courses for Foreigners. Italian language courses for foreigners, from beginner to proficiency, open all year round. Courses: G-20 group courses in the morning 20 hours per week; GK-25 combination courses 25 hours per week; GK-30 combination intensive courses 30 hours per week. Cultural courses: Italian cooking, business Italian, commercial correspondence, history of art, Italian wines. Accommodations: family, flat, small hotels.

Dates: Jan 4, Jan 18; Feb 1, Feb 15; Mar 1, Mar 15; Apr 6, Apr 19; May 3, May 17; Jun 7, Jun 21; Jul 5, Jul 19; Aug 2, Aug 16, Aug 30; Sep 13, Sep 27; Oct 11, Oct 25; Nov 8, Nov 22; Dec 6. Cost: Two weeks: LIT560,000 (G20), 1,130,000 (GK25), 1,640,000 (GK30); 4 weeks: LIT820,000 (G20), 1,880,000 (G25), 2,820,000 (GK30). Contact: Prof. Bruno Fabbri, "I Malatesta," Corso d'Augusto 144, 47900 Rimini, Italy; (011) 39-541-56487, fax (011) 39-541-21088; imalatesta@rn.nettuno.it, www.akros.it/imalatesta.

Italian Studies in Florence. For students interested in intensive beginning and intermediate language courses and cultural studies in literature, cinema, and art history taught in one of the world's most beautiful cities. Numerous cultural opportunities and field trips offer a valuable supplement to class work.

Dates: Jun 8-Jul 17. Cost: Tuition $2,800; housing $1,475; travel $760. Contact: Penn Summer Abroad, College of General Studies, Univ. of Pennsylvania, 3440 Market St., Suite 100, Philadelphia, PA 19104-3335; (215) 898-5738, fax (215) 573-2053.

John Cabot Univ. Located in the center of Rome, JCU offers the most well-rounded study abroad experience. As a 4-year American university in Italy, JCU offers a wide selection of courses taught in a truly international atmosphere represented by Italians, Americans, and students from over 40 different nations. Full student services and college credit transfer assistance.

Dates: Winter term: Jan-Mar; Spring: Apr-Jun; Summer: Jun-Jul; Fall: Sep-Dec. Cost: Application fee: LIT60,000 (approx. $35.50). Tuition per course: LIT1,930,000 (approx. $1,150). Housing: LIT700,000-1,200,000 per month (approx. $420-$700). Contact: Admissions Office, John Cabot Univ. via della Lungara 233 00165, Rome, Italy; (011) 39-6-681-9121, fax (011) 39-6-683-2088; jcu@johncabot.edu, www.johncabot.edu.

Sarah Lawrence College in Florence. Individually designed programs with total immersion in the academic and social life of Florence. Options include enrollment in the Univ. of Florence, studio arts, music, and internships. Frequent field trips and excursions are included. Private tutorials and small seminars with distinguished Italian faculty.

Dates: Sep-Jun. Jan-Jun (option for students

Study Programs

with a minimum 1 year of college level Italian, or the equivalent). Cost: $32,132 (year) Includes all fees, tuition, excursions, field trips, and cultural activities, housing, and most meals. Contact: Prema Samuel, Sarah Lawrence College in Florence, Box CR, Bronxville, NY 10708; (800) 873-4752.

SCSU Summer Program in Urbino. Study language and art history, painting and drawing at Univ. 12 days of travel.

Dates: Jul 1-Aug 5. Cost: $2,100 room and board, excursions. Contact: Dr. Mike Vena, Foreign Languages Department, SCSU, 501 Crescent St., New Haven, CT 06515; (203) 392-6466, fax (203) 392-6136.

Studio Art Centers International. Combine beginning, intermediate, or advanced Italian language studies with courses in studio arts, art history, art conservation, or cultural studies at SACI's central Florence location. Outside the classroom, students are partnered with Italian university students for language and cultural exchange. Programs include year/semester abroad, late spring and summer studies.

Dates: Sep-Dec; Jan-Apr; May-Jun; Jun-Jul. Cost: Fall/Spring tuition $7,725 per term (1998/99); late Spring/Summer (1998) $3,000. Contact: SACI Coordinator, U.S. Student Programs, Institute of International Education, 809 UN Plaza, New York, NY 10017-3580; (800) 344-9186, (212) 984-5548, fax (212) 984-5325; saci@iie.org, www.saci-florence.org.

Summer Study in Florence. Get 8 transferable credits in 7 weeks in downtown Florence. Classes are 3 days per week in English, Renaissance Literature, and Art. Low costs, modern accommodations, time for travel throughout Italy. Top U.S. school offers credits.

Dates: Jun 1-Jul 20 (1998). Cost: All costs $4,500 depending on type of residence (1998). Contact: bernhema@muohio.edu or call (513) 523-2705.

Tech Rome. Tech Rome is a 6-week summer travel study program of Louisiana Tech Univ. It features hotel housing, 3 meals per day, tours, and traditional classroom courses combined with field travel for college credit. Up to 13 semester hours may be earned in a choice of over 40 courses in diverse subject areas. Courses are taught by American professors.

Dates: May-Jul. Cost: $4,328 includes tuition, all housing for 6 weeks, 3 meals per day, tours. Group flights are available. Contact: Tech Rome, P.O. Box 3172, Ruston, LA 71272; (318) 257-4854; http://techrome.latech.edu.

Temple Univ. Rome. Temple Univ. in Rome, established in 1966, offers a semester or academic year and a 6-week summer program of full-time study designed primarily for 3rd year undergraduate students. The semester or academic program is comprised of 4 academic components. Architecture, Liberal Arts and Italian Studies, Visual Arts, and International Business. Except for courses in Italian language and literature, all instruction is in English. The academic program is enriched by course field trips and a broad range of extracurricular activities.

Dates: Fall: Aug 30-Dec 12, application deadline Apr 1; Summer: Jun 4-Jul 16, application deadline Mar 15; Spring: Jan 10-Apr 24, 2000, application deadline Oct 15, 1999. Cost: (1998-99) 1 semester: $7,770-$11,193. Includes tuition and fees, housing, meals.. Contact: Mike Dever, Temple Univ., International Programs, Conwell Hall, 5th Fl., Philadelphia, PA 19122; (215) 204-4684, fax (215) 204-5735; intlprog@vm.temple.edu, www.temple.edu/intlprog.

Wisconsin Summer in Perugia. This intensive Italian language program gives students an opportunity to study at the Università Italiana per Stranieri in Perugia, a train-ride away from Florence and Rome. Students take courses in Italian language, at any level, and a 1-credit cultural survey, taught in

English. No previous knowledge of Italian required. Application deadline: First Friday in Mar. Late applications considered on a space-available basis.

Dates: Late May through Jul (8 weeks). Cost: Call for current information. Contact: Office of International Studies and Programs, 261 Bascom Hall, Univ. of Wisconsin, 500 Lincoln Dr., Madison, WI 53706; (608) 262-2851, fax (608) 262-6998; peeradv@macc.wisc.edu.

Jamaica

Tropical Marine Biology. Intense course studies coral reefs, turtle grass beds, tropical sandy and rocky shores, mangrove swamps. Two field trips per day, 2 or 3 hours of lectures per day. Boats leave at 9 a.m. for coral reefs and other habitats. Room and board in small campus hotel, all Jamaican staff, 3 undergraduate or graduate credits.

Dates: Jul 6-17. Cost: Call for details. Contact: Dr. Eugene Kaplan, Director, HUML, Gittelson Hall 114, Hofstra Univ., Hempstead, NY 11550; bioehk@hofstra.edu.

Japan

BCA Program in Sapporo. Earn 15-18 credits per semester at Hokusei Gakuen Univ. in Sapporo, with a 1-week orientation, homestay with Japanese families, field trips, and extended study tour through Honshu. Year program could include first semester or 2-month interterm in Dalian, China. Students accepted from all U.S. colleges and universities. No foreign language prerequisite. All levels of Japanese language study available. Practica and internships available.

Dates: Fall: Aug-Dec; Spring: Mar-Jul; Summer: Aug-Jul; or Year: Mar-Dec. Cost: $18,845 (academic year); $10,545 (semester). Includes international transportation, room and board, tuition, insurance, group travel in country. Contact: Beverly S.

Eikenberry, 605 E. College Ave., North Manchester, IN 46962; (219) 982-5238, fax (219) 982-7755; bca@manchester.edu, www.studyabroad.com/bca.

Friends World Program. A semester or year program at the Friends World Center in Kyoto includes intensive seminars focused on Japanese culture, language, and the arts. Writing workshops are also offered. Students design internships and independent research projects. Sample topics include: traditional medicine, education, Buddhism, gender studies, peace movements, and environmental policy. Student may earn 12-18 credits per semester.

Dates: Fall: mid-Sep-mid-Dec; Spring: mid-Jan-mid-May. Cost: $13,115 per semester in 1998/1999. Includes tuition, travel, room and board, fees, and books. Contact: Stephanie Pollack, Friends World Program, 239 Montauk Hwy., Southampton, NY 11968; (516) 287-8475; fw@southampton.liunet.edu.

Intensive Language and Culture. This program features high quality instruction with personalized attention at all language levels, full year or more of Japanese language credit, conveniently offered 5 times a year, educational excursions to many cultural, historical, political sites in and around Tokyo. Sponsor universities include Western Washington Univ., the Univ. of Idaho, and Lincoln Univ.

Dates: Spring: Jan 8-Mar 25; early Summer: Apr 5-Jun 24; late Summer: Jul 4-Sep 25; Summer short-term: Jul 4-Aug 21; Fall: Oct 8-Dec 23. Cost: $5,150. Includes tuition, fees, textbooks, excursions, housing (homestay or dorm), local transportation. Contact: Michael Anderson, KCP International, P.O. Box 28028, Bellingham, WA 98228; (888) KCP-7020) or (360) 647-0072, fax (360) 647-0736; kcp@kcp-usa.com, www.kcp-usa.com.

Japan Center for Michigan Univ. (JCMU). JCMU offers intensive Japanese instruction at 4 levels, and courses in Japanese studies (during the academic year). Students may

Study Programs

live with Japanese families or in the Center's apartments, and may enroll for any combination of terms beginning in Sep, Jan, or Jun. Undergraduate credit is granted through Michigan State Univ.

Dates: Sep-Dec, Jan-Apr, Jun-Aug. Cost: $3,500 includes tuition, books, rent, insurance. Contact: John Hazewinkel, Program Coordinator, Japan Center for Michigan Universities, MSU International Center, E. Lansing, MI 48824; (517) 355-4654, fax (517) 432-2659; JCMU@pilot.msu.edu, www.isp.msu.edu/JCMU.

Japan Exchange and Teaching Program. Sponsored by the Japanese Government, the JET Program invites over 1,000 American college graduates and young professionals to share their language and culture with Japanese youth. One-year positions are available in schools and government offices throughout Japan. Apply by early December for positions beginning in July of the following year.

Dates: One-year contracts renewable by mutual consent not more than 2 times. Cost: Participants receive approx. ¥3,600,000 per year in monthly payments. Contact: JET Program Office, Embassy of Japan, 2520 Massachusetts Ave. NW, Washington, DC 20008; (202) 238-6772, fax (202) 265-9484; eojjet@erols.com, www.jet.org.

Minnesota State University - Akita. Accredited university program on residential American-style campus. Courses include Japanese language, area studies, special topics. Typical class size 10-20. Homestays encouraged. Japanese roommate for each student. Program ideal for students in all majors; particularly beneficial for those with career and/or personal interest in Japan.

Dates: Apr and Sep start dates. Dec 15 and May 15 deadlines. One semester or 1 year. Cost: $6,500-$10,500 for 1 semester; $11,300-$18,500 for 1 year. Includes tuition, room and board, fees, airfare, books, misc. expenses. Contact: Dr. Karin Treiber, Akita

Support Office, 550 Cedar Street, Suite 11, Lower Level, St. Paul, MN 55101; (612) 296-8885, fax (612) 296-9946; msuakita@so.mnscu.edu, www. mnscu.edu/html/info/akita.htm.

Teaching English in Japan. Two-year program to maximize linguistic and cultural integration of participants who work as teachers' assistants. Placements twice yearly in April and August. Most positions are in junior high schools in urban and rural areas. Bachelor's degree and willingness to learn Japanese required.

Dates: Hiring for positions every Apr and Aug. Applications accepted year round. Cost: Airfare, salary, housing, healthcare provided. No application fees. Contact: Institute for Education on Japan, Earlham College, D-202, Richmond, IN 47374; (888) 685-2726, fax (765) 983-1553; www.earlham.edu/aet/home.htm.

Temple Univ. Japan. U.S. undergraduate students can study in the heart of Tokyo for a semester, academic year, or summer alongside bilingual Japanese students. The academic program is comprised of an extensive liberal arts curriculum that includes Japanese language at all levels and upper level Asian studies courses. A special engineering program is also offered in the fall semester for sophomore engineering majors. With the exception of Japanese language courses, all courses are conducted in English.

Dates: Fall: Aug 30-Dec 9, application deadline Apr 1; Summer: late May-late Jul; Spring: Jan 4-Apr 9, 2000, application deadline Oct 1, 1999. Cost (1998-99) $9,240 per semester. Includes tuition, housing in shared accommodation, refundable housing deposit, and activity fee. Contact: Mike Dever, Temple Univ., International Programs, Conwell Hall, 5th Fl., Philadelphia, PA 19122; (215) 204-4684, fax (215) 204-5735; intlprog@vm.temple.edu, www.temple.edu/intlprog.

Kenya

Friends World Program. A semester or year program in Kenya at Friends World Center in Machakos. Includes intensive seminars, field study, homestays, travel, and independent study. Seminars are offered in historical and contemporary East Africa and Swahili language. Field projects have been done in the areas of sustainable development, education, traditional medicine, agroforestry, marine ecology, wildlife studies, and music. Students may earn 12-18 credits per semester.

Dates: Fall: mid-Sep-mid-Dec.; Spring: mid-Jan-mid-May. Cost: $12,640 per semester in 1998/1999. Includes tuition, travel, room and board, fees, and books. Contact: Stephanie Pollack, Friends World Program, 239 Montauk Hwy., Southampton, NY 11968; (516) 287-8475; fw@southampton.liunet.edu.

Korea

Penn-in-Seoul. For students interested in East Asia, Korea, international relations and other business disciplines. This program, offered in conjunction with Kyung Hee Univ., includes courses in the area of international relations as well as internships with multinational corporations, government agencies, and think tanks. Field trips exploring Korean history and culture are integral to the program.

Dates: Jun 13-Aug 16. Cost: Tuition $2,968; housing $850. Contact: Penn Summer Abroad, College of General Studies, Univ. of Pennsylvania, 3440 Market St., Suite 100, Philadelphia, PA 19104-3335; (215) 898-5738, fax (215) 573-2053.

Mexico

BCA Program in Xalapa. Earn 15-18 credits per semester at Univ. Veracruzana. Four-week presemester intensive language in Cuernavaca, homestay with families, field trips, and extended study tour. Intermediate college level Spanish required for regular university courses. Students accepted from all U.S. colleges and universities.

Dates: Fall: Sep-Dec or Jan; Spring: Mar-Jun or Jul; Year: Aug-Jun or Jul. Cost: $13,545 (academic year); $7,945 (semester). Includes international transportation, room and board, tuition, insurance, group travel in country. Contact: Beverly S. Eikenberry, 605 E. College Ave., North Manchester, IN 46962; (219) 982-5238, fax (219) 982-7755; bca@manchester.edu, www.studyabroad.com/bca.

Centro de Idiomas/Language Link. The Centro de Idiomas offers intensive Spanish language programs in the exciting Pacific coastal city of Mazatlan, Mexico. Combine a beach vacation with your study. Your choice of 2-4 hours daily of group classes with only 6 students or private classes. Professional adults, college students, and all Spanish levels accommodated in a very well organized school. Programs of 1-12 weeks. Academic credit. Caring homestays and many additional weekly activities include all water sports and excursions with marine biologists.

Dates: Year round. New classes begin every Monday. Cost: $105 registration deposit. Four hours daily group classes and homestay: $280 per week. Includes tuition, insurance, shared room (private $20 extra), and 3 meals daily. Contact: Kay G. Rafool, Language Link Inc., P.O. Box 3006, Peoria, IL 61612; (800) 552-2051, fax (309) 692-2926; info@langlink.com; www.langlink.com.

College of William and Mary. Direct enrollment program offers courses in Spanish language and literature, anthropology, art history, history, political science, or international relations. Taught in Spanish or English. Excursions. Homestays with Mexican families. William and Mary resident faculty direct overseas program.

Dates: May-Jul. Cost: $3,450 (1998) includes international travel, instruction and William and Mary credit, faculty director, excursions, homestays with 2 meals per day. Contact: Ann M. Moore, College of William and Mary, Programs Abroad, Dept. TA, P.O. Box 8795, Williamsburg, VA 23187-8795; (757) 221-3594, fax (757) 221-3597; ammoo2@facstaff.wm.edu, www.wm.edu/academics/reves/mexico.html.

Doing Business in Mexico. Innovative teaching methods combine with cultural immersion at the Autonomous Univ. of Guadalajara and a specialized Beaver-taught class in English, culminating in an extensive field study trip. Semester for beginning and intermediate Spanish speakers with business related major also available. Full range of program services. On-site representative. Need-based scholarships available.

Dates: Fall, Spring, full year, Summer. Cost: Full year: $10,200; Semester: $6,500, Business semester: $6,500; Summer: $1,350. Contact: Meredith Chamorro, Beaver College Center for Education Abroad, 450 S. Easton Rd., Glenside, PA 19038-3295; (888) BEAVER-9, fax (215) 572-2174; cea@beaver.edu, www.beaver.edu/cea.

El Bosque del Caribe, Cancun. Take a professional Spanish course 25 hours per week and enjoy the Caribbean beaches. Relaxed family-like atmosphere. No more than 6 students per class. Special conversation program. Mexican cooking classes and excursions to the Mayan sites. Housing with Mexican families. College credit available.

Dates: Year round. New classes begin every Monday. Group programs arranged at reduced fees. Cost: Enrollment fee $100, $180 per week. One week with a Mexican family $160. Contact: Eduardo Sotelo, Director, Calle Piña 1, S.M. 25, 77500 Cancún, Mexico; (011) 52-98-84-10-38, fax (011) 52-98-84-58-88; bcaribe@mail.cancun-language.com.mx.

Guadalajara Summer School. For the 46th year, the Univ. of Arizona Guadalajara Summer School will offer intensive Spanish in the 6-week session, intensive Spanish in the 3-week session, and upper-division Spanish and Mexico-related courses in the 5-week session. Courses may be taken for credit or audit.

Dates: Jul 5-Aug 19. Cost: $1,057-$2,000 includes tuition and host family housing with meals. Contact: Dr. Macario Saldate IV, Director, Guadalajara Summer School, The Univ. of Arizona, P.O. Box 40966, Tucson, AZ 85717; (520) 621-5137; janeg@u.arizona.edu, www.coh.arizona.edu/gss.

Intensive Language Programs. Intensive Spanish immersion program in groups, 40 class hours per week including Spanish class, lectures, and Hispano-American courses. Executive, semester, and specialized programs for teachers, professionals, nurses, and adults continuing education. Live with Mexican family or in student residence. Excursions to historical and archaeological sites.

Dates: Year round starting every Monday. Cost: Tuition $190 per week; lodging $154 per week. Contact: The Center for Bilingual Multicultural Studies, Javier Espinosa, San Jeronimo #304, Cuernavaca, MOR-62179, Mexico; (011) 52-73-17-10-87, fax (011) 52-73-17-05-33; admin@bilingual-center.com, www.bilingual-center.com.

Intensive Spanish in Cuernavaca. Cuauhnahuac, founded in 1972, offers a variety of intensive and flexible programs geared to individual needs. Six hours of classes daily with no more than 4 students to a class. Housing with Mexican families who really care about you. Cultural conferences, excursions, and special classes for professionals. College credit available.

Dates: Year round. New classes begin every Monday. Cost: $70 registration fee; $650 4 weeks tuition; housing $18 per night. Contact: Marcia Snell, 519 Park Dr., Kenilworth, IL 60043; (800) 245-9335, fax (847) 256-9475; lankysam@aol.com.

Language and Culture in Guanajuato. We work with innovative teaching techniques, tailoring instruction to each student's needs. Spanish, Mexican history, politics, culture-cuisine, folk dancing, and Latin American literature.

Dates: Year round. New classes begin every Monday. Cost: $925. Includes 4 weeks of classes and homestay with 3 meals daily. Contact: Director Jorge Barroso, Instituto Falcon, A.C., Guanajuato, Gto. 36000 Mexico; Tel./fax (011) 52-473-1-0745, infalcon@redes.int.com.mx, www.infonet.com.mx/falcon.

Latin American Studies, Spanish. Intensive Spanish language study in small groups at all language levels, taught by native speakers. Latin American studies courses in history, literature, Mexican arts and crafts, current events, Mexican cuisine, anthropology of Mexico, extensive program of field study excursions led by Cemanahuac anthropologists. Academic credit available; professional seminars arranged; family homestay highly recommended.

Dates: Classes begin each Monday year round. Cost: Registration, tuition, room and board with Mexican family for 2 weeks: $756. Contact: Vivian B. Harvey, Educational Programs Coordinator, Cemanahuac Educational Community, Apartado 5-21, Cuernavaca, Morelos, Mexico; (011) 52-73-18-6407, fax (011) 52-73-12-5418; 74052.2570@ compuserve. com, www.cemanahuac.com. Call (800) 24`7-6641 for a brochure.

Spanish as a Second Language. The Universidad del Mayab offers 3 sessions for international students. The 15-week fall and spring semesters include a 90-hour Spanish language course for 6 college credits and three 45-hour electives, for 3 college credits each one. The 5-week summer program includes 1 45-hour Spanish language course and 1 elective course, for a total of 6 credits. An official transcript is issued upon successful completion of the program.

Dates: Feb, Jun, Sep (1998). Cost: $300 per 45-hour course, $250 registration fee (groups of 8 or more students do not pay a registra-

tion fee). Homestay available upon request. Contact: Universidad del Mayab, School for International Studies, Apdo. Postal 96, Cordemex, Yucatan, Mexico 97310; fax (011) 52-99-22-00-06; lenguas@www.dcc.anahuac. mx.

Spanish in the Land of the Maya. Learn, live and love Spanish in the land of the Maya. Discover Mayan ruins and visit living Mayan Villages. Enjoy the relaxed atmosphere of colonial San Cristóbal de las Casas, Chiapas and experience the lush vegetation of the Chiapas' Highlands and the only tropical forest in North America.

Dates: Year round starting lessons every Monday and homestays any day of the week. Cost: $170 per week (group lessons, double occupancy). For upper scale lodging, single room and private instruction please inquire. Includes stay with a local family, 3 meals per day, 15 hours of Spanish instruction per week, workbooks, participation in cultural activities, access to dark room and screen printing shop, certificate. Contact: Centro Bilingüe Roberto Rivas-Bastidas or Israel Rivas-Bastidas, rrivas@sancristobal.podernet.com.mx, www.mexonline.com/centro1.htm. Centro Bilingüe Calle Real de Guadalupe 55, Centro Cultural "El Puente," San Cristóbal de las Casas, Chiapas, Mexico, 29230; Tel./fax (011) 52-967-8-37-23, fax/voice mail (011) 52-967-8-41-57; spanish@sancristobal.podernet. com.mx.

Spanish Institute of Cuernavaca. Become a participant in Mexican culture by studying Spanish at the Spanish Language Institute in beautiful Cuernavaca on the dates of your choice. Students and professionals from ages 18 to 80 at all language levels study 6 hours daily in classes of 5 students in a small school of excellent reputation dedicated to personal attention and professionalism. U.S. graduate and undergraduate credit available. Caring family stays and full excursion program. Longer stays and additional credits also possible.

Dates: Year round, begin any Monday. Cost: $100 registration, $150 per week tuition, $105 (shared), $144 (private) per week for homestay, all meals, school transportation. Form a group of 12 and your trip is complimentary. Includes insurance. Contact: Kay G. Rafool, Language Link Inc., P.O. Box 3006, Peoria, IL 61612; (800) 552-2051, fax (309) 692-2926; info@langlink. com, www.langlink.com.

Study in Mexico. Beginning to advanced level intensive Spanish language study with a special required seminar in Mexican culture and the opportunity to take integrated courses at the Autonomous Univ. of Guadalajara. Students live in private households. All meals are included.

Dates: Fall, Spring, Summer, academic year. Cost: Summer session I: $1,950, session I and II: $3,000 (1998); Fall or Spring semester $6,200. Contact: Stacy Johnson, Program Coordinator, Beaver College Center for Education Abroad, 450 S. Easton Rd., Glenside, PA 19038-3295; (888) BEAVER-9, fax (215) 572-2174; cea@beaver.edu, www.beaver.edu/cea.

Wisconsin Summer in Oaxaca. Students live in a beautiful and historic setting with local families while they study Spanish language and Latin American literature and culture. All classes are taught in Spanish by local instructors under the direction of a Univ. of Wisconsin director. Includes excursions to local Indian villages and pre-Columbian ruins. Intermediate Spanish language ability required. Application deadline: First Friday in Mar. Late applications considered on a space-available basis.

Dates: Approx. late May-mid-Jul. Cost: Call for current information. Contact: Office of International Studies and Programs, 261 Bascom Hall, Univ. of Wisconsin, 500 Lincoln Dr., Madison, WI 53706; (608) 262-2851, fax (608) 262-6998; peeradv@macc.wisc.edu.

WSU Puebla Summer Program. The WSU Summer Program in Puebla provides an outstanding opportunity for students, teachers, and other interested individuals to study the Spanish language, gain the invaluable experience of living in another country, and earn college credit toward a degree or teaching certification. Students in the program spend 6 weeks in Puebla, either in the Hotel Colonial or in a private home with a Mexican family or both.

Dates: Jun 21-Jul 30. Cost: $1,750. Contact: John H. Koppenhaver, Wichita State Univ., Wichita, KS 67260-0122; (316) 978-3232, fax (316) 978-3777; koppenha@twsuvm.uc.twsu. edu.

Morocco

Passage to Morocco. "Passage to Morocco" is a 3-week study visit consisting of: Standard Arabic study, cultural diversity exploration home stays, lectures on Morocco and related North African issues, as well as visits to historical and cultural attractions.

Dates: Approx. Jun-Jul. Cost: $2,000. Contact: Andrea Akova, National Council on U.S.-Arab Relations, 1140 Connecticut Ave., NW, Suite 1210, Washington, DC 20036; (202) 293-0801, fax (202) 293-0903; pzm@ncusar.org, www.ncusar.org.

Nepal

Sojourn Nepal. Sojourn Nepal is a 12-week program comprised of homestay, language study, lectures, village stay, trekking, and opportunities for apprenticeships in a vast variety of areas. Cultural immersion at its finest.

Dates: Fall and Spring semesters. Cost: $5,000 all inclusive. Airfare not included. Contact: Jennifer Warren, Sojourn Nepal, 2440 N. 56th St., Phoenix, AZ 85008; Tel./fax (602) 840-9197; snepal@aol.com.

Study Abroad in Nepal. Join the Naropa Institute (NCA accredited) program in Nepal. On this program, our students are immersed in Nepali and Tibetan traditions through coursework in meditation, arts and culture, music and dance, Buddhist traditions, language, and independent study/travel. Classes are taught by Nepali and Tibetan scholars and artists, as well as Naropa faculty.

Dates: Early-Sep-mid-Dec. Cost: $7,250 (1998). Includes tuition (12 semester credits), room and board, program expenses. Airfare not included. Contact: Study Abroad Office, The Naropa Institute, 2130 Arapahoe Ave., Boulder, CO 80302; (303) 546-3594, fax (303) 444-0410; peter@naropa.edu.

Wisconsin Year in Nepal. The program provides integrated language training, tutorial instruction, and independent fieldwork projects. Participants attend summer school in U.S. prior to the term abroad for intensive language study and orientation to South Asian life and cultures. The first semester begins with a homestay period, in a 1-month village-study tour. The entire second semester is devoted to fieldwork projects.

Dates: Summer school in Madison: early Jun-mid-Aug; academic program abroad: late Aug-Apr. Cost: One-way airfare from the U.S. West Coast to Nepal, room, board and pocket money while abroad. Summer school and related expenses additional. Call for current information. Contact: Office of International Studies and Programs, 261 Bascom Hall, Univ. of Wisconsin, 500 Lincoln Dr., Madison, WI 53706; (608) 262-2851, fax (608) 262-6998; peeradv@macc.wisc.edu.

Netherlands

School of Child Neuropsychology. Advanced training for graduate students from all countries. Classes (Thursdays and Fridays) are taught in English. Requirement to apply: Master's degree in psychology, medicine, special education, speech pathology, or equivalent qualification. Module A: basics and child neuropsychological syndromes. Module B: child neuropsychological assessment and treatment. Diploma: Satisfactory standards in exams.

Dates: A: Sep-early Nov; B: Jan-early Mar. Cost: A: DFL4,500; B: DFL4,500; A and B: DFL8,200. Contact: Professor Dirk J. Bakker, Ph.D., Director, Paedological Institute, P.O. Box 303, 1115 ZG Duivendrecht, Netherlands; (Tuesday, Thursday, Friday) (011) 31-20-6982131, fax (011) 31-20-6952541.

New Zealand

General Studies in New Zealand. Located in the City of Hamilton at the Univ. of Waikato, students are able to take a variety of courses in several disciplines. The courses concerning New Zealand/Pacific Society and Culture are especially popular with international students. Students are able to enjoy excellent study facilities and participate in organized university activities.

Dates: Semester 1: Jul-Oct; Semester 2: Feb-Jun. Cost: Semester 1 or 2 $4,315; year $7,775. Contact: University Studies Abroad Consortium (USAC), Univ. of Nevada, Reno #323, Reno, NV 89557-0093; (702) 784-6569, fax (702) 784-6010; usac@admin.unr.edu, www.scs.unr.edu/~usac.

Norway

Camp Norway. Camp Norway is an innovative summer program combining fast-paced learning with the direct experience of living in Norway. Camp Norway takes place in Skogn, about a 1-hour drive north of Trond-heim on the beautiful Trond-heimsfjord. Camp Norway provides top-notch language instruction, as well as field trips exploring the spectacular scenery of the area, visits to historic sights and opportunities to develop international friendships. College and high school credit are available.

Dates: Jun 29-Jul 26 (optional post-program tour Jul 26-31). Cost: $2,650 for Sons of Norway members, $2,750 for nonmembers. Cost includes room and board, books, field trips, activities, and transportation from Trondheim to Skogn. (Prices subject to change if significant fluctuations in the exchange rate occur.) Contact: Sons of Norway, 1455 W. Lake St., Minneapolis, MN 55408; (612) 827-3611 or (800) 945-8851; national@sofn.com.

Oslo International Summer School. The International Summer School of the Univ. of Oslo in Norway welcomes qualified participants from all parts of the world from late Jun-early Aug. The ISS is a center for learning in an international context, offering courses in the humanities, social sciences, and environmental protection to more than 500 students from over 80 nations every summer.

Dates: Jun 26-Aug 6. Cost: Approx. $2,425 (basic fees, room and board). Contact: Torild Homstad, Administrator, Univ. of Oslo, International Summer School, North American Admissions-A, St. Olaf College, 1520 St. Olaf Ave., Northfield, MN 55057-1098; (800) 639-0058 or (507) 646-3269, fax (507) 646-3732; iss@stolaf.edu.

Scandinavian Urban Studies Term. Courses include urbanization and development in Scandinavia, Scandinavia in the world, art and literature/perspectives on social change, and Norwegian language. Incorporates many experiential learning activities. Offered in cooperation with Univ. of Oslo, housing in student village with field study-travel to Stockholm, Sweden, and Tallin, Estonia, plus 2 weekend homestays in Norway. Full semester's credit. All majors. No language requirement.

Dates: Sep-Dec. Cost: $9,850 (1998-99). Includes tuition, room and board, field trips. Contact: Rebecca Rassier, Director of Student Services, HECUA, Mail #36, Hamline Univ., 1536 Hewitt Ave., St. Paul, MN 55104-1284; (612) 646-8832 or (800) 554-1089, fax (612) 659-9421; hecua@hamline.edu, www.hamline.edu/~hecua.

Peru

Amauta Language School and Language Link. Become a resident in the former capital of the Incas by studying Spanish at Amauta in Cusco on the dates of your choice. Students and professionals of all ages and all language levels study 4 hours daily in one-on-one classes. Family stays or school residence hotel. Two-week stay includes a trip to incredible Machu Picchu. Also optional loction in Urabamba and study-volunteer packages. Additional weeks possible, from 2-16.

Dates: Start any Monday, year round. Cost: Two weeks $525, includes 4 hours daily private lessons, homestay with all meals or residence hotel without meals, city tour, trip to Machu Picchu, insurance. Contact: Kay G. Rafool, Language Link Inc., P.O. Box 3006, Peoria, IL 61612; (800) 552-2051, fax (309) 692-2926; info@langlink.com, www.langlink.com.

UPC Peru Study Abroad. Study abroad at Universidad Peruana de Ciencias Aplicadas (UPC). Intensive summer language program for beginners and intermediates. Full immersion semester program with coursework conducted at the University in Spanish. Courses include Liberal Arts, Latin American Studies, Communications, Business, Architecture, and Engineering. Features homestays with students' families and trips to Machu Picchu and the Amazon Jungle.

Dates: Spring semester: Feb-Jul; Summer program: Jul-Aug; Fall semester: Aug-Dec. Cost: Semester program: $6,700, includes full room and board, tuition, orientation with daytrips, as well as 2 overnight excursions to Machu Picchu and the Amazon Jungle Summer program: $1,600 includes full room and board, tuition, and visits to museums and ruins, and 1 overnight weekend excursion. Contact: Tal Shaked, Coordinator, UPC-Peru Study Abroad, 65 Williston Rd., Brookline, MA 02146; (617) 731-9276, fax (617) 731-9524; perusa@ici.net, www.upc.edu.pe.

Poland

Penn-in-Warsaw. For students interested in Polish history and culture, as well as international relations, economics, and other business disciplines. Taught in English, this program will acquaint students with the political and economic changes occurring in Poland and provide insight into the conditions for doing business in a changing economy. Short-term internships with Polish or joint-venture institutions will complement class instruction. Dates: May 30-Jul 5. Cost: Tuition $2,968; housing $300. Contact: Penn Summer Abroad, College of General Studies, Univ. of Pennsylvania, 3440 Market St., Suite 100, Philadelphia, PA 19104-3335; (215) 898-5738, fax (215) 573-2053.

Polish Language and Culture. Jagiellonian Univ. (founded in 1364) offers intensive and non-intensive Polish language courses; 8 levels; academic methods. Courses on Polish history, literature, art, film, economy, politics, etc. Cultural program; trips to places of interest. Up to 8 credits for the language and/or 6 credits for other programs (transcripts of studies issued). Dates: Four weeks: Jul 2-29 (arrival Jul 1); 6 weeks: Jul 2-Aug 12 (arrival Jul 1); 3 weeks: Jul 2-22 (arrival Jul 1); Jul 26-Aug 15 (arrival Jul 25). Cost: Four weeks $1,080; 6 weeks $1,410; 3 weeks $800. Plus $30 registration fee. Room, board, and tourist program included.Contact: Ewa Nowakowska, Program Director, Summer School, ul. Garbarska 7a, 31-131, Krakow, Poland; (011) 48 12-4213692, fax (011) 48-12-4227701; plschool@jetta.if. uj.edu.pl; www. if.uj.edu.pl/uj/sl.

Portugal

Wisconsin in Portugal. Study at the Univ. of Coimbra, one of the world's oldest universities, founded in 1285. Students enroll in the Portuguese Language and Culture course for international students in the Faculty of Arts. Courses in Portuguese grammar, conversation, composition, history, art, geography. Advanced study includes linguistics and literature. Students with advanced language skills may register for regular university courses. Application deadline: Second Friday in Oct for spring, first Friday in Feb for fall or year. Dates: Mid-Oct-mid-Jun. Semester or year option. Cost: Call for current information. Contact: Office of International Studies and Programs, 261 Bascom Hall, Univ. of Wisconsin, 500 Lincoln Dr., Madison, WI 53706; (608) 262-2851, fax (608) 262-6998; peeradv@macc. wisc.edu.

Russia and the NIS

ACTR Russian Language Program. ACTR's semester, academic year, and summer programs maximize linguistic and cultural immersion into Russian society. The academic program emphasizes the development of practical speaking, listening, reading, and writing skills, while providing participants with a structured opportunity to learn about contemporary Russian society and cuture in country. Dates: Summer, academic year, Fall, and Spring. Cost: Vary according to program and length of stay. Contact: Margaret Stephenson, ACTR, 1776 Massachusetts Ave., NW, Suite 700, Washington, DC 20036; (202) 833-7522, fax (202) 833-7523; stephens@actr.org.

Scandinavia

University Student Exchange. The Univ. of Jyväskylä, Finland offers graduate and post-graduate degrees and programs within the faculties of Education, Social Sciences, Humanities, Mathematics and Natural Sciences, Sport and Health Sciences, and School of Business and Economics. Dates: Jan-May, Sep-Dec. Cost: Free for degree and exchange students. Contact: Univ. of Jyväskylä, P.O. Box 35, FIN-40351 Jyväskylä, Finland; (011) 358-14-601079, fax (011) 358-14-601061; intl@jyu.fi, www.jyu.fi.

Spain

Academic Year Abroad Madrid. Direct registration at the Universidades Reunids of the Compultense primarily in the Facultad de Filosofia y Letras but including social sciences: advanced (virtually graduate) courses possible at the Compultense. AYA-sponsored orientation and tutorials. Intensive language at Universitas Nebrissensis. Optional room and board with Madrileña families and cultural activities.

Dates: Early Sep-end Jan; late Jan-end May; mid-Jun. Cost: Term $7,550; year $12,800. Includes tuition, tutorials, room and board, cultural activities. Contact: Dr. A.M. Cinquemani, Academic Year Abroad, P.O. 733, Stone Ridge, NY 12484-0733; fax (914) 687-2470; aya@ulster.net, www.studyabroad.com/aya.

BCA Program in Barcelona. Earn 14-16 credits per semester at Universidad de Barcelona, with a fall 4-week intensive language training and orientation, field trips, and an extended study tour to Madrid and Toledo or Andulcía. Internships and practica available. Students from all U.S. colleges and universities accepted. Intermediate level college Spanish required. Courses in all academic disciplines taught by university professors.

Dates: Fall: Sep-Dec or Jan; Spring: Jan-Jun; Year: Sep-Jun. Cost: $18,845 (academic year); $10,545 (semester). Includes international transportation, room and board, tuition, insurance, group travel in country. Contact: Beverly S. Eikenberry, 605 E. College Ave., North Manchester, IN 46962; (219) 982-5238, fax (219) 982-7755; bca@manchester.edu, www.studyabroad.com/bca.

CLIC of Sevilla and Language Link. Your choice of intensive groups of 3-6 students or completely private classes. Professional adults, college students, and all Spanish levels accommodated in a very well organized school. Programs of 2-16 weeks starting on most Mondays. Graduate and undergraduate credit through accredited U.S. university. Earn 6 units in 5 weeks. Homestays or residence hall. In Jul and Aug beach campus on Isla Cristina on the Costa de la Luz. Combine 2 weeks there with 2 weeks in Seville. Summer program also for high school teens in Jul. Additional weekly activities included.

Dates: Year round. New classes begin every Monday. Cost: Four hours daily of group (3-6) classes and homestay: 2 weeks $610; Isla Cristina program combined with Seville: 4 weeks $1,235. Includes registration, tuition, insurance, accommodation arrangements fee, homestay with 2 meals or residence hall. Contact: Kay G. Rafool, Language Link Inc., P.O. Box 3006, Peoria, IL 61612; (800) 552-2051, fax (309) 692-2926; info@langlink.com; www.langlink.com.

Escuela Internacional. Escuela Internacional offers quality programs in Spanish language and culture with U.S. undergraduate credits in Madrid, Salamanca, and Malaga. Our qualified teachers and small classes (maximum 12 students per class) guarantee you a successful program. Stay with a selected family or in a shared apartment. Enjoy our extensive afternoon activities and weekend excursions. Our professionalism, enthusiasm, and personal touch will make your experience in Spain memorable and fun.

Dates: Year round, 2-48 weeks. Cost: From PTS59,000 for 2 weeks (includes 15 hours per week instruction, room and books) to PTS120,000 (includes 30 hours per week instruction, room and full board, books, activities, and excursion). Contact: Escuela Internacional, Midori Ishizaka, Director of Admissions, c/o Talamanca 10, 28807 Alcalá de Henares, Madrid, Spain; (011) 34-91-8831264, fax (011) 34-91-8831301; escuelai@ergos.es, www.ergos.es/escuelai.

Intensive Spanish Courses. CLIC, the newest affiliate for International House, offers intensive Spanish courses for all levels as well as summer courses in Isla Cristina on the coast. Accommodations are carefully selected and we have a varied cultural program and exchanges. The school occupies 2 stately houses in the old part of the city and combines professionalism and a friendly atmosphere. Approved North American academic credits.

Dates: Year round. Cost: Approx. $825 for a 4-week Spanish course and homestay, individual room, 2 meals per day. Contact: Bernhard Roters, CLIC-International House Seville, Calle Santa Ana 11, 41002 Sevilla, Spain; (011) 34-5-4374500, fax (011) 34-5-371806; clic@arrakis.es, www.clic.es.

International Program in Toledo. Participants with 2 years of Spanish select from a wide variety of Spanish language, Latin American, and European studies courses taught in Spanish. Summer term requires only 1 year Spanish. Monday-Thursday classes are enhanced by excursions. Housing available in an historic residence or with Spanish families. Univ. of Minnesota accredited.

Dates: 1998-99 Fall and/or Spring semesters, Summer term. Cost: $8,250 (Fall or Spring), $3,490 (Summer). Includes tuition, study abroad and registration fees, room and board, and 1-day excursions. Contact: The Global Campus, Univ. of Minnesota, 102 Nicholson Hall, 216 Pillsbury Dr. SE, Minneapolis, MN 55455-0138; (612) 626-9000, fax (612) 626-8009; umabroad@tc.umn.edu, www.umabroad.umn.edu.

La Coruña Summer Program. Intensive language program providing participants with the opportunity to study Spanish language, civilization, and culture in one of the most beautiful regions in Spain. Cultural immersion is further achieved through homestays with Spanish families. Cultural excursions include Madrid and nearby Santiago de Compostela, site of the famous pilgrimage of Saint James.

Dates: Approx. Jul 1-31. Cost: Approx. $1,700 (tuition and room and board). Con-

tact: Study Abroad Advisor, Central Washington Univ., Office of International Studies and Programs, 400 E. 8th Ave., Ellensburg, WA 98926-7408; (509) 963-3612, fax (509) 963-1558; goabroad@cwu.edu.

Painting in Barcelona. A celebrated Spanish faculty made up of Tom Carr and Carme Miquel will conduct a 3-week advanced painting workshop at the spacious studio of Escola d'Arts Plastiques i Disseny "Llotja." Included are 3 museum tours to the Antonio Tapies Foundation, the Miro Foundation, and the Picasso Museum. Three credits.

Dates: Jul. Cost: $2,850. Includes airfare, double occupancy rooms, continental breakfast daily, and 3 tours. Contact: Dora Riomayor, Director of International Studies, School of Visual Arts, 209 E. 23rd St., New York, NY 10010-3994; (212) 592-2543.

Penn-in-Alicante. For students interested in the language, literature, and culture of Spain, this program combines classroom instruction with visits to points of cultural and historical interest, including Madrid and Toledo. Students live with local families.

Dates: Jun 29-Jul 25. Cost: Tuition $2,968; room and board $1,650. Contact: Penn Summer Abroad, College of General Studies, Univ. of Pennsylvania, 3440 Market St., Suite 100, Philadelphia, PA 19104-3335; (215) 898-5738, fax (215) 573-2053.

Semester in Spain. Semester, year, summer, and January terms for high school graduates, college students, and adult learners. Beginning, intermediate, and advanced Spanish language studies along with Spanish literature, culture, history, and art. All courses taught in Spanish by native Spaniards. Four courses per semester, 4 credits each. Homestays are arranged for all students. January term and summer terms also.

Dates: Winter: Jan 4-23; Spring: Jan 27-May 21; Summer: May 31-Jun 25 and/or Jun

28-Jul 21; Fall: Aug 26-Dec 18. Cost: Fall or Spring $7,950; year approx. $15,900; Summer and Jan term approx. $2,000 each term. Includes tuition, books, room and board. Contact: Debra Veenstra, U.S. Coordinator, Semester in Spain, Dept. TA, 6601 W. College Dr., Palos Heights, IL 60463; (800) 748-0087 or (708) 239-4766, fax (708) 239-3986.

Spanish and Basque Studies (Bilbao). The Getxo-Bilbao area offers intensive language studies (Spanish or Basque) that fulfill up to 2 years of university language requirements in 1 semester, plus courses in history, political science, art, culture, economics, teacher education, literature, etc. Program organized field trips, housing, and many local university activities at this seaside city.

Dates: Spring semester: Jan-May; Fall semester: Aug-Dec 16. Cost: Fall or Spring semester $4,390; year $7,190. Contact: University Studies Abroad Consortium (USAC), Univ. of Nevada, Reno #323, Reno, NV 89557-0093; (702) 784-6569, fax (702) 784-6010; usac@admin.unr.edu, www.scs.unr.edu/~usac.

Spanish and Basque Studies (San Sebastian). San Sebastian offers intensive language (Spanish or Basque) studies that fulfill up to 2 years of university language requirements in 1 semester, plus courses in history, literature, political science, economics, art, teacher education, etc. Program organized field trips to Madrid and elsewhere, housing, and many local university activities in this beautiful seaside resort.

Dates: Spring semester: Jan-May; Summer sessions: May-Jul, Jun-Jul, Aug; Fall semester: Aug-Dec. Cost: Fall or Spring semester $6,290; year $9,880; Jun or Jul $1,980; Aug $1,610; Jun and Jul $3,680; Jun, Jul or Aug $3,190; Jun, Jul, and Aug $4,680. Contact: University Studies Abroad Consortium (USAC), Univ. of Nevada, Reno #323, Reno, NV 89557-0093; (702) 784-6569, fax (702) 784-6010; usac@admin. unr.edu, www.scs.unr.edu/~usac.

Spanish in Malaga. Widely recognized to be one of Spain's leading language schools, Malaca Instituto offers language and cultural programs at all levels for adults of all ages. Qualifying American students can apply for academic credit; our programs carry the EAQUALS guarantee of quality (see www.eaquals.org). For further details see also www.malacainst-ch.es.

Dates: Courses begin every 2 weeks from Jan 5. Cost: Two-week tuition PTS43,700; 2-week tuition plus accommodations from PTS77,500. Contact: Bob Burger, Malaca Instituto, c/o Cortada 6, Cerrado de Calderon, 29018 Malaga, Spain; (011) 34-5-229-32-42, fax (011) 34-5-229-63-16.

Spanish Language and Civilization. IEMA is known for its excellent teachers and training on practical Spanish and communicative skills. Situated near Madrid, in a famous 11th building, protected by UNESCO. In Avila, unlike in other regions of Spain and South America, standard Spanish is spoken. The best walled city of the world. Carefully selected homestays.

Dates: Year round. Cost: $450 and up. Contact: Dr. Rainer Rutkowski, IEMA, c/o Martin Carramolino, 6, E-05001 Avila, Spain; (011) 34-9-20222773, fax (011) 34-9-20252955; www.worldwide.edu/spain/iema.

Spanish Language and Culture. Offered by a Spanish higher education institution. All grades. Small groups (about 15 students). Three different accommodations options: halls of residence, host family, and shared flats (self-catering). Summer courses (Jul-Aug) and permanent. An attractive cultural-touristic program is also available. Special rates for shorter periods (minimum 1 month).

Dates: Permanent course: Oct 1998-Jun 1999. Summer courses: Jul 1-28, Aug 3-29 (1998). Cost: Summer course: 1 month PTS70,000; 2 months PTS100,000; full academic year PTS190,000; 4 month-session PTS100,000. Contact: Cursos de Español,

Lengua Extranjera, Universidad de León, Avda. Facultad 25, 24071, León, España; (011) 34-87-291646 or 291650, fax (011) 34-87-291693; neggeuri@isidoro.unileon.es.

Study in Seville. Semester, academic year, January and summer terms in Seville. Intensive immersion. Classes taught in Spanish by Spanish faculty. Intermediate and advanced-level courses are offered during Jan and semester programs. All levels are offered during summer. Resident Director, homestays, 35-room mansions, library, computer lab, e-mail, incuded study/tours, "intercambios" with Spaniards, scholarships, internships, credits transferable, free video.

Dates: Jan term; Spring: Feb-May; Summer I: Jun; Summer II: Jul. Fall: Call for details. Cost: Semester $8,175, Jan term $2,060, Summer term $1,995. Includes tuition, double occupancy room and full board, laundry, study visits, orientation, health insurance, enrollment, activity and computer fees including e-mail account. Contact: Dr. Judith Ortiz, Director U.S., Center for Cross-Cultural Study, 446 Main St., Amherst, MA 01002; (800) 377-2621, fax (413) 256-1968; cccs@crocker.com, www.cccs.com.

Summer Study in Spain. Four-week study at host institution in Alicante, on the Mediterranean Southeastern coast. Weekend trips to Valencia, Barcelona, Ibiza, 1-week travel through Granada, Sevilla, Cordoba, Madrid. All levels of language instruction. Courses in literature and culture. Independent studies in various aspects of sociocultural, political life in Spain. Attendance at cultural events.

Dates: May-Jul. Cost: $2,950 includes airfare NY-Madrid-NY, ground transportation and accommodations in Spain; while in Alicante, room and board with host family or in locally rented apartment and central dining facility; 6-credit tuition, transcript, required textbooks, insurance, tickets for visits to museums and historic sites. Contact: Dr. Agustin

Bernal, CB 231, Dept. of Modern Languages, Eastern Connecticut State Univ., Willimantic, CT 06226; (860) 465-5273/4540/4571, fax (860) 465-4575; bernala@ecsu. ctstateu.edu.

Univ. of Salamanca. Founded in the early 13th century, the Univ. of Salamanca is one of the most distinguished centers of learning in Europe. SUNY Cortland is celebrating the 32nd consecutive year in this "City of the Golden Stones." The lives of Cervantes, Lope de Vega, Santa Teresa, and Miguel de Unamuno were all linked to the Univ. of Salamanca. Fields of study include Spanish language and literature, humanities, social sciences. Special course on the Arab influence on Spain is available in the spring semester. Upper division and some qualified sophomores may apply. Requires at least 4 semesters college-level Spanish for fall, 6 semesters for spring. Homestays.

Dates: Fall: early Sep-mid-Dec; Spring: early Jan-mid-Jun. Cost estimate: $4,450, Spring: 1 trimester $3,000, 1 trimester (6 weeks) and special course on Arab Influence in Spain $5,500. Estimates include full-day orientation before departure, application fee, room and food allowance, mandatory Spanish insurance, airfare, transportation from Madrid to Salamanca, books and supplies, insurance, walking tour of Salamanca, 2 excursions, administrative fees and program operation costs. SUNY tuition not included. Contact: Office of International Programs, Box 2000, SUNY Cortland, Cortland, NY 13045; (607) 753-2209, fax (607) 753-5989; studyabroad@ cortland.edu, www.study abroad.com/suny/cortland.

Universidad (Complutense) de Madrid. A graduate and undergraduate program at the Universidad (Complutense) de Madrid for students interested in studying courses in language, literature, culture and civilization, composition, art history, philosophy of Spain. Students are taught by full-time faculty members from the Universidad (Complutense) de Madrid, the most prestigious university in

Spain. A lot of extra activities and excursions are organized for students.

Dates: Summer program: Jul; semester: Fall, Winter, Spring. Cost: Summer: total cost from $1,985 including airfare; year: $10,250 total cost including airfare. Contact: Modern Language Studies Abroad, P.O. Box 623, Griffith, IN 46319; Tel./fax (219) 838-9460.

Sweden

Uppsala Univ. Int'l. Summer Session. Sweden's oldest academic summer program focuses on learning the Swedish language. All levels from beginners to advanced. Additional courses in Swedish history, social institutions, arts in Sweden, Swedish film. Excursions every Friday. Extensive evening program includes both lectures and entertainment. Single rooms in dormitories or apartments. Open to both students and adults. Credit possible.

Dates: Jun-Aug; Jun-Jul; Jul-Aug. Contact program director for exact dates. Cost: SEK22,400 (approx. $2,740) for the 8-week session, SEK12,000 (approx. $1,500) for the 4-week session. Includes room, some meals, all classes, evening and excursion program. Contact: Dr. Nelleke van Oevelen Dorrestijn, Uppsala Univ. Int. Summer Session, Box 1972, 751 47 Uppsala, Sweden; (011) 31-71-541-4955, fax (011) 31-71-541-7705; nduiss@wxs.nl, www.uuiss.uu.se.

Switzerland

American Studies. Two programs of 5 months of studies each at the undergraduate and pre-MBA levels recognized by American accredited universities as one academic year in terms of transfer credits (up to 36). Learn French and get a European background in a truly multi-cultural environment.

Dates: Feb-Jun or Aug-Dec. Cost: Tuition, insurance, lodging, activities approx. $11,500 total. Contact: Lemania College, Ms. E. Perni,

International Admissions Office, Chemin de Préville 3, 1001 Lausanne, Switzerland; (011) 41-21-320-15-01, fax (011) 41-21-312-67-00; info.lemania@lshp1.fastnet.ch.

Univ. of Lausanne, Cours de Vacances. Courses are taught in French in 4 series of 3 weeks each. Beginners courses last at least 6 weeks. One or more series may be attended. Classes are constituted according to the students' tested level of competence. Students can also practice sports at the Sports Centre or use our Multimediacentre (videos, tapes, and Macintosh).

Dates: Series I: Jul 5-23; Series II: Jul 26-Aug 13; Series III: Aug 16-Sep 3; Series IV: Sep 6-Sep 24. Cost: CHF470 for 3 weeks; CHF1,050 for beginners (6 weeks). Contact: Univ. of Lausanne, Cours de Vacances, BFSH2, CH-1015 Lausanne, Switzerland; (011) 41-21-692-3090, fax (011) 41-21-692-3085; CoursDeVacances@cvac.unil.ch, www.unil.ch/cvac.

Geneva Study Abroad. An opportunity for a part-time voluntary work assignment in which the student can earn academic credit. Many times our students find themselves in responsible non-routine assignments. All students are enrolled in a full course load of at least 12 semester hours.

Dates: Fall and Spring semesters each academic year. Cost: $9,338. Includes program fee, transportation package, medical insurance, tuition, and security deposit. Contact: Phyllis L. Dreyer, CICP-Kent State Univ., P.O. Box 5190, Kent, OH 44242-0001; (330) 672-7980, fax (330) 672-4025; pdreyer@kentvm.kent.edu, www.kent.edu/cicp.

Univ. of Geneva Summer Courses. French language and civilization at all levels, beginners to advanced. All instructors have a university diploma. Excursions and visits to Geneva and its surroundings. Class of 15-20 students. Minimum age 17.

Dates: Jul 12-30, Aug 2-20, Aug 23-Sep 10, Sep 13-Oct 1. Cost: SFR470 for 3 weeks (tuition). Contact: Mr. Gérard Benz, Univ. of Geneva, Summer Courses, rue de Candolle 3, CH-1211 Geneva 4, Switzerland; (011) 41-22-705-74-34, fax (011) 41-22-705-74-39; elcfete@uni2a.unige.ch, www.unige.ch/lettres/elcf/coursete/cournet.html.

Syria

Summer in Syria. Summer in Syria is a 6-week study visit. The program consists of 4 weeks of courses at the Univ. of Aleppo that include history, culture, and anthropology of Syria. One week of archaeological site visits, and 1 week exploring Syria's numerous historical and cultural attractions.

Dates: Jun-Jul. Cost: $3,000. Contact: Andrea Akova, National Council on U.S.-Arab Relations, 1140 Connecticut Ave., NW, Suite 1210, Washington, DC 20036; (202) 293-0801, fax (202) 293-0903; sis@ncusar.org, www.ncusar.org.

Thailand

College Year in Thailand. The program at Chiang Mai Univ. features Thai language study, subject tutorials, and a fieldwork project. Students attend summer school in Madison before the term abroad for intensive Thai language study as well as cultural and academic orientation. Application deadline: Second Friday in Feb. Late applications are considered on a space-available basis.

Dates: Summer school in Madison Jun-mid-Aug; academic year abroad late Aug-May. Also fall semester option late Aug-mid Dec. Cost: Call for current information. Contact: Office of International Studies and Programs, 261 Bascom Hall, Univ. of Wisconsin, 500 Lincoln Dr., Madison, WI 53706; (608) 262-2851, fax (608) 262-6998; peeradv@macc.wisc.edu.

Southeast Asian Studies (Bangkok). Diverse courses in culture, language, economics, busi-

ness, society, and religions provide a fascinating, well-balanced approach to Southeast Asia. Program-organized field trips, student residence halls, and many university activities at one of Thailand's most modern universities.

Dates: Spring semester: Jan-May; Summer session: Jun-Aug; Fall semester: Aug-Dec. Cost: One semester: $2,680; year: $4,380; Summer session: $1,480. Contact: University Studies Abroad Consortium (USAC), Univ. of Nevada, Reno #323, Reno, NV 89557-0093; (702) 784-6569, fax (702) 784-6010; usac@admin.unr.edu, www.scs.unr.edu/~usac.

Turkey

Live and Study in Istanbul. Here is your chance to live in Istanbul for 7 weeks while studying at Bosphorous Univ. All courses taught in English by Bosphorous faculty; a wide variety of courses are available. Resident director arranges orientation program and excursions. Housing in residence hall with full board plan. No knowledge of Turkish necessary.

Dates: Late Jun-mid-Aug. Cost: $3,300 (1998) includes tuition in Turkey, registration, room and partial board, orientation, excursions, medical emergency evacuation insurance, support services. Contact: Illinois Programs Abroad, Univ. of Illinois, 115 International Studies Bldg., 910 S. 5th St., Champaign, IL 61820; (800) 531-4404, fax (217) 244-0249; ipa@uiuc.edu, www.uiuc.edu/providers/ips/sao.

Pitzer College in Turkey. This program emphasizes the religious forces that shape personal and communal identity among Turkish villages and includes language study at Middle East Technical Univ. in Ankara and family stays in traditional villages and Istanbul.

Dates: Aug-Dec; Feb-Jun. Cost: 1998-99 costs: $14,720 tuition, room and board, roundtrip airfare, field trips, evacuation insurance. Contact: External Studies, Pitzer College, 1050 N. Mills Ave., Claremont, CA 91711; (909) 621-8104, fax (909) 621-0518; external_studies@pitzer.edu, www.pitzer.edu/academics/ilcenter/external_studies/index.html.

Turkey by Land and Sea. Unique itineraries combine sailing the Turkish coast, touring legendary archaeological sites, and visiting exotic Istanbul. Designed for those who wouldn't normally consider a group tour. Sixteen or 17 days, 8-14 guests, licensed professional guides (fluent in English), excellent accommodations.

Dates: Jun, Sep, Oct. Cost: $2,800-$3,200. Contact: Dick Linford, ECHO: The Wilderness Co., 6529 Telegraph Ave., Oakland, CA 94609; (800) 652-3246, fax (510) 652-3987; echo@echotrips.com, www.echotrips.com.

United Kingdom and Ireland

American College Dublin. Study abroad in Dublin for a summer, semester, or a year to earn U.S. college credit for courses in: business, psychology, sociology, history, literature, liberal arts, and tourism. Opportunities for internship and study tour to Europe are available. Accommodations are provided in a residence hall of Georgian architecture.

Dates: Spring: Jan 11-May 7, Summer and Fall call for details. Cost: Spring $8,150. Summer and Fall. Call for details. Contact: Coordinator, American College Dublin Study Abroad Program, 3601 N. Military Trail, Boca Raton, FL 33431; (800) 453-8306, fax (561) 989-4983; acdinfo@aol.com, www.cybervillage.com/acdireland.

Art and Design in Britain. Studio Art (including painting, sculpture, graphic and industrial design, ceramics, printmaking, film, etc.) programs offered at 6 British universities: Chelsea College of Art and Design, Glasgow School of Art, Norwich School of Art and Design, Univ. of Northumbria, and Univ. of Wolverhampton, and Central St. Martin's College of Art and Design.

Courses integrated with British students. Housing in university residence halls or shared apartments. Resident director organizes orientation program, monitors students' academic progress.

Dates: Sep-Dec, Jan-Jun. Cost: Varies by programs: semester $6,000-$9,800; year $13,900-$14,850 (1998-99). Includes tuition, housing (except Chelsea and Central St. Martin), support services, medical emergency evacuation insurance. Contact: Illinois Programs Abroad, Univ. of Illinois at Urbana-Champaign, 115 International Studies Bldg., 910 S. 5th St., Champaign, IL 61820; (800) 531-4404, fax (217) 244-0249; ipa@uiuc.edu, www.uiuc.edu/providers/ips/sao.

BCA Program in Cheltenham. Earn 15-16 credits per semester at the Cheltenham and Gloucester College of Higher Education with a 2-week orientation in country, field trips, and an extended study tour to Wales or Kent. Courses in all academic disciplines including women's studies. Internships and practica available. Students accepted from all U.S. colleges and universities.

Dates: Fall: Sep-Dec; Spring: Feb-May; Year: Sep-May. Cost: $18,845 (year); $10,545 (semester). Includes international transportation, room and board, tuition, insurance, group travel in country. Contact: Beverly S. Eikenberry, 605 E. College Ave., North Manchester, IN 46962; (219) 982-5238, fax (219) 982-7755; bca@manchester.edu, www.studyabroad.com/bca.

British Studies at Oxford. This program of study in one of the world's most prestigious universities offers undergraduate and graduate credit in Art History, Business, Communication, Drama, Education, English Literature, History, and Political Science taught by Oxford Univ. professors. The participants live in private rooms tidied daily by the college staff, who also serve 3 bountiful and tasty meals a day in the Great Hall. Field trips are an integral part of each course as well as the group trips to the theater in Stratford-upon-Avon and London.

Dates: Contact program director for details.

Cost: $2,995 for 3 weeks; $5,650 for 6 weeks. Includes 4 or 8 credits, travel in Britain for course related events, theater, entrance to museums, dinners in country inns, and many field trips. Overseas travel not included. Contact: Dr. M.B. Pigott, Director, British Studies at Oxford, 322 Wilson Hall, Oakland Univ., Rochester, MI 48309-4401; (248) 652-3405 or (248) 370-4131, fax (248) 650-9107; pigott@oakland.edu, www.oakland.edu/oxford.

College of William and Mary. Summer in Cambridge. Five-week program in English studies with instruction and credit by William and Mary faculty; courses in literature, history, and film studies; lodging in Christ's College, Cambridge with breakfast; excursions with meals include possible weekend trip to France.

Dates: Jul 2-Aug 6. Cost: $3,140 (1998) includes instruction, credit from William and Mary, most books, single room with breakfast in Cambridge Univ. college, excursions with meals and lodging (if overnight). Additional costs include airfare, 2 meals per day in Cambridge, personal travel, and incidentals. Contact: Ann M. Moore, College of William and Mary, Programs Abroad, Dept. TA, P.O. Box 8795, Williamsburg, VA 23187-8795; (757) 221-3594, fax (757) 221-3597; annmoo2@facstaff.wm.edu, www.wm.edu/academics/reves/cambridge.html.

The European Fashion Industry. London College of Fashion is the only college in the British university sector to specialize in fashion. Unique 4-credit summer program; specialist courses in design, marketing and merchandising, cosmetics and beauty; historical and cultural studies; plus optional 4-week internship.

Dates: Jun-Jul. Cost: £1,450 for 4 weeks. London accommodations not included. Contact: Alanah Cullen, Business Manager, DALI at London College of Fashion, 20 John Princes St., London W1M 0BJ, England; (011) 44-171-514-7411, fax (011) 44-171-514-7490; lcfdali@london-fashion.ac.uk.

Fashion Design/Merchandising. London College of Fashion is the only College in the British university sector to specialize in fashion. Located in the center of London, we offer you: a choice of 2 specialist programs, each covering seven subject areas; 16 credits per program; internship opportunities, plus optional Paris field trip.

Dates: Spring semester: Jan-Mar; Fall semester: Sep-Dec. Cost: (1998/1999 tuition fees) £2,425 per 12-week semester. Airfare and accommodations not included. Contact: Alanah Cullen, Business Manager, DALI at London College of Fashion, 20 John Princes St., London W1M 0BJ, England; (011) 44-171-514-7411, fax (011) 44-171-514-7490; lcfdali@london-fashion.ac.uk.

General Studies (Brighton). Brighton offers courses in many disciplines: art, business, sports science, engineering, computing, geography, design, education, math, etc. Organized field trips, housing in student residence halls. Summer graduate program in teacher education. Only 45 minutes from London.

Dates: Spring: Jan-Jun; Summer: late Jun-early Aug; Fall semester: Sep-Dec. Cost: Fall or Spring: $3,140; year: $5,480; Summer: $2,160. Contact: University Studies Abroad Consortium (USAC), Univ. of Nevada, Reno #323, Reno, NV 89557-0093; (702) 784-6569, fax (702) 784-6010; usac@admin.unr.edu, www.scs.unr.edu/~usac.

General Studies (Reading). Reading offers courses in nearly every academic discipline: art, business, literature, performing arts, engineering, computing, geography, education, agriculture, etc. Housing in student residence halls. Only 25 minutes from London.

Dates: Winter: Jan-Mar; Apr-Jul; Fall semester: Sep-Dec 11. Cost: Fall, Winter or Spring semester: $3,480; Winter or Spring quarter: $2,950; year: $8,860. Contact: University Studies Abroad Consortium (USAC), Univ. of Nevada, Reno #323, Reno, NV 89557-0093; (702) 784-6569, fax (702) 784-

Study Programs

6010; usac@admin.unr.edu, www.scs.unr. edu/~usac.

Harlaxton College. Harlaxton College is owned and operated by the Univ. of Evansville in Indiana. Therefore, all courses are U.S. accredited and usually transfer easily. Students live and study in a magnificent 19th-century Victorian manor house in the English Midlands. Assistance is available with air arrangements and airport pickup; optional field trips are available throughout England, Ireland, Scotland, Wales, and the Continent. Harlaxton is a full-service study abroad program with help every step of the way.

Dates: Spring: Jan 7-Apr 20; Fall: Aug 27-Dec 9. Cost: $10,500 per semester (1998-99). Includes tuition, room and board. Contact: Suzy Lantz, Harlaxton Coordinator, Univ. of Evansville, 1800 Lincoln Ave., Evansville, IN 47722; (800) UKMANOR or (812) 488-1040; sl5@evansville.edu.

Internships in Dublin. Interns live with families or in apartments. Two programs available: 6-credit internship plus 9-credit classwork in Irish Studies through the Institute of Public Administration or full-time (15-16 credits) internship. IPA placements may be in Parliament, municipal government, health care administration, radio/TV, and at the *Irish Times*. Full-time placements available in social services, communication, film, advertising and others. Fields: public administration, parliamentary internships, political science, technology, finance, health and communications. Fifteen-16 credits per semester, 10 for Summer. Prerequisites: 2.5 GPA for traditional full-time internships, 3.0 for IPA internships. Adaptability and maturity. Strong performance in major. Junior or senior status. Application materials: SUNY application.

Dates: Fall: early Sep-mid-Dec (application deadline Feb 1); Spring: early Jan-late Apr (application deadline Sep 1); Summer: early Jun-mid-Aug (application deadline Feb 1). Cost: 1998 estimates: IPA $6,737 for Dublin internships (full-time) $5,793; Summer $4,350

(Dublin internships only, IPA not available). Estimates include full-day orientation before departure, application fee, room and board, food allowance, health and accident insurance, roundtrip airfare from N.Y., bus pass. SUNY tuition not included. Contact: Office of International Programs, Box 2000, SUNY Cortland, Cortland, NY 13045; (607) 753-2209, fax (607) 753-5989; studyabroad@cortland.edu, www.studyabroad.com/suny/cortland.

Ireland and Northern Ireland. Twelve program opportunities in the Republic and the North. University study and special subject area programs including internships in the Irish parliament. Program provides a full range of services including a full-time resident director and staff in Dublin, orientation, homestay, and guaranteed housing.

Dates: Fall, Spring, academic year, and Summer. Semesters and terms. Cost: Varies. Call for current fees. Contact: Meghan Mazick, Beaver College Center for Education Abroad, 450 S. Easton Rd., Glenside, PA 19038-3295; (888) BEAVER-9, fax (215) 572-2174; cea@beaver.edu, www.beaver.edu/cea.

Ithaca College London Center. British and international faculty teach undergraduate courses in business, communications, humanities, music, social sciences, and theater. Field trips and excursions to various sites throughout London and the U.K. are an integral part of the curriculum. Internships are available to juniors and seniors majoring in art history, business, communications, economics, English, history, politics, psychology, sociology, and theater arts. A special intensive drama program is also offered.

Dates: Jan 5-May 1. Cost: Approx. $15,500 per semester. Includes tuition, fees, books, room and board, college-sponsored excursions, and airfare. Costs may vary depending on students' lifestyles and spending habits. Contact: Andrea M. Kiely, Coordinator of Study Abroad, International Programs, Ithaca College, 214 Muller Ctr., Ithaca, NY 14850-7150; (607) 274-3306, fax (607) 274-1515.

Junior Year Abroad Program. The Faculty of Arts accepts a limited number of North American students who attend the same courses and sit for the same examinations as Irish students. GPA of 3.0 is required.

Dates: Sep-Dec, Jan-Apr. Cost: Tuition and fees: year £5,550, semester £3,000. Contact: JYA Office, Faculty of Arts, Univ. College Dublin, Belfield, Dublin 4, Ireland; (011) 353-1-706-8248, fax (011) 353-1-283-0328; www.ucd.ie.

Laban Centre London. Program for students outside the U.K. to spend 1 year (2 semesters) in London studying contemporary dance, choreography, and related subjects. Courses are planned for your individual needs and credits are given for subjects taken. Please ask for a booklet.

Dates: Sep-Jul. Contact: Admissions Officer, Laban Centre London, Laurie Grove, London SE14 6NH, U.K.; (011) 44-181-692-4070, fax (011) 44-181-694-8749; info@laban.co.uk.

The London Theater Program. Study with some of Britain's most distinguished actors and directors. Undergraduate program co-sponsored by Sarah Lawrence College and the British American Drama Academy exposes you to the rigor and excitement of professional British training in acting. Frequent trips to West End and fringe productions.

Dates: Sep-Apr (may attend semester or year). Cost: $14,635 (1 semester) includes all academic expenses, field trips, cultural activities, and room. Contact: Prema Samuel, Sarah Lawrence College, Box CR, Bronxville, NY 10708; (800) 873-4752.

North American Institute for Study Abroad. Semester, academic year, or summer term. Two to 6 courses per semester. Graduate credit available in summer courses. Courses taught in English. Typical class size 25. Less than 25 percent of each class are program participants. Other students are from host institution, host country, other programs. Seminars and tutorials also used for instruction. Unstructured time each week to be used at students' leisure.

Dates: Late Sep-mid-Dec (Fall), early Jan-late May (Spring). Approx. dates. Apply by Jul 1 for Fall or full year, by Oct 1 for Spring, and by Apr 1 for Summer. Cost: 1997-1998: semester $6,000-$8,500, year $11,500-$16,500, Summer $1,050-$3,190. Contact: Elizabeth Strauss, Associate Director, or Amy Armstrong, Operations Manager, North American Institute for Study Abroad, P.O. Box 279, Riverside, PA 17868; (717) 275-5099, fax (717) 275-1644.

OASP Visiting Student Program. OASP's students become Visiting Students of the Univ. of Oxford and associate students of Lady Margaret Hall, an undergraduate college. Individual instruction in liberal arts and other subjects plus Univ. lectures. Tuition arranged to meet home university requirements in most cases. Orientation, excursions, single rooms, bursaries, e-mail. Ten years experience.

Dates: Term or academic year. Cost: Term: $8,950; year: $22,400 includes tuition, housing, fees, lectures. Contact: E. Derow, OASP Visiting Student Program in cooperation with Lady Margaret Hall, Oxford, England, 7B Dunstan Rd., Headington, Oxford OX3 9BY, England; Tel./fax (011) 44-1865-762495; 100645.3460@compuserve.com, http://ourworld.compuserve.com/homepages/oasp.

Oxford Advanced Studies Program. The program is an academic and cultural summer course held at Magdalen College, one of Oxford's oldest and most famous colleges. Students select 2 or 3 subjects from a wide choice; teaching is in a combination of small seminar groups and individual tutorials. The social and cultural program is packed with a variety of exciting experiences.

Dates: Jul. Cost: $4,950. Contact: Mrs. J. Ives, U.S. Registrar, Oxford Advanced Studies Program, P.O. Box 2043, Darien, CT 06820; (203) 966-2886, fax (203) 972-3083.

Oxford School of Drama Summer Acting Course. Four-week intensive acting course based

Study Programs

in Oxford, covering voice, movement, improvisation, text analysis, and audition technique.

Dates: Jul 11-Aug 7. Cost: £1,800, includes VAT, accommodations, 2 meals per day, theater tickets. Contact: The Oxford School of Drama, Sansomes Farm Studios, Woodstock, Oxford OX20 1ER U.K.; (011) 44-1993-812883, fax (011) 44-1993-811220.

Oxford Summer Programs. A very wide range of courses including literature, art, philosophy, history, social studies, international relations, creative writing, and environmental studies.

Dates: May-Oct (1998). Minimum stay: 2 weeks. Cost: £400 per week, single room and board. Contact: Carolyn Llewelyn, Centre for International Education, 5 Worcester St., Oxford OX1 2BX, U.K.; (011) 44-1865-202238, fax (011) 44-1865-202241; info@ceninted.demon.co.uk, www.usinternational.com/cie.

Penn-in-London. For students interested in theater and literature, this program offers first-hand opportunities to experience the best in traditional and contemporary British theater, from page to footlights.

Dates: Jun 27-Jul 31. Cost: Tuition $2,968; theater tickets $500; housing $825. Contact: Penn Summer Abroad, College of General Studies, Univ. of Pennsylvania, 3440 Market St., Suite 100, Philadelphia, PA 19104-3335; (215) 898-5738, fax (215) 573-2053.

Regent's College in London. Study at Regent's College gives you the overseas experience so many employers are seeking. You'll live and study in an international community on a full-service campus in the heart of London. Fully accredited courses are taught by primarily British faculty, with a variety of internships available. You'll have opportunities to explore the London area, the British Isles, the continent and beyond.

Dates: Late Aug-May (1998-1999). Cost: Tuition $6,690, room and board (double) $3,310. Contact: Rockford College, Regent's Admissions, 5050 E. State St., Rockford, IL 61108-2393; (800) REGENTS, fax (815) 226-2822; regents@ rockford.edu, www.rockford. edu.

Royal Holloway, Univ. of London (Jr. Yr. Abroad and Visiting Student Program). Royal Holloway is a part of the Univ. of London but is located on a 120-acre campus about 30 km to the west of central London, close to Windsor and Heathrow Airport. Opportunities exist for visiting students to study for the fall, spring/summer, or full year. Subjects cover arts and humanities, social science, and management, science, and performing arts.

Dates: Full year: Sep-Jun; Spring/Summer: Jan-Jun. Fall semester Sep-Dec. Cost: Full year: £7,225 (arts), £8,675 (science); Fall semester: £3,324 (arts), £3,990 (science); Spring/Summer: £3,974 (arts), £4,772 (science). Contact: Robert Walls, Head of Educational and International Liaison, Royal Holloway, Univ. of London, Egham, Surrey, TW20 0EX, U.K.; (011) 44-1784-443399, fax (011) 44-1784-471381; liaison-office@ rhbnc.ac.uk, www.rhbnc.ac.uk.

Sarah Lawrence College at Oxford. Work individually with Oxford scholars in private tutorials, the hallmark of an Oxford education. The only American-sponsored program that gives students from other colleges access to the full range of tutors and disciplines at Oxford Univ.'s 37 colleges. Social and academic privileges with Visiting Student status through Wadham College. Frequent field trips and cultural activities.

Dates: Oct-Jun. Cost: $29,510 includes all academic and housing expenses, field trips, and activities. Contact: Prema Samuel, Sarah Lawrence College at Oxford, Box CR, Bronxville, NY 10708; (800) 873-4752.

Study Abroad at Keele Univ. Keele offers American students the chance to study for a semester or year on one of the largest campuses in England, set in beautiful countryside in the heart of Staffordshire. We offer a flexible, modular curriculum, with accessible modules from 30 different subject areas. Students are guaranteed accommodations in single-study bedrooms.

Dates: Sep 27, 1999-Jan 21, 2000; Jan 24-Jun 9, 2000. Cost: 1998-99 prices: £5,450 full year;

£2,990 for semester tuition only. Accommodations £1,263-£1,909 for year. Contact: Dr. Annette Kratz, International Office, Keele Univ., Staffordshire, ST5 5BG, U.K.; (011) 44-1782-584008; fax (011) 44-1782-632343; aaa29@keele.ac.uk.

Study Abroad in Northern Ireland. The Queen's Univ. of Belfast offers study abroad opportunities in all subject areas except medicine. Attendance can be for 1 or 2 semesters; students usually take 3 modules per semester.

Dates: First semester: Sep 27, 1999-Jan 28, 2000; second semester: Feb 7-Jun 18, 2000 (3 weeks vacation at Christmas and Easter). Cost: Tuition fee for 1998-99 was £2,500 for 1 semester, £4,900 for 2 semesters. Call for 1999-00 rates. Accommodations range from £45-£60 per week. Contact: Mrs. C. McEachern, Administrative Officer, International Liaison Office, The Queen's Univ. of Belfast, Belfast BT7 1NN, Northern Ireland, U.K; (011) 44-1232-335415, fax (011) 44-1232-687297; ilo@qub.ac.uk.

Study Abroad-Strathclyde. Participants will integrate fully into student life at the Univ. of Strathclyde, Scotland's third largest university. Choose from a vast range of courses in engineering, business, science, education, and arts including Scottish history, literature, and politics. Full credit is normally awarded and transferred upon the completion of the course.

Dates: Oct-Jun; Oct-Dec. Cost: $6,200 includes tuition and accommodations for 1 semester; $12,400 includes tuition and accommodations for 2 semesters. Contact: Michelle Stewart, International Office, Univ. of Strathclyde, 50 George St., Glasgow G1 1QE, Scotland, U.K.; m.stewart@mis.strath.ac.uk, www.strath.ac.uk.

Study in Great Britain. Thirty-one program opportunities in England, Scotland, and Wales. University study and special subject area programs, including internships, for fall, spring, academic year and summer. Program provides a full range of services including predeparture advising, orientation, homestay, and guaranteed housing. Need-based scholarships available.

Dates: Fall, Spring, academic year. Summer semester and terms. Cost: Varies. Call for current fees. Contact: Beaver College Center for Education Abroad, 450 S. Easton Rd., Glenside, PA 19038-3295; (888) BEAVER-9, fax (215) 572-2174; cea@beaver.edu, www.beaver.edu/cea.

Study in Wales. Opportunities for either year-long or semester study abroad at the Univ. of Wales Swansea (10,500 students, located by the sea) in fully integrated programs. Host family and summer internship programs are available. University housing, orientation, and cultural events are integral to all programs. Swansea is a lively maritime city with great social life and numerous outdoor activities.

Dates: Sep-Dec/Jan-May/May-Jul. Cost: From $4,500. Contact: Emma Frearson, Study Abroad Swansea, American Studies Centre, Univ. of Wales Swansea, Singleton Park, Swansea SA2 8PP, Wales, U.K.; (011) 44-1-792-295135, fax (011) 44-1-792-295719; e.frearson@swansea.ac.uk, www.swan.ac.uk/sao/saohp.html.

Teach English as a Foreign Language. Courses in central London leading to the Cambridge/RSA Certificate (CELTA), regarded internationally as the ideal qualification in TEFL. International House has 40 years experience in training teachers and can offer jobs to those recently qualified in its 110 schools in 27 countries.

Dates: Four-week (110 hours) intensive courses, contact program director for specific starting dates for each 4-week session. Cost: £944 includes Cambridge/RSA registration. Contact: Teacher Training Development, International House, 106 Piccadilly, London W1V 9FL, England; (011) 44-171-491-2598, fax (011) 44-171-499-0174; teacher@dial.pipex.com.

Temple Univ. London. A student can spend the fall semester or summer in London studying in Temple's London Semester program or British Mass Media Summer program. For the fall semester program, students may choose from courses in liberal arts and/or British Communications and Theater. Students can also obtain resume-enhancing practical experience in internships. Classes and housing are located in the heart of London within minutes of Bloomsbury, the British Museum, and the Univ. of London.

Dates: Fall: Sep-Dec, application deadline Apr 1; Summer: Jul-Aug. Cost: $9,964-$12,405 per semester. Includes tuition, housing, computer lab fee, daily out-of-pocket expenses, flight and transfer. Contact: Debbie Marshall, School of Communications and Theater, Temple Univ., 2020 N. 13th St., Philadelphia, PA 19122; (215) 204-1961; augusta@vm.temple.edu.

TESOL/CELTA Programs. Part-time, 7.5 hours per week for 20 weeks, to gain the widely recognized Trinity College validated Certificate in TESOL to each EFL. Also offer a 5-week intensive full-time course to gain the internationally recognized Cambridge CELTA qualification to teach EFL.

Dates: TESOL program: Jan 11-Jun 25. CELTA program: Jan and Apr. Cost: TESOL program £685; CELTA program £695. Contact: David Kimmins, Southwark College, The Cut, London SE1 8LE; (011) 44-171-815-1682.

UNH Cambridge Summer Program. This program's outstanding reputation rests in its balance between offerings of challenging courses in literature, and history taught by primarily Cambridge Univ. professors and a wealth of activities including fine theater, excursions, lectures, readings, and socializing, all in traditional English style. Courses in creative writing are among the exciting possibilities offered in 1998.

Dates: Jul 6-Aug 14. Cost: $4,325. Contact: Michael Ferber, Director, UNH Cambridge Summer Program, 95 Main St., Durham, NH 03824; Tel./fax (603) 862-3962; cambridge.program@unh.edu.

Univ. College Cork. First opened in 1849, the Univ. College Cork (UCC) is 1 of 3 constituent colleges of the National Univ. of Ireland. Eight faculties comprise the educational offerings of UCC: Arts, Celtic Studies, Commerce, Law, Science, Food Science and Technology, Engineering and Medicine. Enrollment in regular UCC classes with Irish students. Cortland's program specializes in language, history, and culture, but other courses may be available. Housing arranged prior to departure from U.S. in apartments near campus. Fall, spring, summer, academic year.

Dates: Fall: Early Sep-mid-Dec:, Spring: mid-Jan-early Jun; Summer: early Jul-end of Jul. Cost: Fall estimate: $7,409; Spring estimate: $8,128; Summer estimate: $3,215; academic year estimate: $14,872. Estimates include full-day orientation before departure, application fee, apartment rental (including utilities), food allowance, health and accident insurance, roundtrip airfare from NY, books and supplies. SUNY tuition not included. Contact: Office of International Programs, Box 2000, SUNY Cortland, Cortland, NY 13045; (607) 753-2209, fax (607) 753-5989; studyabroad@cortland.edu, www.studyabroad.com/suny/cortland.

Univ. of Cambridge International Summer Schools. Largest and longest established program of summer schools in the U.K. Intensive study in Cambridge as part of an international community. Term I (6 weeks) and Term II (2 weeks) of the International Summer School offer over 60 different courses. Three-week specialist programs: Art History, Medieval Studies, History, English Literature, and Shakespeare. Wide range of classes on all programs. U.S. and other overseas institutions grant credit for study at the Univ. of Cambridge Summer School. Guidelines available.

Dates: Jul-Aug. Cost: Tuition from £460-£625 (2 to 4 weeks), accommodations from £240-£925 (2 to 4 weeks). Six-week period of study also possible by combining 2 summer schools. Contact: Sarah Ormrod, Director, International Division, Univ. of Cambridge

Board of Continuing Education, Madingley Hall, Madingley, Cambridge CB3 8AQ, England; (011) 44-1954-210636, fax (011) 44-1954-210677; rdi1000@cam.ac.uk, www.cam.ac.uk.

Univ. of North London. SUNY Cortland celebrates its 26th consecutive year at UNL, a prestigious public university. Over 400 courses are offered. Fields of study include education, natural sciences, humanities, communications, social sciences, business, health, theater arts, women's studies and more. Credits per semester: 12-16. Pre-arranged housing in flats in the Bayswater district. Internships available.

Dates: Fall: mid-Sep-mid-Dec:, Spring: end-Jan-mid-May. Cost: Fall estimate: $3,771, Spring: $4,192. Estimates include full-day orientation in the U.S., application fee, apartment rental, meals, commuter ticket on underground for semester, London tour and Thames cruise, insurance, roundtrip airfare from N.Y., transportation from airport to downtown London upon arrival, books and supplies, various cultural activities, administrative fees. SUNY tuition not included. Contact: Office of International Programs, Box 2000, SUNY Cortland, Cortland, NY 13045; (607) 753-2209, fax (607) 753-5989; studyabroad@cortland.edu, www.study abroad.com/suny/cortland.

Visual Arts and Crafts Courses. Week and weekend courses. Summer schools in art, ceramics, woodworking, textiles, sculpture, silversmithing, music, and art appreciation. One-, 2-, and 3-year diploma courses in conservation and restoration of antique furniture, clocks, ceramics, fine metalwork, and rare books and manuscripts; tapestry weaving (also 6-week modules); making early stringed instruments. Validation at postgraduate level is by the Univ. of Sussex.

Dates: Diploma courses start each year and end in July. Short courses are year round. Cost: Diploma courses £6,921 per annum; residential accommodations £2,979 per annum; short courses (residential) £359, weekends £150, 7

days £483. Contact: Heather Way, Press and Public Relations Coordinator, West Dean College, West Dean, Chichester, West Sussex, PO18 0QZ U.K.; (011) 44-1243-811301, fax (011) 44-1243-811343; westdean@pavilion.co.uk, www.pavilion.co.uk.

United States

Master of International and Intercultural Management. The School for International Training Master of International and Intercultural Management offers concentrations in sustainable development, international education, and training and human resource development in 1 academic year program. This degree is designed for individuals wishing to make a career change or enter the field. A practical training component enables "on-the-job" training and an opportunity to work internationally.

Dates: Call for details. Cost: Call for details. Contact: Kat Eldred, Director of Outreach and Recruitment, Admissions Counselor, School for International Learning, P.O. Box 676, Kipling Rd., Brattleboro, VT 05302; (802) 257-7751, fax (802) 258-3500; admissions@sit.edu, www.sit.edu.

Venezuela

Pitzer College in Venezuela. The mountain city of Merida and the coastal artisan community of La Vela de Coro provide the program's focus on art, artists, and the mix of cultures. The program features family stays, intensive language study, and internships throughout Venezuela.

Dates: Mid-Aug-mid-Dec; early Feb-early Jun. Cost: 1998-99 costs: $14,720 tuition, room and board, roundtrip airfare, field trips, evacuation insurance. Contact: External Studies, Pitzer College, 1050 N. Mills Ave., Claremont, CA 91711; (909) 621-8104, fax (909) 621-0518; external_studies

@pitzer.edu, www.pitzer.edu/academics/
ilcenter/external_studies/index.html.

Venusa Institute of Int'l. Studies and Modern Languages. Mérida and the Venusa Institute are nestled at the foot of the Sierra Nevada mountain range deep in the heart of the Venezuelan Andes. Fields of study include Spanish language, Latin American history and culture, international business, cross cultural communications, teaching of English as a second language (TESOL), Intl. agriculture, ecology and botany, anthropology and sociology, and more. Internships available in the fall and spring. Homestays. One semester college-level Spanish and overall GPA of 2.5 required. Summer short-term study tours available to different regions of Venezuela, 3 credits per module.

Dates: Fall: late Aug-mid-Dec; Spring: early Jan-end of Apr; Summer: 2 sessions, mid-May-late Jun and late Jun-mid-Aug. Cost: Fall/Spring estimate $4,500 plus SUNY tuition per semester; Summer $2,570 plus SUNY tuition. Estimate includes full day orientation in the U.S., orientation in Venezuela, application fee, room and board with local family, airfare to NY to Mérida roundtrip, 2 full day field trips, insurance, books and supplies, program administration costs. SUNY tuition additional. Contact: Office of International Programs, Box 2000, SUNY Cortland, Cortland, NY 13045; (607) 753-2209, fax (607) 753-5989; study abroad@cortland.edu, www.studyabroad.com/suny/cortland.

Worldwide

ActionQuest Sail/Dive Programs. Summer and semester live-aboard voyages for teens and high school graduates. Multi-level sailing and scuba certification programs with marine science, seamanship, windsurfing, water skiing, and leadership training. Semester voyages (75 days) focus on experiential education, personal growth, and college-level academics. No experience necessary.

Dates: Semester: Jan-Mar, Sep-Dec; Summer: mid-Jun- early Jul, Jul, late Jul-mid-Aug. Cost: Semester: $11,250 not including airfare; Summer: from $2,885-$3,885 not including airfare. Contact: James Stoll, ActionQuest, P.O. Box 5507, Sarasota, FL 34277; (800) 317-6789, (941) 924-6789, fax (941) 924-6075; actionquest@msn.com, www.actionquest.com.

Advanced Diploma in Hospitality (Management). This 3-year program prepares students for careers at junior and middle management levels in the hospitality industry. After 2 years students graduate with a Diploma in Hospitality (Management) with management skills. After 1 1/2 years, students graduate with a Certificate in Hospitality (Supervision).

Dates: Feb 8, Jul 19. Cost: $3,325 tuition per semester plus living expenses approx. $7,500 per year, ($145 per week). Contact: Mr. Vernon Bruce, Manager, International Education, William Angliss Institute of TAFE, 555 La Trobe St., Melbourne, 3000 Australia; (011) 61-3-9606-2139, fax (011) 61-3-9670-9348; vernb@angliss.vic.edu.au, www.angliss.vic.edu.au.

Advanced Diploma in Tourism (Management). This 3-year program prepares students for careers at the junior and middle management levels in marketing, sales, and related administrative areas in the travel and tourism industry. After 2 years students can graduate with a Diploma of Tourism. After 1 1/2 years, students can graduate with a Certificate in Tourism as a supervisor. After 6 months a student can graduate with a Certificate in Tourism as a Tour Guide.

Dates: Feb 8, Jul 19. Cost: $3,150 tuition per semester plus living expenses approx. $7,500 per year ($145 per week). Contact: Mr. Vernon Bruce, Manager, International Education, William Angliss Institute of TAFE, 555 La Trobe St., Melbourne, 3000 Australia; (011) 61-3-

9606-2139, fax (011) 61-3-9670-9348; vernb@angliss.vic.edu.au, www.angliss.vic.edu.au.

AIYSEP. AIYSEP is a nonprofit high school foreign exchange program based in the U.S. which establishes exchange programs for students in Europe, America, and many other foreign countries. Area counselors are located in Europe, U.S., Australia, New Zealand, South America, Peru, Canada, and Japan. AIYSEP believes a greater international understanding is accomplished among people and countries through cultural homestay programs.

Dates: Year, semester, and Summer programs. Cost: Year $3,995-$6,000; semester $3,495-$4,000; Summer $1,900-$3,000. Contact: American International Youth Student Exchange, 200 Round Hill Rd., Tiburon, CA 94920; (800) 347-7575 or (415) 435-4049, (415) 499-7669, fax (415) 499-5651; AIYSEP@compuserve.com.

Antioch Education Abroad. Programs cover Brazilian ecosystems; Buddhist studies in India; comparative women's studies in Europe; European politics; economics and society; Antioch in Germany; Thailand: sustainable development studies; Antioch in Cape Verde, Africa; Field Studies in Japan.

Dates: Call for details. Cost: Call for details. Contact: Antioch Education Abroad, Antioch College, Yellow Springs, OH 45387; (800) 874-7986, (937) 767-6366, fax (937) 767-6469; aea@antioch.college.edu.

Art and Cultural Learning Journeys. Guided excursions with informative lectures bring to life famous sights and artworks in Italy, Spain, England, and Bali. Free workshops in drawing, painting, photography, etc. Limited scholarships available. Travel with A.R.T.I.S., a nonprofit organization of fine art educators dedicated to providing you with unique and rewarding international cultural experiences. College credit available.

Dates: May-Jul, Dec for Rome. Ten, 20, or 30 days. Cost: $2,500 to $3,700. Includes air-

fare, studio space, furnished apartment, workshops, all ground transportation, entry fees, etc. Contact: A.R.T.I.S., 833 E. Holaway Dr., Tucson, AZ 85719; (800) 232-6893, fax (520) 887-5287; dfro@digmo.org, www.artis-tours.org.

Boston Univ. International Programs. Offering internship and language/liberal arts programs in 15 cities on 6 continents and in 9 different languages. Course offerings range from intermediate-level language and liberal arts study through advanced-level, direct enrollment in local universities. Internship programs combine coursework with an academic internship. Application materials: 2 references, transcript, essays, and academic approval.

Dates: Fall, Spring, and Summer (length varies). Application deadline: Mar 15 (Summer and Fall); Oct 15 (Spring). Cost: $4,500-$14,770; application fee: $35. Contact: Boston Univ., International Programs, 232 Bay State Rd., 5th Fl., Boston, MA 02215; (617) 353-9888, fax (617) 353-5402; abroad@bu.edu, http://web.bu.edu/abroad.

Center for Global Education-Undergraduate Semester Programs. The center facilitates cross-cultural learning experiences that prepare students to think more critically about global issues and to work toward a more just and sustainable world. Programs include homestays, community learning, and regional travel. Students explore women's issues and issues of social change, sustainable development, and human rights. Programs in Mexico, Central America, and Namibia/South Africa.

Dates: Semesters (Sep-Dec or Feb-May). Cost: Contact the Center for current costs. Contact: Academic Programs Abroad, Center for Global Education, Augsburg College, 2211 Riverside Ave., Box 307TR, Minneapolis, MN 55454; (800) 299-8889, fax (612) 330-1695; globaled@augsburg.edu, www.augsburg.edu/global.

Center for Northern Studies. Comprehensive undergraduate and graduate program combining formal academic work in natural science, anthropology, political economy, and archaeology with extensive field work throughout the North. CNS is fully licensed by the state of Vermont. Our credits are widely accepted in New England. We offer a winter ecology course in January.

Dates: Fall semester (Sep-Dec); Winter ecology (Jan); Spring (Feb-May). Cost: $13,870 per semester; $3,060 Winter Ecology includes tuition, housing, and field trips. Contact: Scott Jones, Laura Fandos, The Center for Northern Studies, P.O. Box 1860, Wollott, VT 05680; (802) 888-4331, (802) 888-3969; cnsnorth@ together.nct, www.middlebury. edu/~cns.

College Semester Abroad (SIT). A pioneer in study abroad, The School for International Training (SIT) offers over 57 programs in over 40 countries worldwide. For over 40 years SIT has been a leader in offering field-based study abroad programs to U.S. college and university students.

Dates: Fall and Spring semester. Cost: $8,900-$11,900 depending on location. Includes airfare, tuition, room and board, insurance. Contact: School for International Training, P.O. Box 676, Kipling Rd., Brattleboro, VT 05302; (802) 257-7751, fax (802) 258-3500; csa@sit.edu, www.sit.edu.

Columbia Univ. Study-Away Programs. Columbia Univ. in Paris (semester, academic year, and summer); Berlin Consortium for German Studies (autumn, spring, academic year); summer language program in Beijing; summer program in Scandiano, Italy.

Dates: Vary by program and curricular option; contact program for info. Cost: Vary by program and curricular option; contact program for info. Contact: John Sharples, Assistant Director of Overseas Programs, Continuing Education and Special Programs, 2970 Broadway Mail Code 4110, New York, NY 10027; (212) 854-2559, fax (212) 854-5861; studyaway@columbia.edu, www.columbia. edu/cu/ssp.

Cooperative Center for Study Abroad. Study abroad programs in English-speaking countries such as Australia, Canada, England, Ireland, New Zealand, and Scotland. Students can receive higher education credit. Classes taught by faculty from consortium member schools. Five- and 10-week internships available in conjunction with London Summer and Cambridge programs.

Dates: May-Jan. Cost: $1,495-$5,895 includes roundtrip airfare, accommodations, and some meals. Contact: Dr. Michael A. Klembara, Executive Director, CCSA, Northern Kentucky Univ., Highland Heights, KY 41099; (606) 572-6512, fax (606) 572-6650; ccsa@nku.edu, www.nku.edu/ccsa.

Coral Cay Conservation Expeditions. Volunteers needed to join major expeditions to help survey and protect coral reefs and tropical forests in the Caribbean, Asia-Pacific, Philippines, Indonesia, Red Sea. No previous experience required. Full accredited training provided (including scuba certification if required). Thousands of CCC volunteers have already helped establish 8 new marine reserves and wildlife sanctuaries worldwide.

Dates: Expeditions depart monthly throughout the year. Cost: From $995 (2 weeks) to $4,415 (12 weeks) excluding flights. Contact: Coral Cay Conservation Ltd., 154 Clapham Park Rd., London SW4 7DE, U.K.; (305) 757-2955 (U.K. office 011-44-171-498-6248, fax 011-44-171-498-8447); ccc@coralcay.demon. co.uk, www.coralcay.org.

Diploma of Food Technology. This 2-year course provides a broad-based qualification in food technology for paraprofessional staff in the food industry. The course develops the ability to identify, analyze, and resolve food processing problems; leadership and communication skills; an innovative approach to support the development and implementation of company policies and practices, and a total commitment to total quality management. There are streams in nutrition, baking, or confectionery studies. Students can graduate with a Certificate in Food Technology after 1 year of study.

Dates: Feb 8, Jul 19. Cost: $2,975 tuition per semester plus living expenses approx. $7,500 per year ($145 per week). Contact: Mr. Vernon Bruce, Manager, International Education, William Angliss Institute of TAFE, 555 La Trobe St., Melbourne, 3000 Australia; (011) 61-3-9606-2139, fax (011) 61-3-9670-9348; vernb@angliss.vic.edu.au, www.angliss.vic.edu.au.

¿?don Quijote In-Country Spanish Language Schools. Intensive Spanish language courses using the communicative method are combined with an intensive immersion in the social and cultural life of some of Spain's most interesting cities (Salamanca, Barçelona, Granada, Malaga). Airport pick-up service, study counseling, homestay or student flats, excursions, access to recreational facilities, touring, and sightseeing opportunities. donQuijote now offers intensive Spanish language courses through partner schools in Latin America: Cuernavaca and Mèrida, Mexico; Antigua, Guatemala; Alajuela, Costa Rica; and Quito, Ecuador.

Dates: Year round—Fall, Spring, Winter, and Summer. Cost: Inquire. Contact: ¿?don Quijote, Apartado de Correos 333, 37080 Salamanca, Spain; (011) 34-923-268-860, fax (011) 34-923-268-815; donquijote@offcampus.es, www.teclata.es/donquijote.

Duke Foreign Academic Programs. Semester and academic year programs in 9 locations, as well as 14 summer programs. Qualified students may choose a semester or academic year in La Paz (Bolivia), Berlin, Beijing and Nanjing, Paris, Madrid, Venice, Rome, Costa Rica (various sites), or St. Petersburg. Course range from art history, to classical languages to tropical biology.

Dates: Vary by program. Cost: Vary by program. Contact: Office of Foreign Academic Programs, Duke Univ., 121 Allen Bldg., Box 90057, Durham, NC 27708-0057; (919) 684-2174, fax (919) 684-3083; abroad@asdean.duke.edu, www.aas.duke.edu/study_abroad.

Friends World Program. A 9-month program in comparative religion and culture. Students will study for three 10-week terms in Japan, India, and Israel. The field course will be based on experiential approaches, emphasizing participation, observation, and involvement in local religious life. Culture's relation to religion and social change will be emphasized.

Dates: Early Sep-mid-May. Cost: $27,386 for year (1998/1999). Includes tuition, travel, room and board, fees and books. Contact: Stephanie Pollack, Friends World Program, 239 Montauk Hwy., Southampton, NY 11968; (516) 287-8475; fw@southampton.liunet.edu.

The Global Campus. Choose from 11 language, theme, area studies, integrated classroom, and field study opportunities in countries ranging from England to Venezuela. Course topics include language, culture, international relations, and international development. Field placements and internships available for credit in Ecuador, India, Kenya, and Senegal. Open to all students and professionals.

Dates: Academic year, semester, quarter, and Summer options. Cost: From $2,650-$16,500. Includes tuition, study abroad, and registration fees, room and board, and excursions. Contact: The Global Campus, Univ. of Minnesota, 102 Nicholson Hall, 216 Pillsbury Dr. SE, Minneapolis, MN 55455-0138; (612) 626-9000, fax (612) 626-8009; umabroad@ tc.umn.edu, www.umabroad.umn.edu.

Global Ecology and Cities in the 21st Century. Two different academic programs to be offered by the International Honors Program in 1998-99. "Global Ecology" is a 2-semester program of around-the-world study and travel to England, Tanzania, India, the Philippines, and Mexico with academic coursework in ecology, anthropology, economics, and environmental issues.

The "Cities in the 21st Century" program is a 1-semester program of study and travel to South Africa, India, and Brazil with academic coursework in urban studies, anthropology, sociology, economics, and political science.

Dates: "Global Ecology": Sep-May. "Cities in 21st Century": Jan-May. Cost: "Global Ecology": $21,950 plus airfare, includes tuition, room and board. "Cities in the 21st Century": $12,650 plus airfare, includes tuition, room and board. Estimated airfare for each program is $3,900. Contact: Joan Tiffany, Director, International Honors Program, 19 Braddock Pk., Boston, MA 02116; (617) 267-0026, fax (617) 262-9299; info@ihp.edu, www.ihp.edu.

Illinois Programs Abroad. Brazil, Ecuador, Great Britain, Turkey, and Russia. Summer: language, literature, culture, social sciences, business (Brazil only). Semester/year: full university curriculum. Art and design (Great Britain only). Russian language and literature, social sciences (Russia only).

Dates: Summer, Fall, Spring, and year. Cost: Varies by program. Contact: Illinois Programs Abroad, Univ. of Illinois, 115 International Studies Bldg., 910 S. 5th St., Champaign, IL 61820; (800) 531-4404, fax (217) 244-0249; ipa@uiuc.edu, www.uiuc.edu/providers/ips/sao.

International Cooperative Education. Paid internship/employment for college and university students for a period of 8-12 weeks in 4 European (Belgium, Finland, Germany, and Switzerland) and two Asian (Japan and Singapore) countries. Employment depends on foreign language knowledge, major, and previous work experience. Work permits and housing are provided.

Dates: From Jun-Sep. Cost: Students must pay for air transportation and have a reserve of at least $800 for initial expenses. Program fee $800. Contact: Günter Seefeldt, PhD, Director, International Cooperative Education Program, 15 Spiros Way, Menlo Park, CA 94025; (650) 323-4944, fax (650) 323-1104,

ICEMenlo@aol.com, http://members.aol.com/ICEMenlo.

International Internship Program. People to People International coordinates 2-month, unpaid internships for students and professionals for 6 units of graduate or undergraduate (junior level and above) credit, or on an audit-basis, through the Univ. of Missouri-Kansas City. Open to all fields. Positions correspond with academic background, work experience, and career goals. Internships are available in the following countries (subject to change): Kenya, England, Italy, Denmark, Ireland, Argentina, Germany, Russia, and Australia.

Dates: Flexible throughout the year. Apply 3 months in advance. Cost: $1,875 includes tuition and placement fee. Housing and airfare not included. Contact: People to People International, 501 E. Armour Blvd., Kansas City, MO 64109-2200; (816) 531-4701, fax (816) 561-7502; internships@ptpi.org, www.ptpi.org/studyabroad.

International Student Exchange Program. Study abroad for the same cost as study at home through ISEP exchanges between 100-plus U.S. universities and over 100 in 35 countries (many offering courses taught in English). Pay tuition, room and board at your home institution to receive similar services at an institution abroad, without losing financial aid.

Dates: Year round. Cost: $250 placement fee; $37 per month health insurance premium (obligatory). Contact: International Student Exchange Program (ISEP), 1601 Connecticut Avenue, NW, Suite 501, Washington, DC 20009-1035; (202) 667-8027, fax (202) 667-7801; info@isep.org, www.isep.org.

Internationale Teaching Opportunities (I.T.O.). ITO provides information on teaching in foreign countries. Teaching overseas can be a wonderful learning experience. We have information on almost every country.

Dates: Always available. Cost: Information is sold for $3 per country. Contact: I.T.O., P.O.

Box 4701-T, Wheaton, IL 60189; interteach@aol.com.

Language Immersion Programs. Learn a language in the country where it's spoken. Intensive foreign language training offered in Costa Rica, Russia, Spain, France, Italy, Germany, and Ecuador for students aged 16 and older. Classes are taught in up to 8 different proficiency levels and are suitable for beginners as well as people with advanced linguistic skills. All courses include accommodations and meals. Lots of extracurricular activities available. Students can earn college credit through Providence College.

Dates: Courses start every second Monday year round. Year programs commence in Sep, semester programs in Jan, May, and Sep. Cost: Varies with program, approx. $950 per 2-week course. Contact: Stephanie Greco, Director of, Admissions, EF International Language Schools, EF Center, 1 Education St., Cambridge, MA 02142; (800) 992-1892, fax (617) 619-1701; ils@ef.com.

M. Econ. Sc. European Economic and Public Affairs. This interdisciplinary program designed to equip graduates with comprehensive expertise in European economic, political, legal and business affairs, is undertaken by those who will go on to be European specialists in organizations/companies with a significant European role and those intending to pursue further study in European affairs or international relations.

Dates: One-year program Sep-Aug. Cost: EU citizens IR£5,500, nonEU IR£10,000. Possible tuition scholarships available to nonEU citizens. Contact: Dr. Richard Sinnott, The Director, Centre for European Economic and Public Affairs (CEEPA), Univ. College Dublin, Belfield, Dublin 4, Ireland; (011) 353-1-706-7634, fax (011) 353-1-269-2589; ceepa@ucd.ie, www.ucd.ie/~ceepa.

Peace Corps Masters in Forestry. Earn a master's degree in forestry in combination with 2 years of Peace Corps service. Open to students with any undergraduate major. One college-level chemistry course is required, statistics recommended. Students must be accepted into both the Michigan Tech Graduate School and the U.S. Peace Corps. (Michigan Technological Univ. is an equal opportunity educational institution/equal opportunity employer.)

Dates: Fall entry of each year. Cost: Variable by state of residence. Tuition and fees are waived during 2 years of Peace Corps service. Check web site for costs. Contact: Blair Orr, Forest Ecology and Management, Michigan Tech Univ., Houghton, MI 49931; (800) 966-3764; bdorr@mtu.edu, http://forestry.mtu.edu/peacecorps.

Pitzer College. Pitzer College cultural/immersion/field study programs in China, Ecuador, Italy, Nepal, Turkey, Venezuela, Wales, Zimbabwe, and Ontario feature host family stays, intensive language study, independent projects, or internships and study trips. Community service projects and a field journal designed to facilitate critical reflection.

Dates: Fall, Spring, and year programs. Cost estimate: $14,487 includes tuition, room and board, and airfare. Contact: External Studies, Pitzer College, 1050 N. Mills Ave., Claremont, CA 91711; (909) 621-8104, fax (909) 621-051; external_studies@pitzer.edu, www.pitzer.edu/academics/ilcenter/external_studies/index.html.

Programs in European Studies. The Center for European Studies, Maastricht Univ., offers semester, year, and summer programs. Students compose their own "package" of courses—all taught in English, fully integrated with European students in international dormitories. Maastricht, on the border of Belgium, Germany, and the Netherlands is the oldest city of the Netherlands.

Dates: Spring: Jan 5-Apr 30; Summer: Jul 3-Aug 18; Fall: Aug 20-Dec 20. Cost: $300 per credit (1 semester per 16 credits $800). Other:

$600 per month (housing food, miscellaneous). Contact: Karin Quanten, Coordinator Undergraduate Programs, Center for European Studies, Witmakersstraat 10, 6211 JB Maastricht, the Netherlands; (011) 31-43-321-26-27, fax (011) 31-43-325-73-24; k.quantn@ces.unimaas.nl, www.unimaas.nl.

Summer Study Abroad. Summer opportunities in Australia, Austria, England, Ireland, Mexico, and Scotland, including internships, fine arts, drama, history, literature, environmental studies, psychology, and languages. Full range of program services. Guaranteed housing.

Dates: Vary. Call for tentative dates. Cost: Varies. Call for fees. Contact: Beaver College Center for Education Abroad, 450 S. Easton Rd., Glenside, PA 19038-3295; (888) BEAVER-9, fax (215) 572-2174; cea@beaver.edu, www.beaver.edu/cea.

Teaching Internship Program. Global Routes interns are assigned in pairs to remote villages where they teach in local schools and complete at least 1 community service project. Each intern lives separately with a local family in a simple, traditional home. Training, support, and adventure travel are an integral part of the programs. Programs offered in Costa Rica, Ecuador, Kenya, Thailand, Zimbabwe, Navajo Nation.

Dates: Year round in 3-month session. Cost: $3,550 Summer, $3,950 during year. Includes all expenses (room, board, adventure travel) except airfare to and from country. Scholarships and fundraising information available. Contact: Global Routes, 1814 7th St., Suite A, Berkeley, CA 94710; (510) 848-4800, fax (510) 848-4801; mail@globalroutes.org, www.global routes.org.

Up With People. The Up With People Leadership Program accelerates education and career opportunities through the unique combination of international travel, performing arts, and community service. Join 700 college-age students from 30 to 35 countries in this challenging 11-month experiential program. College credit is available.

Dates: Programs start every Jan and Jul. Cost: $13,700 includes all travel, lodging, food, and student program expenses within the 11-month program. Contact: Admissions Department, Up With People, 1 International Ct., Broomfield, CO 80021; (800) 596-7353 or (303) 438-7373, fax (303) 438-7301; uwp-info@upwithpeople.org, www.upwithpeople.org.

World Experience Student Exchange Program. Have the experience of a lifetime. Learn another language and culture. Live as a member of a family and attend a local school. Choose from 30 countries. One- or 2-semester programs. Add a new dimension to your life. Eligibility: 15-18 years, 3.0 GPA.

Dates: Aug or Jan departure for 1 to 2 semesters. Cost: $2,640 plus individual country fees for 1 year; $2,265 plus individual country fees for 1 semester. Travel expenses not included. Contact: World Experience, 2440 Hacienda Blvd #116, Hacienda Heights, CA 91745; (800) 633-6653, fax (626) 333-4914; weworld@worldexperience.org, www.world experience.org.

WorldTeach. WorldTeach is a private nonprofit organization based at Harvard Univ. that contributes to educational development and cultural exchange by placing volunteers as teachers in developing countries. Volunteers teach English, math, science, and environmental education. One-year, 6-month, and summer opportunities. Programs in Costa Rica, Ecuador, Namibia, China, Mexico, and Honduras.

Dates: Year-round departures; deadlines vary depending on program. Cost: $3,600-$5,650. Includes international airfare, health insurance, placement, training, and in-country support. Contact: Admissions Department, WorldTeach, Harvard Institute for International Development, 14 Story St., Cambridge, MA 02138; (800) 4-TEACH-0 or (617) 495-5527, fax (617) 495-1599; info@worldteach.org, www.worldteach.org.

CHAPTER 14

INTERNSHIP
PROGRAMS

The following listing of internship programs was supplied by the organizers in 1998 and is updated in each September/October issue of Transitions Abroad *magazine. Contact the program directors to confirm costs, dates, and other details. Please tell them you read about their programs in this book! Programs based in more than one country or region are listed under "Worldwide."*

Australia

Australian Internships. Interns are placed with research teams, Australian employers, political administrations, etc., for periods ranging from 6 weeks to a year. The positions are unpaid. Homestay (or other) accommodations are included. Placement is arranged to suit the individual provided 4 months notice is given. Most placements are in Queensland or New South Wales.

Fields: marine and wildlife biology, business, etc. No academic credit offered. Unlimited internships. Prerequisites: a) High School Graduates, b) Professional Development for Graduates and Junior/Senior college students.

Dates: Year round. Application deadline: Four months before start date. Cost: $2,455 (includes room and board) for 6-week program. Application fee: $500. Contact: Dr.

Maurice A. Howe, Education Australia, P.O. Box 2233, Amherst, MA 01004; (800) 344-6741, fax (413) 549-0741; edaust@javanet.com.

Custom Designed Professional Development Internships. Placement service in Australia locates suitable programs based on participants' internship needs. Responsibilities vary by placement. Excellent professional development and career building opportunities. Opportunities to travel before and after placement. Flexible duration and start dates. Interns are not usually placed as a group. On-call support service, academic or professional supervisor provided in Australia. Pre-trip support for air travel, visas, and orientation.

Fields: management, marketing, finance and accounting, communications (radio, television, newspaper, public relations), law, politics, the arts, social work, biology, wildlife management, natural resources, and marine science. Academic credit can be arranged through home university. One hundred-200 internships per year. Prerequisites: Pursuing or have obtained a university/college degree. Application materials: application and transcript(s).

Dates: Six, 8, 10, 12, 16 weeks or more (52 weeks maximum) placements. Year-round start dates. Sign up at least 4 months prior to intended departure. Cost: $3,240 (6 weeks) to $4,480 (16 weeks). Includes room, 2 meals per day in homestay (or no meals in an apartment), internship placement, liaison service in Australia, airport transfers. Compensation: placements are typically unpaid due to immigration rules. Application fee: $500 deposit with application. Eighty percent refundable for cancellation after placement is found. Contact: AustraLearn, U.S. Center for Australian Universities, 110 16th St., CSU Denver Center, Denver, CO 80202; (800) 980-0033, fax (303) 446-5955; studyabroad@australearn. org.

Belize

Internships in Belize. Interns live with host families. Following a 1-week orienation, participants work full time in various non-governmental agencies. Must be self-starters. Journals and written projects are submitted at the end of program for assessment. Academic credit offered: 15-16 credits per semester. Required: 2.5 cumulative GPA, strong performance in major, maturity, and adaptability; junior or senior status.

Dates: Fall and Spring, 17 weeks each. Cost: $4,608 includes room and board, health insurance, local transportation, international airfare, and orientation. Contact: Director, Office of International Programs, Box 2000, SUNY Cortland, Cortland, NY 13045; (607) 753-2209, fax (607) 753-5989; study abroad@cortland.edu, www.studyabroad. com/suny/cortland.

Central America

Semester Internship and Research Program. The Institute for Central American Development Studies (ICADS) offers a semester abroad study program, including coursework and structured internship opportunities in Costa Rica, Nicaragua, and Belize in the following areas: women's studies, environment/ ecology, public health, education, human rights, and many others. The program is progressive and aimed at students who wish to work on social justice issues and on behalf of the poor, women, and the oppressed in Central America. Fall and spring with academic credit, summer noncredit Spanish and internship program.

Dates: Fall, Spring, and Summer semesters. Cost: $7,200 Fall and Spring, $3,500 Summer. Includes all travel (except from U.S.), housing, food, books, classes, and study tour to Nicaragua or Panama. Contact: Sandra Kinghorn, PhD, Director, ICADS, Dept. 826, P.O. Box 025216, Miami, FL 33102-5216; (011) 506-225-0508, fax (011) 506-234-1337; icads@netbox.com, www.icadscr.com.

Colombia

Community Internships in Latin America. Emphasis on community participation for social change. Students work 3 days a week in an internship, meet together for core seminar and internship seminar, and carry out independent study project. Wide range of internship opportunities in community development and related activities. Based in Bogotá. Family homestay. Latin American faculty. Full semester's credit, U.S. transcript provided. All majors, 2 years Spanish language required.

Dates: Early Feb-mid-May. Cost: $9,000 (1998-99). Includes tuition, room and board, field trips. Contact: Rebecca Rassier, Director of Student Services, HECUA, Mail #36, Hamline Univ., 1536 Hewitt Ave., St. Paul, MN 55104-1284; (612) 646-8832 or

(800) 554-9421, fax (612) 659-9421; hecua@hamline.edu, www.hamline.edu/~hecua.

Costa Rica

Intensive Spanish Immersion. The Institute for Central American Development Studies (ICADS) offers 30-day programs of intensive Spanish languages—4 1/2 hours daily, 5 days a week. Small classes (4 students or less) geared to individual needs. Extra lectures and activities emphasize environmental issues, women's studies, economic development, and human rights. ICADS offers optional afternoon internship placements in grassroots organizations. Supportive informal learning environment. Homestays and field trips.

Dates: Programs begin first day Monday of each month. Cost: One month $1,225. Includes airport pick-up, classes, books, homestay, meals, laundry, lectures, activities, field trips, and internship placements (10 % discount after first month). Contact: Sandra Kinghorn, Ph.D., Director, ICADS, Dept. 826, P.O. Box 025216, Miami, FL 33102-5216; or ICADS, Apartado 3-2070, Sabanilla, San Jose, Costa Rica; fax (011) 506-234-1337; icads@netbox.com, www.icadscr.com.

Learn Spanish While Volunteering. Assist with the training of Costa Rican public school teachers in ESL and computers. Assist local health clinic, social service agencies, and environmental projects. Enjoy learning Spanish in the morning, volunteer work in the afternoon/evening. Spanish classes of 2-5 students plus group learning activities; conversations with middle-class homestay families (1 student per family). Homestays and most volunteer projects are within walking distance of school in small town near the capital, San Jose.

Dates: Year round, all levels. Classes begin every Monday, volunteer program is continuous. Cost: $345 per week for 28 hours of classes and group activities plus Costa Rican dance and cooking classes. Includes tuition, 3 meals per day, 7 days per week, homestay, laundry,

all materials, and airport transportation. $25 one-time registration fee; $100 additional one-time registration fee for volunteer program. Contact: Susan Shores, Registrar, Latin American Language Center, 7485 Rush River Dr., Suite 710-123, Sacramento, CA 95831; (916) 447-0938, fax (916) 428-9542; lalc@madre.com.

Czech Republic

Penn-in-Prague. For students interested in Jewish studies and Czech culture, this program, located amidst the fairy tale beauty of Prague and affiliated with Charles Univ. and the Jewish Museum of Prague, offers an insight into the rich history and urgent contemporary problems of this important region, as well as an opportunity to learn beginning and intermediate Czech. Some internships can be arranged with the Jewish Museum.

Dates: Jul 6-Aug 14. Cost: Tuition $2,968; housing and excursion $850. Contact: Penn Summer Abroad, College of General Studies, Univ. of Pennsylvania, 3440 Market St., Suite 100, Philadelphia, PA 19104-3335; (215) 898-5738, fax (215) 573-2053.

Dominican Republic

Internship and Study Program. English-speaking program exposes students to career opportunities in business, human service organizations, and government agencies in conjunction with academic program featuring study of Spanish language, Latin American and Caribbean Studies, and African-American Studies. Direct enrollment for fluent Spanish speakers. Internships. Host families. Field trips.

Dates: Fall, Spring, or year (dates vary with the type of program). Cost: $5,374 per semester, in-state tuition and fees, housing, meals, insurance, airfare, books. Contact: International Programs, Univ. of Albany, LI66, Albany, NY 12222; (518) 442-3525, fax (518) 442-3338; oipua@csc.albany.edu.

Internship Programs

Ecuador

Academia Latinoamericana. Ecuador's top private Spanish language institute in former diplomat's mansion with gardens, swimming pool, hot tub, in lovely residential area of Quito. Small group classes, executive courses, high school groups, exclusive "SierrAzul Cloud Forest" extension program. Select host family accommodation. Excursions to haciendas, Indian markets, other activities. USA college credit and internships available.

Dates: Year round. Cost: $296 per week. Includes 20 hours of one-on-one lessons, 7 days with host family, 2 meals per day, transfer, services at the school and teaching material. Contact: Suzanne S. Bell, Admissions Director, USA/International, 640 East 3990 South, Suite E, Salt Lake City, UT, 84107; (801) 268-4608, fax (801) 265-9156; academia@juno.com, delco@spanish.com.ec, www.ecua.net.ec/academia.

Europe

Internships/Homestays. Large variety of internships available in France, Germany, Spain, Italy, and Britain. Also family stays to boost language ability and provide safe, comfortable environment. Seventeen years experience.

Dates: Year round. Cost: Registration $400, family accommodations and half board $220 per week. Contact: Interspeak Ltd., The Coach House, Blackwood, Lanark ML11 0JG, U.K.; (011) 44-155-894-219, fax (011) 44-155-894-954; interspeak@mcmail.com, www.interspeak.mcmail.com.

France

Internships in Francophone Europe. IFE is an academic internship program—accredited at a number of schools—that places student interns in mid to high levels of French public life including government, politics, the press, social institutions, NGOs, etc. IFE is a selective admissions program for motivated students, proficient in French, who are interested in immersion in the working life of a French institution and in today's France. The program includes intensive preparatory course work in French history, sociology, politics, language training, and the completion of a research project related to the internship. Open to undergraduates and recent graduates.

Dates: May 1 deadline for Fall semester (Aug 21-Dec 22); Nov 1 deadline for Spring semester (Jan 22-May 24). Cost: $5,950 (tuition only); tuition plus housing (approx.) $7,660. Need-based scholarships available, especially for post BA's. Contact: Bernard Riviere Platt, Director, Internships in Francophone Europe, 26, rue Cmdt. Mouchotte J108, 75014 Paris, France; (011) 33-1-43-21-78-07, fax (011) 33-1-42-79-94-13; ifeparis@compuserve.com.

Penn-in-Compiegne. For students with some proficiency in French who are interested in international relations, economics, or business. The program, affiliated with The Université de Technologie de Compiegne, also offers a 2-week internship in a French enterprise. Students live with local families.

Dates: May 23-Jul 2; with internship: May 23-Jul 18. Cost: Tuition $2,968; room and board, and activities $960 (study only) or $1,280 (full program). Contact: Penn Summer Abroad, College of General Studies, Univ. of Pennsylvania, 3440 Market St., Suite 100, Philadelphia, PA 19104-3335; (215) 898-5738, fax (215) 573-2053.

Germany

German as a Foreign Language. Various levels of German year round; intensive, crash, and long-term courses, individual tuition. Special feature: German and theater. Special programs: business German for professionals, German for teachers, German in a teacher's home, German for special purposes. Academic year for high school students, international study year, internship, guest studentship, homestays for groups, courses for firms and other institutions (banking, insurance, doctors, lawyers, etc.), residential language camps for juniors, examination preparation. Various types of accommodations. Full range of activities.

Dates: Year round. Cost: Contact school for details. Contact: GLS Sprachenzentrum, Barbara Jaeschke, Managing Director, Kolonnenstrasse 26, 10829 Berlin, Germany; (011) 49-30-787-41-52; fax (011) 49-30-787-41-92; gls.berlin@t-online.de, www.gls-berlin.com.

Mannheim Program for Bilingual Careers. A professional program abroad for young Americans who wish additional language training, university study in Germany, and option of a paid internship under the auspices of AGABUR Foundation, Inc. Designed for undergrads, graduating seniors, and young professionals. See web site for application form and information.

Dates: Spring: Mar-Aug; Summer: Jun-Aug; Fall: Sep-Feb. Cost: Six months $7,935 (plus $500), 3 months $4,500 (plus $500). Contact: Prof. Gerhard Austin, AGABUR Foundation, Inc., 9 Eastwood Rd., Storrs, CT 06268-2401; (860) 429-1279, fax (860) 487-7709; austin@uconnvm.uconn.edu, www.mannheim-program.necaweb.com.

India

Penn-in-India. For students interested in South Asian studies, performing arts, religion, economics, and traditional medicine, PSA's newest program offers students a survey of both India's rich cultural history and its burgeoning industrial life. The program is located in Pune, a cosmopolitan city of 4,000,000 which is a thriving arts center, a hub of scholarship, and a growing economic presence. Students will live with Indian families in the area and be involved in community projects.

Dates: Jun 25-Aug 7. Cost: Tuition $2,968; program cost $1,790. Contact: Penn Summer

Abroad, College of General Studies, Univ. of Pennsylvania, 3440 Market St., Suite 100, Philadelphia, PA 19104-3335; (215) 898-5738, fax (215) 573-2053.

Japan

IES Toyko Program. IES Tokyo students participate in a field experience in a Japanese organization and its accompanying seminar as part of the IES Tokyo program. With permission from the student's home school, the field experience may be considered an internship. Placement depends on availability, a student's background and skills, and language requirements.

Dates: Fall semester: Aug 24-Dec 20, 1999; academic year 1999-2000: Aug 24-Jul 30. Cost: Semester fee $10,700; year: $19,200. Includes tuition, housing, orientation, international health insurance, visa processing, field trips, and 2 meals a day for those living with families. Students living in dormitories pay an additional fee of $1,000 per semester and receive 2 meals a day, 6 days a week. Contact: Institute for the International Education of Students, 223 W. Ohio St., Chicago, IL 60610-4196; (800) 995-2300 or (312) 944-1750, fax (312) 944-1448; info@iesabroad.org, www.iesabroad.org.

Japan Exchange and Teaching Program. Sponsored by the Japanese Government, the JET Program invites over 1,000 American college graduates and young professionals to share their language and culture with Japanese youth. One-year positions are available in schools and government offices throughout Japan. Apply by early December for positions beginning in July of the following year.

Dates: One-year contracts renewable by mutual consent not more than 2 times. Cost: Participants receive approx. ¥3,600,000 per year in monthly payments. Contact: JET Program Office, Embassy of Japan, 2520 Massachusetts Ave. NW, Washington, DC 20008; (202) 238-6772, fax (202) 265-9484; eojjet@erols.com, www.jet.org.

Internship Programs

Teaching English in Japan. Two-year program to maximize linguistic and cultural integration of participants who work as teachers' assistants. Placements twice yearly in April and August. Most positions are in junior high schools in urban and rural areas. Bachelor's degree and willingness to learn Japanese required.

Dates: Hiring for positions every Apr and Aug. Applications accepted year round. Cost: Airfare, salary, housing, healthcare provided. No application fees. Contact: Institute for Education in Japan, Earlham College, D-202, Richmond, IN 47374; (888) 685-2726, fax (765) 983-1553; www.earlham.edu/aet/home.htm.

Korea

Penn-in-Seoul. For students interested in East Asia, Korea, international relations and other business disciplines. This program, offered in conjunction with Kyung Hee Univ., includes courses in the area of international relations as well as internships with multinational corporations, government agencies, and think tanks. Field trips exploring Korean history and culture are integral to the program.

Dates: Jun 13-Aug 16. Cost: Tuition $2,968; housing $850. Contact: Penn Summer Abroad, College of General Studies, Univ. of Pennsylvania, 3440 Market St., Suite 100, Philadelphia, PA 19104-3335; (215) 898-5738, fax (215) 573-2053.

Mexico

El Bosque del Caribe, Cancun. Take a professional Spanish course 25 hours per week and enjoy the Caribbean beaches. Relaxed family-like atmosphere. No more than 6 students per class. Special conversation program. Mexican cooking classes and excursions to the Mayan sites. Housing with Mexican families. College credit available.

Dates: Year round. New classes begin every Monday. Group programs arranged at reduced fees. Cost: Enrollment fee $100, $180 per week. One week with a Mexican family $160. Contact: Eduardo Sotelo, Director, Calle Piña 1, S.M. 25, 77500 Cancún, Mexico; (011) 52-98-84-10-38, fax (011) 52-98-84-58-88; bcaribe@mail.cancun-language.com.mx.

Intensive Language Programs. Intensive Spanish immersion program in groups, 40 class hours per week including Spanish class, lectures, and Hispano-American courses. Executive, semester, and specialized programs for teachers, professionals, nurses, and adults continuing education. Live with Mexican family or in student residence. Excursions to historical and archaeological sites.

Dates: Year round starting every Monday. Cost: Tuition $190 per week; lodging $154 per week. Contact: The Center for Bilingual Multicultural Studies, Javier Espinosa, San Jeronimo #304, Cuernavaca, MOR-62179, Mexico; (011) 52-73-17-10-87, fax (011) 52-73-17-05-33; admin@bilingual-center.com, www.bilingual-center.com.

Internship Program. Internship and field experience are available in a wide variety of public and private facilities in the areas of social work, health, criminal justice, law enforcement, education, and more. CMI will make arrangements for you to work in your specific area and schedule Spanish classes around your work hours.

Dates: 1998: Year round. Begin any Monday. Cost: 1998: $369 per week includes Spanish classes, homestay, and internship program. Contact: Becky Alfaro, CMI, Fray Antonio de San Miguel, #173, Morelia, Michoacan, Mexico; (011) 52-43-12-45-96, www.spanish-language.com.

Poland

Penn-in-Warsaw. For students interested in Polish history and culture, as well as international relations, economics, and other business disciplines. Taught in English, this pro-

Choosing an Internship
Doing Your Own Search Saves Thousands in Fees
By Erika L. Weidner

The time is right and you have decided to gain field experience for a possible future career while learning the culture of a new country. Making the decision to be an intern is the simple part; the actual process of finding the right internship is likely to be more tedious. Careful research and asking the right questions will dramatically increase your chances of finding the position that provides the experience you need.

The first question is whether to take the independent search approach or go through an organization that connects interns with employers. Either way may be appropriate; it depends upon your needs and budget.

If you do your own search you have two options: you can either search for an already existing internship position, or you can approach a company or organization and propose that they employ you (paid or unpaid). Both choices require research and time—the second even more than the first. Both bypass the middleman and ultimately save you money.

Choosing a company that suits you in a location you prefer and then convincing them to employ you may seem like an easy and even enjoyable task—especially for an outgoing and resourceful individual. But don't do the work of finding the right company to employ you and stop there. My experience is that if a company does not have a specific position for interns, then taking you on as a "free" employee leaves you with nothing to do unless someone volunteers to invest their time in creating a project for you. The chances of a paid employee in a large organization spending time putting together a project for you are remote.

So if you approach a company or organization that does not have existing internship positions, be adamant about obtaining a clear description of what you will be doing. The larger the company, the less likely it is that you will receive guidance. Remember, the success of an internship does not depend upon the name of the organization but upon what you do and how well you work with your immediate supervisor.

Placement Organizations. You may assume that organizations arrange the placement themselves. However, an independent third party often does the search and uses the same approach I described as an independent option: they approach companies and organizations that may or may not have intern positions and convince them to take you on as an intern. When you send in your application, you receive a bill for placement fees before you are placed.

Unfortunately, you may not have the option of declining the position found for you. Thus, you may pay someone else a great deal of money to do the same thing you could have done yourself with much more care and attention.

Placement by a third party or agency or program may be the best choice for you: if you are more concerned with location than the type of internship, if you feel you are not experienced enough to act on your own, if the placement organization provides a support system that would help you, if you are pressed for time, if the cost of the placement is not a major concern.

Choosing a Location. Geographic location obviously makes a huge difference in the experience you will have as an intern. Internships are almost unheard of in Central and East

European countries that were formerly communist. The best method is to seek an existing position through an American, West European, or international organization or company. Internships are becoming more common throughout Eastern Europe, but do not expect people you meet to understand why you are working for free.

Always assume that the internship placement organization that you are using is doing what is financially best for them, not academically best for you. Ask specific questions to avoid later frustration: Who is organizing the internship? Is it an existing position or a new one?

Request a specific job description; if none seems to be available, insist.

Although most internship placement organizations say that fees are non-refundable, you may be able to regain some of your money should you have a negative experience. If you spend any of your designated time in a foreign country not working in an internship because you could not be placed, you should demand a partial refund. Too often we do not behave as consumers when engaged in educational travel.

An unpaid internship is exactly that, unpaid. But it is likely that your employer would be willing to pay for your travel expenses to and from your workplace. They may also pay for your lunch. Propose this after you have been working in the position for a week and have shown that you are productive. You may also want to ask local students in the area about the customary perks for interns. However, you should never count on perks when calculating your budget.

Researching and choosing an internship may take longer than the internship itself, but the time is well invested. Reflecting on what you are and are not comfortable doing and carefully considering which method is best for you will come close to ensuring a positive experience.

Checklist for Arranging Your Own Internship

1. Compile a list of organizations for which you would like to intern, with phone numbers and addresses. Go through publications related to your industry or country of choice to obtain names and ideas. To search on the web use key words like "internship" or "education," and see "Key Internet Resources" in the September/October issue of *Transitions Abroad*.

2. Decide which division you want to intern in by researching the organization; obtain the name of the assistant director of that department.

3. Write a letter stating your interest and describing what you want to achieve while interning at the organization. Come up with a goal or game plan prior to contact. This is the most important aspect of creating your own internship. Outline what it is you will be doing; do not simply ask for an unpaid position.

4. Follow up with a phone call a few weeks after you have sent the letter.

5. If the person to whom you wrote the letter is receptive to the idea, obtain a clear outline and written or verbal agreement on your tasks, who your supervisor will be, and your hours. Discuss his or her goals as well as your own.

6. Contact your potential supervisor and discuss the same thing you discussed with your original contact. This way you get a feel for their personality. If they cannot make time to talk with you at this stage, they will most likely not have time to deal with you during the internship either. Make sure the other people you will work with know what you will be doing and are receptive as well.

7. Use your intuition and go for it if it feels right. Set a date both parties agree on and make sure you know your contact name for day one. Call them a few days prior to your start date to remind them you are coming.

gram will acquaint students with the political and economic changes occurring in Poland and provide insight into the conditions for doing business in a changing economy. Short-term internships with Polish or joint-venture institutions will complement class instruction.

Dates: May 30-Jul 5. Cost: Tuition $2,968; housing $300. Contact: Penn Summer Abroad, College of General Studies, Univ. of Pennsylvania, 3440 Market St., Suite 100, Philadelphia, PA 19104-3335; (215) 898-5738, fax (215) 573-2053.

Spain

Seville Internship Option. A 3- or 6-credit internship may be requested by students attending the CC-CS academic program during the Fall or Spring semester. Applicants must have completed 1 advanced college-level Spanish course. Internships are unpaid and not guaranteed. Many potential areas available. An internship-application must be requested in addition to the program application.

Dates: Spring: Jan 26-May 21. Fall: Call for details. Cost: Semester $8,175. Includes tuition, double occupancy room and full board, laundry, study visits, orientation, health insurance, enrollment, activity and computer fees including e-mail account. Contact: Dr. Judith Ortiz, Director U.S., Center for Cross-Cultural Study, 446 Main St., Amherst, MA 01002; (800) 377-2621, fax (413) 256-1968; cccs@crocker.com, www.cccs.com.

The Center for Cross-Cultural Study. A 3- or 6-credit internship may be requested by students attending the CC-CS academic program during the fall or spring semester. Applicants must have 1 semester of Spanish past the intermediate level and must be accepted into the academic program. Internships are unpaid and not guaranteed. Potential areas: banking, finance, accounting, general business, marketing, health related fields, education and student-teaching, public relations, museums and cultural centers. An internship application must be requested in addition to the program application.

Dates: Fall: Sep-Dec; Spring: Feb-May. Cost: Fall/Spring $8,705; academic year $16,100. Includes tuition, double occupancy room and board, laundry, study visits, orientation, health insurance, e-mail and computer lab fees. Contact: CC-CS, Dept. T, 446 Main St., Amherst, MA 01002; (413) 256-0011 or (800) 377-2621, fax (413) 256-1968; cccs@crocker.com, www.cccs.com.

United Kingdom and Ireland

Fashion Design and Merchandising. London College of Fashion is the only college in the British Univ. sector to specialize in fashion. Located in the center of London, students enroll in a selection of semester and summer programs with internship options. While studying in regular classes during part of the week, you can earn credits 2 days a week in professionally oriented internships in public relations, design, marketing, retailing, trend forecasting, and design companies.

Six credits offered. Twenty-four internships per year. Prerequisites: prior work experience is helpful, although it is not mandatory. Application materials: completed application form and resume.

Dates: Fall or Spring: 12 weeks. Summer: 4 weeks. Application deadline: Rolling admission. Cost: £2,425 12-week program, £1,450 4-week program. Contact: Jan Miller, London College of Fashion, 20 John Princes St., London W1M 0BJ, U.K.; (011) 44-171-514-7411, fax (011) 44-171-514-7490; lcfdali@london-fashion.ac.uk.

Hansard Scholars Programme. An opportunity for students to become involved in the workings of the British government and British politics, accompanied by a comprehensive study of British politics and British public policy. Students are mainly assigned internships with Members of Parliament, but also to political parties, think tanks, and pressure groups.

Prerequisites: 2 or more years of college. Application materials: transcript, 2 letters of recommendation, and an essay.

Dates: Spring 1999: Jan 11-Apr 2; Summer 1999: May 17-Jul 23; Fall 1999: Sep 28-Dec 18. Cost: 1998: £4,500 per semester (includes housing and London travel costs). Contact: Penny O'Hara, Programme Manager, The Hansard Society, St. Philips, Building North, Sheffield St., London WC2A 2EX, U.K.; (011) 44-171-955-7478, fax (011) 44-171-955-7492; hansard@lse.ac.uk.

IES London Work-Study Program. The first 4 weeks consist of an orientation from BUNAC and IES, and an intensive study period where students select 2 courses totaling 6 credits. During the 5th week, students find their own accommodations and paid job. Students spend the final 7 weeks working and taking a 4-credit evening tutorial.

Dates: May 19-Aug 13, 1999. Cost: $2,400. Includes tuition (maximum 10 credits), housing, and a Tube pass for the first 5 weeks, international health insurance, and visa processing. Contact: Institute for the International Education of Students, 223 W. Ohio St., Chicago, IL 60610-4196; (800) 995-2300 or (312) 944-1750, fax (312) 944-1448; info@ iesabroad.org, www.iesabroad.org.

Internships in Dublin. Interns live with families or in apartments. Two programs available: 6-credit internship plus 9-credit classwork in Irish Studies through the Institute of Public Administration or full-time (15-16 credits) internship. IPA placements may be in Parliament, municipal government, health care administration, radio/TV, and at the Irish Times. Full-time placements available in social services, communication, film, advertising and others. Fields: public administration, parliamentary internships, political science, tech-

nology, finance, health and communications. Fifteen-16 credits per semester, 10 for Summer. Prerequisites: 2.5 GPA for traditional full-time internships, 3.0 for IPA internships. Adaptability and maturity. Strong performance in major. Junior or senior status. Application materials: SUNY application.

Dates: Fall: early Sep-mid-Dec (application deadline Feb 1); Spring: early Jan-late Apr (application deadline Sep 1); Summer: early Jun-mid-Aug (application deadline Feb 1). Cost: 1998 estimates: IPA $6,737 for Dublin internships (full-time) $5,793; Summer $4,350 (Dublin internships only, IPA not available). Estimates include full-day orientation before departure, application fee, room and board, food allowance, health and accident insurance, roundtrip airfare from N.Y., bus pass. SUNY tuition not included. Contact: Office of International Programs, Box 2000, SUNY Cortland, Cortland, NY 13045; (607) 753-2209, fax (607) 753-5989; studyabroad@cortland.edu, www.studyabroad.com/suny/cortland.

Internships in London. Undergraduates and graduates and those wishing to explore career choices are able to participate in a full-time internship for a summer, fall, or spring term. Skills, experience, and interest will be matched as closely as possible to the internship. Applications in all fields will be considered.

Dates: Call for details. Cost: 1998: Six weeks $2,375, 12 weeks $3,275, 24 weeks $5,275. Includes accommodations, orientation, placement, support. Contact: Study Abroad Office, Univ. of Pittsburgh, 802 William Pitt Union, Pittsburgh, PA 15260; (412) 648-7413, fax (412) 383-7166; stdyabrd+@pitt.edu.

Ireland and Northern Ireland. Twelve program opportunities in the Republic and the North. University study and special subject area programs including internships in the Irish parliament. Program provides a full range of services including a full-time resident director and staff in Dublin, orientation, homestay, and guaranteed housing.

Dates: Fall, Spring, academic year, and Summer. Semesters and terms. Cost: Varies. Call for current fees. Contact: Meghan Mazick, Beaver College Center for Education Abroad, 450 S. Easton Rd., Glenside, PA 19038-3295; (888) BEAVER-9, fax (215) 572-2174; cea@beaver.edu, www.beaver.edu/cea.

Study in Great Britain. Thirty-one program opportunities in England, Scotland, and Wales. University study and special subject area programs, including internships, for fall, spring, academic year and summer. Program provides a full range of services including predeparture advising, orientation, homestay, and guaranteed housing. Need-based scholarships available.

Dates: Fall, Spring, academic year. Summer semester and terms. Cost: Varies. Call for current fees. Contact: Beaver College Center for Education Abroad, 450 S. Easton Rd., Glenside, PA 19038-3295; (888) BEAVER-9, fax (215) 572-2174; cea@beaver.edu, www.beaver.edu/cea.

Study in Wales. Opportunities for either year-long or semester study abroad at the Univ. of Wales Swansea (10,500 students, located by the sea) in fully integrated programs. Host family and summer internship programs are available. University housing, orientation, and cultural events are integral to all programs. Swansea is a lively maritime city with great social life and numerous outdoor activities.

Dates: Sep-Dec/Jan-May/May-Jul. Cost: From $4,500. Contact: Emma Frearson, Study Abroad Swansea, American Studies Centre, Univ. of Wales Swansea, Singleton Park, Swansea SA2 8PP, Wales, U.K.; (011) 44-1-792-295135, fax (011) 44-1-792-295719; e.frearson@swansea.ac.uk, www.swan.ac.uk/sao/saohp.html.

Univ. of North London. Interns live in apartments in central London with other participants. Part-time interns also take classes at the Univ. of North London. Opportunities in Par-liament, hospitals, promotional agencies, schools, and radio/TV. Supervision by on-site personnel. Journals and essays or projects submitted at end of program. Fields: health, communications, political science, publicity, marketing. Three-16 credits. Full and part-time internships available. Application deadline: Spring: Sep 1; Fall: Feb 1. Prerequisites: 2.5 GPA, strong performance in major, and junior or senior status.

Dates: Fall and Spring semester, 12 weeks each. Cost: $4,100 for Fall and $4,592 for Spring (includes room and board, health insurance, local transportation, international airfare, orientation). Application fee: $20. Contact: Office of International Programs, Box 2000, SUNY Cortland, Cortland, NY 13045; (607) 753-2209, fax (607) 753-5989; studyabroad@cortland.edu, www.study abroad.com/suny/cortland.

United States

Fourth World Movement. The Fourth World Movement is the U.S. branch of the international organization ATD Fourth World, which is devoted to fighting extreme poverty. Two 3-month internships are held in the U.S. each year for Americans as an orientation program for those considering volunteering for at least 2 years. Minimum age is 19. A 2-month summer program may be available.

Dates: Internships held from mid-Sep-mid-Dec, and mid-Feb-May. Cost: Interns receive free housing; they pay food and spending costs. Contact: Jill Cunningham, Fourth World Movement, 7600 Willow Hill Dr., Landover, MD 20785. Send SASE. (301) 336-9489, fax (301) 336-0092; fourworl@his.com.

Master of International and Intercultural Management. The School for International Training Master of International and Intercultural Management offers concentrations in sustainable development, international education, and training and human resource de-

Internship Programs

velopment in 1 academic year program. This degree is designed for individuals wishing to make a career change or enter the field. A practical training component enables "on-the-job" training and an opportunity to work internationally.

Dates: Call for details. Cost: Call for details. Contact: Kat Eldred, Director of Outreach and Recruitment, Admissions Counselor, School for International Learning, P.O. Box 676, Kipling Rd., Brattleboro, VT 05302; (802) 257-7751, fax (802) 258-3500; admissions@sit.edu, www.sit.edu.

Summer Internship and Seminar Programs. Internship program in Washington, DC with Middle East organizations, dealing with such issues as Palestine, U.S.-Arab relations, and trade. Supplementing the internship are lectures from scholars and government employees familiar with the issues facing the Arab world.

Dates: Jun-Aug, 1999. Cost: Call for information. Contact: National Council on U.S.-Arab Relations, (202) 293-0801; internship@ncusar.org.

Sustainable Living Skills Internships. Intensive 10-week internships in sustainable living skills. Daily classes focus on sustainable forestry, appropriate technology, and organic gardening.

Dates: Spring, Summer, and Fall. Cost: $1,800 for room and board, and tuition. Contact: Internship Coordinator, Aprovecho Research Center, 80574 Hazelton Rd., Cottage Grove, OR 97424; (541) 942-8198; www.efn.org/~apro.

Venezuela

Venusa Institute of Int'l. Studies and Modern Languages. Mérida and the Venusa Institute are nestled at the foot of the Sierra Nevada mountain range deep in the heart of the Venezuelan Andes. Fields of study include Spanish language, Latin American history and culture, international business, cross-cultural communications, teaching of English as a second language (TESOL), Intl. agriculture, ecology and botany, anthropology and sociology, and more. Internships available in the fall and spring. Homestays. One semester college-level Spanish and overall GPA of 2.5 required. Summer short-term study tours available to different regions of Venezuela, 3 credits per module.

Dates: Fall: late Aug-mid-Dec; Spring: early Jan-end of Apr; Summer: 2 sessions, mid-May-late Jun and late Jun-mid-Aug. Cost: Fall/Spring estimate $4,500 plus SUNY tuition per semester; Summer $2,570 plus SUNY tuition. Estimate includes full day orientation in the U.S., orientation in Venezuela, application fee, room and board with local family, airfare to NY to Mérida roundtrip, 2 full day field trips, insurance, books and supplies, program administration costs. SUNY tuition additional. Contact: Office of International Programs, Box 2000, SUNY Cortland, Cortland, NY 13045; (607) 753-2209, fax (607) 753-5989; studyabroad@cortland.edu, www.study abroad.com/suny/cortland.

Worldwide

¿?don Quijote In-Country Spanish Language Schools. Intensive Spanish language courses using the communicative method are combined with an intensive immersion in the social and cultural life of some of Spain's most interesting cities (Salamanca, Barçelona, Granada, Malaga). Airport pick-up service, study counseling, homestay or student flats, excursions, access to recreational facilities, touring, and sightseeing opportunities. donQuijote now offers intensive Spanish language courses through partner schools in Latin America: Cuernavaca and Mèrida, Mexico; Antigua, Guatemala; Alajuela, Costa Rica; and Quito, Ecuador.

Dates: Year round—Fall, Spring, Winter, and Summer. Cost: Inquire. Contact: ¿?don Quijote, Apartado de Correos 333, 37080

Salamanca, Spain; (011) 34-923-268-860, fax (011) 34-923-268-815; donquijote@offcampus.es, www.teclata.es/donquijote.

Boston Univ. International Programs. Students enroll in 3 academic courses in conjunction with a professional internship experience. Students choose from internships in advertising and public relations, the arts, business and economics, health and human service, hospitality administration, the media (journalism, film, and television), politics, and prelaw. The internship experience allows students to explore organizations from multi-national corporations to local businesses, from hospitals to community service centers, from major magazine publishers or film production studios to local radio or advertising agencies.

Academic credit offered. Prerequisites: good academic standing, 3.0 GPA; language depending on site. Application materials: 2 references, transcript, essays, academic approval, interview for upper-level language programs.

Dates: Fall, Spring, and Summer (length varies). Application deadline: Mar 15 (Summer and Fall); Oct 15 (Spring). Cost: $4,400-$8,900. Application fee: $35. Contact: Boston Univ., International Programs, 232 Bay State Rd., 5th Fl., Boston, MA 02215; (617) 353-9888, fax (617) 353-5402; abroad@bu.edu, www.bu.edu/abroad.

Brethren Colleges Abroad. Opportunities vary by location. Examples include: business at Siemens Corp. in Germany; social work at a shelter in England; political science at the Council of Europe and The Human Rights Institute in France; business in import-export companies and an international hotel chain in China and Japan; village development with The Resource Foundation in Ecuador; women's advocacy in India.

Fields: business, teaching, political science, social work. Academic credit offered. Prerequisites: participation in BCA's academic program overseas for at least 1 semester.

Dates: Before, after, or during academic semesters. Cost: Living expenses. Application

fee: $150. Contact: Tamula Drumm, Brethren Colleges Abroad, 605 College Ave., N. Manchester, IN 46962; (219) 982-5045, fax (219) 982-7755; bca@manchester.edu; www.studyabroad.com/bca.

Fine Arts Intern. Unpaid internship at a non-profit organization that supports alternative artists, fights censorship by providing censored artists with legal counsel and by educating the public on freedom of special issues. Interns participate in fundraising, supporting artists, data entry, general office work. Also places interns with artists and organizations overseas.

Dates: Ongoing, no deadline. Cost: None. Contact: Institute for Unpopular Culture, Internship Coordinator, 1850 Union St., #1523, San Francisco, CA 94123; (415) 986-4382, fax (415) 986-4354.

IAESTE-U.S. IAESTE-U.S. arranges reciprocal exchanges among more than 60 member countries for students of engineering, architecture, and the sciences to obtain on-the-job practical training with host employers in other countries. The IAESTE program is administered in the U.S. by the Association for International Practical Training (AIPT) in Columbia, MD.

Fields: Technical Fields. Seventy-five to 100 internships per year. Two hundred-300 applicants. Prerequisites: Junior level standing, enrolled full-time at time of application. Application materials: application, reference, transcript, language certification.

Dates: Summer placements (other periods available). Application deadline: Dec 16. Cost: $150 placement. Compensation: cost of living. Application fee: $50. Contact: Jeff Lange, Program Assistant/Eric Haines, Program Director, IAESTE-U.S., 10400 Little Patuxent Pkwy., Suite 250 L, Columbia, MD 21044-3510; (410) 997-3068, fax (410) 997-5186; iaeste@aipt.org, www.aipt.org.

International Cooperative Education. Paid internship/employment for college and university students for a period of 8-12 weeks in

4 European (Belgium, Finland, Germany, and Switzerland) and two Asian (Japan and Singapore) countries. Employment depends on foreign language knowledge, major, and previous work experience. Work permits and housing are provided.

Dates: From Jun-Sep. Cost: Students must pay for air transportation and have a reserve of at least $800 for initial expenses. Program fee $800. Contact: Günter Seefeldt, PhD, Director, International Cooperative Education Program, 15 Spiros Way, Menlo Park, CA 94025; (650) 323-4944, fax (650) 323-1104, ICEMenlo@aol.com, http://members.aol.com/ICEMenlo.

International Exchange Opportunities. International Agricultural Exchange Association (I.A.E.A.) organizes agricultural exchange programs to foreign countries for men and women 18-30 years old. I.A.E.A. makes the travel and housing arrangements to approved host families. Fees cover airfares, work permits, seminars, supervision, travel, and medical insurance.

Dates: Mar, Apr, Jul, Aug, Sep, Oct, Nov. Cost: $2,550-$6,655 (1998). Contact: International Agricultural Exchange Assn., 1000 1st Ave. S., Great Falls, MT 59401; (406) 727-1999, fax (406) 727-1997.

International Internship Program. People to People International coordinates 2-month, unpaid internships for students and professionals for 6 units of graduate or undergraduate (junior level and above) credit, or on an audit-basis, through the Univ. of Missouri-Kansas City. Open to all fields. Positions correspond with academic background, work experience, and career goals. Internships are available in the following countries (subject to change): Kenya, England, Italy, Denmark, Ireland, Argentina, Germany, Russia, and Australia.

Dates: Flexible throughout the year. Apply 3 months in advance. Cost: $1,875 includes tuition and placement fee. Housing and airfare not included. Contact: People to People International, 501 E. Armour Blvd., Kansas City, MO 64109-2200; (816) 531-4701, fax (816) 561-7502; internships@ptpi.org, www.ptpi.org/studyabroad.

Internships International. Quality, non-paying internships in London, Paris, Dublin, Cologne, France, Shanghai, Santiago, Budapest, Melbourne, Bangkok, Hanoi, and Ho Chi Minh City. Internships in all fields, from 6 weeks to 6 months. Open to college graduates and seniors requiring an internship to graduate.

Dates: Based on individual's needs. Cost: $700 program fee. Contact: Judy Tilson, Director, Internships International, 1116 Cowper Dr., Raleigh, NC 27608; (919) 832-1575, fax (919) 834-7170; intintl@aol.com, http://rtpnet.org/~intintl.

MAST International. Offers young people between the ages of 18 and 30 the opportunity to participate in 3- to 12-month practical training internships in the areas of agriculture, horticulture, and forestry. Participants must have at least 6 months work experience in their chosen area; some post-secondary education is preferable.

Dates: Open, applications due 4 months prior to start date. Cost: $400 program fee ($25 non-refundable application fee). Contact: Susan Von Bank, MAST International, 1954 Buford Ave., #240, St. Paul, MN 55108; (800) 346-6278, fax (612) 625-7031; svonbank@coa1.agoff.umn.edu, www.mast.agri.umn.edu.

Syracuse Internships Abroad. All internships are supervised by Syracuse faculty or approved adjuncts who teach in Syracuse programs abroad. Actual work experience is assigned by an agency supervisor. Interviews and final placements take place overseas. Most internships are part of a varied semester experience including coursework, field trips, and social activities.

Fields: business, advertising, political science, social agencies, drama, human development, social work, education, photography, communications. Academic credit offered. Three-6 internship credits, up to 18 total credits. One hundred internships per year. Ninety applicants. Prerequisites: Sophomore status, essays, recommendations, good academic standing. Application materials: application and recommendation forms.

Dates: Fall, Spring, Summer (6 weeks or longer). Application deadline: Mar 15 (Summer), Apr 1 (Fall), Oct 15 (Spring). Cost: $3,500-$15,000 (includes room, food, international airfare, tuition). Compensation: none. Application fee: $50. Contact. Syracuse Univ., 119 Euclid Ave., Syracuse, NY 13244-4170; (800) 235-3472, fax (315) 443-4593; suabroad@syr.edu, http://sumweb.syr.edu/dipa.

The Global Campus. Choose from 11 language, theme, area studies, integrated classroom, and field study opportunities in countries ranging from England to Venezuela. Course topics include language, culture, international relations, and international development. Field placements and internships available for credit in Ecuador, India, Kenya, and Senegal. Open to all students and professionals.

Dates: Academic year, semester, quarter, and Summer options. Cost: From $2,650-$16,500. Includes tuition, study abroad, and registration fees, room and board, and excursions. Contact: The Global Campus, Univ. of Minnesota, 102 Nicholson Hall, 216 Pillsbury Dr. SE, Minneapolis, MN 55455-0138; (612) 626-9000, fax (612) 626-8009; umabroad@tc.umn.edu, www.umabroad.umn.edu.

For more listings of internship opportunities and programs, and for bargains worldwide, travel tips, and all sorts of information on learning, living, working, and traveling abroad, see *Transitions Abroad* magazine. To order a single copy or a subscription, please call 1-800-293-0373 or visit the *Transitions Abroad* web site at www.transabroad.com.

"Our mission is to produce well trained, culturally aware teachers who contribute to the ideals of the global community"

TEACH AND TRAVEL WITH TRANSWORLD

We are dedicated to providing high quality courses and continuing the development of English language training services.

- Courses taught by experts with 25+ years of program directing, curriculum design and teacher training experience
- Bi-monthly start dates, full and part time courses available
- Unique modular courses to accommodate individual experience
- Maximum 12 students per class, 6 per teaching group
- Exposure to a wide variety of exciting teaching approaches, contemporary materials and fun activities

- On-site practical training with foreign students
- Hands-on Computer Assisted Language Learning in our Multi-Media Computer Lab with current software library
- No second language, teaching or computer experience required
- Job preparation courses and placement assistance through Transworld's International Teaching Career Network
- Beautiful school, conveniently located in downtown San Francisco

Visit our website: www.transworldschools.com

Transworld Schools
701 Sutter Street, 2nd floor
San Francisco, CA 94109 USA
Tel: +1 415-928-2835
Fax: +1 415-928-0261
email: transwd@aol.com

Transworld CTEFL is internationally recognized as the most innovative and comprehensive TEFL course in the US

CHAPTER 15

TEEN
STUDY & TRAVEL
RESOURCES

Never before have teens been so fortunate in the choice of overseas educational travel options. Gone are the days when a student eager to travel overseas had only a few creative alternatives to a whirlwind bus and train tour of Europe.

Teen Organizations

Alliance for International Educational and Cultural Exchange, 1776 Massachusetts Ave., Suite 620, Washington, DC 20036; (202) 293-6141, fax (202) 293-6144. Publishes the **International Exchange Locator: A Guide to U.S. Organizations, Federal Agencies, and Congressional Committees Active in International Exchange**. Annual. $11.95 plus $4 s/h. Lists high school and college exchange organizations and others involved in international exchange at all levels.

American Association of School Administrators (AASA), 1801 N. Moore St., Arlington, VA 22209; (703) 528-0700; www.aasa. org. AASA conducted a study released in 1996, titled "Preparing Students for the 21st Century." A booklet containing results is available for purchase from AASA. The study pointed out the need for students to develop an international perspective. In 1999, the association will release results of another study titled "Preparing Schools and School Systems for the 21st Century." That study will focus on "the characteristics of schools and school systems capable of preparing students for a global knowledge/information age." AASA also has related publications on these studies, plus a booklet titled, "Education Around the World ... Snapshots from the Global Village."

AmeriSpan Unlimited, P.O. Box 40007, Philadelphia, PA 19106; (800) 879-6640; info@ AmeriSpan.com, www.AmeriSpan.com. Family, teen, senior, and adult language programs in 12 countries in Mexico, Spain, Central and South America. Housing with a host family.

Council on International Educational Exchange (Council), Council-Pubs Dept., 205 E. 42nd St., New York, NY 10017-5706; (888)-COUNCIL, fax (212) 822-2699; info@ciee.org, http://www.ciee.org. Publishers of materials on work, study, and travel abroad, especially for students; also administers the Council Work Abroad Program and Council Workcamps.

Council on Standards for International Education Travel (CSIET), 212 S Henry St., Alexandria, VA 22314; (703) 739-9050, fax (703) 739-9035. CSIET is a nonprofit organization committed to quality international educational travel and exchange. It establishes standards for organizations operating international educational travel and exchange programs at the high school level and monitors compliance with those standards by annually reviewing those programs that submit themselves for evaluation. It also disseminates information on international educational travel organizations. **Advisory List of International Educational Travel & Exchange Programs**, published annually ($15 postpaid, $20 overseas), lists programs for high school students which adhere to CSIET's standards and provides valuable information for prospective exchange students, host families, and schools.

EF Foundation for Foreign Study (known internationally as EF High School Year), 1 Education St., Cambridge, MA 02141; (617) 619-1400, fax (617) 619-1001; http://ef.com/hsy/. Nonprofit organization dedicated to encouraging cultural awareness and mutual respect between nations through cultural exchange. Over 40,000 students from 25 countries since 1979.

Institute of International Education (IIE). IIE Books, Institute of International Education, P.O. Box 371, Annapolis Junction, MD 20701-0371; (800) 445-0443, fax (301) 206-9789; iiebooks@pmds.com. Free catalog. Publisher of authoritative directories for study or teaching abroad and financial aid, and distributor of Central Bureau (U.K.) publications on working abroad.

Intercultural Press, P.O. Box 700, Yarmouth, ME 04096; (800) 370-2665, or (207) 846-5168, fax (207) 846-5181; interculturalpress@ internetmci.com, www.bookmasters.com/ interclt.htm. Intercultural Press publishes numerous books on international living, travel, study, and cross-cultural experiences. Titles include: **Host Family Survival Kit: A Guide for American Host Families, Survival Kit for Overseas Living, Exchange Student Survival Kit.**

International Youth Exchange Staff (USIA), 301 4th St., Room 314, SW, Washington, DC 20547; (202) 619-6299. The International Youth Exchange Staff of USIA oversees activities initiated under the President's International Youth Exchange Initiative and works closely with other organizations involved in international educational exchange activities.

Mobility International USA (MIUSA), P.O. Box 10767, Eugene, OR 97440; (541) 343-1284 (voice and TDD), fax (541) 343-6812; miusa@igc. A national not-for-profit organization that promotes and facilitates opportunities for people with disabilities to participate in international educational exchange and travel. Resources include: **Looking Back, Looking Forward**, a 17-minute video of interviews with exchange program participants including some high school students; **A World of Options for the 1990's: Guide to International Educational Exchange, Community Service, and Travel for Persons with Disabilities.**

NAFSA: Association of International Educators, P.O. Box 1020, Sewickley, PA 15143; (800) 836-4994, fax (412) 741-0609. Essential publications for advisers and administrators in international educational exchange. For membership information, contact NAFSA: Association of International Educators, 1875 Connecticut Ave. NW, Suite 1000, Washington, DC 20009-5728, (202) 939-3103 or (202) 462-4811, fax (202) 667-3419; inbox@nafsa.org, www.nafsa.org.

National Association of Secondary School Principals, 1904 Association Dr., Dept. CS, Reston, VA 20191-1537; (703) 860-0200, fax (703) 476-9319; jacksonr@nassp.org. A professional association of more than 43,000 school administrators. Administers School Partnerships, International, a short-term, school-to-school pairing program designed to foster long-term academic and cultural partnerships between secondary schools in the U.S. and other countries. A U.S. secondary school is "linked" with a similar secondary school abroad. The partner schools exchange information, educational and cultural materials, and, ultimately, groups averaging 6 to 15 students, accompanied by a faculty member, for 2 to 3 weeks. Students live with a host family, attend classes, and participate in school activities. Cultural orientation is provided upon arrival in the host country before transferring to the partner school location. Cost to participants is $650 to $1,995, including transportation and insurance.

National Federation of State High School Associations, 11724 NW Plaza Cir., Kansas City, MO 64153; (816) 464-5400, fax (816) 464-5571. Can answer questions about athletic and activity eligibility issues.

National School Boards Association, 1680 Duke St., Alexandria, VA 22314; (703) 838-6722, fax (703) 683-7590. A broad-based, not-for-profit organization. Publishes *The American School Board Journal* and *The Executive Educator*, monthly magazines.

NIS/Secondary School Initiative Staff, USIA, 301 4th St., SW, Rm. 320, Washington, DC 20547; (202) 619-6299. The NIS/Secondary School Initiative Staff initiated overseas activities under the Freedom Support Act of 1992 and works closely with other organizations involved in international educational exchange activities.

U.S. Information Agency (USIA), Exchange Visitor Program Services, 301 4th St., (FEMA Room 200), SW, Washington, DC 20547; (202) 475-2389. The USIA evaluates not-for-profit organizations to determine whether they meet Criteria for Teenage Visitor Programs. It grants authorization to issue Forms IAP-66 for securing J-1 visas to enter the U.S.

For more listings of teen study and travel resources, and for bargains worldwide, travel tips, and all sorts of information on learning, living, working, and traveling abroad, see *Transitions Abroad* magazine. To order a single copy or a subscription, please call 1-800-293-0373 or visit the *Transitions Abroad* web site at www.transabroad.com.

Exchanges: The Outbound Experience
Opportunities Abound for High School Students

By Vanessa Relli-Moreau

Every year the parents of thousands of international high school students send them to the U.S. not only to learn in school but to learn to be citizens of a multicultural world. Three times as many foreign students as American students take advantage of the opportunity for an international exchange. Too many American high school students let this world of opportunities pass them by. The U.S., so ardent about competition and emphatic about getting an edge in global commerce, still doesn't recognize the value in travel and study abroad.

Study abroad is not only one of life's most memorable and rewarding adventures, it is often the first real opportunity for the independence that high school kids crave. Students come back to their home country as global citizens with skills that can not be taught in the classroom. They learn about different values and ways of thinking and being. They learn to be open-minded, flexible, and tolerant of differences. High school students who come back from their experiences abroad are more centered and mature than their counterparts without a study-abroad experience, with coping and decision-making skills that others their age may lack when entering college or the job market.

Exchange students can live in another country for an academic year, semester, or summer. Many attend intensive language courses and the local high school and live with host families. They receive support from local coordinators who provide a counseling and emergency support network. For most exchange programs the participant must be between 15 and 18, have at least a C average, and be in reasonably good health.

Many exchange organizations offer financial aid, scholarships, fundraising information, and loan opportunities. Often the cost for expenses overseas are equal to or less than what would be spent at home. Exchange organization fees cover activities in your home country and while overseas, field trips coordinated by local representatives, orientation and screening (for the students, host families, local coordinators, and instructors), a 24-hour emergency network, locating a host family and school, and obtaining the student's visa.

Once it is decided that study abroad is an affordable dream, you can begin your search for your perfect exchange program. Both parents and students should ask the following questions to make sure that an organization is sound and that you feel comfortable with them:

• Is the organization accepted by the Council on Standards for International Educational Travel (CSIET)?
• What is their track record?
• What kind of expertise does the staff bring to the organization?
• Are you able to check references from former students, host families, and schools?
• How do they handle emergencies?
• Do they offer cross-cultural training to students, area representatives, and host families?
• What does tuition include?
• What other services do they offer?
• Do they seem responsive to questions?

- Do they give out this information in writing?
- Are host families screened?
- What type of visa will the student travel on and does the organization help arrange this visa?
- What kind of insurance coverage will the student have, if any?
- Who makes the travel arrangements?
- Are travel costs included in the exchange organization's fee?
- Are there language requirements?
- Will the student lose any academic credit?
- What types of financial aid are available to the student?

Summer Abroad Opportunities

Imagine being 16 years old and arriving in Paris for the first time on a hot June morning. Your host family for the next month is waiting to take you by train to a small village called Oradour-sur-Glane. It is in the heart of France, where there are green hills and shimmering lakes, porcelain is made, and the villagers are some of the friendliest in the world.

This is the new trend for high school students—spending their summers traveling, learning, sightseeing, and experiencing cultures overseas. These students take their once idle summers and turn them into the adventure of a lifetime.

The Choice of Programs

There are many different programs from which to choose. Students may choose an adventure that lasts a week or one that lasts the entire summer. They may choose programs that focus on everything from academics and language enrichment to outdoor adventures such as camping, rock climbing, skiing, and canoeing. Or they may pick a travel program devoted to sightseeing and daily excursions. The programs also vary greatly in price. A student may pay anywhere from a few hundred dollars to several thousand.

Picking Your Best Option

Because short-term summer programs vary so much, it is important to choose carefully. Even though the stay is for a short time, students and parents should research the program as thoroughly as if it were for an academic year. Certain programs house students in supervised dorms; others place students with host families. Which situation feels more comfortable?

If you're looking to gain academic enrichment, check with your high school advisers before leaving. Some programs may include arranging and paying for transportation abroad and for the excursions. Some do not. It is important to note what you will need to pay for and what services are included.

All programs should provide an orientation and thoroughly screen students as well as host families. Ask what their procedures are. Does a student need to have prior language experience? Ask for references of individuals who have participated in the program. Finally, ask if the program been accepted for listing with the Council on Standards for International Educational Travel (CSIET).

Why Study Abroad in Summer?

The academic year program is the ultimate experience in studying abroad. You are immersed every day in another culture. Students experience holidays, school, friends, family, their day-to-day life all from the perspective of their host country. But sometimes it's a good idea to begin building up to this experience by getting your feet wet first in a short-term adventure abroad. If you are perhaps not quite ready to handle a full academic year abroad, this is an opportunity to grow and mature into the experience.

With a short-term summer abroad there is no worry about missing credits. In fact, many students earn extra credits. Students should speak to their high school administrators about gaining credit for language study if they are not staying in an English-speaking country.

A summer excursion is like a honeymoon. You are not there long enough to fight with friends or their host families. Yet you are able to get a taste of what everyday life might be like. The short experience is planned so that every day is a wonderful adventure—of new foods, new friends, and traveling. The purpose of these programs is to see as much as possible. Knowing that students will only be with their host families a short while, oftentimes the families like to take their student to see something new every day.

The Best of All Worlds

For the price of a good summer camp, high school students have the opportunity to broaden their horizons and accomplish something productive with their summer. As with any experience abroad, universities and potential job employers look favorably upon a student with international experience. You will come back with new knowledge and appreciation of your world. Hopefully the next step will be an academic year abroad, and you will be ready for it.

Where to Get Information

The Advisory List of International Educational Travel, published annually by the Council on Standards for International Educational Travel (CSIET), is a resource from which prospective exchange students and their parents and school leaders can learn about the scope, background, and operations of programs abroad. The Advisory List describes 64 international youth exchange organizations that comply with CSIET's standards.

To order the Advisory List send a check for $15 (Virginia residents add 4.5 percent sales tax) to: CSIET, 212 S. Henry St., Alexandria, VA 22314; (703) 739-9050, fax (703) 739-9035. Overseas orders cost $20, including postage and handling.

CHAPTER 16

TEEN
STUDY & TRAVEL
PROGRAMS

The following listing of teen study and travel programs was supplied by the organizers in 1998 and is updated in each July/August issue of Transitions Abroad *magazine. Contact the program directors to confirm costs, dates, and other details. Please tell them you read about their programs in this book! Programs based in more than one country or region are listed under "Worldwide."*

Africa

African American Studies. One- to 3-week educational programs in Africa, Cuba, and Brazil based on a theme: culture, race, economics, politics.

Dates: Feb, Jul, Aug. Cost: From $1,000 to $5,000. Contact: Harold Rogers, AASP, 19 S. La Salle St., #301, Chicago, IL 60603; (312) 443-0929, fax (773) 684-7309.

Asia

Youth For Understanding (YFU). YFU, established in 1951, prepares young people, aged 15-18 years, for their responsibilities and opportunities in a changing, interdependent world through homestay exchange programs. YFU offers year, semester, and summer study

abroad and scholarship opportunities in Japan and South Korea.

Dates: Semester: Jan-Jun, summer: 4, 6, 8 weeks (Jun, Jul, Aug). Cost: $3,775-$5,975. Contact: Program Information Office, Youth For Understanding (YFU) International Exchange, 3501 Newark St., NW, Washington, DC 20016; (800) TEENAGE or (202) 966-6800, fax (202) 895-1104; pio@yfu.org, www.yfu.org.

Australasia

Youth For Understanding (YFU). YFU, established in 1951, prepares young people, aged 15-18 years, for their responsibilities and opportunities in a changing, interdependent world through homestay exchange programs. YFU offers year, semester, and summer study abroad and scholarship opportunities in Australia and New Zealand.

Dates: Year: Jan-Dec, Semester: Jan-Jun, summer: 4, 6, 8 weeks (Jun, Jul, Aug). Cost: $3,475-$6,175. Contact: Program Information Office, Youth For Understanding (YFU) International Exchange, 3501 Newark St., NW, Washington, DC 20016; (800) TEENAGE or (202) 966-6800, fax (202) 895-1104; pio@yfu.org, www.yfu.org.

Australia

The Adventure Company. The Adventure Company, Australia specializes in top quality adventure and nature tours for individuals and groups. We run a variety of scheduled trips, all of which involve a strong nature element. Many of the tours take place in World Heritage Listed National Parks. Assist marine scientists with their research, explore the ecology of the ancient rainforest of far North Queensland, study flora and fauna, or examine Aboriginal art sites dating back 40,000 years, with highly experienced specialist guides.

Dates: Call program for information. Join 1- to 12-day trips. Cost: $50-$1,500, including all trips departing from Cairns. Contact: Gary Hill, The Adventure Company, Australia, P.O. Box 5740, Cairns, Queensland 4870, Australia; (011) 61-7-4051-4777, fax (011) 61-7-4051-4888; adventures@adventures.com.au, www.adventures.com.au. In U.S.: (800) 388-7333.

Central Europe

Youth For Understanding (YFU). YFU, established in 1951, prepares young people, aged 15-18 years, for their responsibilities and opportunities in a changing, interdependent world through homestay exchange programs. YFU offers year, semester, and summer study abroad and scholarship opportunities in Czech/Slovak Republics, Hungary, Poland, Russia, and Ukraine.

Dates: Year: Aug-Jun, semester: Aug-Jan, summer: 4, 6, 8 weeks (Jun, Jul, Aug). Cost: $3,075-$5,775. Contact: Program Information Office, Youth For Understanding (YFU) International Exchange, 3501 Newark St., NW, Washington, DC 20016; (800) TEENAGE or (202) 966-6800, fax (202) 895-1104; pio@yfu.org, www.yfu.org.

Costa Rica

Enjoy Learning Spanish Faster. Techniques developed from ongoing research enable students to learn more, faster, in a comfortable environment. Classes of 2-5 students plus group learning activities; conversations with middle-class homestay families (1 student per family). Homestays are within walking distance of school in small town near the capital, San Jose.

Dates: Year round. Classes begin every Monday at all levels. Cost: $345 per week for 28 hours of classes and group activities plus Costa Rican dance and cooking classes. Includes tuition, 3 meals per day, 7 days per week, homestay, laundry, all materials, and airport transportation. $25 one-time registration fee. Contact: Susan Shores, Registrar, Latin American Language Center, 7485 Rush River Dr., Suite 710-123, Sacramento, CA 95831; (916) 447-0938, fax (916) 428-9542; lalc@madre.com.

Rainforest Study Program. Ten-day learning trip includes: Arial Tram, rainforest lodge, guided rainforest hikes (emphasis on natural history), birding, exotic flowers, insect observation, horseback riding, tree climbing, tours of small and large farms in rainforest ecosystem, beach day, volcano, city tours, lectures, discussions, full-time bilingual guides, and more.

Dates: Apr-Nov. Arranged individually with each group. Cost: $1,170-$1,400. Group reservations only (15-24). One free leader for every 9 enrolled. Includes all expenses and taxes in Costa Rica. Airfare not included. Contact: Karin Stein, Forum International Univ.,

850 Juniper Ave., Kellogg, IA 50135; Tel./fax (515) 236-3894 or (925) 671-2900; costari@netins.net, www.selvabananito.com/schools.html.

Europe

AIFS Foundation, Study Abroad Programs. For over 30 years, the American Institute For Foreign Study (AIFS) has been a leader in the field of international education. We offer academic year and semester homestay programs in Spain, Germany, France, and Holland to high school students 15-19 years old, with an overall GPA of at least a C, and have studied 2 years of a foreign language. Summer programs to Chile and Australia.

Dates: Varies by program. Cost: $5,600 academic year, $2,500 summer. Includes airfare, orientation, insurance, homestay, and school enrollment. Contact: Amy Mullen, AIFS Foundation-AYA, Greenwich Office Park, 51 Weaver St., Greenwich, CT 06851; (800) 322-4678; www.aifs.com.

AIFS, Pre-College Summer Study Abroad Program. For over 30 years, the American Institute For Foreign Study (AIFS) has been a leader in the field of international education. Each year AIFS organizes cultural exchange programs throughout the world for more than 40,000 students. Programs are offered on college campuses throughout Europe to students who have completed their junior or senior year of high school. All students are issued transcripts from the host institution.

Dates: Jun-Aug, varying by location. Cost: $3,000-$6,000 includes tuition, meals, and airfare (cost varies by location). Contact: Stacey Millen, ACIS, 19 Bay State Rd., Boston, MA 02215; (800) 888-2247; stacey_millen@acis.com, www.acis.com.

Homestays Abroad. A great way to become fluent in another language and discover another culture. You live with a host family and attend the local high school for a semester or a full academic year. A local coordinator is available at all times for assistance and guidance. Programs available in France, Germany, and Spain.

Dates: Aug, semester, and year programs, Jan semester program. Cost: TBA. Includes coordinator, insurance, and transportation. Contact: James Rolen, International Education Forum, 20 W. Main St., Ste. 2, Bay Shore, NY 11706; (800) 356-8818, fax (516) 968-5973, jmr@iefny.ief.org.

Rassias Programs. Rassias Programs offers French and Spanish study and homestay programs for high school students. Tours and Arles, France; Gijón and Segovia, Spain. Instruction uses the famed Rassias Method® developed by Prof. John Rassias of Dartmouth College.

Dates: Jun 25-Jul 31; Jun 20-Jul 20; Jul 9-Aug 8. Cost: $5,500-$6,200 includes airfare. Contact: Bill Miles, Rassias Programs, P.O. Box 5456, Hanover, NH 03755; (603) 643-3007, fax (603) 643-4249; rassias@sover.net, www.sover.net/~rassias.

Tennis: Europe and More. See the world like a touring pro. Tennis tournament circuits for high school varsity players or better in 4-6 European countries or California and Hawaii. Match play, social activities, sightseeing, meeting and living with tennis friends. A unique way to gain insights into other cultures. Ten itineraries, 16-34 days, ages 14-18 years.

Dates: Jun 24-Aug 9. Cost: Call for details. Contact: Dr. Martin Vinokur, Director, Tennis: Europe, 73 Rockridge Ln., Stamford, CT 06903; (800) 253-7486; tenniseuro@aol.com, http://members.aol.com/tennis euro.

Youth For Understanding (YFU). YFU, established in 1951, prepares young people, aged 15-18 years, for their responsibilities and opportunities in a changing, interdependent world through homestay exchange programs. YFU offers year, semester, and summer study abroad and scholarship opportunities in Belgium, France, Germany, Greece, Italy, Netherlands, Spain, and Switzerland.

Dates: Year: Aug-Jun, semester: Aug-Jan, summer: 4, 6, 8 weeks (Jun, Jul, Aug). Cost: $3,475-$6,175. Contact: Program Information Office, Youth For Understanding (YFU) International Exchange, 3501 Newark St., NW, Washington, DC 20016; (800) TEENAGE or (202) 966-6800, fax (202) 895-1104; pio@yfu.org, www.yfu.org.

France

France Langue Schools in Paris/Nice. Delightful private language institute blocks from the Champs Elysees, Paris, or the sunny beaches of the French Riviera. Year round, all ages and levels. Specialty classes: commerce, cuisine, business, au pair, tourism, DELE, DALF. Custom-designed programs for teachers and high school groups. University credit available. Family stay, residence halls, apartments, or hotel accommodations.

Dates: Contact for information. Cost: Contact for information. Contact: Mr. De Poly, France Langue, 22 ave. Notre Dame, 06000 Nice, France; (011) 33-4-93-13-7888, fax (011) 33-4-93-13-7889; frlang_n@club-internet.fr, www.france_langue.fr.

Germany

German as a Foreign Language. Various levels of German year round; intensive, crash, and long-term courses, individual tuition. Special feature: German and theater. Special programs: business German for professionals, German for teachers, German in a teacher's home, German for special purposes. Academic year for high school students, international study year, internship, guest studentship, homestays for groups, courses for firms and other institutions (banking, insurance, doctors, lawyers, etc.), residential language camps for juniors, examination preparation. Various types of accommodations. Full range of activities.

Dates: Year round. Cost: Contact school for details. Contact: GLS Sprachenzentrum, Barbara Jaeschke, Managing Director, Kolonnenstrasse 26, 10829 Berlin, Germany; (011) 49-30-787-41-52; fax (011) 49-30-787-41-92; gls.berlin@t-online.de, www.gls-berlin.com.

Greece

Junior Year. Junior Year boarding program for students interested in exploring Greek culture and language in the framework of a traditional college preparatory program. Boarding unit close to campus in 5 acres of pine forest, with pool and riding stables nearby.

Dates: Sept 1-Jun 15. Cost: Comprehensive fee of $20,800 not including travel to and from Greece. Contact: Tasis Hellenic International School, Xenias and Artemidos Kefalari, Kifissia, Greece, P.O. Box 51025, 145 10 Kifissia; (011) 30-1- 8081426 or 8012362, fax (011) 30-1-8018421; bhani@hol.gr, www.tasis.com.

India

Studies Abroad for Global Education (SAGE). Year-abroad program in India for high school students in grades 9-12 at accredited international schools offering college preparatory courses and many extracurricular activities. Includes a winter tour of India and volunteer opportunities between semesters.

Cost: Fee $11,000. Does not include travel to and from India. Contact: Jane Cummings, KWI, 159 Ralph McGill Blvd., #408, NE, Atlanta, GA 30308; (404) 524-0988, fax (404) 523-5420.

Latin America

Youth For Understanding (YFU). YFU, established in 1951, prepares young people, aged 15-18 years, for their responsibilities and opportunities in a changing, interdependent world through homestay exchange programs. YFU offers year, semester, and summer study abroad and scholarship opportunities in Argentina, Brazil, Chile, Ecuador, Mexico, Uruguay, and Venezuela.

Dates: Year: Aug-Jun, semester: Aug-Jan, Jan-Jun summer: 4, 6, 8 weeks (Jun, Jul, Aug). Cost: $3,075-$5,775. Contact: Program Information Office, Youth For Understanding (YFU) International Exchange, 3501 Newark St., NW, Washington, DC 20016; (800) TEENAGE or (202) 966-6800, fax (202) 895-1104; pio@yfu.org, www.yfu. org.

Mexico

Intensive Language Programs. Intensive Spanish immersion program in groups, 40 class hours per week including Spanish class, lectures, and Hispano-American courses. Executive, semester, and specialized programs for teachers, professionals, nurses, and adults continuing education. Live with Mexican family or in student residence. Excursions to historical and archaeological sites.

Dates: Year round starting every Monday. Cost: Tuition $190 per week; lodging $154 per week. Contact: The Center for Bilingual Multicultural Studies, Javier Espinosa, San Jeronimo #304, Cuernavaca, MOR-62179, Mexico; (011) 52-73-17-10-87, fax (011) 52-73-17-05-33; admin@bilingual-center.com, www.bilingual-center.com.

Intensive Spanish Language (Cuernavaca). The Cemanahuac Educational Community offers intensive Spanish language study taught by native speakers. Special classes on history, literature, art, and anthropology of Mexico and Latin America, with field study excursions led by Cemanahuac anthropologists. Group programs with special fees. College credit available for juniors and seniors. Family homestay highly recommended.

Dates: Classes begin each Monday, year round. Advanced placement (AP) classes available. Cost: Registration, tuition, room and board with Mexican family for 2 weeks: $756. Contact: Vivian B. Harvey, Educational Programs Coordinator, Cemanahuac Educational Community, Apartado 5-21, Cuernavaca, Morelos, Mexico; (011) 52-73-18-6407, fax (011) 52-73-12-5418; 74052. 2570@compuserve. com, www.cemanahuac. com.

Scandinavia

Youth For Understanding (YFU). YFU, established in 1951, prepares young people, aged 15-18 years, for their responsibilities and opportunities in a changing, interdependent world through homestay exchange programs. YFU offers year, semester, and summer study abroad and scholarship opportunities in Denmark, Finland, Norway, and Sweden.

Dates: Year: Aug-Jun, semester: Aug-Jan, Jan-Jun, summer: 4, 6, 8 weeks (Jun, Jul, Aug). Cost: $3,075-$5,775. Contact: Program Information Office, Youth For Understanding (YFU) International Exchange, 3501 Newark St., NW, Washington, DC 20016; (800) TEENAGE or (202) 966-6800, fax (202) 895-1104; pio@yfu.org, www.yfu. org.

United Kingdom and Ireland

Irish Way Program. The Irish Way is a 5-week travel-study program for American high school students. Participants take classes in Irish culture, history, dance, sports, Gaelic, and go on field trips and stay with an Irish host family for 1 week. The Irish Way has sent over 2,500 students to Ireland since 1976.

Dates: Jun 30-Aug 1. Cost: $2,955 includes roundtrip, transatlantic airfare. Contact:

Katie Finn, Irish American Cultural Institute, 1 Lackawanna Pl., Morristown, NJ 07960; (973) 605-1991; irishwaynj@aol.com, www.irishaci.org.

Worldwide

ActionQuest Sail/Dive Programs. Summer and semester live-aboard voyages for teens and high school graduates. Multi-level sailing and scuba certification programs with marine science, seamanship, windsurfing, water skiing, and leadership training. Semester voyages (75 days) focus on experiential education, personal growth, and college-level academics. No experience necessary.

Dates: Semester: Jan 9-Mar 25, Sep 25-Dec 9. Summer: Jun 21-Jul 11, Jul 13-Aug 2, Aug 4-21. Cost: Semester: $11,250 not including airfare. Summer: $2,885-$3,885 not including airfare. Contact: James Stoll, ActionQuest, P.O. Box 5507, Sarasota, FL 34277; (800) 317-6789, (941) 924-6789, fax (941) 924-6075; actionquest@msn.com, www.actionquest.com.

AIYSEP. AIYSEP is a nonprofit high school foreign exchange program based in the U.S. which establishes exchange programs for students in Europe, America, and many other foreign countries. Area counselors are located in Europe, U.S., Australia, New Zealand, South America, Peru, Canada, and Japan. AIYSEP believes a greater international understanding is accomplished among people and countries through cultural homestay programs.

Dates: Year, semester, and Summer programs. Cost: Year $3,995-$6,000; semester $3,495-$4,000; Summer $1,900-$3,000. Contact: American International Youth Student Exchange, 200 Round Hill Rd., Tiburon, CA 94920; (800) 347-7575 or (415) 435-4049, (415) 499-7669, fax (415) 499-5651; AIYSEP@compuserve.com.

The ASA Group. The ASA Group offers programs for American students to Spain, Germany, and Japan. Programs include short-term summer camps, 5-month and 10-month academic year programs. We also have sports programs where teams made up of members from the U.S. travel abroad and compete against foreign teams.

Dates: Call for details. Cost: Call for details. Contact: Grant Miller, ASA, 7119 Church Ave., Pittsburgh, PA 15202; (800) 303-4100, fax (412) 734-0903; asa@asa.ls.org, www.asa.ls.org.

ASA Pre-College and Language Study Programs. Since 1984 ASA has offered pre-college summer enrichment programs for high school students at Stanford Univ., the Univ. of Massachusetts-Amherst, and Oxford Univ. in England. ASA also has language programs in France and Spain, and a program for middle school students at Amherst College.

Dates: Call for details. Cost: Call for details. Contact: David Evans, ASA, 355 Main St., Armonk, NY 10504; (800) 752-2250 or (914) 273-2250, fax (914) 273-5430; www.asaprograms.com.

ASPECT Foundation Outbound Program. The ASPECT Foundation offers programs in Brazil, Uruguay, France, Germany, Japan, Spain, Ireland, and England. Students aged 15-18 experience another culture first-hand by being a member of a host family. They gain language fluency, international friendships, and lifetime memories.

Dates: Inquire. Cost: Inquire. Contact: Outbound Coordinator, ASPECT Foundation, 350 Sansome St., Ste. 900, San Francisco, CA 94104; (800) 879-6884, fax (415) 228-8051; exchange@aspectworld.com.

AYUSA International. AYUSA International is an educational student exchange organization dedicated to promoting peace and personal growth through international exchange. U.S. high school students, ages 15 to 18, participate in an academic year, semester, or summer language and homestay program abroad. Students live with host families and attend local schools. Academic credit depends on home school policies. Orientation is provided in the U.S. and upon arrival in the host country. Summer group travel, language study, community service, and environmental adventure programs are also available. AYUSA has been selected by Kiwanis International to administer its international youth exchange programs. Various country specific scholarships are available for semester and academic year programs as well as awards for families who host an international student. Scholarships are also available to Kiwanis and Key club members.

Dates: Varies by country. Cost: $2,600 to $5,700 including transportation and insurance. Contact: AYUSA International, 1 Post St., 7th Fl., San Francisco, CA 94104; (800) 727-4540, fax (415) 986-4620; studyabroad@ayusa.org, www.ayusa.org.

CCI Teen Homestay Programs Abroad. CCI provides both long- and short-term homestay opportunities for teens interested in traveling abroad. High school abroad (3, 5, or 10 months), language-travel programs, international youth camps, or independent homestay programs are available in Europe, Asia, Africa, South America, Australia, and Mexico.

Dates: Rolling admissions. Cost: $680 and up. Contact: Kathleen Baader, CCI, 17 North 2nd Ave., St. Charles, IL 60714; (888) ABROAD1, fax (630) 377-2307; info@cci-exchange.com, www.cci-exchange.com.

Global Works, Inc. Global Works is an environmental and community service-based travel program, with language immersion and homestay options available. A grassroots, not-for profit organization for students ages 14-18. Experienced leadership. Four-week trips to Ireland, Ecuador, France, the Pacific Northwest, Costa Rica, Puerto Rico, Czech Republic, and the Fiji Islands.

Dates: Late-Jun-mid-Aug, 1998. Cost: $2,550-$3,475. Includes all but airfare. Contact: Global Works, Inc., Pam and Biff Houldin, Directors, RD2, Box 356-B, Huntingdon, PA 16652; (814) 667-2411, fax (814) 667-3853; info@globalworksinc.com, www.globalworksinc.com.

Musiker Tours. Student travel and adventure programs throughout the U.S., Canada, and Europe. Camping, hotel, and college dorm stays available. Activities include: biking, hiking, visits to national parks and monuments, whitewater rafting, and visits to movie studios and theme parks, to name a few. An action-packed summer for 3-6 weeks for students ages 12-17, in compatible coed groupings.

Dates: Jun-Aug (variable dates). Cost: $3,199-$6,499. Contact: Musiker Tours, 1326 Old Northern Blvd., Roslyn, NY 11576; (888) 878-6637 or (516) 621-0718 in NY, fax (516) 625-3438; www.summerfun.com.

O.C.E.A.N. Outbound Program. U.S. secondary school students, ages 15-18, travel abroad for a summer, semester, or academic year. Participants are selected on basis of language proficiency and academic excellence. They are placed with host families and attend host schools. Prior to their departure from the U.S., students are provided with an orientation.

Dates: Summer, school semester, academic year. Cost: $1,500-$12,000 depending on country and duration of stay. Contact: Jose DePontes and Laura Stahl, O.C.E.A.N. (Organization for Cultural Exchange Among Nations), 2101 E. Broadway Rd., Ste. 2., Tempe, AZ 85282-1735; (800) 28-OCEAN, (602) 784-4891; ocean.intl@worldnet.att.net, www.oceanintl.org.

People to People Student Ambassador Program. The People to People Student Ambassador Program selects students from sixth grade through high school to participate in 2- to 3-week educational programs in Costa Rica, Europe, Australia, New Zealand, China, and South Africa. Participants live with families for periods of 2 to 5 days in several of the countries visited. High school and university credits are available. Students must complete an application and interview prior to acceptance.

Dates: Students depart early-Jun to late-Jul. Cost: Tuition ranges from $2,900 to $4,500. Includes transportation. Contact: Ellie Emmanuel, People to People Student Ambassador Program, South 110 Ferrall, Spokane, WA 99202-4861; (800) 669-7882 or (509) 534-0430 or (509) 534-5245.

Rock the World with AFS. Make a world of difference in your high school career with AFS, celebrating 50 years of providing intercultural learning opportunities in more than 45 countries. Programs include year and semester academic homestays and summer programs for students aged 15-18, and interim programs for recent graduates.

Dates: Varied. Cost: Varied. Contact: Call (800) AFS-INFO or visit our web site at www.afs.org/usa.

Rotary Youth Exchange. Rotary International is a worldwide service organization that encourages and facilitates international youth exchange as one of the many activities of its member clubs. Rotary short- and long-term Youth Exchange programs are open to students, generally between 15-18 1/2 years of age. Accepted students must be sponsored by a local Rotary club or district. Selection criteria include a written application and personal interviews with the applicant and the parents at local club and district levels.

Dates: Ongoing. Cost: Student responsible for their flight and insurance. Contact: Rotary International, Intercultural Programs Section, 1Rotary Ctr., 1560 Sherman Ave., Evanston, IL 60201-3698; (847) 866-3421, fax (847) 866-6116; www.rotary.org.

SHARE! High School Exchange Program. Foreign students, ages 15 to 18, live with a volunteer American host family and attend a local public school for a full academic year (10 months, mid-Aug to mid-Jun) or a semester (5 months). Students must demonstrate proficiency in written and spoken English to be accepted.

Dates: Arrive Aug 1999, depart Jun 2000. Cost: $3,000-$6,000, excluding transportation and personal expenses. Contact: Beth Schumann, ERDT, Director of Program Development, 475 Washington Blvd., Suite 220, Marina del Rey, CA 90292; (310) 821-9977, fax (310-) 821-9282; erdtshare@earthlink.net, www.glyfix.com/erdt.

Summer Discovery Pre-College Programs. Summer Discovery Pre-College Enrichment Programs at UCLA, Univ. of Michigan, Univ. of Vermont, Georgetown Univ., and Cambridge Univ., England. Helping to prepare students from high school to college and beyond. Students learn to balance their academic, social, and recreational activities for 3-6 weeks during the summer. Appropriate for students completing grades 9-12. Courses offered: college-credit, enrichment courses, SAT preparation, driver education, ESL/TOEFL, community service, etc. Trips, sports, and excursions offered daily.

Dates: Jun-Aug (variable dates). Cost: $2,900-$5,400. Contact: Summer Discovery, 1326 Old Northern Blvd., Roslyn, NY 11576; (888) 878-6637 or (516) 621-0718 in NY, fax (516) 625-3438; www.summerfun.com.

Travel/Study Programs for All Ages. High school, academic semester and year, language school, summer immersions, school and general group tours for teens or adults, internships, au pair, teaching positions—these and much more available. Call for current listings and prices.

Dates: Vary. Cost: Vary according to destination and length of program. Contact: Cultural Homestay International, 2455 Bennett Valley Rd., #210B, Santa Rosa, CA 95404; (800) 395-2726, fax (707) 523-3704; chigaylep@msn.com, www.chinet.org/outbound.html.

World Experience Student Exchange Program. Have the experience of a lifetime. Learn another language and culture. Live as a member of a family and attend a local school.

Choose from 30 countries. One- or 2-semester programs. Add a new dimension to your life. Eligibility: 15-18 years, 3.0 GPA.

Dates: Aug or Jan departure for 1 to 2 semesters. Cost: $2,640 plus individual country fees for 1 year; $2,265 plus individual country fees for 1 semester. Travel expenses not included. Contact: World Experience, 2440 Hacienda Blvd #116, Hacienda Heights, CA 91745; (800) 633-6653, fax (626) 333-4914; weworld@worldexperience.org, www.world experience.org.

For more listings of teen study and travel programs, and for bargains worldwide, travel tips, and all sorts of information on learning, living, working, and traveling abroad, see *Transitions Abroad* magazine. To order a single copy or a subscription, please call 1-800-293-0373 or visit the *Transitions Abroad* web site at www.transabroad.com.

LIVING
ABROAD

*Obviously, the better your grasp of the local language, the easier you will find it
to "get by." But language is far more than a practical tool. It's the key to understanding the way people think and behave and thus your main gateway to feeling
a part of the ambient culture. Even if you are nowhere near fluent, your faltering
efforts to communicate—if just to say hello, please, and thank you—will ingratiate you to people almost anywhere in the world.*

—GINA DOGGETT, PAGE 360

From Coping to Thriving

A Wealth of Tools for Living Overseas

By Gina Doggett

It's Monday, and you have to go personally to hand in a deposit for your phone. "Why do they have to make everything so difficult?" you mutter. Cursing the rain, you head out to catch a bus. You brighten as the bus arrives. A few stops later, you realize that the bus is going in the wrong direction.

The swirl of thoughts and feelings that follow will be familiar to you if you have lived in a foreign country and can remember the exciting—but disorienting—first few weeks, when you were operating under the combined effects of euphoria, frustration, and culture shock. Achieving mental equilibrium is a subtle process with few obvious landmarks.

The following list of resources contains a wealth of tools for understanding a new culture and finding your place in it as a foreigner. If you can, you should start using them before you go. Several, such as the Culture Shock! series, are country- or culture-specific, while others, such as the **Art of Crossing Cultures**, provide general guidance for adapting to a new culture. And no matter how much assistance you receive from your employer or your sponsor, you will be hungry for the practical and logistical guidance contained in books such as the **Living and Working in . . .** series.

Obviously, the better your grasp of the local language, the easier you will find it to "get by." But language is far more than a practical tool. It's the key to understanding the way people think and behave and thus your main gateway to feeling a part of the ambient culture. Even if you are nowhere near fluent, your faltering efforts to communicate—if just to say hello, please, and thank you—will ingratiate you to people almost anywhere in the world. Granted, the ability to learn a second language is not evenly distributed. If you are one of those who feel passed over by this gift, at least consider that a multitude of language-learning strategies exist that you may not have tried. Check out **How to Learn a Foreign Language** or **How to Master Languages** to discover the method—or methods—that might work best for you. And, if possible, start boning up before you go.

While you may be wrapped up in a work assignment, your partner and children are likely to have totally different experiences related to the move. Some excellent resources are available for helping them cope with the peripatetic life style. The new **Relocating Spouse's Guide to Employment and**

Moving Your Family Overseas provide useful advice and inspiration. In addition, many local organizations offer help for trailing spouses.

For children, the workbook **Of Many Lands: Journal of a Traveling Childhood** offers exercises that will help them focus on experiences and transitions that they may otherwise suppress, to their detriment. Two other valuable resources in this domain are **Notes from a Traveling Childhood** and **Where in the World Are You Going?**

One day, no doubt, you will return home. Your reentry will be unique, but one that has bottom-line similarities with that of anyone else who has lived in, and returned from, a foreign culture: you will have a feeling of being different, even special, for having had the experience; of pride for the special knowledge you have acquired; and of strangeness for having missed out on the prevailing culture at home for the past (how many?) years—and for being unable to fully communicate your experience to a home-country audience whose attention, sharp at first, wanes quickly.

The stories you bring back are part and parcel of your life experience. This is crucially true for your children, thrown among peers who have difficulty fathoming a life in which samosas, falafel, or goat's eyes are normal. Aletheia Publications specializes in books treating this topic, such as **The Absentee American**, based on interviews with former foreign service brats, and **Strangers at Home**.

If you have children, you will have noticed with a mixture of admiration and jealousy how easily they picked up the local language during your stay abroad. Their natural fluency is a treasure that should be preserved and protected in every way possible, not just because bilingualism is a highly marketable skill but also because a second language is an invaluable personal asset. You might even consider enrolling them in a bilingual school, if one exists in your community.

As for you, options include continuing education at the local university, getting involved with the local Italian or Thai or Ethiopian community, or using self-instructional tools such as a Champs-Elysées audio-cassette magazine. Strategies for maintaining a language should be just as personalized as those for learning one.

So, now you know the bus routes. You've made special friends whom you'll always cherish. And you've had an experience that no one can take away from you. You've been challenged to tackle practicalities, to understand a foreign culture and language, and to abandon your native life. At the same time, through being away from home, you've learned things about your own culture. One way and another, living abroad has enriched your life. Bravo! Encore!

CHAPTER 17

LIVING ABROAD RESOURCES

As more Americans choose to work, live, and retire overseas the resources and support organizations for expatriates have become better and better. A selection of the best resources follows to help you as you make your own transitions abroad.

Organizations for Americans Abroad

Association of American Residents Overseas, BP 127, 92154 Suresnes Cedex, France. (011) 33-1-42040938; fax (011) 33-1-42020912; aaroparis@aol.com; http://members.aol.com/aaroparis/ aarohome. htm. An organization founded in 1974 to fight for legislation affecting the interests of U.S. citizens overseas. Offers 2 group insurance plans, a quarterly newsletter, seminars.

Association of American Wives of Europeans BP 127, 92154 Suresnes Cedex, France; (011) 33-1-42040938; fax (011) 33-1-42020912; aaroparis@aol.com; http://members.aol.com/aaroparis/aarohome. htm.

Democrats Abroad, 7900 Rebecca Dr., Alexandria, VA 22307; (703) 768-3174. An organization with affiliates around the world dedicated to getting out the vote among absentee Americans and promoting Democratic Party causes.

Federation of American Women's Clubs Overseas. Ruetistrasse 30, 8906 Bonstettem, Switzerland.

Republicans Abroad, 310 1st St., SE, Washington, DC 20003; (202) 662-1390. An organization with affiliates around the world dedicated to getting out the vote among absentee Americans and promoting Republican Party causes.

World Federation of Americans Abroad, 49 rue Pierre Charron, 75008 Paris, France.

Country Specific Publications

Background Notes Series. Published irregularly throughout year. Available from Superintendent of Documents, U.S. Government Printing Office, Washington, DC 20402; (202) 512-2250; fax (202) 512-2250; www.access.gpo.gov/su_docs. $2.50 per copy, $19 per year in U.S. More than 150 pamphlets by country about the people, land, history, foreign relations, etc., from Afghanistan to Zambia.

Bloom Where You're Planted (in Paris). $25 includes s/h from The American Church in Paris, 65 quai d'Orsay, 75007 Paris; (011) 33 1 40620500. Updated each year to accompany an annual orientation program in October, it's full of practical information on living in Paris.

Country Reports from the Economist Intelligence Unit. Quarterly overviews of 180 countries in 99 periodicals covering politics and economics, as well as the outlook for next 12-18 months. Annual subscription £175. Also, Country Forecasts on 55 countries, four reports annually for £360 from The Economist Intelligence Unit Limited, Subscriptions Department, P.O. Box 154, Dartford, Kent DA1 1QB, U.K. (011) 44 1 322 289194, fax 223803.

Craighead's International Business Travel and Relocation Guide to 78 Countries. (Gale Research Inc.). Annual, 3 vols. Available in large libraries.

Culturgrams by David M. Kennedy Center for International Studies. Brigham Young Univ., Publication Services, P.O. Box 24538, Provo, UT 84602; (800) 528-6279. Four-page summaries of the basic features of over 160 cultures worldwide.

Encountering the Chinese by Hu Wenzhong and Cornelius L. Grove. 1991. $17.95 plus $3 s/h from Intercultural Press. Jennifer Hoopes,

P.O. Box 700, Yarmouth, ME 04096; (800) 370-2665; www.bookmasters.com/intercult.htm.

Europe the European Way: A Traveler's Guide to Living Affordably in the World's Great Cities by James F. Gollattscheck. 1996. $13.95 from Globe Pequot, P.O. Box 833, Old Saybrook, CT 06475; (860) 395-2855.

From Nyet to Da: Understanding the Russians by Yale Richmond. Rev. ed., 1996. $17.95 plus $3 s/h from Intercultural Press (above).

How to Books: Living and Working Abroad. Over 40 books offering country-specific information on immigration formalities, education, housing, health, law, economy, and leisure. All books are regularly updated and some are into their 6th edition. Prices from $15 to $20, excluding shipping charges. Customer Services, Plymbridge Distributors Ltd., Estover Rd., Plymouth PL6 7PZ, U.K.; (011) 44-1-752-202301, fax (011) 44-1-752-202331; www.howtobooks. co.uk.

How to Live and Work in Germany by Christine Hall (2nd ed.). £9.99 plus £4 s/h from How To Books (above).

How to Live and Work in Greece by Peter Reynolds. £9.99 plus £4 s/h from How To Books (above).

How to Live and Work in the Gulf by Hamid Atiyyah. Country-by-country expert advice. £9.99 plus £4 s/h from How To Books (above).

How to Live and Work in Italy by Amanda Hinton. £8.99 plus £4 s/h from How To Books (above).

Live and Work in . . . (Vacation Work). A series of guides written with the British reader in mind covering Europe and beyond. Most of the practical information also applies to North Americans considering work or retirement abroad. Titles to date: France, Spain and

Portugal, Italy, Germany, Belgium, The Netherlands, and Luxembourg, U.S. and Canada, Scandinavia, Australia and New Zealand. Available for $16.95 plus $3.50 s/h for first book and $0.75 for each additional book from Seven Hills Book Distributors, 49 Central Ave., Cincinnati, OH 45202; (800) 545-2005.

Living and Making Money in Mexico. 1998. $15 plus $2.50 s/h from Living Overseas Books, P.O. Box 2062, Vashon Island, WA 98070; (800) 341-2510, ext. 27; sales@livingoverseas.com, www.livingoverseas.com. Created by overseas entrepreneur Robert Lawrence Johston III who also publishes **Living and Making Money in Costa Rica** and **The Official Guide to Living and Making Money in Central America**.

Living and Working in Australia by Laura Veltman (6th ed. 1998). £12.99 plus £4 s/h from How To Books (above).

Living and Working in Britain by David Hampshire ($21.95, Survival Books). The most comprehensive source of practical information about everyday life in Britain. Similar titles by same author on France, Spain, Australia, Switzerland; also, **Buying a Home Abroad,** $16.95, and **Buying a Home in France and Spain,** $16.95. Can be ordered through Seven Hills Book Distributors (above).

Living and Working in Britain by Christine Hall. £8.99 plus £4 s/h from How To Books (above).

Living and Working in China by Christine Hall. £9.99 plus £4 s/h from How To Books (above).

Living and Working in France by Alan Hart. £9.99 plus £4 s/h from How To Books (above).

Living and Working in Hong Kong by Jeremy Gough. £10.99 plus £4 s/h from How To Books (above).

Living and Working in Israel by Ahron Bregman. £10.99 plus £4 s/h from How To Books (above).

Living and Working in New Zealand by Joy Muirhead. £9.99 plus £4 s/h from How To Books (above).

Living and Working in Saudi Arabia by Rosalie Rayburn and Kate Bush. 2nd ed. £12.99 from How To Books (above).

Living and Working in Spain 3rd. ed. £8.99 plus £4 s/h from How To Books (above).

Living and Working in the Netherlands by Pat Rush. £9.99 plus £4 s/h from How To Books (above).

Living, Studying, and Working in Italy by Travis Neighbor and Monica Larner. 1998. $14.95. From Henry Holt and Co.: (212) 886-9268, fax (212) 647-1874; academic@hholt.com. Essential new step-by-step guide through all phases of planning the move and settling in.

The Newcomer: An Introduction to Life in Belgium. Available free from the Belgian National Tourist Office, 780 3rd Ave., #1501, New York, NY 10017-2024; (212) 758-8130, fax (212) 355-7675; info@visitbelgium.com; www.visitbelgium.com. Valuable information for people who are preparing to move to Belgium.

Cross-Cultural Adjustment

Art of Crossing Cultures by Craig Storti. 1990. $16.95 plus $3 s/h from Intercultural Press (above). A clear and compelling analysis of the personal challenges inherent in the cross-cultural experience.

Cross-Cultural Adaptability Inventory by Colleen Kelley and Judith Meyers. 1993. $17-$55 for various components sold separately from Intercultural Press (above). Preparing people to go abroad, returning from abroad, or interacting with other cultures. May also be used as a tool to assess cultural adaptability.

Cross-Cultural Dialogues: 74 Brief Encounters with Cultural Differences by Craig Storti. 1994. $16.95 plus $3 s/h from Intercultural Press (above). Conversations between peoples of two different cultures.

Do's and Taboos Around the World: A Guide to International Behavior by Roger Axtell (John Wiley & Sons). Advice for the business and pleasure traveler on what to do and not to do in other cultures. Titles include: Gestures: **Do's and Taboos of Body Language Around the World, Do's and Taboos of Using English Around the World.**

Global Nomads International (GNI) assists the internationally mobile family. The organization publishes *Global Nomad Perspectives*, a journal for this population and the professionals who work with them. GNI's annual conference, titled "The Global Village—A Global Nomad's Home Town," will be held this year at the American University in Washington, DC, October 9-11. Global Nomads International, P.O .Box 9584, Washington, DC 20016-9584; (202) 466-2244; info@gni.org; http://globalnomads.association.com.

Living Overseas: A Book of Preparation by Ted Ward. 1984. $149.95. Simon & Schuster, (800) 832-7479, fax (800) 445-6991. A sophisticated and readable study of cultural differences and how to cope with them. $19.95 plus 6 percent s/h. from Free Press, a division of Simon & Schuster, 200 Old Tappan Rd., Old Tappan, NJ 07675;

Managing Cross-Cultural Transition by Steven Shepard.1997. $19.95 plus $3 s/h from Aletheia Publications (above). Subtitled "A Handbook for Corporations, Employees, and Their Families," this book examines each stage of the expatriation and repatriation process in detail

New Relocating Spouse's Guide to Employment: Options and Strategies in the U.S. and Abroad by Frances Bastress. 1993. $14.95 plus $4 s/h from Impact Publications, 9104 N. Manassas Dr., Manassas Park, VA 22111; (703) 361-7300, fax (703) 335-9486; www. impactpublications.com. Addresses the unique career challenges of the men and women who accompany relocating employees.

Transcultural Odysseys: The Evolving Global Consciousness by Germaine W. Shames (Intercultural Press). Real people's stories about cultural adjustment.

Transcultural Study Guide. Volunteers in Asia. 1987. $7.95 plus $1.70 postage from VIA Press, P.O. Box 4543, Stanford, CA 93409; www.volasia.org. Hundreds of questions that lead a traveler toward an understanding of a new culture.

Travel That Can Change Your Life: How to Create a Transformative Experience by Jeffrey A. Kottler (Jossey-Bass Publishers). Practical tips for life-changing travel.

Understanding Arabs by Margaret K. (Omar) Nydell. Rev. ed., 1997. Crosscultural guide to all 19 Arab countries. $17.95 plus $3 s/h from Intercultural Press (above).

Understanding Cultural Differences: Germans, French, and Americans by Edward T. Hall and Mildred Reed Hall. 1989. $16.95 plus $3 s/h from Intercultural Press (above).

Guidebook Series

*Culture Shock! Series (Graphic Arts). Guides to customs and etiquette of various cultures. Titles include: Thailand, China, Pakistan, France, Britain, Israel, India, South Africa,

Health Insurance Abroad
Are You Well Insured? If Not, What Should You Do?

By Leslie Papppas

When Finn Torjensen moved his family to China's Shanxi province to start a medical training program, he thought he'd covered everything.

Then the car he was riding in rolled off a cliff.

After weeks in a Chinese hospital, doctors recommended that Torjensen be flown back to the U.S. for treatment. Out of necessity, his family went with him.

"There was no way I could have gone back by myself. I had a broken neck," Torjensen said.

Worst-case scenarios happen. And when they happen overseas, things can get complicated.

Language barriers make communication difficult. Medicines are sometimes different. When hospitals within the country do not provide the required care, a medical evacuation may be necessary.

All of this means that if you live abroad, insurance companies consider you high maintenance. So if you need to buy health insurance overseas, it's going to be difficult to get. If you have insurance, you may need to purchase additional coverage. And if you think you're completely covered, read the fine print: some companies won't cover you if you leave the country.

Luckily for Torjensen, he had done his research. But are you that well covered? And if not, what should you do?

Option 1: Continue your insurance from home. Your insurance needs will vary depending upon your destination and the length of time you plan to be outside of the U.S. Most people will simply continue the policy they already have; for U.S. citizens, a major medical plan offers the most comprehensive health insurance available. Many plans have a wide range of benefits and will continue to cover you as long as you pay your premiums. However, they probably won't cover you forever.

Jackie Abrams, an insurance broker and director of American Citizens Abroad (ACA), a nonpartisan, nonprofit, Geneva-based organization that works to improve the status of American expatriates, has scoured the market to find insurance policies for her overseas clients.

"I don't know of any U.S. policies that will cover you permanently out of the U.S.," Abrams said.

In fact, many companies will cancel their coverage if the policyholder lives outside of the country for more than 90 days. Even if you maintain an address in the States and continue to pay the premiums, some companies may dispute a claim or cancel a policy if they discover you have been living abroad.

If you have already moved overseas and discover that the policy you have does not actually cover you, your first reaction may be to find another insurance company. But that may be tricky. If you use an overseas address, many companies based in the U.S. will reject your application regardless of how healthy you are.

So before you sign up for an American insurance policy, ask very specific questions about the extent of the coverage. If you already have a policy, read the fine print. Finally, make sure your coverage starts before you leave the U.S.

The disadvantage of keeping a policy from back home is that it does not take an expat's special needs into account. Most policies in the U.S. will not cover major medical evacuation, for example. And it may be difficult to put in a claim if all receipts are in a foreign language.

Luckily, there are emergency medical assistance companies to fill in the gap.

Option 2: Supplement your insurance. Emergency medical assistance companies do not offer comprehensive health insurance, but they can supplement an insurance policy by providing medical assistance in the event of an emergency.

Most offer 24-hour medical consultation via multi-lingual crisis phone lines, refer members to the nearest appropriate doctor or clinic, help fill prescriptions, monitor hospitalization, and, if needed, arrange an emergency medical evacuation to the nearest Western-standard hospital.

Two of the most widely-used medical assistance companies are AEA and SOS. AEA was founded in 1985 and is based in Singapore. SOS was founded in Switzerland in 1974 and is now headquartered in Philadelphia. Both have a worldwide network of doctors, hospitals, ambulances, administrative personnel, and inter- national-standard clinics.

Medical assistance and evacuation insurance is virtually useless, of course, if you don't have a major medical policy to back it up. If you are already living abroad and need to buy insurance, there is one last option.

Option 3: Buy a special expatriate health insurance policy. A number of insurance companies offer such policies. The good news is that they will accept virtually any healthy person who applies, so if you've already moved overseas and are having trouble finding coverage, you aren't completely out of luck.

Expat policies will usually offer worldwide coverage in addition to some type of evacuation insurance. When you apply for this type of insurance, you must specify a "usual country of residence" in addition to your country of citizenship. Most expat policies will discontinue coverage if you stay in your home country for more than 90 days.

If you are ever in need of a medical evacuation, expatriate policies will work in conjunction with an assistance company to send you to the nearest Western-standard hospital. This may or may not be in your home country. In other words, if you break your neck in Shanxi, the company would fly you to Hong Kong and pay your hospital bills. They probably won't fly you back to the U.S., however.

There are other advantages to an expatriate plan. It is often cheaper than doubling up on several policies. It includes evacuation insurance. And it will cover shipping your mortal remains home if you happen to die.

But as a wise insurance guru once said, "Don't look at the benefits. Look at the exclusions." Many so-called "international" policies are really temporary travel policies in disguise. If there is a maximum time frame, or if the plan requires that you reapply after one year, you are really buying a temporary policy.

The biggest problem with a temporary travel policy is that you may not be able to find another company to cover you when the plan expires. Many policies will allow you to reapply, but few guarantee that they will accept you. If you have put in a large claim, or if the condition of your health has deteriorated, you may be rejected. Even minor skin cancers will put a black mark on your record. A car accident may require a month in the hospital, but what if you need three years of physical therapy?

"If you get temporary insurance for six months and you get anything that will be considered pre-existing, you probably will not be able to obtain any insurance [after the plan expires]," Abrams said. "Depending on the illness, you could possibly never be insurable again."

Permanent Policies for Expats

Unfortunately, finding a reliable and permanent expatriate policy is no easy task.

To start, contact the medical assistance companies in your area. As most assistance companies work in conjunction with global insurance providers, representatives may be able to provide you with a list of companies that sell expatriate plans.

Second, look for insurance brokers who specialize in insurance for Americans overseas. Don't rely on just one: put two or three of them to work.

Most importantly, when shopping around, ask tough questions. Think up a dozen worst-case scenarios and grill your insurance agent before investing in a policy.

Insurance While Abroad

It is impossible to provide a complete list of global insurance providers. The few listed below are good starting places, but be sure to conduct your own wide search to find the provider that's right for you.

Insurance Providers

AEA International-Seattle, Columbia Seafirst Ctr., 701 5th Ave., Seattle, WA 98104-7016; (206) 340-6000; www.aeaintl.com.

Cultural Insurance Services International (CISI), 102 Greenwich Ave., Greenwich, CT 06830; (800) 284-3577; www.aifs.org/aifscisi. htm.

Dave Tester Expatriate Insurance Services, 18a Hove Park Villas, Hove BN3 6HG, England; (011) 44-1273-703469, fax 777723.

Goodhealth Worldwide Ltd., Mill Bay Ln., Horsham, W. Sussex, England RH12 1TQ; fax (011) 44-1403-268429.

International Medical Group, Inc., 135 North Pennsylvania, Suite 1700, Indianapolis, IN 46204; (800) 628-4664 or (317) 636-4721; insurance@imglobal.com, www.imglobal.com.

International SOS Assistance, 8 Neshaminy Interplex, Suite 207, Trevos, PA 19053; (215) 244-1500; www.intsos.com.

Wallach and Co., Inc., 107 W. Federal St., P.O. Box 480, Middlebury, VA 20118-0480; (800) 237-6615, fax (540) 687-3172; wallach_r@ mediasoft.net.

Worldwide Assistance, 1133 15th Street NW, Suite 400, Washington, DC 20005-2710; (800) 821-2828, fax (202) 828-5896; wassist@aol.com.

Other Companies and Additional Information

American International Group, Blue Shield International, Ltd., BUPA International (England), **Commercial Union Insurance Company, International Health Insurance** (Denmark). **American Citizens Abroad**, Jackie Abrams, Director, Washington Office, 1051 North George Mason Dr., Arlington, VA 22205; (703) 276-0949, fax (703) 527-3269; Jacabr@aol. com, www.aca.ch.

Burma, Canada, Philippines, Australia, Korea, Nepal, A Globe-Trotter's Guide, Ireland, Morocco, Switzerland, Syria, Vietnam, Successful Living Abroad: Wife's Guide, Turkey, Germany, Denmark, Bolivia, United Arab Emirates, Czech Republic, Living and Working Abroad. New this year: Mexico, Netherlands, Egypt.

Customs and Etiquette in... (Global Books). Pocket guides to customs, manners, and culture of individual countries. Available for: Arabia and the Gulf States, China, Germany, Russia, Greece, Hungary, Japan, England, India, Israel, Thailand, Singapore, Holland, Italy, Ireland, Vietnam.

Health and Safety

Staying Healthy in Asia, Africa, and Latin America. $11.95 plus s/h from VIA Press, P.O. Box 4543, Stanford, CA 94309; www.volasia.org. Provides an overview of health problems common to Asia, Africa, and Latin America. Sections on prevention of illness, as well as guidelines in case of illness.

Where There Is No Doctor: A Village Health Care Handbook by David Werner. 1992, rev. ed. This simply written, heavily illustrated, comprehensive health manual is particularly useful for those working or living in a semi-isolated or isolated location. Other Hesperian books include **Where Women Have No Doctor** ($20) and **A Book for Midwives** ($22). $17 plus s/h from the Hesperian Foundation, 1919 Addison St., Suite 304, Berkeley, CA 94704; (510) 845-4507, fax (510) 845-0539; hesperianfdn@igc.apc.org.

Home and Hospitality Exchanges

Ambassador Exchange Travel and Hospitality Club, 34 Southport St., Box 88585, Toronto, ON M6S 4Z8, Canada; (416) 760-9617;

amexclb@io.org, www.io.org/~amexclb. Registry and complementary services for people wanting to partake in travel, vacation, and hospitality exchanges.

American International Homestays. Arranges visits any time with different English-speaking families for 3 nights minimum each in 25 countries. Visitors have private rooms and opportunities to learn from hosts about local culture. American International Homestays, Inc., P.O. Box 1754, Nederland, CO 80466; (800) 876-2048, fax (303) 642-3365; www.commerce.com/homestays.

Bells' Home Hospitality. A 9-year-old homestay service with a small network of middle class families exemplifying the good nature of the Costa Rican people. The Bells will help you develop your itinerary based on their and their guests' experiences over the years. Brochure from: Vernon and Marcela Bell, P.O. Box 185, 1000 San Jose, Costa Rica; (011) 506-225-4752, fax 224-5884; homestay@sol.racsa.co.cr, www.ilisa.com/bells.

Home Base Holidays, Lois Sealey, 7 Park Ave., London N13 5PG, England; (011) 44-181-886-8752, fax (011)44-181-482-4258; homebase@cableinet.co.uk, www.homebase-hols.com. Exchange in over 40 countries with a particularly large choice of offers throughout Great Britain. Home Base Holidays is a member of the International Home Exchange Association (IHEA). Three directories published annually plus access to all listings on the web site. Directory membership: £50 per year, Internet membership £40 (Major credit cards and U.S. checks accepted.)

Homelink International. America's oldest and largest home exchange organization. P.O. Box 650, Key West, FL 33041; (800) 638-3841, (305) 294-1448; fax (305) 294-1448; homelink@swapnow.com, www.swapnow.com.

Hostelling International (AYH), 733 15th St. NW, Suite 840, Washington, DC 20005; (202)

783-6161; www.iyhf.org or www.hiayh.org. Plan your own hosteling trip: many hostels have private family rooms. Advance reservations are required.

International Home Exchange. Extensive worldwide listings. For $30, they'll list your home for one year. Browsing their listings is free; www.homeexchange.com.

International Home Exchange Association (IHEA), P.O. Box 1562, Santa Clarita, CA, 91386-0562; (800) VHU-SWAP or (805) 298-0376, fax (805) 298-0576. IHEA is a union of 18 independently owned and operated home exchange clubs worldwide.

International Home Exchange Network, P.O. Box 915253, Longwood, FL 32779; (407) 862-7211; fax (407) 869-7992; linda@ihen.com, www.ihen.com. Extensive worldwide home and hospitality exchange listings. Cost is $29.95 to list.

INTERVAC U.S., P.O. Box 590504, San Francisco, CA 94159; (800) 756-HOME or (415) 435-3497, fax (415) 435-7440; intervacus@aol.com. It publishes 5 catalogs a year, containing 10,000 homes in more than 50 countries. Members contact each other directly. The $78 cost includes the purchase of 2 of the company's catalogs, plus the inclusion of your own listing. Hospitality and rentals are also available.

Latitudes Home Exchange, P.O. Box 436, South Perth 6951, Western Australia, Australia; (011) 61-8-9367-9412, fax (011) 61-8-9367-9576; homeswap@iinet.net.au, www.iinet.net.au/~homeswap. Membership includes directory of thousands of members worldwide (AUS$100 per year) and custom matching to suit the member's criteria (AUS$50 life-time membership plus AUS$250 once an exchange has been agreed upon).

Mi Casa Su Casa Gay Home Exchange, P.O. Box 10327, Oakland, CA 94610; (800) 215-CASA or (510) 268-8534, fax (510) 268-0299;

homeswap@aol.com, www.well.com/user/homeswap. International lesbian and gay home and hospitality exchange networks. Bi-annual member journal describes houses and apartments available in more than 15 countries, primarily for short-term vacations. Annual membership fee less than $100.

Teacher Swap, P.O. Box 454, Oakdale, NY 11769-0454; (516) 244-2845, fax (516) 244-2845; tswap@aol.com.

Vacation Homes Unlimited P.O. Box 1562, Santa Clarita, CA, 91386-0562; (800) VHU-SWAP or (805) 298-0376, fax (805) 298-0576; vhusap@scv.net or info@vacation-homes.com; www.vacation-homes.com. Founder member of International Home Exchange Association (see above). Directory and internet service with opportunities in more than 40 countries. Visiting browsers welcome.

Language Learning

Audio Forum, 96 Broad St., Guilford, CT 06437; (800) 243-1234, (203) 453-9794; fax (203) 453-9774; 74537.550@compuserve.com. The world's largest selection of self-instructional language courses: 275 courses in 96 languages.

Audio-Magazines from Champs-Elysées, Inc., P.O. Box 158067, Nashville, TN 37215-8067; (615) 383-8534; www.champs-elysees.com. Lively audio-cassette magazine with transcript and glossary, in Spanish, French, German, and Italian at annual subscriptions ranging from $79 to $129.

Center for Applied Linguistics. 1118 22nd St., NW, Washington, DC 20037; (800) 276-9834; www.cal.org. Research, data bases, encouragement – lots of resources for language learning.

How to Learn a Foreign Language by Graham Fuller. 1997. $9.95 from Audio-Forum (above).

How to Master Languages by Roger Jones. £8.99 plus £4 s/h from How to Books (above).

How to Study and Live in Britain by Jane Woolfenden. £8.99 plus £4 s/h from How to Books (above).

Surf's Up! A Website Workbook for Basic Language Learning, available in French, German, and Spanish. Audio-Forum (see above).

Whole World Guide to Language Learning by Terry Marshall, 1990. How to learn a language while abroad. $16.95 plus $3 s/h from Intercultural Press (above).

Living Abroad Publications

Adventures Abroad by Allene Symons and Jane Parker (Globe Pequot), 1991. A comprehensive overview of retirement abroad drawn from interviews with 56 people living abroad who share their opinions and advice.

The Adventures of Working Abroad by Joyce Sautters Osland. 1995. Author draws from 14 years of living abroad to help prospective, current, and potential expatriates adjust. $25 from Jossey-Bass, Inc. (a division of Simon & Schuster), 350 Sansome St., 5th Fl., San Francisco, CA 94104; www.josseybass.com.

The Canadian Guide to Working and Living Overseas by Jean-Marc Hachey. 1998, 1,000 pp, US$40, CAN$54.40, covers every facet of international work and living overseas. Features 1,870 profiles, 1,670 web sites, and 700 resources in 58 bibliographies, web updates until the year 2001. Indispensable for students, recent graduates, managers, and world travelers. Order by phone (800) 267-0105, fax (800) 221-9985; www.workingoverseas.com. Checks payable to Univ. Toronto Press (UTP), 5201 Dufferin St., North York, ON M3H 5T8, Canada.

Fact Sheets. Free from Office of Overseas Schools, U.S. Department of State, Washington, DC 20522-2902; www.state.gov/www.about_state/schools. Fact sheets on overseas elementary and secondary schools assisted by the Department of State.

Guide to Living Abroad by Louise M. Guido. Annual. Published in 11 volumes, each containing practical information of interest to expatriates, such as health, buying a house, immigration matters, personal security, and education. The guides also have a section on regional travel. $30 from Living Abroad Publishing, 32 Nassau St., Princeton, NJ 08542; (609) 924-9302, fax (609) 924-7844.

Handbook for Citizens Living Abroad. 1990. $10. Practical information on moving and living abroad in question and answer format. American Citizens Abroad, 1051 North George Mason Dr., Arlington, VA 22205; jacabr@aol.com, acage@aca.ch.

Hidden Immigrants: Legacies of Growing up Abroad by Linda Bell. 1997. Cross Cultural Publications, Cross Roads Books, PO Box 506, Notre Dame, IN 46556; fax (219) 273-5973.

How to Emigrate by Roger Jones. £9.99. How To Books Ltd., Plymbridge House, Estover Rd., Plymouth, PL6 7PZ, U.K.; (011) 44-1-752-202301, fax 202331; orders@plymbridge.com, www.howtobooks.co.uk. Essential advice and information on weighing up your prospects, choosing the right location, coping with immigration, and so on.

The Insiders' Guide to Relocation by Beverly Roman. Order by calling (800) 582-2665 or sending a check for $14.95 plus $4 s/h to: Falcon Publishing, P.O. Box 1718, Helena, MT 59624. Available in bookstores nationwide. Whether moving across town or across the globe, The Insiders' Guide to Relocation shares tried and true methods to make the transition easier. An entire section entitled International Relocation includes chapters on Business Strategies Abroad, Overseas Pre-move Planning, Insurance Overseas, International

Finances, Kidstuff Overseas, Settling in Overseas and Repatriation.

Intercultural Press publishes numerous books on international living, travel, study, and cross-cultural experiences. Titles include: **Host Family Survival Kit: A Guide for American Host Families, Survival Kit for Overseas Living, Exchange Student Survival Kit.** (see above).

The ISS Directory of Overseas Schools (International Schools Service). American-style elementary and secondary schools overseas.

Living Abroad. Magazine for international executives. Annual editions for 11 regions. Working with a network of 80 local-country writers, *Living Abroad* offers timely, practical information on life in another country including culture, housing, financial, educational, medical, business and employment. $30 per issue. Living Abroad Publishing (see above).

Living Abroad: Keeping Your Life, Family and Career Intact While Living Abroad by Cathy Tsang-Feign (Hambalan Press, GPO Box 6086, Hong Kong). 1996. Self-help for expatriates.

Notes from a Traveling Childhood: Readings for Internationally Mobile Parents and Children by Karen Curnow McCluskey (ed.). 1994. $5.95 plus s/h from the Foreign Service Youth Foundation, P.O. Box 39185, Washington, DC 20016.

Of Many Lands: Journal of a Traveling Childhood by Sara Mansfield Taber. 1997. A personal notebook with useful questions prompting children and adolescents to record their feelings and observations about the country-hopping life style of the foreign service. $8.50 plus s/h from the Foreign Service Youth Foundation (above).

Schools Abroad of Interest to Americans (Porter Sargent Publishers). Lists 800 elemen-

tary and secondary schools in 130 countries for young Americans.

Spending a Year Abroad by Nick Vandome (3rd ed.) Sets out the numerous options. £8.99 plus £4 s/h from How To Books (above).

Survival Kit for Overseas Living by L. Robert Kohls. 3rd ed., 1996. Best-selling guide to adaptation to living abroad. $11.95 plus $3 s/h from Intercultural Press (above).

The Unknown Ambassadors by Phyllis Michaux. 1996. Traces the history of efforts to establish and improve the rights of Americans living abroad, including citizenship rights of children of dual-national couples, Social Security and Medicare benefits for Americans living or traveling overseas; equitable tax treatment and voting rights. $15.95 plus $3 s/h from Aletheia Publications (above).

Where in the World Are You Going? by Judith M. Blohm. 1996. $9.95 plus $3 s/h from Intercultural Press (above). An activity book for children ages 5-10 who are moving abroad with their families.

Women's Guide to Overseas Living by Nancy J. Piet-Pelon and Barbara Hornby. 2nd ed., 1992. $15.95 plus $3 s/h from Intercultural Press (above). Examines issues critical to women (and their families) who relocate abroad.

Reentry Publications

The Absentee American by Carolyn D. Smith. 1991. $12.95 plus $3 s/h from Aletheia Publications, 3815 Corporal Kennedy St., Bayside NY 11361; (718) 224-6303; fax (718) 281-0403; alethpub@aol.com; http://members. aol.com/alethpub. Describes the impact of overseas living on Americans who spent some of their formative years in other countries and returned to the U.S. during their high school or early college years. Based on a survey and interviews of more than 300 returnees, the book describes overseas life, reentry, and the long-term effects of living abroad.

Art of Coming Home by Craig Storti. 1997. $17.95 plus $3 s/h from Intercultural Press (above). Understanding cultural differences and easing reentry shock.

Strangers at Home by Carolyn Smith (ed.). 1996. $15.95 plus $3 s/h from Aletheia Publications (above). An anthology of perspectives on the effects of living overseas and coming "home" to a country that seems just as foreign as the one left behind. Includes useful advice for parents seeking to help their children—especially teenagers—cope with the experience of reentry and fitting in.

Retirement Abroad

How to Retire Abroad by Roger Jones. 1993. Written by an English specialist in expatriate matters, with a country-by-country guide. £8.99 plus £4 s/h from How To Books (above).

Web Sites

American Citizens Abroad, www.aca.ch. Web site for a non-profit association dedicated to serving and defending the interests of U.S. citizens world-wide. Features their newsletter.

Cultural Homestay International, www.chinet.org. Cultural Homestay International is a non-profit public benefit organization founded in 1980 to promote international understanding, friendship, and goodwill through cultural homestays. Their web site has information on how you can host a foreign exchange student, become one yourself, their internship programs, and other opportunities.

Ecola Newsstand, www.ecola.com. Published on the World Wide Web since March, 1995, Ecola has links to more than 6,600 English language newspapers and magazines world wide.

Escape Artist, www.escapeartist.com/going/home.htm. Expatriate resources include an impressive collection of web links, immigration resources, general expat resources, expatriate taxpayer resources, printed resources, world wide moving companies, overseas jobs, Index of World Wide Embassy and Consulate Resources, and a bulletin board. Almost a glut of information here.

Expat Exchange, www.expatexchange.com. Extensive site with chat rooms, tax assistance, links, information on international careers, plus the *Overseas Digest*, a free newsletter.

Expat Forum, www.expatforum.com. A good deal of practical resources of general and some of more specific interest to expatriates and other international types.

First Point International, www.firstpointinter.com. An established worldwide relocation specialist with an important difference. Relocation organisations traditionally work for companies that are relocating to different regions or countries. First Point International, however, was established to assist private individuals who would like to try life in a different country.

Haney's Home Exchange, www.sima.dk/haneys. Haney's Home Exchange establishes contact between families from all over the world who want to exchange their homes during the summer holidays, or any other period during the year. Look past the imperfect English—for $81, they'll connect you with a family who wants to exchange their home with yours.

Holi-Swaps, www.holi-swaps.com. Worldwide vacation home exchange listings and advice.

Home Free, www.homefree.com/homefree/index.html. Home Free offers Home Exchange and Travel Companion Matching Services.

International Home Exchange, www.HomeExchange.com. A big database of homes for exchange. Extensive worldwide listings. For $30, they'll list your home for one year. Browsing their listings is free.

International Home Exchange Network, www.ihen.com. IHEA member site. Extensive worldwide home exchange listings. Cost is $29.95 to list.

Internet Home Exchange, www.NetHomeXchange.com. The Internet Home Exchange is the oldest, and claims to be the largest, Internet-based home exchange service in the world. They have over 700 listings in over 40 countries.

Invented City, www.invented-city.com. With over 2,000 listings, this is one of the largest databases in the home exchange business, and it's updated on a daily basis. You can browse through the listings without photographs or contact information, but you'll have to pay their $75 fee for listing your own home to get their full information.

Living Abroad, www.livingabroad.com. Web site of Living Abroad Publishing, publishers of *Living Abroad* magazine. The "Relocation Services" section provides resource information on relocating to about 40 different countries.

Living in Indonesia, www.expat.or.id. Loads of information covering all aspects of relocating to Indonesia, from preparing before you go, to where to buy groceries in Jakarta.

Relocation Journal, www.relojournal.com/main.htm. *The Relocation Journal* aims to help you get a clear grasp of the big picture of moving abroad, even the stuff you don't want

to deal with, like taxes. Clicking on "Inside This Issue" is a good place to start.

RIDEF Home Exchange Service, www.cyberlab.ch/exchange. This non-commercial-looking site has several hundred home exchange or vacation rental listings worldwide. A $39 membership includes your own listing and access to all contact information for one year.

Taxi's Newspaper List, http://users.dcltanet.com/users/taxicat/e_papers.html. What better way to keep yourself informed than by reading the local newspaper? This site has links to the web sites of hundreds of newspapers, inside the U.S. and abroad.

Terra Cognita, www.terracognita.com. Terra Cognita produces videos and workbooks for international transitions and business. Their web site is a good introduction to their services and has links to some good resources.

Trading Homes International, www.tradinghomes.com. Online home exchange service with over 1,300 listings, constantly updated. Basic membership is $65.

Vacation Homes Unlimited, www.vacationhomes.com. Vacation Homes Unlimited has been promoting the concept of home exchange vacationing since 1986. They offer home exchange opportunities in 40+ countries worldwide.

For more listings of resources for living abroad, and for bargains worldwide, travel tips, and all sorts of information on learning, living, working, and traveling abroad, see *Transitions Abroad* magazine. To order a single copy or a subscription, please call 1-800-293-0373 or visit the *Transitions Abroad* web site at www.transabroad.com.

Living Abroad Resources

About the Contributors

Editors and Contributing Editors

DIANNE G. BRAUSE is an educator and educational and ecotravel advocate and the author of *Forever Green: An Ecotourist's Guide to Lane County*. She can be reached c/o Lost Valley Educational Center, 81868 Lost Valley Ln., Dexter, OR 97431, www.efn.org/~lvec.

DAVID CLINE is the Managing Editor of Transitions Abroad Publishing.

GINA DOGGETT was a Foreign Service brat, spent some years as a closet foreigner in Washington, and is now a journalist in Paris.

ANDREW GERARD is the Database Manager and Webmaster at Transitions Abroad Publishing. If it's on the Internet and it has to do with alternative travel, Andy will find it.

SUSAN GRIFFITH is the author of *Work Your Way Around the World* and *Teaching English Abroad: Talking Your Way Around the World*, both available from Peterson's Guides.

CYNTHIA HARRIMAN is the author of *Take Your Kids to Europe* and a passionate advocate of family travel. She welcomes readers' input at charriman@masongrant.com.

CLAY HUBBS is the founder, editor, and publisher of *Transitions Abroad*. He taught Modern European and American literature and served as Director of International Studies at Hampshire College from 1972-1998.

DEBORAH McLAREN is the author of *Rethinking Tourism and Ecotravel: The Paving of Paradise and What You Can Do to Stop It* and the director of the Rethinking Tourism Project. She works with communities worldwide designing alternative tourism projects. Send information about your environmental travel experiences, tips, and recommended educational programs and ecotour operators to: Deborah McLaren, RTP, P.O. Box 581938, Minneapolis, MN 55458; RTProject@aol.com.

WILLIAM NOLTING is the Director of the Univ. of Michigan Overseas Opportunities Office (603 E. Madison St., Ann Arbor, MI 48109) and International Education Editor for *Transitions Abroad*.

VANESSA RELLI-MOREAU is Membership Director for the Council on Standards for International Educational Travel (CSIET), Alexandria, VA. For information on high school study abroad, contact CSIET at (703) 739-9050.

SUSAN SYGALL is the Director of Mobility International USA, a nonprofit organization whose purpose is to promote international educational exchange and travel for persons with and without disabilities. Contact her at P.O. Box 10767, Eugene, OR 97110.

KATHY WIDING is a freelance travel writer and the Travel Books Editor for *Transitions Abroad*. She and her husband Jerry are authors of *Cycling the Netherlands, Belgium, and Luxembourg*. She is also a part owner of Wide World Books and Maps, a travel bookstore in Seattle, WA, www. travelbooksandmaps.com.

ARLINE K. WILLS is the Seniors Travel Editor for *Transitions Abroad*. Since her first flight to Cuba in 1958, she has made dozens of trips abroad. She lives in Lynnfield, MA.

Contributing Writers

STARLETT R. CRAIG is the Director of Pre-College Enrichment Programs at Clemson Univ. and the national chair of Black and Multicultural Professionals in International Education.

MIKE DANEN lives in Agoura Hills, CA. He and his wife Doris recently traveled to the former Yugoslavia to meet distant relatives.

ROGER L. EDWARDS, SR. is an electrical engineer and technical writer who lives in Memphis, TN. He is developing a screenplay inspired by his recent travels in Latin America.

KATE GALBRAITH, a managing editor for the 1998 *Let's Go* travel guide series, is a writer for the online journal *Slate* and a frequent contributor to *Transitions Abroad*.

MARIE GASPER is a French major at Xavier Univ. in Cincinnati.

CHRIS GRANT-BEAR, a native Scot, is Elementary Principal at the TASIS Helenia International School in Greece. Her work has been published in Britain, the U.S., and Greece.

WILLIAM HOFFA is an international education consultant based in Amherst, MA. He teaches in the Master's in International And Intercultural Management program at the School for International Training in Brattleboro, Vermont.

JOANNA HUBBS is Professor of Russian Cultural History at Hampshire College and the author of *Mother Russia*.

BRAD JENSEN is a graduate student in Information Technology for Development in the School of Information at the Univ. of Michigan. He is currently a Rotary Scholar in Pretoria, South Africa.

SARAH MEEKER, who writes from Seattle, WA, has traveled through Europe, Asia, and the former USSR. Since becoming a parent, she has enjoyed the new pace and perspective that children bring to travel.

LESLIE PAPPAS has lived in China since 1994. Comments on this article may be addressed to her at lesliepp@public2.bta.net.cn.

ROB RAMER is a journalist in Minneapolis, MN. He was recently married to Deborah McLaren and works with the Rethinking Tourism Project

TERRY REDDING is a world traveler and frequent contributor to *Transitions Abroad*. He would like to receive comments and suggestions on independent, low-budget travel. He can be reached at 901 W. Braddock St., Tampa, FL 33603.

RICK STEVES (425-771-8303 or www.ricksteves.com) is the host of the PBS series "Travels in Europe" and the author of 21 European travel guidebooks, including *Europe Through the Back Door*, all published by John Muir.

ERIKA L. WEIDNER graduated from the Univ. of Oregon with a degree in International Studies. As a student, she completed internships in both Budapest and London.

Special Thanks to **VICTORIA HUBBS** and **ANDY GERARD** for helping to facilitate the gathering of much of the information in this volume and to **JANIS G. SOKOL** for patiently typing and retyping it.

Index to Advertisers

Geographical

Index